Political
Terrorism

Political Terrorism

Edited by Lester A. Sobel

Contributing editors: Hal Kosut, Joseph Fickes, Joanne Edgar, Myrna Lebov, Chris Hunt, Steve Orlofsky, Maurie Sommer, Gerry Satterwhite

FACTS ON FILE, INC.   NEW YORK, N.Y.

Political
Terrorism

Library of Congress Catalog Card Number 74-84438
ISBN 0-87196-232-2

9 8 7 6 5 4 3 2 1
PRINTED IN
THE UNITED STATES OF AMERICA

Contents

INTRODUCTION 1
THE MIDDLE EAST 9
    Arab-Israeli Antagonism 9
    Israel Acts Vs. Terrorists.. 10
    Israeli Attacks in Jordan 11
    Terrorists Clash with Jordanians 16
    Terrorists Bomb Israeli Targets 17
    Arabs Attack Planes 19
    Arab States & Terrorists 29
    Guerrilla Attacks, Israeli Retaliation 38
    Terrorism in Israel & in Occupied Areas.................. 42
    Guerrilla-Arab State Tensions................................. 44
    Lebanon Suffers Retaliation 47
    Terrorists Hijack Planes, Slay Tourists at Airport 51
    Mid-East Terrorists Strike in Europe & Other Areas... 53
    Strife Embroils Israel, Arab States & Commandos 69
LATIN AMERICA 82
    Action Against Terrorism Urged 82
    ARGENTINA: Recent Terrorists & Their Activities .. 83
        Diplomats & Officials Become Kidnap/Terrorist
            Targets 83
        Trelew Prison Break & Killings 89
        Assassinations & Kidnappings Continue............ 89
        Peronists Return to Power............................... 91
        Action Against Terrorists................................ 98

Terrorism After Peron's Death........................ 101
BOLIVIA: Che Guevara Slain as
     Guerrilla Campaign Fails 106
   Struggle Continues 109
BRAZIL: Assassinations & Kidnappings 113
CHILE: Unrest & Terrorism 118
COLOMBIA: Terrorist-Government Clashes........... 122
CUBA: Exile Attacks 127
   Action Against Hijackings 129
DOMINICAN REPUBLIC: Unrest & Terrorism 130
GUATEMALA: Terrorism & Repression 135
HAITI: Repression & Exile Activity........................ 143
MEXICO: Many Guerrilla Bands Active.................. 145
PERU: Terrorism Curbed 151
URUGUAY: Tupamaros Suppressed...................... 151
   Foreign Diplomats Attacked 153
   Security Tightened... 157
VENEZUELA: Terrorism Declines 163
THE UNITED STATES 167
RACIAL TERRORISM: Terrorists' Diverse Goals... 167
   The Black Panthers... 167
   San Rafael Judge Killed,
     Angela Davis Acquitted 174
   Other Black Militants..................................... 174
   The Ku Klux Klan & Similar Terrorists............. 178
'NEW LEFT' & ANTIWAR ACTIVISTS............. 181
PUERTO RICO: Terrorism in
   Name of Independence.............................. 200
OTHER AREAS 203
CANADA: Separatists Blamed for
     Bombings & Kidnappings.......................... 203
   Cross & Laporte Kidnapped, Laporte Slain 204
CYPRUS: Enosis Demand Spurs Terrorism 209
ETHIOPIA: Eritrean Terrorist Attacks.................... 212
FRANCE: Minor Terrorism, Many Causes 213
GREAT BRITAIN: Scattered Terrorist Acts............ 216
GREECE: Terrorists Oppose Junta........................ 218
IRAN: Muslim & Communist Terrorists.................. 220
ITALY: Rightist & Leftist Terrorism...................... 221
JAPAN: United Red Army Strikes........................ 225

NORTHERN IRELAND: War Against Partition..... 227
    Londonderry Killings & Aftermath.................... 232
    Violence Spreads to London 233
    Anti-Terror Action 234
    Attacks in London & Abroad 238
PORTUGAL & AFRICA: African Territories
    Promised Freedom After Coup in Portugal... 243
THE PHILIPPINES: Red & Muslim Terrorism........ 250
RHODESIA: African (Black) Struggle
    for Majority Rule..................................... 254
SOUTH AFRICA & SOUTH-WEST AFRICA
    (NAMIBIA): Stern Action
    Curbs Terrorism 259
SOVIET UNION: Jewish Militants Active.............. 263
SPAIN: Basques Fight Regime............................. 267
TURKEY: Leftist Terrorism 271
WEST GERMANY: Baader-Meinhof
    Group Accused.. 274
YUGOSLAVIA: Croatians Attack Regime 276
INTERNATIONAL ACTION................................... 279
    U.N. Discusses Problem 279
    No Action on 'Skyjackings' 282
INDEX 285

Introduction

ASSASSINATIONS, THE CAPTURE OF HOSTAGES, the destruction of property and other politically motivated violence short of war have been relatively common occurrences since the early days of man's experiments in political action. Only since the late 1960s, however, has terrorism become so widespread as to constitute a significant cause of international concern.

The word terrorism is employed to specify acts of violence for political coercion. But there seems to be no definition that will satisfactorily cover all uses of the term. According to an academic quip, terrorism is "what the other fellow does." Yet, even this is not always so, since some activists (the late Brazilian urban guerrilla theorist Carlos Marighella, for example) seem quite willing to describe their behavior as both idealistic—and terroristic. In general, the word terrorism is used today to define almost all illegal acts of violence committed for political purposes by clandestine groups.

The lawyer William A. Hannay, writing in the April 1974 issue of *International Lawyer* about United Nations debate on terrorism, asserted that "recent contemporary usage tends to curb its [the term's] meaning to either random or extortionate violence, aimed ultimately at the target state of a guerrilla, resistance or liberation movement but which strikes at unarmed civilians, diplomats or non-combatants."

Martha Crenshaw Hutchinson of the University of Virginia refined the use of the term by describing a concept called "revolutionary terrorism." In an article in the September 1972 issue of

The Journal of Conflict Resolution, Professor Crenshaw wrote that "revolutionary terrorism is a part of insurgent strategy in the context of internal warfare or revolution." Such terrorism, she noted, "is manifested in acts of socially and politically unacceptable violence. . . . There is a consistent pattern of symbolic or representative selection of the victims or objects of acts of terrorism. . . . The revolutionary movement deliberately intends these actions to create a psychological effect on specific groups and thereby to change their political behavior and attitudes."

In 1933, the *Encyclopaedia of the Social Sciences* listed terrorism as a word for "the method whereby an organized group or party seeks to achieve its avowed aims chiefly through the systematic use of violence." It held that "terroristic acts are directed against persons who as individuals, agents or representatives of authority interfere with the consummation of the objectives of such a group." According to the *Encyclopaedia,* the "cardinal point in the strategy of terrorism" was the "publicity value of the terrorist act." It said that "the terrorist does not threaten; death or destruction is part of his program of action, and if he is caught, his behavior during trial is generally directed primarily not toward winning his freedom but toward spreading a knowledge of his doctrines."

In the late 1960s and early 1970s, however, terrorists acting on behalf of the Palestinian Arab cause have frequently made no attempt to direct their violence toward representatives of authority or even toward individuals who were less obvious in their interference with Arab objectives. Instead, as Hannay indicated, they often killed victims or seized hostages at random. But their stated purposes, in keeping with the *Encyclopaedia* description, usually were to bring political grievances to the world's attention and to win the release of imprisoned comrades. Latin American terrorists of the same period also frequently chose victims who did not seem to constitute serious impediments to their cause. While some victims of Latin American terrorists were linked with regimes the activists were fighting, many of their kidnap targets seemed to be picked on the basis of the ransom for which they could be bargained.

Col. Roger Trinquier noted in *Modern Warfare* (1954) that "the goal of modern warfare is control of the population, and terrorism is a particularly appropriate weapon, since it aims directly at the inhabitant. In the street, at work, at home, the citizen lives continually under the threat of violent death. In the presence of this permanent danger surrounding him, he has the depressing feeling of being an isolated and defenseless target. The fact that public authority and the police are no longer capable of ensuring his security adds to his distress. . . . He is more and more drawn to the side of the terrorists, who alone are able to protect him."

This expression of at least one rationale for terrorism seems to be an apt explanation of, for example, the Viet Cong's use of this weapon in South Vietnam. It provides little insight, however, into the activities of terrorists who kill or kidnap foreign diplomats, who hijack airliners far from home or who rob banks or kidnap wealthy people for ransom.

Leila Khaled, who took part in more than one Arab skyjacking, gave further, if perhaps unwitting, illumination. She told a *Time* correspondent in October 1970 (as reported in the issue dated Nov. 2, 1970): "If we throw bombs, it is not our responsibility. You may care for the death of a child, but the whole world ignored the death of Palestinian children for 22 years. We are not responsible." The implication is that "the whole world" is responsible for her group's attacks and that "the whole world" could end the terrorism by yielding to the terrorists' demands.

What might be described as a more authoritative justification of Arab terrorism was elicited by staff members of the U.S. Senate Committee on Foreign Relations during a survey trip to the Middle East in November–December 1973. It was summarized by staff member Seth Tillman in a staff report published March 5, 1974:

> Terrorist activities, say top Palestinian leaders, have not been carried out for the sake of their immediate results, or for the purpose of terror in itself, or for personal revenge, or as acts of random criminality. Their purpose, they say, has been broadly political, to draw the attention of the world, and most especially of the United States, to the Palestinian movement and to its purposes. Terrorism, they say, has been used by other patriotic movements which lacked other effective means, including the Israelis before 1947, or for that matter, the Americans before 1776.

The modern brand of terrorism, striking in almost any non-Communist country, bears the trademark of a new variety of political activist—the urban guerrilla. The new terrorists have discarded the dicta of Mao Tse-tung, Ernesto (Che) Guevara and the other classic revolutionary theorists that guerrillas must win their first victories in the countryside. As far as many Latin American revolutionaries are concerned, this proposition received its death-blow in 1967 when Guevara was defeated and slain in his unsuccessful effort to put the theory into effect in the mountains of Bolivia. Since Guevara's death, revolutionaries have increasingly concentrated on the large population centers, and the cities and suburbs have become the principal locale of their terroristic acts.

An early advocate of urban guerrilla tactics was the American black militant Robert Williams. Williams, credited with exerting a strong influence on both black and New Left activists, wrote in the February 1964 issue of his publication *The Crusader:*

"The new concept of revolution . . . is lightning campaigns conducted in highly sensitive urban communities with the paralysis reaching the small communities and spreading to the farm areas. The old method of guerrilla warfare, as carried out from the hills and countryside, would be ineffective in a powerful country like the USA. . . . The new concept is to huddle as close to the enemy as possible so as to neutralize his modern and fierce weapons. The new concept creates conditions that involve the total community, whether they want to be involved or not. . . . During the hours of day sporadic rioting takes place and massive sniping. Night brings all-out warfare, organized fighting and unlimited terror against the oppressor and his forces. . . ."

Perhaps the most influential of the urban guerrilla theorists was the late Brazilian revolutionary Carlos Marighella, who was ambushed and slain by the Brazilian police in 1969. His instructions for conducting campaigns of terrorism in the cities of Brazil were reduced to 55 pages of a handbook published in numerous languages as *Minimanual of the Urban Guerrilla.* The *Minimanual* was circulated among rebels in almost every part of the world.

Marighella disdained the definition of terrorism as "what the other fellow does." "The accusation of assault or terrorism no longer has the pejorative meaning it used to have," Marighella declared. ". . . It does not factionalize, it does not discredit; on the contrary, it represents a focal point of attraction. Today, to be an assailant or a terrorist is a quality that ennobles any honorable man because it is an act worthy of a revolutionary engaged in armed struggle against the shameful military dictatorship and its monstrosities."

In the *Minimanual,* Marighella described the principal task of the urban guerrilla as being "to distract, to wear out, to demoralize the militarists, the military dictatorship and its repressive forces, and also to attack and destroy the wealth and property of the North Americans, the foreign managers and the Brazilian upper class." "Thus," he continued, "within the framework of the class struggle, as it inevitably and necessarily sharpens, the armed struggle of the urban guerrilla points toward two essential objectives: (a) the physical liquidation of the chiefs and assistants of the armed forces and of the police; (b) the expropriation of government resources and those belonging to the big capitalists, latifundists and imperialists, with small expropriations used for the maintenance of individual urban guerrillas and large ones for the sustenance of the revolution itself."

Marighella defined and prescribed in the *Minimanual* a variety of terrorist/urban guerrilla activities. For example:

Terrorism—"Terrorism is an action, usually involving the placement of a bomb or fire explosion of great destructive power, which is capable of effecting irreparable loss against the enemy. Terrorism requires that the urban guerrilla should have an adequate theoretical and practical knowledge of how to make explosives. The terroristic act, apart from the apparent facility with which it can be carried out, is no different from other urban guerrilla acts and actions whose success depends on the planning and determination of the revolutionary organization. It is an action the urban guerrilla must execute with the greatest cold-bloodedness, calmness and decision. . . ."

Execution—"Execution is the killing of a North American spy, of an agent of the dictatorship, of a police torturer, of a fascist personality in the government involved in crimes and persecutions against patriots, of a stool pigeon, informer, police agent or police provocateur. . . . Execution is a secret action in which the least possible number of urban guerrillas are involved. In many cases, the execution can be carried out by one sniper, patiently, alone and unknown, and operating in absolute secrecy and in cold blood. . . ."

Kidnapping—"Kidnapping is capturing and holding in a secret spot a police agent, a North American spy, a political personality or a notorious and dangerous enemy of the revolutionary movement. Kidnapping is used to exchange or liberate imprisoned revolutionary comrades, or to force suspension of torture in the jail cells of the military dictatorship. . . . The kidnapping of North American residents or visitors in Brazil constitutes a form of protest against the penetration and domination of United States imperialism in our country. . . ."

The objective of the type of action advocated by Marighella was made clear by the Brazilian urban guerrilla Ladislas Dowbor in an interview with Sanche de Gramont in Algiers in the summer of 1970. De Gramont quoted Dowbor in the New York Times Magazine Nov. 15, 1970 as saying that "you cannot build the revolutionary consciousness of a population through political explanations. But military actions can create this consciousness." Although discontent in Brazil is widespread, people "have not yet reached the stage of holding the system responsible," Dowbor asserted. He said: Terrorists, therefore, "attack the targets they [the people] consciously identify," "their visible enemies—the farm overseer, or the shop foreman, or the landowner who throws squatters off his land." This "provokes a reaction of the system. . . . [W]e provoke the army, the police, the press and the clergy into taking positions against us and in support of the visible enemy. It is then that the workers are able to identify the system as the enemy. . . . [A]rmed action, which means living in small, clandestine cells, reduces the possibility of contact with the population. We must rely on the repercussions of our actions. If it is a violent action, it will appeal to those parts of the population that are sensitive to violence—that is the marginal masses, the unemployed, the *favelados*."

Assertions that most terrorists belong to a worldwide network taking orders from some secret, high-ranking power center are childishly far-fetched. Terrorist groups seem more frequently to be small, autonomous units not infrequently at ideological odds with each other even though they seldom know each other. Some, however, do seem to keep in touch in formal or informal ways by the circulation of the *Minimanual* and other underground publications, by broadcasts from Havana, Cairo and other revolutionary centers, by occasional personal contacts and reciprocal aid and even by attending international meetings of revolutionaries or terrorist/guerrilla training sessions said to have taken place in such diverse places as Cuba, the Soviet Union, China, North Korea, Algeria, Lebanon, Syria, West Germany and Italy.

An example of how terrorists of different countries have made contact with and cooperated with each other is the case of three Japanese who massacred 26 tourists at Lod airport in Israel in 1972. Nine members of the Japanese United Red Army, a terrorist group, had hijacked an airliner in Japan in 1970 and had forced it to land in North Korea. There they met Arab terrorist leader George Habbash and agreed to aid the Arabs. As a result of this contact, a Habbash agent contacted three United Red Army members in Japan early in 1972. The three flew to Lebanon for training, then were armed in Rome by Italian terrorists, who sent them on to Israel by Air France for the brief shooting attack that brought death or serious injury to 100 people, many of them Puerto Ricans with no previous involvement in the Arab-Israeli dispute.

Although terrorists are found among adherents of almost every brand of left-wing or right-wing ideology, the overwhelming majority of today's terrorists can be described as leftists. Most have a New Left or Trotskyist character. Establishment Communists and other members of the "Old Left" generally deplore terrorism under current conditions as "adventurist" (or "romantic") and counter-productive. Following a meeting of the U.S. Communist Party National Committee, party leader Gus Hall was quoted in *Daily World* July 13, 1971 as asserting that "masses have largely rejected the tactics of anarchism and acts of individual terror. This rejection of wrong tactics has isolated many groups of petty bourgeois radicals such as Students for a Democratic Society, Progressive Labor, to an extent the Black Panther Party, the Weathermen and many varieties of Trotskyism."

Orthodox Communists sometimes cite Lenin as the authority for opposing terrorism. Yet Lenin did not reject terrorism under all circumstances. Frequently quoted is Lenin's letter of Oct. 16, 1905 to the St. Petersburg Committee:

... [I]t horrifies me to find that there has been talk about bombs for over six months, yet not one has been made! ... Form fighting squads at once everywhere, among the students, and especially among the workers, etc., etc. Let groups be at once organized of three, ten, thirty, etc., persons. Let them arm themselves at once as best they can, be it with a revolver, a knife, a rag soaked in kerosene for starting fires. . . .

The propagandists must supply each group with brief and simple recipes for making bombs, give the man elementary explanation of the type of the work, and then leave it all to them. Squads must at once begin military training by launching operations immediately, at once. Some may at once undertake to kill a spy or blow up a police station, others to raid a bank to confiscate funds for the insurrection, others again may drill or prepare plans of localities, etc. But the essential thing is to begin at once to learn from actual practice: have no fear of these trial attacks. They may, of course, degenerate into extremes, but that is an evil of the morrow, whereas the evil today is our inertness, our doctrinaire spirit, our learned immobility, and our senile fear of initiative. Let every group learn, if it is only by beating up policemen: a score or so victims will be more than compensated for by the facts that this will train hundreds of experienced fighters, who tomorrow will be leading hundreds of thousands. . . .

This book is intended as a record of the wave of violence described as terrorism that achieved worldwide proportions toward the latter half of the 1960s and continued on into the 1970s. The material comes largely from the reports printed by FACTS ON FILE in its weekly coverage of world events. Although much that is here is highly controversial, a conscientious effort was made to set it all down without bias and to make this volume, as far as possible, a reliable and balanced reference work.

The Middle East

Arab-Israeli Antagonism

Arabs and Jews have been fighting over their conflicting claims to Palestine since long before the 1948 conflict from which Israel emerged as an independent Jewish state. The struggle has been characterized by frequent recourse to terrorism.

The Balfour Declaration of Britain in 1917 had expressed that government's decision to "facilitate" "the establishment in Palestine of a national home for the Jewish people," and the declaration's principles were incorporated by the League of Nations in the mandate that the League of Nations gave to Britain to govern Palestine. Arab reaction to the declaration and to Zionist aspirations in Palestine were manifested in such actions as the riots of 1920 and 1921, a series of murderous attacks on Jews in Palestine in 1929 and the terrorism of 1936-9, in which Arab bands attacked Jewish settlements, murdered Jews, mined roads, burned crops and ambushed vehicles.

Terrorism by Jews against Britain followed World War II, when the British continued to restrict the entry of Jews into Palestine despite pleas for the admission of the survivors of Hitler's death camps.

After the establishment of Israel, Arab terrorism was considered in part responsible for the Arab-Israeli warfare of 1956 and 1967.

Israel's military success in these two conflicts brought no peace to the Jewish state. Israel faced continued attacks from Arab fedayeen (self-sacrificers) and other terrorists—not all of them necessarily Palestinian. Israelis, their friends and innocent third parties were subject to aircraft hijackings, bombings, machine-gunnings and indiscriminate homicidal attacks in virtually any part of the world. The Israeli armed forces retaliated by striking at Arab commando bases.

The major Arab terrorist groups operated, nominally at least, under the guidance of the Palestine Liberation Organization (PLO), which had been formed by the Arab governments at a summit meeting in Cairo in 1964. Arab terrorist groups included: Al (or El) Fatah, the largest of the Arab guerrilla organizations, which was headed by Yasir Arafat, the PLO chairman; the Popular

9

Front for the Liberation of Palestine (PLFP), an independent Marxist-Leninist group opposed to Al Fatah and Soviet policies; the Popular Democratic Front For the Liberation of Palestine (PDFLP), a group that had split away from the PLFP, the Popular Front for the Liberation of Palestine-General Command (PFLP-GC), an independent group; Al Saiqah, a group controlled by the Syrian government; Arab Liberation Front, a unit controlled by the Iraqi government. The name Black September has been used for what some observers consider ad hoc *terrorist operations in which, it has been said, recruits from the PLFP and PDFLP have participated.*

The events described below were among the significant developments in the post-1967 terrorism involved in the Arab-Israeli dispute.

Israel Acts Vs. Terrorists

Fatah Men Seized. Israeli police officials in Jerusalem announced Oct. 12, 1967 the arrest of 24 members of Al Fatah (the Syrian-based terrorist organization that had perpetrated raids against Israel before the June war) and the capture of large quantities of arms. The police commissioner of Jerusalem, Shaul Rosolio, said that "by these arrests we have thwarted a wave of planned sabotage that would have been carried out in the next few weeks." The weapons taken in and around East Jerusalem included machineguns, light mortars, explosives and anti-tank guns.

The 24 Arabs had been accused of participating in a sabotage campaign in the Jerusalem area since Sept. 17. Prior to their arrests, more than 100 other suspects had been seized throughout the Israeli-occupied west bank of the Jordan River.

Israeli army sources were reported Sept. 28 to have linked the Syrian government, and to some extent Algeria, with the guerrilla operations. Captured Arab terrorists were reported to have told Israeli authorities that they had been trained by Syrian and Algerian officers at camps at Duma and Hamma near Damascus and at Zebdani near the Syrian-Lebanese border. The Duma camp was said to be a base of the Palestine Liberation Front, whose members had carried out widespread raids against Israel before the war. Trucks of the Palestine Battalion of the Iraqi army, stationed in Jordan, were said to have moved the saboteurs from Syria to Jordanian territory near the Jordan River.

Syrian Foreign Min. Ibrahim Makhous had denied Sept. 26 that Syria was involved in the outbreak of anti-Israeli guerrilla attacks. In a note circulated to foreign diplomatic representatives in Damascus, Makhous charged that Israel had accused Syria "to prepare world public opinion for launching new Israeli aggression" against the Arabs. Makhous' remarks followed statements by Israeli officials earlier in the week that the Arab terrorists should be fought "not only on Israeli soil but at the source."

Terror Base Wiped Out. Israeli forces Dec. 7, 1967 wiped out an Arab terrorist base in a cave near the west-bank town of Nablus. Army, border police and security personnel killed 6 Arabs, captured an undisclosed number of prisoners and seized a cache of arms that included Soviet and Chinese Communist weapons.

The Jordanian government charged Dec. 8 that the Israelis Dec. 7 had expelled 200 Jordanians of the Nuseirat tribe from the west bank near Jericho to the east bank of Jordan. Saleh Nazhan, muktar of the tribe, told Jordanian authorities that prior to their eviction, the Israelis had destroyed almost all of the victims' homes, the local school and a mosque and had killed several men. The Israelis claimed the raid was in retaliation for the inhabitants' hiding of Arab saboteurs, Nazhan said.

Arab Terror Ring Smashed. Israeli officials announced Dec. 21 the smashing of an Arab attempt to revive a widespread sabotage campaign against Israeli control of the west bank.

Israeli military authorities said that 54 Arab suspects had been seized and that 2 had been shot in a roundup that had started in Ramallah Dec. 15. Subsequent arrests were carried out in Jenin, Nablus and East Jerusalem. The 2 slain Arabs were killed in an exchange with Israeli security forces while resisting arrest in the Beit Haran area near Latrun.

The Israeli newspaper *Maariv* reported Dec. 22 that the 54 captured Arabs had confessed to receiving orders to stir up trouble in East Jerusalem and Bethlehem during Christmas observances.

Israel Battles Raiders. Israeli authorities Mar. 7, 1968 reported the seizure of 2 suspected Al Fatah commanders in a round-up of Arab infiltrators Mar. 2–4. The search followed the slaying Mar. 1 of an Israeli Druse in Abu Ghosh, a village west of Jerusalem. The 2 alleged Al Fatah leaders were identified as William Naguib Nasser, arrested in Jerusalem Mar. 3, and Kamal Nammer.

Israeli officials said that Nasser, whom they described as the highest-ranking Al Fatah officer caught so far, had trained terrorists in Algeria and West Germany, then had become a terrorist instructor in Syria. After his capture, the Israelis said, Nasser helped the Israelis capture Nammer and other terrorists. In addition to Nasser and Nammer, 15 alleged terrorists were seized, and 2 alleged terrorists were slain. Israeli security forces also captured several arms caches near Ramallah and Hebron and in the Gaza Strip.

The Defense Ministry had reported Mar. 3 that Israeli troops had killed 35 of about 50 Arab infiltrators trying to cross the Jordan River to the west bank in the previous 10 days. 5 had been slain Feb. 23 4 miles north of the Allenby Bridge, near Jericho; an Israeli statement said they carried sabotage equipment and Russian and Chinese submachineguns.

Israeli Reprisals. The Israeli military practice of blowing up the homes of suspected Arab terrorists was extended Mar. 6 to East Jerusalem, the former Jordanian sector of the city annexed by Israel after the June 1967

war. The action was deplored by Jerusalem Mayor Teddy Kollek.

The building blasted by explosives was the residence of Kamal Nammer, a suspected Al Fatah terrorist who had been captured Mar. 3. The structure was destroyed and several nearby homes in the Arab quarter were heavily damaged. Kollek and his aides visited the neighborhood Mar. 7, apologized for the incident and offered immediate compensation for the damage.

UAR Aids Guerrillas. A report from Cairo Apr. 12 said the UAR had begun to help Arab guerrillas attacking Israel by giving them arms, training and intelligence information.

The report followed a statement Apr. 10 in which UAR Pres. Gamal Abdel Nasser had declared that Egypt was "fully prepared to support, train and arm the Palestine resistance movement because it is part of the battle for destiny."

In its first broadcast, Al Fatah said May 11, 1968 that its objective was to free all of Palestine and not only to terminate Israeli occupation of Arab areas seized in June 1967. The announcement, apparently beamed from Cairo, said that Al Fatah would broadcast an hour a day and direct its messages largely at Palestinian Arabs under Israeli rule.

The Palestine National Council, consisting of the Palestine Liberation Organization, Al Fatah and a number of smaller Arab guerrilla groups, held its first meeting in Cairo July 10 to plan a coordinated strategy against Israel. UAR Labor Min. Kamal Rifaat told the conferees that the "Arab nation rejects defeat and demands victory." "You have chosen to wage a holy war of liberation," he declared.

Israeli Attacks in Jordan

Israeli troops and planes made several attacks on targets in Jordan during 1968 in what was described as operations against infiltrators and terrorist bases.

Israeli Raid in Jordan. A force of about 15,000 Israeli troops entered Jordan Mar. 21 and carried out a day-long massive retaliatory raid against alleged Arab terrorist bases used for guerrilla attacks on Israel. Jordanian army troops also entered the fray and clashed with the Israelis. Israeli Premier Levi Eshkol said the operations were designed to forestall an expected "new wave of [Arab] terror" against Israel. The UN Security Council convened in emergency session Mar. 21 and unanimously adopted Mar. 24 a resolution condemning Israel.

The Israeli raid, the first major ground thrust into Arab territory since the June 1967 war, was spearheaded by armor, paratroop drops and air strikes. The major assault was directed primarily at an Arab *fedayeen* (commando) camp at Karameh, 3 miles east of the Jordan River, and at nearby Shune, north of the Dead Sea. Another Israeli force crossed the Jordan River south of the Dead Sea to strike at suspected Arab guerrilla bases in the Jordanian towns of Safi and Dakal.

Israeli and Jordanian authorities both claimed victory and gave conflicting versions of the number of casualties and damage inflicted. According to the Israelis: "At least 150 saboteurs were killed, and there were substantial Jordanian army losses. Israeli casualties were 21 killed and 70 wounded" (a revised Israeli report Mar. 23 said: 23 Israelis had been killed, and 3 Israelis were missing; 138 Arabs had been taken prisoner, and nearly 1,000 weapons, mostly of Soviet and Chinese Communist make, had been seized). About 30 Jordanian tanks were hit and 2 captured. 6 Israeli armored vehicles were hit. Terrorist bases and buildings, and other installations were destroyed in both areas, and Jordanian artillery had been demolished. One Israeli plane was downed by Jordanian gunfire, but it crash-landed in Israeli territory and the pilot was saved.

Before withdrawing from Jordanian territory, an Israeli force occupied Karameh, searched its houses for terrorists and blew up several installations.

Jordan's account of the fighting, as given in various army communiqués and broadcasts by Amman radio: 20 Jordanian soldiers were killed and 65 wounded. 15 Jordanian civilians were slain by the Israelis at Shimat Nimrin, 7 miles east of the Allenby Bridge, the Israelis' deepest penetration into Jordan. 30 Arab commandos in Karameh were killed. Israeli forces suffered more than 200 casualties, including more than 100 killed. Jordanian forces destroyed 45 Israeli tanks and 50 other vehicles and downed 5 Israeli planes. Israeli forces, pursued by Jordanian troops, retreated to the occupied west bank after having "abandoned equipment."

It was reported Mar. 22 that the Arab commandos, believed to be members of the Al Fatah terrorist organization, had returned to their Karameh base following the withdrawal of the Israeli troops. According to the commandos' version of the fighting: The Israelis had first tried to cross the Jordan River by throwing up a temporary bridge opposite Karameh, but Jordanian artillery destroyed the span. The Israeli force then employed a pincer movement, crossing the Allenby Bridge and the Damiya Bridge to the north. The southern column was the first to reach Karameh, but by then the commando force had withdrawn to the hills because their ammunition was running low. Another Israeli unit of 400–500 men landed by helicopter about ½ mile east of the Karameh camp and engaged the commandos. More than 100 of the Israelis were killed.

In an address to the Knesset (parliament), Eshkol Mar. 21 justified Israel's attack on Jordan. He assailed the Amman government for not having "acted to stem the terrorist acts" against Israel. Eshkol said: "The terrorist bases are well known to the Jordanian government. Members of the gangs appeared openly wearing their uniforms and bearing arms. According to highly authoritative information, a new wave of terror was about to take place. Since political contacts did not bring about cessation of the murders, we had no other choice but to act in self-defense to avert these dangers."

Eshkol noted that since mid-February 6 Israelis had been killed and 44 injured by Arab terrorists. In the latest incident, 2 Israeli adults had been killed and 28 children injured when a school bus had been blown up by a mine Mar. 18 in the Negev desert, 12 miles north of Elath.

King Hussein declared Mar. 23 that his government was not responsible for the security of Israel and therefore would do nothing to inhibit the activities of guerrillas stationed in Jordan.* Commenting on the losses suffered in the Karameh attack, Hussein said 50 Arabs had been killed, but it was "difficult to distinguish" how many were commandos. The Jordanian army death toll was considerably higher than the 20 fatalities first announced since many of the wounded had eventually died, the king said. (Jordanian officials reported later that army fatalities totaled 40.) Hussein said that, according to an Israeli message intercepted by Jordan Mar. 21, the number of Israeli soldiers killed was 73, not 21 as announced by the Israelis.

Artillery Duel on Border. Israeli and Jordanian forces engaged in a 6-hour artillery duel along 85 miles of the Jordan River Mar. 29. The fighting, the 2d major clash on the cease-fire line in 8 days, was marked by Israeli air strikes.

The fighting followed the killing earlier Mar. 29 of 4 Israeli farm workers and the injuring of several others when their tractor ran over a mine near Massada, a communal settlement south of the Sea of Galilee in the Beisan Valley. The incident first led to an exchange of light arms fire nearby between Jordanian and Israeli soldiers across the Jordan River. The fighting intensified as both sides employed artillery and tank guns. Israel claimed that Jordanian shells struck the 5 nearby settlements of Shaar Hagolin, Ashdot Yaakov, Kfar Ruppin, Tel Katzir and Gesher. No casualties were reported. Israeli forces retaliated by carrying out air strikes 7 miles inside Jordan. 4 Jordanian long-range artillery pieces were reported destroyed. The artillery exchanges extended as far south as the Dead Sea. Some Israeli shells struck Karameh, the Arab commando base raided by Israeli troops Mar. 21. Israeli losses were listed at one soldier killed and 8 wounded. One plane was

*An Al Fatah member captured by Israel told reporters in Tel Aviv Mar. 23 that the Jordanian army gave Al Fatah military intelligence and provided covering fire for river crossings but otherwise did not work directly with the guerrillas. The Syrian and Iraqi armies gave Al Fatah most of its help, he said.

downed by Jordanian anti-aircraft fire, but the pilot bailed out safely, and the plane crashed in Israeli territory.

Amman claimed the Israelis had started the fighting with machinegun and tank fire directed at Jordanian positions near the Sea of Galilee. Other Jordanian targets came under Israeli fire from the occupied Golan heights on the Syrian border. Amman communiqués claimed that Jordanian forces had shot down 7 Israeli planes and inflicted heavy losses on Israeli tanks, half-tracks and other vehicles.

'Copter Raid in Jordan. Israeli army authorities reported Apr. 8 that a few dozen Israeli helicopter-borne soldiers had crossed 18 miles into Jordan that day to pursue Arab *fedayeen* infiltrators. All of the guerrillas, "about half a dozen," were killed and the Israelis suffered no casualties, the report said.

According to the Israelis: The guerrillas had been spotted east of the Israeli Negev settlement of Ein Yahav, near the Jordanian border, 35 miles south of the Dead Sea. After firing at a circling Israeli helicopter, the Arabs fled back to Jordan. Several other helicopter patrols joined the chase, and some landed behind the fleeing band to bar their escape. The operation culminated in a gun clash between the Arabs and their pursuers on the cliffs of the Hills of Moab. In addition to wiping out the infiltrators, the Israeli patrol destroyed a granite house used as a terrorist base. The infiltrators were members of the Egyptian 141st Commando Battalion, receiving its orders from the Egyptian embassy in Amman, Jordan. The Israelis found documents telling of imminent attacks against the Israeli Negev towns of Elath, Sdom and Timna.

The Israeli raid followed the killing earlier Apr. 8 of 2 Israeli soldiers and a Bedouin scout when their jeep ran over a mine.

According to Jordan's version of the fighting south of the Dead Sea, an Israeli armored force, supported by helicopters and planes, crossed the cease-fire line following an exchange of artillery and tank fire. But the Israeli raiders were repelled by Jordanian troops and were forced to withdraw to their own territory without "achieving their aims."

Israel's possible use of counter-terrorism was suggested in a statement made Apr. 9 by Maj. Gen. Chaim Bar Lev, Israeli chief of staff. Bar Lev said Israel had not yet "adopted all possible methods against terrorism." "Counter-terrorist activity cannot be excluded, although it would not be the reply par excellence," he said.

Israeli-Jordanian Clashes. An Israeli patrol Apr. 28 killed 13 Arab infiltrators on the occupied west bank in one of the bloodiest encounters since the June 1967 war. The skirmish was one of several fought by Israeli troops with Arab guerrilla raiders and regular Jordanian forces on the west bank and on the Jordan-Israel cease-fire line. As a result of the clashes, the Israeli government Apr. 26 issued one of its sternest warnings to Jordan about possible armed retaliation for the continued incursions into Israeli-held territory.

The Apr. 28 clash occurred several miles north of Jericho in Wadi Auja, a dry river bed that led from the Judean Hills north of Jerusalem to the Jordan River. In addition to the 13 Arabs killed, one was captured and 2 escaped. Israeli authorities reported that 2 Israeli soldiers had been killed and one wounded.

Israeli and Jordanian forces June 4 engaged in an all-day clash along the northern sector of the Jordan River near the Sea of Galilee. The fighting was marked by Israeli air attacks on Jordan.

The clash was described by Amman as the most serious since the Israeli incursion into Jordan Mar. 21. Heavy casualties were reported on both sides.

Israel reported that 3 Israeli farmers in the border area had been killed and 5 wounded. Jordan claimed that 45 Israeli soldiers had been killed or wounded in the day's action, that Jordanian antiaircraft had shot down 4 Israeli planes and that 4 Israeli tanks and 3 artillery positions had been destroyed. Jordan said that Israeli air strikes on Irbid, a Jordanian village 12 miles east of the cease-fire line, had resulted in the killing of 34 civilians and the wounding of 134.

According to Israeli military authorities: The fighting started when Jordanian mortars shelled the Israeli settlement of Kfar Ruppin, in the Beit Shean Valley, about midnight the night of June 3–4. About 11 hours later Jordanians on the east bank opened up with small-arms fire. The Israelis returned the fire. The Jordanians replied with long-range artillery. Jordanian tanks pulled up near Israeli-occupied El Hamma, on the Golan Heights (in Syria), and fired at Israeli targets. Israeli jets attacked Jordanian artillery positions around Irbid until a *de facto* cease-fire went into effect.

According to a Jordanian account of the fighting, as narrated in a complaint filed with UN Security Council Pres. Arthur J. Goldberg of the U.S. by Jordanian Amb. Muhammad H. El-Farra: Israel carried out a "surprise attack" on Jordan about 9 miles south of the Sea of Galilee. The attack opened with machinegun and artillery fire followed by artillery and air strikes on Irbid and surrounding villages. "For the first time the Israelis are using land-to-land rockets, shelling Jordanian villages and the city of Irbid and its suburbs. Several quarters of . . . Irbid were destroyed."

Israeli military officials speculated that the fighting had been started by members of Al Fatah and that regular Jordanian army troops had entered the fighting after the Israelis returned fire.

Israel reported June 22 that its forces had killed 11 Arab guerrillas of an Al Fatah unit near Jericho. One Israeli soldier was killed.

Israelis Battle Guerrillas. Israel reported taking a heavy toll of Arab guerrillas in clashes along the west bank of the Jordan River July 17–28.

The Israelis said their forces killed 13 Arab saboteurs July 17 in a brief engagement northwest of the Dead Sea. One Arab was captured and an Israeli wounded. The guerrillas, who were reported to have crossed the Jordan River from the east bank July 16, carried Soviet assault rifles, bazookas, grenades and explosives.

All 6 members of an Arab guerrilla force were killed July 22 in a clash with an Israeli patrol between the Damiya and Allenby bridges. The slayings brought to 59 the number of Arab guerrillas killed since the beginning of June, according to

Israeli army figures. 2 Israelis were killed and 10 wounded in the engagements.

7 Arab guerrillas, identified as members of Al Fatah, were killed July 26 in a 2-hour clash with Israeli troops near Jericho. 2 Israeli officers—a brigade commander (Col. Arie Regev, 35) and a lieutenant—were killed.

An Israeli patrol killed 2 guerrillas July 28 as it repulsed a guerrilla unit that crossed the Jordan River. Jordanian army guns on the east bank opened fire to provide cover for the retreating infiltration force.

Israelis Raid Jordan. Israeli planes carried out a heavy raid Aug. 4 on Arab guerrilla bases 10 miles inside Jordan. The air strike was followed by an Israeli ground incursion into Jordan Aug. 6 by troops pursuing a band of Arab guerrillas.

Reporting on the Aug. 4 incident, a Jordanian communiqué said: Israeli planes had bombed positions in the vicinity of Salt, about 13 miles northwest of Amman. 23 civilians and 5 soldiers were killed; 76 civilians and 6 soldiers were wounded. One Israeli plane was claimed shot down by ground fire in the Jericho area. (Israel said all of its planes returned safely.) During the 3-hour air strike, Jordanian and Israeli tanks and artillery exchanged fire across the Jordan River. Amman reported that 2 Israeli tanks and 2 artillery positions were destroyed and Israeli forces suffered casualties in the Jericho area.

Gen. Haim Bar-Lev, the Israeli chief of staff, called the air strike a "substantial and unexpected blow to the terrorist organizations. I hope this will help the authorities in Jordan to finally realize that violations of the cease-fire will bring unpleasant consequences." Bar-Lev said he was certain that Al Fatah's 2 bases to the south and west of Salt had been destroyed. He was unable to say how many of the 300–400 guerrillas stationed in the area had been killed in the raid. (The Israeli army said Al Fatah had chosen the mountainous area around Salt as "a substitute base for Karameh," which had been destroyed in a similar Israeli strike Mar. 21. About 12 bases and command posts had been shifted to the Salt area, with the southern sector serving as Al Fatah's command center, the Israelis said.)

Bar-Lev described the air raid as "an answer to 3 violations of the cease-fire per day" by terrorists based in Jordan. According to an army press report, the Arab guerrillas had carried out 98 forays against Israeli territory in July; 3 Israelis and 44 guerrillas were slain in the raids.

In the Israeli ground incursion into Jordan Aug. 6, the first since Apr. 8, helicopter-borne troops intercepted an escaping band of Arab guerrillas, killing 5 and wounding 2. 2 others escaped. The engagement occurred a few miles east of the Israeli settlement of Ein Yahav, about 30 miles south of the Dead Sea. According to Israel, the helicopters began combing the area after the guerrillas had fired 3 bazooka shells into Ein Yahav. No one was injured. The settlement's infirmary, empty at the time, was shattered. After spotting the Arabs escaping in a jeep, the helicopters landed and the Israeli troops destroyed the force. A further search turned up a cave apparently used as a guerrilla base. It contained food, weapons and ammunition. The Israelis returned to their own territory after blowing up the Arab jeep and cave.

An Al Fatah broadcast from Cairo Aug. 8 warned that "Israeli civilians should not hope to be safe if Arab civilians are subjected to genocide" attacks by Israeli troops. Another Arab commando group, the Popular Front for the Liberation of Palestine, also threatened reprisals against Israeli civilians. The front claimed it had set off an explosion in an Israeli bar in Jerusalem in retaliation for the death of Arab civilians in the Israeli attack on Salt.

(The Palestine Liberation Organization had reported Aug. 1 that its commandos that day had killed 6 Israeli soldiers in a rocket attack on a patrol vehicle near the Jordan Valley settlement of Maoz Haiyim. An Israeli army spokesman's account of the incident said one soldier had been killed and 3 wounded in an ambush.)

Israelis Attack in Jordan. Israeli commandos, attacking targets 37 miles inside Jordan Dec. 1, 1968, destroyed 2 bridges in retaliation for infiltration attacks on Israel. The raid precipitated heavy Israeli-Jordanian artillery and aerial bombardments, which continued through Dec. 3. Iraqi troops, stationed in Jordan since the June 1967 war, were involved in the clashes.

The Israelis said the Dec. 1 commando attack centered on targets east of Sodom (Israel), at the southern end of the Dead Sea. The UPI reported that the Israelis had destroyed a highway bridge at Wadi el Abyad, about 60 miles north of Maan, and the Hejazi railway bridge, 6 miles farther north.

An Israeli army spokesman said the raid was in retaliation for 50 Arab infiltration attacks against Israel since the signing of a pact Nov. 16 by Jordanian officials and Arab commandos based in Jordan. The incidents included bazooka and rocket attacks on Israeli civilian settlements and industrial facilities. The heaviest assault took place Nov. 23, when guerrillas, believed to be Al Fatah members, launched 15 rockets against the Sodom potash works.

In a simultaneous engagement Dec. 1, Israeli and Jordanian forces traded the heaviest artillery fire to the north since the June 1967 war. The 5-hour gun duel ended at dawn Dec. 2 with an Israeli air attack on Irbid, about 40 miles north of Amman. At one point, Israeli tanks and artillery fired along a 20-mile front against Iraqi and Jordanian forces as well as at Arab guerrillas. The guerrillas fired rockets, some of which landed in the Israeli settlement of Deganya "A." Jordan said Israeli artillery had shelled the Jordanian towns of El Shuna, Asad, Taiviba and Irbid.

A 3-hour Israeli-Arab artillery duel along the Jordan Valley the night of Dec. 2 was climaxed by a 2d Israeli air strike on targets in Jordan early Dec. 3. The fresh fighting erupted with a coordinated Jordanian-Iraqi artillery barrage along the 25-mile front north of the Israeli-held west bank.

Terrorists Clash With Jordanians

Although the Arab governments gave material as well as verbal support to the guerrilla-commando-terrorist groups attacking Israel, it became obvious that the Arab host countries—primarily Jordan, Syria and Lebanon—were having trouble controlling the often undisciplined armed irregulars. The guerrillas were accused of acting as quasi-governments, levying tribute from citizens of the host country, fighting with police and armed forces of the host country and terrorizing fellow Arabs.

Jordan Quells Commandos. Tension between Jordan and a minor Arab commando group based in Jordan erupted into an open clash between the 2 sides in and around Amman Nov. 3, 1968. At least 25 civilians and 5 soldiers were killed. About 70 persons were arrested.

The dissident commando unit was identified as Kataeb al Nasr (Contingents for Victory), also called Al Saiqah. Its leader, ex-Syrian army officer Taher Dablan, 37, had formed the group in June after he had been expelled from the Palestine Liberation Organization.

The fighting followed the arrest of Dablan Nov. 2 for Kataeb al Nasr's alleged link to a mob attack that day on the U.S. embassy in Amman.

Angered by Dablan's arrest, his followers Nov. 3 ambushed a police car and seized 4 policemen as hostages. 3 of the policemen were reportedly killed. Jordanian security officials then raided Kataeb al Nasr's headquarters in the Wahdat refugee camp outside Amman and seized large supplies of arms. Firing broke out, and many of Dablan's men broke out through a police encirclement. They made their way into Amman, where further fighting ensued. Kataeb al Nasr urged Amman residents to rally to its cause on the ground that the government was out to crush the commando group. In response to the appeal, more than 10,000 persons, including students, commandos and townspeople, staged an antigovernment demonstration Nov. 4. Security forces moved in and suppressed the uprising after a bloody clash.

During the fighting Nov. 4, King Hussein had assailed "phony elements" among the commandos in Jordan. He charged in a broadcast that their target was "not [Israeli] occupied territory but the [Jordanian] east bank itself."

The 2 largest commando groups in Jordan, the Palestine Liberation Organization (PLO) and Al Fatah, agreed to government demands to submit to official checkpoints, to abolish their own checkpoints and to keep their armed followers out of Amman. A smaller commando group, the Popular Front for the Liberation of Palestine (PFLP), rejected the government demands.

At a meeting of Al Fatah, PLO and PFLP representatives in Cairo Nov. 5, the commando groups accused Jordan of attempting to break up the guerrilla forces and to make peace with Israel. An Al Fatah broadcast charged the Jordanian government with staging the Amman unrest Nov. 4 to weaken and discredit the guerrilla fighters.

Jordan's previous confrontation with Kataeb al Nasr (when it was known as Al Saiqah) had occurred following the kidnaping Oct. 7 of rightwing Druse leader Hassan al-Atrash. Suspecting the commando group of having seized Atrash and of having taken him to Damascus, the Jordanian government had established roadblocks on the outskirts of Amman and on roads to the Jordan Valley and the north. Al Fatah had charged that the roadblocks were an excuse to harass the commandos and keep them out of Amman.

Jordan-Commando Pact. A 7-point agreement governing the relations between Jordan and the Arab commando groups operating from Jordan was reached Nov. 16, 1968.

Terms of the agreement (some of which formalized previous government-commando understandings): (1) Commandos were forbidden to carry arms or wear uniforms in Jordanian towns; (2) commandos had no right to search civilian cars; (3) commando vehicles were to carry Jordanian license plates; (4) commandos were to carry identity cards of their organizations; (5) a crime committed by a commando was to be investigated by Jordanian authorities in the presence of a representative of the guerrilla's organization; (6) commandos were forbidden to enlist Jordanians subject to conscription or deserters from Jordan's armed forces; (7) commando-Jordanian government disputes were to be handled

by a council made up of 4 major commando groups based at the Amman headquarters of the Palestine Liberation organization (PLO).

The council's formation had been confirmed in an Al Fatah broadcast Nov. 20. Represented on the council were Al Fatah, PLO, the Popular Front for the Liberation of Palestine and the Syrian Baath-dominated Al Saiqa, also known as Kataeb al Nasr.

(Al Fatah leader Yasir Arafat was elected at a PLO meeting in Cairo Feb. 3, 1969 as chairman of a newly formed PLO executive committee.)

Terrorists Bomb Israeli Targets

Blasts Kill Jews & Arabs. A bomb explosion in the Jewish section of Jerusalem Nov. 22, 1968 killed 12 persons and injured 55. The fatalities comprised 10 Israeli Jews and 2 Arabs.

The blast ripped through Jerusalem's crowded Mahane Yehuda market place, destroying fruit and vegetable stalls and several nearby shops, apartments and automobiles. Police said the explosives were hidden in a car parked in the market place 2 hours before the blast. 500 Arabs were rounded up for questioning; by Nov. 25 all but 30 were released.

One of the Arab commando groups that had carried out raids against Israel —The Popular Front for the Liberation of Palestine—announced Nov. 22 that its members were responsible for the Jerusalem incident. The front said the explosion was "in retaliation for Israeli terrorist actions against our people" in Arab occupied territories.

A bomb exploded in a Jerusalem supermarket Feb. 21, 1969, killing two youths and wounding nine other persons.

Hundreds of shoppers were in the Jerusalem supermarket, during its busiest period, the hours before the Jewish Sabbath, when the bomb exploded. Fifteen minutes after the blast, and after the store had been cleared of customers, another bomb was found on the premises and defused. Among the injured was Maj. Roy Skinner of Australia, a U.N. truce observer.

(A third bomb had been found earlier Feb. 21 in front of the British consulate in East Jerusalem; it was disarmed in a nearby field.)

The Popular Front for the Liberation of Palestine said Feb. 21 that it was responsible for that day's bombing.

A bomb heavily damaged the British consulate in East Jerusalem Feb. 25, 1969.

The blast caused slight injury to a consulate secretary. British officials said they believed Arab guerrillas had decided to attack British targets because of "highly exaggerated" reports that Britain was planning to sell tanks to Israel. The East Jerusalem consulate had been the target of an unsuccessful bomb attack Feb. 21. The Popular Front for the Liberation of Palestine Feb. 25 claimed responsibility for the bombing. The PFLP said it had decided on the attack because of the alleged British decision to supply Israel with tanks.

A bomb exploded in Lydda, Israel Feb. 25, injuring one person. Three Arabs were detained for questioning. One of them was said to have been carrying the bomb on a tricycle and it was believed to have detonated accidentally. The rider was wounded.

The arrest of 80 Arabs on charges of conducting an extensive guerrilla operation against Israel was announced March 5 by Daniel Bareli, the Israeli police chief in Jerusalem. Twenty of those arrested had been seized March 4. Bareli said the group, most of whom were suspected PFLP members, would specifically be charged with the bombings of the Jerusalem supermarket Feb. 21 and of the British consulate in East Jerusalem Feb. 25. Bareli said the group had operated in Jerusalem, the west bank and the Gaza Strip and received instructions from the Egyptian embassy in Amman, Jordan. Among those arrested were Wodet Komeri, a woman, who reportedly had directed the operations, Bashir el-Hirri, a prominent lawyer from the west-bank town of Ramallah, accused of having organized the terrorist network, and Illya el-Khouri, an Arab Anglican priest from Ramallah, who was said to have crossed the Jordan River several times in recent months to contact the ring's leaders in Amman.

A bomb exploded in the cafeteria of the Hebrew University in Jerusalem March 6, wounding 29 Israelis, most of them students. About 200 students were in the room, which was heavily damaged.

In Beirut, two Arab guerrilla groups, the Popular Democratic Front for the Liberation of Palestine and the Popular Front for the Liberation of Palestine (PFLP), claimed credit for the attack.

A branch of the Israeli National Bank in the west-bank town of Al Bireh was damaged by a guerrilla hand grenade earlier March 6. One person was injured.

Israeli security forces March 6 destroyed five Arab houses in East Jerusalem that had been found to contain arms, explosives and other terrorist equipment. After permitting the families to leave, an Israeli demolition squad razed the buildings. Previously, the Israelis had blown up buildings suspected of harboring Arab terrorists. But they were said to have discontinued the practice because of damage to surrounding structures.

Three bombs exploded on a street leading to the Western (Wailing) Wall in Jerusalem June 20. The blasts killed one Arab and wounded five other persons, including two American tourists and an Israeli soldier. At least 20 suspects were arrested.

The Popular Front for the Liberation of Palestine (PFLP) said in Amman June 21 that its members were responsible for the explosions. The PFLP statement said the attack was not aimed at injuring Jewish worshippers "but to remind the world and tourists of the Zionists' barbaric and Nazi-like acts and to warn the enemy to stop these actions."

Gaza Violence. Arab students staged riotous demonstrations in the Israeli-occupied city of Gaza Feb. 2-3, 1969.

The violence was precipitated by the sentencing Feb. 2 of three Arab girls as members of a terrorist group in the Gaza Strip. One received a three-year jail sentence; the two others were given terms of two years each for having served as messengers for terrorist bands. Israeli authorities released the three girls Feb. 3 on the condition that they end their connections with the guerrillas.

About 2,000–3,000 Arab girls, protesting the sentences, poured out of three high schools Feb. 2 and rampaged through the streets of Gaza, blocked traffic and hurled stones, injuring several persons, including an Israeli woman soldier. Israeli troops, armed with nightsticks, drove the rioting girls back to their schools. More than 90 were injured and almost half required hospitalization.

Tensions in Gaza were further heightened Feb. 3 when a grenade, hurled by an unknown assailant into a crowded square, killed two Arab boys (aged 9 and 16) and wounded 10 others.

An Israeli lieutenant was killed June 15 when a terrorist tossed a grenade at his patrol vehicle in Gaza city. Two grenades thrown at Israeli vehicles in Gaza city June 16 and 20 missed their marks and exploded among groups of Arab civilians. One Arab was killed and 21 others were injured in the first incident; another Arab was killed and 16 were wounded in the other attack.

Arabs Attack Planes

A new tactic in the terrorist war on Israel was unveiled in 1968 when Arabs began a series of seizures of Israeli airliners in flight or of attacks on passenger-laden planes on the ground. As time went on, the attacks were not confined to Israeli planes but were directed against aircraft of almost any nationality.

Israeli Plane Hijacked. An Israeli commercial airliner, en route from Rome to Tel Aviv, was hijacked over Italian territory July 23, 1968 by 3 armed members of the Popular Front for the Liberation of Palestine (PFLP). The plane landed in Algiers.

The Algerian government immediately released 19 non-Israeli passengers, who were flown to Paris later July 23 in an Algerian plane. 10 Israelis—4 women passengers, 3 children and 3 of the plane's air hostesses—were released July 27 and were flown to Geneva before going on to Tel Aviv. The Algerian government temporarily held the plane —an El Al Boeing 707 jet—7 crew members and 5 Israeli male passengers.

A PFLP statement issued in Beirut July 23 claimed that members of its "specialized unit" had taken over the Israeli airliner without the advance knowledge of the Algerian government. The front urged Algeria to hold the plane and its Israeli passengers and crew but to release the non-Israelis. PFLP officials said July 24 that the organization had asked the International Red Cross to supervise the exchange of the Israeli crew and passengers in Algiers for captured Palestinian guerrillas imprisoned in Israel.

Algerian Foreign Min. Abdelaziz Bouteflika, arriving in Paris July 24 on a diplomatic visit, denied that his government was "involved, either directly or indirectly" in the hijacking.

Algeria Aug. 31 released the last 5 passengers and 7 crewmen of the Israeli airliner. The plane was released a few hours later and was flown to Rome by a French pilot. The Israelis were flown to Rome in an Italian jet and returned to Israel Sept. 1. The Israeli plane arrived in Israel the same day.

Italy had negotiated with Algerian officials for the release of the Israeli plane.

Israel informed the Red Cross Sept. 2 that it would free 16 convicted Arab infiltrators, captured prior to the June 1967 war, in exchange for the release of the hijacked plane.

A PFLP spokesman Sept. 2 criticized the release of the plane. He said Algeria had not consulted his group.

Plane Attacked in Athens. 2 Arab terrorists attacked an Israeli commercial jetliner in Athens the day after Christmas 1968.

The Israeli jetliner, an El Al Boeing 707 carrying 41 passengers, was attacked at the Athens airport Dec. 26 as it was about to take off on a flight to New York from Tel Aviv. The 2 Arab assailants fired a submachinegun at the plane and its passengers and tossed incendiary grenades at one of the plane's engines, setting it ablaze. One passenger was shot to death and the plane's hostess was seriously injured when she jumped out of the plane with the passengers. Greek police arrested the 2 suspects, identified as Mahab H. Sleiman, 19, of Tripoli, Lebanon and Mahmoud M. Mohamad, 25, a Palestinian Arab refugee. The 2 men had arrived at the Athens airport earlier Dec. 26 on an Air France flight from Beirut. They said they were members of the Syrian-based Popular Front for the Liberation of Palestine (PFLP) and were under orders of a PFLP official in Beirut "to destroy an Israeli plane and kill Jews." Their statement was made to Greek Deputy Premier Stylianos Patakos, who had hurried to the airport to question the captives.

The PFLP Dec. 26 claimed credit for the Athens airport attack. Charging that El Al was no longer "an airline undertaking innocent civilian transport," the statement said that El Al planes, "in secret flights under supervision of the Israeli Defense Ministry," had transferred "air force pilots trained in flying Phantom jets in preparation for a surprise attack and new aggression against the Arab states."

Israeli Transport Min. Moshe Carmel asserted Dec. 26 that Israel could not "relieve the government of Lebanon from responsibility for acts of sabotage organized on Lebanese soil with governmental encouragement."

The Lebanese government Dec. 27 denied Carmel's charge of Lebanese complicity in the Athens airport shooting. The statement said the allegation was an Israeli "attempt to justify its repeated aggressions against Lebanese territory."

The two terrorists were convicted and sentenced by a Greek criminal court March 26, 1970.

Mahmoud Mohammad was sentenced to 17 years and five months, Maher Suleiman to 14 years and three months. Both were convicted of interfering with air traffic, arson and illegal use and possession of explosives. The original charge of premeditated murder against Mohammad, for wielding a machinegun that had killed an Israeli passenger, was revised to a lesser count of manslaughter by negligence.

Israelis Raid Beirut Airport. Helicopter-borne Israeli commandos carried out a one-hour raid on the Beirut International Airport in Lebanon Dec. 28, destroying 13 civilian planes belonging to 3 Arab airlines. The assault was in retaliation for the Athens attack.

According to Lebanese accounts: The attack was carried out by 8 Israeli helicopters. 5 landed at the hangar area and one on a runway, while 2 others hovered overhead. The Israeli commandos destroyed the aircraft by planting explosive charges in the nose-wheel well and the undercarriage-wheel well of each plane.

The 13 planes destroyed were estimated to be worth $43.8 million. 8 of the aircraft belonged to Trans-Mediterranean Airways, Lebanese-owned; 3 to Lebanese International Airways; 2 to Middle East Airlines, 30%-owned by Air France.

The Israelis were under orders to confine their attack to Arab-owned planes and not to inflict casualties. The commandos were reported to have made sure that no passengers were aboard the planes destroyed; aircraft of non-Arab carriers were parked at the airport but none were touched.

A Jerusalem communiqué said all the Israeli helicopters returned safely. An Israeli government announcement on the raid Dec. 28 said that the Arab terrorists who had struck the Israeli jet in Athens had "come from Beirut airport and belonged to the branch of the sabotage organization in Lebanon." The statement warned that "Arab governments that allow the activities of sabotage organizations from their territories must know they bear responsibility for terrorist acts."

In defending the raid, Israeli Premier Levi Eshkol declared Dec. 29 that "on no account can we accept the idea that the waging of war against Israel should be permitted if those who wage it call themselves an organization and not a government."

Lebanese Premier Abdullah Yaffi said Dec. 30 that the Israeli attack on the Beirut airport "has had no effect on our stand regarding the commandos" who operate against Israel. This was interpreted to mean that Lebanon would continue to refuse to adopt a stronger anti-Israeli policy. Yaffi, however, asserted that "we consider commando action as a legitimate and sacred action."

Every people whose ... land has been taken away must resort to every means to get it back."

The Israeli army reported Dec. 30 that Arab commandos had shelled 5 Israeli settlements Dec. 29 in apparent reprisal for the Beirut attack. Al Fatah reported that it already had started "the first rain" of retaliation raids by shelling an Israeli town, Beisan, Dec. 29.

Israel reported that 2 civilians were killed Dec. 31 when Arab guerrillas from Lebanon shelled the Israeli settlement of Kiryat Shmona in the upper Galilee.

Lebanese authorities denied that rocket fire against Israel had come from Lebanon. Al Fatah asserted that its forces had fired on Kiryat Shmona from inside Israel.

UN Censures Israel. The UN Security Council Dec. 31 approved by 15-0 vote a resolution condemning Israel for the attack on the Beirut airport, favoring Israeli compensation for the damage inflicted and hinting at possible sanctions if such assaults were renewed. The Council had convened Dec. 29 at the request of Lebanon and Israel.

After the vote, Israeli delegate Yosef Tekoah assailed the resolution, which, he said, "fails to take account of Israel's rights under the cease-fire, disregards the rights of its citizens to be free from Arab attacks, overlooks and slights the Israeli dead and wounded, is an affront to the basic values of the United Nations." Referring to Soviet delegate Yakov A. Malik's criticism of Israel's actions, Tekoah said: "As long as this Arab war of aggression against Israel continues, Israel will insist on its right to defend itself in the best way it finds it necessary, whether the guardians of international law in Moscow are pleased or not."

Malik earlier had denounced other Council members for refusing to invoke sanctions under Chapter VII of the Charter.

In explaining his vote on the resolution, U.S. representative J. R. Wiggins said that although the U.S. delegation had supported it, the American representatives dissociated themselves "from the sweeping generalizations, ... the reckless attacks upon Israel [in Council debate Dec. 29 and 30] for alleged policies and acts having nothing to do with the episodes properly before us."

In debate Dec. 30, Israeli delegate Tekoah asserted that the Arab terrorist attack on the Israeli plane in Athens "was of the same character" as Arab assaults against Israeli territory. Since the Arabs were defeated by Israeli forces in 1967, they had engaged in a policy of "bleeding Israel by murder, of the innocent and defenseless, by terror and sabotage," Tekoah said. The Athens incident left Israel with no alternative but to take action "against this menace threatening to bring chaos and catastrophe to international life" Tekoah said. He chided world governments for having remained "strangely silent" in the face of the Athens incident and recalled how these governments had "remained passive when Israeli shipping was barred from the Suez Canal for 20 years."

Lebanese ex-Foreign Min. Fouad Boutros, who had flown to New York to attend the Council meeting, said Israel was not justified in raiding Lebanon in retaliation for the attack on the Israeli plane in Athens. "Lebanon can certainly not be held responsible for acts which were committed outside its territory by Palestinian refugees whose intent was not known to Lebanon, and whose acts were due to the fact that they were refugees thrown out by Israel."

In a message Dec. 30 to Lebanese Pres. Charles Helou, Pope Paul VI deplored the Israeli attack and expressed hope that Lebanon would not be "drawn along the path of violence."

Israeli Religious Affairs Min. Zerah Warhaftig Dec. 31 criticized the pope for his expressions of sympathy to Lebanon over the loss of its planes while saying nothing about the "murder of innocent Jews" by Arab terrorists. Warhaftig particularly cited the Arab attack on a Jerusalem marketplace Nov. 22 in which 13 Israelis were killed. Speaking at a memorial service for the 6 million Jews killed by the Nazis, Warhaftig said: "We must learn the lesson from what happened during the period of genocide, not only concerning those who perpetrated the crime but those who kept their peace and raised no voice in protest.

The policy of silence continues in our day."

Plane Attacked in Zurich. An Israeli El Al Boeing 720 commercial airliner with 17 passengers and 10 crewmen was attacked Feb. 18, 1969 by four Arab terrorists with submachine guns as it was about to take off from the airport at Zurich, Switzerland.

Three passengers and three crewmen were injured in the attack. An Israeli security guard aboard the plane jumped out and shot and killed one of the assailants. The three other terrorists, including a woman, were captured immediately by Swiss policemen and airport personnel. The Arabs had fired 60 bullets at the plane and also hurled three incendiary grenades, which fell short.

A statement issued Feb. 18 by the Popular Front for the Liberation of Palestine (PFLP) at its headquarters in Amman, Jordan, claimed responsibility for the attack. The PFLP said the raid was in retaliation for what it called Israeli acts of torture and brutality against "unarmed and innocent civilians in occupied Arab territory." The statement said the raid was in accordance with PFLP policy to track down and strike the El Al fleet, which it called a military arm of Israel.

The PFLP identified the attackers as all Palestinians: Ammah Ahmed Dahbour, the woman, and Ibrahim Tewfik, Mohammed Abu el Haja and Abdel Mohsen Hassan. Hassan was the one killed.

Israeli Foreign Minister Abba Eban asserted that the raid "demonstrates the character of the terrorist organizations which the president of Egypt [Gamal Abdel Nasser] praised unreservedly only a few days ago." "There is no doubt," Eban said, "that the executors of this act of terrorism as well as their masters drew encouragement from the climate of forgiveness shown to them after the attack on the El Al plane at Athens airport." He recalled that the UN resolution condemning Israel for its retaliatory raid on the Beirut airport "did not devote a single word of condemnation to the Athens attack."

The Israeli government's ministerial-level Security Committee held a four-hour meeting Feb. 19 on the crisis resulting from the Zurich attack.

A statement drawn up at the meeting was delivered later in the Knesset (parliament) by Communications Minister Moshe Carmel. Carmel warned the Arabs that Israel "retains the moral right and the operational ability to take any necessary means of protection, whenever required to break the strength of those scheming against us and our planes and to secure the free aerial traffic of Israel's air routes." "Compliance [by Arab government] with hijacking and with scheming against and assault upon our air routes will cause serious damage to all, including the Arab states," Carmel said.

Carmel linked Beirut to the Zurich attack, to the Arab commando assault on an Israeli airliner in Athens Dec. 26, 1968 and to the hijacking of an Israeli commercial plane July 23, 1968. "Information at our disposal," Carmel said, indicated that plans for the three incidents had been plotted in Lebanon and that the raiders had left from Beirut for each attack.

Support for the Zurich raiders was expressed Feb. 20 by the Cairo newspaper Al Ahram, which said the attack "proved that the will of the resistance will not falter despite all the enemy's counterblows." In further support of the Arab guerrillas, Al Ahram disclosed that the Egyptian government would provide health insurance for the commandos and their families. Under the plan, wounded or sick Arab commandos would be flown without charge to Egyptian hospitals "if they are unable to obtain treatment in Jordanian medical institutions."

Two newspapers in Beirut Feb. 20 criticized the commando raid in Zurich. One, the conservative Al Jarida, wrote that "loyalty to commando activity prompts us to say that this raid at Zurich has been an embarrassment to the commandos. It would have been better from the beginning to leave civil aviation out of the battle." Al Amal, journal of Lebanon's Phalangist party, said that "no matter how daring and courageous this attack is said to have been, there is no doubt that it exposes the legality and integrity of commando activity to a challenge, and will provide Israel with a golden opportunity to spread her propaganda against the Arab cause."

The Soviet Communist Party newspaper Pravda Feb. 27 defended the Arab commando attacks on Israeli airliners as acts "carried out by patriots defending their legal right to return to their homeland." At the same time, the newspaper assailed Israeli reprisal raids for these attacks as "acts of undisguised aggression."

A court in Winterthur, Switzerland Dec. 22 convicted and sentenced the three Arab terrorists to 12 years in prison on a charge of murder.

Switzerland sent notes Feb. 28 to Jordan, Syria and Lebanon, protesting against the attack on the Israeli plane.

The notes called on the three Arab governments to take measures "to prevent any new violations of Swiss territory." According to a Swiss Foreign Ministry communique issued in Berne, the three surviving Arab raiders had told Swiss investigators that they had been "trained in Jordan and some of them left Syria to carry out their attack in Zurich."

U.S. Jet Hijacked to Syria. A U.S. Trans World Airlines passenger jet, en route from Rome to Athens and Tel Aviv, was hijacked over southern Italy Aug. 29, 1969 by two armed Arabs and was forced to fly to Damascus, Syria. Moments after the plane landed, the cockpit was heavily damaged by a bomb that had been planted by the hijackers. Warned of the impending blast, the passengers jumped out of an emergency exit minutes before the explosive device went off.

The plane carried a crew of 12 and 101 passengers, including six Israelis. The others were mostly Americans, Greeks and Italians. The Syrians, holding all six of the Israelis, freed 105 passengers and crewmen Aug. 30; most of them were flown to Athens and Rome on an Italian plane. Four of the Israelis, all women, were released Sept. 1 and were flown back to Israel via Athens. The two remaining Israelis, both men, were held in custody.

The Popular Front for the Liberation of Palestine (PFLP), which claimed responsibility for the hijacking, declared in a communique from Cairo Aug. 30 that the two Israeli men would be held hostage in Damascus for "the release of Syrian comrades in Israeli prisons."

The two hijackers, PFLP members, were identified as Leila A. Khaled, a 20-year-old woman, and Selim al-Eisawi, about 30. Both were taken into Syrian custody after the landing in Damascus. Rome police said the two had come from Beirut Aug. 28.

Seizing control of the plane shortly after it took off from Rome, the hijackers had told the occupants that "the Che Guevara Commando Unit of PFLP" had taken command of the flight. They announced that "among you is a passenger responsible for the death and misery of Palestinian children, women and men, on behalf of whom we are carrying out this operation. This assassin will be brought before a Palestinian revolutionary court." The statement did not identify the accused Israeli official.

U.S. Secretary of State William P. Rogers expressed hope Aug. 29 that Syria would not "associate itself with this irresponsible act and will take immediate steps to arrange the release of the aircraft, its crew and its passengers."

Rogers Aug. 30 deplored Syria's "forcible detention of some of the innocent civilian passengers." He said the U.S. was "astonished that a government [Syria], which is a member of the United Nations, having its own international airline and obviously benefitting from and dependent upon the freedom and safety of air travel, would choose to condone and associate itself with this act of piracy."

The International Federation of Air Line Pilots Associations (IFALPA) voted Sept. 1 to call a 24-hour worldwide strike against airlines manned by its 44,000 pilot members unless Syria released the two Israeli passengers.

IFALPA said that the organization "urgently calls upon the U.N. to . . . secure the immediate release of the two passengers . . . and, further, the imposition of suitable punishment on the hijackers." The detention of the two Israelis and the failure to prosecute the hijackers gave "overt encouragement to further criminal acts of this nature," the statement said.

Leila Khaled and Selim al-Eisawi, the two hijackers, were freed by the Syrian government Oct. 13.

The two Israelis, whom Syria had held as hostages, were exchanged by Syria Dec. 5 for 13 Syrian prisoners in Israel.

The two Israelis freed Dec. 5 were Hebrew University Prof. Shlomo Samueloff and Salah Muallem. They returned to Israel via Athens, flying first to the Greek capital on the TWA plane, which had been repaired following the bomb damage it had suffered during the hijacking.

Centers Bombed in Europe. Arab youths Sept. 8, 1969 hurled bombs at the Israeli El Al Airlines office in Brussels, Belgium and tossed hand grenades at the Israeli embassies in The Hague, Netherlands and in Bonn, West Germany.

A spokesman for the Popular Front for the Liberation of Palestine (PFLP) in Amman said the coordinated attacks were carried out by teen-age members of the "Young Tigers" of the "Ho Chi Minh Section" of the PFLP. Four persons were slightly injured in the Brussels incident—three El Al employes and a passerby. Police arrested two Arab youths. No one was injured in the embassy blasts. Two had grenades, thrown at the rear of the embassy in Bonn, exploded under the window of Ambassador Asher ben Nathan. One Arab youth was arrested.

A PFLP spokesman said Sept. 9 that its forces planned an all-out war against Israeli commercial interests around the world and warned travelers not to use Israeli planes or ships. The spokesman said the embassies had been bombed because they "are the centers of espionage and collection points for mercenaries and immigrants to our occupied Palestine." The Hague and Bonn were singled out because Israeli pilots had been trained to fly the newly-acquired U.S. Phantom jets in the Netherlands and West Germany, the statement said.

A bomb planted by Arab terrorists had injured two persons Aug. 25 at the London office of Zim, the Israeli shipping company. PFLP leader George Habbash warned in Amman Aug. 29 that other Jewish-owned firms in London faced similar assaults.

El Al Office Bombed in Athens. Two Jordanian members of an Arab commando group tossed a hand grenade into Israel's El Al airline office in Athens Nov. 27, wounding 15 persons and causing heavy damage. One of the injured, a 2-year-old Greek boy, died Nov. 29. The other injured were three Americans, 10 Greeks and a Briton employed by El Al.

The Jordanians were seized and admitted their guilt. The two, Elie Karabetian, 23, and Mansur Seifeddin Mourad, 21, were formally charged in Athens Criminal Court Nov. 28 with "attempted premeditated murder."

The Palestine Popular Struggle Front, an Arab guerrilla organization based in Amman, Jordan, claimed responsibility for the attack.

Greek Premier Stylianos Patakos condemned the attack Nov. 28 as a "cowardly act by unscrupulous criminals." His statement followed an Israeli protest to the Greek government contending that its failure to repudiate the first Arab armed attack on an Israeli jet airliner in in 1968 had encouraged the Nov. 27 incident. Israeli sources said Nov. 28 that Israeli officials had warned Greek authorities of a possible bombing by Arab terrorists against the El Al office in Athens but said the Greeks had taken no precautions.

Arab Hijacking Thwarted. Greek police Dec. 21, 1969 arrested three Arabs, including a young woman, suspected of planning to hijack a U.S. Trans World Airlines passenger jet at the Athens airport.

They were seized as they were about to board the plane, bound from Tel Aviv for Rome and New York, after a TWA clerk became suspicious. A subsequent search revealed that the trio possessed two guns, three hand grenades and mimeographed announcements that the plane was being seized by the Popular Front for the Liberation of Palestine (PFLP). One of the suspects, Issam Doumidi, 18, was said to have confessed that he and his colleagues planned to hijack the aircraft to Tunis, evacuate the passengers and then blow it up "to warn the Americans to stop providing air communications with Israel."

Attack in Munich.

Three Arab terrorists Feb. 10, 1970 killed one Israeli and wounded 11 other persons in a grenade attack on a bus and lounge at an airport in Munich, West Germany. The three assailants were arrested and charged with murder.

The Israeli was killed by one of the grenades thrown onto an airport bus that 19 passengers of an El Al plane had boarded to return to the airliner from the terminal. The plane had landed earlier on its way from Tel Aviv to London.

Two of the guerrillas had boarded the bus with the others and ordered the driver at gunpoint to open the door before it pulled out. The third Arab outside hurled a grenade into the vehicle when the bus driver tried to drive away. The Arab then threw another grenade into the lounge where the remaining passengers were waiting to return to their plane.

Police identified the assailants as Mohammed el-Hanafi, an Egyptian, and Rahman Saleh Abder and Mohammed Hadidi, both Jordanians. Police said they had flown into Munich airport earlier Feb. 10 from Paris. During the attack, Hanafi's right hand was almost blown off by a grenade. His arm was later amputated. Abder was wounded when he crashed through a skylight attempting to flee.

Responsibility for the Munich attack was claimed Feb. 11 by two guerrilla groups in Amman, Jordan—the Popular Front for the Liberation of Palestine and the smaller Action Organization for the Liberation of Palestine. An Action spokesman said, "We did not intend any harm to these Israelis, . . . but intended" to capture them "in exchange for some Palestinian commando captives" held by Israel.

The Action statement was confirmed in Bonn Feb. 12 by Bavarian Interior Minister Bruno Merk, who said Munich police concluded that the three Arabs had originally planned to hijack the Israeli plane. Merk said the police based their findings on two texts of Arab commando orders discovered at the airport lounge.

Israel-bound jet crashes.

A Swissair passenger plane bound from Zurich to Israel crashed after takeoff Feb. 21, 1970, killing all 47 persons aboard, including 14 Israelis and six Americans. An Arab guerrilla group at first claimed responsibility for the crash, but another group later denied Arab involvement. The Swiss government Feb. 22 officially cited sabotage as the suspected cause of the incident.

The Swiss plane, enroute to Tel Aviv, was carrying 38 passengers and a crew of nine when it crashed near Wurenlingen 15 minutes after takeoff. The aircraft was returning to Zurich after the pilot reported an explosion aboard, apparently in the rear luggage compartment. Smoke from the resultant fire filtered into the crew's compartment, obscuring the pilot's vision, and he crashed.

A communique read Feb. 23 by Swiss President Hans-Peter Tschudi said it was not yet possible to "draw conclusions of the causes of the catastrophe." The chief of the Zurich crime laboratory, however, said he was "already convinced it was a bomb."

The Arab claim of credit for the crash was issued in Beirut Feb. 21 by a spokesman for the Popular Front for the Liberation of Palestine-General Command. Its alleged attack on the aircraft was said to be its first operation abroad.

The denial of Arab connection with the incident was announced Feb. 23 by the unified command of Palestinian guerrilla organizations, which comprised 10 Arab guerrilla groups based in Jordan. The statement, broadcast from Cairo by Al Fatah, the largest of the units, said an investigation had shown "beyond a shadow of a doubt" that none of the commando groups had anything to do with the incident. The statement added: "The [Arab] revolution strongly condemns such barbaric action. No commando contingent would have carried out such action."

Al Fatah leader Yasir Arafat said in Amman Feb. 27 that "the unified command of the commando organizations is now seriously reviewing the entire question of attacks on international airlines." Arafat, however, again denied Arab involvement in the incident, saying that "the Palestine revolution's policy is against endangering all civilians wherever they are."

Swiss authorities investigating the crash reported March 3 that they had found parts of an altimeter in the wreckage of the plane. They said that this altimeter had probably set off the explosion that caused the crash. Meanwhile, police in Frankfurt, West Germany reported March 3 that a Feb. 21 explosion aboard an Austrian Airlines plane had also been set off by an altimeter. Nobody was injured in the Austrian Airlines incident.

(Police had arrested three armed Arabs at the Munich, West Germany airport Feb. 17, thwarting a possible attempt to hijack an Israeli airliner. The three Arabs —two Iraqis and a Jordanian—arrived in Munich aboard a Yugoslav plane from Paris enroute to Belgrade. Acting on the pilot's suspicions, police seized the Arabs and found several pistols in their luggage and two statements indicating they planned to hijack an El Al plane. Police said the leaflets identified the men as members of an Arab commando group.)

Airline curbs—Several European airlines suspended cargo flights to Israel Feb. 22. They were Swissair, Air France, Austrian Airlines and Royal Dutch Airlines. British Overseas Airways Corp. and British European Airways imposed a 48-hour ban on all freight service to Israel. BOAC continued to accept mail bound for Israel. Olympic Airways of Greece announced Feb. 23 a "temporary suspension" of cargo and mail deliveries to Israel.

Aharon Remez, Israel's ambassador to Britain, criticized the flight restrictions of BOAC and BEA in a letter to the two carriers Feb. 22. He said their action "can only be interpreted as a capitulation to intimidation and encouragement to continue air piracy and indiscriminate attacks against airlines of all nationalities." The British government came in for attack in the House of Commons Feb. 23 for permitting the two airlines to curb flights to Israel.

■Ground crews at London's airport refused Feb. 24–25 to service airlines of eight Arab countries and Israel's El Al airline for safety reasons. British Overseas Airways Corp. and British European Airways, which had suspended freight and mail service to Israel Feb. 22, lifted the ban Feb. 26. Other airlines that had imposed similar restrictions eased them, but Lufthansa of West Germany continued the curbs. Swissair announced that it would resume mail and cargo deliveries to Israel March 5.

Arabs hijack 4 planes. Members of the Popular Front for the Liberation of Palestine hijacked three jet airliners bound for New York from Europe Sept. 6, 1970 and diverted them to the Middle East. The attempted seizure of a fourth, an El Al plane bound from Amsterdam, was thwarted when security guards aboard the aircraft shot and killed one hijacker and wounded his companion. The plane then made an unscheduled landing in London and later flew on to New York. The wounded hijacker, held by British police, was identified as Leila Khaled, who had been involved in the hijacking of a TWA 707 to Syria in 1969 and who had been released by the Syrians.

The other planes seized were: a Swissair DC-8, bound from Zurich, with 155 passengers and crew; a TWA Boeing 707 from Frankfurt, with 151 passengers and crew; and a Pan American World Airways 747 jumbo jet, bound from Amsterdam with 152 passengers and a crew of 17. The Swissair and TWA planes were flown to what was described as a "revolution airport" in the desert at Zerqa, Jordan. The Pan Am plane was first flown to Beirut and after refueling, flew to Cairo, where the aircraft was blown up on the runway minutes after the passengers and crew were evacuated. The passengers were later flown to Rome on another plane.

The PFLP held the occupants of the two planes in Jordan as hostages for imprisoned commandos in Israel, Great Britain, Switzerland and West Germany. The Popular Front warned that it would blow up the two planes with its passengers if the guerrillas, jailed for attacks involving planes, were not freed by 10 p.m. (New York Time) Sept. 9.

Switzerland and West Germany at first agreed to meet the commando demands to release six Arab guerrillas held in the two countries but reversed their decisions Sept. 8 in favor of joint international efforts to negotiate the passengers' release.

The guerrillas removed 127 passengers from the two planes in Jordan, mostly women and children, and housed them in two hotels in Amman. A commando spokesman said they were free to leave Amman. The remaining passengers on the two aircraft, all males, were of American, Israeli, British and West German nationality. The planes were surrounded by the commandos and by an outer ring of Jordanian army troops, including more than 50 tanks and armored cars.

A PFLP spokesman in Beirut said Sept. 6 that the TWA and the Pan Am planes had been seized "to give the Americans a lesson after they supported Israel all these years" and in retaliation for the U.S. peace initiative in the Middle East. The spokesman said the Swissair hijacking was in reprisal for the sentencing of three terrorists for their 1969 attack on a plane in Zurich.

The Brussels newspaper Le Soir had reported Sept. 5 the interception by amateur radio operators of a message from Interpol, the international police organization, saying that a Palestinian commando force was on its way from Beirut to Europe. El Al officials in Amsterdam Sept. 6 refused to allow onto the plane whose hijacking was attempted later that day two men holding Senegalese passports. When El Al informed Pan American Airways that suspected hijackers were aboard its 747 jumbo jet, ground controllers warned the captain, who searched the two men but found nothing. They had hidden weapons under their seats. (According to the New York Times Sept. 13, all hijackings carried out by the PFLP since July 1968 were directed by Dr. Wadi Haddad, second in command of the PFLP.)

International efforts were begun Sept. 8 to seek the release of the passengers held in Jordan. Meanwhile, security was tightened at airports around the world in the wake of bomb threats against planes and in an attempt to prevent further plane seizures.

Meanwhile, another plane, a British Overseas Airways Corp. (BOAC) VC-10 jet, was seized Sept. 9. It was hijacked after takeoff from Bahrein, a stop on its regular Bombay-London route. The VC-10, with 105 passengers and a crew of ten, was ordered to land at Beirut for fuel and to pick up a woman commando. Following orders relayed by commandos at the Beirut control tower radio, the plane circled southern Lebanon and was flown to the desert airstrip near Amman later Sept. 9.

The PFLP said Sept. 9 in Beirut that the VC-10 and those aboard would be hostages for the release of Leila Khaled, the commando woman jailed in London after her capture during the abortive hijacking attempt on the El Al 707 Sept. 6.

The U.S., Britain, Switzerland and West Germany agreed to joint action by working through the International Committee of the Red Cross. Three Red Cross officials, named by the four governments as a liaison group, arrived in Amman to confer with officials of the Popular Front for the Liberation of Palestine to seek release of the hostages.

U.S. Secretary of State William P. Rogers met in Washington Sept. 8 with ambassadors of 10 Arab countries. A spokesman for the group, Kuwaiti Ambassador Talat al Ghoussein, said after the meeting that the hijackings "do not serve the cause of the Palestinian people." He said the Arab governments would "try to contact the guerrillas and convince them of this."

The Egyptian newspaper Al Ahram asserted Sept. 8 that the hijacking of the four airliners was harmful to the guerrillas' cause. "One of the main goals of the battle is to gain world public opinion on the side of the Palestinian struggle and not to lose it," Al Ahram said. "It is evident that the attack on international civil aviation," the newspaper said, "does not encourage world feeling of solidarity with the Palestinian cause." Another Egyptian newspaper, Al Akhbar, also expressed opposition to the commandos' action Sept. 9, asserting that international reaction "reflects the denunciation and disgust of people against those who carry out such acts."

The TWA, Swissair and BOAC planes were blown up by the terrorists at the "revolution airport" in Jordan Sept. 12.

The destruction of the planes came at the end of a week of international efforts to secure release of the more than 300 passengers and crewmen seized aboard the jets. The efforts were made more complicated by a renewal of fighting between Jordanian troops and commandos.

Despite the commandos' initial threats to blow up their captives with the planes, none was harmed and most of the passengers and crews were permitted to leave Jordan soon after the jets were destroyed. However, at least 54 passengers and crewmen remained in commando hands Sept. 15, hostages to the demands for the release of commandos held by Great Britain, West Germany, Switzerland and Israel.

The destruction of the three jetliners was carried out by PFLP demolition men 15 minutes after the last of the passengers had left. Passengers reported that after the planes had been blown up, Jordanian armored units, which had surrounded the desert airstrip for the past week, moved to circle the passengers and their armed commando escorts. The troops withdrew, however, after the guerrillas warned that the passengers would die with them if there was any interference with the convoy.

The PFLP spokesman in Amman told a news conference later Sept. 12 that the planes had been destroyed earlier than planned because of "a conspiracy by various imperialist powers to abort this operation." The PFLP originally had set a 10 p.m. Sept. 12 deadline for destruction of the planes if its demands for the release of imprisoned commandos had not been met.

The Palestine Liberation Organization's main coordinating body, the commando Central Committee, suspended the Marxist PFLP from membership Sept. 12 for its destruction of the aircraft. A statement broadcast by the committee said the PFLP had pledged to follow policy guidelines set by the Central Committee Sept. 10 on the release of the jets and passengers,* and that "the Central Committee was surprised by the PFLP's violation of the afore-mentioned decisions."

Relations between the PFLP and the more moderate commando elements heading the Central Committee had been increasingly strained during the week the airliners and passengers were held at the desert airstrip. The committee leadership, especially Yasir Arafat, head of the committee and of the dominant Al Fatah commando organization, had criticized the PFLP's actions, and particularly its failure to move the passengers to Amman, as bringing discredit on the entire commando movement. The situation was made more difficult by the absence of the PFLP leader, Dr. George Habash, who was reported to be visiting Communist China and North Korea to seek new arms supplies.

Israeli Foreign Minister Abba Eban announced Sept. 15 that his government would not be party to a unified agreement with European governments to free Arab prisoners in exchange for the hostages. His statement was understood to have been motivated by the inconclusive nature of Red Cross talks with the commandos. Israel was reported Sept. 11 to have agreed "in principle" to the release of some Arab guerrilla prisoners in exchange for all the hostages and an unspecified number of Israeli prisoners of war.

Eban declared that the Arab terrorists held in Britain, West Germany and Switzerland were common criminals whose sole aim was "assault on the lives of Israelis." "If the three governments involved," he said, "are prepared to consider, out of dire distress, purchasing the liberation of all the hijacked persons by these releases, it must under no circumstances be claimed that the contribution is in any other coin than that of the safety of Israelis."

---

*Commando radio broadcasts from Baghdad, recorded Sept. 11 by the BBC Monitoring Service, gave the following text of the Central Committee policy statement on the hijacked aircraft: "The committee has decided the following: (1) To transfer all the passengers to Amman. . . . (2) To release all passengers of various nationalities with the exception of Israelis of military capacity. These passengers will be released when an official statement is issued by the foreign countries concerned that they are ready to free the Palestinian girl and other fedayeen held . . . in Western Germany, Switzerland and Britain. (3) To release the three aircraft and their crews as soon as the fedayeen in question arrive in Jordan or in any other Arab country. . . . (4) To hold the Zionist passengers of military capacity in Amman until an agreement is reached in the current negotiations with the Red Cross on the release by the Zionist authorities occupying Palestine of a number of Palestinian men and women fedayeen imprisoned in enemy jails."

The remaining hostages were freed by the guerrillas in separate groups Sept. 25, 26 and 29 as part of a deal for the release of Arab terrorists held in Europe.

Sixteen Swiss, German and British nationals, abandoned by their guerrilla captors in the Wahdat refugee camp near Amman, were discovered by Jordanian army troops Sept. 25.

Thirty-two American hostages were released to Red Cross custody Sept. 26, after being held in various places around Amman.

The final six American hostages—three U.S. government officials, two Jewish rabbis and a teacher—were handed over Sept. 29 to the Red Cross, whose Geneva headquarters announced their release.

A Swiss government official Sept. 29 said that Switzerland, Britain and West Germany would release a total of seven Arab guerrillas when the six Americans had safely left Jordan. According to the New York Times Sept. 29, Swiss authorities expected Israel to release as a "humanitarian" gesture 10 captured Lebanese soldiers and two Algerians taken from an airliner Aug. 14. The seven terrorists held by Western governments were freed Sept. 30.

Arab States & Terrorists

UAR Linked to Raiders. An Israeli protest to the U.N. Security Council Feb. 12, 1969 charged that Egypt had "come out openly in full support" of Arab guerrillas in their campaign against Israel.

Israeli delegate Yosef Tekoah asserted in a message to Council President Armand Berard of France that Cairo was organizing and directing the commandos.

Israeli sources reported that between June 6, 1967 and Dec. 31, 1968 Israel had been subjected to 1,288 acts of sabotage and border incidents: 920 in the Jordan-Israel sector, 166 in the Egyptian sector, 37 in the Syrian sector, 35 in the Lebanese sector, 130 in the Gaza Strip. These incidents reportedly had claimed the lives of 234 Israeli soldiers and 47 civilians and had wounded 765 Israeli soldiers and

330 civilians. (Israel's combat fatalities in the June 1967 war had been listed as 759.) According to the Israelis, guerrilla losses were "close to 600 killed" near the truce lines, and hundreds more in the west bank area. About 1,500 guerrillas had been arrested or captured.

Commando Shift to Jordan. Al Fatah leader Yasir Arafat, chairman of the Palestine Liberation Organization's (PLO) executive committee, announced plans to shift a large part of his guerrilla force from Egypt and Syria to Jordan, the Cairo newspaper Al Ahram reported Feb. 6, 1969. The force was said to consist of three battalions: 3,800 men in Egypt, 3,000 in Syria and 1,200 attached to an Iraqi division in Jordan.

Arafat and the PLO's executive committee conferred in Amman Feb. 16 with Jordanian King Hussein. It was believed to be the first meeting between Hussein and a PLO executive chairman.

Al Fatah officials had reported in Cairo Feb. 13 that Israeli Defense Minister Moshe Dayan had sent a message to Arafat informing him that he was ready to meet with the guerrilla leader. Arafat had not responded to the request. The Al Fatah officials said Dayan had released an Arab prisoner to carry the message to Arafat.

Iraq Curbs Commandos. The Lebanese Communist newspaper Al Nida reported April 17, 1969 that Iraq had curbed the activities of commandos operating there.

In a note dated March 31, the secretary of Iraq's ruling Revolutionary Command Council, Chafic al-Daraji, had ordered the Palestine Liberation Organization (PLO) to work through a newly established Iraqi-controlled "Arab Liberation Front." The note complained that PLO members had ignored Baghdad's orders to keep Iraqi military intelligence authorities informed of "matters pertaining to their presence in Iraq." Specifically the PLO was accused of holding unauthorized rallies and fund drives and of establishing contacts with "certain Iraqi political organizations." The note suggested that the PLO establish training camps at Al Rutbah, close to the Jordanian border. It said the guerrillas must not operate outside the battle ground "and must concentrate in Jordan. There is no reason for them to be in Iraq."

In another anti-guerrilla action, the Iraqi radio was reported to have discontinued Al Fatah's daily one-hour program from Cairo.

Ibrahim Bakr, deputy chairman of the PLO's executive committee, said in Beirut April 18 that as a result of meetings he had held with Iraqi leaders in Baghdad, Iraq's restrictions against the commandos could be disregarded. Iraq, he said, had agreed to support increased guerrilla operations.

Lebanon Fights Commando Backers. Lebanese Premier Rashid Karami resigned April 24, 1969 following clashes between security forces and demonstrators demanding an end to government restrictions against guerrillas who sought to use Lebanon as a base for attacks on Israel.

The pro-commando demonstrations were called by the Progressive Socialist Party, the Arab Nationalist Movement, the Baath party and the Communist Party. All were illegal except the Socialists.

Karami submitted his resignation after two ex-premiers, Abdullah Yaffi and Saab Salal, had charged in parliamentary debate April 24 that the government was unduly harsh in suppressing the demonstrators. (A resolution adopted April 25 by the Council of the Ulemas, the Moslem religious teachers, demanded a parliamentary investigation of the "tough methods" used by the government to quell the riots. The group called on the government to release arrested demonstrators and to permit guerrillas in Lebanon to attack Israel.)

Alluding to fears of Israeli retaliation against Lebanon for guerrilla attacks, Karami told parliament: "There are two sides in Lebanon, one saying commando action should be carried out from Lebanon, whatever the circumstances," and another saying "the commandos represent a danger to Lebanon. . . ."

An Al Fatah statement April 25 demanded that the Beirut government permit "freedom of commando activity" in Lebanon and "freedom of movement and supply" in the country.

Pierre Gemayel, head of the Phalangist Party, Lebanon's largest political organization, proposed April 26 that Al Fatah leader Yasir Arafat mediate the dispute between the commandos and the Lebanese government. Expressing fears of Israeli retaliation, Gemayel said of the guerrillas: "Their crossing of Lebanese territory would cost us the occupation of a large part of our southern district," which bordered Israel.

Lebanese Army Post Besieged. Palestinian commandos surrounded an army post in Lebanon April 29, but Lebanese troops lifted the siege April 30. Several men were wounded. The operation was part of Lebanon's drive to prevent guerrilla attacks against Israel.

The attackers were members of Saiqah, the commandos of the Palestinian branch of Syria's Baath party, and were said to be controlled by the Damascus government. The Lebanese army post, situated between the villages of Merj Ayun and Hasbeya, six miles from the Israeli frontier and 11 miles from the Syrian border, was astride a commando infiltration route from Syria. It was reported that since the Israeli attack on the Beirut International Airport Dec. 28, 1968, Saiqah and other guerrilla units, totaling about 1,000 men, had massed on the southern Lebanese border facing Israel. Lebanese police and troops reportedly had sought to curb their operations.

The siege of the army post followed weeks of friction between the government forces and commandos in the area, including a guerrilla attempt to kidnap a police officer. The army garrison's radio appeal for outside help brought armored units to the scene, and the Saiqah men were driven off after some shooting.

Yasir Arafat, leader of Al Fatah, conferred with Lebanese officials in Beirut May 8-12 in an attempt to mediate the dispute between the government and the commandos. Arafat reportedly failed to persuade Beirut to permit the free movement of guerrillas from Lebanon into Syria and to allow them to use Lebanese territory to attack Israel. Lebanon, however, was said to have offered several concessions. It agreed to recognize the "presence" of the commandos in Lebanon.

The commando delegation said May 12 that in the talks it had rejected any "tutelage of the Palestinian revolution," and "limitation of the area of operation of the commandos."

Taking part in the Beirut talks until May 11 was Dr. Hassan Sabry al-Kholy, special representative of U.A.R. President Gamal Abdel Nasser.

An Al Fatah broadcast May 9 had appealed to the "Lebanese masses, the army and students" not to "stand by idly while the conspiracy against the commandos is fulfilled."

Lebanon Battles Commandos. Lebanon's stepped-up campaign to curb the activities of anti-Israeli Palestinian commando groups operating in Lebanon precipitated a major military confrontation between the government and the guerrillas. Scores were killed and wounded in fighting between both sides and in guerrilla-instigated riots and clashes in Beirut and Tripoli Oct. 18–25, 1969.

In submitting his resignation for the second time in just under six months, Karami Oct. 22 dissociated himself from government forces' attacks on the guerrillas. Karami praised the commandos and appealed to Lebanese to maintain their national unity and not to permit "imperialist and Zionist agents" to undermine the country's security.

Syria exerted pressure against Beirut Oct. 21 by closing its borders with Lebanon and prohibiting Syrian citizens from traveling to Lebanon. Damascus threatened "firmer and more effective measures" to stop Lebanese army attacks on the guerrillas. A Baghdad announcement Oct. 22 pledged that Iraq would provide the guerrillas with material and diplomatic support.

The clashes threatened an open break between Lebanon and Syria (which vowed strong support for the guerrillas), prompted the resignation of Lebanese Premier Rashid Karami Oct. 22 and further embroiled Israel, the Soviet Union and the U.S. in the growing Middle East crisis. The crisis appeared to ease as a tacit cease-fire went into effect throughout Lebanon Oct. 27.

Damascus denounced Lebanon Oct. 24 for announcing the previous day that tanks and armored cars were massing on its Syrian frontier and that a force of 200 men had been seen climbing a hill toward the Lebanese border. These reports, the Damascus broadcast charged, were meant to give the erroneous impression that Syria was about to attack Lebanon. Syria assailed Beirut for its drive against the guerrillas in the south and vowed that it would intensify the measures it had taken against Lebanon.

A force of about 300 men, reported to be Al Fatah, crossed into Lebanon from Syria Oct. 25 and occupied the village of Yanta, six miles inside the country, astride the Damascus-Beirut highway. The invaders also laid siege to the nearby village of Deir Al Ashaer. In announcing the incursion, the Lebanese government said the force included 20 trucks, eight military vehicles towing 120-mm. mortars and five tanks. The statement said Lebanese troops had taken up positions a few miles west of Yanta to prevent a further guerrilla advance. Beirut held Syria responsible for permitting the guerrilla force to enter Lebanon.

An Al Fatah broadcast from Cairo Oct. 25 appealed to "honest elements" in the Lebanese army to revolt against their officers and "imperialist agents" in the armed forces who "carry out the instructions of the CIA." Al Fatah insisted that it wanted to use Lebanese territory as "a base and a passageway for commandos" in their military actions against Israeli villages and military positions on the Lebanese border.

The clashes were halted by a secret Lebanese-commando peace agreement Nov. 3, but serious new commando attacks on Lebanese forces broke out again Nov. 20.

At least 30 persons were killed and more than 80 were wounded March 24–27, 1970 in clashes in Lebanon between commandos and armed civilian followers of the Christian Phalangist Party, which opposed the presence of the guerrillas in the country. Lebanese army troops were involved in some of the fighting.

U.S. centers hit in Lebanon. The extremist Popular Front for the Liberation of Palestine carried out seven rocket and bomb attacks against U.S. property in Beirut and southern Lebanon March 28–29, 1970. There were no casualties and little damage.

A PFLP statement March 29 said the raids were in retaliation for "plans of the United States embassy in Beirut to foment religious strife and create civil massacres in Lebanon aimed at paralyzing the Palestine resistance movement." The statement referred to the March 24–27 clashes between the Palestinian commandos and armed civilian followers of the Christian Phalangist Party.

The PFLP attacks were directed near the U.S. embassy and the American Insurance Co. in Beirut March 28 and the U.S.-owned Medreco oil refinery near Sidon and the John F. Kennedy Library and the Bank of America in Beirut March 29.

Lebanese Curbs. Palestinian commandos were reported Oct. 31, 1970 to have agreed to reorganize their movement in Lebanon in order to improve relations with the Beirut regime. The commando decision followed demands by the Lebanese that the guerrillas stop using Lebanon as a base for firing rockets into Israel.

The government pressure came after residents of the Marjyun border district in southern Lebanon staged an unusual anti-commando demonstration in protest against a guerrilla rocket attack into Israel from the neighboring border village of Qaliah Oct. 25. The protesters feared that the shelling would provoke Israel into more retaliatory attacks on Lebanon. The demonstrators set up roadblocks in the area and called on Lebanese troops and policemen to stop the commando raids.

The controversy was reported Oct. 27 to have been discussed at a meeting of Lebanese Premier Saeb Salam and Yasir Arafat, leader of the guerrillas. These talks were followed by a conference of commando leaders in Lebanon Oct. 30. In the talks, presided over by Arafat, the commandos agreed to these measures restricting their activities in the country: the offices set up by the 10 separate commando groups in Lebanon's 15 Palestinian refugee camps would be replaced by centers in each camp under the authority of the Palestine Liberation Organization, the commandos' coordinating group headed by Arafat; the commandos would establish a centralized fund-raising office in Beirut; the commandos would no longer wear uniforms and carry arms in public.

Jordan-Commando Clashes. At least 30 persons were killed or wounded in clashes between Jordanian troops and Palestinian guerrillas in the Amman area Feb. 10–12, 1970.

The fighting was precipitated by commando violation of a government decree issued Feb. 10, restricting their activities in order to prevent a possible challenge to King Hussein's rule. The directive barred commandos from carrying arms in towns, gave them two weeks to turn in caches of weapons and explosives, banned demonstrations and unauthorized publications and outlawed political party activity.

Al Fatah, speaking for all 10 Palestinian guerrilla groups in Jordan, declared in a broadcast Feb. 10 that the decree was a U.S.-supported attempt to disarm the Palestinians in preparation for a settlement with Israel. Al Fatah reported Feb. 11 that all the commando units had agreed to be represented by a Unified Command to insure unity in their dealings with Hussein.

The clashes were ended by a suspension of the government decree agreed to in talks between Hussein and commando representatives Feb. 11–12. The accord provided for immediate discussions to resolve all outstanding differences between the two sides.

A further government-commando accord reached Feb. 22 said that both sides were in "full understanding on strengthening national unity and on mobilization of the masses in Jordan so they may stand united with the gallant Jordanian forces and the struggling resistance organizations."

Although specific provisions of the agreement were not made public, they were said to permit the commandos to exercise their own discipline, with the understanding that they refrain from carrying arms in public and not appear in uniform in the main cities.

Maj. Gen. Mohammed Rassoul Kilani, who reportedly advocated a tough policy against the commandos, was removed as Jordanian interior minister Feb. 23.

Jordan Troops Fight Guerrillas. About 200 persons were killed and 500 were wounded in clashes between Jordanian army troops and Palestinian guerrillas in and around Amman June 6–10, 1970; 90% of the victims were civilians. The fighting stopped when King Hussein yielded to commando demands that he oust two top army officers accused by the commandos of plotting with the U.S. against the Palestinian cause.

The Syrian government June 11 proclaimed support for the Palestinian commandos in their fighting with the Jordanian government. Damascus radio called on Jordanian soldiers to stop shooting at the commandos.

The underlying cause of the violence remained commando opposition to Jordanian government attempts to restrain their operations against Israel.

In an outgrowth of the disturbances, the U.S. military attache in Amman was shot to death, another American aide was abducted and then released, a number of foreigners, including Americans, were held hostage but later freed, and pro-commando mobs in Beirut burned the Jordanian embassy.

The brunt of the fighting for the commandos was believed conducted by the Popular Front for the Liberation of Palestine (PFLP).

King Hussein was the target of an assassination attempt June 9. A government broadcast said his motorcade came under "criminal attack" near Suweilih, a small town west of Amman, where the king had a summer villa. Hussein was reported returning to his palace in Amman to deal with the crisis at the time. An Amman broadcast

June 11 said Hussein disclosed that his bodyguard was killed and five other persons were wounded in the attack. Reuters news service reported Hussein was wounded in the ambush.

The truce pact was reached in negotiations between Hussein and Yasir Arafat, leader of Al Fatah. It called for the return of all guerrilla forces to their barracks, the establishment of joint controls and checkpoints, the release of prisoners and the formation of two committees to investigate the cause of the clashes and to prevent their recurrence. Lt. Gen. Hammad Shehab, the Iraqi chief of staff, acted as mediator in the Hussein-Arafat talks.

The PFLP rejected the truce agreement and demanded instead the abolition of what it called the government's anti-commando organizations and the dismissal of officials believed to be hostile to the commandos.

Following further talks with Arafat June 11, Hussein yielded to PFLP demands and dismissed his uncle, Maj. Gen. Nasser Ben-Jamil as commander in chief and Maj. Gen. Zaid Ben-Shaker as commander of the Third Armored Division, which surrounded Amman.

The commandos accused Ben-Jamil of collaborating with U.S. intelligence officials. An Al Fatah broadcast from Cairo June 10 had labeled him as "the head of the anticommando conspiracy" and called Ben-Shaker a co-conspirator. The commandos had assailed Ben-Shaker for harsh repression of the guerrillas. Hussein reportedly rejected a commando demand to deport Ben-Jamil and Ben-Shaker along with Rasoul al-Kallani, the former chief of security, and former Premier Wasfi Tell. Kallani had been accused by the Al Fatah broadcast of being a co-conspirator. These men reportedly had been members of an intelligence board whose aim was to undermine the commandos.

Premier Bahjat al-Talhouni reported June 13 that a government motorcade carrying Maj. Gen. Mashur Haditha, army chief of staff, had been fired on that day near Amman. Five of the general's guards were wounded, he said. According to a commando broadcast of the incident, joint action by commandos and troops loyal to King Hussein had blocked an advance on Amman of tanks operated by a dissident force. The broadcast said the dissidents were followers of Gen. Ben-Jamil.

U.S. aide slain—Maj. Robert Perry, 34, U.S. military attache in Amman, was shot to death by commandos in his home in the Jordanian capital June 10. A State Department statement said Perry was killed by automatic-weapons fire at close range through the locked doors of his house when guerrillas attempted to enter.

In other incidents involving members of the U.S. embassy, Morris Draper, 42, head of the embassy's political division, was kidnaped by commandos June 7 as he drove to a dinner party in Amman. He was released unharmed June 8 following contacts between the Jordanian government and the commandos. The guerrillas had said Draper was being held for the release of commandos captured in the fighting with Jordanian troops.

Sixty foreigners held hostage by the commandos in two Amman hotels for three days were released June 12 as peace was restored in the capital. Most of those freed were Americans and Britons. In announcing their release, Dr. George Habash, head of the PFLP, told a gathering of the hostages in one of the hotels: "Believe me—and I am not joking—we were determined to blow up the hotels with the hostages in them if we had been smashed in our camps." A guerrilla spokesman had said June 10 that the hostages were being held to force the Jordanian army to halt the shelling of guerrilla positions in refugee camps.

Arab commandos reorganize. A new 27-man Central Committee of the 10 Palestinian commando organizations was formed at an emergency meeting of all the guerrilla groups in the Palestine Armed Struggle Command in Jordan June 9, 1970. Yasir Arafat was elected commander in chief of all Palestinian forces.

The decision to reorganize the commando leadership had been made at a meeting of the Palestine National Council May 29–June 4 in Cairo. The council consisted of 112 members, representing the commandos, students, workers and individual leaders of the Palestinian community in various Arab countries.

The Supreme Military Council, composed of the 10 commando groups, divided Jordan into several military zones and appointed a separate command for guerrillas operating from each zone.

The Central Committee constituted the highest political authority for the commandos.

The 10 commando groups in the Central Committee were: Al Fatah, the largest of the groups; As Saiqah, the second largest group, sponsored by the ruling Baath party of Syria; the Popular Front for the Liberation of Palestine; the Popular Democratic Front for the Liberation of Palestine; the Popular Front for the Liberation of Palestine (General Command); and the Palestine Arab Organization (the last three had broken away from the PFLP); the Action Group for the Liberation of Palestine, an offshoot of Al Fatah; the Arab Liberation Front, sponsored by the Iraqi Baath party; the Popular Liberation Forces, the military branch of the PLO; and the Popular Struggle Front.

Only four of the 10 groups were represented on the PLO executive committee. They were Al Fatah, As Saiqah, the Popular Democratic Front for the Liberation of Palestine and the Popular Liberation Forces.

The Palestine National Council also established a joint committee of commandos and leftist organizations in Jordan and Lebanon. The inclusion of the PFLP on the Central Committee was the first time that organization became involved in any overall commando group.

Jordan-commando accord. An agreement aimed at settling the long-standing dispute between Jordan and the Palestinian commandos was signed in Amman July 10, 1970. It had been worked out by representatives of Egypt, Libya, Sudan and Algeria.

The accord, signed by Jordanian Premier Abdel Moneim Rifai and by Yasir Arafat, chairman of the Central Committee of the Palestine Liberation Organization, reasserted most of the terms of the agreement reached after previous Jordanian-commando clashes in February. Its principal points:

The commandos would remove their forces from Amman and other major towns, but a civilian militia would be permitted to remain under supervision of a joint government-commando committee.

The commandos would refrain from: carrying arms in public places, using unlicensed vehicles, military training with live ammunition, storing heavy weapons and explosives in populated centers and maintaining bases in towns.

The commandos would obey Jordanian statutes, hand over law violators and refuse to accept recruits liable for service in the Jordanian army.

The Amman government pledged to support the Palestinian guerrilla movement and to bar any government body from carrying out acts detrimental to the commandos.

Palestinians urge war. Arab guerrillas called for a continued military struggle against Israel at a meeting of the Palestinian National Council in Amman Aug. 27–28.

Resolutions adopted by the delegates Aug. 28 denounced a U.S. peace initiative that had brought about negotiations between Israel, Jordan and Egypt. The council said that anyone opposed to the Palestinians' campaign to destroy Israel "is a traitor to his cause and the revolution and deserves severe punishment."

Hussein escapes assassination. Jordanian King Hussein escaped injury when would-be assassins fired on his motorcade in Amman Sept. 1, 1970.

The incident was followed by an exchange of gunfire between Jordanian army troops and Palestinian commandos hostile to Hussein in and around Amman.

A government communique issued after the attack declared: "The Jordanian government assures the Jordanian people and the Arab nation that the situation in the capital and the kingdom is under full control. Any rumors by the army of a crackdown on the commandos are completely untrue, and the aim of these rumors is to create confusion."

The attempt on Hussein's life pointed up the continued opposition of the Palestinian commandos to Jordan's decision to enter peace talks with Israel. The incident followed clashes Aug. 26-30 between Jordanian army troops and the commandos in Amman.

Clashes resume in Jordan. Two weeks of sporadic but heavy fighting between commandos and Jordanian toops led to the installation of a military government by King Hussein Sept. 16. The prior government, headed by Premier Abdel Moneim Rifai, was reported to have been dismissed by Hussein Sept. 15 when he learned terms of a truce agreement negotiated with the commandos—an agreement that reportedly would have turned control of Jordan's major cities over to the guerrilla leaders. The truce negotiated by the Rifai government was the fourth to be concluded with the commandos during the two week period.

The fighting had broken out following the attempt to assassinate Hussein.

The fourth truce agreement was worked out with the aid of Arab League mediators and was signed Sept. 15 by Rifai and PLO Central Committee Chairman Yasir Arafat. The agreement called for replacing army guards by police units throughout Amman, reductions in army strength near the capital and the evacuation of all new positions by both sides.

In addition, the commandos were to remove roadblocks and stop all interception, interrogation and arrest procedures. The army agreed not to intercept commandos. The post office, power plant and water stations would continue to be guarded by units of both sides.

The agreement, to go into effect Sept. 16, was presented by Rifai to King Hussein, who reportedly declared that he "had been betrayed." The king immediately dismissed the Rifai government.

Hussein announced the formation of the military cabinet Sept. 16.

The new government was headed by Brig. Mohammed Daoud as premier and minister of foreign affairs and justice and included five other generals, two colonels and three majors. However, Hussein simultaneously named Field Marshal Habes al-Majali to replace Maj. Gen. Mashur Haditha as commander in chief of the army and military governor of Jordan. Real authority was believed to be in Majali's hands.

Hussein's letter appointing Daoud ordered him to implement the cease-fire agreement negotiated with commando leaders by Rifai. Government spokesmen said Sept. 16 that the military leaders were aiming at a "Lebanese" solution under which commandos would be concentrated in border areas adjacent to Israel. A spokesman for Al Fatah, the largest guerrilla group, said Sept. 16 that the commandos would not leave their strongholds in the cities of northern Jordan.

The Central Committee of the Palestine Liberation Organization rejected the military government Sept. 16 as the product of "a fascist military coup." It ordered commandos to hold their positions and fortify them against attack by the army.

Central Committee statements broadcast that day by the commando radio stations in Baghdad and Damascus said that the Popular Front for the Liberation of Palestine had been readmitted to the committee and that all guerrilla units were now under the command of Yasir Arafat. The committee called for a general strike Sept. 17 to help it topple the government.

The Baghdad and Damascus broadcasts made it clear that the commandos had the backing of the Iraqi and Syrian governments. The Damascus broadcasts said that Syria considered the new Jordanian government the puppet of an imperialist plot to destroy the Arab commando movement.

Columns of tanks and troops under orders of the new military government entered Amman at dawn Sept. 17 and immediately engaged Palestinian guerrillas emplaced in buildings throughout the Jordanian capital. The fighting quickly spread to other parts of the country.

The fiercest fighting was in the capital, where Jordanian tanks and infantry units surrounded and attacked the Al-Husseini and Wahdat refugee camps, sites of commando operational headquarters.

Hussein's military government charged in a broadcast that the guerrillas began the fighting by firing on the army's general staff headquarters shortly before dawn. The commando radio denied the account, asserting that the army started the shooting by opening fire on the two Palestinian refugee camps.

By 5 p.m. the official Amman radio announced that the government troops were in command of the city except for scattered pockets of guerrilla resistance.

As the fighting ebbed in the capital at sunset, the clashes in the north increased in intensity. At Zerqa, 13 miles northeast of Amman, government forces overran a guerrilla redoubt that had once been the staging area for commando forays against Israel.

Fierce house-to-house fighting continued in Amman Sept. 18.

A large force of the guerrillas, fighting from behind a column of Syrian tanks, Sept. 21 routed Hussein's forces in northern Jordan. The guerrilla radio reported that all the cities in the north, except Amman, had fallen to the commandos.

Jordanian tanks rolled across the desert Sept. 23, pushing back a guerrilla force that had driven a wedge between government forces in the north and south. Syrian tanks that had spearheaded the guerrilla advance were chased back across the border into Syria after constant pounding from a squadron of Jordan jets. Field Marshal Majali announced a cease-fire order in Amman. The order was ignored, however, as both sides continued to exchange small-arms fire throughout the city. King Hussein said Sept. 23 that most of the capital was under government control. He said he believed "the brunt of the problem" was over.

Hussein later noted an agreement between his government and four captured commando chiefs that he said amounted to capitulation by the guerrillas. The accord was repudiated in a broadcast from Damascus by Arafat who called it a "conspiracy." He said the four guerrilla officers, two of them line officers in his chain of command, "do not represent the Palestine Resistance at this time."

The level of fighting ebbed Sept. 24 as Arafat announced shortly after midnight that he would meet with four envoys representing the Arab chiefs of state who were meeting in Cairo to seek an end to the civil war.

Fighting ends in cease-fire accord— Peace returned to Jordan for the first time in 10 days Sept. 25 as King Hussein's government and the Arab commando leadership jointly ordered an immediate nationwide cease-fire.

At the time of the cease-fire, Jordanian forces controlled nearly all of Amman and had pushed north to encircle guerrilla forces holding Irbid, Ramtha and Jarash. A Jordanian general told newsmen that the Arab commando leadership had agreed to the cease-fire to freeze the military position and prevent a worsening of their situation.

Hussein forms new government—King Hussein Sept. 26 appointed a new civilian-military government of "national reconciliation" to replace the all-military government he installed 11 days before on the eve of his drive to crush the Arab commando movement.

The new cabinet of seven civilians and six army officers was to be headed by Ahmed Toukan.

The military retained the key defense and interior ministries in the new government. A senior army officer, Brig. Mazen Ajluni, the deputy military governor under Majali, was also retained in the new cabinet as minister of state for the premier's office.

The commandos assailed Hussein and his new cabinet through a spokesman in Damascus. The spokesman for the Central Committee said the appointment of the new cabinet "does not change our attitude in the least. Nor will it make any change in the situation, as long as the royal regime exists and the real criminals, first and foremost King Hussein, are in power."

Agreement ends Jordanian civil war. King Hussein of Jordan and Yasir Arafat met with Arab chiefs of state in Cairo Sept. 27 and joined them in signing a 14-point agreement that called for an immediate end to the fighting in the 10-day Jordanian civil war.

The two key provisions in the 14-point agreement provided that (1) Hussein would continue in control but under the supervision of other Arab nations until the situation in Jordan could be normalized and (2) the guerrillas would have full support of the Arab world until "full liberation and victory over the aggressive Israeli enemy." The accord also included the following major points:

■ Withdrawal of Jordanian forces to areas three miles outside of Amman.

■ Withdrawal of guerrilla forces from Amman to a new position suitable for staging commando raids against Israel.

■ The transfer of power and responsibility for the administration of internal security from military to civilian authorities.

Jordan recognizes Al Fatah—Jordanian Information Minister Adnan Abuh Odeh said Oct. 1 that in the future his government would recognize only one of the 10 Arab guerrillas organizations— Al Fatah, headed by Yasir Arafat. Asserting that all other guerrilla groups were illegal, Odeh said "We are not going to suppress anyone, but we want to deal only with Fatah." He suggested that members of the other commando forces join Al Fatah.

Commandos quit north Jordan. Palestinian commandos began withdrawing from towns in northern Jordan Oct. 6 in accordance with the Sept. 27 agreement. The guerrillas were moving to encampments in the countryside and some were reported going to Syria.

Both guerrillas and Jordanian troops had begun moving out of Amman Sept. 30 in implementation of the Cairo accord; the pullout was reported complete Oct. 4. The government forces took up positions along the front line with Israel. The troop withdrawals were supervised by a truce team of 100 Arab officers from Egypt, Sudan, Saudi Arabia, Kuwait and Tunisia.

A truce pact to restore peace in northern Jordan, supplemental to the Sept. 27 Cairo agreement, had been signed Oct. 1 by Jordanian army officers and guerrilla representatives in Ramtha. Principal points of the agreement:

■ Both sides were to withdraw their armored units from the Ramtha-Irbid-Jerash triangle.

■ All unarmed units would be permitted to go south to Amman or other towns.

■ Guerrillas must keep their weapons at their bases or in their homes and must not carry them in the streets.

■ All prisoners were to be set free. (Jordan reported Oct. 6 that at least 10,400 guerrillas had been released from detention camps the previous day, bringing to a total of 18,882 the number of commandos freed since the Cairo agreement.)

The cease-fire continued to be punctuated by clashes. A Jordanian tank force advancing toward Ramtha was attacked by guerrillas Sept. 30. One tank was blown up by a commando mine.

Guerrilla Attacks, Israeli Retaliation

Israeli Jets Bomb Syria. In the first air raid on Syria since the 1967 war, Israeli jets Feb. 24, 1969 bombed sites on the Damascus-Beirut road allegedly used as bases for Al Fatah.

Israeli authorities reported that the planes bombed guerrilla camps at Halma and Maisalun, in the vicinity of Damascus. The report said that hundreds of commandos were caught in their buildings and tents in the 30-minute strike and that two Syrian MiG-21s were downed by Israeli pilots in four air clashes during the operations. Israel said all its planes returned safely, refuting Syrian claims that 3 Israeli Mirages had been shot down.

Israeli military authorities said the air strike was in retaliation for increased terrorist attacks from Syrian bases on the Israeli-held Golan Heights. The Israelis charged that 12 such raids had occurred in the previous two weeks. Syria had always supported the commandos but only recently had permitted them to infiltrate across the border into Israel. According to the Israelis, Halma was the principal Al Fatah training base in Syria and Lebanon and served as the group's logistic headquarters. Halma also was said to be the staging area for guerrillas trained in the U.A.R., Algeria and Communist China.

New Arab Commando Group. A new commando group, called the Arab Organization of Sinai, was reported by Cairo to have carried out its first raids behind Israeli lines in the Sinai Peninsula March 23, 1969. In one raid, the attackers, using portable rockets, were said to have destroyed an Israeli command center and radar site at El Borg, 10 miles east of the Suez Canal in the northern part of the peninsula. In another raid, the guerrillas reportedly struck at Israel artillery and supply positions at Ein Moussa, on the eastern shore of the Red Sea.

Israel Bombs Jordan. Jordan charged March 26, 1969 that 18 civilians had been killed that day when four Israeli jets bombed roadside rest houses at Ein Khanzir, on the outskirts of the town of Salt, 16 miles north of Amman. The U.N. Security Council, at Jordan's request, took up the incident March 27 and April 1 censured Israel for the raid.

France and the Soviet Union joined the majority in voting for the resolution. The U.S., Britain, Colombia and Paraguay abstained.

The vote by the Council was the first since the 1967 war that failed to take a unanimous stand on a cease-fire violation. Yosef Tekoah, the Israeli representative, said this was a clear indication that the U.S. and Britain were opposed to Arab guerrilla and terrorist attacks on Israel, while the Soviet Union backed the Arab "terror organizations."

U.S. Ambassador Charles Yost said that the U.S. could not vote for a resolution that did not hold Arab terrorists equally to blame. "Death is just as final and as shocking if it comes from a bomb in a supermarket or from a bomb from the air."

Yoseph Tekoah charged that Amman was playing a major role "in warfare by terror against the people of Israel" "since Jordanian territory serves as the main jumping-off ground for attacks against Israel." Jordan, he charged, "is the central base of the terror operations." Thus, the Israeli attack on the Salt area "was an act of self-defense," Tekoah said. Tekoah warned that if the Arab governments were "unwilling to stop" guerrilla raids on Israel, then Israel "must take itself all the necessary measures to put an end to it."

Vowing to avenge the killing of the Jordanian civilians, the Popular Front for the Liberation of Palestine March 27 urged foreigners not to travel on Israeli planes or ships "so we may have a free hand in striking at Israeli communications lines."

Israeli jets attacked Jordanian positions again March 30, bombing targets south of the Sea of Galilee. The raid followed the wounding of four Israeli soldiers by bazooka rockets.

Israel was reported June 1 to have warned Jordan that Israeli forces would strike at Jordanian soldiers unless Amman's troops stopped aiding Arab guerrillas in their attacks on Israel. The warning, the second reported in a week, was said to have been transmitted to King Hussein through U.S. channels.

Israeli jets struck Jordan June 18 and 19. The June 18 strike, heavier of the two, was directed against an area extending 45 miles from the Dead Sea to the Gilead Hills, on the east bank of the Jordan. A Jerusalem communique said among the targets hit were Jordanian artillery batteries near El Zahadane and positions near two bridges crossing the Jordan River. Amman reported four Jordanian soldiers killed and seven wounded in the air attack. Israeli military officials said the aerial assault was in retaliation for 600 "acts of aggression" against Israel from Jordanian territory since Jan. 1. In the past two months the Israelis listed 40 attacks by artillery, 107 by mortars, 17 by tanks, 17 by Soviet-made Katyusha rockets and 7 by antitank rifles. The Israelis reported killing 66 guerrillas and taking 20 prisoners during the two-month period. An Israeli Defence Ministry statement said "Jordanian aggression is increasing—with the participation of the terror-

ists and the Iraqi expeditionary forces and without them."

Israeli jets attacked Jordan June 22. The 45-minute raid against targets at Arab el Hassan and Khirbet el Barka were described by Israeli officials as retaliation for the Arab shelling earlier June 22 of a settlement near Beison in northern Israel.

Israeli Deputy Prime Minister Yigal Allon had warned June 16 that unless the guerrillas halted their attacks Israel "will stop drawing the distinction between the terrorists and the Arab regular armies."

Israeli Attacks in Jordan. Israeli officials disclosed May 9, 1969 that Israeli commandos had been crossing the Jordan River for the past year to attack Arab guerrilla forces in Jordan.

The assaults on the east bank of the Jordan came to light when Israeli newspapers were permitted to publish accounts of one of the heaviest of these raids, carried out May 8. Striking one mile east of the river in the area of Wadi Yavesh, opposite the Israeli settlement of Tirat-Tsvi, an Israeli commando unit destroyed 12 guerrilla structures and killed three Jordanian civilians in an abandoned village. Amman reported that the civilians were killed when their car ran over mines planted by Israelis before they withdrew.

The Israelis reportedly divulged the commando activities when it was felt they could no longer be concealed because of the widespread damage caused by the latest raid.

Guerrillas Attack Jericho. Arab guerrillas, apparently firing from Jordan, shelled Jericho in the Israeli-held west bank May 27 and 28. It was the first attack on the all-Arab city since the 1967 war.

In the May 27 incident, an Arab policeman was injured, several stores were burned and other structures were damaged. Israeli authorities reported that one civilian was wounded and a building destroyed in the May 28 shelling.

A spokesman for Al Fatah charged May 29 that Israeli forces had fired on

Jericho in an effort to force the Arab population to flee.

Arabs Damage Pipeline. Arab guerrillas of the Popular Front for the Liberation of Palestine May 30, 1969 blew up and heavily damaged a section of the Trans-Arabian Pipeline, owned by the Arabian-American Oil Co. (Aramco), in the Israeli-occupied Golan Heights of Syria.

The explosion and resultant fire blocked the flow of oil through the 1,000-mile pipeline connecting Dharan, Saudi Arabia on the Persian Gulf to Sidon, a Lebanese port on the Mediterranean. The pipeline provided Saudi Arabia, Jordan, Syria and Lebanon with millions of dollars in royalties and transit fees each year.

A PFLP spokesman in Amman, Jordan said May 31 that an explosive charge had been placed in the Baniyas River where the pipeline runs along the river bed. The purpose of the blast, the spokesman said, was to spill oil into the river and pollute the water it supplied to Israeli settlements and fisheries in the Huleh Valley. As a result of the blast, oil was reported seeping into the northern part of the Sea of Galilee, an important water source for Israel, but without causing dangerous pollution. Oil slicks also were observed on the Jordan River. Israelis fought the pipeline blaze 14 hours before extinguishing it May 31.

The PFLP was sharply criticized in the Arab world June 1 for having blown up the pipeline. The Egyptian newspaper Al Ahram said the PFLP's "incomprehensible" action had inflicted no harm on Israel but had violated a "logical framework of Arab principle and interests." The Saudi Arabian government, which stood to lose most from the pipeline attack, charged in a Mecca radio broadcast that the PFLP commandos had served Zionism by their sabotage.

The Beirut newspaper Al Hayat said the PFLP was serving Israeli interests by its attack.

Israeli Jets Raid Jordan. Israeli jets carried out heavy attacks on targets in Jordan Aug. 6–10, 1969 following raids on Israeli territory by Jordan-based Arab guerrillas and by regular Jordanian forces. Israeli jets also launched a reprisal raid on guerrilla camps in Lebanon Aug. 11.

The heaviest of the Israeli strikes, Aug. 10, blasted sections of northern Jordan's Ghor Canal, which drew water from the Yarmuk River for the irrigation of 180,000 acres of land in the Jordan Valley.

Israeli jets struck at targets southeast of the Sea of Galilee Aug. 6, about 20 minutes after Jordanian artillery had shelled the settlement of Ashdot Yaakov.

Israeli jets Aug. 7 penetrated up to 15 miles across the Jordan border south of the Yarmuk River, hitting camps, fortified positions, command posts and transportation equipment. Israeli tanks joined in the attack but did not cross into Jordanian territory. The assault followed an Arab guerrilla attack earlier Aug. 7 in which an Israeli bus was blown up near El Hamma, killing the civilian driver and a soldier and wounding 12 soldiers. A commando group, the Popular Front for the Liberation of Palestine, claimed its forces had killed 50 Israeli soldiers in the bus attack.

The Palestine Armed Struggle Command, representing seven guerrilla organizations, said a joint commando force had attacked and occupied for three hours the Israeli settlements of Neve-Ur, Yardena and Beit Yossef and three Israeli military posts in the northern Jordan Valley Aug. 7. The command said many Israelis had been killed and four tanks were destroyed. Commando losses were listed as six wounded in the three-hour attack. The Israelis dismissed the Arab claims, saying that the guerrilla assault had been confined to a bazooka attack on Yardena in which one woman was injured.

A guerrilla attack on the Israeli potash works at Sodom on the Dead Sea Aug. 7 prompted Israeli jets to pound Jordanian positions in the area the following day.

The air strike on Lebanon Aug. 11 was directed at seven guerrilla bases east of the Hasbani River, a tributary of the Jordan River. An Israeli spokesman said the 30-minute mission, the first air attack on Lebanon, had been ordered "as a result of the increase in terrorist activities emanating from Lebanese territory." The statement said 21 such attacks had occurred in the past month.

Al Fatah reported that its commandos Sept. 11 had blown up the Mahraniah irrigation dam, at the confluence of the Jordan and Yarmuk Rivers.

Northern Jordan's East Ghor Canal, damaged by Israeli attacks, was repaired Sept. 22 for the second time in two months under an unofficial agreement between Israel and Jordan negotiated with the aid of U.S. officials in Amman. An Israeli spokesman said Jerusalem had agreed not to interfere with the repair work if the cease-fire agreement in the area south of the Sea of Galilee was observed. But within four hours after the repairs were completed, the Israeli settlements of Tirat Zvi, Neve Ur and Gesher, across the Jordan River from the canal, came under Arab guerrilla fire.

Israelis Strike at Lebanon. Increasing Arab commando attacks along the Lebanese frontier prompted Israeli forces to carry out heavy air strikes against Lebanon Sept. 3–5, 1969 as well as the 'first commando attack on Lebanon since Oct. 28, 1966.

The Sept. 3 air strike was directed at suspected guerrilla concentrations on the slopes of Mount Hermon from which rockets the previous day had shelled the northern Israeli villages of Kiryat Shmona and Kfar Giladi. Three civilians were killed and four others were wounded at Kiryat Shmona.

The target of the Israeli commando strike the night of Sept. 4 was the village of Halta, two miles inside Lebanon. The Israelis emptied 12 houses of occupants and destroyed the structures, reportedly containing weapons and uniforms. Five Arab guerrillas were killed and four Israelis were wounded in the operation.

A Beirut communique Sept. 5 said the Israeli commandos had been transported to Halta by helicopters but that Lebanese forces had repulsed them.

Israeli troops moved into southern Lebanon Oct. 3 and blew up buildings in the villages of Mazraat Deharjat and Aitrun, suspected of housing Arab guerrillas. According to the Israelis, guerrillas had

launched a raid from the first village against the Israeli settlement of Ramat Shalom Sept. 30, killing an Israeli Druze watchman.

Israeli commandos Dec. 3, attacking less than one mile inside Lebanon, reported destroying an Arab guerrilla base near the villages of Chabaa and Kifar Chouba in the foothills of Mount Hermon.

The raiding party claimed that 12 Arab guerrillas were killed and "many more" wounded in the attack. One Israeli was reported killed. Before leaving, the raiders blew up equipment and ammunition. Lebanon said the Israelis were brought in by helicopters.

The Israelis said the raid was in retaliation for an attack by Arab guerrillas Dec. 2 on their positions near Massada, in the Golan Heights, six miles southeast of the commando base struck by the Israelis. As Saiqa, the Syrian-supported guerrilla group, claimed credit for the raid, saying in Damascus Dec. 3 that its forces had ambushed a patrol and killed 15 Israelis' and wounded 30 others.

U.N. acts on Israeli raid. An Israeli attack on Arab guerrilla bases in Lebanon was condemned by the U.N. Security Council Sept. 5, 1970. A resolution calling for "complete and immediate withdrawal" of Israeli forces from Lebanon was approved by a vote of 14–0, with the U.S. abstaining.

Israeli representative Shabtai Rosenne acknowledged that Israeli forces had "carried out a search-and-comb mission" around Mt. Hermon in Lebanon Sept. 4 and 5, but that the troops had "completed their mission a few hours ago and have since evacuated the territory." Rosenne dismissed the operation as "a minor action ... directed solely against terrorists in the area affected."

In a report on the Israeli incursion, Lebanon had said Sept. 5 that its tanks and guns had stopped an Israeli advance toward Rashaya. The village had come under Israeli air attack along with the adjacent communities of Suba and Haiariya in the Mt. Hermon area. An Al Fatah spokesman said its commando forces had been engaging the Israeli forces in the area for the past 36 hours.

Commandos score truce. Palestinian guerrillas Aug. 7, 1970 reiterated opposition to any truce in the Middle East and followed up their pronouncement with attacks against Israel from Jordan, Syria and Lebanon. Israeli forces struck back. The guerrillas acted in defiance of a U.S.-proposed truce accepted by Israel and the Arab governments.

In Amman, a spokesman for the Central Committee of the commando movement, which comprised 10 commando groups, said the Palestinians "reject the cease-fire; we want to liberate our land and the decision of the United Arab Republic to accept a cease-fire does not change our position—and will prompt us to step up our military operations until final victory."

A Central Committee statement issued in Beirut said the Palestinians would continue their struggle until all of Palestine had been "liberated."

Commando sources reported rival Palestinian groups reached agreement Aug. 6 on preventing further clashes between the guerrilla organizations opposed to the American peace plan and those commandos who supported Cairo's acceptance of it. In one action Aug. 5, a member of the Popular Front for the Liberation of Palestine was killed in an exchange of fire with the pro-Nasser Action Group for the Liberation of Palestine at Irbid in northern Jordan. Injuries were reported on both sides. Fighting broke out again Aug. 6 when PFLP commandos raided the Amman office of the pro-Nasser Palestine Arab Organization.

Terrorism in Israel
& in Occupied Areas

Gaza & West Bank Hit. About 35 Arab residents of the Israeli-occupied Gaza Strip, many of them women, were injured May 15, 1969 by grenades and other explosive devices that were thrown into market areas by Arab terrorists. (Since the June 1967 Arab-Israeli war, hundreds of residents of Arab areas had been injured by terrorist bombs.)

The incidents occurred before dawn in the towns of Gaza, Jabaliya, Khan Yunis, Rafa and Deir el Balah. They were related to a general Arab protest marking Israel's Independence Day, which coincided with the lunar Hebrew calendar anniversary of Jordanian Jerusalem's capture by the Israelis in 1967.

An Israeli military court in the Gaza Strip April 13 had sentenced an 18-year-old girl to 20 years in prison—the stiffest penalty imposed on a woman since the war. The girl had been found guilty of hurling grenades at an Israeli patrol vehicle and injuring four soldiers.

Israeli forces May 27 arrested 10 members of an Arab guerrilla group, the Popular Front for the Liberation of Palestine, accused of terrorizing Gaza Strip residents suspected of collaborating with the Israelis. The arrests followed the May 26 shooting of an Arab member of Israel's Gaza border police.

Beirut reported another Israeli attack inside Lebanese territory Sept. 6. A communique said an Israeli armored column had advanced from the Golan Heights toward the Lebanese villages of Haman and Rashaya, about three miles northwest of the border. The report said the Israeli force withdrew three hours later in the face of Lebanese artillery fire. Al Fatah claimed its men fought with the Israelis in the same area.

A grenade thrown by an Arab terrorist Nov. 19 killed an Arab boy in the Gaza Strip town of Khan Yunis. Five other Arabs were wounded in the attack, which was directed at the branch of an Israeli bank.

Israeli authorities Nov. 20 announced the arrest of more than 50 members of five Arab groups suspected of major terrorist incidents in Israel and in the occupied areas in the past few months. Two of the groups operated out of the west-bank town of Hebron, one in Gaza, one in Acre, north of Haifa, and the other in Taiyibe, an Arab village between Tel Aviv and Haifa. The Acre group was believed responsible for the dynamiting of five Haifa apartment houses in October. Six of its seized members, all Israeli Arabs, were said to have links with the El Asifa, an arm of Al Fatah.

The arrest of the Acre suspects and the demolition of a car in the town Nov.

22 prompted Jewish youths to attempt to break into the Arab quarter there Nov. 23. The car, containing explosives, blew up as it entered Acre, killing its two Israeli Arab occupants.

One of the victims of the car explosion was said to have provided Israeli authorities with information before his death leading to the arrest later Nov. 22 of Capt. Abdul Latif Rsheid, a key figure in Arab terrorist groups. Rsheid, a former Jordanian army intelligence officer who was believed to have organized the Acre terrorist groups and similar organizations in the Galilee, was seized in Sir, a village south of the west-bank town of Jenin.

An Arab was killed and five injured by a grenade thrown into a crowded marketplace in Jerusalem Jan. 1, 1970. Another grenade thrown at an Israeli army vehicle in Hebron that day missed its target and killed two Arab bystanders. They were identified as Moho Hilbi el Moukhtasseb, 28, son of the mufti of Jerusalem, and the mufti's uncle.

Six Arab terrorist suspects were killed and 24 captured in a series of Israeli anti-guerrilla operations along the Jordan River in the west-bank area Jan. 8. Two were slain near Umsutz, three in two separate operations in the Arava area, south of the Dead Sea, and one in Beit Fajar, south of Bethlehem. In the latter clash, 20 suspects were captured and a huge arms cache was uncovered.

Israeli Police Minister Shlomo Hillel said Jan. 5 that 120 Israeli Arabs had been found guilty of collaboration with Arab guerrillas since the 1967 war.

Terrorist grenade attacks in the Gaza Strip in March 1970 killed 27 persons and injured 132, making it the bloodiest month in the Israeli-occupied strip since the 1967 war. Most of the attacks were directed against Arabs accused of collaborating with Israel.

Israeli miliary authorities reported Jan. 3, 1971 that 39 Arabs in the occupied areas had been killed and 734 wounded by Palestinian guerrilla action, largely in the Gaza Strip, during 1970.

Rockets Aimed at Jerusalem. The Israeli army sealed off a six-square-mile area southeast of Jerusalem Aug. 29, 1969 following the discovery Aug. 26 of 16 guerrilla rockets aimed at the Israeli capital.

Three shells fired from three of the rockets had struck the southern Jerusalem suburbs Aug. 25 but caused no casualties or damage. The 13 other rockets had failed to go off. Israeli army helicopters searching for the rocket emplacements spotted them on a barren hill, two miles east of Bethlehem, between the Arab villages of Sur Bahir and Beir Sahhour.

Israeli planes Aug. 26 bombed Arab guerrillas bases in Jordan south of the Dead Sea in retaliation for the Jerusalem shelling.

516 Arab Homes Destroyed. Defense Minister Moshe Dayan disclosed Dec. 16, 1969 that Israel had destroyed 516 homes in the occupied areas since the 1967 war in retaliation for Arab cooperation with suspected guerrilla terrorists. Of this number, 265 were demolished in the west bank, 227 in the Gaza Strip and 24 in East Jerusalem, Dayan said. Fourteen of the 24 East Jerusalem houses had been "closed up," a recent action in which doors and windows were bricked up to avoid destroying nearby houses, according to Israeli authorities.

Arab leaders claimed that more than 7,500 dwellings had been blown up by the Israelis in the occupied territories since the 1967 war.

Haifa Blasts Kill 2. Two Israeli civilians were killed and 20 were wounded when Arab terrorist bombs exploded under five apartment buildings in Haifa Oct. 22 and 23, 1969. Police attributed the blasts to the Popular Front for the Liberation of Palestine.

Tel Aviv Blasts. Bomb explosions in Tel Aviv Nov. 6, 1970 killed one person and injured 34. Al Fatah took credit for the blasts and said a large number of Israelis were killed or wounded.

The two explosions, spaced 20 minutes apart, occurred in the city's central bus station. (The terminal had been the target of a similar Arab bomb attack Sept. 4, 1968, in which one person was killed and 51 wounded.)

An Al Fatah statement issued in Amman Nov. 8 by Abu Iyad, the guerrilla group's second-in-command, boasted that the Tel Aviv blasts were "the start of more and bigger operations within our occupied homeland."

Arab Rocket Attack. Arab guerrilla rockets July 7, 1971 struck the Israeli town of Petah Tiqva, seven miles northeast of Tel Aviv, killing four persons and wounding 30. Targets of the attack were a hospital and a schoolyard. Al Fatah, the commando group, claimed credit for the shelling.

Six Arab guerrillas linked by Israeli authorities to the Petah Tiqva raid were killed in an encounter with an Israeli patrol July 14, according to a Tel Aviv communique. A seventh was reported to have escaped into Jordan. The guerrillas were intercepted in the west bank 12 miles north of Jericho.

Terrorists Attack Arabs. Arabs under Israeli control were victims of several Arab terrorist strikes during 1971.

Palestinian commandos inflicted casualties on other Arabs in retaliation for suspected cooperation with Israeli authorities in a series of hand grenade attacks in the Gaza Strip June 6, 11 and 23. Two Arabs were shot to death following a grenade assault June 6.

Arab laborers waiting for Israeli buses to take them to work were the target of grenade attacks June 11. Two Arabs were killed and 81 injured. The incident occurred near the Muwazzi refugee camp in south Gaza.

Two Arabs were killed and 44 persons were wounded June 23 by a hand grenade tossed into a market place at Khan Yunis.

Bombs by Mail. Explosive parcels were mailed to Israel from Europe Jan. 2–9, 1972. Thirteen mail-bombs were sent to individuals in Israel in the seven-day period. Most were sent from Vienna. The only casualty was a bomb disposal expert who was injured while dismantling an explosive package in a Tel Aviv police station Jan. 3. A number of prominent Israelis, including Gen. Ezer Weizman, former air force commander, were recipients of the packages.

(A British decision to permit the Palestine Liberation Organization to open an office in London was assailed by Israel July 4, 1972.)

Guerrilla-Arab State Tensions

Commandos curb forces in Lebanon. The Palestinian commandos in Lebanon Jan. 3, 1971 announced new actions designed to curb the "bourgeois appearance" of the movement in the country, to restore the secrecy of the guerrilla organization and to create greater efficiency.

Al Fatah announced that it would withdraw arms from its men in Lebanon to achieve closer cooperation with the Beirut government and close its four offices in the country's refugee camps. The Beirut office would remain open.

The guerrillas also were said to be concerned over a recent outbreak of violence among their followers. In one incident, an Al Fatah man had been slain by three other guerrillas in Beirut Dec. 31, 1970. Al Fatah's own military police arrested two of the three suspects and turned them over to Lebanese authorities. The alleged assailants were identified as members of the extreme Action Organization for the Liberation of Palestine (AOLP), an offshoot of Al Fatah. Al Fatah also seized AOLP leader Issam Sartawi, closed AOLP's office in Beirut and seized its arms.

Jordan in anti-commando drive. Jordanian troops launched a major attack against Palestinian commando bases north of Amman Jan. 8, 1971. Fighting continued in the area and in the capital itself until Jan. 13 when a truce was agreed to by both sides.

The fighting broke out Jan. 8 around the towns of Jarash, Salt and Ruseifa. The government said the clashes in the Jarash area followed the kidnaping Jan. 7 by commandos of two noncommissioned army officers and the killing of a Jordanian soldier. Guerrilla statements asserted that government forces had shelled commando bases and confiscated their arms. Al Fatah claimed that a hospital at El Rumman had been shelled and that the al-Baqaa refugee camp, a few miles west of Amman, had been bombed. (Amman had reported Jan. 6 that three persons were killed and nine wounded in clashes in the capital that day following guerrilla attacks on two police stations in the city.)

A clash in Amman Jan. 11 resulted in the deaths of three civilians and a policeman. Meanwhile, Ibrahim Bakr, a member of the Central Committee, the coordinating group of the 10 guerrilla organizations, said Jan. 11 that the latest Jordanian attacks had paralyzed the commando movement and made it impossible for them to mount raids against the Israelis.

Government and commando representatives, assisted by the inter-Arab truce officials, met Jan. 12 to negotiate a truce that was agreed to the following day. A 13-point agreement that went into effect Jan. 14 reportedly contained nothing new except a timetable to implement the unfulfilled pledges outlined in the pact that had ended the September 1970 fighting. The latest treaty called on the guerrillas to withdraw to bases outside the cities and towns and for both sides to release all prisoners by Jan. 20.

Other points of the agreement: The government was to return guerrilla weapons and provide for free commando movement. It also was required to return the office of the Palestine Armed Struggle Command at Ramtha seized during the September fighting. The commandos were to be permitted to reopen within a month their closed offices and bases specified under previous agreements.

Jordan-commando clashes. Jordanian troops and Palestinian commandos engaged in sharp fighting in Amman and in the northern sector around Irbid March 26–April 6, 1971. Fighting broke out for the first time along the border with Syria from which some guerrilla units were believed to have moved into Jordan. The commando forces displayed their most aggressive stance since the September 1970 civil war, initiating offensive actions and carrying out widespread acts of sabotage against government facilities.

The Interior Ministry reported that 10 civilians and eight government soldiers had been killed in the fighting at Irbid March 26.

Fighting spread to Amman March 28 as government troops fired on a crowd of demonstrating women, killing three of them. The government charged that the guerrillas were using the demonstrators as a shield to fire on Jordanian policemen. A spokesman for the Palestine Liberation Organization charged that the troops had first opened fire on the women, who were protesting government policy. Fighting quickly spread to other parts of the city.

A guerrilla announcement April 2 declared that the fedayeen were fighting to force King Hussein to replace Wasfi Tell as premier and to oust the high-ranking officers whom they regarded as responsible for starting the latest round of fighting. An Al Fatah newspaper published in Damascus and distributed in Amman said the commandos would not sign a new peace agreement with the government as long as Tell remained in office. It charged that he and some army officers were planning to "finish off the commando movement once and for all."

Amman press reports April 5 told of a meeting of commando leaders in the border town of Dera, Syria April 1 in which they had decided on a "scorched earth" policy to force King Hussein to accede to their demands for freedom of action and movement in Jordan.

Syria was reported April 4 to have warned Jordan that the 6,000 regular troops of the Palestine Liberation Army stationed south of Damascus would be permitted to move into Jordan "unless harassment of guerrillas was quickly stopped."

Hussein orders commando purge. Hussein gave orders June 2, 1971 for a "final crackdown" against the Palestinian commandos, whom he charged with attempting "to establish a separate

Palestinian state and destroy the unity of the Jordanian and Palestinian people."

Hussein's directive, given to Premier Wasfi Tell, demanded "bold, decisive action against the handful of professional criminals and conspirators who use the commando movement to disguise their treasonable plots."

A statement issued by the central committee of the Palestine Liberation Organization (PLO) in Beirut June 1 had accused Jordan of mounting an offensive against commando bases in Jordan "in a conspiracy against the Palestine revolution." The PLO charged that "for the third day running the first and second divisions of government troops have been attacking our bases in Jerash and Salt with heavy artillery, armored vehicles and machine guns." The statement called Amman's drive "an extension of the intrigue begun by the Jordanian authorities last September." This was in reference to the 10-day clashes between government and commando forces in which hundreds were killed and thousands wounded.

The statements of King Hussein and the PLO came after four days of renewed fighting between government and guerrilla forces and were followed by a fresh outburst of clashes.

Seven commando groups June 5 called for the overthrow of King Hussein's government and the formation of a national union government. A joint statement broadcast by Baghdad radio said "this is the only way to prevent a unilateral peace agreement between Jordan and Israel." The statement was signed by Al Fatah, the Popular Front for the Liberation of Palestine, the Popular Democratic Front, the Popular Front-General Command, the Palestine Liberation Organization, the Arab Liberation Front and the Popular Struggle Liberation Front.

The Jordanian army began an all-out attack against the commandos in northern Jordan July 13, 1971. After several days of heavy fighting, the government claimed the guerrillas had been crushed and that more than 2,000 of them were captives.

The government announced July 14 that it had launched the assault to oust the guerrillas from inhabited areas following attacks they had made on Jordanian troops in the Jarash area. The fighting was centered in the Ajlun-Jarash area, 25 miles north of Amman, stronghold of the commando movement. The main Palestinian resistance was reported quelled by July 15.

Palestinian sources reported July 18 that scores of commandos had fled across the Jordan River into Israeli-occupied territory to escape capture by the Jordanian forces. Israeli officials, confirming the unprecedented development, reported July 19 that 72 guerrillas had crossed into the occupied west bank July 17–19 and surrendered to Israeli authorities.

In a review of the latest fighting, Jordanian Premier Wasfi Tell told newsmen July 19 that the commandos had lost all their bases in Jordan. He said Jordan's troops had captured 2,300 fedayeen and that only about 200 others were at large, but were being rounded up by "routine patrols." Tell said casualties totaled 50 guerrillas killed and 31 Jordanian soldiers slain and 96 wounded.

The new outbreak of clashes caused a further deterioration in relations between Amman and Egypt, Syria and Iraq, which assailed the crackdown against the Palestinian guerrillas.

The Jordan-commando fighting briefly flared along the Syrian border July 19. Damascus radio charged that Jordanian artillery shelled the Syrian town of Dera and other settlements near the border, burning crops and causing civilian casualties. Jordan claimed commandos from Syria crossed the border into Jordan and kidnapped two farmers and wounded two civilians in a rocket attack on the border town of Ramtha.

A government announcement July 21 said 2,000 captured Arab commandos had been released. An Amman spokesman said several hundred had left for Iraq and Syria the previous day. The spokesman said most of the others would remain in Jordan, having agreed to surrender their weapons and return to civilian life. Authorities July 20 had freed 831 guerrillas in Amman and in the northern city of Irbid. Another 500 were set free in Amman July 21.

Bomb alert in Cairo. The imposition of a bomb alert in Cairo earlier in September and the distribution of anti-Soviet pamphlets in the city by an unknown organization was disclosed in Beirut Sept. 29, 1971 by travelers from Cairo.

The bomb alert followed the discovery of an explosive device near the office of Information Minister Abdel Kader and elsewhere, including a ship in a district inhabited by Russians.

The anti-Soviet literature was signed by a group called the Egyptian National Front. The tracts, circulated by mail, denounced "Soviet imperialism" in Egypt and called for the ouster of "Soviet imperialism from our land."

Egyptian officials were reported Oct. 3 to have accused Israeli intelligence of having distributed the leaflets in order to create suspicion between Egypt and the Soviet Union.

Jordanian premier assassinated. Premier Wasfi Tell of Jordan was shot to death by three Palestinians while entering a hotel in Cairo Nov. 28, 1971. Jordanian Foreign Minister Abdullah Sallah was slightly injured and an Egyptian policeman accompanying the two men was seriously wounded. At least 10 shots were fired. The three gunmen and another Palestinian acting as lookout were arrested.

Tell was assassinated as he was returning to his hotel from a meeting of the Arab League's Joint Defense Council discussing strategy against Israel. In Beirut, the Popular Front for the Liberation of Palestine claimed responsibility for his death.

The gunmen described themselves as members of a Palestinian commando faction called the Black September organization. It had been formed in July to avenge the slaying of Palestinian guerrillas in the Jordan civil war in September 1970. A statement issued by the group at the time vowed a "scorched earth" policy against the Jordanian government. The commandos considered Tell a prime enemy after their forces were crushed during that conflict.

The three assassins were identified as Monzer Suleiman Khalifa, 27; Gawad Khali Boghdadi, 23; and Ezzat Ahmad Rabah, 23. The fourth man was not identified. The police said all had en-

tered Egypt several days prior with Syrian passports. All four were freed on bail (to be provided by the Palestine Liberation Organization) Feb. 29, 1972.

A medical-ballistics report said the bullets fatal to Tell had not been fired from the guns carried by the four defendants.

Jordan aides attacked. The Jordanian ambassadors to Britain and Switzerland were the targets of assassination attempts Dec. 15 and 16, 1971.

Ambassador Zaid al-Rifai was shot and wounded in the hand Dec. 15 when a gunman waiting in ambush near a London street intersection fired at his car.

In Geneva, two Swiss policemen were seriously injured Dec. 16 when a package left at Jordan's U.N. mission and addressed to Ambassador Ibrahim Zreikat exploded as they were opening it. The reception room of the mission was destroyed. Zreikat was in another room and escaped unhurt. Police and firemen had been called to examine the parcel by mission authorities.

The Black September organization said it was responsible for the attempt on Rifai's life. An Al Fatah broadcast from Cairo Dec. 16 expressed approval of the effort to kill Rifai and charged that he was King Hussein's liaison with U.S. intelligence.

A Jordanian government statement of Dec. 17 charged that the Black September group did not exist and was "only a mask used by Fatah to hide its treacherous schemes" against Jordan. The statement said "We know very well those in Fatah who are in charge of these schemes" and warned "they shall not escape punishment."

Lebanon Suffers Retaliation

Israeli forces raid Lebanon. Israeli forces crossed the border into Lebanon June 28, 1971 to attack a guerrilla base at Blida. The 200 troops involved in the operation were said to have blown up three houses apparently used by the commandos for attacks on Israel.

A Beirut military spokesman reported another Israeli incursion into Lebanon June 29. The spokesman said government troops fought the Israelis about one mile inside Lebanon as they attacked the villages of Taybeh and Al Adassiyae, north of Blida.

Israeli forces crossed into Lebanon Jan. 10, 1972 for retaliatory attacks against commando bases in the towns of Bint Jbail and Kfar Hamam, three miles north of the border. The operation followed guerrilla raids on Israel from Lebanon Jan. 6–10.

According to an Israeli announcement Jan. 11, two guerrilla buildings were blown up in Bint Jbail and "a number of terrorists were killed." Two other commandos and an Israeli soldier were killed in an exchange of fire. In the Kfar Hamam raid, Israeli soldiers "also blew up two buildings with the terrorists inside them." One Israeli soldier was killed in the engagement.

According to the Lebanese government's version of the attack, a force of 100 Israeli soldiers struck at Bint Jbail, blew up two buildings and withdrew. In the second operation later that night, 150 Israelis struck out from the Golan Heights and pounded Kfar Hamam and the nearby village of Rashya Fakhar on the slopes of Mount Hermon. Three houses in Kfar Hamam were blown up and a number of buildings in Rashya Fakhar were destroyed by shelling. Three commandos and a Lebanese civilian were killed in the two attacks.

An Israeli force crossed into Lebanon Jan. 13 for a reprisal raid on a commando base in Kafra. They reported blowing up two houses used by guerrillas. The incursion followed guerrilla shelling Jan. 8, 10 and 12 of the Israeli town of Kiryat Shmona.

Lt. Gen. David Elazar, Israeli chief of staff, warned Lebanon Jan. 14 that the recent commando attacks from its territory were "liable to bring disaster upon the villages of south Lebanon." He called on the Beirut government and its army to "do their best to prevent such a grave development." Elazar attributed the recent upsurge of commando raids, following months of calm, to the massing of nearly 4,000 commandos at Lebanese bases near the Israeli border. He said intelligence reports told of Libyan instructors or advisers with the commandos. Elazar's statement was transmitted to Beirut in writing through the U.N. Mixed Armistice Commission.

The Palestinian commandos were reported Jan. 15 to have decided to refrain from firing on Israel while inside Lebanon. The guerrillas, whose leaders had conferred with Lebanese officials, agreed instead to operate from "mobile bases" and fire only when inside Israeli territory. The arrangement was worked out following a meeting Jan. 14 between commando leader Yasir Arafat and Lebanese military officials. The Lebanese reportedly feared an Israeli occupation of the Arkub region aimed at neutralization of the commandos' main military bases.

Israeli air and ground forces carried out heavy reprisal operations against commandos in Lebanon Feb. 25–28. The Israelis claimed about 60 guerrillas killed and more than 100 wounded. Israel placed its losses at 11 slightly wounded. The guerrillas admitted that 20 of their men had been slain and 36 wounded.

The attackers pulled out after the U.N. Security Council had adopted a resolution earlier Feb. 28 demanding Israeli withdrawal from Lebanon.

Jerusalem said the operation was in retaliation for the recent infiltration of commandos into northern Israel from Lebanon. Three Israeli soldiers and a civilian couple were killed and several others were wounded in guerrilla ambushes Feb. 22–23.

The Israeli thrust was centered on a number of guerrilla strongholds in the Arkoub Valley, an area between the Hasbani River and the western flank of Mount Hermon.

An Israeli report Feb. 28 said the four-day offensive had left the guerrilla forces in disarray and that much of their equipment had been captured. Buildings, installations, base camps and headquarters were destroyed from the air or dynamited on the ground.

Some of the Israeli ground patrols had come under fire by guerrillas from nearby Syria Feb. 27.

Lebanese troops Feb. 28 quickly moved into the commando areas evacuated by the Israelis. "This time we intend to occupy the guerrilla positions and keep them," a high-ranking Lebanese officer was quoted as saying.

A guerrilla spokesman Feb. 29 acknowledged the Lebanese army's right to control the area, saying "under no circumstances will we infringe on this sovereignty."

Golan Heights clash. Israeli forces followed up their four-day attack on Palestinian commandos in Lebanon with air and artillery strikes March 1 on suspected guerrilla bases in the southern and central part of the Israeli-occupied Golan Heights. Syrian planes retaliated later in the day with raids on Israeli settlements about two miles inside the heights.

An army spokesman in Jerusalem said the bombing of the suspected commando strongholds was in response to mortar attacks on Israeli settlements during the night. A Damascus broadcast said the Syrian air assaults were in retaliation for Israeli shelling of three Syrian villages in the heights and an air raid on a guerrilla camp near Dera in Syria, close to the border with Jordan.

Israel Warns Lebanon. Israeli Defense Minister Moshe Dayan warned March 3, 1972 that Israel "reserves the option" of maintaining an indefinite presence in Lebanon if Beirut failed to curb attacks by Palestinian commandos on Israel from Lebanese soil.

Speaking in a television interview, Dayan described as a "fundamental change" in Lebanon's policy to have its army take control of former commando areas on the slopes of Mount Hermon from which the guerrillas had been operating against Israel since 1968.

The executive committee of the Palestine Liberation Organization was reported to have decided at meetings in Beirut March 1–2 to order their guerrilla forces out of populated centers in southern Lebanon and to abandon their fixed bases. The action was aimed at avoiding confrontations with the Lebanese army, which had moved into the areas formerly controlled by commandos.

Israelis Seize Captives. An Israeli armored force struck into Lebanon June 21, 1972 and captured five Syrian officers, a Lebanese officer and three military policemen. The strike coincided with an Israeli air and artillery attack against a suspected Palestinian commando base at Hasbeya in southeastern Lebanon. The Israeli military action followed by a day resumption of guerrilla attacks across the border after a four-month lull. Two civilians were killed in the ambush of a tourist bus.

According to Beirut's account of the incident: Four Lebanese policemen were killed and two civilians were wounded during the capture of the Syrians and Lebanese at the village of Ramieh about 100 yards from the Israeli border. The Syrians and their Lebanese escorts were ambushed by five Israeli tanks and three other armored vehicles.

Reporting on the Hasbaya attack, the Lebanese said the Israeli planes and artillery killed 14 civilians and wounded 25 others. Commando sources reported that 30 of their men had been killed and 30 wounded in the raid.

A Syrian communique broadcast by Damascus radio said the captured Syrian officers were in Lebanon "as part of the visits exchanged" by the Syrian and Lebanese armies.

An Israeli military spokesman said the Israeli operations against Lebanon were "connected with information we had in recent weeks of preparation" for more guerrilla attacks against Israel from Lebanese territory. The capture of the Syrians came as a surprise and was "evidence of joint Syrian-Lebanese planning against Israel," the spokesman said.

In a previous encounter, Israel reported that its forces June 15 had killed four Arab infiltrators in the occupied Golan Heights. The men were said to have worn uniforms largely identical with Syrian army uniforms.

Lebanon Raided Again. Israeli planes and artillery June 23, 1972 struck at suspected Palestinian commando bases in Lebanon for the second time in three days, inflicting heavy casualties.

The June 23 Israeli attack followed the commando shelling earlier June 23 of Qiryat Shemona, an Israeli town.

A Lebanese communique said 18 Lebanese civilians were killed and 12 wounded in the Israeli assaults. The Palestinian Resistance Movement in Beirut reported "scores of guerrillas" killed or wounded in the attacks. Seventeen of the Lebanese fatalities occurred during Israeli jet strikes on Deir el Ashayer on the Syrian border, according to Lebanese authorities. The communique said the other Lebanese was killed by an Israeli rocket attack near Marjoun, directly opposite Kiryat Shmona.

Justifying the Israeli action, Premier Golda Meir said June 23 "if the danger [to Israeli lives] is from over the border and the Lebanese government is unable to handle it, we don't have any choice but to do it ourselves."

U.N. condemns Israel—The U.N. Security Council, called into emergency session June 23 at Lebanon's request, approved a resolution June 26 condemning "the repeated attacks of Israeli forces on Lebanese territory and population." The vote was 13-0, with the U.S. and Panama abstaining.

The resolution, sponsored by Belgium, Britain and France, called on Israel to refrain from future attacks on Lebanon and urged it to release the five Syrian officers and one Lebanese officer captured June 21.

The U.S. and Panama explained that their abstentions were based on the resolution's failure to also condemn the Arabs for their attacks on Israel.

Israeli delegate Yosef Tekoah deplored the Council's action, charging that the resolution "ignores the murderous attacks on innocent civilians, the assaults on villages and towns, the crimes of air piracy perpetrated by Arab terrorist organizations."

Commando-Lebanese Accord. Beirut sources reported June 26, 1974 that the commandos in Lebanon had agreed to a government request to temporarily suspend attacks on Israel to spare Lebanon from reprisal attacks by Israel. The decision was confirmed by Premier Saeb Salam, who said "we are in an understanding with the commandos and we

shall remain so." He refused to give further details.

Salam had said June 24 that his government had no intentions of cracking down on the commandos. He declared: "Let Israel hear this: There will not be a clash between Lebanon and the Palestinians in any way."

Salam made his statement after conferring three times in the previous 24 hours with commando leader Yasir Arafat.

Three right-wing and Christian leaders opposed to the guerrillas had urged abrogation of the 1969 Lebanese-commando pact that had ended several weeks of bloody fighting between government and commando forces and provided for cooperation between the two sides. The opponents of the guerrillas were former President Camille Chamoun, Deputy Raymond Edde, head of the National Bloc party, and Deputy Pierre Gamiel, head of the Phalangist party.

A formal agreement barring commando raids on Israel from Lebanon was reached June 27 by Salem and Arafat.

Although neither side gave details in announcing the accord the following day, informed sources reported that the commandos had agreed to pull back from a number of Lebanese villages and towns near the Israeli border. The guerrillas also were said to have acceded to a Lebanese request to establish a unified information office in Beirut that would not be permitted to issue its own military communiques.

The Popular Front for the Liberation of Palestine-General Command announced June 28 that it would not abide by the Beirut accord for freezing operations against Israel. The PFLP-GC said its forces would continue attacks on Israeli-held areas but would carry out the raids "in the depth of enemy territory" and not near the cease-fire lines.

Commando leader assassinated. A leader of the Popular Front for the Liberation of Palestine, Ghassan Kanafani, 36, was killed in an explosion in a car in Beirut July 8, 1972. Also killed was his 17-year old niece.

A statement by the PFLP accused "Zionist and imperialist quarters" of the deaths and pledged retaliation.

Kanafani had been a spokesman for the front but recently had said he no longer held that position. He had said he was only editor of its weekly journal, Al Hadaf.

Commando sources, linking Israeli intelligence with Kanafani's death, said their investigators had found at the blast site a card bearing the official Israeli emblem with the sentence: "With the compliments of the Israeli embassy in Copenhagen."

A spokesman for Israel's National Police Headquarters in Jerusalem said July 9 that the bomb or explosive device that killed Kanafani probably had gone off accidentally and that it apparently was intended for Israel as part of a guerrilla plot to send parcels containing explosive devices to kill Israelis. The spokesman, Mordechai Tavor, said the card found at the blast site was a type commonly used by the Israeli embassy in Copenhagen that was sent out with publicity material and invitations. He noted that Kanafani's brother lived in Denmark.

The PFLP July 11 claimed credit for a grenade explosion that day at the central bus terminal in Tel Aviv. Nine people were wounded. The front said the attack was in reprisal for Kanafani's death.

Russians arm commandos. A New York Times dispatch from Geneva Sept. 17, 1972 reported that the U.S.S.R. for the first time had begun sending arms directly to Al Fatah, the chief Palestinian guerrilla organization. Sources in the Swiss city said the first shipment had arrived within the last few weeks. The Soviet Union was said to have pledged the weapons during talks in Moscow in July with a delegation of commando groups led by Yasir Arafat.

The Soviet arms shipment was confirmed by pro-commando sources in Beirut Sept. 21. Its destination, according to the sources, was Syria where Al Fatah maintained its military headquarters. One Arab informant was quoted as saying that the Russians had sent "only light weapons this time—but there will be more deliveries."

Terrorists Hijack Planes, Slay Tourists at Airport

German airliner seized, then freed. A West German Lufthansa jumbo jet airliner enroute from New Delhi to Athens was hijacked by five Palestinians Feb. 21, 1972 and was diverted to Aden, Southern Yemen Feb. 22. All 172 passengers held hostage, including Joseph P. Kennedy 3rd, son of the late Sen. Robert F. Kennedy, were released later Feb. 22. The 16 crewmembers were freed Feb. 23, and the hijackers surrendered to Yemeni authorities.

The plane was commandeered one-half hour out of New Delhi when the guerrillas, armed with hand grenades, dynamite and pistols, broke into the cockpit. The pilot said the Arabs did not say they wanted to fly to any specific country, but submitted compass readings that would have brought the aircraft to the desert along the Red Sea on the coast of the Arabian Peninsula. He said the hijackers were persuaded to have the plane fly to Aden instead. On landing, the hijackers wired the doors of the jet with explosives and threatened to blow it up.

The Palestinians described themselves as members of the Organization for Victims of Zionist Occupation, based in a refugee camp in the Israeli-occupied Gaza Strip.

Baghdad radio broadcast a political message which it claimed had been read by the hijackers to the passengers over the plane's public address system. The statement assailed "the flagging and defeatist attitude certain Arab regimes are adopting" on Israel and on West German aid to Israel. It pledged that "we will pursue the enemy everywhere and strike him and uproot him throughout the world."

The Bonn government disclosed Feb. 25 that it had paid $5 million in ransom for the release of the Lufthansa jet airliner and its crew.

Transport Minister Georg Leber said the Palestinian commandos had demanded the money in a letter addressed to Lufthansa and mailed at Cologne Feb. 22. It had stipulated that the ransom be carried by messenger to a secret meeting place outside Beirut, Lebanon.

The West German government, which was a majority shareholder in the airline, complied with the request.

Leber identified the hijackers as members of the Popular Front for the Liberation of Palestine.

The Middle East News Agency reported that the five hijackers were released by the Yemen authorities Feb. 27.

Israel thwarts Arab hijackers. Israeli paratroopers broke into a hijacked Belgian airliner at Lod Airport in Tel Aviv May 9, 1972, killing two of four Palestinian commandos and rescuing 90 passengers and 10 crewmen. (But one woman passenger shot accidentally died May 18.)

The plane, operated by Sabena Airlines, had been seized May 8 by the four Arabs, including two women, after taking off from Vienna en route to Tel Aviv. The hijackers, armed with guns and grenades, were identified as members of the Black September organization.

On landing at Lod, the Arabs, with International Red Cross representatives acting as intermediaries, began negotiating with Israeli authorities in the field's control tower. They demanded the release of 317 Palestinian guerrillas in Israeli prisons in exchange for the safety of the plane and its passengers and crew. The Arabs threatened to blow up the aircraft with all its hostages unless their demands were met. The negotiations and subsequent rescue operation were directed by Defense Minister Moshe Dayan, who was in the control tower with Lt. Gen. David Elazar, chief of staff, and other Israeli officials.

After the rescue had been carried out, Elazar disclosed that the negotiations with the commandos had been a ploy to gain time for preparing the plan to take over the plane, that Israel had no intention of meeting the hijackers' demands.

According to witnesses, Israelis crawled under the aircraft in the darkness and damaged it, making it unable to take off. They offered to repair the airliner so it could fly on to Cairo with the hostages, as the hijackers later demanded. Eighteen Israeli paratroopers, disguised in the overalls of aircraft repairmen, were driven to the plane in an airlines service vehicle. The soldiers climbed ladders onto the wings, opened two emergency doors and burst into the jet. A 10-second exchange of gunfire with the Arabs ensued. Two of the hijackers were shot to death, one of the women commandos was wounded and the second woman hijacker surrendered.

Tourists slain at Israeli airport. Three Japanese terrorists used by an Arab commando group attacked the Lod International Airport near Tel Aviv the night of May 30, 1972, killing 24 persons and wounding 76. The death toll was 28 by June 24. One attacker was slain by his own grenade, another was shot to death, apparently by bullets fired by his own companions, and the third was captured by an El Al airliner mechanic.

The captured attacker told Israeli authorities he was a member of "the Army of the Red Star" (also referred to as the United Red Army), a left-wing Japanese group recruited by the Arab guerrilla movement. In Beirut, the Marxist Popular Front for the Liberation of Palestine claimed credit for the assault.

The three Japanese had debarked with 116 other passengers from an Air France flight from Rome. Entering the passenger lounge, the three men picked up two valises from a conveyor belt, unzipped them and whipped out machineguns and grenades. Then they began firing and lobbing grenades indiscriminately at a crowd of about 300 in the waiting room. One of the terrorists fired at aircraft on the runway from an opening of the baggage conveyor, and the other, who eventually was captured, raced out to the tarmac, shooting at anyone in sight.

The Japanese embassy in Israel identified the captured men as Daisuke Namba, 22, and the others as Ken Torio, 23, and Jiro Sugizaki, 23.

Tokyo police June 1 reported that Daisuke Namba's name actually was Kozo Okamoto, brother of another Red Army member who had taken part in the hijacking of a Japanese airliner to North Korea in 1970. The two slain terrorists were correctly identified later as Rakeshi Okudeira and Yoshuyiki Yasuda.

Among the dead were 16 Puerto Ricans who arrived on a pilgrimage to the Christian holy places. Eight Israelis were slain, including Dr. Aharon Katzir-Katchalsky, 58, one of the country's leading scientists.

Arab commandos claim credit—In a statement issued from its Beirut headquarters May 31, the Popular Front for the Liberation of Palestine said it was responsible for the Tel Aviv airport attack.

The PFLP "announces its complete responsibility for the brave operation launched by one of its special groups tonight in our occupied land," the statement said. The announcement identified the three attackers as Bassem, Salah and Ahmed, and said they belonged to a group called the "Squad of the Martyr Patrick Uguello." Uguello was identified by the PFLP as a Nicaraguan who had been shot to death during an attempt to hijack an El Al plane over London September 1970.

The front said the Tel Aviv airport attack also was in reprisal for the Israeli killing of two Arab guerrillas during an aborted hijacking of a Belgian plane at the Lod airfield May 9.

PFLP spokesman Bassam Zayid said in Beirut May 31 that the front had instructed the three Japanese gunmen not to fire on the Air France plane passengers but on those debarking from an El Al flight due to arrive 10 minutes later and those waiting for them. "We were sure that 90%-95% of the people in the airport at the time the operation was due to take place would be Israelis or people of direct loyalty to Israel," Zayid said. "Our purpose was to kill as many people as possible at the airport, Israelis, of course, but anyone else who was there."

An Egyptian broadcast from Cairo May 31 boasted that "the heroes proved they can penetrate the conquered territories to avenge the blood of others. Now Israel has no alternative but to close down Lydda [Lod] Airport and to prevent tourist visits if she wishes to protect her borders."

According to Japanese press reports, sources close to the United Red Army said the three Japanese terrorists could have been among several "soldiers" sent by the group several months ago to Middle East camps to receive guerrilla training.

Mid-East Terrorists Strike in Europe & Other Areas

11 Israelis slain at Olympics. Seventeen persons, among them 11 members of the Israeli Olympic team, were shot to death Sept. 5, 1972 in a 23-hour drama that began when Arab terrorists broke into the Israeli dormitory at the Olympic village in Munich, West Germany. Nine of the Israelis, seized by the Arabs as hostages, were killed along with five of their captors in an airport gun battle between the Arabs and West German police.

The Arabs and their hostages had been taken by helicopter to the airport 15 miles west of Munich where a jet was being made ready to fly them all to Cairo.

The other two Israelis were killed in the initial Arab attack on their living quarters. The 17th victim was a West German policeman.

In Cairo, the organization called Black September claimed responsibility for the attack.

The bloody drama began at 4:30 a.m. Sept. 5, when the commandos scaled an eight-foot wire fence that surrounded the Olympic village compound. The raiders made their way to Building 31, which housed the Hong Kong, Uruguayan and Israeli teams.

At about 5:30 a.m. the commandos burst into the quarters where the Israeli athletes were staying. As they rushed in, they were intercepted by Moshe Weinberg, the Israeli wrestling coach, who held a door against the commandos while shouting for the Israeli athletes to flee. Seconds later the Arabs broke in, killing Weinberg, 33, and Joseph Romano, 33, a weight lifter.

Six of the fifteen Israelis managed to escape the building. The nine, who were trapped inside their quarters, were reported to have fought the attackers for a time with knives. The Arabs, however, overpowered the Israelis, seizing them as hostages.

Once in control of the Israeli quarters in Building 31, the Arabs made known their demand: they wanted the release of 200 Arab commandos imprisoned in Israel.

Throughout the late morning and afternoon, West German officials negotiated with the Arabs on the patio of the Israeli dormitory.

The stalemate was broken at about 9 p.m. when the West Germans succeeded in persuading the terrorists to move out of Building 31 with the hostages. As part of the bargain, the West Germans agreed to have three helicopters transport the Arabs and the nine Israelis to the military airport at Furstenfeldbruck.

Munich authorities then cleared a path around the building, from which the Arabs and Israelis emerged at about 10 p.m. Using underground passageways, the group was moved by bus out of the Olympic village to the waiting helicopters.

When the convoy arrived at the airport, two of the terrorists walked from the helicopters to inspect a Boeing 707 jet that was to take them to Cairo. As they walked back to the helicopters, German riflemen reportedly opened fire. The Arabs, armed with automatic weapons, returned the fire.

Israeli leaders warned the Palestinian guerrillas Sept. 6 that they would pay for the Munich deaths.

At the same time, the Israeli government indirectly linked the governments of the Arab world to the murders.

The Israeli government issued a statement warning that "Israel will persevere in her struggle against the terrorist organizations and will not absolve their accomplices from responsibility for terrorist actions." Government sources later identified those "accomplices" as the Arab nations that gave sanctuary to the guerrillas, specifying Egypt, Syria and Lebanon. An unidentified Israeli official said "the Egyptians are the prime party in this incident. They have the power and influence to stop these groups, and instead they encourage them." The official said Egypt "shares the responsibility" with the Black September guerrillas for the attack.

PLO disavows responsibility—The executive committee of the Palestine Liberation Organization declared in a statement issued in Damascus Sept. 14 that its group was not responsible for the Black September group linked to the Munich killings. The statement insisted that the PLO's objective "was only aimed at pressuring Israel to release detained guerrillas from Israeli jails."

Arabs force release of Munich slayers. Two Arab guerrillas of the Black September group hijacked a West German airliner over Turkey Oct. 29, forcing the Bonn government to release the three Arabs held for the Munich murders. The freed killers were flown to Libya.

The released Arabs who faced trial for the killings were Mahmud el-Safadi, 21, Samer Mohammad Abdullah, 22, and Ibrahim Badran, 20.

The aircraft, a Lufthansa Boeing 727 with 13 passengers and seven crewmen, was commandeered by the two guerrillas after it left Beirut, Lebanon for Ankara, Turkey. Threatening to blow up the plane and its occupants unless their demands were met, the commandos forced the pilot to fly to Munich, with fuel stopovers at Nicosia, Cyprus and Zagreb, Yugoslavia. As the plane circled the heavily-guarded Munich airport, however, the hijackers ordered it flown back to Zagreb. It circled the airfield there for an hour and did not land until a smaller jet carrying the three guerrillas released by the West Germans arrived at the Yugoslav airport. The three freed prisoners then boarded the hijacked airliner, which flew to Tripoli, Libya.

The Israeli government reacted sharply to the release of the Munich commandos. A Foreign Ministry spokesman said Oct. 29 that "every capitulation encourages the terrorists to continue their criminal acts."

Lufthansa chairman Herbert Culmann and the pilot of the hijacked plane assumed responsibility Oct. 30 for capitulating to the terrorists. Culmann told a news conference in Cologne that refusal to accede to the hijackers' demands would have "sealed the fate of the people" aboard the commandeered aircraft.

Israeli Foreign Minister Abba Eban protested to Bonn Oct. 30. The message, conveyed through West German Ambassador to Israel Jesco von Puttkamer, charged "capitulation to terrorists " and said Israel questioned whether "there has been a change in German policy regarding terrorists and their actions."

In reply to Eban's charge of "capitulation," a West German government spokesman said Oct. 30 that the foreign minister had "missed the point" that 20 lives were at stake.

The U.S. State Department Oct. 30 criticized the West German decision in freeing the Arab terrorists. Spokesman Charles W. Bray 3rd expressed "regret that known terrorists can secure their freedom as a result of extortion and blackmail and can find safe haven."

Letter bombs go to many countries. An envelope bomb apparently mailed by Arab guerrillas exploded and killed a diplomat in the Israeli embassy in London Sept. 19, 1972. This was followed by the discovery of similar boobytrapped envelopes destined for Israeli officials in at least eight other cities. All bore Amsterdam postmarks. None of these detonated.

The man killed was Dr. Ami Shachori, counselor for agricultural affairs. Three more explosive devices in envelopes addressed to senior Israeli embassy members were discovered by Israeli security men. Israelis told police that one of them contained a leaflet from Black September.

Four more explosive letters addressed to members of the Israeli embassy staff were found in a London post office later September 19.

A security check of mail at the Israeli embassy in Paris Sept. 19 turned up two large envelopes containing explosives. They were defused.

Additional bomb letters were intercepted Sept. 20 in New York, Montreal, Ottawa, Brussels and Jerusalem. All were addressed to Israeli officials.

Ten more letter bombs, postmarked from Amsterdam, were intercepted in a Jerusalem post office Sept. 21. Others were received at the Israeli embassies in Kinshasa, Zaire; Brussels and Buenos Aires.

Amsterdam police theorized Sept. 21 that the Arabs had slipped into the Netherlands the previous week and fled the country after carrying out their mission.

Amsterdam police said Sept. 22 that the British police would coordinate international efforts to investigate the letter-bomb activities. Authorities in the Netherlands and other countries agreed to forward pertinent information to Scotland Yard in London.

A Jordanian government spokesman said Sept. 23 that the Amman post office that day had intercepted and defused four letter bombs addressed to four Jordanian officials. The spokesman said the letters bore Amsterdam postmarks.

Dutch authorities Oct. 25 detained and then released a Jordanian with an Algerian diplomatic passport who was found to be carrying unaddressed letter bombs, hand grenades and explosives in his luggage. The Jordanian, intercepted at the Amsterdam airport, told a magistrate that he was unaware of the contents of the suitcases. He said he thought his luggage contained documents for an Algerian embassy in South America. In response to an Israeli query as to why the Jordanian was freed, the Dutch Justice Ministry repeated the statement made by the Arab.

A letter bomb delivered Oct. 4 to the Rome office of United Hias Service, a Jewish immigration office, was defused by Italian explosive experts. The letter, mailed from Malaysia, bore inscriptions which said "Black September."

A postal clerk was seriously injured Oct. 14 when a letter bomb exploded in a New York post office.

The letter, bearing a Malaysian postmark, was addressed to an unidentified former national officer of Hadassah, the women's Zionist organization.

Two other New York women also active in American Zionist circles had received letter bombs Oct. 10. The recipients opened the envelopes, but the bombs did not explode. Both letters bore Malaysian postmarks. Similar letters were mailed Oct. 10 to Jewish families in Bulawayo, Rhodesia.

Letter bombs were sent Oct. 24–27 to U.S. officials, including President

Nixon, and to Palestinian Liberation Organization leaders and other Palestinians in four Arab countries. Several of the latter bombs were opened and exploded, injuring a number of Arabs.

Israeli postal authorities in the northern town of Kiryat Shmona Oct. 24 intercepted three letter bombs intended for President Nixon, Secretary of State William P. Rogers and Defense Secretary Melvin R. Laird.

Letter bombs bearing Belgrade, Yugoslavia postmarks were received Oct. 25 in Lebanon, Libya, Algeria and Egypt. A letter opened in Beirut exploded and injured the secretary of a trading company known to have arranged arms deals with Arab countries. The envelope was addressed to a Palestinian partner in the firm who was traveling outside Lebanon. A Beirut postman was blinded after one of the letters he was sorting exploded in his face. Palestine Liberation Organization official Abu Khalil was injured in Algiers when he opened a booby-trapped parcel. Another PLO official, Mustafa Awad Abu Zeid, the organization's secretary in Libya, was blinded by a parcel bomb opened in Tripoli. Two other persons received less serious injuries. Egyptian authorities intercepted a parcel bomb at the Cairo airport. The package was addressed to a PLO official.

Three other letter bombs exploded at the Cairo airport Oct. 26, seriously injuring an Egyptian security officer, who was examing the envelopes after intercepting them. The letters were intended for three officials of the PLO office in Cairo.

The Beirut office of the newspaper of the Popular Front for the Liberation of Palestine was the intended target of a letter bomb Oct. 27. The device was intercepted at the city's post office and rendered harmless.

The Malaysian Home Affairs Ministry confirmed Nov. 1 that 15 letter bombs meant for Jewish groups in London, Rome and the U.S. had been discovered in the Kuala Lumpur post office Oct. 31 and defused by army experts. Malaysian officials said Nov. 2 that a local Malay-Arab group was responsible for sending out 35 letter bombs, including the 15. The same group was said to have mailed out nine other explosive devices from Penang in October.

A letter bomb received by the Egyptian embassy in London Oct. 31 was rendered harmless. London police Nov. 2 defused a letter bomb destined for the British Technion Society, which was connected with the University of Haifa in Israel. It was postmarked Penang.

Another 19 letter bombs intended for Jews in London and Glasgow were received Nov. 10–13 bearing postmarks from New Delhi and Bombay, India. One of the devices that had not been intercepted was opened Nov. 10 at a London diamond trading company, exploding and wounding an official of the firm.

Swiss authorities intercepted five letter bombs at the airport postal center in Geneva Nov. 10. All bore New Delhi postmarks and were addressed either to the Israeli mission to U.N. agencies in Geneva or to Jews and Jewish organizations.

The Indian government was criticized by opposition leaders in parliament Nov. 13 for allegedly being lax in preventing dissemination of the letter bombs. Rightwing Jan Sangh party members charged that New Delhi's "pro-Arab policy" hindered government action in the matter. Communications Minister H. N. Bahgunua denied the allegations, saying that more than 50 letter bombs had been caught by Indian authorities.

Israel opposes anti-terror groups. Following the Sept. 19 letter bombing in London, the Israel branch of the Jewish Defense League (JDL) announced the formation of an anti-terrorist organization to combat Arab guerrilla groups and institutions in Europe and the U.S. The Israeli government immediately cracked down on the JDL and individuals attempting to take action on their own.

Israeli authorities Sept. 21 disclosed the arrest of Amihai Paglin, a former leader in the underground struggle against British rule in Palestine, in connection with a secret shipment of arms that had been intercepted at the Tel Aviv airport. The weapons, including machine guns and grenades, were meant for use against Arabs abroad. The JDL claimed responsibility for the arms shipment, but its leader, Rabbi Meir Kahane, was later said to have told Justice Minister

Yacov Shapiro that it was wrong to involve Israel. Israeli authorities also arrested JDL member Abraham Hershkowitz on charges of attempting to ship the arms out by air.

Police Sept. 22 raided JDL's Jerusalem headquarters, seized documents connected with the alleged arms smuggling operation and arrested the league's secretary, Joseph Schneider. He was charged with illegal possession of weapons.

Israeli police acknowledged Sept. 26 that some arms shipments meant for the anti-terrorist campaign against Arabs had slipped out of the country and reached their destinations.

The Israeli government issued an injunction Sept. 22 against Kahane and 19 other JDL members ordering them to keep out of the West Bank and the Gaza Strip. The order was said to be aimed at preventing the JDL from conducting "any activities liable to disrupt order or endanger security in those areas."

Kahane, who had planned to leave Israel Oct. 2 for a visit to the U.S., was arrested by Israeli police Oct. 1. They said he had in his possession detonators for the grenades in the arms shipment seized Sept. 14 at the Tel Aviv airport.

(A group in West Germany calling itself the International Anti-Terror Organization warned Sept. 20 that it planned to bomb Arab airlines, organizations and embassies in retaliation for Arab attacks on Israelis.)

Arab bookstore bombed in Paris. A bookstore in Paris serving as the French headquarters of the Palestine Liberation Organization was slightly damaged by a bomb blast Oct. 4. Police said an extremist Jewish group had taken responsibility for the explosion. Shortly after the incident, a Paris newspaper received an anonymous message signed by the "Massada action and defense movement." It said the bombing was the organization's first response to terrorism against Israelis and Jews and vowed retaliation against future acts of Arab terrorism.

U.S.-Israeli talks on terrorism. The U.S. Sept. 22, 1972 backed Israel's view that priority must be given to combatting international terrorism, although "options must be kept open" for a Middle East peace settlement. The announced American position followed a report Sept. 21 that Israel had informed friendly governments that it would refuse to participate in further peace negotiations until all Arab terrorism was crushed.

The U.S.-Israeli agreement on terrorism was reached in talks in Washington between Secretary of State William P. Rogers and Foreign Minister Abba Eban. After the meeting a State Department spokesman said Rogers had agreed with Eban that "individual governments must act effectively to combat this challenge to world social order." Eban, the spokesman said, had outlined the measures Israel was taking to fight terrorism.

After meeting with Rogers, Eban emphasized to newsmen that his country was determined to combat terror tactics because "it has always been our policy to hit where we can those who make war against us."

"It is not our policy or duty," he said, "to wait for the saboteurs to kill us or our children." Eban charged that Egypt, Syria and Lebanon had engaged "in a new form of warfare" against Israel by supporting the Arab commandos.

(Rogers discussed the issue of terrorism later Sept. 22 with French Foreign Minister Maurice Schumann. Rogers, the department later disclosed, had informed Schumann that the U.S. "will press hard for sanctions in the case of civil aviation and for other practical responses to terrorist acts.")

The Sept. 21 report that Israel would refuse to negotiate pending the elimination of the Arab terrorist threat also said that Israel was preparing new blows against the Palestinian commandos. According to the Israeli source, in the coming months Israel would launch a "major military effort" in the Middle East to destroy the terrorist groups. It would also take preventive action anywhere in the world if necessary, particularly in Europe, where the Arab guerrillas were becoming more active. The "Europeans are less capable of coping with them [the guerrillas] than the Israelis," the source said.

U.S. tightens security. The U.S. government announced Sept. 27 that henceforth all foreigners in transit through the U.S. would be required to have transit visas.

State Department officials said the move was prompted by the increasing threat of terrorist activities.

Under the rule, foreigners, even those changing planes at U.S. airports, must have transit visas. Exempted were naturalized Canadians, British subjects living in Bermuda and Mexicans holding valid border-crossing cards.

Formerly, foreign visitors had been permitted to remain in the U.S. for up to 10 days without a visa on condition that they presented evidence to airlines or shipping lines that they would leave the country by that time.

U.S. seeks to bar Arab terrorists. The Nixon Administration had begun a major effort to identify Arabs in the U.S. suspected of planning terrorist acts against Israeli citizens in the country and to carry out a more careful check of travelers from Arab countries, it was reported Oct. 4. The security measures were in accord with a promise by President Nixon to prevent terrorist attacks on Israelis in the U.S.

Bonn bans Palestinian groups. West Germany announced Oct. 4 that it had outlawed two Palestinian organizations in the country after receiving "concrete evidence that new terrorist acts are being planned for Germany." Police started a nationwide search for followers of the groups, identified by Interior Minister Hans-Dietrich Genscher as the General Union of Palestine Students, with 800 listed members, and the General Union of Palestinian Workers, with 1,000 members.

Genscher said "well under 100 Arabs" with suspected ties to terrorists had been expelled from West Germany since the Sept. 5 guerrilla attack in Munich and that 1,900 other Arabs had been barred from entering West Germany for lack of proper papers or because of suspicious connections. Among those listed as having been ousted from West Germany was Abdullah Hassan Yums el-Frangi, 30,

chief of the Palestinian Student Union. He and eight other Arabs were deported Sept. 27. Hesse Interior Minister Hans Heinz Bielefeld had said earlier in the week that the Munich attackers had tried to telephone Frangi's apartment on the day of their assault. Bielefeld said police had found evidence in Frangi's apartment indicating that he had helped plan Arab terrorist moves against the Israeli and Lebanese embassies in Bonn.

Arab & El Al man slain in Rome. An Libyan embassy clerk believed to have been an official of Al Fatah was shot to death in Rome Oct. 16, 1972. The victim, Abdel Wael Zuaiter, a Jordanian, reportedly was Al Fatah's top agent in Italy.

An Al Fatah statement issued in Beirut Oct. 17 charged that Zuaiter's assassination had been engineered by Israel's secret service and was carried out by Israeli terrorists.

Rome police said Oct. 18 that they believed Zuaiter's killing was the result of a feud between Black September and other Palestinian commando groups.

An Italian employe of the Israeli El Al airline office in Rome was shot to death April 27, 1973. The victim was Vittorio Olivares. His accused assailant, who was arrested, was identified as Zaharia Abou Saleh, a Lebanese.

Saleh told Italian police he was a member of the Palestinian Black September and was sent to Rome by the organization on a mission to kill Olivares because he was an Israeli spy responsible for the slaying of Zuaiter.

Arabs seize Israelis in Thailand. Four armed Palestinian commandos seized the Israeli embassy in Bangkok, Thailand Dec. 28, 1972 and held six Israeli occupants hostage for 19 hours before releasing them. The Arab guerrillas, described as members of the Black September group, freed the Israelis Dec. 29 after negotiations with Thai officials. The guerrillas were flown to Cairo in a Thai plane.

The seizure of the embassy began when two of the commandos climbed the wall of the compound and opened the gate for the two others. The guerrillas walked into the building and held the six Israelis at gunpoint, threatening to kill them and blow up the embassy unless 36 Palestinian prisoners held in Israel were freed by 8 a.m. Dec. 29.

Two Thai officials—Marshal Dawee Chullaspaya, the armed forces chief of staff, and Deputy Foreign Minister Chartichai Choonhavan—entered the embassy and conferred with the guerrillas while hundreds of Thai soldiers and police surrounded the building. They were assisted in the negotiations by Egyptian Ambassador Mourtafa el-Essaway. After the guerrillas were persuaded to give up the hostages and leave the country, the commandos, the negotiators and the six Israelis left by bus for the Bangkok airport, 18 miles away. The commandos, the two Thais and the Egyptian ambassador boarded the plane and arrived in Cairo later Dec. 29. The Israelis remained in the bus at the Bangkok airport.

Thai officials said the guerrillas had been shamed into releasing their captives. A Thai officer said the Egyptian ambassador had told the commandos that Dec. 27 and 28 "were very important days for the Thai people," because ceremonies were being held for the investiture of the son of King Phumiphol Aduldet as crown prince, and "if anything happens it would make things very difficult."

Arab & Israeli slain in Cyprus. A representative of the Palestine Liberation Organization in Cyprus was killed by a bomb explosion in a Nicosia hotel room Jan. 25, 1973. Police said that the victim, Hussain al-Bathis, must have been handling a number of bombs. Police said Bathir had arrived in Nicosia Jan. 22 from Beirut and carried a Syrian passport and Lebanese identification documents.

An Israeli was shot to death March 12 in a Nicosia hotel by a man said to be a Jordanian, Cyprus police reported. The murdered Israeli, Simha Gilzer, 59, was described by police as a businessman.

The Iraqi news agency reported March 13 that Black September had claimed credit for Gilzer's slaying. According to the report, the Palestinian commando group said Gilzer was an Israeli intelligence officer responsible for Bathir's death.

Israeli agent slain in Madrid. An agent of the Israeli security services was shot and killed by a Palestinian commando in Madrid Jan. 26, 1973. Black September claimed credit for the killing.

The Israeli government Jan. 30 acknowledged the death of the agent and identified him as Baruch Cohen, 37.

Western diplomats slain in Saudi embassy in Sudan. Three diplomats—two U.S. and one Belgian—were murdered March 2, 1973 in Sudan by Black September terrorists who had seized the Saudi Arabian embassy the previous day during a reception for one of the men later slain.

The Arab terrorists took over the Saudi Arabian embassy in Khartoum March 1 and held six diplomats hostage, demanding the release of Arab prisoners in various countries. When the terrorist demands were refused during negotiations that followed, they murdered three of the hostages—U.S. Ambassador Cleo A. Noel, Jr.; George C. Moore, the departing U.S. charge d'affaires; and Guy Eid, the Egyptian-born charge at the Belgian embassy.

The terrorists ended their three-day occupation of the embassy at dawn March 4, surrendering to Sudanese authorities, who promised only that they would not be killed immediately.

The attack began about 7 p.m. March 1 when a Land Rover with diplomatic plates, later identified as belonging to Al Fatah, drove up to the gates of the embassy, where a party celebrating Moore's departure was in progress. The eight invaders, led by Abu Salem, second-ranking official at the Fatah office in Khartoum, crashed the gate and entered the building firing machine-guns and revolvers. No police guards were on duty.

Many of the guests escaped by jumping over the embassy wall. Others hid and then fled, while some identified themselves and were released. Noel suffered an ankle-wound from a ricocheting bullet and Eid was shot in the leg. According to Shigeru Nomoto, the Japanese charge d'affaires who described the attack in a March 3 statement, the commandos "tightly bound Ambassador Noel and Mr. Moore with ropes they had brought with them and punched and kicked them unmercifully." Also held in the attack were Sheik Abdullah el-Malhouk, Saudi ambassador and host to the party; his wife and four children and Adli el-Nazir, the Jordanian charge d'affaires.

Several hours later the guerillas issued an ultimatum that they would kill the six hostages within 24 hours unless certain demands were met. They insisted on the release of Abu Daoud and other members of Fatah imprisoned in Jordan as well as of Maj. Rafeh Hindawi, a Jordanian officer under life sentence for plotting against the Amman government. They also demanded the release of Sirhan Sirhan, convicted assassin of U.S. Sen. Robert F. Kennedy; all Arab women detained in Israel; and members of the Baader-Meinhof urban guerrilla group in West Germany "because they supported the Palestinian cause."

Telephone contact with the commandos was maintained by Sudanese Interior Minister Mohammed el Baghir who informed them early March 2 that the Jordanian government had refused demands for the release of Daoud, Hindawi and the others.

Shortly after the Jordanian refusal, the commandos read a statement in which they gave up their demand for the release of prisoners in Israel, "since Sudan cannot contact the Zionist enemy," and for the "German comrades," because the West German ambassador, who left the party early, "was not present as we had hoped." The dispatch concluded: "We insist and reconfirm that we will not leave the embassy or release the hostages or even guarantee their lives except if the Palestinian prisoners held in the prisons of the reactionary regime of Jordan are freed."

At a Washington news conference March 2, President Nixon said that while the U.S. would "do everything we can" to have the hostages released, it would "not pay blackmail."

The three Western diplomats were killed March 2 at about 9:30 p.m., the Sudanese government announced the following day. A Sudanese officer, who entered the embassy with permission from the terrorists, confirmed that the men had been taken to the basement and shot repeatedly.

The commandos remained in the embassy throughout March 3, occasionally speaking through a bullhorn to Sudanese soldiers outside and refusing to hand over the bodies of the slain diplomats unless the government guaranteed the commandos safe conduct to an unspecified Arab capital. Baghir told the terrorists later in the day that an emergency Cabinet session had rejected their request for an airplane and that they would be given until dawn the following morning to surrender. The commandos surrendered on that schedule.

(According to the Washington Post March 6, Sudanese Information Minister Umar al-Hag Musa confirmed that a major role in the surrender of the commandos had been played by Yasir Arafat, leader of Al Fatah. The Post quoted Musa as having said: "He helped in the last part, when it became clear they had no way out.")

In Lebanon, Prime Minister Saeb Salam expressed March 3 "the regret" of his government but noted that the Palestinians "have an issue of fate which should be dealt with from its roots" and that the international community should "embark on finding positive solutions for this issue based on right, justice and the dignity of man."

Baghir reported March 10 that a confession by one of the terrorists had revealed that the attack had been directed from the Beirut headquarters of Al Fatah and that the terrorists had maintained radio contact with Al Fatah.

The eight terrorists were convicted of murder and were given life sentences by a Khartoum court June 24, 1974, but Sudanese President Gaafar el-Nimeiry immediately commuted the sentences to seven-year terms and announced that the convicted men would be turned over to the Palestine Liberation Organization (PLO), headed by Arafat, who had been accused of complicity in the case. The eight men were released to the PLO June 25 and flown to Cairo.

Jordan thwarts commando plot. The Jordanian regime announced that it had arrested in Amman Feb. 15, 1973 a number of men "who infiltrated into the country to commit acts against the security of the state." It was subsequently disclosed that the Jordanians had seized 17 Palestinian commandos, including Abu Daoud, a member of Al Fatah's executive unit, the Revolutionary Council, thwarting a reported plan to assassinate King Hussein and overthrow his government. The men had entered Jordan from Kuwait and Syria.

Amman radio announced March 4 that the 17 men had been tried by a court-martial and were sentenced to be executed. Hussein March 6 offered to suspend the death sentences if the guerrilla groups agreed to "put an end once and for all to their plots against Jordan." Hussein's offer followed a plea by the ruler of Kuwait, Sheik Sabah al-Salem al-Sabah, who had sent an emissary to Amman to ask the king for clemency.

(The Palestinian news agency in Beirut had reported Dec. 17, 1972 that Hussein had expelled the last unit of the Palestine Liberation Army from Jordan. The agency said the commandos' 4th Battalion had crossed into Syria that day. The major part of the PLA was thus in Syria.)

Fatah linked to Black September. Jordan reported March 24, 1973 that Al Fatah leader Abu Daoud had confessed that Black September was a "fictitious entity, a camouflage" for commando operations conducted by Fatah.

Daoud was quoted by Amman radio as having named Fatah leaders who had planned a number of raids in the past 18 months in the name of the Black September organization. Daoud was quoted as saying that Saleh Khalef (also known as Abu Ayad) had masterminded the Black September attack on Israeli Olympic athletes in Munich and the slaying of an Israeli agent in Madrid in January. Amman radio said Khalef was believed to be second in command to Al Fatah chief Yasir Arafat. Daoud was said to have told his captors that another Fatah leader, Abu Youssuf, had engineered the 1971 assassination of Jordanian Premier Wasfi Tell and the 1972 hijacking of a Belgian airliner to Tel Aviv and the seizure of the Israeli embassy in Bangkok, Thailand. Daoud said the Munich attack had been planned by Fatah leaders in Sofia, Bulgaria and that all participants of the assault had left for Munich from Libya.

In a British television interview broadcast March 27, Daoud reiterated his charges that Black September "is not a separate organization" but "a group of people from Al Fatah." He also said that Fatah, and not Black September, was responsible for the March 1 attack on the Saudi Arabian embassy in Khartoum.

Bombs defused in New York. Police in New York March 7, 1973 discovered and defused three bombs in parked cars next to Israel's El Al Airlines terminal at Kennedy International Airport and near two Israeli-owned banks.

A U.S. federal warrant was issued March 15 for a suspected Black September terrorist believed to have escaped the country after planting the bombs. Federal Bureau of Investigation agents identified the suspect as Khalid Danham Al-Jawari, an Iraqi.

An FBI official said the bombs were set to explode March 4 during Premier Golda Meir's visit to New York but failed to go off because of "an error in the circuitry system."

Israeli aide slain in U.S. The air and naval attache of the Israeli embassy in Washington, Col. Yosef Alon, 43, was murdered July 1, 1973 by unknown assailants who escaped in a car. Alon was shot five times as he was parking his auto outside his suburban home in Chevy Chase, Md. after returning from an embassy party.

A broadcast later July 1 by the Voice of Palestine Radio in Cairo said Alon had been "executed" in reprisal for the "assassination" June 28 of an alleged Palestinian Black September representative in Paris. Identified by French police as an Algerian, Mohammed Boudia, 41, was killed when his automobile exploded as he started the engine. The Cairo broadcast said Boudia was murdered "at the hands of the Zionist intelligence element." Boudia had been sought by Italian police in connection with the sabotage of petroleum installations in Trieste in 1972.

France deports guerrilla suspects. Two suspected Black September members who reportedly were part of a plan to blow up the Israeli and Jordanian embassies in Paris were arrested there March 16, 1973. Dianne Campbell-Lefevre, a Briton, was deported to London March 22, and Jamil Abdelhakim, was flown to Damascus March 23.

Information on the two suspects and the reported bomb plot had been provided by two Arabs who had been arrested March 14 by French authorities near the Italian border with explosive equipment in their car.

Attack fails in Cyprus. A group of Arab guerrillas April 9, 1973 blew out the entrance to the Nicosia apartment building housing Israeli Ambassador Rahamim Timor and then attacked an Israeli El Al airliner in a futile attempt to hijack it before takeoff. Nine men participated in the raid.

No residents of the building were injured. The ambassador's family, but not Timor himself, and others were in their apartments at the time. The bomb exploded after it was placed at the entrance by an Arab who ran to a waiting car. Cypriot security guards opened fire as the automobile sped away and its three occupants were later arrested.

Shortly afterward, Arabs in two cars crashed through the gates of the Nicosia airport. One of the vehicles was stopped by police, but the other made its way to the Israeli plane about to leave with passengers for Tel Aviv. The Arabs began exchanging fire with Cypriot policemen and an Israeli security agent. The Israeli wounded three of the Arabs with automatic weapons fire; one of them later died. Two Cypriot policemen were wounded. One Arab assailant escaped and a total of seven were taken into custody. Dynamite and grenades were tossed at the plane but failed to explode.

The nationality of the captured raiders was not certain. Six carried passports—two each from Oman, Saudi Arabia and Ras al Khaima, a Persian Gulf emirate. President Makarios of Cyprus condemned the Arab attack April 10 and called on the Arabs and Israelis not to use his country "as a battlefield in the Arab-Israeli conflict."

The seven Arabs were sentenced in Nicosia July 27 to seven years in prison for the April 9 attack, but they were granted amnesty by Makarios, were freed Dec. 6 and were flown to Cairo.

Japanese jet hijacked, destroyed. A Japan Air Lines 747 passenger jet en route to Tokyo were hijacked July 20, 1973 by four armed terrorists shortly after takeoff from Amsterdam and was diverted to the Persian Gulf sheikdom of Dubai, a state in the Union of Arab Emirates. The plane remained on a desert airstrip for three days and was then flown July 24 to Benghazi, Libya, where it was blown up by the hijackers minutes after they and the 137 passengers and crew evacuated the aircraft.

The hijackers had boarded the plane earlier July 20 in Paris. They commandeered the aircraft 30 minutes out of Amsterdam. Shortly afterward a woman hijacker was killed and the plane's Japanese purser was wounded when the hand grenade she was holding exploded accidentally.

The terrorists first tried to have the plane land in Beirut, but Lebanese officials refused permission. Then they flew on to Basra, Iraq, where the runway was regarded as too short for a jumbo jet. The plane headed for Bahrain in the Persian Gulf, but authorities there also denied the hijackers the right to land. The plane finally touched down at the Dubai airport.

Sheik Mohammed bin Rashid, defense minister of the Union of Arab Emirates, boarded the plane July 21 to negotiate for the release of the hostages. The terrorists rejected this request.

The Dubai control tower July 23 relayed to the hijackers a message reported by authorities to have been sent by a clandestine terrorist group in West Germany. The message said: "If you intend to kill the passengers on board ... do it at once, otherwise be human enough to release them... Please give up your intentions. There are other means of unbloody possibilities to reach your political aims."

Shortly after receiving the message, the hijackers demanded and Dubai authorities agreed to refuel the plane. The plane took off July 24. The hijackers' request to land at Baghdad was rejected by Iraqi officials. Syrian officials granted the plane permission to land at Damascus, where it refueled and took off a few hours later for Benghazi.

The plane landed at the Libyan field later July 24, all on board slid down the emergency escape chute. Two minutes later, the aircraft was rocked by an explosion, starting a fire that quickly destroyed the jet. The hijackers were captured by Libyan troops.

The captain of the plane, Kenzi Konuma, said the hijackers had received a relayed message from other guerrillas in Amsterdam to blow up the plane on landing in Benghazi. The message had been sent via the air control towers in Bahrain and Kuwait, the captain said.

The hijackers, identified as three Palestinians and one member of the terrorist Japanese Red Army, were arrested by Libyan authorities.

During the flight to Dubai, the hijackers variously described themselves as members of the Organization of Sons of Occupied Territories, the Mount Carmel Martyrs, "the Japanese Red Army acting for the People of Palestine," and "Palestine commandos and members of the Japanese Red Army."

The major Palestinian commando groups in Beirut disclaimed any knowledge of these groups and disassociated themselves from the hijacking.

Although the hijackers publicly made no specific demands, they were reported to have said during the flight to Dubai that they sought the release of Japanese Red Army terrorist Kozo Okamoto, serving a life sentence in Israel for the 1972 massacre at Tel Aviv's Lod International Airport.

Israeli Transport Minister Shimon Peres declared July 21 that his government would not turn Okamoto over to the hijackers. "The position of Israel that we don't give in to blackmail still holds," he said.

Israeli officials said July 24 that unspecified precautions had been taken to prevent the Japanese plane from entering Israeli air space in preparation for a possibility that the hijackers might carry out previous commando threats to crash such a plane into an Israeli city.

A statement signed and distributed clandestinely by the Organization of Sons of Occupied Territories in Beirut July 26 said the Japanese plane was hijacked and destroyed in retaliation for the $6 million the Japanese government had paid Israel in compensation for the victims of the Lod incident.

A PLO spokesman confirmed Aug. 14, 1974 that Libya had released the four terrorists and that they had arrived in Damascus Aug. 13. A Beirut newspaper said that Libyan leader Muammar el-Qaddafi had personally decided to free them following requests from Yasir Arafat and other Palestinian guerrilla leaders.

Arab blocked in Athens raid. An armed Arab terrorist who failed in an attempt to attack an El Al Israeli airlines office in Athens July 19 was later flown out of Greece in exchange for the release of 17 hostages he had held in a nearby hotel for more than five hours.

The gunman was prevented from entering the El Al office by a guard inside who pressed the security lock that closed the inner glass doors. The Arab then fled to the hotel with two policemen giving chase. Armed with a submachine gun and grenades, the Arab threatened to kill the hostages in the lobby unless Greek Deputy Premier Stylianos Patakos escorted him to the Athens airport for safe conduct out of the country. Patakos refused.

The release of the hostages was negotiated by the ambassadors in Athens of Egypt, Libya and Iraq, who spoke with the gunman in the lobby for two and a half hours. The gunman was taken to the airport and flown to Kuwait.

Arabs raid Athens airport terminal. Two Arab terrorists attacked the crowded Athens airport terminal with machine guns and grenades Aug. 15, 1973, killing three people and wounding 55. (Two more victims died later.) The terrorists, identifying themselves as Black September guerrillas, surrendered to Greek police after releasing 35 hostages they had seized following the killings.

The two Arabs were identified as Shafik el Arida, 22, of Palestine and Tallal Khaled Kaddourah, 21, of Lebanon. They told the court Aug. 7 that they were obeying "orders to hit at emigrants to Israel because they kill our wives and children." Court officials said Arida and Kaddourah had flown to Athens from

Benghazi, Libya Aug. 3 to survey the transit lounge. Then they took off for Beirut and returned Aug. 5 to carry out the attack.

Police said the two Arabs drew guns and started shooting as they were about to undergo a routine search by a Greek security inspector. The terrorists fired at a line of passengers about to board a Trans World Airlines plane bound for New York and others waiting in the terminal. Arid and Khantouran admitted to police Aug. 6 that they had meant to fire at the passengers of another TWA flight for Tel Aviv. Those Israel-bound travelers had already boarded the aircraft when the two Arabs entered the terminal.

An Athens court Jan. 24, 1974 sentenced the two terrorists to death.

Arida, who with his companion had pleaded guilty, said "We are sorry in our hearts that we injured Greeks, but orders are orders and we do not question them. Any plane of any country that flies to Israel is a target for us."

In an operation connected with the case, three Pakistanis seized a Greek freighter in Karachi Feb. 2, 1974 and threatened to blow up the ship and kill its two crewmen unless Greece freed the two Arabs.

The gunmen released the hostages Feb. 3 after receiving assurances from the Greek government that it would commute the death sentences.

The hijackers described themselves as members of the Moslem International Guerrillas, a group known to be active in the Philippines and Indonesia. They were flown to Cairo Feb. 4 and threatened to commit suicide unless they were given safe conduct to Libya.

The Arabs were deported from Greece to Libya May 5. Greek Justice Minister Stylianos Triandafyllou said the men were being handed over at the request of the Libyan government, which had pledged they would be "held answerable for their actions."

The death sentences of the terrorists had been commuted to life imprisonment April 30, and then President Phaidon Gizikis granted them a full pardon. Greece had pledged to treat the two men leniently following threats of further attacks in Greece unless the two commandos were freed.

The Israeli government expressed shock May 5 at the release of the two commandos, saying that "freeing murderers under pressure of threats" would lead to more terrorism.

The U.S. State Department May 6 also was critical of the Athens government's action, stating that "deporting individuals convicted of murdering innocent people is not the answer to deterring further terrorist activity."

Arab slain in Norway. A Moroccan suspected of being a member of the Palestinian Black September organization was killed by two gunmen July 21, 1973 in the Norwegian town of Lillehammer, 115 miles north of Oslo.

Oslo police said six persons of various nationalities, including two Israelis, were arrested in connection with the slaying of Ahmed Bouchiki, 30.

An Oslo newspaper (Aftenposten) reported Aug. 1 that Bouchiki had been killed after being mistaken for a Black September leader by an extremist Israeli counterterrorist group called the Wrath of God, an offshoot of the militant Jewish Defense League. The newspaper said that two Israeli undercover agents had infiltrated the group and had been in telephone contact with diplomat Yigal Eyal and other Israeli officials in Oslo. The two Israelis were arrested in Eyal's Oslo apartment July 25.

The Israeli counterterrorist group was believed to have carried out the killing of Bouchiki as part of an Israeli plan to thwart a Black September effort to assemble a group in Norway and then hijack an El Al Israeli airlines jet in Denmark.

An Oslo court Feb. 1, 1974 convicted five Jews, including two Israelis, in connection with Bouchiki's murder. A sixth defendant, an Israeli, was acquitted. The prosecution said Bouchiki was mistaken for a Palestinian agent.

The defendants were charged with being accessory to murder and with spying for Israel. Sylvia Rafael of South Africa and Abraham Gehmer of Israel each received a 5½-year prison term. Dan Aerbel of Denmark was given a five-year sentence.

Ethel Marianne Gladnikoff of Sweden received a 2½-year sentence and Zwi Steinberg of Israel a one-year sentence.

Commandos to get East Berlin office. Allied officials in West Berlin reported Aug. 18 that the Palestine Liberation Organization (PLO) would open an office in East Berlin under an agreement reached there earlier in 1973 between PLO leader Yasir Arafat and East German Communist party secretary Erich Honecker.

An East German statement said the purpose of the commandos' office would be "to further mutual understanding" between East Germans and Palestinians and "to increase solidarity in their joint struggle against imperialism and Zionism."

Arabs raid Saudi embassy in Paris. A group of five armed Palestinian commandos entered the Saudi Arabian embassy in Paris Sept. 5, 1973 and seized 13 diplomats and employes as hostages. After 28 hours of protracted negotiations, the guerrillas agreed to release all but four Saudi hostages, and left Paris Sept. 6 with their captives aboard a plane provided by Syria. The aircraft landed in Kuwait Sept. 7 after a refueling stop in Cairo.

The commandos described themselves as belonging to a hitherto unknown group called Al Icab. After storming the embassy, they threatened to blow up the building or kill the hostages unless their demands were met. They called for the release of Abu Daoud, an Al Fatah leader serving a life term in Jordan for terrorism. The gunmen later dropped this demand and insisted only that they be given safe passage by plane to an Arab country.

The impasse was finally broken Sept. 6 when Syrian President Hafez al-Assad agreed to put a Syrian Arab Airlines plane at the disposal of the commandos. The aircraft arrived at Paris' Le Bourget airfield later in the day.

The French government agreed to safe passage for the commandos and their Saudi hostages in exchange for the release of four women held hostage.

The French dropped their original demand that the commandos must not leave with their arms and the hostages.

The terrorists with the four hostages transferred later Sept. 7 to a Kuwaiti Boeing 707 plane and circled over Riyadh, Saudi Arabia, threatening to throw their captives out of the aircraft unless the Saudis took action to help secure Abu Daoud's release. Saudi officials refused. Jordan announced Sept. 7 that it would not free Daoud.

Returning to Kuwait, the gunmen asked for another Syrian plane to fly them to Damascus. Ali Yassin, PLO representative in Kuwait, who was serving as mediator between the commandos and the Kuwaitis, was seized as a hostage by the commandos. In further negotiations Sept. 8 Kuwait offered to give the commandos safe passage to Iraq in a car if the commandos freed all the hostages. The guerrillas insisted on taking Yassin or a Kuwaiti security official with them. This demand was refused. Yassin was freed two hours later. The commandos surrendered later Sept. 8, released the four Saudis and were taken into custody.

Italy thwarts commando air attack. Italian military police Sept. 5 arrested five Arabs whom they said planned to shoot down an Israeli El Al airliner at Rome's international airport at Fiumicino.

One of the Arabs was seized in an apartment at Ostia, four miles from the airport, along with two light-weight launchers for ground-to-air missiles, according to the police. The four others were arrested later in Rome.

Two of the Arabs were soon released in their own recognizance and presumably left Italy. The other three were convicted and sentenced in a Rome court Feb. 27, 1974. They received prison terms of five years and two months each and were fined $2,500 each. Then they were freed on bail. (Observers noted that Italy was then negotiating for oil from Arab oil states, which had imposed a cutback in oil production and had raised oil prices in what was described as retaliation for Western failure to support the Arabs against Israel.)

Hostages used to curb Austrian transit of Soviet Jews. Yielding to terrorists, the Austrian government announced Sept. 29, 1973 it would no longer allow group transit of Soviet Jewish emigrants through Austria and would close Israeli-run facilities for emigrants awaiting transfer to Israel. The decision was made in return for the release of one Austrian and three Soviet Jewish hostages, whom Arab guerrillas had held at the Vienna airport.

The three Jewish hostages were seized Sept. 28, along with a woman who later escaped with her infant son, on a Moscow-Vienna train carrying 40 Jewish emigrants in Czechoslovak territory at the Austrian border. The two heavily armed guerrillas, who said they were members of a group called the Eagles of the Palestinian Revolution, left the train at the Austrian customs station, where they seized a customs official, commandeered a car and drove to Vienna's Schwechat airport.

During several hours of negotiations, the Austrian Cabinet offered to fly the guerrillas to the Middle East but refused their demands to take the hostages with them. The hostages were released early Sept. 29, after Austrian Chancellor Bruno Kreisky agreed to close the Schoenau Castle transit facility outside Vienna, run by the Jewish Agency of Israel, and to bar "group transports" of Jews through Austria.

The guerrillas were given a twin-engine plane with two Austrian pilots and were allowed to land in Libya only after they had been refused by Tunisia and Algeria and had threatened to blow up the plane. The plane had made refueling stops in Yugoslavia and Italy. In a statement issued at Schwechat, the guerrillas said they had acted "because we feel that the immigration of Soviet Union Jews constitutes a great danger to our cause."

Austria's government-run television said Sept. 29 that the offer to close Schoenau had been a compromise suggested by Arab governments, "especially Iraq." Kreisky, in several interviews that day, said he had refused demands to bar all future Jewish emigrants from entering Austria and said "all people with proper papers" would be allowed to pass through. Nearly all the 70,000 Jewish emigrants who had left the European Communist countries since 1971 had passed through Austria in groups, without Austrian visas.

Kreisky, Jewish-born, said he had acted solely to prevent loss of life but said Austria "would sooner or later have had to order a modification" of the emigration procedures because of the threat of violence and the presence of "armed men from both sides."

Austria had been criticized by Arab and Communist governments for permitting the transit facilities. Three Arabs had been arrested as suspected terrorists early in 1973, only to be released after the Austrian embassy in Beirut received a terrorist bomb threat. Austrian security officials were reported to have opposed the Schoenau operation, in existence for 11 years.

Israeli officials condemned Austria's decision on the transit issue. Israeli Ambassador Yitzhak Patish, recalled to Tel Aviv Sept. 29, said this was the first success by Arab terrorists in forcing a government to change its policy.

Israeli Premier Golda Meir asked the Austrian government to reconsider its decision in an Oct. 1 address to a meeting of the Assembly of the Council of Europe in Strasbourg, France. She called the Austrian decision "the greatest encouragement to terrorism throughout the world."

But Meir failed to convince Kreisky to reverse his decision when she met with him in Vienna Oct. 2.

The 17-nation Council of Europe voted unanimously Oct. 2, after hearing Meir, to advise Austria that it considered no government bound by pledges obtained through blackmail.

After their meeting, Kreisky told newsmen that resisting the terrorists would have not discouraged future terrorism, since "by now, even if they are indicted and convicted, terrorists know the events that follow—that they will be liberated anyway."

President Nixon Oct. 3 also criticized what was seen as an Austrian capitulation to terrorism.

Nixon said "we simply cannot have governments—small or large—give in to international blackmail by terrorist groups."

Arabs hijack, free Dutch plane. A KLM Royal Dutch Airlines 747 passenger jet en route from Amsterdam to Tokyo was seized over Iraq Nov. 25, 1973 by three Palestinian hijackers. The plane and the last of its 11 hostages were released by the gunmen after landing in Dubai Nov. 28.

The plane, carrying 18 crew members and 247 passengers, mostly Japanese, was taken over by the hijackers Nov. 25 shortly after taking off from Beirut. The gunmen identified themselves as members of a little-known group called the Arab Nationalist Youth for the Liberation of Palestine. KLM said the men demanded that the airlines halt the transporting of arms to Israel, and that the Dutch government drastically alter its "pro-Israel stance" and cease providing mediation or assistance in the emigration of Soviet Jews to Israel. They threatened to blow up the plane if their demands were not met.

The commandos forced the plane to turn back and land in Damascus, Syria, where it was denied refueling. It then flew to Nicosia, Cyprus Nov. 26. It took off again after Cypriot officials rejected the hijackers' demand for release of seven Arabs jailed for the April attack on the home of Israel's ambassador to Cyprus and on an Israeli airliner. (The seven were granted amnesty by Cypriot President Makarios and flown to Cairo Dec. 6.)

The aircraft stopped briefly at Tripoli, Libya and then landed Nov. 27 at Valletta, Malta, where the gunmen freed all 247 passengers and eight stewardesses. Their release followed a Dutch government announcement Nov. 26 pledging not to "allow the opening of offices or camps for Soviet Jews going to Israel" and banning "transportation of weapons or volunteers for Israel."

The plane left Malta with 11 hostages—10 crewmen and a KLM vice president, A.W. Withholt. It arrived in Dubai Nov. 28, then left for Aden, South Yemen and returned to Dubai later Nov. 28 after Yemeni authorities discouraged a landing. The three gunmen surrendered the plane and its 11 hostages in return for safe-conduct guarantees.

Commando massacre at Rome airport. Five armed Palestinian commandos attacked a U.S. airliner at Rome's international airport Dec. 17, 1973, killing 29 persons aboard the plane. Two other persons, including an Italian policeman, were shot to death as the gunmen were hijacking a West German Lufthansa airliner nearby. The hijacked plane was flown to Kuwait Dec. 18 after short stopovers at Athens and Damascus. The guerrillas released 12 hostages and surrendered.

The Palestinians began shooting as they removed submachineguns from luggage in the lounge of the airport at Fiumicino, 15 miles from Rome. The men made their way to a Pan American Boeing 707 that was preparing to take off for Beirut and Teheran. They hurled incendiary bombs inside the aircraft, killing the 29 people aboard and heavily damaging the plane. Among the dead were four Moroccan government officials en route to Teheran for a state visit and 14 U.S. employes of the Arabian-American Oil Co.

The guerrillas herded five Italian hostages into the Lufthansa plane and killed a sixth, the Italian customs policeman, as he tried to escape. The second man shot outside the plane died on the way to the hospital. The plane, carrying the guerrillas, the Italians and the crew, took off, and the pilot was ordered to head for Beirut. Lebanese authorities, however, refused landing permission, and the jet was flown to Athens, where it landed Dec. 18.

In negotiations by radio with Greek authorities 'n the Athens airport control tower, the guerrillas reportedly demanded the release of two Arab terrorists held since August for an attack on the Athens airport. The terrorists killed one of their Italian hostages and dumped his body from the plane before leaving Athens.

The plane's pilot, Capt. Joe Kroese, had urged the Greek authorities to meet the commandos' demands, reporting that four other hostages had been shot dead. Kroese was unaware at the time that the shootings were a hoax, that the guerrillas were merely firing their guns in the air to give the false impression that they were killing the other prisoners.

The plane then flew to Damascus, where Syrian authorities permitted the loading of food and fuel.

On landing in Kuwait later Dec. 18, the five guerrillas released their hostages in return for "free passage" to an unknown destination. But Kuwait announced Dec. 23 that they would be turned over to the

Palestine Liberation Organization (PLO) for trial.

The PLO had said Dec. 17 that the assault was against the interests "of our people." A PLO official said Dec. 18 his group would "do everything in our power to stop such acts."

U.S. officials Dec. 26 identified the terrorists as members of the Popular Front for the Liberation of Palestine. They said Libya had provided and transported the weapons used.

Guerrillas attack in Singapore, Kuwait. A combined operation of guerrilla actions by the Popular Front for the Liberation of Palestine (PFLP) and the radical Japanese Red Army was carried out in Singapore Jan. 31, 1974 and Kuwait Feb. 7. The nine terrorists involved were flown to Aden, South Yemen Feb. 8 after agreeing to release all their hostages. The PFLP claimed credit for the entire operation.

In the first raid, in Singapore Jan. 31, four guerrillas—two of the PFLP and two of the Red Army—seized a ferryboat in the harbor with five hostages aboard after making an unsuccessful attempt to blow up the refineries of Royal Dutch Shell. Two of the hostages managed to escape Feb. 1 by jumping overboard.

The guerrillas threatened in a note to Singapore authorities to kill themselves and their hostages unless they were given safe-conduct to an Arab country. One of the three storage tanks they attempted to blow up was set afire but was quickly extinguished. The men said they had set off the blast to support the "Vietnam revolutionary people and for making a revolutionary situation after considering the

situation of today's oil crisis." They demanded a plane to fly them to an Arab country.

The Singapore government rejected their request but offered the gunmen sanctuary Feb. 4 in any of the 42 diplomatic missions in Singapore.

Later, in Kuwait, five PFLP guerrillas broke into the Japanese embassy Feb. 7 and seized Ambassador Ryoko Ishikawa and nine members of his staff at gunpoint. Four non-Japanese staff members were permitted to leave the building. The PFLP raiders threatened to kill the hostages unless the four guerrillas in Singapore were freed and flown to Kuwait aboard a Japanese airliner.

Kuwait refused to allow landing of a Japanese plane but offered the gunmen safe-conduct out of the country if they surrendered the Japanese hostages unharmed.

Japan appealed to the Kuwaiti government later Feb. 7 to meet the PFLP demand. Kuwait at first rejected this plea but accepted it Feb. 8. A Japan Air Lines plane carrying the four guerrillas from Singapore landed in Kuwait later Feb. 8, picked up the other four PFLP commandos and flew to Aden, South Yemen.

Arabs hijack British plane. A British Airways jetliner was hijacked by two Arab terrorists March 3, 1974 shortly after takeoff from Beirut. The plane was forced to land at Amsterdam's Schiphol airport, where it was set afire after all 92 passengers and 10 crewmen were permitted to evacuate the aircraft. The two hijackers were arrested.

Arab Terrorists Captured in Europe
January 1972 through January 1974

	Number captured	Release secured by threat	Released for other reasons	Convicted and sentenced	Awaiting or on trial
Italy	12		7	2	3
France	2			2	
Britain	5		4	1	
Austria	8	2	6		
West Germany	7	3			4
Greece	3	1		2	
Turkey	2		2		
Cyprus	10	7	3		
Holland	1		1		
	50	13	23	7	7

Source: The Economist

The jet had landed at Beirut on a scheduled flight from Bombay to London. On seizing the plane, the hijackers first ordered the pilot to fly to Athens, but Greek authorities refused authorization to land.

The guerrillas were said to have identified themselves as members of the Palestine Liberation Army. The Palestine Liberation Organization (PLO) in Beirut March 3 disavowed any connection with the hijacking.

Amsterdam police reported March 6 that the two guerrillas had said under interrogation that the arms and explosives for their operation were hidden in the plane by accomplices before they boarded it in Beirut.

A Dutch court June 6 convicted the terrorists of air piracy and arms charges and sentenced them to five-year prison terms.

The British Airline Pilots' Association criticized the sentences as "ineffectual." It favored the death penalty for hijacking.

West Berlin frees 2 guerrillas. West Berlin authorities released two jailed Arab terrorists June 10, 1974 after receiving threats that other guerrillas would attack at the World Cup soccer matches in the city and in West Germany.

The two men were flown to Egypt. They had been convicted April 22 of plotting to blow up the West Berlin office of El Al, the Israeli airline, and the city's police registration office for foreigners.

West German police June 13 reported they had smashed a Palestinian terrorist ring planning to launch raids during the World Cup matches that opened that day. Five Palestinians were arrested, including a student in Saarbrucken whose group, according to police, had plotted assaults against the Israeli embassy in Bonn and Israeli passenger planes.

3 Paris offices bombed. Three car bombs exploded outside the offices of two right-wing, pro-Israeli publications and a Jewish welfare organization early Aug. 3, 1974. Two people were injured. The police defused a fourth bomb outside the office of the national television network.

The Popular Front for the Liberation of Palestine Aug. 5 took credit for the attacks. In a message to two publications, the newspaper L'Aurore and the weekly Minute, it said they "have consciously made themselves into instruments of criminal actions by Israeli secret agents."

Strife Embroils Israel, Arab States & Commandos

Israeli air-ground raid on Lebanon. Israeli forces carried out a major ground and air attack against Palestinian commando bases in southern Lebanon Sept. 16–17, 1972. Some 3,000 troops, spearheaded by about 50 tanks and other armored vehicles and with air support provided by about 25 jets, thrust 15 miles across the border in the deepest penetration of southern Lebanon.

Israeli authorities reported that during the 33-hour operation "at least 60" guerrillas were killed, 16 Arab villages were searched for terrorists and more than 150 houses believed to have quartered the commandos were destroyed. Israel placed its losses at three killed and six wounded. The Lebanese army as well as the guerrillas put up strong resistance.

Lt. Gen. David Elazar, Israeli chief of staff, Sept. 17 described the operation as "a major battle" in "our continuing war against the terrorists." It followed the killing of two Israeli soldiers Sept. 15 by Arab raiders in the Golan Heights.

Arab sources said the Israelis killed at least 35 guerrillas, 18 Lebanese soldiers and 23 Lebanese civilians. A Beirut communique said Israeli jets had destroyed two major bridges over the Litani River, which cut across Lebanon about 15 miles north of the Israeli frontier.

Describing the ground action, the Lebanese said the Israeli troops and armored units struck in the southeast up to Adiesse and Taiybe in the direction of Marjioun and drove past Bin Jbail up to Tibnine and Ghandouniye. In a second thrust to the west, the Israeli force pushed as far as Kana, 15 miles south of the port of Tyre, according to the report.

Beirut curbs commandos. In the aftermath of the Israeli foray, Lebanon

Sept. 17 ordered the commandos to evacuate all villages in southern Lebanon. The Palestine Liberation Organization (PLO) was reported Sept. 20 to have acceded to the Beirut government's demands. The agreement followed mediation moves by Mahmoud Riad, secretary general of the Arab League, who had arrived in the Lebanese capital on short notice Sept. 18.

According to the text of a Lebanese directive released Sept. 17 by the Al Fatah office in Cairo, the guerrillas were to remain confined to their camps in sectors where they had previously been restricted. They were to carry arms and wear their battle dress only after coordination between their command and the Lebanese army.

Al Fatah leader Yasir Arafat was reported at first to have challenged the commando curbs in a meeting with Premier Saeb Salam.

Shortly after the Israeli forces withdrew from southern Lebanon, government troops moved back into the area to block guerrilla reoccupation of their former bases.

Rival commando factions clash. Two Al Fatah factions clashed Oct. 14, 1972 with machine guns and mortars in the Bekaa Valley region of eastern Lebanon near the Syrian border.

The clash occurred between a dissident group that sought to defy the Lebanese government-commando agreement curbing guerrilla raids into Israel from Lebanon and the main faction of Al Fatah leader Yasir Arafat. The dissidents were said to number about 1,000 men and were led by Abu Youssef el Kayed.

Lebanon & Syria bases bombed. Israeli planes bombed Al Fatah bases in Syria and Lebanon Oct. 15, 1972. This was the first time Israel attacked targets in Arab countries without immediate provocation. In explaining the new policy, an Israeli spokesman said "we are no longer waiting for them to hit first. This is the operative phase of our pledge to hit the terrorists wherever they are, and they are in Lebanon and Syria."

The new Israeli strategy was further stated in a broadcast by Chaim Herzog, former chief of staff. He said: "We are not engaged in reprisal but a war against terror. The very presence of terrorists in the area between the border and the Litani River is a provocation" and Israel, therefore, considered itself "free to act against them."

Premier Golda Meir said the attacks on Syria and Lebanon were carried out because it was in those countries that the guerrillas had planned the Munich killings, the Tel Aviv airport massacre and the mailing of letter bombs to Jews.

Israelis strike deep in Lebanon and kill 3 Fatah leaders. An Israeli force struck deep into Lebanon April 10, 1973, attacking Palestinian commando bases in the center of Beirut and in the coastal town of Saida to the south. The raids followed the terrorist attack on the home of the Israeli ambassador to Cyprus and on an Israeli airliner there.

Lebanese Premier Saeb Salam submitted his resignation April 10 following the Israeli raid.

Operating under cover of darkness, the Israeli units drove into Beirut after landing on the coast in small boats and killed three prominent Al Fatah leaders in the capital. They were Abu Youssef (whose real name was Mohammed Yussef Najjar), one of two Fatah representatives on the PLO Executive Committee, Kamal Adwan, an organizer of Palestinian resistance in the occupied West Bank; and Kamal Nasser, former Jordanian parliament member and official spokesman of the PLO.

All three men and Youssef's wife were shot to death in separate apartments in two guarded houses that were entered by the attackers. The buildings were located in the Sabra refugee camp in the heart of Beirut, where most of the commando groups were headquartered. Other guerrilla targets struck in the city were the central offices of the Democratic Popular Front and workshops reportedly used to prepare explosives.

In the operation at Saida, the Israelis blew up a garage allegedly used to repair vehicles of guerrillas stationed in southern Lebanon.

After coming ashore near Beirut, the Israeli units were reportedly met by six Israeli agents, who were said to have entered Lebanon a week earlier as tourists with false British, Belgian and West German passports. They drove the raiders into Beirut in automobiles they had rented earlier in the week.

Lebanon said 12 persons were killed in the Israeli attack—four Palestinians, two Lebanese policemen, two Lebanese civilians, three Syrians and an Italian woman.

A PLO statement in Beirut charged April 10 that the Israeli raiders had "relied on elements of American military intelligence" provided by the U.S. embassy in Beirut. The U.S. State Department denied the allegation in Washington.

Lt. Gen. David Elazar, Israeli chief of staff, told a news conference in Tel Aviv April 10 that the raid was carried out in retaliation for "the intensification of terrorist acts in Europe and other places in the last months." He said that although most of those commando raids had failed, "we had to act."

Elazar said that "there is no possibility of honoring the sovereignty of Lebanon and its capital as long as it is serving as a complete haven for terrorists."

Arafat takes political powers. The Iraqi news agency reported April 21 that Al Fatah leader Yasir Arafat had taken over the leadership of the combined commando movement's political and governmental relations in the wake of the Israeli slaying of three Fatah leaders in Beirut April 10. Arafat replaced Abu Youssef, one of the slain men, as head of the political department of the Palestine Liberation Organization. The department was responsible for relations with Arab and foreign governments.

Israel thwarts Arab 'suicide' mission. Israeli troops April 21 captured three Palestinian guerrillas from Lebanon who were said to have planned an attack on civilians at a bus station at Safad, Israel. Identified as members of Al Fatah, the three were seized two miles south of the Lebanese border and 14 miles northwest of their intended target.

One of the captured men, Shehada Ahmed Mustafa, told a news conference in Tel Aviv April 22 that he and his companions were on a "suicide mission to sabotage the bus station, a restaurant and other public places" and were under orders "to kill as many as we could and not permit ourselves to be captured."

Lebanese, commandos clash in Beirut. Lebanese army troops, using planes and tanks, engaged in heavy fighting with Palestinian commandos May 2–3, 1973. The fighting began in Beirut and soon spread to other parts of Lebanon.

The fighting was halted briefly May 2 by a cease-fire agreed to by Al Fatah leader Yasir Arafat and Premier Amin Hafez. However, the truce broke down and the battle resumed May 3 following a guerrilla ambush of a Beirut police barracks in which three policemen were killed and seven wounded. Another cease-fire was arranged May 3, but reports said the conflict was continuing.

The latest outbreak was precipitated by a breakdown in negotiations for the release of two Lebanese officers kidnapped by guerrillas May 1. The two officers were released after the first day's fighting. The men had been held as hostages for the release of seven Palestinian commandos arrested April 27 for carrying explosives at the Beirut International Airport. The fighting reflected the long-standing dispute between the two sides—commando demands for freedom of movement in Lebanon to carry out operations against Israel.

The hostilities began May 1 near Beirut's Shatila camp, which housed 5,000 Palestinian refugees, and spread to the nearby Burj-al-Barajineh camp, which housed 7,700 refugees. The fighting was first confined to the camp areas but soon extended to other parts of the city. Guerrilla rockets set fire to an army depot near the Beirut airfield and struck army barracks at Hasmiyeh along the highway toward Damascus.

The clashes expanded to southern Lebanon May 3 and were particularly fierce in the Arkub region, a commando stronghold which had been used for operations against Israel. Capt. Riad Awad, guerrilla commander in the Arkub region, and three other commandos were reported to have been killed when their jeep attempted to run through an army roadblock at Hasbeya. Other clashes in the south raged in the Yanta and Rasheiya areas between government forces and the Syrian-backed As Saiqa guerrilla group.

Two large groups of Palestinian forces crossed from Syria into Lebanon to join the combat. The first group, numbering several thousand men, entered Lebanon May 3 and skirmished with government soldiers, but withdrew to Syria after the May 4 truce was worked out. The second commando thrust into Lebanon occurred May 9.

The collapse of a May 4 cease-fire precipitated the resignation May 8 of Premier Amin Hafez and his Cabinet.

Lebanese President Suleiman Franjieh told Arab mediators in Beirut May 5 that his government would not permit the guerrillas in his country to terrorize and kidnap people "as if they were above the official authority." Franjieh informed the representatives of the presidents of Syria, Egypt and Iraq that the Palestinian refugee camps in Lebanon harbored illegal arms and served as the headquarters of subversive guerrilla organizations. He said Beirut was opposed to giving the commandos special privileges to organize attacks against Israel from Lebanon.

The hostilities in Beirut were largely curtailed by a new cease-fire negotiated May 8, but incidents continued in southern Lebanon.

Syria closed its border with Lebanon May 8, accusing Beirut of complicity in an anti-Palestinian plot of "foreign design." A government statement broadcast by Damascus radio threatened intervention, saying that Syria would "carry out its full commitment in confronting and foiling this conspiracy."

Libya May 8 pledged to give the commandos its "entire potential" in their struggle with Lebanon. The offer was contained in a cable sent by Col. Muammar el-Qaddafi to Al Fatah leader Yasir Arafat.

A guerrilla force from Syria moved into Lebanon May 9 for the second time in eight days. The commandos, said to number several thousand, took up positions in the southeastern Rasheiya area

and set up gun emplacements between Rasheiya and Massna, about 15 miles to the north. The guerrillas came under rocket and strafing attacks later in the day by Lebanese planes.

Government jets May 10 bombed commando positions in northern Lebanon and in the Rasheiya sector in the south. An army communique said the raids followed commando assaults on three army positions on the eastern bank of the Hasbani River in the south and on a government checkpoint at Arida and on an airbase at Klaitat, near the Syrian frontier in the north.

Lebanese security forces arrested 35 persons in Beirut May 12 on charges of stirring up trouble between the Lebanese army and the guerrillas. Among those seized as "agents provocateurs" were a number of West Europeans and citizens of other Arab states. During the fighting in Beirut both sides had claimed that a "third force" was firing at government and Palestinian forces to provoke more clashes.

Lebanon-commando accord. The Lebanese government and the Palestinian commandos announced May 17 an agreement that ended two weeks of fighting in which at least 250 persons were reported killed. In another development that reflected a return to normal conditions, Amin Hafez agreed May 19 to withdraw his resignation as premier and again head the Cabinet.

The peace agreement was worked out in two days of talks between a team of three Lebanese army officers and representatives of three major guerrilla organizations—Al Fatah, the Popular Front for the Liberation of Palestine and the Popular Democratic Front. Terms of the accord were kept secret, but according to Lebanese press reports and diplomatic sources in Beirut it was known to contain the following points:

■ The Palestine Liberation Army's 5,-000-man Yarmuk Brigade and other guerrillas who had entered Lebanon from Syria at the height of the fighting were to leave the country. (Their withdrawal was completed May 18.)

■ The 15 camps housing 90,000 Palestinian refugees were brought under Lebanese sovereignty and their status as "isolated zones" on Lebanese territory was ended.

■ Guerrillas were barred from carrying arms or wearing uniforms outside the refugee camps.

■ The commandos were banned from establishing roadblocks, making arrests or conducting interrogations.

■ Joint Lebanese army and guerrilla inspection teams were to see to it that no heavy weapons were stored in the refugee camps.

Three guerrilla leaders denounced the accord May 20 and warned they would not abide by the key demands that the commandos withdraw from populated areas and that heavy weapons be prohibited in the camps. The opponents of the agreement were identified by the semi-official Palestine News Agency as Salah Khalef, Abu Maher and Yasir Abeid Rahboh.

Israelis force down Iraqi jet, Habash escapes. An Iraqi airliner en route from Beirut to Baghdad was intercepted Aug. 10, 1973 by two Israeli fighters 25 miles north of Beirut and was forced to land at a military airfield in northern Israel near Haifa. The plane was permitted to continue its scheduled flight to Baghad after a two-hour security search by Israeli authorities.

The U.N. Security Council, meeting at Lebanon's request, unanimously condemned the Israeli action Aug. 15.

Israeli Defense Minister Moshe Dayan said Aug. 11 that the purpose in forcing down the Iraqi plane was to capture several commando leaders, including George Habash, head of the Popular Front for the Liberation of Palestine (PFLP), believed to be aboard. Dayan called Habash a "master of murder."

An Israeli military spokesman had conceded earlier Aug. 11 that the wrong plane had been intercepted.

Israel's chief of staff, Lt. Gen. David Elazar, warned Aug. 15 that Israel would carry out further plane interceptions. He said Israel had the "right of self-defense" to "get those that advocate the liquidation of Israel."

Syria vs. Fatah. Syria was seen as cracking down on the Al Fatah movement on its territory. The group's Voice of Palestine radio station at Deraa near the Jordanian border was shut by Damascus Sept. 14, 1973, and its six staff members were arrested. The closure followed the station's attack the previous week on a Syrian-Jordanian-Egyptian agreement to adopt a common policy at the U.N.

Syria's arrest of 16 more Al Fatah guerrillas was reported Sept. 18. The Syrians also were said to have closed Al Fatah training bases and border trails used to infiltrate supplies into Lebanon.

Jordan grants amnesty to commandos. King Hussein of Jordan declared an amnesty Sept. 18, 1973 for 1,500 political prisoners, including 754 Palestinian commandos imprisoned after fighting with Jordanian forces in 1970 and 1971.

A total of 347 guerrillas were let out of the Amman jail Sept. 19 and another 400 were released Sept. 20. Among those freed Sept. 19 was Abu Daoud.

Hussein said his amnesty covered "all convicts, detainees and wanted people within and outside the kingdom who had committed political crimes against state security with the exception of murder and espionage." He said the move was taken in the interest of national unity "now that life has returned to stability and normality" in Jordan. (The amnesty also applied to 2,500 commandos outside Jordan who had been sentenced in absentia or were wanted for trial.)

Gaza Arabs score terror. Gaza Arabs Feb. 15, 1973 had protested a recent outbreak of Palestinian commando terrorism in the Israel-occupied area.

Six members of the Shatti refugee council resigned to protest the murder of the council chairman Feb. 11. Other Gazans were circulating a petition calling on Arab world leaders to persuade the commandos to halt their attacks in the Gaza Strip. The petition followed an unsuccessful attempt Feb. 13 to assassinate former Gaza Mayor Rashid Shawa. Shawa was ambushed by gunmen but escaped with minor injuries.

Israel expels 8 Arabs. Israel Dec. 10, 1973 expelled eight Palestinians from the West Bank and East Jerusalem and sent them to Jordan in connection with an upsurge of terrorist bombings the previous week.

The men were charged with incitement and atempting to undermine security, law, order and normal life and with advocating cooperation with Palestinian terrorist groups. Among those ousted were Mayor Abed Salah Ita of El Birah in the West Bank and Abed Abu Messager, a member of East Jerusalem's Supreme Moslem Council, which administrated the city's Moslem community affairs.

In related actions, Israeli forces Dec. 9 had demolished the homes of five Arabs in the West Bank town of Abu Daif in connection with a grenade attack in November.

Col. Eliezer Segev, the Israeli military governor of Nablus (West Bank), and a soldier were wounded Dec. 8 when their car was hit by a grenade.

Eight West Bank Arabs were wounded when a guerrilla threw a hand grenade into a crowd at Hebron Dec. 12.

18 slain in Kiryat Shmona. Three Arab guerrillas, apparently coming from Lebanon, crossed the border April 11, 1974 into the Israeli town of Kiryat Shmona, less than a mile away, stormed a four-story apartment building, forced their way into apartments and began shooting indiscriminately, killing 18 persons, including eight children and five women. Two of the dead were Israeli soldiers who had taken part in the assault on the terrorists after the commandos attacked a second building in the town. All three infiltrators were killed when explosive-laden knapsacks they were carrying ignited after being hit by Israeli fire, according to Israeli accounts. Sixteen persons were wounded, mostly soldiers.

Credit for the attack was claimed April 11 by the Lebanese-based Marxist Popular Front for the Liberation of Palestine-General Command (PFLP-GC). A photo showing the three terrorists was distributed by the PFLP-GC. They were identified as a Palestinian, a Syrian and an Iraqi.

The PFLP-GC issued three communiques, apparently while the attack was in progress. The first said the attack was being carried out by a "suicide squad based in Israel." It said hostages had been seized and warned their lives would be in danger if Israeli forces attempted to storm the buildings that were under siege. A second communique demanded the release of 100 prisoners from Israeli jails. (Israel denied that any hostages had been taken in the Kiryat Shmona attack.) A final communique said shortly after the guerrillas had died that "Our men carried out their instructions. They set off explosive belts they wore for the operation when the enemy stormed the building they were holding. They died along with their hostages."

A member of the PFLP-GC Politburo, identifying himself as Abdul Abbas, said in Beirut April 12 that "this operation was just the beginning of a campaign of revolutionary violence within Israel that is aimed at blocking an Arab-Israeli peace settlement."

Insisting that the guerrillas had infiltrated from Lebanon, Premier Golda Meir warned April 11 that Israel regarded the Lebanese government and its people "who collaborated with the terrorists, as responsible for these murders."

Lebanese Premier Takieddin Solh April 11 supported the commandos' claim that they had launched their assault against Kiryat Shmona from inside Israel. Solh repeated this view April 12 in a meeting with the ambassadors of the U.S., France, China, Britain and the Soviet Union.

Israelis attack 6 towns in Lebanon—In retaliation for the Kiryat Shmona attack, Israeli forces crossed into southern Lebanon April 12 and raided the villages of Dahira, Yaroun, Muhebab, Blida, Ett Taibe and Aitarun, west and north of Kiryat Shmona. An Israeli communique said buildings in the towns were blown up after their inhabitants were evacuated. The communique said "the action was intended to harm villages whose residents had given assistance to terrorists."

A Lebanese communique said the Israeli raiders had blown up 24 houses and a power station in Ett Taibe, kidnapped 13 civilians and killed two women in blowing up a house in Muhebab. According to reports from Ett Taibe, the Israelis had informed the villagers that the 13 hostages they were taking would not be returned until Lebanon freed the two Israeli pilots forced down in Lebanon after a raid on Syrian forces April 8.

Defense Minister Moshe Dayan said April 13 that the raid into Lebanon was "political, not military," that it had been purposely limited in size and damage as a warning to the Beirut government that it must prevent commandos from crossing into Israel if it wanted to be spared future Israeli incursions. Dayan said "The Lebanese villagers will have to abandon their homes and flee if the people of Kiryat Shmona cannot live in peace. All of southern Lebanon will not be able to exist."

The Israeli raid, Dayan explained, was part of a new government policy to pressure Lebanon to curb the commandos. "We are trying to explain that we are not the police of Lebanon," that Lebanon was "responsible for what is taking place inside its territory."

Terrorists kill 25 in Maalot. Twenty-five Israelis, all but four of them teen-aged school children, died as a result of an attack by three Palestinian commandos May 15, 1974 on the Maalot village, five miles from the Lebanese border.

The Beirut-based Popular Democratic Front for the Liberation of Palestine, headed by Nayef Hawatmeh, took credit for the attack. The three guerrillas, who were said by Israel to have infiltrated from Lebanon, burst into a high school at Maalot, where about 90 students from other towns on an excursion were sleeping.

Israeli troops stormed the building after a breakdown in negotiations with the guerrillas,who were seeking the release of 20 commandos imprisoned in Israel in return for the lives of the youths. Sixteen

children were killed immediately, and five of 70 injured students died later. Israel claimed the children were shot by the guerrillas, all of whom were slain themselves in the exchange of fire with the soldiers. One Israeli soldier was killed.

Before taking over the school, the commandos had burst into an apartment in Maalot and killed a family of three. Police said that prior to arriving in Maalot, the guerrillas had killed two Arab women and wounded several others after firing on a van carrying workers.

After the terrorists broke into the school, they began to herd the students into classrooms. Seventeen children and three accompanying adults escaped by jumping through windows. Later in the morning, the commandos freed a woman officer with the group and sent her out with their ultimatum demanding the release of the 20 Arab prisoners by 6 p.m. By that time the freed prisoners were to be in Damascus or Cyprus along with Francis Hure, French ambassador to Israel, and Red Cross representatives.

The commandos threatened to blow up the school with wired charges unless the deadline was met. Israeli officials said they agreed to the demands.

Defense Minister Moshe Dayan and Lt. Gen. Mordechai Gur, army chief of staff, arrived on the scene to take command of the rescue operations. The guerrillas asked that Ambassador Hure and Rumanian Ambassador Ion Covaci be brought to the school to act as mediators. The negotiators were to bring a code word to the terrorists signifying the arrival of the freed 20 prisoners in Damascus or Cyprus, at which time half of the hostages were to be released. The others, Covaci and the three terrorists would depart in another aircraft, with the release of the remaining youths contingent upon the arrival of the plane in an Arab capital, preferably Damascus. The code word never arrived, and after the terrorists refused an Israeli demand to extend their deadline, the Israelis decided to storm the building.

Premier Meir vows protection—Premier Golda Meir declared in a television broadcast May 15 that the Arab raid on Maalot was a "bitter day" for Israel and pledged to do everything possible to prevent future attacks.

Mrs. Meir said: "I can't promise they will let us live in peace. But I want to and can promise that the government—any government of Israel—will do everything in its power to cut off the hands that want to harm a child, a grown-up, a settlement, a town or a village."

Israeli jets attack Lebanon—In reprisal for the commando attack on Maalot, Israeli jets May 16 carried out two separate attacks in southern Lebanon, bombing and strafing Palestinian targets from the foothills of Mount Hermon to the coastal city of Saida. Initial casualty figures reported by Lebanese and Palestinian commando authorities said 21 were killed and 134 wounded. It was the heaviest Israeli air attack ever carried out in Lebanon.

A Lebanese Defense Ministry communique said that severe damage was done to the Ein el Halweh refugee camp, the largest in Lebanon, and that the Nabatieh camp was hit.

The Defense Ministry said that at least five areas were attacked by the Israeli aircraft in the Mount Hermon sector, which served as a hideout and staging area for commando operations against Israel's northern border.

Announcing the raids, an Israeli military spokesman said they had been directed at commando storehouses, work shops and training camps largely in the Nabatiyah, Saida and Tyre regions.

Israel crackdown on commandos. A security alert was imposed on Jerusalem and most of northern Israel May 22 to prevent Palestinian terror attacks against civilian targets. The decision followed a report of infiltration into Israel by a group of commandos from Lebanon. Six guerrilla infiltrators were killed and two captured in northern Israel May 23.

Troops and police were deployed on the streets of Jerusalem, particularly in Arab East Jerusalem. In a separate action, police announced destruction of a "terrorist" cell in East Jerusalem in which "considerable quantities of arms and sabotage material were found in possession of three members of a gang."

Several hundred armed volunteers were aiding police and troops in the northern region around Nazareth and Afula and nearby areas in searching schools, factories and other sensitive centers for infiltrators.

One infiltrator was killed near the Lebanese border by Israeli forces May 22 and the other six were slain May 23 after they had moved across the Syrian-Israeli lines into the Golan Heights. The interrogation of two guerrillas captured in the area earlier led to the interception and clash with the six other commandos. According to the Israelis, the two captives said they belonged to the Popular Democratic Front for the Liberation of Palestine and were on a mission similar to the May 15 Maalot massacre. They told newsmen they were under orders to take civilian hostages at the kibbutzim of Ein Gev and Haon near the Sea of Galilee in exchange for the release of 30 terrorists held in Israeli jails and the return of the bodies of the three guerrillas killed at Maalot.

Israeli police reported June 4 they had captured two Arab terrorists on a mission to kill persons at random in Haifa. The terrorists, Israeli citizens from Galilee, had slipped across the Lebanese border June 3 and were seized after a suspicious taxi driver tipped off the police.

Arabs raid Israeli settlement. Four Palestinian terrorists were killed after slaying three women June 13, 1974 in a raid on Shamir, a northern Israeli kibbutz.

The Popular Front for the Liberation of Palestine-General Command claimed credit for the attack on Shamir.

According to the Israeli version of the incident: The four guerrillas entered Shamir after crossing into Israel from Lebanon, six miles away. They shot to death a woman volunteer worker from New Zealand and wounded a man leaving a dining hall. Six armed men of the settlement gave chase and shot one commando to death. The three other guerrillas took refuge in a factory building, where they exchanged fire with the Israelis. The three men blew themselves up with their own grenades and explosives after shooting two more women to death inside the building.

The Israelis said the terrorists were carrying leaflets demanding the release of 100 guerrillas in Israeli prisons "within six hours" in exchange for hostages they had planned to seize.

The guerrilla command in Damascus said 31 Israeli hostages and four of its own men had been killed in the Shamir attack, which it described as lasting 6½ hours. The statement said 15 Israeli soldiers also had been killed or wounded by the terrorists. The command said the attackers came from within Israel, and not from Lebanon.

Israeli jets raid Palestinians. Israeli planes carried out heavy raids June 18–20 against suspected Palestinian guerrilla bases in southern Lebanon in retaliation for the June 13 commando attack on Shamir in northern Israel and for other terrorist assaults emanating from Lebanon.

The raids, the heaviest on Lebanon since the October 1973 war, were directed against commando installations near Mount Hermon and other Palestinian targets to the west, including at least a dozen refugee camps and settlements.

An Israeli spokesman said the targets in the June 19 strike included a command post of the Popular Front for the Liberation of Palestine-General Command near the coastal town of Saida. A Jerusalem communique conceded that the planes that day had bombed in the vicinity of the Rashidya refugee camp in the Ras el Ein region but insisted that "all possible steps were taken to prevent harming the residents of the refugee camps."

It was reported that the guerrillas fired shoulder-carried SA-7 Strella missiles at Israeli planes attacking Saida June 20 but scored no hits.

Israeli government sources reported June 20 that the latest series of raids on Lebanon represented a new policy of pre-emptive attacks against the commandos. Its purpose was to disrupt the guerrilla forces by striking at their headquarters and to pressure the Lebanese government to curb the commando activities, the government sources said.

In a further move against guerrilla attacks, the Israelis were building a security fence along the northern frontier to prevent infiltration.

The Israeli Foreign Ministry said June 20 that Israel would continue attacking Palestinian groups responsible for "the murder of Israeli civilians," while continuing to seek peace.

Israel had informed the United Nations Security Council June 18 that it would take all necessary measures to defend itself against guerrilla attacks from Lebanon. The letter also rejected a Lebanese complaint that Israel was using Lebanon as a scapegoat for the commando raids, which Beirut claimed came from within Israel.

Israeli Defense Minister Shimon Peres urged Lebanon June 21 to "take constructive steps toward sealing her frontier with Israel against the passage of terrorists setting out to commit murderous acts."

Lebanese Premier Takieddin Solh had said that his country had no intention to curb the Palestinians, that Israeli attempts to divide the Palestinians and the Lebanese were bound to fail.

Libyan leader Col. Muammar el-Qaddafi cabled PLO leader Yasir Arafat June 24 that Libya "places all its capabilities at your disposal."

U.S.S.R. linked to terror group. Antony Terry reported in the London Sunday Times June 16, 1974 that "Western intelligence sources [had] confirmed that Russian secret service officers of the KGB and ... GRU have trained, equipped and financed" the Popular Front for the Liberation of Palestine-General Command. According to the article:

The man behind the PFLP(GC) is Ahmed Jibril, a former Syrian army demolition officer who has been to Russia several times for training.

Soviet support for him dates back five years and he now has a base in Moscow as well as supply and communications centres in several East European capitals, including Sofia and East Berlin.

Many of his Palestinian recruits have also gone through Soviet sabotage and subversion courses run by KGB and GRU officers....

The master-minding of Jibril's organisation is effected directly by Soviet diplomats stationed in the Middle East who are also KGB officers. One of these is Yuri Ivanovich Starchinov, a 35-year-old officer who joined the Soviet embassy in the Lebanon as deputy military attache three years ago....

The guerrilla warfare and sabotage training of the Jibril terrorists by the Russians is said in Western circles to be both thorough and effective. The chain of command from Moscow goes through the Soviet Ambassador in Beirut, Sarvar Azimov....

For some reason, the Russians have always preferred to ship their arms supplies to Jibril's guerrillas through Polish ports rather than direct from Bulgaria, where the organisation has its main headquarters in Eastern Europe.

Jibril has been receiving Soviet consignments of arms and equipment for the last four years. He has a "logistics and liaison officer," Abu Umar, who, like Jibril himself, is a former Syrian army officer....

Palestinians get Syrian arms—PLO leader Yasir Arafat said Syria had shipped "sophisticated weapons" to his forces in Lebanon in recent weeks and would continue to send the arms, the Beirut newspaper Al-Yom reported July 10. Western intelligence sources in Beirut had reported July 4 that the Syrians had sent the guerrillas shoulder-launched Strela SA-7 missiles.

Palestinians clash in Lebanon. At least 20 guerrillas were killed and 17 wounded June 23 in several hours of fighting at three refugee camps in and around Beirut between members of the Popular Democratic Front for the Liberation of Palestine (PDFLP) and the Popular Front for the Liberation of Palestine-General Command.

The clashes first erupted at a camp at Sabra, in a suburb of Beirut, and spread to the Shatila and Tal Zattar camps outside the city. Al Fatah assumed control of security at the camps after the fighting subsided.

The Palestinian news agency Wafa said the clashes were "the result of a misunderstanding." A PDFLP spokesman charged that the violence had started when "suspect and seditious elements" of the General Command fired a rocket at a PDFLP office at the Shatila camp. The statement said General Command members had carried out "provocative and suspect" acts the previous week, including the abduction of some PDFLP men who were still being detained.

The two groups held conflicting views. The General Command favored all-out war against Israel to liquidate the state. The PDFLP advocated establishment of a Palestinian state in the Israeli-occupied West Bank and Gaza Strip.

Terrorist raid in Nahariya. Israeli troops June 24, 1974 killed three Palestinian commandos after the guerrillas had slain three civilians in a raid on an apartment house in Nahariya, four miles south of Lebanon. An Israeli soldier was killed and five were wounded in the clash. The dead civilians were a woman and her two children.

Al Fatah claimed credit for the attack on Nahariya in a statement issued in Baghdad June 25. It was believed to be the first time that Al Fatah, regarded as one of the more moderate Palestinian commando groups, publicly acknowledged responsibility for such a mission.

According to Israeli accounts, the terrorists apparently reached Nahariya by water from Lebanon. A small boat was found beached just south of the coastal town. As the gunmen made their way into the center of Nahariya at night, they were spotted by an armed volunteer guard who opened fire, alerting police and troops. The Israeli force quickly surrounded the apartment house the guerrillas had entered and then stormed the building, killing the three Palestinians in an exchange of gunfire and hand grenades. The terrorists had killed the family of three after bursting into one of the apartments.

The Israelis retaliated for the Nahariya raid by firing artillery shells at Palestinian targets in southern Lebanon June 25.

Israel filed a complaint with the United Nations Security Council June 25, charging that Lebanon must be held responsible for the attack on Nahariya because it continued to permit the terror groups to operate freely on its territory. The Israeli letter charged that the commando leaders held frequent meetings with "the heads of the Lebanese government."

Terrorists to halt raids from Lebanon. The PLO was reported to have informed Lebanese Premier Takieddin Solh June 30, 1974 that its forces would stop using Lebanon as a base for attacks against Israel to spare the country retaliatory Israeli raids. Solh had told Parliament members June 27 that Lebanon would not act as a "sentry for Israel's security," but said the Palestinians had displayed a readiness to work out "the best solutions in order to avoid further losses in lives and property."

Egypt and Syria were said by Palestinian sources July 1 to have pressured the guerrillas to halt their forays across the Lebanese-Israeli border in a move to preserve the cease-fire with Israel.

Arabs to aid Lebanon, PLO. The Arab League defense council was reported to have agreed at a meeting in Cairo July 3–4 to provide Lebanon and the Palestine Liberation Organization (PLO) in Lebanon with financial assistance to strengthen their defenses against Israeli air and ground attacks.

Cairo newspapers reported July 5 that Lebanon had rejected a PLO plan submitted to the council meeting July 4 that would permit the Palestinian forces to establish missiles and antiaircraft guns in the 15 refugee camps in Lebanon.

Lebanese Premier Takieddin al-Solh had declared at the opening session July 3 that the protection of Palestinians in his country was not the exclusive responsibility of his country. The burden had to be shared collectively by all Arab nations, he said.

Israelis raid Lebanese ports. Israeli naval commandos raided the southern Lebanese ports of Tyre, Saida and Ras a-Shak the night of July 8 and sank 30 fishing boats in retaliation for the Palestinian guerrilla attack on the Israeli town of Nahariya June 24. The raid also was aimed at forestalling future guerrilla naval actions against Israel.

The foray was carried out by divers brought in by missile boats that slipped in from the sea. The raiders landed on shore in rubber rafts, blew up the fishing boats and returned to their ships undetected.

The Israeli army July 9 published an English translation of warning leaflets left behind by the naval force. They reminded the Lebanese fishermen that Israeli retaliatory attacks against the Palestinian terrorists had caused great damage to Lebanese villages and that these terrorists were "now using your fishing harbors, your boats and were hiding behind your peaceful civilian activity to sow death and destruction." The leaflets noted that the guerrillas who had attacked Nahariya had "come from your harbors." The statement warned that if the Palestinians were permitted to continue to operate from Lebanese harbors, Israel would not allow the fishermen to conduct their activities off the Mediterranean coast as in the past.

Israeli army authorities disclosed July 9 that the guerrillas had been undergoing diving and sabotage training for several years, that their supplies and weapons had been kept in camps not far from the shore, and that fishing jetties and motor boats had been used for attacks against Israel.

Israeli Information Minister Aharon Yariv disclosed July 9 that some of the boats destroyed in the Lebanese ports had belonged to terrorists or to Arabs who cooperated with them.

Israeli attacks continue. Israeli ground and air forces attacked suspected Palestinian guerrilla targets in southern Lebanon July 18 and 23.

In the July 18 action, Israeli troops crossed the border and blew up three houses in Bustan, about six miles east of the Mediterranean coast. The Israeli command said the buildings were used by "Arab terrorists."

Israeli military authorities did not specify the targets struck by Israeli planes July 23.

An Israeli spokesman said the raids were part of Premier Yitzhak Rabin's policy to attack the guerrillas "anytime, anywhere."

Israeli planes bombed the towns of Khreibe and Rachaya el Fakkhar Aug. 7, killing two civilians and wounding 17, the Lebanese Defense Ministry reported. The Palestine news agency Wafa said 10 guerrillas had been wounded in the second attack.

Israel reported the raids were against "terrorist" targets.

The air strikes followed the abduction Aug. 6 of six Lebanese civilians by Israeli troops that crossed the border. Their seizure was in retaliation for the kidnapping that day of four Druse employed by Israel to build a security fence between Lebanon and Israeli-occupied areas in the Golan Heights. The Popular Front for the Liberation of Palestine (PFLP) claimed credit for the kidnapping.

Israeli jets Aug. 9 bombed a tent encampment and two buildings at Rachaya el Fakkhar, a town used by the guerrillas as a supply base and assembly point, the Israeli military command reported.

An Israeli patrol boat Aug. 9 sank a guerrilla motorized rubber dinghy in Israeli territorial waters just south of Lebanon, preventing a commando raid on Israel, the Israeli command reported. A Palestinian military spokesman Aug. 10 conceded the loss of the boat, but said before sinking, the guerrilla craft scored a direct hit on the Israeli patrol boat.

Israeli gunboats Aug. 13 shelled the Rashidieh refugee camp near Tyre, killing one civilian and damaging a number of houses, the Palestinian news agency reported. The report claimed that one of the Israeli boats was hit and set afire by Palestinian guns. An Israeli military report on the operation said the principal target at the camp was a building used by the guerrillas as their naval headquarters from which the Palestinian boat had set sail Aug. 9.

Lebanese Premier Takieddin Solh disclosed Aug. 13 that guerrilla units were being withdrawn from Rachaya el Fakkhar on orders of Palestine Liberation Organization (PLO) leader Yasir Arafat. The pullout had started Aug. 12 after more than 300 villagers and their families, in protest against the government for failing to provide them with protection from Israeli air strikes, closed their shops, moved out of their homes and drove to another village 20 miles away.

PLO to open office in Moscow. The U.S.S.R. announced Aug. 4, 1974 that the Palestine Liberation Organization (PLO) had been granted permission to open an office in Moscow. The disclosure was contained in a joint communique based on talks PLO leader Yasir Arafat had held in Moscow with Soviet officials July 31–Aug. 4.

Pro-guerrilla newspapers in Beirut Aug. 3 said the Soviet Union had agreed to supply the Palestinians with defensive weapons, including ground-to-air missiles and anti-armor weapons.

Soviet policy in the Middle East had been assailed by George Habash, leader of the Popular Front for the Liberation of Palestine (PFLP), Lebanese newspapers reported Aug. 2. The PFLP, a member of the PLO umbrella group, had been excluded from the Moscow talks. Habash said: "There is an imperialist American scheme for the region but the Soviet line is ineffective because the Russians base their policies on Israel's right to exist."

Archbishop Capucci accused. Israeli police Aug. 18, 1974 arrested Archbishop Hilarion Capucci, leader of the Greek Catholic Church in East Jerusalem, and charged him with smuggling arms and weapons to Palestinian guerrillas in the West Bank and with serving as a link between Al Fatah and guerrilla groups on the West Bank.

Capucci was seized at his home in Jerusalem as he was about to leave for a religious conference in Beirut. Police disclosed he had been under surveillance since 1973. They said he had first been detained and then released Aug. 8 after being intercepted by police as he was about to leave for Nazareth, in northern Israel. A search of his car turned up large quantities of weapons and dynamite. It was thought he had brought back the weapons after a visit to Lebanon.

Capucci was indicted by an Israeli district court in Jerusalem Sept. 3 on three counts of arms smuggling for terrorists.

Capucci was charged with maintaining contacts with foreign agents, carrying and possessing illegal weapons and performing service for an unlawful association. Also named in the indictment were the prelate's contacts, Abu Jihad, head of the Black September organization, and Abu Firas, leader of Al Fatah operations in the West Bank. Demolition materials transported by Capucci from Lebanon in April, May and July had been "used for sabotage activities in Jerusalem," the indictment said.

According to Israeli officials, Capucci had told his interrogators that he had been forced into Al Fatah service through blackmail, it was reported Aug. 23. The archbishop was said to have claimed that Al Fatah officials in Lebanon had threatened him with physical violence and with disclosure of actions that might jeopardize his position in the church.

Israelis intercept guerrillas—An Israeli patrol Sept. 4 clashed with a Palestinian guerrilla detachment it intercepted near the Israeli Arab village of Fasuta, three miles south of the Lebanese border, thwarting a plan to free Capucci. A communique said that two infiltrators and two Israeli soldiers were killed.

According to Israeli military spokesmen, the infiltrators had entered from Lebanon for the purpose of seizing Israeli hostages in exchange for the release of Capucci and 11 guerrillas in Israeli jails.

The Popular Democratic Front for the Liberation of Palestine (PDFLP) claimed credit, saying its forces had captured an Israeli installation, taken hostages and were negotiating through foreign diplomats, presumably the French and Finnish ambassadors in Israel, for the exchange. The statement said a number of the hostages had been killed by attacking Israeli troops. The Israelis denied the claim and said the clash was over in minutes.

Another PDFLP communique from Damascus conceded that two of the infiltrators were killed in the operation.

PDFLP leader Nayef Hawatmeh, vowing Sept. 5 that the raids into Israel would continue, reaffirmed that the previous day's foray was aimed at securing Capucci's release and that hostages were taken.

The Israelis had intercepted a similar Arab infiltration unit Sept. 2 at Hanita near the western end of the Lebanese frontier, killing two.

West Bank terror group emerges—The emergence of a Palestinian terror group seriously resisting Israeli rule in the West Bank for the first time since Israel's occupation of the territory in 1967 was reported by the New York Times Aug. 22.

The new movement, known as the Palestinian National Front (PNF), had sur-

faced since the October 1973 war and launched a terror campaign in the West Bank in March, it was reported. According to Israeli government officials, 896 West Bank Arabs had been arrested recently on security charges. Of the total, 549 had been tried and were serving jail terms; 314 were awaiting trial; and 33 were being held under administrative detention.

Israeli officials said the core of the PNF was the Jordanian Communist Party, outlawed by King Hussein. They said the PNF had decided to embark on a terror campaign before the October war, when the Soviet Union began to improve its ties with the Palestine Liberation Organization (PLO). The PNF's objective was to assume the leading resistance role on the West Bank and thus place itself in the forefront in any future negotiations on the territory, according to the Israelis.

Militant group quits PLO. The militant Popular Front for the Liberation of Palestine (PFLP) announced its withdrawal Sept. 26 from the Executive Committee of the Palestine Liberation Organization (PLO).

In making the announcement in Beirut, Ahmed Yamani, PFLP representative in the Executive Committee, accused the PLO of "deviation from the revolutionary course" by joining in U.S.-sponsored moves for political settlement of the Arab-Israeli conflict. He said he had "accurate information" of PLO contacts with the U.S. through a third party. Denouncing the PLO policy of seeking to establish a Palestinian state in the West Bank and Gaza Strip if and when those territories were given up by Israel, Yamani asserted that the PFLP would continue the struggle until all of Palestine was "liberated," Israel destroyed and King Hussein overthrown in Jordan.

Yamani disclosed that two other PLO factions supporting the PFLP's decision, the Popular Front for the Liberation of Palestine-General Command and the Iraqi-sponsored Arab Liberation Front, had also decided to withdraw from the Executive Committee.

Latin America

Action Against Terrorism Urged

Terrorism has a long history in Latin America. The North American epithet "banana republic" refers specifically to politically and economically insecure countries of old Central and South America in which U.S. pressure and domestic armed bands had found it not difficult to enforce their will on government and society. Beginning in the mid-1960s, the more traditional terrorism endemic in Latin America has been supplemented by the terrorism of a new kind of revolutionary—the urban guerrilla.

Latin America in the 1960s was the home ground of several prominent theorists of political violence—for example, Ernesto (Che) Guevara, Carlos Marighella, Gen. Alberto Bayo—as well as the scene in which their theories were put into practice. In this period and in the years that followed, such developments as attacks on diplomats and hijackings of aircraft began to give terrorism in Latin America an increasingly international coloration— and made it increasingly a matter of international concern.

Although most Latin American terrorists seem to be concerned almost exclusively with their own domestic struggles, instances have been reported of international cooperation by Latin American urban guerrilla groups that share similar political orientation. In 1973, it was reported, a mutual cooperation agreement was signed by the Tupamaros of Uruguay, the ERP (People's Revolutionary Army) of Argentina, the MIR (Movement of the Revolutionary Left) of Chile and the ELN (National Liberation Army) of Bolivia.

OAS assails political terrorism. The General Assembly of the Organization of American States June 30, 1970 unanimously adopted a resolution condemning terrorism and political kidnapings as "common crimes whose gravity converts them into crimes against humanity."

In condemning "terrorist acts," the OAS assembly urged those states that had not already done so to adopt "criminal legislation that prevent or punish such crimes." In addition, the Inter-American Juridical Committee was ordered to present a plan within 120 days on how the purposes of the resolution might be effected. The resolution was unanimously passed when Brazil dropped its proposal to define terrorist acts as "a threat to peace and security" in the hemisphere.

82

(The OAS Permanent Council had strongly condemned terrorism and kidnaping June 15, leaving the adoption of methods to deal with it to the General Assembly.

(Four Latin American embassies in Washington, D.C. were firebombed early July 2. No injuries were reported, and the bombings caused only minor damage to the embassies of Argentina, Haiti, Uruguay and the Dominican Republic. A firebomb had been thrown at the Inter-American Defense Board headquarters the previous day; a group identifying itself as "Revolutionary Force Seven" claimed credit for the bombing, which left no injuries and little damage.)

ARGENTINA

Recent Terrorists & Their Activities

The current wave of terrorism in Argentina, which started in 1970, was preceded by a shorter period of terrorism in 1958-60. The French leftist Regis Debray, a specialist in revolution, analyzed this earlier wave briefly in the September-October 1965 issue of New Left Review. He described it as proof "that terrorism is not just the 'spontaneity of the intellectual.'" Debray noted that:

... This terrorist outbreak erupted from the base, from the Peronist unions and youth organization....

Between 1958 and 1960 there were at least 5,000 terrorist incidents. The movement was of considerable importance, but it was only the work of isolated groups or even individual terrorists, without any common programme or leadership.

The movement first appeared in the form of support for strike actions, at the time illegal. Militants would plant a bomb against an industrial establishment . . . to force it to close down or as a reprisal. This spread rapidly and became almost a daily occurrence, without any very clear point: bombs in the road, underneath vehicles, against the front of buildings, more or less anywhere. Towards the end, some groups of young workers managed to introduce some direction into this wave of spontaneous protests, and bombs were placed at the various agencies representing imperialist interests.... But the police had little difficulty in picking up the terrorists who had no underground organization. . . . and the movement was broken by the adoption of the 'Conintes Plan' (a sort of siege. . .); the terrorists were arrested and sentenced by emergency trials. Such terrorism obviously has nothing in common with the Venezuelan 'terrorism,' systematically directed against the imperialist economic infrastructure (pipe-lines, oil-wells, large warehouses, banks, the American military mission and so on).... In Argentina, terrorism led to a decline after 1960 in working-class militancy and a marked falling off in revolutionary combativity.

The current wave of Argentine terrorism took form with the strengthening of the movement for the return of Peron. It has been characterized by terroristic activity by groups with often clashing ideology. Their political orientations range from far left to far right, but these often antagonistic groups frequently claim the same short-term goal— originally the return of Peron, later the continuation of his presumed program.

The ERP (Ejercito Revolucionario Popular, or Ejecerito Revolucionario del Pueblo, People's Revolutionary Army), an allegedly Trotskyist organization, is the largest, best known, most active and best organized terrorist group in Argentina. The FAL (Frente Argentino de Liberacion, also identified as Fuerzas Argentinas de Liberacion, Fuerzas Armadas de Liberacion and Argentine [or Armed] Liberation Forces [or Front]) is a terrorist group formed by dissident Communist Party members and described as both "Marxist" and "with no clearly defined ideology." Two terrorist groups, the Montoneros (which described itself as "Peronist and Christian") and the FAR (Fuerzas Armadas Revolucionarias, or Revolutionary Armed Forces), merged in November 1973 and kept the name Montoneros. Another Trotskyist terrorist group is known as the Red Faction (Partido Revolucionario de los Trabajadores [Fraccion Roja]). A rightwing terrorist group was identified as MANO (Movimiento Argentina Nacional Organizado, or Argentine National Organized Movement).

Diplomats & Officials Become Kidnap/Terrorist Targets

Paraguayan consul kidnaped. Joaquin Waldemar Sanchez, Paraguayan consul in the town of Ituzaingo in Corrientes Province, was abducted in Buenos Aires March 24, 1970 by a group of men who identified themselves as members of the FAL (Argentine Liberation Front). Sanchez was released by his kidnapers March 28 after the Argentine government refused to release two political prisoners. Argentina became the first Western Hemisphere government to defy kidnapers' demands in a recent wave of terrorist kidnapings in Latin America.

The kidnapers had demanded the release of two political prisoners—Car-

los Della Nave and Alejandro Baldu—
in exchange for Sanchez.

However, in an apparent attempt to
force a showdown, the Argentine government announced March 25 that Baldu
was "a fugitive from justice" who had
not yet been captured and that Della
Nave was being "processed for common
crimes" and would not be released.

The kidnapers replied that they would
execute Sanchez "by firing squad" and
"begin the execution of all managers of
American business" if their demands
were not met. They also announced that
they were extending their deadline for
Sanchez' execution, originally set for
10 p.m. March 25.

Sanchez was released unharmed early
March 28 in a suburb of Buenos Aires.
His kidnapers said "humanitarian
reasons" were behind their decision to
spare his life. In an earlier statement,
the kidnapers had cited their organization's previous unwillingness to shed
unnecessary blood. "But now," they continued, "there has been killed, not in
combat, but in cold blood, one of our
dearest comrades [Baldu]. This changes
our position and obliges us to adjust to
circumstances." In a statement March
28 they warned that they were prepared
to "undertake the execution of an undetermined number of police and officials."

Interior Minister Francisco Imaz
hailed Sanchez' release March 28 and
maintained that the government's decision to reject the kidnapers' demands
was the only position possible. Any
other position would have been tremen-
dously dangerous for the future of the
country."

Soviet diplomat escapes. Right-wing kidnapers failed in an attempt to abduct
Soviet diplomat Yuri Pivoravov March 29,
1970, when Pivoravov escaped from the
getaway car as it was being pursued by
police. Pivovarov, assistant commercial
attache at the Soviet embassy in Buenos
Aries, apparently was not seriously hurt
in the incident. Police, alerted by the
screams of Pivovarov's wife, shot and
injured three of the kidnapers, who were
later captured when the car crashed.

Argentine officials revealed March 30
that a deputy federal police inspector,
Carlos Benigno Balbuena, was one of the
three wounded kidnapers. The other two
men, Guillermo John Jansen and Albert
Germinal Borrell, were unconnected
with the police, the government said.

Earlier, the right-wing Argentine National Organized Movement (MANO)
had claimed responsibility for the kidnaping attempt and described the three
wounded men as "war heroes." (MANO
had threatened March 27 to kill Soviet
Ambassador to Argentina Yuri Volski
and his family in reprisal for the Sanchez
kidnaping.)

Aramburu kidnaped & slain. Lt. Gen.
Pedro Eugenio Aramburu, 67, a former
provisional president of Argentina, was
kidnaped from his home May 29, 1970 by
four men, two of them wearing army officers' uniforms. Aramburu's body was
found July 16 in the cellar of an old farmhouse near Timote, about 300 miles west
of Buenos Aires. He had been shot twice
in the chest.

Following the abduction, at least a
dozen communiques had been received
from political organizations claiming
credit for the abduction, but the Juan Jose
Valle-Montoneros Command, named for
a Peronist army general executed in 1956,
offered what was called convincing evidence that it held Aramburu.

A communique June 1 from the Valle
Command said Aramburu had been
found guilty and would be shot by a
Peronist firing squad. The statement
said it was "impossible to negotiate his
release."

A month-long search for Aramburu
and clues to the kidnapers reportedly
failed to turn up any substantial evidence
until a July 1 terrorist raid on La Calera,
a suburban town near Cordoba. Fifteen
terrorists claiming to be members of the
Montoneros group took over the town for
about two hours, robbed a bank and
occupied police and telephone offices.
In a shootout with police following the
raid, several of the terrorists were seriously injured, among them Emilio Angel
Maza, 24, who died July 6. Maza was
later identified as one of the Aramburu
kidnapers. More than 10 arrests were

made in connection with the La Calera raid, and these reportedly led to other arrests and the discovery of Aramburu's body near Timote.

Fernando Abal Medina, 23, described as having "received Communist training in Cuba," was identified by Argentine police July 11 as the mastermind of the abduction.

Inspector Osvaldo Sandoval, a key witness in the trial of five persons charged in connection with Aramburu's murder, was shot and killed in Buenos Aires Nov. 14. A group that identified itself as the Argentine Liberation Forces claimed responsibility for Sandoval's death.

(Carlos Raul Capuano Martinez, sought for alleged involvement in the Aramburu kidnap-murder, was killed in a shootout with Buenos Aires police Aug. 17, 1972.)

British consul kidnaped. Stanley Sylvester, honorary British consul in Rosario, was kidnaped May 23, 1971 by ERP (People's Revolutionary Army) members.

A message from the group said that the kidnaping was carried out "in homage" to Luis N. Blanco, a left-wing university student killed in riots in Rosario in May 1969. The guerrillas said Sylvester would be "tried before a people's court of justice."

Sylvester was the director of a Swift Co. meat packing plant in Rosario, Swift de la Plata. The firm had been the target of considerable leftist criticism.

A demand by the kidnapers for distribution of $62,500 in food to the poor of Rosario was carried out by the de la Plata meat-packing plant May 29. Sylvester was released unharmed May 30.

Assassination foiled. More than a dozen young men and women were arrested after police discovered a plot to kill both Argentine President Alejandro Lanusse and Uruguayan President Jorge Pacheco Areco while they reviewed a military parade on Argentine Independence Day, July 9, 1971.

The youths, members of a self-proclaimed Revolutionary Peoples' Army composed of both Argentines and Uru-

guayans, were found with arms and explosives, according to police reports July 11. Police said a tank truck loaded with gasoline was to have been exploded near the reviewing stand.

An attempt by 10 youths to kidnap Julio Rodolfo Alsogaray, ex-commander in chief of the army, failed Aug. 17 in Buenos Aires.

Blast leads to bomb factory. An explosion April 4, 1970 in Buenos Aires led to what was believed to be a terrorist bomb factory. Two persons were injured in the apparently accidental explosion. An address book found at the site led to more than 100 arrests April 5.

The Parke Davis pharmaceutical plant near Buenos Aires was severely damaged by an explosion June 18; according to unconfirmed reports three employes were reported missing and feared dead. Nine bombs exploded June 27 in Buenos Aires, Rosario and Cordoba; U.S.-owned firms were among the targets.

Terrorism & counter-terrorism. Various other acts of terrorism were reported as well as actions to counter terrorism.

The U.S. embassy said Nov. 27, 1970 that the Buenos Aires homes of three U.S. military advisers had been "entered simultaneously by three armed groups." The three groups, who left leaflets identifying themselves as the Peronist Armed Forces, "demanded U.S. currency, official documents, firearms and uniforms," the embassy spokesman said.

The New York Times Aug. 9, 1971 reported estimates of Argentine authorities that armed subversive groups in Argentina had 6,000 active members. The report said evidence indicated that, as in Brazil and Guatemala, "death squads" linked to security forces had been responsible for the killing of persons suspected of subversive activities.

Members of a subversive command unit of the Revolutionary People's Army Aug. 18 raided an armory in Cordoba, fleeing with a large quantity of arms.

A 27-year-old navy canteen maid became the first Argentine to be sentenced by a special military tribunal to combat rising left-wing guerrilla activity.

Louisa Velosa, who told the tribunal that police had tortured her with electric shocks, was given a seven-year sentence Nov. 3 after being found guilty of participating in an armed attempt by guerrillas to seize weapons from the Buenos Aires police July 20.

'Third World' priests arrested. Four priests, members of the Third World Priests Movement, were arrested by the army in Rosario Aug. 3, 1971 with 13 other suspects in a roundup of "terrorist elements." The priests were Jose Maria Ferrari, Nestor Garcia, Juan Carlos Arroyo and Ruben Dri. Army officials said they had seized arms, explosives, subversive literature and narcotics in raids on the priests residences.

In a related development, the permanent commission of the Argentine Episcopate in Rome issued a statement, reported in the French newspaper Le Monde Aug. 19, affirming that the country's problems "have engendered violence on the attitudes, remarks and acts [kidnapings, crimes, tortures and assassinations] that are absolutely unjustifiable and condemnable."

The statement was understood as marking a schism in the Argentine church, with the Catholic bishops condemning both the violence of the "oppressors" and that of the "oppressed."

La Prensa of Buenos Aires reported Jan. 7, 1972 that naval authorities had abducted from their homes businessman Ricardo Beltran and the Rev. Albert Fernando Carbone, a member of the Third World Priests Movement, for questioning about an aborted Peronist plot to attack a coast guard post in the city of Zarate Jan. 3.

Beltran was reported active in Peronist circles, and Carbone had previously been given a two-year suspended sentence in connection with the slaying of former President Pedro Aramburo.

Despite protests from Third World Movement priests that Carbone had no knowledge of military tactics, federal authorities were reported Jan. 11 to be holding the men custody in a Buenos Aires jail.

ERP robs bank. Fifteen ERP members stole perhaps $800,000 from the state-owned National Development Bank in Buenos Aires Jan. 30, 1972. It was called the biggest bank robbery in Argentina's history.

According to newspaper accounts, the guerrillas held 13 bank employes hostage for eight hours while they bored a hole in the bank's vault. A police report implicated two bank employes.

Notices distributed later in Buenos Aires bars said the money was "expropriated for the people's cause, and will be used to continue the revolutionary war."

(Montonero members had robbed a Buenos Aires automobile company Jan. 23, burning several vehicles in an adjacent lot.)

Wave of terrorist attacks. A wave of political assassinations and kidnapings was sweeping Argentina, the New York Times reported March 22, 1972.

Participating in the terrorist campaign, the Times noted, were Peronist urban commandos, who defied a recent plea from Gen. Juan Domingo Peron to his followers for a halt to violence.

Among incidents reported:

In early January, two bombs damaged the headquarters of the women's branch of the Peronist movement, where Isabel Martinez Peron, wife of Peron, had an office. Mrs. Peron had come from Spain to try to unify the Peronist movement in Argentina.

Four police bomb disposal experts were killed Jan. 14 when a bomb they were defusing exploded in the Buenos Aires home of former Justice Minister Jaime Perriaux. A communique issued later by the Armed Liberation Forces (FAL) said the group had left the bomb in Perriaux's home because he had introduced the death penalty and state of siege regulations during his administration (July 1970–mid-1971).

Members of the terrorist Revolutionary Armed Forces (FAR) set off explosives in the Buenos Aires social building of the Argentina Association of Hereford Raisers Jan. 22, causing structural damage to the building.

Police arrested 43 suspected subversives in Buenos Aires, Salta and Bahia

Blanca Jan. 13 and 14, confiscating arms, munitions, wigs and masks and discovering documents in which guerrilla attacks were allegedly planned.

Six leftist guerrillas in Tucuman, 665 miles northwest of Buenos Aires, commandeered a milk truck Feb. 7 and delivered its 1,000-gallon load of bottled milk to poor people in two shantytowns.

A policeman was killed and the owner of a refrigeration concern was seriously wounded March 13 in Buenos Aires when about 10 terrorists fired on them.

An executive of a leading wine company was kidnaped March 17 and released after payment of $37,000 ransom. The kidnapers identified themselves as members of the Armed Forces of Liberation.

A leader of the New Force party was killed by Monteros members March 18, the same day that Montoneros set fire to a New Force office in Buenos Aires.

At least 10 members of the Armed Forces of Liberation were reported March 19 to have blown up the clubhouse of the exclusive Buenos Aires San Jorge Polo Club with three bombs.

Alleged ERP terrorists attacked a police station in Rio Tala April 27, killing two officers and seriously wounding the San Pedro police commissioner.

Seven youths disarmed two guards and then blew up a coast guard installation about five miles from Buenos Aires, the Miami Herald reported May 2.

Terrorists set off explosives at the homes of several police officers in the northwestern city of Tucuman May 5. No one was reported injured.

The offices of five U.S. companies in Buenos Aires were bombed in apparent response to the U.S. escalation of the Vietnam war, the Washington Post reported May 12.

Sixteen bombings were reported in Buenos Aires, Cordoba, Rosario and Santa Fe June 9, on the 16th anniversary of an abortive Peronist military coup. Among the sites bombed were the offices of the Buenos Aires newspaper La Opinion and a steel plant near the capital.

A renewed outbreak of terrorist attacks in Buenos Aires, Rosario, La Plata, Salta, Sante Fe and several smaller communities was reported Aug. 20. The actions followed the explosion of 15 bombs in Cordoba Aug. 18.

Fiat executive slain. Oberdan Sallustro, 56, president of Argentina's Italian-owned Fiat automotive industries, was kidnaped by ERP terrorists March 21, 1972 as he drove to work in Buenos Aires. He was found shot to death in a suburban house April 10.

The body was found after a police car searching for Sallustro discovered the ERP hideout. It was fired on by several guerrillas, and Sallustro was reportedly executed during the shootout that ensued. One of the guerrillas was captured.

According to the New York Times April 11, the ERP had sought a $1 million ransom for Sallustro and the release of 50 of the more than 500 political prisoners held in Argentina. Fiat had reportedly been willing to pay the ransom, but President Lanusse had barred any form of negotiations with the ERP.

El Nacional of Caracas reported April 11 that Lanusse had also rejected a plea for negotiations with the ERP from Italian President Giovanni Leone. Lanusse had maintained that Sallustro's kidnaping was an internal Argentine matter.

After the government's refusal to allow negotiations, the ERP had announced that it would execute Sallustro "at the appropriate moment."

The army announced April 18 that it had captured the eight-member ERP team that had kidnaped and murdered Sallustro.

Eighteen other alleged ERP members, 15 of them women, were also arrested in connection with the case, and six other accomplices were said to be at large.

Two of the men arrested in the Sallustro case, Andres Ernesto Alsina Bea and Ignacio Ikonicoff, charged in the Montevideo weekly Marcha May 12 that they had been tortured in Buenos Aires jails.

(Alsina Bea, a journalist for the Buenos Aires newspaper La Opinion, said he was kicked severely and electric shock was applied to his genitals and mouth. Ikonicoff, a journalist for Inter Press, was also beaten and claimed other prisoners were burned with acid.)

Three of the defendants were given life sentences March 16, 1973 for their roles in Sallustro's kidnap-murder, and seven received terms of one to 12 years. (A three-judge court agreed that two of the defendants had been tortured.)

General assassinated. Gen. Juan Carlos Sanchez, commander of the army's 2nd Corps, was machine-gunned to death April 10, 1972 as he rode to his office in the city of Rosario. Unidentified attackers also seriously wounded Sanchez' chauffer and accidentally killed a news vendor.

The People's Revolutionary Army (ERP) and the Revolutionary Armed Forces (FAR) issued a joint communique April 10 claiming responsibility for Sanchez' death and promising further assassinations. The communique said Sanchez had been killed in reprisal for his anti-guerrilla campaign.

(According to El Nacional of Caracas April 11, the 2nd Corps had pursued terrorists vigorously, extending military repression over groups not directly connected with urban guerrillas, such as progressive Roman Catholic priests. Soldiers under Sanchez' command had been accused of torturing persons they arrested, but authorities had dismissed the charges.)

The ERP-FAR document also denounced President Alejandro Lanusse for "threatening a fascist coup" and for promoting "an electoral farce" by declaring general elections for March 1973. Numerous sources said Lanusse's election plan and his recent negotiations with ex-President Peron had caused the latest wave of terrorist attacks in Argentina.

The National Security Council, meeting late April 10, decreed that all trials for kidnaping, violating the public peace and attacking institutions would henceforth be transferred to military tribunals.

Authorities announced June 24 that Dr. Luis Alejandro Gaitini, 27, had been arrested in connection with Sanchez' assassination. Gaitini, an alleged member of FAR, reportedly confessed participation in Sanchez' murder and other terrorist activities.

Gaitani and two other defendants were sentenced to life imprisonment and two others to terms of nine and 11 years Feb. 9, 1973 for alleged participation in the affair.

Torture reports grow. More than 50 persons reportedly had been tortured at prisons and military installations during the past year, and accounts of political torture were growing in magazines and newspapers, according to the Miami Herald May 26, 1972.

The most publicized recent case of political torture involved Norma Morello, a Roman Catholic schoolteacher and rural organizer, who returned to her home in Goya May 14 after being held without charge for nearly six months. After her release, Miss Morello signed an affidavit saying she had been tortured for three days with electric devices, repeatedly threatened with rape and denied sleep for 15 days while she was interrogated at a military installation outside Rosario.

Miss Morello said May 15 that she had been tortured because police wanted her to link the Catholic movement in Goya to Argentina's guerrilla movements.

Two other women, arrested in connection with a kidnaping, claimed they had been tortured by federal police with an electric needle, the Herald reported May 26. Police denied the charge.

The army issued instructions May 25 intended to prevent the mistreatment and torture of political prisoners.

Members of the Third World Priests movement charged at a press conference in Buenos Aires Jan. 10, 1973 that Argentine political prisoners were subjected to "inhuman treatment." Rev. Osvaldo Catena, a movement official who had been jailed for nine months, said he and all other prisoners had been "underfed and deprived of medical care."

Hugo Norberto D'Aquila, chief of psychiatric services at Buenos Aires' Villa Devoto prison, was kidnapped Jan. 11 by members of the Liberation Armed Forces (FAL) and released unharmed Jan. 13. The FAL said D'Aquila had been interrogated on conditions among political prisoners in Villa Devoto.

Trelew Prison Break & Killings

16 killed after prison break, hijack. Sixteen suspected guerrillas, including at least three women, were shot to death Aug. 22, 1972 in an alleged break-out from the prison at the naval air base near Trelew, in the southern province of Chubut. Three other alleged subversives were reportedly wounded.

According to police officials, all of the victims had been arrested Aug. 15 at the Trelew airport, where they had helped 10 other alleged terrorists hijack an Austral Airlines jet with 96 aboard.

The hijacking was carried out in conjunction with a mutiny at an army maximum security prison at Rawson, 15 miles from Trelew, during which a group of inmates escaped. Some escapees were reportedly among the hijackers, who commandeered the jet to Santiago, Chile, where they surrendered to police and requested political asylum.

News of the killings at Trelew caused large demonstrations in several cities in which hundreds of persons were arrested. In the industrial city of Cordoba 600 protestors were arrested Aug. 22.

Lawyers for the slain guerrilla suspects Aug. 22 denounced their clients' deaths as "a virtual execution," charging it would have been impossible for them to try to escape because they were held in separate cells under heavy guard.

Those killed included 12 members of the left-wing People's Revolutionary Army (ERP), one of the Revolutionary Armed Forces and two of the Peronist Montoneros. They had surrendered to military authorities after helping in the hijacking. Their deaths were widely assumed to be a retaliatory execution ordered by the government.

Trelew hijackers reach Cuba. The 10 Argentine guerrillas who hijacked an airliner from Trelew to Santiago were sent to Cuba by the Chilean government Aug. 25.

The Argentine government, which had demanded extradition of the guerrillas, angrily recalled its ambassador from Santiago Aug. 26 and delivered what it called a "very severe" protest to Chile Aug. 27.

In a nationwide radio and television message Aug. 25, Chilean President Salvador Allende said his government's decision to grant the guerrillas political asylum and then send them to Cuba was motivated by "profound humanity and morality" and followed "international conventions and principles and the dispositions of our internal laws."

Upon arrival in Havana Aug. 26, the 10 guerrillas told newsmen that armed Marxist and Peronist groups in Argentina would step up their offensive against the government of President Alejandro Lanusse. ERP leader Roberto Mario Santucho, whose wife was among the 16 killed at Trelew, accused Lanusse of direct responsibility for the "assassination" of his fellow guerrillas.

In Argentina, meanwhile, the government reportedly gave two conflicting versions of the Trelew killings, one on an "off the record" basis to newsmen, and an official version released Aug. 25. According to the London newsletter Latin America Sept. 1, journalists were originally told that the prisoners had escaped from their cells early Aug. 22 and after seizing the second-in-command of the base, Capt. Luis Sosa, were proceeding toward the armory when they were engaged in fierce combat by guards.

The later version, however, held that Sosa had ordered the prisoners out of their cells and was inspecting them in a narrow passage—some five feet wide—when he was seized by a guerrilla, who took his submachine gun and began shooting at the guards. The weakest part of the version, the newsletter noted, was that the guerrilla had missed his targets while Sosa alone had escaped unharmed from a fusillade that cut down 16 guerrillas and wounded three of their comrades.

Assassinations & Kidnapings Continue

Admiral assassinated. Rear Adm. Emilio R. Berisso, plans and strategy officer for the naval chief of staff, was shot to death near Buenos Aires Dec. 28, 1972. The assassins escaped.

The FAR (Revolutionary Armed Forces) later claimed credit for Berisso's death.

Berisso's position in the Navy reportedly linked him to the armed forces security network responsible for repression of the country's guerrilla groups. His assassination followed a number of other terrorist actions.

Terrorism preceding assassination— Three kidnaped businessmen were freed unharmed in Buenos Aires Sept. 6 after ransoms reportedly totaling $850,000 were paid to their captors.

Jan J. Van de Panne, a Dutch citizen who headed the Philips Argentina electronics firm, was released by alleged Peronist Montonero guerrillas after his company paid them $500,000. He had been held since Sept. 5. Two Argentine businessmen—Adolfo Kaplun and Eduardo Falugue, both abducted Sept. 4—were freed after their families reportedly ransomed them for $150,000 and $250,000. Police arrested nine "common criminals" in connection with Kaplun's kidnaping, La Prensa of Buenos Aires reported Sept. 15.

A wealthy landowner, Eden Ronald Bongiovani of La Pampa province was reportedly kidnaped Sept. 6 and held for $200,000 ransom.

Felix Azpiazu, a Spanish industrialist kidnaped Dec. 6, was freed unharmed Dec. 8 after his firm paid a reported $100,000 ransom.

Ronald Grove, managing director of Great Britain's Vestey industrial group in South America, was kidnaped in Buenos Aires Dec. 10 and released unharmed Dec. 19 after Vestey paid a reported $1 million ransom.

Vicente Russo, an executive for a Buenos Aires subsidiary of the International Telephone and Telegraph Corp., was kidnaped in the capital Dec. 27 and released unharmed Dec. 29. Company officials refused to comment on local newspapers reports that a ransom of $500,000–$1 million had been paid.

(Police in La Plata announced Feb. 21, 1973 that they had captured a seven-person FAR cell implicated in, among other crimes, the kidnapings of Ronald Grove and Enrico Barella. The group was said to be led by Francisco Urondo, a journalist and poet.)

A series of bomb blasts took place Oct. 17, the anniversary of Peron's release from prison in 1945 under the pressure of popular demonstrations. The blasts, which disrupted train services in Rosario and damaged buildings and installations throughout the country, followed the bombing Oct. 16 of the new U.S.-owned Sheraton Hotel in Buenos Aires. A Canadian woman was killed in the blast and two other persons were injured.

Buildings were damaged by bombs Oct. 11 in Cordoba and Corrientes. Ten Cordoba buildings had been bombed Oct. 7.

An armed band blew up an exclusive social club in Santa Fe Oct. 13 after clearing the building. Bombings were reported Oct. 12 in Buenos Aires and other cities and at the farms of several military officers.

A guerrilla was shot to death in a gunfight with Buenos Aires police Oct. 18 following the explosion of a bomb at the home of the father of a Cabinet minister, according to police.

The wife of a leading radical Peronist theoretician was seriously wounded Oct. 19 by a bomb set off in their Buenos Aires apartment. The Buenos Aires office of a lawyer who defended left-wing guerrillas was bombed the same day.

Fifteen bombs exploded in Argentina Dec. 22, damaging buildings used by the armed forces, labor unions, political parties, banks and businesses, but causing no casualties. Bombs were set off at six businesses in Rosario early Dec. 20.

(The government June 2 had reinstituted the death penalty, abolished in 1886, for kidnaping and terrorism.)

Peronists assassinated. An aide to Jose Rucci, secretary general of the Peronist-dominated General Labor Confederation, was shot to death in Buenos Aires Feb. 14, 1973 by gunmen attempting to break up a FREJULI (Justicialista Liberation Front) party meeting. This was the fifth politically motivated slaying in four weeks.

Gunmen in the Buenos Aires suburb of Lanus Jan. 22 had killed Julian Moreno, a Metallurgical Workers Union official and FREJULI candidate for Lanus municipal intendant, and fatally wounded his chauffeur. FAR took responsibility for the killings and for the earlier assassination of two other Peronists, Jose Alonso and Augusto Vandor. The FAR said its victims—members of the labor sector that, led by Rucci, had sought to cooperate with the government—were traitors to the Peronist movement.

Policemen assassinated. Unidentified gunmen killed two policemen in separate attacks in the Buenos Aires suburbs of Lanus and San Justo Feb. 21 and 22. A third policeman and a civilian were wounded in the second attack.

Separate attacks against five policemen and assaults on three police headquarters, all attributed to the ERP, were reported by the Miami Herald March 28.

Peronists Return to Power

FREJULI sweeps elections. Ex-President Juan Peron's Justicialista Liberation Front (FREJULI) swept the first round of general elections March 11, 1973 and the runoff round April 15. FREJULI won the presidency, a majority of provincial governorships and control of both houses of Congress. The armed forces commanders March 30 declared FREJULI candidate Hector J. Campora president-elect for a four-year term beginning May 25.

Radical senatorial candidate Fernando de la Rua defeated FREJULI candidate Marcelo Sanchez Sorondo in the Buenos Aires race.

According to the Washington Post April 17, the defeat of FREJULI in the capital might be due to the recent wave of terrorism by left-wing guerrillas, which voters had come to associate with Peronism. Peronist guerrillas remained active despite a peace call by Campora.

According to the London newsletter Latin America April 13, the continuation of Peronist terrorism was intended to ensure the release of political prisoners and institution of revolutionary changes by the new government, which could not easily disavow its guerrilla supporters.

More than 100,000 soldiers had been reported mobilized April 12 to forestall possible guerrilla violence coinciding with the April 15 runoff. The move followed

an increase in killings, bombings and kidnapings by terrorist groups in the wake of the March 11 round of elections.

Most of the violence was attributed to the Trotskyist People's Revolutionary Army (ERP), which contended that election of a Peronist government would delay an Argentine revolution. The ERP, it was reported, was again under the leadership of Roberto Santucho, who escaped from prison and fled to Chile and then Cuba in August 1972. He had reportedly returned to Argentina.

Peronist guerrillas were said to have halted most operations to insure that the armed forces transferred power to Campora May 25. However, the assassination of an army intelligence officer April 4 was laid to the Peronist Montonero group.

Campora said April 8 that the popular verdict in the March 11 elections rendered all terrorist activities "inadmissible." He had appealed earlier to guerrillas to "think and give us a sufficient truce so that we can prove whether or not we are on the path of liberation."

Adm. Aleman kidnaped. Retired Rear Adm. Francisco Agustin Aleman, a former naval intelligence chief and merchant marine under-secretary, was kidnaped from his Buenos Aires apartment April 1, 1973 by three ERP terrorists, including his own nephew.

An ERP communique April 3 said Aleman was being held "as a prisoner of war" to further "the people's struggle for the liberation of all political and social prisoners."

Aleman's abductors painted a number of ERP slogans in his apartment, including "Popular Justice for Trelew."

Aleman, held 68 days, was freed June 7 after he admitted wrongdoing by the navy in the August 1972 killing of 16 imprisoned revolutionaries at the naval air base prison near Trelew, Chubut Province. Aleman said in a statement released by the ERP that the killings "were a sad affair" and that the version presented by his captors indicated the navy's role in them was "ignominious."

Col. Iribarren Assassinated. Col. Hector A. Iribarren, chief of intelligence of the army's 3rd Corps, headquartered in Cordoba, was shot to death April 4 by two gunmen who crashed their truck into his car. Iribarren, a key figure in anti-guerrilla efforts in the area, apparently was killed when he resisted an abduction attempt.

The murder was later blamed by authorities on the Montoneros, according to the Miami Herald April 8.

Terrorists in La Plata Feb. 16 set off bombs at the homes of a government official, a former governor of Buenos Aires province and a Peronist candidate for Congress. Similar explosions were reported in Santa Fe, Cordoba and Tucuman Jan. 26.

Widespread terrorism. Among other reported incidents of terrorism during the early months of 1973:

About 40 members of the left-wing People's Revolutionary Army (ERP) temporarily occupied a military installation in Cordoba Feb. 18, disarming 70 soldiers and officials and escaping with an army truck carrying arms and ammunition. Other ERP guerrillas simultaneously occupied a nearby police installation to prevent police from intercepting the commandeered truck, which the guerrillas later burned.

Naum Kacowicz, a prominent Buenos Aires businessman, was kidnapped Feb. 16 and reported freed Feb. 21 after a record $1.5 million ransom was paid.

Pinucela Cella de Callegari, wife of a Zarate industrialist, was kidnapped March 19 and released three days later after payment of a $250,000 ransom.

Gerardo Scalmazzi, Rosario branch manager of the First National Bank of Boston, was kidnapped March 28 and freed April 4 after the bank paid a ransom estimated at $750,000-$1 million.

A bomb explosion killed one person and injured others March 30 in the Buenos Aires building housing the naval commander's offices. The blast was one of four that day in the capital and Rosario. One Rosario explosion, apparently directed against Peronist leader Ruben Contesti, killed Contesti's mother.

The technical operations manager of Kodak Argentina S.A., a subsidiary of the U.S.-based Eastman Kodak Co., was kidnapped in Buenos Aires April 2 and freed unharmed April 7 after Kodak paid a $1.5 million ransom. The executive, Anthony R. DaCruz, reportedly was the first U.S. businessman kidnapped in Argentina. His abductors were identified as members of the Liberation Armed Forces.

The New York Times reported April 3, before DaCruz' release, that about 50 business executives had been kidnapped in Argentina during the past two years, and almost $5 million in ransom money had been paid for their release. Many observers asserted that a growing proportion of the kidnappings were the work of common criminals interested only in money rather than that of terrorists acting for political motives.

Angel Fabiani, son of a Buenos Aires businessman, was abducted April 2 and freed April 5 after payment of a "large ransom," according to press reports.

A shootout April 4 between Cordoba police and two men attempting to kidnap jeweler Marcos Kogan resulted in the deaths of Kogan and the abductors, La Prensa reported April 5.

The daughter of one of the nation's most powerful army commanders, Gen. Manuel A. Pomar, was kidnapped by presumed urban guerrillas April 5, according to military sources.

Alberto Faena, a Buenos Aires textile executive, was kidnapped by Liberation Armed Forces guerrillas April 6 and freed April 10 after payment of a reported $500,000 ransom.

Francis V. Brimicombe, a British tobacco company executive kidnapped April 8, was freed unharmed April 13 after his company paid a reported $1.5 million ransom.

Santiago Soldati, son of a Swiss businessman, was kidnapped in Buenos Aires April 29 and freed unharmed May 4. The newspaper Cronica reported the next day that his family had paid a $1.5 million ransom.

Col. Nasif abducted. ERP terrorists April 26, 1973 kidnapped Lt. Col. Jacobo Nasif, the third-ranking officer of the Cordoba frontier guard, which had been reorganized to combat guerrillas.

Nasif was freed June 5 after 40 days in captivity. An ERP communique said he had been released only after the guerrillas determined that recently pardoned political prisoners were in good health.

Adm. Quijada assassinated. Retired Rear Adm. Hermes Quijada was assassinated April 30, 1973.

Quijada was shot to death by two men disguised as policemen as he rode to work in Buenos Aires. His chauffeur,who was injured in the incident, fatally wounded one of the assailants, later identified as an ERP leader.

The ERP sent a communique to the press April 30 taking credit for the assassination. Quijada had chaired the joint chiefs of staff in August 1972, when 16 guerrillas were killed at the naval prison near Trelew.

Emergency declared. The military government declared a state of emergency in the Federal District and the five most populous provinces April 30 after Quijada's assassination.

The decree placed the armed forces in direct control of the capital and the provinces of Buenos Aires, Santa Fe, Cordoba, Mendoza and Tucuman. It said assailants of military or police personnel would be prosecuted in special military courts and sentenced to death, without the right of appeal. It also decreed the death penalty for persons making, selling or possessing unauthorized arms, ammunition or explosives.

Military commanders took control of the capital and provinces May 1, and subsequently decreed other severe measures.

President Alejandro Lanusse cabled President-elect Hector Campora soon after Quijada's murder, urging Campora to return from Madrid, where he was conferring with his political mentor, ex-President Juan Peron. Campora complied, returning to Buenos Aires May 2.

Campora met May 3 with Lanusse and the other armed forces commanders, navy Rear Adm. Carlos Coda and air force Brig. Carlos Alberto Rey.

It was well known that Campora previously had refused to condemn Argentina's five guerrilla groups, seeking the continued support of the Peronists among them and of the Peronist youth movement, which supported the guerrillas. However, he was reported May 4 to have assured the commanders he would not tolerate guerrilla attacks on the armed forces after May 25.

The state of emergency was ended by the government May 19.

Terrorism continues. Incidents of terrorism continued both during the 19-day state-of-emergency period and after it was lifted May 19, 1973.

Armed men in Buenos Aires May 1 kidnapped the son of the Swiss chairman of the Italo-Argentine Electric Co. After payment of $1.5 million, the youth was released May 4.

The Buenos Aires businessman Jose Marinasky, who had been kidnapped May 14 but who was freed May 18, was an uncle of Mario Raul Klachko, sought in connection with the 1972 kidnap-murder of Fiat executive Oberdan Sallustro. Klachko's wife, Giomar Schmidt, who had been accused of killing Sallustro, had been acquitted of all charges, La Prensa of Buenos Aires reported May 16.

About 20 guerrillas attacked a police radio station near Buenos Aires May 20, leaving one officer dead and three wounded. Some of the attackers also were reported wounded.

Dirk Kloosterman, secretary general of the powerful Mechanics Union, was killed by gunmen in La Plata May 22. He was identified with conservative Peronist labor leaders who had been under attack by left-wingers in and out of the Peronist movement.

In another shooting reported the same day, two Argentine executives employed by the Ford Motor Co.'s Buenos Aires subsidiary were wounded by unidentified gunmen in an unsuccessful kidnap attempt. One of the injured executives, Luis Giovanelli, died of his wounds June 25.

Oscar Castells, president of the Coca-Cola Bottling plant in Cordoba, was kidnapped May 22. After payment of $100,000 ransom, he was released June 4.

The ERP released Argentine business executive Aaron Beilinson June 3, after 10 days' captivity, in payment for $1 million ransom. At a press conference, Beilinson read a statement in which the ERP pledged to use the money to "help finance the revolutionary struggle."

Terrorism condemned. By May 1973 many previously uncommitted political figures had started to oppose the terrorism so prevalent in Argentina.

Terrorism was also assailed by many Peronists. Former President Juan Peron condemned guerrilla "provocations" in a statement published May 31. President Hector Campora met June 14 with 20 recently pardoned guerrilla leaders and told them he wanted peace in Argentina by June 20, when Peron was scheduled to return from Spain.

The Peronist youth movement also attacked the ERP, with one group vowing to kill 10 guerrillas "for every Peronist that falls."

The ERP, for its part, vowed to fight on against "all injustice and postponements, against the exploitation of the worker, against all suffering by the people," until capitalism was "definitely eliminated" and "workers' power" established. In a statement May 29, the guerrillas attacked the government's attempts to reach a "national accord," and called on "progressive and revolutionary Peronist and non-Peronist" groups to join them in attacking "imperialist firms and the army oppressors."

The ERP and the major Peronist guerrilla groups—the Montoneros and the Revolutionary Armed Forces—held clandestine conferences with selected newsmen June 8. The Peronists issued a statement afterwards vowing a continued battle against "the military imperialist clique" but also pledging to destroy any guerrilla group that opposed the Campora government.

Newsmen reportedly met four ERP leaders, including Roberto Santucho. Santucho said "the causes of social exploitation and the political-economic dependency of the country have not disappeared or even been touched by the new government," but he pledged that the ERP would not attack the government or the police "if they do not repress the people."

The ERP leaders reportedly denied their organization had kidnapped a British businessman, Charles Agnew Lockwood, held since June 6 for a reported $2 million ransom. They also denied responsibility for extortion threats against Ford Argentina and subsidiaries of the U.S. firms Otis Elevator Co. and General Motors. (Lockwood was freed July 29 after the payment of a ransom that he agreed was "pretty close" to $2 million. He said he did not know to which group his kidnappers belonged.)

(According to the London newsletter Latin America June 8, the ERP was suffering from internal problems. There was an open split between the ERP majority and the August 22 column, with the latter reportedly supporting the government and criticizing continued guerrilla activities as rigid and sectarian.)

Ford grants ERP demands. The Argentine affiliate of the Ford Motor Co. agreed May 23, 1973 to distribute $1 million worth of medical items, food and educational materials to prevent further attacks on its employes by guerrillas of the ERP's August 22 column.

Ford Argentina May 28 began payment of $400,000 to be shared equally by two hospitals in Buenos Aires and Catamarca. A company spokesman said construction of ambulances for use in various provinces had begun in Ford factories, and $200,000 had been allocated for dried milk to be distributed in shantytowns around the capital. A further $300,000 would be spent on supplies for needy schools in the Buenos Aires area.

The ERP had sent Ford and the press communiques May 22 claiming responsibility for a machinegun attack earlier that day on two Ford executives, and warning of further attacks if Ford did not provide $1 million in welfare donations.

Edgar R. Molina, Ford's vice president for Asian, Pacific and Latin American operations, said at the company's U.S. headquarters May 23 that Ford believed "we have no choice but to meet the demands."

Campora inaugurated, prisoners freed. Hector Jose Campora was inaugurated as president of Argentina May 25, 1973.

Campora declared an immediate amnesty for political prisoners late May 25 after 50,000 Peronists threatened to break down the gates of Buenos Aires' Villa Devoto prison and prisoners belonging to the People's Revolutionary Army (ERP) occupied prison offices.

Prisoners began leaving the jail soon after the decree was announced, but the demonstration continued, resulting in clashes in which two persons were killed and about 65 arrested.

At least 375 prisoners from different jails were released early May 26, and some counts put the total at more than 500. Those released included guerrillas jailed in connection with the killings of Fiat executive Oberdan Sallustro, ex-President Pedro Aramburu and army Gen. Juan Carlos Sanchez.

An amnesty bill for political prisoners was passed by Congress May 27 and signed by Campora the same day. The president also signed legislation dissolving the military regime's special "anti-subversive" courts and repealing the ban on the Argentine Communist party.

The ERP issued a statement May 27 saying that despite the amnesty, it would continue to attack businesses and the armed forces.

Shootouts greet Peron's return. At least 20 persons were killed and 300 wounded near Ezeiza international airport June 20, gunfire in a crowd of nearly two million people awaiting the arrival of ex-President 1973 when rival Peronists exchanged Juan D. Peron from exile.

Machinegun and handgun fire broke out shortly before Peron's plane landed, and continued sporadically into the evening. Several reporters said the initial fire came from snipers in woods near the stage from which Peron was to speak. Neither troops nor police were near the scene, since security had been entrusted to armed members of the Peronist youth wing.

According to the Washington Post June 22, much of the fire was exchanged between rival factions of Peronist youths, who had been bitterly divided over which would direct security operations.

According to another report, the shooting erupted when young left-wing Peronists tried to mount the stage to place guerrilla banners in full view of the crowd. They were blocked by conservative trade unionists, who had played a key role in organizing Peron's homecoming. A trade unionist reportedly fired a warning shot into the air, and then volleys were unleashed from both sides.

Snipers and gunmen reportedly stalked each other and terrorized thousands of bystanders for more than an hour, and indiscriminate shooting continued even after ambulances began removing the dead and wounded, according to the report.

The left-wing Peronist Youth (JP) June 22 accused right-wing Peronists and U.S. Central Intelligence Agency infiltrators of provoking the Ezeiza shootouts. It alleged that retired Lt. Col. Jorge Osinde, who organized the homecoming, had directed an "ambush" by "three hundred armed mercenaries" to keep Peron from speaking.

The JP asserted Osinde's men opened fire when one of its columns tried to join the crowd near the stage. It also charged unnamed persons had tried to remove wounded JP members from hospitals, and had tortured others at Ezeiza's international hotel.

Another group, the Peronist Working Youth, also blamed Osinde and other homecoming organizers for the bloodshed.

Leonardo Favio, a movie actor and director who witnessed the bloodshed, said at a press conference June 24 that the shooting was begun by thugs hired by leaders of the General Labor Confederation and Osinde. Favio added that he had seen prisoners taken by the thugs beaten and tortured at the airport's hotel. (Favio had said previously that the JP had started the violence.)

A special government commission investigating the shootouts had received overwhelming evidence that the violence was initiated by right-wing Peronists, it was reported June 29.

ERP presents views. The People's Revolutionary Army (ERP) charged at a news conference June 27 that the government was responsible for the Ezeiza killings and that Campora was defrauding the people who elected him.

Roberto Santucho, the guerrilla group's leader, told 22 selected newsmen that fascist gangs organized by "the Social Welfare Ministry under the immediate supervision of the torturer Osinde" had carried out the "unexpected and ferocious attack against revolutionary Peronists" near the airport.

Santucho denied that the ERP was Trotskyist, as was widely assumed. He asserted: "The ERP is Socialist, with a broad program attracting comrades of distinct tendencies—Marxists, Peronists, Catholics, but no Trotskyists."

Santucho said the government should be modeled after Cuba's socialism, but he stressed that Cuba had given the ERP only moral support.

The guerrilla leader noted that two factions had split off from the ERP but were still using that name. One of them, the ERP-August 22, appeared to have seceded because of the majority faction's intransigence regarding Peronism.

Santucho asserted the ERP had been incorrectly held responsible for several recent kidnappings and extortions. He admitted his group had carried out kidnappings since Campora's investiture.

Kidnappings continue. John R. Thompson, president of the Argentine affiliate of the Firestone Tire & Rubber Co., was kidnapped June 18, 1973, then released July 5. The ERP confirmed July 10 that it had abducted Thompson and that his firm had paid a record $3 million "revolutionary tax" for his release.

It was reported that bargaining for Thompson's release had taken place openly at the Presidents Hotel in downtown Buenos Aires. An undisguised ERP negotiator was said to have haggled with Firestone officials there before the ransom figure was agreed on. The ransom, in bundles of 500-peso notes, was reported to have filled an armored car provided by the ERP.

At least 16 major kidnappings were reported in different parts of the country June 27–Aug. 7, and other abductees were ransomed. Hans Gebhardt, a businessman kidnapped June 19, was ransomed for $80,000 July 2. Mario Baratella, an Italian banker seized June 25, was reported ransomed July 5. Raul Bornancini, assistant manager of First National City Bank of New York in Cordoba, was abducted July 2 and reported released July 13.

The government took a number of steps to end the kidnapping wave, including establishment of a special kidnapping unit in the federal police July 2.

The U.S.-based Coca-Cola Export Corp. began removing its executives and their families to Uruguay and Brazil Aug. 11, after professed ERP guerrillas demanded that the firm pay $1 million to specified charities or face attacks on its executives.

Tucuman police chief slain. The ERP appeared to be responsible for the machinegun killing Aug. 5 of the Tucuman police chief, Hugo Tamagnini, accused by the guerrillas of torturing political prisoners. Before dying, Tamagnini reportedly identified one of his slayers as ERP member Carlos Santillan. An ERP communique later claimed responsibility for the murder, according to press reports.

Peron & wife elected. Ex-President Juan Peron and his third wife, Maria Estela (Isabel) Martinez, were elected president and vice president of Argentina Sept. 23, 1973. They were inaugurated Oct. 12.

Peron, just short of his 78th birthday, had campaigned little, sending his wife on provincial campaign tours.

Peron vowed in a radio and television address to use "emergency" measures to combat any violence that might persist after the election.

Peron attributed recent political and criminal violence in Argentina partly to "a political and economic disturbance" in which he saw "the foreign influence of imperialism, which has never stopped working against freely elected governments."

ERP outlawed. The People's Revolutionary Army (ERP), the nation's strongest guerrilla group, was outlawed by provisional President Raul Lastiri Sept. 24, 1973.

A group of asserted ERP guerrillas had captured a military supply center in Buenos Aires early Sept. 6 and held it under police and army siege for five hours, killing one officer before surrendering. Police said 11 guerrillas had been arrested at the scene and others detained elsewhere.

Professed members of the ERP's breakaway August 22 column Sept. 9 kidnapped a director of the Buenos Aires newspaper Clarin and held him until Sept. 11, after Clarin published documents by the guerrillas urging support for the Peron-Peron ticket in the Sept. 23 elections and sharply criticizing Lastiri and Social Welfare Minister Lopez Rega. An unidentified armed group threw firebombs and shot into Clarin's offices later.

Rucci slain, other terrorism. Secretary General Jose Rucci of the Peronist-dominated General Labor Confederation (GCT) was assassinated Sept. 25.

Rucci, his driver and a bodyguard were cut down by unidentified gunmen as Rucci left the house of a relative in western Buenos Aires. The government blamed the ERP for the attack, but there was also speculation it might be the work of left-wing Peronists, who had bitterly opposed Rucci's conservative union leadership. The ERP Sept. 27 denied having killed Rucci.

A left-wing Peronist, Enrique Grimberg of the JP, was murdered Sept. 26, causing fear of open warfare between conservative and radical Peronists.

Marcelino Mancilla, leader of the Mar del Plata CGT and an orthodox Peronist, had been murdered Aug. 27, apparently by guerrillas of the FAR.

Constantino Razzetti, a Peronist leader in Rosario, was shot to death Oct. 14, presumably by right-wing Peronists. Razzetti, a biochemist and vice president of the Rosario municipal bank, was killed soon after delivering a speech at a Peronist luncheon severely criticizing the conservative Peronist labor bureaucracy.

Another conservative Peronist, Julian Julio, leader of a bus drivers' union in Mar del Plata, had been killed by unidentified gunmen Oct. 9.

In another apparently political murder, Jose Domingo Colombo, political and union news editor of the San Nicolas (Buenos Aires Province) newspaper El Norte, was shot to death by gunmen who invaded the paper's offices Oct. 3. El Norte's director said fliers distributed in the city a few days earlier quoted the JP as charging the newspaper employed "Communists and Trotskyists."

There were several attacks on radical Peronists. Jorge Lellis, a JP leader in Rosario, narrowly escaped assassination Oct. 4 when gunmen in a passing vehicle fired on him. In Cordoba the same day, two construction union members were reported wounded when gunmen fired on local headquarters of the General Labor Confederation, dominated by left-wing Peronists.

In Buenos Aires, offices of the JP magazine Militancia were severely damaged by a bomb explosion Oct. 9. JP headquarters in Formosa were fired on Oct 17, with no injuries reported. And in Mendoza, a bomb explosion Oct. 22 nearly destroyed the offices of provincial Gov. Alberto Martinez Baca, who had been criticized by conservative Peronists for not ridding his administration of radical Peronists.

Pablo M. Fredes, a leftist leader of the Transport Workers Union, was taken from his Buenos Aires home Oct. 30 and shot to death by unidentified gunmen.

Antonio J. Deleroni, a leftist lawyer, and his wife, Nelida Arana de Deleroni, were killed in Buenos Aires Nov. 27 by a gunman later identified as a member of a right-wing Peronist youth group and former bodyguard for the Social Welfare Ministry.

A member of the left-wing Peronist Youth (JP) was stripped and beaten by right-wing Peronists Nov. 2, and a leftist member of the Transport Workers Union was kidnapped and tortured Nov. 21. Following the first incident, leaders of the JP obtained an audience with Interior Minister Benito Llambi and Federal Police Chief Miguel Antonio Iniguez to protest the right-wing campaign against Peronist leftists, which included not only murders and torture but almost daily bombings of leftist offices.

In a related development, Sen. Hipolito Solari Yrigoyen, a member of the Radical party, was wounded Nov. 1 when a bomb exploded in his automobile. Solari had represented combative labor unions and political prisoners accused of guerrilla activities.

Foreign executives kidnapped. Kidnappings of foreign executives continued during the latter half of 1973. Although most perpetrators apparently were members of terrorist groups, it was assumed that at least a few of the kidnappers were common criminals whose sole objective was ransom.

David Heywood, an executive of Nobleza Tabacos, a subsidiary of the British-American Tobacco Co., was kidnapped Sept. 21 and freed by police Oct. 20. Police said they arrested four of the abductors, all "common criminals," and recovered more than $280,000 in ransom money.

David B. Wilkie Jr., a U.S. citizen and president of Amoco Argentina, a subsidiary of Standard Oil Co. of Indiana, was kidnapped in suburban Buenos Aires Oct. 23 and ransomed by his company Nov. 11. The company said the payment was "well below" the $1 million reportedly demanded by the kidnappers.

Swissair said Nov. 29 that its Latin American director Kurt Schmid, abducted in Buenos Aires Oct. 22, was freed Nov. 28 and immediately left the country. The airline refused to say whether it had paid a ransom.

U.S. executive murdered. John A. Swint, general manager of a Cordoba subsidiary of Ford Motor Argentina, was assassinated Nov. 22. The Peronist Armed Forces (FAP), one of several terrorist groups supporting President Juan Peron, later took credit.

Swint and two bodyguards were killed in an ambush in suburban Cordoba by about 15 gunmen. A third bodyguard was seriously wounded. Eyewitnesses said there was no attempt to kidnap the U.S. executive.

The FAP claimed credit for the assassination in a communique to newspapers Nov. 28, and warned Ford headquarters in Buenos Aires that day that it planned to "knock off" other foreign executives and their families "one by one," and to blow up the main Ford plant in suburban Buenos Aires. Ford reportedly moved some 25 U.S. executives and their families out of the country Nov. 28–29.

Action Against Terrorists

Terrorism curbs approved. The Chamber of Deputies passed President Juan Peron's controversial anti-terrorism bill Jan. 25, 1974 less than a week after an ERP attack on an army garrison.

The bill, reforming the Argentine penal code, was approved 128–62, over the opposition of virtually all non-Peronist legislators and members of the leftist Peronist Youth (JP).

The bill virtually doubled prison sentences for convicted kidnappers, conspirators and armed extremists, and turned over internal security functions to the federal police rather than local law enforcement officers. It also outlawed "illicit" political associations and "incitement to violence," but defined the terms ambiguously.

Peron and the right wing of his movement had demanded swift approval of the bill after 60–70 ERP members attacked an army tank garrison at Azul, 170 miles south of Buenos Aires, the night of Jan. 19–20. The guerrillas occupied the garrison and fought a seven-hour gun battle with troops, leaving two guerrillas, a soldier, the base commander and his wife dead. The terrorists escaped with a hostage, Lt. Col. Jorge Ibarzabal.

Peron appeared on nationwide television after the attack, wearing his army general's uniform, and called on the armed forces, police, labor unions and his Justicialista Party to unite "to annihilate as soon as possible this criminal terrorism." He accused left-wing Peronists of being "complacent" about terrorism and indirectly criticized Buenos Aires Province Gov. Oscar Bidegain, a left-wing Peronist, by asserting terrorists were "operating in the province with the indifference of its authorities."

A majority of Peronist senators and deputies demanded Bidegain's resignation late Jan. 21, and the governor acceded Jan. 23. He was replaced Jan. 26 by the vice governor, Victorio Calabro.

Police and soldiers carried out widespread raids in search of the Azul attackers, and announced the arrest of 13 suspects Jan. 23, including several persons allegedly wounded at the garrison.

$14.2 million ransom for Samuelson.

Victor Samuelson, manager of the Esso Argentina oil refinery at Campana, north of Buenos Aires, was kidnapped Dec. 6, 1973 by ERP members. He was freed April 29, 1974, seven weeks after his employer had paid a record $14.2 million ransom.

An ERP communique Dec. 8 had said Samuelson would be "submitted to trial" on unspecified charges. A subsequent message Dec. 11 demanded a $10 million ransom.

The $10 million was demanded in food, clothing and construction materials to be distributed in poor neighborhoods across Argentina "as a partial reimbursement to the Argentine people for the copious riches extracted from our country by [Esso] in long years of imperialist exploitation."

The company announced March 13, 1974 that it had actually paid a $14.2 million ransom. The terrorists had also demanded that a communique they issued on the kidnapping be printed by 12 newspapers in Buenos Aires and some 30 in the provinces, but all but three papers in the capital declined in fear of reprisals from the government.

The ERP communique said Esso had agreed originally to pay $4.2 million in supplies to victims of recent floods in Argentina, plus $10 million in cash as "indemnization" for "the superprofits that Esso has obtained in the country, thanks to the exploitation of its workers." However, the message stated, "existing obstacles" had made distribution of the supplies unfeasible, so the entire $14.2 million had been paid in cash.

Esso repatriated its remaining U.S. executives March 14–15 to avert any new kidnappings. Fear of abduction or murder had caused more than 500 U.S. business executives to leave Argentina during the past few months, the Miami Herald reported March 22. The estimated 300 U.S. businessmen who remained in the country reportedly headed small concerns.

(The government May 28 created a special industrial police force to guard Argentine and foreign factories against guerrilla attacks.)

ERP, Latin guerrillas unite.

Leaders of the ERP said at a clandestine news conference in suburban Buenos Aires Feb. 14 that they would step up their attacks on the Argentine military and form a "common front" with leftist guerrillas of Chile, Bolivia and Uruguay.

One of the leaders, who identified himself as Enrique Gorriaran, said: "We consider that to halt or diminish the fight against the oppressor army would allow it to reorganize and to pass over to the offensive."

Another of the leaders, identified as Domingo Mena, said the ERP and the Revolutionary Left Movement of Chile, the National Liberation Army of Bolivia and the Tupamaro guerrillas of Uruguay were "prepared to do combat under a joint command." A joint declaration by the four groups pledged to overthrow "imperialist-capitalist reaction, to annihilate counterrevolutionary armies, expel Yankee and European imperialism from Latin American soil, country by country, and initiate the construction of socialism in each of our countries . . ."

The ERP June 12 made public documents asserting that it had distributed $5 million among the other members of the Latin American guerrilla "Revolutionary Coordination Board," the coordinating organization set up by the Argentinian, Bolivian, Uruguayan and Chilean terrorist groups. The ERP documents, signed by Mario Roberto Santucho, reported that the money was part of the Samuelson ransom. The ERP said the guerrillas were using the money to finance "a new stage of military development," the establishment of rural guerrilla movements to mobilize and organize the masses and complement the operations of the existing guerrilla units.

Peronists assassinated.

Intra-Peronist violence continued.

Rogelio Coria, former secretary general of the national Construction Workers Union, was shot to death in Buenos Aires March 22.

Luis A. David, a supporter of Peron and head of the right-wing Nationalist Liberation Alliance, had been found shot to death March 21 near San Nicolas (Buenos Aires Province). The adjunct secretary of the San Nicolas Construction Workers Union, Roberto Jose Kusner, had been shot dead the day before.

Another right-wing Peronist, Miguel Angel Castrofini, of the Nueva Argentina university faction, was assassinated March 8.

Juan Manuel Abal Medina, ex-secretary of the National Justicialista Movement and an organizer of radical Peronist youth groups, was wounded in the arm in an assassination attempt in Buenos Aires March 23. Presumed rightists fired on him from a passing car and threw two grenades into the apartment building into which he retreated.

Maria Liliana Ivanoff of the leftist Peronist Youth (JP) was kidnapped and shot to death by presumed Peronist rightists outside Buenos Aires April 26. Carlos Mugica, a leader of the Third World Priests Movement with close ties to the JP, was gunned down as he left his church in the capital May 11.

The government news agency TELAM charged May 14 that Mugica had been killed by the Peronist Montoneros guerrilla group, presumably for his recent appeals to leftists to moderate their attacks on the orthodox Peronist leadership and remain loyal to President Peron. However, the London newsletter Latin America noted May 17 that Mugica had first gained prominence by defending two dead Montoneros, and that the guerrillas never killed a person for making appeals such as Mugica's.

JP leader Carlos Castelacci was killed May 10 in a gun battle with other leftist Peronists over possession of one of the JP's Buenos Aires offices.

U.S. diplomat attacked. ERP guerrillas April 12, 1974 wounded and kidnapped Alfred A. Laun III, director of the U.S. Information Service in Cordoba. The first U.S. diplomat kidnapped in Argentina, Laun was freed within hours.

The guerrillas invaded Laun's home outside Cordoba in the morning and wounded him in the head, abdomen and shoulder when he resisted abduction. They released him that evening, apparently for fear he would die in captivity.

Laun underwent surgery in a Cordoba clinic, and was reported "out of danger" April 15. He was flown to Panama for further treatment April 17.

Shortly after the kidnapping, the ERP sent a message to a Cordoba radio station claiming credit for the abduction. The guerrillas said Laun would be "interrogated on counterrevolutionary activities in Vietnam, Santo Domingo, Brazil and Bolivia, and for his active participation as a liaison in the fascist military coup against our brother people in Chile. He will also be interrogated on his ties with the Central Intelligence Agency."

(The U.S. embassy in Buenos Aires denied Laun had ever worked for or with the CIA, or served in Brazil or Bolivia. It also denied he had participated in any activities connected with Chile. Laun previously had served in the Dominican Republic, South Vietnam and Thailand.)

Anti-guerrilla offensive. Hundreds of persons were arrested in Tucuman Province May 18–21 as federal police mounted a campaign against the ERP.

The action followed further violence by the ERP and by members of the opposing Peronist political factions and a warning by President Juan Peron that Argentina faced civil war. Peron was quoted May 16 as saying that because of "revolutionary infantilism," Argentina might have "reached a situation of unavoidable confrontation."

The Tucuman anti-guerrilla hunt was abandoned May 25. Security forces said that bad weather had enabled the guerrillas to escape encirclement.

The task force of more than 1,000 policemen and soldiers reportedly captured only 27 alleged guerrillas, none of them major ERP leaders. The failure of the anti-guerrilla effort was dramatized May 31 when more than 40 ERP members briefly occupied the town of Acheral, which had served as a center of operations for the campaign.

ERP members had assassinated Jorge Quiroga, a former judge of the disbanded anti-subversive court, in downtown Buenos Aires April 28. Quiroga had interrogated and sent to prison the 16 ERP and Peronist guerrillas who were killed by authorities at the Trelew naval air base prison in August 1972.

Buenos Aires police claimed May 6 that the ERP was also responsible for the murder of Manuel R. Garcia, a moderate Peronist labor leader, outside the capital May 4.

Claudio Alberto Luduena, sought in the ERP's recent kidnapping of U.S. Information Service official Alfred Laun, was killed in Cordoba April 28 as he attempted unsuccessfully to kidnap Antonio Minetti, a business executive.

New security unit. Bombings, political assassinations and kidnappings continued in Buenos Aires and other cities, leading President Juan Peron to set up a new committee to command all security operations. The committee, reported June 7, 1974, consisted of Peron, the ministers of defense, interior and justice, and the armed forces commanders. Its orders would be carried out by a new security secretariat headed by Brig. Gen. Alberto Caceres, the frontier police chief who had served as federal police chief under the supplanted military dictatorship.

Terrorism After Peron's Death

Peron dies, wife assumes presidency. President Juan Domingo Peron died of a heart attack July 1, 1974.

The presidency was assumed by Peron's widow, Maria Estela (Isabel) Martinez de Peron, who became the first woman chief of state in the Americas.

Mrs. Peron had assumed executive powers June 29, when doctors ordered Peron to take "absolute rest" while they treated him for what they said was infectious bronchitis with heart complications.

Most political groups and military leaders had pledged their support for Mrs. Peron June 29–30, citing the Constitution's provisions for the vice president to rule if the president was incapacitated.

The 250,000-member left-wing Peronist Youth Organization announced its unconditional support for Mrs. Peron June 29, and the Montoneros guerrilla group, also on the Peronist left, said it backed the vice president "as long as Gen. Peron is not in the physical condition to continue exercising the presidency." Both groups previously had criticized Mrs. Peron for favoring her husband's most conservative advisers, including Social Welfare Minister Jose Lopez Rega, whom the Peronist left called a "fascist."

It soon became clear that Peronist guerrilla factions were prepared to mount terrorist actions in opposition to Mrs. Peron.

An alleged Montoneros internal document disseminated among journalists Aug. 3 said the guerrillas should restructure their ranks for a "resistance stage" because there was no longer any "reason" to support Mrs. Peron. A "formal break" with her government would "depend on circumstances," the document stated.

Montoneros leader Mario Firmenich asserted Aug. 12 that Mrs. Peron was not the "heir" of her late husband because "the leadership of the masses cannot be inherited."

Former Interior chief slain. Arturo Mor Roig, who organized the March 1973 presidential elections when he served as interior minister under the supplanted military dictatorship, was shot to death in suburban Buenos Aires July 15, 1974.

Mor Roig had been in office in August 1972, when officers at the Trelew naval air base in Patagonia killed 16 leftist guerrillas, many of them members of the ERP.

At least six persons were killed and 28 arrested as police mounted an intense search for Mor Roig's assassins.

Police in Buenos Aires reported July 16 that two men and a woman had been killed when they exchanged gunfire with officers seeking to search their automobile.

Interior Minister Benito Llambi announced July 18 that four suspects had been killed and 28 arrested since the assassination, and all were members of the ERP or of other left-wing extremist groups. However, the ERP denied responsibility for Mor Roig's death in a press communique July 18.

(Ex-President Alejandro Lanusse, in whose Cabinet Mor Roig had served, charged the Peronist Montoneros organization had committed the assassination, the French newspaper Le Monde reported July 21.)

Two more suspects were killed July 20 in a shootout with police.

Montoneros resume guerrilla warfare. The Montoneros went underground again as violence by feuding Peronists and ERP members mounted.

Hundreds of bombings and numerous assassinations occurred throughout Argentina Aug. 13–Sept. 18, seriously threatening the ability of President Maria Estela Martinez de Peron to govern. Terrorist attacks had claimed one victim every 19 hours since Aug. 1, according to the New York Times Sept. 18.

Montoneros leader Mario Firmenich said at a clandestine press conference Sept. 6 that his movement had begun a "people's war" against the government, which, he claimed, had been "captured by imperialists and oligarchs" since the death of President Juan Peron July 1. Mrs. Peron's administration had made it impossible for leftists to operate legally, leaving armed warfare as their only alternative, Firmenich charged.

Firmenich said the Montoneros had assassinated two anti-guerrilla security officers, kidnapped an engineer and carried out a number of machinegun and bombing attacks against automobile dealerships and other targets in recent days. Montoneros in Tucuman claimed credit for the murder of sugar executive Jose Maria Paz Sept. 7.

Firmenich said the Montoneros were not yet strong enough to battle police and military units, but he expected they would be strong enough "in several weeks." He did not rule out the possibility of joining forces with the ERP, which was leftist but not Peronist. "There is no need to confuse political ideologies," he said. "We will have to see what their policy is . . . if it is like ours, we can act together . . ."

The Montoneros' decision to resume guerrilla warfare was supported by the other organizations of the Peronist left, although they chose to remain aboveground. It was denounced by the right-

wing Peronist newspaper Mayoria, which asserted the Montoneros were now out of the Peronist movement, and by the independent daily La Opinion, which said the guerrillas were out of touch with reality.

The strongest support for the Montoneros came from leftist students at Buenos Aires University, where Peronist youths had occupied all but one of the faculties since Aug. 14. The University's interim rector, Raul Laguzzi, openly backed the Montoneros. Laguzzi and his wife were seriously injured and their four-month-old son was killed Sept. 7 when their home was bombed by presumed right-wing Peronists.

President Peron met with the commanders of the armed forces and leaders of anti-guerrilla operations Sept. 7 in an apparent effort to devise a strategy against the Montoneros and militant students.

Meanwhile, bombings and assassinations of Peronist leaders continued. An estimated 50 bomb explosions were reported in Buenos Aires and other parts of the country Aug. 22, the second anniversary of the killing of 16 leftist guerrillas at the naval air base at Trelew, and more than 100 bomb blasts were reported Sept. 16–17. Other bombings occurred daily, many at dealerships of IKA-Renault, an automobile company involved in a bitter labor dispute.

Four members of the left-wing Peronist Youth organization were killed in suburbs of Buenos Aires Aug. 22–23. At least seven Peronists were killed in a wave of assassinations Sept. 16–18.

ERP-Montonero collaboration. It was reported that the ERP and Montoneros had agreed at least to coordinate their terrorist strikes.

The ERP magazine The Combatant announced Sept. 26 that the ERP was "prepared to collaborate with the Montoneros in the military field, to stage joint attacks against the armed forces, the police and the repressive forces in general, and the imperialist corporations." However, the ERP said the two groups could not form a "joint military force" because the Montoneros were not a "revolutionary organization" but a group with "erroneous populist concepts at the service of a bourgeois illusion."

ERP leader Roberto Santucho had said Sept. 18 that his group would stage "indiscriminate executions" of army officers in retaliation for the alleged execution by the army of 14–16 guerrillas captured during an ERP raid on an infantry post in Catamarca Province in August.

(The ERP had acknowledged Aug. 28 that it had suffered a "serious defeat" at the hands of police and soldiers in Catamarca Province earlier in the month, after guerrillas attacked an infantry post outside the city of Catamarca. Combined security forces pursued a guerrilla column in the province's mountains Aug. 13–15, killing or arresting at least 27 insurgents. Police in a suburb of Buenos Aires claimed Sept. 9 to have found and confiscated the printing press on which the guerrillas allegedly printed 80% of their propaganda. The ERP continued terrorist attacks despite these setbacks, blowing up a police station in suburban Buenos Aires Aug. 16).

The Montoneros killed two persons Sept. 19 in kidnapping Juan and Jorge Born, directors of Bunge & Born Co., one of the largest international trading conglomerates in Latin America. A Montoneros communique later demanded $50 million in ransom for the Born brothers and said they would be "tried for the acts committed against the workers, the people and the national interest by the monopolies to which they belong." The communique said the two persons killed— the Borns' chauffeur and the manager of one of their companies—had tried to prevent the kidnapping.

Rightists form AAA. Right-wing elements in September threatened armed violence to counter the leftist terrorism.

A right-wing group calling itself Argentine Anticommunist Alliance threatened Sept. 5 to "execute" 10 liberal and leftist federal deputies for "infamous treason against the fatherland."

The AAA's terrorists assassinated Julio Troxler, a leftist former deputy police chief of Buenos Aires, Sept. 20. In a communique Sept. 21, the group said it was responsible for the murders of four other prominent leftists, including Atilio Lopez, former vice governor of Cordoba Province, and that it intended to kill 12

more leftists, including ex-President Hector Campora, former Buenos Aires University Rector Raul Laguzzi and Congressman Hector Sandler. A report in El Nacional of Caracas Sept. 28 said the AAA had a "black list" of 49 persons to be assassinated, most of them left-wing Peronists.

The AAA communique said Troxler had been killed because he was "a commie and a bad Argentine." It added: "Five are down and the lefties will continue to fall wherever they are."

The AAA was held responsible for the murders of a leftist construction worker in Bahia Blanca Sept. 22; a magazine editor, a television employe and a third person in Buenos Aires Sept. 26; and two relatives of former President Arturo Frondizi Sept. 27. Silvio Frondizi, brother of the ex-president, was dragged from his Buenos Aires home and later found dead outside the city. His son-in-law, Luis Mendiburu, was killed trying to prevent the abduction. Frondizi was a Marxist lawyer and essayist; his brother ran a small political party that, according to the newsletter Latin America Sept. 27, was near a break with the government.

Several people who were on the AAA's death list or feared they might eventually appear on it fled Argentina. Rodolfo Puiggros, the liberal former rector of Buenos Aires University, took asylum in the Mexican embassy Sept. 24—an unusual step since he was not being sought by the government—and was flown to Mexico City the next day. Laguzzi, who had recently been wounded in a terrorist attack, fled to Mexico Sept. 28. (The current rector of Buenos Aires University, Eduardo Ottalagano, a rightist, survived an assassination attempt in Villaguay Sept. 23. Ottalagano was unharmed, but his assailant and a local hotel owner were killed and two policemen were wounded in the incident. The assailant's political affiliation was not revealed.)

Two prominent actors, Norman Briski and Nacha Guevara, fled to Peru Sept. 28, two days after the AAA threatened to kill them and three other well-known performers. The Argentine Actors Association struck Sept. 27 to protest the threat.

The AAA then added several more persons to its death list Sept. 30–Oct. 1, threatening to kill each if he did not leave

the country. Army Gen. Juan Carlos
Sosa, leftist union leader Armando Cabo
and former Bishop Jeronimo Podesta
were threatened by the AAA Sept. 30.
The next day the rightists threatened
three legislators from the Radical Party—
Deputy Mario Amaya and Senators Hipolito Solari Yrigoyen and Humberto
Perette—and a dean and three professors
at the state university in Rosario. With
these the AAA had passed "death
sentences" on 61 persons, 19 of whom had
been killed in the past two months, according to El Nacional of Caracas Oct. 2.

According to the London newsletter
Latin America Oct. 11, it was generally
assumed that AAA members included
soldiers and police, with the police in ulti-
mate control. Montoneros leader Roberto Quieto charged at a clandestine
press conference Oct. 4 that the AAA was
"organized by the federal police chief,
Alberto Villar," and that its "inspiration
and political orientation" came from the
government itself.

Quieto said Oct. 4 that the Montoneros
were prepared to negotiate a truce with
the government if it would grant
emergency wage increases, end its intervention in the trade unions, restore
freedom of political expression, repeal
repressive security legislation, stop the
AAA assassination campaign and fire
Villar and his deputy chief, Luis Mar-
garide. The ERP offered a truce of its own
Oct. 6, asking the government in return to
free all political prisoners, repeal the new
anti-subversion act and restore the ERP
to legality.

The government ignored these offers
and the bloodshed resumed Oct. 7 with
the assassination of army Maj. Jaime Gi-
meno.

The AAA killed two more persons Oct.
8—Rodolfo Achem, administrative secretary at La Plata National University,
and Carlos Miguel, director of the
university's planning department. Army
Lt. Juan Carlos Gambande was assassinated in Santa Fe Oct. 11. Two
newsmen were found shot to death outside
Buenos Aires Oct. 13, and a Peronist
leftist, Juan Carlos Leiva, was murdered
in La Plata Oct. 14.

Anti-terrorism bill. Congress Sept. 28
passed an anti-terrorism bill submitted by

President Maria Peron and backed by
the armed forces. The law provided stiff
prison terms for persons who disseminated subversive propaganda or tried
to change the nation's political structure "by means not laid down by the
Constitution," and it restricted news
reporting of activities by illegal groups.

Observers said the wording of the bill
indicated it was designed primarily to fight
leftist guerrillas, although the government
said Sept. 27 that it would also be used
against rightist assassins.

Mrs. Peron had charged Sept. 26 that
leftist guerrillas were trying to provoke a
military coup, and she pledged to the
armed forces that her government would
press a full battle against subversives.

In an attempt to gather support amid
the increasing violence, Mrs. Peron held a
rally in Buenos Aires Sept. 20. Only 30,-
000-50,000 persons attended even though
the huge General Labor Confederation
called an eight-hour nationwide strike to
enable workers to see the president. The
crowd, composed almost exclusively of
conservative Peronists, chanted slogans
against the Montoneros as Mrs. Peron
denounced "those who only know how to
kill, . . . those who obstruct the road to
liberation and national pacification."

Terrorist actions. Among other incidents of terrorism during 1974:

Douglas Roberts, administrative director of Pepsi-Cola S.A., local affiliate of
the U.S. firm PepsiCo, was abducted in
suburban Buenos Aires Jan. 4 but released Feb. 2 on the payment of a ransom
of undisclosed size. Some of the kidnappers were arrested by the police, who
had followed them after they picked up
the ransom.

A bomb explosion Jan. 7 seriously
damaged the Buenos Aires printing works
that produced El Mundo and the
semiofficial Peronist organ Mayoria.

Unknown terrorists attacked a police
station in Rosario Jan. 16, seriously
wounding one officer before setting fire to
the building.

The ERP announced the release of Julio
Baraldo, director of the local affiliate of
Italy's Bereta arms factory, in exchange
for an undetermined quantity of arms, it
was reported Jan. 19.

Nineteen separate bombings of offices and homes of leftists were reported early Jan. 26. Police said bombs exploded in Buenos Aires at seven JP offices, the office of a JP-dominated union, and a cafe frequented by leftists; a woman was seriously injured by the last explosion. Other bombs exploded at the homes of leftist militants in suburban Buenos Aires and Rosario and at offices of the Communist Party and the Young Socialist Movement in Bahia Blanca.

U.S. engineer Charles Hayes was freed Jan. 31 after a month in captivity, when his A. G. McKee construction company reportedly paid a $1 million ransom.

Enrique (Henry) Nyborg Andersen, Danish regional manager of the Bank of London & South America, kidnapped in Buenos Aires Nov. 17, 1973, was released Feb. 19, 1974 after payment of a ransom estimated at $1,145,000.

Mario Reduto, a retired naval petty officer kidnapped Feb. 22, was found dead in a garbage dump in Zarate (Buenos Aires Province) March 14. The ERP admitted "executing" Reduto, whom it had accused of heading a parapolice group that allegedly attacked and tortured leftists.

Members of the ERP Feb. 23 kidnapped Antonio Vallocchia, an executive of Swift & Company in Rosario, whom they held responsible for the "unjustified dismissal of 42 workers demanding decent salaries." Swift said Feb. 26 that it would reinstate the 42 employes and pay them for the days they were out of work, in accordance with ERP demands.

ERP members stole firearms in attacks staged on police stations in Ciudadela (Buenos Aires Province) March 8, Resistencia (Chaco Province) March 15 and Melincue (Santa Fe Province) March 23. The guerrillas killed a police officer in the Resistencia raid and freed two imprisoned comrades in the Melincue attack.

The French-based Peugeot auto firm announced March 18 that its Argentina production manager, Yves Boisset, had been released by kidnappers who had held him since Dec. 28, 1973. French sources in Buenos Aires said the abductors had demanded a $4 million ransom. Jose Chohelo, a Peugeot representative in the capital, was kidnapped June 3 and ransomed for $200,000 June 11.

The personnel manager at the Fiat-Concord automobile plant in Cordoba, Roberto Francisco Klecher, was shot to death on a downtown street April 4. The Peronist Armed Forces later claimed credit.

Antonio Magaldi, secretary general of the regional General Labor Confederation in San Nicolas (Buenos Aires Province), was shot to death April 4. The next day a leftist Peronist organizer, Fernando Quinteros, was dragged from his Buenos Aires home and shot dead by two men claiming to be policemen.

Three young members of the Socialist Workers Party were kidnapped from a meeting in suburban Buenos Aires May 30 and later found shot to death. The unidentified abductors, who were armed with machine guns, also kidnapped, beat and later released three other party members, all women.

More than 20 bombs exploded in Buenos Aires May 29–30, most at automobile dealers, according to the Miami Herald June 1. At least 10 bombings were reported the same days in Cordoba.

A bomb had blown up the Buenos Aires headquarters of the General Labor Confederation May 28. Other explosions had damaged a department store and two branches of the Bank of Commerce in the capital May 25.

Gregorio Manoukian, president of the Tanti supermarkets, was killed in a kidnap attempt in Buenos Aires June 7.

Police authorities in Buenos Aires announced June 11 that Remo Crotta, head of the paper industry union, and Francisco Oscar Martinez, of the Peronist Youth organization in La Plata, had been found dead. Both had been reported kidnapped earlier.

Herbert Pilz, production manager of the Argentine affiliate of Mercedes Benz, was kidnapped in suburban Buenos Aires June 17 and released July 12 for what a Mercedes spokesman called a large ransom.

David Kraiselburd, chairman of the board of the news agency Noticias Argentinas and publisher of the La Plata newspaper El Dia, was shot to death July

17 as police closed in on the house in La Plata where he was held by kidnappers. Police wounded and captured one abductor, identified as Carlos Starita, an alleged member of the left-wing Peronist University Youth. Kraiselburd had been kidnapped June 25, but his captors had not contacted his family nor made a ransom demand.

Jorge H. Ferrari, an official in the Economy Ministry, was assassinated by unidentified persons in the Buenos Aires suburb of San Justo July 20.

More than two dozen persons were killed July 31–Aug. 12 as intra-Peronist violence increased and the ERP stepped up its attacks on military and police installations.

Rodolfo Ortega Pena, the leading left-wing Peronist congressman, was assassinated in Buenos Aires July 31. Martin Salas, a young right-wing Peronist, was shot to death in La Plata Aug. 5, and four leftist Peronists in that city were killed in apparent retaliation Aug. 6–7.

A group calling itself "Montoneros Soldiers of Peron" claimed responsibility for Ortega Pena's murder in a communique to the press Aug. 3. A United Press International report Aug. 3 said the group was an offshoot of the left-wing Peronist Montoneros guerrillas, but the London newsletter Latin America reported Aug. 9 that the group was right-wing Peronist and had no connection with the Montoneros. Another communique to the press Aug. 7 claimed Ortega Pena had been assassinated by a rightist group calling itself "Argentine Anti-Imperialist Action."

Eleven persons were injured Aug. 4 when bombs exploded at the Buenos Aires headquarters of the left-wing Peronist Youth, the Communist Party and the Communist Youth.

Retired Gen. Carlos Prats Gonzalez, the former Chilean Army commander, and his wife were killed early Sept. 30 when a bomb exploded in or under their car as they drove to their Buenos Aires home.

A close friend of Prats, quoted by the Washington Post Oct. 1, said Prats had said recently that he had received information of a plan to kill him. Prats had said the assassination would be made to look like the work of the AAA but would

be staged by Chilean or U.S. rightists.

BOLIVIA

Che Guevara Slain as Guerrilla Campaign Fails

The death of Ché Guevara while leading a guerrilla campaign in Bolivian mountains in 1967 was said to have had a profound effect on revolutionary movements in Latin America and elsewhere. Since he was so prominent a supporter of the theory that guerrillas must first win in the countryside, the defeat of his campaign strengthened the argument of those who urged revolutionaries to become urban guerrillas and to employ such weapons as terrorism in the cities.

Guevara Falls in Clash. The Bolivian army high command confirmed Oct. 10, 1967 that Maj. Ernesto (Ché) Guevara de la Serna, 39, Argentine-born Cuban revolutionary leader who had been leading Bolivian guerrillas, had been fatally wounded Oct. 8 during a clash with army troops near Higueras and died Oct. 9.

Gen. Alfredo Ovando Candia, Bolivian armed forces commander, said that Guevara had admitted his identity before dying from his wounds and that further identification had been provided by fingerprints. (Guevara's fingerprints were on file in Argentina and had been taken when he received a passport in 1952.) Later medical examinations, however, indicated that Guevara could not have survived for 24 hours with his wounds but had apparently been captured alive and, possibly, executed the following day. According to Ovando's report, Guevara told his captors: "I am Ché Guevara, and I have failed."

Guerrillas Were Losing. There was evidence that the Guevara-led guerrillas, after some initial success, were on the brink of defeat even before Guevara's death. Guevara, who had arrived in the rebel area Nov. 7, 1966, reportedly had complained of the indifference of the local peasants to the revolution he was leading. Ill with arthritis and chronic asthma and often in pain, Guevara was reported to have been making plans to try to escape from Bolivia but was blocked by the stepped-up army counter-insurgency campaign in which he was finally killed.

A 16-man U.S. Special Forces (Green Berets) training team from the Panama Canal had come to Bolivia to train the Bolivian 2d Ranger Battalion in counter-insurgency techniques, and 600–1,000 Bolivian troops had been operating in the southeast area against an estimated 60–100 guerrillas.

The Bolivian army scored its first major battle success against the guerrilla forces Aug. 31 when a patrol ambushed and wiped out a 9-man guerrilla group. The action took place near Masiguri Bajo in the southeast. The dead included 2–3 Cubans including the band's leader, known as Joaquín. Also killed was a Bolivian girl, Laura Gutierrez, known as Tania. The earlier reports indicated that a prisoner, José Carillo, taken during the action, had disclosed that Guevara had been instructing the rebels.

It was reported in mid-August that Bolivian army units had found 4 jungle caches of guerrilla arms in the Nancahuazá River area. This loss of arms was said to have seriously crippled the guerrilla campaign.

The Bolivian government announced Sept. 18 that it had arrested 15 people accused of aiding the guerrillas. The 15 included university teachers in La Paz and Loyola Guzmán Lara, 25, a philosophy student at La Paz' San Andrés University. Miss Guzmán, who called herself a Moscow-leaning Communist, was accused of being a key figure in supplying matériel and moral aid to the rebels.

Bolivian Pres. René Barrientos Ortuño said at a press conference Sept. 22 that Guevara had entered Bolivia to "establish the guerrilla center of South America" and "to create a focus that was later to be extended." Speaking at a news conference in La Paz, Barrientos insisted that the guerrilla movement was an "adventure financed, inspired and led from the outside."

Gen. Alfredo Ovando Candia, the armed forces commander, said at the Sept. 22 news conference that the guerrillas had been scattered in recent weeks because of heavy pressure from Bolivian army patrols. He said that since the previous enemy contact Sept. 2, the patrols had been pursuing several guerrilla units, each having no more than 4 persons, and that Guevara was in charge of the principal group.

Ovando said that Guevara and 7 Cubans with him had been "virtually Fidel Castro's general staff" during the early days of the Cuban revolution. He said Guevara, Cmndr. Juan V. Acuna and Capt. Eliseo Reyes Rodríguez of the Cuban army and the other Cubans had entered Bolivia in November–December 1966. Ovando reported that the Bolivian army as of then had suffered 35 killed and 13 wounded during the 5-month-old guerrilla campaign. He said that 19 rebel bodies (13 Bolivian, 5 Cuban and 1 Argentine) had been recovered and that about 20 other guerrillas had been killed by then. (The army announced Sept. 27 that 3 more rebels, including Roberto [Coco] Peredo, had been killed Sept. 26.)

Following Guevara's death, Bolivian military sources said Oct. 16 that the number of Bolivian guerrillas had been reduced to 6 following a battle with army units Oct. 14 in which 4 rebels (2 Bolivians, 1 Cuban and 1 Peruvian) were killed. The 6 were said to consist of 3 Cubans and 3 Bolivians and to be led by Guido (Inti) Peredo.

Debray Trial. A military trial of Jules Régis Debray, 27, French Marxist writer who had been captured Apr. 20 after spending 1½ months with the Bolivian guerrillas, began in secret Aug. 18 in the southern town of Camiri. The trial was opened to the press Sept. 26 but then adjourned indefinitely Sept. 27 to await a decision as to whether the 5-officer military tribunal was competent to try Debray and 6 co-defendants. Debray was charged with entering Bolivia to assist the guerrillas and with "rebellion, murder, robbery, assault and other crimes" during his stay in Bolivia.

The trial was resumed Oct. 10 after the tribunal was declared competent. But Debray, in tears, abandoned his defense Oct. 11 after hearing of Guevara's death. He announced to the tribunal Oct. 12 that he wished to be regarded as equally responsible—"politically and morally"—as Guevara for guerrilla acts in Bolivia although he had done no fighting.

Debray had told newsmen July 20 that Guevara had come to Bolivia to organize the guerrillas but had since left. Debray said Guevara's mission was "to say no to the oppression and humiliation which confront the people because of the power of the United States." Debray, who had supported Fidel Castro and had taught at the University of Havana, insisted that he had entered Bolivia only to get material for a journalistic account of the guerrilla movement.

Debray told a group of foreign correspondents Aug. 20 that 90% of the guerrillas he had seen in Bolivia were Bolivians and that during his interrogation he had been questioned by U.S. Central Intelligence Agency (CIA) officers.

Debray was given a 30-year sentence Nov. 17 on his conviction of having been an active member in the guerrilla band. (He was freed under an amnesty decree Dec. 23, 1970.)

Guevara's Diary. Guevara's Bolivian war diary was published in 1968. A photographic reproduction of the diary, captured by the Bolivian army Oct. 9, 1967, had been sent secretly to Havana by Bolivian Interior Min. Antonio Argüedas. The text of the diary was published July 1 in Cuba and the following day in the U.S. by *Ramparts* magazine, which had acquired the publishing rights from the Castro government.

The diary had been kept by Guevara from his arrival in Bolivia Nov. 7, 1966 until Oct. 7, 1967. Initially optimistic, the diary reflected Guevara's growing disillusion with the political apathy, and even hostility, of the Bolivian peasants and the alleged hindrance of the Moscow-leaning Bolivian Communist Party. Guevara's secret papers also revealed that he had kept in radio contact with Cuban Premier Fidel Castro.

The Complete Bolivian Diaries of Che Guevara and Other Captured Documents,

a book published in New York Aug. 6 by Stein & Day, Inc., revealed that 13 guerrillas killed in Bolivia while members of Guevara's band were Cuban army officers and that 4 were members of the Cuban Communist Party's Central Committee. The 4 committee members were identified as (aliases in parentheses): Maj. Juan Vitalio Acuña (Joaquín), Maj. Antonio Sánchez Díaz (Marcos), Maj. Alberto Fernández Montes de Oca (Pachungo) and Capt. Eliseo Reyes Rodríguez (Rolando).

CIA's Aid Confirmed. President Barrientos April 1, 1969 confirmed reports that U.S. Central Intelligence Agency personnel had been sent to Bolivia in the guise of army officers to train units fighting guerrillas led by Che Guevara.

Barrientos asserted, however, that "All these things which are now becoming known are a surprise to me." He added, "I never met these gentlemen as members of the CIA but as officers present to train our troops. I never gave any documents to CIA agents."

Barrientos' comments came in response to disclosures contained in a series of articles in Presencia, the La Paz Christian Democratic newspaper. A London Times account April 3 said that the articles were based partly on information from Gen. Joaquin Zenteno Anaya, former commander of the army division that captured Guevara. Zenteno, who had become Ambassador to Lima, reported that the CIA agents included two former Cuban army captains, Felix Ramos and Edguardo Gonzalez, both of whom possessed credentials from Barrientos on the basis of an agreement reached "at high level." Zenteno's information was given in testimony to a military tribunal investigating the case of Antonio Arguedas, who had admitted being a CIA agent while serving as interior minister and who had sent Guevara's diaries to Cuba.

(True magazine March 9 had published an article by Andrew St. George charging that Guevara's capture was the result of a top-secret plan formulated by White House advisers and approved by President Lyndon B. Johnson.

Guevara Associates Identified. In the first official identification of Cuban army regulars who fought in Bolivia with Che Guevara, Havana Oct. 8, 1969 identified the 13 Cubans—12 army officers and one civilian—who had been killed in Bolivia fighting with Guevara.

The announcement from Havana listed three majors (the highest officer rank in the Cuban armed forces), three captains and six lieutenants. Majors Antonio Sanchez Diaz Pinares and Juan Vitalio Acuna Nunez and Capt. Eliseo Reyes San Luis, three of the 13 named, had been Central Committee members of the Cuban Communist Party.

Struggle Continues

Guerrilla Leader Slain. Interior Minister Eufronia Padilla announced Sept. 10, 1969 that Guido (Inti) Paredo, who reportedly had assumed the leadership of the Bolivian guerrilla movement following Guevara's death, had been killed in a police raid Sept. 9. Padilla said that Peredo was fatally injured when a grenade exploded in his hand.

Peredo had proclaimed the resumption of guerrilla warfare throughout Latin America Sept. 4. In a statement broadcast by six Bolivian radio stations and published in newspapers, Peredo vowed that the "guerrillas are going to resume the movement. The war will be long and cruel and more violent than in 1967." He added that the battle would not be finished until "Bolivia and the continent are free from oppression." In the wake of Peredo's manifesto and an upsurge of terrorist bombings in La Paz and other major cities, the Bolivian government had mobilized troops Sept. 6.

Le Monde of Paris reported Sept. 17 that the ELN (Ejercito de Liberation Nacional, or National Liberation Army) had vowed to continue the fight despite Peredo's death. Padilla said that the group was now led by a former Guevara lieutenant from Cuba, Harry Villegas Tamayo, also known as Pombo.

The army Oct. 21, 1970 announced the capture of Inti's younger brother, Osvaldo (Chato) Peredo. Chato and seven other guerrillas captured in Bolivia arrived in Chile Nov. 11.

Chato Peredo said: "The guerrilla has not died in Latin America; on the contrary, the movement continues growing. Conditions are propitious to push the fight on all fronts."

(The Bolivian government exiled five prisoners to Chile Feb. 13, 1971. The five, said to have led guerrilla activities in and around Santa Cruz, included Oscar Zamora Medinacelli, head of the Peking branch of the Bolivian Communist party.)

Hostages Used to Free Prisoners. The ELN successfully used hostages in July 1970 to win the release of imprisoned guerrillas.

ELN guerrillas had invaded the town of Teoponte, 95 miles north of La Paz, July 19. Occupying the town for several hours, they burned the offices of the U.S.-owned gold mining firm South American Placers, Inc., stole $5,000 and fled into the jungle with two West German technicians as hostages.

In a letter delivered to a radio station July 21, the ELN warned that the two technicians—Gunter Lerch and Eugene Schulhauser—would be shot unless Bolivian authorities released 10 prisoners within 48 hours. The Bolivian government yielded to the guerrillas' demands July 22 and flew the 10 prisoners to Arica, Chile. The two technicians were set free at Teoponte July 23.

The 10 freed prisoners included persons arrested and jailed for participation in guerrilla warfare with the late Ernesto Guevara. They were Loyola Guzman, the only woman in the group, Enrique Ortega, Gerardo Bermudez, Felix Melgar Antel, Oscar Busch, Victor Cordoba, Roberto Moreira, Rodolfo Saldana, Juan Sanchez and Benigno Coronado. They were reported to have reached Cuba by way of Mexico Aug. 30.

Envoy in West Germany killed. Former Bolivian Consul General to Hamburg Roberto Quintanilla was shot and killed in the Hamburg consulate April 1, 1971.

The ELN issued a communique April 2 claiming responsibility for Quintanilla's death. The ELN charged that

Quintanilla, who had retired as consul general but was remaining in Germany until his replacement arrived, was responsibile for the death of guerrilla leader Inti Peredo in 1969.

Alberto Larrea Humerez, economic minister under former President Rene Barrientos, was assassinated April 19.

Selich escapes assassins. Col. Andres Selich, who became interior minister in the rightist government formed by Col. Hugo Banzer Suarez Aug. 22, 1971, after the forcible overthrow of leftist President Juan Jose Torres, escaped assassination twice within a month. A bomb was thrown Aug. 22 into a room where Selich was holding a meeting, but Selich emerged unhurt. The Interior Ministry then reported Sept. 15 that a woman had delivered a package asking that it be handed to Selich. Aides discovered a bomb inside the package, dismantled it and arrested the woman. In questioning the woman, officials said they had uncovered an ELN conspiracy.

Selich was reported Nov. 2 to have accused Cuban Premier Fidel Castro of intervening in Bolivian affairs.

Selich announced the discovery of a "guerrilla arsenal" and the arrest of a number of persons linked to "extreme leftist organizations."

"We are engaged in a war to the death against Castro-communism," said Selich, "and that war has not yet ended."

Selich also accused the Torres government of having hired "between 250 and 300 foreigners to organize extremist fighting groups."

The Bolivian government restored the death penalty for terrorism, kidnaping, attempts against the lives of "state dignitaries," and the organization of urban or rural guerrillas, it was reported in the London newsletter Latin America Nov. 12. The death penalty had been abolished in 1967.

Bolivian guerrillas believed in Chile. The Bolivian government believed that hundreds of exiled citizens were being trained as guerrilla fighters in Chile, the Miami Herald reported Feb. 17, 1972.

Interior Minister Mario Adett Zamora charged that "Bolivian exiles in Chile are receiving military and subversive instruction with the consent of the [Chilean] government and with the support of Cuba and . . . the countries behind the Iron Curtain." Officials were said to believe the guerrillas would return to Bolivia to commit acts of urban terror and to foment labor uprisings in the nation's economically vital tin-mining regions.

As evidence of subversive preparations, the government cited the presence in Chile of known revolutionaries and enemies of the regime of Hugo Banzer Suarez (including deposed President Gen. Juan Jose Torres) and the formation in Santiago of the Bolivian Anti-imperialist Revolutionary Front.

Guerrillas slain. Interior Minister Mario Adett Zamora announced March 25, 1972 that the police had killed two members of the National Liberation Army (ELN), arrested six other alleged guerrillas and found a large supply of arms and explosives in the central city of Cochabamba.

Adett Zamora said one of the slain guerrillas, Oscar Nunez Reyes, was the ELN regional commander in Cochabamba, which he said was the group's most important area of operations after La Paz. Adett Zamora claimed police had wiped out 90% of the extremists in Cochabamba and 80% of those in La Paz.

ELN's leaders. Interior Minister Adett Zamora April 8, 1972 revealed the names of the three men who, along with Osvaldo (Chato) Peredo, allegedly commanded the ELN.

They were: Lisimaco "Guillermo" Gutierrez, a former university professor; Pedro "Adrian" Morant Saravia, a university student; and Gerardo "Miseria" Bermudez Rodriguez, a Marxist theorist.

Adett Zamora claimed that 120 "extremists" had been arrested in recent days, foiling plans for an urban guerrilla uprising, the Times of the Americas reported April 12.

The French newspaper Le Monde reported June 25 that Gutierrez and two other guerrillas had been shot to death a few weeks earlier while "attempting to escape."

The ELN had virtually been eliminated as an effective threat to the government, according to the London newsletter Latin America June 9. Recent arrests and killings of suspected guerrillas and the tone of current government propaganda suggested the group was infiltrated and informed upon at all levels, the newsletter said.

Soviet diplomats ousted. Bolivia announced April 19, 1972 that 62 Soviet diplomats and dependents had left the country on orders of Bolivian President Banzer after Bolivia accused the embassy of promoting Castroite subversion.

The government claimed April 13 that captured ELN documents showed embassy First Secretary Igor Sholokov and Third Secretary Aleksei Smirnov were in contact with the guerrilla movement.

'Death Squad' appears. A communique issued in Santa Cruz March 23 announced that a Brazilian-style political "death squad" had been formed to eliminate subversives, and that "for every nationalist killed, 20 traitors will die."

Adett Zamora declared the death squad "outside the law" April 20 after it claimed its fifth victim.

2 women quit ELN. The Interior Ministry July 14, 1973 released letters in which two women announced that they were breaking with the ELN. The women—Loyola Guzman, reputedly the guerrilla group's top female leader, and Sonia Montano Virreira—had both been arrested April 4 in a gun battle in which Guzman's husband was killed.

In her letter, Guzman admitted that recent government operations had hurt the ELN badly, virtually eliminating the leaders with whom she had fought.

Priests & nuns accused. Interior Minister Mario Adett Zamora charged May 16, 1972 that certain priests were aiding subversive organizations.

Adett Zamora's claim followed a gun battle May 16 between security forces and alleged ELN members at a con-vent about 45 miles from La Paz. One policeman and one guerrilla were reported killed.

Archbishop Clemente Maurer, head of the Bolivian church, had accused the government May 1 of confusing any call for social justice with leftist extremism. Maurer attributed the deterioration of church-state relations to the government and police.

Msgr. Luis Rodriguez, bishop of the eastern city of Santa Cruz, had warned April 26 that attempts were being made to divide and discredit the church. Rodriguez, who had protested the recent arrest in Santa Cruz of a Belgian priest, had been severely criticized by the prefect of the city, who warned that any priest suspected of aiding revolutionaries would be "treated as he deserves."

Three Colombian nuns were arrested May 16 on charges of cooperating with the ELN. The arrests followed a shootout between security forces and suspected guerrillas at a convent in the highland town of Achacachi. The nuns were later deported.

Mary Elizabeth Harding, a U.S. citizen and former nun arrested Dec. 5, 1972 for alleged guerrilla activities, was released from jail Jan. 13, 1973 and deported Jan. 15. Adett Zamora said that Ms. Harding had confessed belonging to the ELN and had supplied the government with information which "proved valuable for learning the plans of the extreme left and the guerrillas with respect to Bolivia."

Guerrilla 'plot' reported. Interior Minister Mario Adett Zamora claimed Dec. 20, 1972 that exiled Bolivian guerrillas had plotted to assassinate President Hugo Banzer Suarez and "Vietnamize" Bolivia. He said more than 30 persons had been arrested in connection with the plot, which allegedly had Cuban financial backing and support from guerrilla movements in Chile, Argentina and Uruguay.

According to Adett, exiles under the leadership of Ruben Sanchez, a former army major living in Chile, had planned to invade Bolivia from Chile, Argentina and Brazil to sabotage mining centers and organize peasants against the government. The plan was supported by a number of exiled Bolivian politicians, including ex-President Hernan Siles, Adett charged.

The plotters allegedly also had planned to assassinate Banzer during his visit to a town near Cochabamba Dec. 20. Adett said four would-be assassins, all members of the left-wing National Liberation Army (ELN), had been arrested in Cochabamba Dec. 20 after killing a soldier.

New leftist plot alleged. The government claimed Jan. 11, 1973 to have discovered a new subversive plot and arrested its principal leaders. The alleged conspiracy, the latest of a series reported by the regime since it seized power in August 1971, was supposedly directed by two leftist groups—the ELN and the Revotionary Left Movement—and aimed at infiltrating the armed forces.

According to Interior Minister Mario Adett Zamora, the plot was discovered in documents found in raids on "guerrilla hideouts" in La Paz. The documents allegedly revealed that a leftist agent named "Vicente" was "operating in military circles" in an attempt to "break the ironlike unity of the armed forces." Adett said "Vicente" still had not been identified, but "the principal ringleaders of the conspiracy are under arrest."

Adett's announcement followed a series of arrests in La Paz and Cochabamba. About 60 persons reportedly were arrested in Cochabamba Jan. 10, including a number of teachers accused of belonging to the Communist party and of having met secretly to "prepare actions to disrupt the public peace and . . . the security of the government."

In a related development, the chief of staff of the second army based at Oruro, Col. Humberto Cayoja Riart, was relieved of his command and appointed military attache in Washington only hours after flatly denying there were any guerrillas in his area, the London newsletter Latin America reported Jan. 19. His denial conflicted with repeated statements by Adett about guerrilla activity between Oruro and La Paz.

New plots alleged; Selich killed. The government claimed to have broken up two subversive plots in April and May 1973. An alleged leader of the second conspiracy, ex-Col. Andres Selich, was beaten to death by security officials.

Selich was reported arrested May 14 along with seven army colonels said to have conspired against President Hugo Banzer Suarez. Other military officers and prominent politicians also were reported detained.

The government said May 16 that four of Selich's co-conspirators had escaped from custody earlier in the day in the southern town of Tarija, near the Argentine border. Officials said the plotters, members of "the extreme right," had sought to seize power May 25, while Banzer was in Argentina for its presidential inauguration. They also allegedly planned to "execute a series of violent acts to drench the country in blood."

Selich, a leader of the 1971 military coup that brought Banzer to power, had lived in Argentina since May 1972, when he was dismissed as Bolivia's ambassador to Paraguay and accused of plotting against the president.

Selich's death coincided with the killing in La Paz of two ELN members. Authorities said Oswaldo Ucasqui, an Argentine citizen, and Monica Ertl, the alleged killer of a Bolivian consul in West Germany in 1971, were killed in a shootout with police May 13.

Valverde plot. The government said Aug. 18, 1973 that it had crushed a planned uprising by right-wing Bolivian Socialist Falange (FSB) dissidents led by ex-Health Minister Carlos Valverde.

Interior Minister Walter Castro said the revolt was planned to take place during a visit by President Hugo Banzer Suarez to Santa Cruz. He linked the plot to Bolivian exiles in Chile and Peru.

Valverde, a guerrilla leader during the last MNR government, was reported Aug. 18 to have dug in at a farm outside Santa Cruz with some 190 armed followers. Troops were sent from La Paz to the area, and the subversives reportedly fled the next day. Valverde was reported in Paraguay Aug. 21.

'Leftist plot' crushed. The government announced Sept. 23, 1973 that it had crushed an alleged left-wing plot against President Banzer and that 89 political and labor union leaders had been arrested in La Paz, Cochabamba, Santa Cruz and Oruro.

Interior Minister Walter Castro said the alleged conspiracy, by exiled Bolivians and radicals from Cuba, Chile, Argentina and other countries, was "a desperate action by the extreme left to try and regain ground on the continent" following the overthrow of the late Chilean President Salvador Allende Gossens.

Castro claimed the conspirators included ex-Presidents Hernan Siles Zuazo—to have been installed as president after Banzer's ouster—and Juan Jose Torres, as well as labor leader Juan Lechin Oquendo and ex-guerrilla leader Oswaldo "Chato" Peredo, all currently in exile.

Officials said Salustio Choque, a conspirator and former member of the Bolivian guerrilla group led by the late Ernesto "Che" Guevara, had been arrested Sept. 22, and arms were found in his house.

Castro held a second press conference Sept. 26 to give more details of the alleged plot. He said the government had obtained from a Communist party member, at a "high" cost, a 13-page "operating plan" that included projected subversion in La Paz and other cities, simultaneous invasions from Chile and Argentina, and flying in of arms to Santa Cruz and Beni departments in planes with Cuban registrations.

Castro asserted the plotters, including members of Argentina's outlawed People's Revolutionary Army, had founded the Nationalist Left Liberation Alliance, with headquarters in Santiago and in Salta, Argentina. He said they planned to make Siles interim president of Bolivia and then to remove him and institute socialism in the country.

Another 'plot.' Interior Minister Juan Pareda Asbun said July 4, 1974 that a guerrilla group calling itself the Black Condor was preparing to attack the Banzer regime under the leadership of ex-Presidents Alfredo Ovando and Juan Jose Torres and of French radical journalist Regis Debray.

Pereda said Torres had given Ovando money he allegedly received from the People's Revolutionary Army, an Argentine Marxist guerrilla group, which recently had collected millions of dollars in ransom money for foreign businessmen it had kidnapped.

Ovando, who lived in Spain, denied Pereda's charges "categorically" July 5.

BRAZIL

Assassinations & Kidnappings

The major short-term objective of terrorists in Brazil during the late 1960s and early 1970s appears to be the overthrow of the country's military government, long accused of oppression, the torture of political prisoners and other excesses. Assassinations and kidnappings have been the most widely publicized actions of the terrorists, who also claim credit for numerous robberies, raids on military and police installations, bombings and acts of sabotage.

The best-known of the terrorist groups is the ALN (Acão Libertadora Nacional, National Liberation Action or National Liberation Alliance), founded in 1967 by the late urban guerrilla leader and theorist Carlos Marighella. Other terrorist/urban guerrilla groups include MR-8 (Movimiento Revolucionario-8, Revolutionary Movement-8 or Revolutionary Movement of October)*, Molipo (Movimiento Libertador Popular, or People's Liberation Movement) and the VPR (Vanguardia Popular Revolucionaria, or Popular Revolutionary Vanguard).

Assassinations. U.S. Army Capt. Charles Rodney Chandler, 30, was killed Oct. 12, 1968 by two gunmen as he was leaving his São Paulo home. The assassins, who had used machineguns, sped away in a car after leaving pamphlets describing Chandler as a "Vietnam war criminal" who had come "to Brazil to train war criminals and show them the most ad-

---

*Signifying Oct. 8, 1967, the date on which Ernesto (Che) Guevara was killed in Bolivia.

vanced techniques of torture and cruelty." The leaflets termed the killing "a warning to all his followers who one day or another will answer for their actions to the revolutionary tribunal." Chandler, who had served a year in Vietnam, had been in Brazil "strictly on civilian status," the U.S. consul said, to study Portuguese language and Brazilian history at the University of São Paulo.

Brazilian police Oct. 14 arrested José Luis Andrade Maciel, a São Paulo dentist, on charges of masterminding Chandler's killing.

The Rev. Henrique Pereira Neto, 28, aide to left-wing Archbishop Helder Camara, was found murdered May 28, 1969 in a remote area of the Recife University campus. A professor of sociology at the university, Pereira Neto had carried out liaison between Archbishop Helder and student organizations. Archbishop Helder charged May 28 that Pereira Neto had been lynched by right-wingers who planned to murder other priests and student leaders as well.

Valter Lino de Matos, brother of the leader of the opposition Brazilian Democratic Movement in the state of Sao Paulo, was murdered May 28.

Sao Paulo Attacks. Terrorists destroyed installations at three radio and television stations in Sao Paulo July 13–16, 1969. Officials asserted that the attacks, part of a wave of recent terrorist activities, were the work of leftist terrorists led by Carlos Marighella, head of the ALN, and Carlos Lamarca, head of MR-8, a former army captain specializing in anti-terrorist measures. When Lamarca deserted to the guerrillas, he brought them 70 light machine guns.

Increase in Terrorism. Government sources reported a significant increase in terrorist activities during 1968–69, particularly in Sao Paulo and Rio de Janeiro. In more than 60 holdups since January 1969, hundreds of thousands of dollars had been stolen. In addition, the number of bombing attacks, attacks on arms supplies depots and attacks on radio and TV stations had also increased.

American Ambassador Kidnapped. U.S. Ambassador to Brazil C. Burke Elbrick was kidnapped by Brazilian terrorists in Rio de Janeiro Sept. 4, 1969 but released Sept. 7 after the Brazilian government yielded to his captors' demands by publishing a revolutionary manifesto and releasing 15 political prisoners.

Elbrick had been returning to the U.S. Embassy in his limousine following lunch at his residence when he was taken captive Sept. 4 by four armed men. He had been accompanied only by his Brazilian chauffeur, an embassy employe for four years, who was left behind.

In a manifesto left in Elbrick's limousine, the kidnappers gave two conditions for his release: publication and broadcast of their manifesto throughout Brazil, and the release of 15 political prisoners and their transfer to asylum in another country. Asserting that "the life and death of the ambassador are in the hands of the dictatorship," the kidnappers warned that if the demands were not met within 48 hours they would "be forced to carry out revolutionary justice" and "execute Ambassador Elbrick."

The manifesto stressed that Elbrick's kidnapping was "not an isolated act. It is another one of the innumerable revolutionary acts already carried out: bank holdups, where funds for the revolution are collected, returning what the bankers take from the people and their employes; raids on barracks and police stations, where arms and ammunitions are obtained for the struggle to topple the dictatorship; invasions of jails when revolutionaries are freed to return them to the people's struggle; the explosion of buildings that signify oppression; the execution of hangmen and torturers."

The note continued: "With the kidnap of the ambassador we want to demonstrate that it is possible to defeat the dictatorship and the exploitation if we arm and organize ourselves. We show up where the enemy least expects us, and we disappear immediately, tearing out the dictatorship, bringing terror and fear to the exploiters, the hope and certainty of victory to the midst of the exploited. Mr. Elbrick represents in our country the interests of imperialism, which, allied to the great bosses, the big ranches and the big national bankers, maintain the regime of oppression and exploitation."

The note was signed by the National Revolutionary Movement of October (MR-8), two of the 10 or more guerrilla and terrorist groups said by government authorities to be operating in Brazil. (Brazilian government spokesmen had announced July 27 that it had dismantled the MR-8 with the arrest of 29 of its key members. Seven more MR-8 members were reported arrested Aug. 7, and the arrests of several dozen more terrorists were announced Aug. 10.)

Following an emergency meeting of key military and cabinet officials Sept. 4, the government announced Sept. 5 that it would meet the kidnappers' demands. Foreign Minister Jose de Migalhaes Pinto confirmed Sept. 5 the government's decision to "order the transfer overseas of the 15 prisoners whose names are to be furnished to it." Two hours later, the kidnapers placed the 15 names in a suggestion box at a suburban supermarket. Their message said Elbrick would be released when the prisoners were safely in Mexico. Mexico announced the same day that it would grant asylum to the 15 prisoners. (Chile also offered asylum Sept. 5.)

A Brazilian air force transport plane with the prisoners aboard left Rio Sept. 6, after a delay of several hours beyond the deadline set by the kidnappers. The government attributed the delay to a difficulty in rounding up the prisoners. Reports indicated, however, that radical military officers had objected to the government's decision to meet the kidnap demands and had made efforts to hold up the prisoners' release. In addition, a group of about 200 navy men was reported to have surrounded the airport in an attempt to block the plane's takeoff at the last minute. A captain in the navy group called the prisoners' release a "national disgrace" but said that the men let the plane depart when they "received orders from above...."

Following the arrival of the plane in Mexico City Sept. 7, Elbrick was released in Rio.

At a news conference Sept. 8, Elbrick said that his captors were "all young, very determined, intelligent fanatics" who be-lieved that violence was the only workable political alternative in Brazil. "They seemed to ascribe all the troubles and difficulties they saw in Brazil to what they called North American imperialism," he said.

Prisoners Granted Asylum. Arriving in Mexico City Sept. 7, the 15 political prisoners were immediately granted asylum by the Mexican government.

In a statement Sept. 8, the group called the kidnapping a "natural act of resistance" to the "imprisonments, tortures and violences" committed by the Brazilian government. They charged that the Brazilian military had created a "climate of tension and anxiety, insecurity and violence, extending to all levels of society" and that Brazil's 90 million people consequently lived in a "police state."

The 15 freed prisoners were:

Gregorio Bezerra, 70, a leading member of the clandestine Communist Party, who had been in prison since 1964, when he had been arrested in Recife and dragged by army troops through the streets. Wladimir Palmeira, 24, former president of the Metropolitan Student Union in Rio, arrested in 1968 and sentenced in August to three years imprisonment for leading student demonstrations against the government; Flavio Tavares, a newspaperman charged in 1966 with organizing guerrilla activities and recently arrested on charges of membership in a terrorist group called the Revolutionary Movement of July 26 (the anniversary of the Cuban revolution); Ricardo Zarattini, former National Student Union officer, jailed for subversive activities among peasants; Luiz Travassos, former National Student Union president who was also active in the radical movement of the Roman Catholic Church; Jose Dirceu de Oliveira e Silva, also a former president of the National Student Union; Ricardo Villas Boas de Sarego and Maria Augusta Carneiro, both student leaders arrested May 1 for allegedly firing at a policeman who was attempting to prevent them from distributing anti-government literature; Onofre Pinto, a former air force sergeant, arrested and charged with murder in the killing of U.S. Army Capt. Charles R. Chandler; Ivens Marchetti, a Sao Paulo architect, also charged in connection with Chandler's murder; Jose Ibrahim and Rolando Prattes, labor leaders in the Sao Paulo area; Argonauto Pacheco da Silva, labor leader and former Sao Paulo legislator; Joao Leonardo da Silva Rocha, a Sao Paulo lawyer; Mario Galgardo Zanconato, 22, former medical student, who said in Mexico City Sept 8 that he had organized eight bank robberies in Minas Gerais to raise funds for the revolutionary movement.

Thirteen of the freed prisoners flew to Cuba Sept. 30.

Government Restrictions. The military government announced Sept. 8 that it was preparing restrictive measures to stem the tide of urban guerrilla activities. "The nation is now aware that the process of revolutionary and subversive war is now in full evolution," the government statement asserted. "At all costs, order and tranquility will be preserved."

The restrictive measures were not immediately made public. The government announced Sept. 9, however, that it had reinstituted the death penalty for acts of subversion and terrorism. (Capital punishment had been abolished in Brazil, except during periods of foreign wars, since 1891, according to Brazilian lawyers.) The decree, which amended the constitution to permit capital punishment, was issued as Institutional Act No. 14 and was dated Sept. 5; it was signed by the ruling military triumvirate and Justice Minister Luis Antonio Gama e Silva.

Institutional Act No. 13, issued Sept. 5, had authorized the banishment of any Brazilians considered "manifestly harmful and dangerous to national security," while a complementary act that day had banished the 15 prisoners.

Marighella Killed. Brazilian police ambushed urban guerrilla leader Carlos Marighella in Sao Paulo Nov. 4, 1969 and shot him to death.

In announcing Marighella's death, police charged the Catholic Church's Dominican order with involvement in his terrorist activities and announced that several Dominican priests had led security forces to the spot where Marighella was killed.

Archbishop Felicio Cesar da Cunha Vasconcelos of Ribeirao Preto in Sao Paulo State excommunicated the city's police chief and his assistant for being "directly responsible for the violence committed against members of the clergy and religious of the archdiocese," Le Monde reported Nov. 16. The archbishop specifically cited the arrest and alleged torture of Sister Maurina Borges da Silveira, the mother superior of a convent in Ribeirao Preto. (Ribeirao Preto authorities had previously announced the arrests of 40 persons in the dissolution of 22 "terrorist cells," the Miami Herald reported Nov. 16.)

Archbishop Vicente Scherer of Rio Grande do Sul said Nov. 17 that the government had not proved anything against the priests but added that "whoever participates in a common program with terrorists who kill innocent people in cold blood, assault and rob, becomes an accomplice to such crimes and participates in their responsibility."

Bishops denounce terrorism. Brazilian bishops, gathered in Brasilia for their 11th general assembly, adopted a resolution May 27, 1970 denouncing torture and terrorism. Adopted by a vote of 159–21, the statement was a compromise between liberal and conservative bishops.

'Anti-terrorist' activities. The London Times said Feb. 4, 1970 that an Operational Center for Internal Defense had been established in Rio de Janeiro to coordinate the government's fight against "Communist subversion." The center, headed by First Army Commander Gen. Syseno Sarmento, incorporated the security and intelligence activities of the three armed services and the political police.

The Second Army headquarters in Sao Paulo announced Jan. 28 that a special military police unit had ended a five-month anti-terrorist campaign with arrest of 320 persons, the discovery of 66 terrorist cells and the confiscation of a large quantity of weapons. Officials claimed that the National Liberation Alliance and the Palmares Armed Revolutionary Vanguard had been almost completely dismantled in the campaign.

Japanese consul abducted. Nobuo Okuchi, 56, Japanese consul general in Sao Paulo, was kidnapped March 11, 1970 and held for four days until the government met the abductors' demand for the freeing of five prisoners.

The kidnappers, who identified themselves as members of the Popular Revolutionary Vanguard, announced March 12 that Okuchi would be freed following the release and transportation out of Brazil of five political prisoners held in Sao Paulo. The abductors also demanded that the government pledge to take no retaliation against remaining political prisoners after Okuchi's release and that the government call off a massive search for the kidnappers and Okuchi.

The Brazilian government March 12 called off the massive search it had undertaken to find the kidnappers and announced that it would release and grant asylum to five political prisoners in exchange for Okuchi's freedom.

The prisoners, whose names were sent to the government March 13, arrived in Mexico City March 15. They were: Sister Maurina Borges da Silveira, mother superior of a convent in Ribeirao Preto who had been charged with aiding terrorists; Mrs. Damaris Oliveira Lucena, wife of a guerrilla leader who was reportedly killed Feb. 20 by Sao Paulo police; Shizuo Ozawa, a member of the Popular Revolutionary Vanguard who had been arrested Feb. 26 for bank robbery; Otavio Angelo, a mechanic arrested Dec. 20, 1969 in what the government called a raid on a terrorist arms factory; and "Diogenes" Jose Carvalho de Oliveira, about whom the government gave no details, although a man of the same name had been arrested in 1969 on charges of murdering U.S. Army Capt. Charles R. Chandler. (Four of the freed prisoners flew to Cuba March 27. Only Sister da Silveira decided to remain in Mexico.)

Okuchi was released unharmed March 15, about 10 hours after the five prisoners had arrived in Mexico.

U.S. consul in Brazil foils attempt. Curtis C. Cutter, 41, U.S. consul in Porto Alegre, foiled a kidnapping attempt in that city April 5, 1970. Cutter, his wife and a friend were driving home after a late dinner when four or five armed men blocked his car in an apparent attempt to kidnap him. However, Cutter stepped on the accelerator and sped off, hitting at least one of the would-be abductors. Cutter was shot in the back when the men opened fire, but his injuries were not serious. The terrorists reportedly fled with their wounded comrade.

German envoy kidnapped. West German Ambassador to Brazil Ehrenfried von Holleben, 61, was kidnapped by terrorists June 11, 1970. He was freed June 16.

Von Holleben was abducted from his car in Rio de Janeiro June 11 by terrorists who killed a Brazilian security agent protecting the ambassador and wounded two others during the incident. The kidnappers left a note demanding a halt to the torture of political prisoners. "We regret we have once more to resort to methods which we have always tried to avoid," the note said. "However, as long as patriots are being tortured and killed in the prisons we will not have any other choice, even knowing that the physical integrity and the lives of people not directly involved in the revolutionary struggle are at risk." The kidnappers, identifying themselves as members of the Popular Revolutionary Vanguard and the National Liberation Alliance, also warned that "all search for and attempted imprisonment of revolutionary combatants should cease immediately."

In a June 12 letter, the kidnappers demanded release of 40 political prisoners in exchange for the release of von Holleben.

The Brazilian government announced June 13 that it would release the 40 political prisoners and publish a revolutionary manifesto, meeting the ransom demands set by the kidnappers for the release of von Holleben. The kidnappers' manifesto, made public by the presidential palace and published in daily newspapers June 13, called for a "fight to the death" to overthrow the Brazilian government. "Only revolutionary war, guerrilla actions and rural guerrilla warfare will lead the Brazilian people to free themselves," the declaration read. The goals stated by the kidnappers included expropriation of all foreign firms and large landholdings in the country, an independent and anti-imperialist foreign policy and guarantee of human rights and civil liberties.

The 40 prisoners were gathered from various prisons June 14 and flown to Algeria June 15. The prisoners—34 men, six women and four children—included four accused in the kidnapping of Ambassador C. Burke Elbrick. They were listed as Fernando Paulo Nagle Gabeira, a former newsman who had pleaded guilty to the charge; Cid de Queiroz Benjamin, a student; Daniel de Arao Reis Filho, a student leader; and Vera Silvia de Araujo Magalhaes, a student. A spokesman for the prisoners, former army officer Apolonio de Carvalho, said in Algeria that the kidnappings would continue since it was "the only way to get political prisoners freed."

Swiss envoy kidnapped. Swiss Ambassador Giovanni Enrico Bucher was kidnapped in Rio de Janeiro Dec. 7, 1970 but freed Jan. 16, 1971 in exchange for the government's release Jan. 14 of 70 political prisoners, who were flown to Chile.

(Bucher's bodyguard, Helio Carvalho de Araujo, who had been shot during the kidnaping Dec. 7, died Dec. 10.)

Among the prisoners released was the Rev. Tito de Alencar Lima, a Dominican priest who reported that he was arrested and tortured for a period of 15 months.

Ransomed rebels return. Military sources said that at least half of the prisoners released by Brazil in exchange for the freedom of kidnapped diplomats, had returned secretly to the country to carry out anti-government activities, it was reported Feb. 9, 1971. One ex-prisoner, Aderval Alves Coqueiro, released in July 1970 with 39 others in exchange West German Ambassador Ehrenfried von Holleben, was killed by police Feb. 6 when he reportedly resisted arrest. ALN member Carlos Eduardo Fleury, freed with Coqueiro, was reported Dec. 10 to have been killed by police in Rio de Janeiro.

Lamarca killed by police. One of the major leaders of the Brazilian revolutionary movement, Capt. Carlos Lamarca, 33, leader of the Popular Revolutionary Vanguard, a group composed of three far-left revolutionary factions, was killed Sept. 17, 1971 in a shoot-out with police in Bahia.

Police kill terrorists. Police Oct. 24, 1970 revealed the arrest and death of Joaquim Camara Ferreira, head of the clandestine terrorist National Liberation Alliance (ALN). Ferreira was said to have died of a heart attack suffered when he fell into police hands Oct. 23. Ferreira had taken command of the ALN after Carlos Marighella died.

Following Ferreira's capture, police announced that they had discovered a master plan for future terrorist activities.

Juarez Guimares de Brito, head of the Popular Revolutionary Vanguard in Rio and assistant to Carlos Lamarca, had committed suicide May 3 as he was on the point of being captured by police. Yoshitama Fujimori, a chief lieutenant of Lamarca, was shot and killed by police Dec. 5.

Jose Raimundo da Costa, suspected of being a national leader of the Popular Revolutionary Vanguard, was reported by the police Aug. 8, 1971 to have been shot and killed while resisting arrest.

Security officials announced Jan. 13, 1972 that guerrilla leader Jeova de Assis Gomes had been killed by police in the interior state of Goias when he resisted arrest and tried to set off a hand grenade.

Vanguard reported smashed. Authorities announced Jan. 10, 1973 that security forces had virtually "dismantled" the Popular Revolutionary Vanguard, an urban guerrilla movement once considered the best-organized in Brazil.

Security sources said six alleged Vanguard terrorists, including two foreign women, had been killed in shootouts in Paulista, eight miles north of Recife. The Vanguard movement, they said, had been preparing for a national congress at Paulista, where a guerrilla training center reportedly had been set up.

CHILE

Unrest & Terrorism

Bombings, assassinations and other incidents of terroristic violence marked the 1960s and early 1970s in Chile.

Terrorism precedes elections. Authorities expressed alarm at an upsurge of terrorism preceding the 1970 elections.

In a speech to the nation June 28, Interior Minister Patricio Rojas blamed the violence on "militants of the Socialist Party" and the Movement of the Revolutionary Left (MIR). Citing 11 incidents of terrorism since June 20, Rojas asserted that the "escalation of violence" was a "coordinated and systematic action . . . designed to upset the institutional order and create a psychological climate of insecurity and confusion" before the Sept. 4 national elections.

Allende elected; Schneider killed. A joint session of Congress elected Salvador Allende Gossens president of Chile Oct. 24, 1970. The election ·was preceded by the shooting Oct. 22 of Army Commander in Chief Rene Schneider Chereau, who died Oct. 25.

Schneider, 57, was shot at least three times by an unknown assailant after three cars halted his limousine as he was being driven to work.

Schneider had taken a strong stand of political neutrality by the armed forces during the current left-right tensions in Chile and had pledged to honor Congress' choice of president. Speculation in Chile indicated that his assassination may have been part of a right-wing plot to prevent Allende from assuming the presidency.

Ex-minister assassinated. Edmundo Perez Zujovic, 59, former Interior minister and head of the rightist wing of the Christian Democrat party, was assassinated June 8, 1971. He died of bullet wounds in a car ambush outside his home by three men firing submachine guns.

Police announced June 8 that they had implicated Ronald Rivera Calderon, 24, in connection with the slaying. Rivera Calderon was identified by Perez Zujovic's daughter, Maria Angelica Perez, who was with her father at the time of the attack. Rivera Calderon was a member of the extremist Marxist group, the Organized People's Vanguard.

Rigntists arrested. Interior Minister Herman del Canto announced March 24, 1972 that police had raided offices of the right-wing Fatherland and Liberty organization and had arrested 12 alleged members of the party. Among those arrested was Pablo Rodriguez, leader of Fatherland and Liberty.

Del Canto said the raid had netted pamphlets, Molotov cocktails, firearms, clubs, gas masks, fire extinguishers and vials of sulphuric acid. Calling Fatherland and Liberty members "a group of crazy fascists," Del Canto said "it is an evident fact that they intended and still intend to act against the security of the country."

The Washington Post reported March 27 that a Santiago judge had formally charged Rodriguez and another leader of Fatherland and Liberty with violating Chile's internal state security.

Del Canto further charged March 28 that right-wing conspirators had planned to assassinate President Allende, free Gen. Roberto Viaux (who awaited trial on charges of complicity in Gen. Rene Schneider's kidnap-murder) and seize power March 24–26.

Del Canto said the main instigator of the plot was retired army Major Arturo Marshall Marchesse, whom he claimed had close links with Fatherland and Liberty. A warrant was issued for Marshall's arrest. Retired Gen. Alberto Green Baquedano, also accused of participating in the plot, was detained March 27.

An army judge June 16 sentenced Gen. Viaux to 20 years in prison for complicity in Schneider's assassination. (Schneider's attempted kidnapping and assassination were described as part of a right-wing plot to keep Allende from taking office.) Thirty-three others were sentenced to prison terms ranging from three years to life or to expulsion from the country in connection with the assassination. But the Military Tribunal Dec. 7 unexpectedly reduced the prison sentences of all those convicted in the Schneider case. Viaux' sentence was reduced from 20 to two years, but he was ordered to serve a one-year sentence for leading a 1969 military rebellion and, after that, to leave Chile for a minimum of five years.

Del Canto impeached. Interior Minister del Canto was suspended by the Chamber of Deputies July 5, 1972, then censured and dismissed by the Senate July 27.

Charges against Del Canto, initiated by the right-wing National party and supported by the liberal Christian Democrats, included abetting violence by extreme leftists.

Del Canto denied the charges before the Senate July 27, saying the proceedings against him were "political" and not constitutional.

Opposition charges increase—Del Canto's impeachment came amid growing opposition charges that the government tolerated illegal activities by armed extreme leftist groups.

In a special Senate session July 26, Christian Democratic Sen. Rafael Moreno exhibited a suitcase containing a pistol, ammunition and several urban guerrilla manuals, which he called "proof" of government tolerance of subversion. Right-wing Sen. Victor Garcia added a tape recording of an alleged conversation between the Socialist civil police chief and a man accused of killing a worker.

The Senate debate followed the arrest July 20 of 18 members of the extremist July 16th National Liberation Movement, including two Nicaraguans, a Brazilian and a Mexican, for violation of the state internal security law. President Salvador Allende ordered a full investigation into leftist terrorist activities July 21.

'Extremist' plan charged. Santiago riot police were placed on alert April 10, 1973 against what the government called a plan by the extreme right and left to block roads and occupy factories.

Earlier in the day, members of the extremist Revolutionary Left Movement (MIR) had led residents of Constitucion, on the coast south of Santiago, in blocking the roads and railway into the town to demand government solutions to local housing and food problems.·

Government Secretary General Anibal Palma charged extremists planned the Santiago occupations to disrupt food distribution, create a climate of agitation and embarrass the government, which they would then criticize for lack of authority. The plan had been originated by the extreme right, which had duped the MIR into cooperating, Palma asserted.

President Salvador Allende had warned April 3 that MIR activists were planning assaults on private and state food distributors, and that strong measures would be taken against such actions. MIR militants surrounded the warehouse of the private distributor CENADI the next day but were dispersed after a battle with police.

Santiago merchants April 5 praised the government's action against the MIR. The MIR denounced it as "police repression", and asserted occupations of factories and food distributors were not provocations but attempts by the people "to defend themselves against inflation and the shortage of essential articles." The MIR urged formation of "commando groups in each factory, farm, village and school" to combat government repression.

Rightist 'plot.' About 40 or 50 members of the right-wing Fatherland and Liberty party were arrested May 11, 1973 in connection with an alleged plot against the government. Most were released after questioning. Vergara said May 13 that the arrests were ordered for violation of the internal security and press laws. He said arms and ammunition held by detainees had been confiscated in Concepcion, Osorno and Chillan.

The alleged plot was reported in the left-wing press after two Fatherland and Liberty leaders, Walter Robert Thieme and Miguel Juan Sessa, were detained in Mendoza, Argentina, where they had flown in a private plane.

La Prensa of Buenos Aires reported May 9 that Thieme and Sessa had admitted to Argentine officials that they had plotted against Allende. They reportedly produced documents and plans for action against the government to begin May 15.

Thieme said at a Buenos Aires press conference May 12 that if "the price of liberation [in Chile] is civil war, we will have to pay it."

(The president of Fatherland and Liberty's Valparaiso organization, Claudio Fadda Cori, had been arrested June 4 on charges of possessing various arms, Prensa Latina reported.)

Fatherland and Freedom members were accused of complicity in an abortive military coup that was crushed easily June 29.

A truck-owners strike, accompanied by acts of terrorism, added to growing unrest in Chile in August. Fourteen members of the Fatherland and Liberty party were reported arrested Aug. 22, and seven others, including Thieme, were reported seized Aug. 26. The Santiago police chief said that with Thieme's arrest "we have accounted for nearly all recent terrorist acts."

Thieme had admitted that his men had staged numerous terrorist attacks recently, including the dynamiting of a pylon which interrupted a nationwide address by Allende, it was reported Aug. 27. Their purpose, Thieme said, was to "accelerate the country's chaos and provide a military takeover as soon as possible." "If we have to burn this country to save it from [Allende], then we'll do that," Thieme asserted.

Strike-related terrorism and sabotage continued at an apparently diminished rate after the arrest of Thieme. Bombings of private homes in Santiago and electricity installations in the southern town of Temuco were reported Aug. 28; an army lieutenant was murdered Aug. 30; and two oil pipelines were reported dynamited Sept. 4. Interior Minister Carlos Briones said Aug. 30 that there had been more than 500 terrorist attacks and eight related deaths since anti-government strikes had begun July 26.

Allende aide murdered. President Salvador Allende's naval aide-de-camp, Capt. Arturo Araya, was assassinated by unidentified gunmen at his home in Santiago early July 27, 1973.

Military coup, Allende dies. The armed forces and national police ousted the Popular Unity government Sept. 11, 1973 after months of strikes, unrest and terrorism.

Police officials in Santiago said President Salvador Allende Gossens had committed suicide rather than surrender power. A newspaper photographer allowed to see the body, and a military communique Sept. 12 confirmed that the president was dead, but there was some confusion over whether he had taken his own life.

A four-man military junta seized control of the government and declared a state of siege, imposing censorship and a round-the-clock curfew. The junta members were the army commander, Gen. Augusto Pinochet Ugarte; the air force chief, Gen. Gustavo Leigh Guzman; the acting navy commander, Adm. Jose Toribio Merino Castro, and the national police chief, Gen. Cesar Mendoza. Pinochet was sworn in as president of Chile Sept. 13.

Altamirano in Cuba. Ex-Sen. Carlos Altamirano, the leftist most sought by the junta, appeared Jan. 2, 1974 in Havana, where he attended celebrations marking the 15th anniversary of the Cuban revolution.

Altamirano said at a press conference the next day that he had not taken political asylum in Cuba. He asserted he had left Chile with the approval of leaders of his outlawed Socialist Party and would return when the anti-junta resistance needed him.

Altamirano said that since the September 1973 coup two-thirds of the Socialist national and regional leadership had been killed or imprisoned, but the party remained alive and committed "to fight until the complete defeat of the fascist military junta." He added, however, that until now the different groups opposed to the junta had been unable to unite.

Altamirano charged that since the coup, more than 15,000 persons had been "assassinated," more than 30,000 arrested for political reasons, thousands tortured. more than 200,000 dismissed from their jobs and more than 25,000 expelled from universities.

He charged that many priests had been killed or imprisoned and 175 had been deported.

Resistance continues. Le Monde Jan. 5 reported a number of acts of resistance against the military government, including the bombing of a factory in the northern city of Calama Jan. 2, which killed one person and injured another.

The junta leader, President Augusto Pinochot, said Feb. 6 that 45 home-made grenades and enough material to assemble

76 other grenades had been found in a house in Santiago. He said a "gigantic" explosives factory allegedly discovered in the Santiago suburb of Maipu a week before was "one of at least five arms and explosives deposits of terrorists."

A spokesman for the junta said May 25 that it had broken up a subversive group of priests and members of the outlawed Revolutionary Left Movement who allegedly received coded orders from Moscow. The junta said the next day that a leader of the group, Deacon Mario Irarrazabal, had been arrested and expelled from Chile, and four other priests, all members of a group called "Christians for Socialism," had been ordered seized and deported.

Extremists executed—Authorities Jan. 19 announced the execution of six extremists for their part in an armed attack the day before on a military jeep outside the northern city of Quillota.

Six other alleged extremists, being transported in the jeep from one prison to another, were allegedly killed in the attack, and two prisoners, identified as lawyer Ruben Cabezas and former Quillota Mayor Pablo Gac, both Socialists, allegedly escaped.

Other executions, torture and political arrests were reported by refugees from Chile arriving in Cuba, according to the Cuban press agency Prensa Latina Jan. 3.

Two members of the outlawed Socialist Party were sentenced to death by a military court in Osorno, the Cuban newspaper Granma reported March 30. The charges against them were violation of the arms control law and "terrorism and political activism."

Death penalty expanded—The military junta July 11 decreed that the death penalty henceforth could be ordered in cases of kidnapping, terrorist acts, illegal trafficking in arms and explosives, and inciting sabotage against production and public services.

MIR leader killed. Miguel Enriquez, secretary general of the Revolutionary Left Movement (MIR), died Oct. 5, 1974 in a shootout with police and soldiers who surrounded the house where he was hiding in the Santiago suburb of San Miguel.

Carmen Castillo, a MIR militant and daughter of Fernando Castillo, former rector of the Catholic University, was wounded in the action and captured. Her ex-husband, Andres Pascal Allende, a member of the MIR central committee and nephew of the late President Salvador Allende, was wounded but escaped.

Enriquez' death reportedly left the armed resistance to the military junta in disarray. Enriquez was the only major leftist leader not in jail or exile, and he had devoted himself since the September 1973 military coup to organizing militant opposition. A number of MIR members took asylum in the Italian embassy in Santiago after his death, the government reported Oct. 11.

Security forces claimed to have found Enriquez' hideout while searching for the MIR militants who robbed a branch of the Bank of Chile in Santiago Oct. 1. Most of the stolen money was found in the San Miguel hideout, and the rest was recovered with the arrest of two MIR members Oct. 11, according to officials.

Security officers also claimed to have found in Enriquez' hideout 26 Soviet automatic weapons, six submachine guns and a "great quantity" of hand grenades and ammunition.

COLOMBIA

Terrorist-Government Clashes

Frequent clashes between terrorist-guerrilla forces and Colombian authorities took place during the late 1960s and early 1970s. The main terrorist-guerrilla groups, generally described as leftist, were the ELN (Ejercito de Liberacion Nacional, or National Liberation Army), the EPL (Ejercito Popular de Liberacion, or People's Liberation Army) and the FARC (Fuerzas Armadas Revolucionarias de Colombia, or Revolutionary Armed Forces of Colombia). A fourth group, the pro-Peking MOIR (Movimiento Obrero Independiente Revolucionario), was reported to engage in clandestine subversion as well as to participate in elections.

6 die in mountain clash. The Colombian army reported Jan. 31, 1968 that troops had killed six ELN guerrillas in the Santander mountains. The report claimed, erroneously as it later proved, that the army thus had virtually eliminated the ELN. One of the dead was identified as José Angel Gómez Leon, a leader in the hijacking of a Colombian airliner to Cuba Aug. 6, 1967. The army reported that about 12 guerrillas were still active in the mountains.

Arenas Surrenders. Le Monde reported Feb. 27, 1969 that Jaime Arenas Reyes, an ELN leader, had surrendered to the authorities in the department of Santander, north of Bogota. Arenas, who was slightly wounded, was reported to have said that he had killed several fellow guerrillas in self defense. According to military authorities, he recounted that other liberation army leaders had been killed by guerrilla commandos; Victor Medina Moron was among those reported killed.

(Arenas, who had ultimately taken an Education Ministry job, was shot and killed by unidentified gunmen outside his home in Bogota March 28, 1971.)

Venezuelan agreement. The governments of Colombia and Venezuela were reported to have reached a formal agreement on a joint campaign to combat guerrilla infiltration on their common border, according to the London publication Latin America Feb. 13, 1970.

ELN cuts Cuba tie, enlists priests. The ELN, led by Fabio Vasquez Castano, was reported in early 1970 to have broken its ties with Cuba because of decreasing aid from the Castro government.

The ELN announced Feb. 15, 1970 that the Rev. Domingo Lain, a Spanish priest expelled by the government in 1969 for "subversive activities," had joined its ranks. In a statement released over his signature Feb. 16, Lain said: "I have taken the road of armed struggle because in the face of reactionary violence of the system in force in Colombia and Latin America there is no alternative to revolutionary violence." Violence, Lain added, "is a right to escape from exploitation." (Lain, who became an ELN leader, was reported killed in a clash with

army troops in Antioquia department Feb. 20, 1974.)

Military sources reported Feb. 27 that a second priest, the Rev. Gilberto Rueda Angarita, had joined the ELN after leaving his parish in eastern Colombia. (Both Lain and Rueda were reported to be members of the Golconda Group, a group of radical priests whose views had brought them into open conflict with the Catholic hierarchy and the Colombian government; the Golconda Group was currently urging a boycott of the nation's April 19 presidential elections.)

Pre-election deaths. Several killings were reported prior to the 1970 election.

A group of about 35 armed men killed four civil servants in Santa Fe March 18 after ordering the townspeople to abstain in the April presidential elections.

Luis Fernando Uribe Bernal, son of the Belgian consul in Medellin, and his fiance, Gloria Piedrita Diaz, were found shot to death March 18 in Medellin.

'Death squad.' A release given March 20, 1970 to the Colombian press announced the formation of a "death squad" for the execution of "undesirable elements in the Colombian society." Such elements, according to the group, included "priests who betray divine principles, students with no patriotic spirit, political demagogues, false intellectuals, Communists, terrorists, activists who sell their country, thieves."

Guerrilla leaders' deaths reported. The London newsletter Latin America reported Jan. 7, 1972 that the Colombian army claimed to have destroyed one of Colombia's three major guerrilla groups, the Popular Liberation Army (EPL) by killing two of its leaders. They also claimed to have killed Joaquin Aroca, top leader of the guerrilla group Revolutionary Armed Forces of Colombia (FARC).

Luis Carlos Hernandez Catano, an ELN leader, was reportedly killed May 23 in a gun battle with soldiers in the state of Antioquia.

Guerrillas raid towns. Some 200 guerrillas identified as ELN members seized the mountain town of San Pablo Jan. 7, 1972 and held it for several hours, killing two policemen, wounding four others and fleeing in stolen trucks with four hostages.

According to a report in the Buenos Aires newspaper La Prensa, guerrillas also took $400,000 from public offices, safes at the city hall, the farm credit office and the telephone company.

The assault was reportedly carried out by ELN members Ricardo Lara Parada and the Rev. Domingo Lain under the direction of ELN leader Fabio Vasquez Castano.

(In early 1971 the army had said that ELN deserters had reported that Vasquez Castano had been killed by his colleagues.)

Three people were killed and eight wounded Jan. 16 in simultaneous guerrilla raids on the northeastern towns of Remedios, Santa Isabel, El Tigre and Yali.

According to the New York Times Jan. 23, ELN members had opened the Remedios jail, robbed banks and set several fires. They were also held responsible for the murder of Oscar Saldarriaga Velez, vice president of the Colombian Industrial Bank, at his farm.

As they had in many of their raids, the guerrillas assembled townspeople to lecture them on their plans to seize political power in Colombia.

The Times reported that since the beginning of 1972 guerrillas had killed a dozen persons and kidnaped four others and stolen the equivalent of $500,000 in food, medicine and cash.

Seven soldiers and two civilians were killed April 20 when ELN members ambushed a military patrol in the northwest state of Antioquia. The patrol was accompanying a public works truck.

About 100 ELN guerrillas occupied the town of Vengache in Antioquia May 6.

Two persons, one a Catholic priest, were killed May 7 when a group of ELN commandos attacked a government building in San Jeronimo in Antioquia.

In a related development, authorities claimed May 23 that a group of ELN terrorists had executed seven peasants in the coastal town of Santa Marta.

Peasant leader killed. Miguel Suarez, a Communist and one of the major leaders of Colombia's peasant movement, was reported shot to death in the town of Yacopi March 24.

According to Le Monde April 5, a group of rightist commandos opened fire on Suarez and several companions as they entered the Yacopi mayoralty building to request permission to hold a campaign rally.

Guerrillas reported captured. Police had arrested between 80-100 persons allegedly connected with leftist terrorist activities, further weakening Colombia's guerrilla movement, according to reports July 12, 1972.

The arrests followed the capture July 5 of eight alleged leaders of the small left-wing Popular Liberation Army, including two of its founders, in Cordoba.

Swedish diplomat killed. The first secretary of the Swedish embassy, Kjell R. Haeggloef, was shot to death by unidentified gunmen in Bogota July 17.

'Swedish-Soviet spy' caught. Colombian security authorities asserted July 22, 1972 that Karl Staf, expelled from Colombia July 18, was a "Soviet-Swedish reporter and spy" who had met with FARC leader Tiro Fijo (real name: Manuel Marulanda Velez) in the town of La Cima and had given the guerrilla $70,000, which Staf had brought with him when he entered Colombia illegally from Ecuador May 5. The statement said that according to documents found on Staf, the alleged spy "proposed to evaluate the power and the true strength of the FARC and the ... [ELN] in order to obtain Moscow's support."

Urban guerrilla network discovered. The army said Sept. 13, 1972 that it had uncovered a vast urban guerrilla network which had infiltrated schools and universities to foment disturbances similar to those in Mexico and France in 1968. The network was said to consist of members of the Maoist Popular Liberation Army, the

Castroist National Liberation Army (ELN) and the pro-Moscow Colombian Revolutionary Armed Forces.

The announcement followed a military report Aug. 25 claiming that 16 ELN urban guerrillas had been captured along with documents detailing plans to create disturbances to gain international attention. Gen. Alvaro Herrera Calderon, army commander, said the guerrillas imitated the style of Uruguay's Tupamaros, infiltrating the government and planning kidnapings and assassinations of prominent foreign and Colombian industrialists.

According to Herrera, the chief of technical assistance in the government's Planning Department, Camilo Cardenas Giraldo, and department engineer Fernando Chacon Castillo were both ELN leaders. Another government official and guerrilla leader, Hernan Mahecha, had been hindering judicial procedures against captured guerrillas, Herrera said.

Kidnappings. The ELN was reported to have raised large sums by kidnapping wealthy men for ransom.

Jairo Duque Perez, ex-dean of law at the University of Antioquia, was abducted by presumed guerrillas from his farm in the northern municipality of Maceo Dec. 6, 1972. A wealthy rancher, Guillermo Castro, had been freed after a month in captivity, following payment of $250,000 in ransom, it was reported Dec. 6.

ELN members killed one person and kidnapped six others in Antioquia and Cordoba Jan. 6–8, 1973. All of the captives, it was reported, were ultimately ransomed.

Emergency measures adopted. The government adopted a series of emergency measures Jan. 26, 1973 following a number of bloody guerrilla actions and the attempted kidnapping of a prominent Cali industrialist and publisher. Among the provisions:

■ All persons convicted by military authorities of kidnapping, extortion and related crimes would serve their sentences in the island prison of La Gorgona, in the Pacific Ocean, considered the most secure in the country.

■ The governors of the nation's 22 departments (states) were authorized to set rewards for persons who provided information detailing crimes and leading to the capture of criminals.

■ Special groups were formed within the armed forces to pursue guerrilla bands operating in rural areas.

■ The mass media were warned that the government would "regulate information" wherever accounts and rumors did not "conform to reality" and tended to create alarm and anxiety.

The measures were set at a Cabinet meeting called late Jan. 26, only hours after Alvaro Caicedo, a wealthy Cali industrialist and publisher, was wounded in a thwarted kidnapping attempt.

The day before, an estimated 50 guerrillas had taken temporary control of the village of San Pedro de Uraba, in the northern department of Antioquia, sacking stores and granaries, robbing the local bank and killing four policemen.

Guerrillas in the Santa Barbara emerald region of eastern Boyaca ambushed a police patrol Jan. 25, killing five officers and wounding another 10, police reported.

Guerrillas belonging to the Castroite National Liberation Army (ELN) clashed with soldiers in the department of Santander Jan. 25. First reports said two soldiers had been killed, several guerrillas wounded and one subversive, Maria Teresa Echeverria, had been killed. Echeverria reportedly was the first female guerrilla to die in combat. Later reports from the Defense Ministry said Luis Jose Solano Sepulveda, second in command of the ELN, had also been killed in the clash.

The army was reported March 9 to have captured Jesus Ariza Gomez, an important EPL leader in Antioquia.

The army claimed to have discovered a large cache of ELN arms in Santander, and to have captured an important ELN urban guerrilla leader near Cali, Latin America reported March 16.

Guerrilla cooperation reported. There was strong evidence the country's three main guerrilla groups were trying to coordinate their activities in the face of the government's determined anti-guerrilla campaign, the London newsletter Latin America reported March 9, 1973.

Elements of the three groups—the pro-Cuban National Liberation Army (ELN), the pro-Soviet Colombian Revolutionary Armed Forces and the pro-Chinese People's Liberation Army (EPL)—had staged a joint attack March 2 on Florian, a small township in the eastern department of Santander.

Two guerrillas were reported killed at Florian. Despite this and heavy ELN casualties in February, the guerrillas were making considerable progress, Latin America reported. They were said to be active in contiguous territory, instead of isolated areas, and to be concentrating on agricultural areas in the north and northwest, where peasant discontent was high.

Guerrillas kill Liberal leader. German Gomez Pelaez, a landowner, journalist and Liberal party leader in the department of Cordoba, was kidnapped May 6, 1973 and then killed by members of the People's Liberation Army (EPL), a Maoist guerrilla group, according to a military communique May 11.

Guerrillas reported smashed. Army Commander Gen. Alvaro Herrera Calderon said Oct. 10, 1973 that recent military operations had all but destroyed two of the nation's three left-wing guerrilla groups, the EPL and ELN.

Herrera said the EPL had lost 25 guerrillas killed by troops and 68 captured since the beginning of 1973. He alleged the group was "practically wiped out, and only its chief and a small band of combatants" remained at large.

The ELN, Herrera said, had been partly destroyed by an army offensive begun Aug. 25 against the guerrillas' main column in the mountainous Anori region of Antioquia department.

Military sources had claimed July 22 that an estimated 60–75 deserters from the ELN and EPL had surrendered to troops fighting the guerrillas in the Alto Sinu region of Cordoba department.

In a development reported July 6, the army confirmed the death of Celso Osma, a reputed ELN leader. Officials specu-

lated Osma may have been killed by other ELN guerrillas, according to the Miami Herald.

ELN leaders slain or seized—The commander of the army's 4th Brigade, Col. Alvaro Riveros Abello, said Oct. 19 that the brigade's 48-day campaign against the ELN in Antioquia had resulted in the capture of 32 guerrillas and the death of 42 others including Antonio and Manuel Vasquez Castano, brothers of ELN founder Fabio Vasquez Castano.

The brothers reportedly were killed in a clash with troops Oct. 19. (Earlier reports of Antonio's death apparently were erroneous.) A third ELN leader, Ricardo Lara Parada, was reported arrested Nov. 25. The army claimed that the ELN had been reduced to one small group led by Fabio Vasquez Castano.

FARC 'only' terrorists still active. Army sources said that the FARC remained relatively untouched by recent military operations, continuing to control territory in the south where they had established two "independent republics." The army had admitted in May that a recent FARC raid on the township of Colombia in Huila department had been led by FARC chief Manuel (Tirofijo) Marulanda, whose death the army had announced previously.

(Tirofijo was pardoned Sept. 27 by a court in Popayan, Cauca department, which reversed a 21-year prison sentence in absentia against the guerrilla leader for allegedly heading a FARC attack on the town of Inza, northeast of Popayan, in 1965. The guerrillas had killed some 20 persons, looted the local bank and several stores, and burned down the court building where insurgents were prosecuted.)

Guerrillas seized. Army spokesmen announced the capture of three guerrillas of the Communist Colombian Revolutionary Armed Forces (FARC) and of two mistresses of FARC leader Manuel Marulanda, it was reported Jan. 4, 1974.

Government sources in Medellin revealed that Jose Manuel Martinez, a founder of the National Liberation Army (ELN), had surrendered after a battle in which soldiers killed three ELN guerrillas, the Miami Herald reported Feb. 8.

CUBA

Exile Attacks

Cuban exiles mounted several ineffectual attacks in Cuba as well as terrorist strikes at Cuban diplomatic targets abroad.

The most spectacular exile terrorist effort was the firing of a bazooka-type shell that exploded harmlessly in the East River in New York about 200 yards from United Nations headquarters Dec. 11, 1964. Argentine-born Cuban revolutionary Ernesto (Che) Guevara was addressing the UN General Assembly when the shell exploded. Three anti-Castro Cubans, arrested Dec. 22, reportedly said that they had deliberately missed hitting the UN and had tried merely to divert public attention from Guevara.

Cuba was accused repeatedly of aiding terrorist/guerrilla movements in Latin American countries.

Cuba was the goal of many aircraft hijackers, but Cuban authorities quickly found that the hijackers often were criminals or demented people rather than useful supporters of the Castro revolution. Cuba ultimately signed a series of agreements designed to curb hijackings.

Bombings & Other Attacks. A bomb exploded in front of the Cuban embassy in Ottawa Sept. 22, 1966, splintering its door and shattering windows. Later Sept. 22, Felipe Rivero, head of the Cuban Nationalist Association, a Miami-based exile group, claimed that his association was responsible for the blast. After the Cuban Nationalist Association threatened in 1967 to bomb the Cuban pavilion at Montreal's Expo 67 fair, Rivero was arrested by U.S. immigration authorities in Miami May 12 and ordered deported July 11.

Nicolas Rodriguez Astiazarain, 30, acting chief of Cuba's UN mission in New York, was burned April 3, 1967 when a package in the mail exploded as he was opening it.

A package allegedly mailed from New York exploded in a Havana post office Jan. 9, 1968; 5 postal workers were injured.

Nine Cuban exiles were arrested in New York Oct. 23, 1968 and charged with 6 bombings of offices of countries that traded with Cuba. The arrest of the exiles and the police seizure of a supply of arms in Johnsonburg, N.J. Aug. 13 followed about 17 bombings and bombing attempts in major cities. All the blasts occurred in front of offices of nations trading with the Castro regime, and leaflets found at some of the scenes proclaimed "Cuban Power" or "United Cuban Power."

Among major bombing incidents involving offices of countries trading with Cuba:

New York—Mexican Consulate and Spanish Tourist Office Apr. 22; Spanish Tourist Office May 30 and June 21; Canadian Tourist Bureau July 4; Japanese National Tourist Office July 7 (2 passersby were slightly injured by flying glass); Bank of Tokyo Trust Co. Aug. 3. A bomb was dismantled July 15 in front of the French Government Tourist Office 2 minutes before it was set to explode.

Chicago—Mexican Government Tourist Office July 14.

Newark, N.J.—A bomb was deactivated July 16 outside the Mexican Consulate and the offices of Aeronaves de Mexico, the Mexican national airline.

Los Angeles—Mexican National Tourist Council, Mexican Travel Agency, Air France, Shell Oil Building and Japan Air Lines July 19; British Consulate-General July 30.

Miami—A bomb blast seriously damaged a British cargo ship, *Caribbean Venture*, in Biscayne Bay Aug. 8. A spokesman for an organization named Cuban Power announced afterwards that a mine had been planted by the group.

The 9 Cubans arrested Oct. 23 were charged with the New York bombings, with plotting to assassinate Cuban officials and embassy personnel and to invade Cuba, and with arson, reckless endangerment, criminal mischief and the illegal possession of weapons and explosives. The 9 arrested, said to be members of the Cuban Power organization: Carlos Fernández, 24, Oscar L. Acevedo, 38, Gabriel Abay, 49, Guillermo Miguel, 38, Arturo Rodríguez Vives, 25, José Rodone, 55, Ivan Acosta, 24, Ramiro Cortez, 18, and Edgar Rivas, 21.

In the raid on the Johnsonburg farm, 13 miles east of the Delaware Water Gap, early Aug. 13, the police found ½ ton of dynamite, automatic weapons and crates of ammunition. They also found a uniform of the 2506th Cuban Assault Brigade of the Bay of Pigs, an anti-Castro secret military organization. The farm's owner, Michael A. DeCarolis, 32, was arrested.

9 Cuban exiles were found guilty by federal court in Miami Nov. 15, 1968 of conspiring to damage ships of countries that traded with Cuba. One of the defendants, Dr. Orlando Bosch, 41, a Cuban Power leader, was also convicted of sending threatening telegrams to the heads of state of Spain, Mexico and Britain. Bosch, Barbaro Balan and José Díaz Morejon were convicted of firing on the Polish freighter Polanika Sept. 16 in the port of Miami. The other 6 convicted: Aimée Miranda, Andrew González, Marco Rodríguez Ramos, Jorge Luiz Gutierrez Ulla, Paulino Gutierrez and Jesus Dominguez Benitez. Bosch, also convicted of sending bomb threats to the heads of state of Spain, Britain and Mexico, received a 10-year sentence Dec. 13. The other 8 were given terms ranging from one to 6 years.

Three Cuban exiles were indicted by a federal grand jury in Newark, N.J. June 4, 1969 on charges of conspiring to bomb Cuban government property in Montreal. FBI officials said that the three Cuban National Movement members had conspired to blow up the Cuban Consulate, the Cuban Trade Commission and Cuban steamships. Indicted were Guillermo Novo Sampol and Felipe Martinez y Blanca, arrested May 20, and Hector Diaz Limontes, arrested June 3.

Two bombs exploded Apr. 4, 1972 at the Cuban Trade Commission offices in Montreal. The blasts killed a Cuban guard and damaged the building.

The Washington Post reported the following day an anonymous caller had informed United Press International in Miami that the bombings had been carried out by a group called the Young Cubans "in the name of Alejandro Del Valle, who died in the [1961] Bay of Pigs invasion."

The "Cuban Secret Government" Dec. 12, 1972 said it had placed bombs that had destroyed a travel agency and three office handling packages for Cuba in Miami, New York and Montreal. No persons were injured by the explosions, but the group warned of further attacks against persons and concerns doing business with Cuba.

In New York, a pro-revolutionary Cuban political and cultural exposition begun July 26, 1973 was closed July 28, a day ahead of schedule, because of day-long demonstrations, a late-night bombing, egg and brick throwing and repeated bomb threats by anti-Castro Cuban exiles.

A Cuban embassy spokesman in Lima said Feb. 5, 1974 that a package bomb had exploded in the embassy the day before, wounding a woman attache and damaging the building. Stamps and postmarks on the package indicated the bomb was sent from Mexico.

Cuban refugee leader slain. Jose de la Torriente, 69, former Cuban minister of agriculture, was fatally wounded by a sniper's bullet in his Miami home April 13, 1974. A leader of Cuban exiles living in Miami, Torriente had been accused by Cuban Premier Fidel Castro of working for the U.S. Central Intelligence Agency (CIA). A Cuban group calling itself "Zero" took responsibility for Torriente's killing April 17.

Action in Cuba. The Cuban government announced Dec. 16, 1968 the capture of 5 armed Cuban exiles Dec. 4, 2 days after they had landed at the northwestern port of Cabānas, 38 miles southwest of Havana.

The announcement said the men had arrived in a launch "of a type used by the CIA in its incursions against our country." Havana said that 2 of the captured exiles—Ernesto Diaz Rodriguez and Emilio Nazario Perez Sargent—were members of Alpha 66 and the 2d Front of Escambray, 2 anti-Castro exile organizations that had merged their operations.

A Miami-based Cuban exile group, the Cuban Representation in Exile

(RECE), reported that one of its military leaders had been captured in Cuba after landing in Oriente Province with a group of anti-Castro infiltrators, the Miami Herald reported June 14, 1969. The RECE identified the leader as Angel Luis Castillo, a former captain in Castro's army. (The Herald report cited rumors that a 10-man infiltration team led by Amancio [El Yarey] Mosqueda Fernandez had been crushed by Cuban forces shortly after its arrival in Cuba in May; all of the team's members were reported killed, wounded or captured.)

Radio Havana announced Dec. 7, 1969 that four Cuban exiles had been executed by a firing squad the previous night. The executed, including El Yarey Mosqueda Fernandez, were said to have been among a group of "10 enemy agents who infiltrated Cuba from the United States May 3" with "instructions to sabotage economic installations" in Oriente Province. The other members of the group were given 20-year prison sentences. (In announcing the arrests of the 10 exiles Oct. 18, the government had identified them as members of the RECE.)

Radio Havana said Feb. 23, 1970 that Jose Antonio Quesada Fernandez, leader of the 2d Front of Escambray, had been executed by a firing squad; Quesada Fernandez had led a small military expedition to Cuba in September 1969 to establish contact with the Cuban anti-Castro underground.

Alpha 66 claimed Nov. 7, 1970 that one of the two of its infiltration groups that had invaded Cuba in September had reached its destination in Oriente province. The Cuban government had claimed Sept. 23 it had killed or captured all the members of a nine-man invasion party, but Alpha 66 reported Sept. 28 that two separate groups of infiltrators had landed.

Cuba charged Oct. 14, 1971 that U.S-backed commando "mercenaries" had attacked a small fishing village on the northern coast Oct. 12, killing two persons and injuring four others.

Radio Havana, in a broadcast monitored in Miami, said the night attack was carried out by two boats and blamed it on "the government of the U.S. and its accomplices." The broadcast said a border patrol guard and an Interior Ministry policeman were killed in the raid. Havana Radio said the "mercenaries" immediately fled out to sea, heading north" after machine-gunning the town.

In New York, Guillermo Martinez Marquez, a spokesman for a Miami-based exile organization headed by Jose de la Torriente, claimed responsibility for the raid, called it a success and said it was the beginning of a series of actions by the group "to free Cuba from its Communist yoke."

(The Miami Herald reported Oct. 20 that the Cuban exile group had claimed that it had seized the small fishing village for more than an hour during the raid. The head of the Cuban Liberation Front claimed its goal had been a military installation outside the town and that the commandoes had torn down telephone lines and sabotaged the village electrical plant.)

Action Against Hijackings

Antihijacking law. The Cuban government Sept. 19, 1969 announced a new law that would provide for the extradition of persons who hijacked planes or boats. However, in announcing the law, a communique explained that it "will be applied in accordance with the attitude assumed by other nations and on the basis of equality and reciprocity."

Under the new law, Cuba reserved the right to determine whether a hijacker was a common transgressor or a political refugee and maintained that it would grant asylum to "those persons, who, for political reasons, arrive in our country having found themselves in the necessity of using this extreme means to elude a real danger of death or grave repression." In addition, the communique indicated that hijackers would be extradited only to those nations that "bilaterally agree with Cuba on the application of an equal policy." The announcement added that Cuba was "unwilling to abide by multilateral agreements adopted by international organizations."

Agreement proposed. Cuban Foreign Minister Raul Roa said Sept. 26, 1970 that Cuba would enter into an agreement with the U.S. for the joint extradition of all sea and air hijackers if no exceptions to the accord were made.

In a speech broadcast on Radio Havana, Roa said: "If the U.S. government really wishes to discuss in a serious and definitive way that problem [hijacking], the Cuba government is willing to subscribe right away." He added: "We also wish to express in a final and categorical way that we do not accept and we do not respect any international agreement about the hijacking of planes, unless it concretely includes all piracy forms and violations without any exception."

In an address before the U.N. General Assembly Oct. 2, Cuban representative Ricardo Alarcon de Quesada repeated Roa's offer to negotiate agreements with individual countries. "We reject any multilateral accord but reiterate our willingness to conclude bilateral treaties that provide strict reciprocity" on the joint return of hijackers, Alarcon said.

(A U.S. State Department official had disclosed March 9 that the U.S. had contacted Cuba regarding the possibility of negotiation of a bilateral agreement on hijackers.)

Cuba returns hijacker—Cuba, for the first time, directly returned a hijacker to the U.S. Sept. 24. Cuban authorities allowed U.S. officials to fly to Varadero, Cuba and pick up Robert Labadie, an Army private who had hijacked a Trans World Airlines jet to Havana.

In his Sept. 26 radio statement, Roa had pointed out that Labadie's return was negotiated through secret diplomatic channels and was initiated by the U.S. Aug. 27.

Antihijacking accords signed. The U.S. and Cuba Feb. 15, 1973 signed a five-year agreement, effective immediately, to curb the hijacking of aircraft and ships between the two countries.

The agreement, officially a "memorandum of understanding" rather than a formal treaty requiring Senate confirmation, was signed simultaneously by U.S. Secretary of State William P. Rogers in Washington and Cuban Foreign Minister Raul Roa in Havana. It committed both countries to either try hijackers

"for the offense punishable by the most severe penalty" or extradite them.

The accord also permitted both nations to grant political asylum to hijackers under carefully defined terms but committed each to punish anyone who used its territory to organize attacks against the other. The latter provision was of particular importance to Cuba because U.S.-based Cuban exile groups had conducted raids against their former homeland, and had committed random violence against Cuban citizens.

The agreement stated that each country would promptly return stolen airplanes or vessels and protect innocent persons and goods on board, and would send back "without delay" any ransom collected by the hijackers. Cuba previously had not returned hijacking ransom money.

Similar antihijacking accords were signed by Cuba with Canada Feb. 15, 1973, Mexico June 7, 1973, Venezuela July 6, 1973 and Colombia July 22, 1974.

DOMINICAN REPUBLIC

Unrest & Terrorism

The Dominican Republic continued to suffer recurrent unrest and incidents of terrorism in the years following the 1965 crisis and the U.S.-OAS intervention. Organizations accused of terrorism included the PRD (Partido Revolucionario Dominicano, or Dominican Revolutionary Party), the leftist PSP (Partido Socialista Popular, or Popular Socialist Party) and the MPD (Movimiento Popular Dominicano, or Dominican People's Movement).

Cuba accused. President Joaquin Balaguer charged May 9, 1967 that terrorist activities in his country were the work of "hundreds of well-trained Communist agents" who, with Cuban support, were attempting to overthrow the government. During the previous week, one terrorist had been killed in a clash between army units and a rebel band. Sen. Rafael Casimiro Castro had been severely wounded May 4 by a terrorist fire bomb.

Fresh terror wave. As terrorism again flared, President Joaquin Balaguer April 21, 1969 dismissed two cabinet officials—national police chief Gen. Braulio Alvarez Sanchez and Education Minister Luis Alfredo Duverge Mejia.

Alvarez' dismissal followed a resurgence of terrorism in which at least seven persons were killed. Two of the dead were followers of former Gen. Elias Wessin y Wessin, right-wing leader. Balaguer blamed the terrorism on "violence preached by the radio and press." Leon Bosch, son of former President Juan Bosch, was arrested in connection with the shootings. As a result, Bosch's PRD, the Dominican Revolutionary Party, had boycotted Congress and called for Braulio Alvarez' dismissal.

Francisco de los Santos, a leader of PRD, and Francisco Cartagena, a provincial leader of the ruling Reformist Party, were shot to death by unknown assailants Sept. 20.

Antigovernment demonstrations and terrorist attacks against police continued in Santo Domingo and spread to other cities in November.

At least two people were killed in terrorist attacks in Barahona the week of Nov. 16–22.

President Balaguer Oct. 29 banned PRD demonstrations. In a national address, he charged that the PRD espoused theories of "civil disobedience and collective subversion" and attacked PRD leaders who had "pleaded for the overthrow of the government and for an armed rebellion to take over the country's rule."

Army Maj. Edmundo Cuello was assassinated Nov. 20 by unknown terrorists in Santo Domingo.

Student unrest & terrorism. Students clashed with police in Santo Domingo Jan. 28–29, 1970 following protests over the disappearance of three youths from Hato Mayor in early January. Demonstrations over the unexplained disappearances also took place in Santiago and San Francisco de Macoris.

Student unrest accompanied by terrorist incidents continued for the next two weeks. More than 200 students were reported arrested Feb. 2 and 3, and most high schools in Santo Domingo and Santiago were closed. At least three persons were reported to have been killed in terrorist incidents.

U.S. officer kidnapped. Lt. Col. Donald J. Crowley, U.S. air attache in the Dominican Republic, was abducted by Dominican terrorists March 24, 1970. He was held until March 26 when his release was granted in exchange for the government's release of 20 political prisoners.

Crowley was abducted by six armed men early March 24 on the grounds of the Embajador Hotel. The kidnappers identified themselves as members of the Unified Anti-Re-election Command, an organization seeking to prevent the re-election of President Balaguer.

Threatening to take Crowley's life if their terms were not met by March 25 at 10 a.m., the kidnappers demanded the release of 21 prisoners in a public ceremony in downtown Santo Domingo. The kidnappers later increased their ransom to 24 prisoners, but the government agreed to release only 20. In addition, the government refused to release the prisoners in Santo Domingo, insisting that they be flown out of the country. Police used tear gas to disperse crowds which had gathered in downtown Santo Domingo early March 25 to await the release of the prisoners.

Crowley was freed March 26, shortly after the 20 prisoners had boarded a jet airliner at the Santo Domingo airport. The plane left for Mexico City after Crowley's release had been verified.

The prisoners, most of whom were under arrest for common crimes but who were also identified with radical antigovernment organizations, included Maximiliano Gomez, secretary general of the left-wing Dominican Popular Movement (MPD). In Mexico, Gomez expressed his intention to return to the Dominican Republic to "help whatever faction or candidate who will lead the fight against Balaguer."

Otto Morales, an MPD leader and a suspect in the kidnapping, was shot and killed by police July 16.

Unrest continues. Violence continued to plague the Dominican Republic following the elections of May 16, 1970, in which President Joaquin Balaguer was reelected to a second term. At least 10 persons were killed in terrorist attacks the week of June 8-14, and an unsuccessful attempt was made against the life of Balaguer June 13. In addition, another 20 persons were reported to have been killed in attacks during the first two weeks of July.

In response to the violence, the government July 3 promulgated a law imposing a maximum sentence of 30 years imprisonment for authors and accomplices of terrorist acts. At the same time, Balaguer signed a law increasing the sentences for violation of regulations governing possession of firearms. In a speech reported by the Miami Herald July 17, Balaguer warned that the government would "adopt whatever measures the people and the circumstances warrant." He added that it was necessary to continue intensive police searches of homes and autos in an attempt to locate suspects.

■ Amin Abel Hasbun, a leader of the outlawed Dominican Popular Movement, was shot to death by police during a raid on his home, it was reported Sept. 26.

■ Jose Florencio, a militant leftist, was sentenced to the maximum penalty of 30 years' imprisonment Dec. 6. Florencio, found guilty of the murder of a policeman in 1969, received the most severe penalty imposed in the country in 1970.

Leftists unite. Two leftist groups allegedly signed an agreement pledging to work together for the overthrow of the Balaguer government. According to a text of the agreement, published in the Santo Domingo paper El Caribe Feb. 25, 1971, the Dominican Popular Movement (MPD) and the April 24 Revolutionary Movement agreed to "work together to achieve the unity of all revolutionary organizations and progressive and anti-imperialist groups and persons throughout the country." The MPD, however, stressed that "the sectors of the right which are in contradiction with the government" could participate in the struggle as "tactical allies," while the April 24 Movement rejected any union with the "pro-imperialist forces of the right who are against the Balaguer government, because any type of alliance with those forces is against the struggle for national liberation."

(Maximiliano Gomez, 28, exiled MPD secretary general, was found dead in Brussels May 23. Le Monde reported May 27 and June 4 that Gomez' friends in Paris thought he had been murdered by killers sent by political allies of President Balaguer.)

Wessin coup fails. After police sealed off Santo Domingo June 27, 1971 because of the death of five persons in a wave of unrest, President Joaquin Balaguer announced June 30 that his government had put down an attempted right-wing coup headed by former General Elias Wessin y Wessin who was immediately placed under arrest.

Balaguer made the announcement in an unprecedented television speech in which Wessin appeared at his side. At least 41 military men were reported to be under arrest, accused of taking part in the conspiracy. A court-martial decided July 1 to deport the former general, who arrived in Spain July 5.

La Banda kills leftists. The New York Times reported Aug. 28, 1971 that at least 50 leftists had been murdered and others jailed and beaten since the formation in April of an anti-Communist terrorist organization known as La Banda (the Band).

Although President Joaquin Balaguer had denied the existence of such a group, which appeared similar to the "death squads" of Brazil, Uruguay and Guatemala, the Times reported Sept. 1 that La Banda was organized by National Police Chief Maj. Gen. Enrique Perez y Perez, on instructions from President Balaguer, to conduct an offensive against the extreme left and eradicate the Communist leadership in the country.

The main targets of the right-wing terrorists were reported to be the Marxist Popular Dominican Movement and the smaller Maoist Communist party, although other more moderate government opponents had been targets of La Banda's campaigns.

The Times quoted political sources as stating that the organization had 400 members in Santo Domingo under the command of Lt. Oscar Nunez Pena, a close friend of Gen. Perez y Perez. Members were described as youths in their late teens and early 20s who were trained in the use of arms. The movement had reportedly spread to interior cities.

In a surprise move, the Miami Herald reported Sept. 14, the government arrested 250 members of La Banda. Balaguer also forced Lt. Nunez Pena's resignation.

It was reported Sept. 17 that about 100 members of La Banda had been released by police due to lack of evidence.

Five students aged 16–21 were shot and killed Oct. 9 as they were celebrating the death several days before of a member of La Banda. Initial reports blamed La Banda for the killings.

In response to intensifying public demands to end the terrorism plaguing the country, President Balaguer Oct. 15 switched the positions of his two top military officers, naming Gen. Neit Nivar Seijas, commander of the 1st Brigade, to succeed Gen. Enrique Perez y Perez as national police chief.

According to observers, Gen. Nivar quickly ended La Banda's activities.

12 die as police battle guerrillas. A day-long battle between police forces using bazookas and mortars and a band of leftist guerrillas wanted in a $50,000 robbery from the Royal Bank of Canada in November 1971, was reported to have resulted in the deaths of eight policemen and four guerrillas Jan. 12, 1972.

A Communist lawyer accused of leading the band, Plinio Matos Moquete, and an associate, Harry Jiminez Castillo, escaped. President Joaquin Balaguer promised them an impartial trial if they surrendered.

The battle, which began at a guerrilla hideout 14 miles east of the capital, touched off riots in Santo Domingo. Students supporting the terrorists took to the streets, throwing rocks and smashing windows.

University occupied. 10 persons were wounded and more than 150 were arrested April 4, 1972 as police and soldiers seeking a guerrilla leader occupied the Autonomous University of Santo Domingo (UASD) and fired on students and teachers.

According to the Miami Herald April 6, authorities said they had learned early April 4 that Tacito Perdomo Robles, leader of the extremist Dominican Popular Movement (MPD), was hiding in the university. Police invaded the campus after demanding that UASD rector Jotin Cury produce Perdomo. Cury, who refused to allow the police to enter the university, was detained along with the vice rector, Tirso Mejia.

200 arrested. More than 200 people were arrested by policemen and soldiers following terrorist attacks in which one policeman was killed and four wounded, the Miami Herald reported June 4, 1972.

Government authorities July 9 discovered a cache of weapons that, they said, had been collected for a leftist revolt.

PRD leader wounded. Arturo Guzman, secretary general of the Santiago construction workers union and a leader of the PRD labor faction, was shot and wounded by unidentified assailants Jan. 2, 1973. This was the second attack on Guzman in less than three months.

Guerrilla invasion fails. A small band of guerrillas landed on the southern coast Feb. 4, 1973 and moved quickly into the central mountain range. The group was spotted by an army patrol Feb. 6 and a series of clashes ensued. By the end of March, according to Dominican authorities, all the guerrillas had been killed or captured.

Tanks and armored cars moved into Santo Domingo Feb. 8 as the government instituted a series of strict security measures following the guerrilla landing.

The measures, amounting to a state of emergency, included tight military surveillance of the major cities, censorship of broadcasting, raids on hundreds of homes and the detention of "suspicious" persons. The French newspaper Le Monde reported Feb. 10 that hundreds of persons were arrested. Other sources reported that the raids on homes were ordered to insure the capture of ex-President Juan Bosch and Jose Francisco Pena Gomez, leaders of the opposition Dominican Revolutionary party (PRD), who were in hiding.

Bosch issued a message late Feb. 7 denying that he or any other PRD leader knew anything of the alleged guerrilla operation and demanding that the government publish alleged documents implicating the PRD in the operation, which the government claimed to have found in the boat in which the guerrillas were said to have landed.

In Santo Domingo, meanwhile, newspapers received a communique Feb. 10 in which an organization calling itself Commandos of the Resistance took credit for the guerrilla operation, which it claimed was led by former Col. Francisco Caamano.

According to the army, Caamano was killed by soldiers in the central mountains Feb. 16 and buried there Feb. 17.

Editor slain. Gregorio Garcia Castro, editor of the Santo Domingo newspaper Ultima Hora and a critic of the government, was shot to death by unidentified persons as he left his office March 28, 1973.

Garcia Castro, one of the most widely read columnists in the country, was said to have sharply criticized not only the government but most political groups. He had reportedly warned Balaguer that there was a police plot to kill him, according to the London newsletter Latin America April 6.

Leftist abductor reaches France. Left-wing revolutionary Manfredo Casado, who took political asylum in the Mexican embassy in Santo Domingo in 1972, was given safe-conduct to travel to France Sept. 27, 1973 after he seized the 12-year-old son of Mexican Ambassador Francisco Garcia and threatened to kill himself and the boy.

The government, which had denied Casado safe-conduct before, acceded when Casado threatened to use a gasoline cache and a grenade to blow up the room in which he held the boy. Casado released the boy unharmed at the Santo Domingo airport. He arrived in France Sept. 28.

In a related development, police in Santo Domingo announced the arrest Nov. 2 of Plinio Matos Moquete, leader of the outlawed leftist "January 12" movement, the Cuban press agency Prensa Latina reported Nov. 4. Matos was sought on charges of bank robbery, illegal possession of arms, and "political subversion." His brother Manuel had been arrested in June on similar charges, according to Prensa Latina.

Terrorists free U.S., Venezuela aides. A U.S. official and six other hostages held by left-wing guerrillas for two weeks in the Dominican Republic were freed Oct. 9, 1974 when the terrorists accepted a government offer of safe-conduct to Panama.

The seven insurgents, who claimed membership in the January 12th Liberation Movement, had kidnapped U.S. Information Service Director Barbara Hutchison outside her office in Santo Domingo Sept. 27 and taken her to the nearby Venezuelan consulate, where they took control of the building and seized seven more hostages—the Venezuelan consul and vice consul, a Spanish priest, and four Dominican employes of the consulate.

Radhames Mendez Vargas, the guerrillas' leader, told reporters over the telephone that his group would kill the hostages one by one unless the U.S. paid them $1 million in ransom and the Dominican government released 38 political prisoners. He said his men had mined the consulate and would blow it up if police tried to storm it.

Security forces cordoned off the area and began the long siege, allowing two daily deliveries of food to the terrorists and their hostages. The deliveries were cut to one a day Oct. 1 on orders of President Joaquin Balaguer, who, with the support of the U.S., Venezuelan and Spanish governments, refused to meet the guerrillas' demands.

Mendez Vargas, a convicted airplane hijacker released from prison earlier in 1974, said Sept. 27 that the terrorist action was a response to the government's rejection of "demands for democratization" and an attempt "to free patriots who are rotting in jail under the Balaguer dictatorship." The only political prisoner Mendez Vargas named was Plinio Matos, his movement's leader; the guerrillas later issued a list of 32 other prisoners whose release they demanded.

At least 10 of those prisoners and the entire organized Dominican left, including the Dominican Popular Movement, of which Matos' group was supposedly an offshoot, condemned the guerrilla action, according to press reports.

Intermittent negotiations were held among the guerrillas, government representatives and U.S. Ambassador Robert Hurwitch. The terrorists dropped the $1 million ransom demand Oct. 3 and asked for release of the political prisoners and safe-conduct for all to either Mexico or Peru. This was rejected by Balaguer and reportedly by the Mexican and Peruvian governments. Balaguer made an "absolutely final" offer of safe conduct out of the country Oct. 7, and the guerrillas accepted this the next day.

Panama agreed to grant the terrorists asylum to help the Dominican government "end this unfortunate case," according to Panamanian Ambassador Alejandro Cuellar Arosemena Oct. 9. The guerrillas were flown to Panama City immediately after they freed the seven hostages.

GUATEMALA

Terrorism & Repression

Guerrilla violence and terrorism have flared repeatedly in Guatemala in the 1960s and 1970s. Such activity has been fought by U.S.-aided counterinsurgency methods that, according to some critics, have resulted in wholesale repression and in "blood-baths" that in the Oriente in the 1967–68 period took the lives of at least 2,000 Guatemalans, of whom relatively few were guerrillas. (Some estimates of the deaths were as high as 6,000.) Norman Gall reported in the

May 20, 1971 edition of the New York Review of Books that:

... only a part of the [counterinsurgency] killing ... has been done by the government's official forces. In 1967 more than 20 right-wing para-military terrorist groups went into action with weapons supplied ... under the U.S. military aid program. . . . They first circulated leaflets carrying the names and sometimes the photographs of their announced victims, whose corpses—and those of many others—were later found grotesquely mutilated. ...

Gall quoted Mario Sandoval Alarcon, secretary-general of the right-wing MLN (Movimiento de Liberacion National, or National Liberation Movement) as telling him in 1967:

We of the Liberacion were the vanguard group that got this started. The army was demoralized by the guerrillas last year [1966] until we organized the White Hand. . . . In the systematic elimination of the guerrillas a series of injustices apparently have been committed. Several hundred persons have been killed, but between January and March [1967] the guerrillas have almost been completely eliminated from the Guatemalan Oriente. The terrorism of the guerrillas, which has resulted in the death of many of our [MLN] people, has forced the government to adopt a plan of complete illegality, but this has brought results.

Georgie Anne Geyer, who had visited the FAR (Fuerzas Armadas Rebeldes, or Rebel Armed Forces) in the Sierra de las Minas in 1966, "right at the height of the FAR's popularity and effectiveness," reported in the July 4, 1970 issue of the New Republic that, after the counterinsurgency campaign, "the FAR has become a fractured, blood-let group of urban guerrillas to whom terrorism has largely become an end in itself." "They have decentralized—reorganized into cells of five persons, which barely know the other cells"—in accordance with Carlos Marighella's prescription, she reported, and thus were left to act "without any real leader."

2 U.S. Aides Slain. 2 U.S. military attachés of the U.S. embassy in Guatemala were shot to death and 2 other embassy aides were wounded Jan. 16, 1968 during an upsurge of terrorism.

The Rebel Armed Forces (FAR), the major Communist group operating in Guatemala, announced in leaflets distributed in Guatemala City later Jan. 16 that it was responsible for the slaying of Col. John D. Webber Jr., 47, head of the U.S. Military Advisory Group, and of Lt. Cmndr. Ernest A. Munro, 40, head of the mission's naval section, and for the wounding of Sgt. Maj. John F. Forester, 42, of Salem, Ore. and Chief

Petty Officer Harry L. Greene, 41, of Omaha.

The Americans had been returning by car to Guatemala City from the Guatemalan Air Force headquarters when another auto pulled up alongside, and its occupants opened fire.

In its announcement of the slayings, the Rebel Armed Forces said they were in retaliation for the killing by rightists Jan. 12 of Rogelia Cruz Martínez, Miss Guatemala of 1950, who had been suspected of leftwing guerrilla sympathies. The Rebel Armed Forces accused the U.S. mission of assisting in the organization of Guatemalan army killer teams, an apparent reference to rightwing counterterrorist groups that had been combatting the leftwing forces since the spring of 1967.

In other shootings in Guatemala City Jan. 16: (a) leftwing lawyer and ex-mayoral candidate Alejandro Silva Falla and his bodyguard were shot to death; (b) ex-labor Min. Manuel Villacorta (in the rightwing government of Carlos Castillo Armas) was fired on in his auto but escaped. A soldier guarding the Guatemala City home of Col. Carlos Arana had been shot to death by guerrillas Jan. 15. Arana had been the military chief of counterinsurgency operations in Zacapa. Conservative businessman Alfonso Alejos, 80, was shot to death in Guatemala City Jan. 17. His slaying was attributed to the Rebel Armed Forces.

U.S. Clerics Linked to Rebels. A U.S. Roman Catholic missionary order operating in Guatemala—the Maryknoll Fathers—said Jan. 21, 1968 that 7 of its missionaries in the country—3 priests and 4 nuns—had been ordered back to Maryknoll headquarters in Ossining, N.Y. in Dec. 1967 because 3 of them had been involved in FAR's activities.

A spokesman for the order, the Rev. Donald J. Casey, managing editor of *Maryknoll* magazine, charged that one of the 3 accused, Sister Marian Peter, 39, was the "ringleader" and had attended a meeting in Escuintla, Guatemala in Dec. 1967 with 5 priests and 4 nuns and a leader of the guerrilla force to map plans for smuggling arms into the country.

The 2 other missionaries linked with the rebels were the Rev. Thomas Melville, 38, and his brother, the Rev. Arthur Melville, 35. The Melvilles and Sister Peter were suspended (the priests were deprived of the right to celebrate mass and hear confession). The 3 had boarded a plane in Dec. 1967, ostensibly to return to New York, but had disappeared on arriving in Miami and were believed to be in Mexico at the Guatelan border. All 3 had admitted contacts with the guerrillas. But they insisted that their purpose was to attempt to direct the revolutionary fervor of the rebels into more peaceful directions.

Archbishop seized. The Catholic archbishop of Guatemala, the Most. Rev. Mario Casariego, 58, was kidnaped by members of a rightwing dissident terrorist group Mar. 17, 1968, then freed Mar. 20.

Casariego and his chauffeur had been seized in Guatemala City while driving from the papal nuncio's home after returning that day from a trip to Mexico. According to an account of the incident given Mar. 21 by national police chief Col. Manuel Sosa Avila: The archbishop and his driver were stopped, taken from their car and driven in another vehicle to a house at Quinta Olga, 135 miles from the capital. (The house belonged to Dr. Carlos Cifuentes Díaz, 1954-6 presidential press chief in the rightist regime of Col. Carlos Castillo Armas.) The abductors' car was driven by Raúl Estuardo Lorenzana, leader of a rightwing terrorist group that was conspiring to overthrow the regime of Pres. Julio César Méndez Montenegro. He was accompanied by 2 other plotters identified as Otto Thiel Cobar and Gilberto Valenzuela. Police Mar. 20 seized the kidnap car in nearby Quezaltenango with 3 other members of the gang (who had been guarding Casariego) as they were fleeing Quinta Olga.

The government Mar. 18 had suspended constitutional guarantees for 30 days in the wake of Casariego's abduction. Casariego, considered socially and politically progressive, had been accused by the rightists of being a "guerrilla bishop."

Siege State Ends. The Guatemalan government was reported June 20 to have lifted the nationwide state of siege, in effect since Mar. 18, and to have restored constitutional rights, suspended since Jan. 16.

The government's action reflected an easing of terrorist activities that had prompted the restrictions.

The slackening of rightwing terrorism was believed attributable to Pres. Méndez' dismissal in March of 3 top military officials: Col. Rafael Arriaga Bosque, defense minister; Col. Carlos Arana Osorio, commander of the Zacapa area east of Guatemala City, a stronghold of Communist guerrilla movement; Col. Manuel Sosa Avila, national police chief. All 3 were given diplomatic posts abroad. They had all been popularly identified with rightist terrorist groups.

U.S. Envoy Slain. John Gordon Mein, 54, U.S. ambassador to Guatemala since Sept. 1965, was killed Aug. 28, 1968 by terrorists who had stopped his car and who opened fire when Mein ran. Mein's chauffeur was not hurt. A statement issued Aug. 29 by the Rebel Armed Forces (FAR) said FAR members had planned to kidnap Mein in retaliation for the Aug. 24 capture of Camilo Sánchez, an FAR leader, by the Guatemalan government.

According to several reports, Mein's limousine was forced to stop by 2 cars as the ambassador was riding to the embassy after attending a luncheon. Several armed youths jumped from the cars and ordered Mein to leave the limousine. Mein was hit with machine-gun and pistol fire as he tried to escape from the attackers. Mein was the first U.S. ambassador murdered at his post.

Guatemalan Pres. Julio César Méndez Montenegro imposed a 30-day state of siege throughout Guatemala Aug. 29.

MLN leader slain. Mario Lopez Villa-toro, a leader of the anti-Communist National Liberation Movement (MLN), was shot and killed June 1, 1969 while campaigning for the party's presidential candidate, Col. Carlos Arana Osorio. (The leftist FAR had "condemned" Arana to death.)

Violence increases. As the March 1, 1970 elections approached, increased terrorist bombings and assassinations led President Julio Cesar Mendez Montenegro Jan. 29 to suspend constitutional rights for 15 days.

Among the incidents reported: Justo Lopez Castanaza, head of the nation's intelligence service, was killed by machine gun fire Jan. 13 in Guatemala City.

Seven leaflet bombs exploded Jan. 22 in different parts of Guatemala City; the bombs contained chlorate and leaflets of the clandestine Guatemalan Labor Party and the Rebel Armed Forces.

Isidoro Zarco, associate editor of the pro-government newspaper Prensa Libre, was shot to death Jan. 28 in Guatemala City. Constitutional guarantees were suspended Jan. 29 following his death, and security forces were authorized to make arrests and inquiries without a warrant.

The Christian Democratic presidential candidate, Jorge Lucas Caballero, was fired on the same week but escaped unharmed, the New York Times reported Feb. 1.

Col. Oscar Giron Perrone, who had participated in the coup overthrowing President Jacob Arbenz Guzman in 1954, was found shot to death Jan. 30 outside of Guatemala City. Giron Perrone had supported Col. Carlos Arana Osorio, presidential candidate supported by the National Liberation Movement and the Institutional Democratic Party.

In a related development, President Mendez Montenegro requested the Organization of American States to send observers to supervise the March 1 elections, the New York Times reported Feb. 4. Ruling Revolutionary Party candidate Mario Fuentes Pieruccini had asked the government to request observers in order to "assure the liberty and purity of suffrage."

Arana wins presidency. Col. Carlos Arana Osorio, 51, won a plurality—42%—of the valid votes cast in Guatemala's presidential election March 1, 1970, and Congress March 21 declared him president-elect.

With armed police guarding the polls March 1, the voting was orderly. The election concluded a tense, violence-torn campaign in which 20 persons were reported to have been killed in political assassinations and urban guerrilla clashes.

Arana, who pledged during the campaign to rid Guatemala of rural guerrillas and urban terrorism, had gained national notoriety in 1966–68 as leader of an anti-guerrilla campaign in the eastern area of Zacapa. In a victory speech March 2, he vowed to act "with energy and without restraint" in pacifying the country. "We have a program which does not contain stop-gap measures," he said. "The stage of speeches is finished and the stage of action has begun . . . Whoever steps outside the law will suffer the full weight of the law."

Sporadic violence had continued to mar the election campaign during its final weeks. Foreign Minister Alberto Fuentes Mohr was kidnapped Feb. 27 by four persons who identified themselves as FAR members. The terrorists, who pulled Fuentes Mohr from his car at gunpoint, announced that he would be killed unless the government, within 24 hours, published an FAR policy statement and turned over Jose Vicente Giron Calvillo, an imprisoned FAR leader, to the Mexican embassy with a safe conduct authorization for travel to Mexico.

Fuentes Mohr was released unharmed Feb. 28 after Giron Calvillo had been delivered to the Mexican embassy. Mexican Ambassador to Guatemala Delfin Sanchez Juarez acted as an intermediary in the exchange. Following his arrival in Mexico City March 1, Giron Calvillo said that the FAR was a nationalist rather than Communist organ and had 20,000 active members in Guatemala. He expressed hope that they could provoke U.S. intervention "to unite the people of Guatemala behind us and start a full-scale revolution."

Among other pre-election developments: Walfred Orlando del Valle, president of the National Electoral Registry, was shot and wounded by terrorists as he was driving through Guatemala City Feb. 24; the driver of the car was also slightly wounded in the shooting.

U.S. envoy kidnapped. The Rebel Armed Forces (FAR) said March 6, 1970 that it had kidnapped U.S. diplomat

Sean M. Holly and threatened to execute him if the Guatemalan government did not release four imprisoned members of the guerrilla group within 48 hours. Holly, a political secretary in the U.S. embassy, was released unharmed March 8, following the government's release of three of the guerrillas; the fourth was already in Mexico.

In response to the kidnapping, the Guatemalan government March 7 released two of the guerrillas—Jose Antonio Aguirre Monzon and Vidalina Antonieta Monzon—into the custody of the Costa Rican embassy, where they were granted political asylum. Aguirre Monzon, who had been arrested March 4, was reported to have served as an intermediary between the FAR and the government in the Fuentes Mohr kidnapping. The government reported March 7 that the third prisoner whose release had been demanded—Jose Antonio Sierra, a bakery workers union organizer—had been freed earlier in the week and allowed to go to Mexico. However, the police denied that the fourth member—Mario Leonel del Cid Garcia—could be found in prison.

Del Cid appeared at the Costa Rican embassy March 8. The three freed prisoners flew to Mexico City that day, where Del Cid reported to newsmen that police had shifted him from one place to another while denying that he was imprisoned.

German envoy slain by FAR kidnappers. Count Karl von Spreti, West German ambassador to Guatemala, was kidnapped March 31, 1970 by armed men in Guatemala City. He was found slain April 5 after the Guatemalan government had refused to meet his kidnappers' terms.

The kidnappers, identified as members of the Rebel Armed Forces (FAR), had demanded April 1 that Guatemala release 17 prisoners in exchange for the freedom of von Spreti.

In reply to the government's intransigence, the kidnappers increased their demands April 3. The new terms for freeing Count von Spreti were the release of 22 political prisoners and payment of $700,000. The West German government issued a strong protest April 3 against the Guatemalan refusal to meet the kidnappers' terms.

In a statement released April 2, the Guatemalan government announced that it was "impossible legally to accede to the demands" since some of the prisoners named had already been convicted and sentenced and could not be freed by executive orders. The government also decreed a state of siege.

(A delegation of foreign diplomats to Guatemala met with Guatemalan Foreign Minister Alberto Fuentes Mohr April 3 to protest the government's defiance of the kidnappers' demands and to request better protection for themselves. The government agreed to provide them with armed guards.)

William Hoppe, special West German envoy sent to Guatemala to mediate in the case, conferred with Guatemalan President Julio Cesar Mendez Montenegro April 4 in an attempt to persuade the government to grant the kidnappers' demands. West German Chancellor Willy Brandt made a similar plea.

Reacting to the news of von Spreti's death, Chancellor Brandt April 5 denounced the Guatemalan government for the "infamous murder," charging that it had "shown itself unable to give the accredited diplomatic representative the necessary security." He added that the German government had been willing to pay the $700,000 in ransom demanded by the kidnapers.

A Guatemalan government spokesman said April 6 that four of the prisoners on the kidnappers' list had confessed to complicity in the August 1968 killing of U.S. Ambassador John Gordon Mein," and "we could not let those go."

In an interview in the West German magazine Der Spiegel April 14, Papal Nuncio Gerolamo Prigione, who served as an intermediary between the kidnappers and the government, charged that much time had been lost in the effort to save von Spreti by the "very inflexible" attitudes of both the government and the kidnappers. Prigione cited Foreign Minister Fuentes Mohr's assertion that Guatemala had to risk von Spreti. "For our government it is a matter of survival. If we yield, we will sign our death warrant," Fuentes Mohr was quoted as saying.

Revenge for von Spreti death. Members of a right-wing group called La Mano (The Hand) claimed responsibility for the April 8 murder of Cesar Montenegro Paniagua, a member of the outlawed Guatemalan Labor (Communist) Party. La Mano stated that Montenegro Paniagua's death was only "the beginning of retaliations against revolutionary groups" responsible for von Spreti's kidnap-murder and other leftist violence.

Francisco Barreno, 40, was found dead April 26 south of Guatemala City. Attached to his clothing was a note that said he had been killed for "belonging to the Guatemalan Labor Party [Communist Party] and diverse labor organizations, for kidnapping and assassinating honorable citizens, for traveling to Cuba, Russia and other Socialist countries. . . .An eye for an eye." Eligio Rodas, 30, was found dead April 27 on the same road. A note attached to his body declared: "Thus will die all the members of the Rebel Armed Forces [FAR]."

Guatemala police announced May 5 the assassination by right-wing terrorists of three victims—Rogelio Zermeno, Rigoberto Ramirez and Lisandro Ortega. On each body a note was found stating that he had been "executed" for belonging to FAR and the Guatemalan Labor Party; the notes were signed "Eye for eye."

Yon Sosa killed in Mexico. The Mexican government announced May 19 that Guatemalan guerrilla leader Marco Antonio Yon Sosa and two of his followers had been shot to death May 16, 1970 by Mexican soldiers on the Mexican side of the Guatemala border.

According to a Mexican government spokesman, "a routine army patrol, which was investigating reports of the presence of armed persons in the area, Saturday encountered a cabin which, at first view, appeared unoccupied. But when the soldiers approached it, they were received with small-arms fire. They responded to the fire." Several of the guerrillas were reported to have escaped. Yon Sosa, a lieutenant in the Guatemalan army until 1960 when he joined the rebellion against President Miguel Ydigoras Fuentes, had headed the Maoist MR-13 (Movimiento Revolucionario de 13 Noviembre, or Revolutionary Movement of Nov. 13).

Other terrorist action. Among other 1970 terrorist actions:

Rudy Weissenberg Martinez, 60, one of the nation's most important coffee exporters, was released by kidnapers April 26 after payment of a large ransom. Weissenberg had been abducted April 23 by members of the Revolutionary Movement of November 13 (MR-13).

A policeman was killed and a bodyguard of President-elect Carlos Arana seriously wounded in a terrorist attack April 29. Arana's bodyguard was driving in his car when two youths in another car opened fire; Col. Arana was not present.

Marco Antonio Marroqui, mayor of Jocotan, Chiquimula, was shot in an ambush, it was reported May 6; he was the second mayor in the area to be killed by unknown assailants.

Rafael Horacio Sanchez, an active supporter of President-elect Arana, was machine-gunned to death May 11 in Guatemala City.

The British publication Latin America reported June 12 that about 30 people had been warned to leave Guatemala or face death by right-wing terrorist organizations.

Victor Rodriguez, active supporter of Arana during his election campaign, was assassinated by a group of armed men in Chiquimula, Le Monde reported July 8.

Aldana Sanchez, mayor of Zacapa, was shot to death July 12; he had received several threats from the FAR.

The home of Uruguayan Ambassador to Guatemala Atilio Arrillaga was bombed Sept. 10. The ambassador was not at home when the incident occurred.

Two Guatemalan police and a civilian, an alleged FAR deserter, were shot and killed Sept. 24.

Mario Sandoval, leader of the right-wing National Liberation Movement and president of the Guatemalan assembly, was reported Oct. 23 to have escaped

injury in an attempt to assassinate him. Two of three dynamite charges which had been placed in his car exploded.

Julio Caney Herrera, a law professor and left-of-center politician was shot to death Nov. 16 while driving to work in Guatemala City.

Three Guatemalans were found shot to death in a canyon north of Guatemala City, it was reported Dec. 10. The three persons, missing since Nov. 28, included the owner of the nation's largest radio station, a businessman and a secretary.

National Liberation Movement Deputy Arnaldo Otten Prado was shot and killed Dec. 18 while driving in his car in Guatemala City.

Jaime Monge Donis, secretary-general of the Guatemalan Labor Federation and an official of the National Social Security Institute, was shot and killed Dec. 23 as he was leaving his home in Guatemala City.

Arana takes office. Col. Carlos Arana was sworn in July 1, 1970 as president of Guatemala and pledged to the nation that he would end terrorism.

In his inaugural speech to Congress, President Arana noted that Guatemala had been faced with "an internal war that sometimes confronts fathers and sons" and promised to bring about "political pacification" in the nation.

Arana also called for a "national crusade" towards social reform. "If the peasant masses continue without land, without technical assistance and without sufficient credit, with misery and sickness as their only birthright, we will all suffer the consequences of their frustration," he said.

State of siege. President Arana imposed a 30-day state of siege Nov. 13, 1970 in response to recent acts of terrorism. In a nationwide radio address, Arana explained that the measure was taken due to the "manifest abuse of personal guarantees established in the constitution and the wave of violence." He cited kidnapings, murders and bombings during the previous two months as examples of the violence. Four policemen were reported killed Nov. 9-12, presumably by members of the terrorist Rebel Armed Forces (FAR).

Under the state of siege, or modified martial law, Arana assumed virtual dictatorial powers for a month. All political activities were suspended, and police duties were turned over to the army, which was authorized to enter and search homes and arrest persons without warrants. In addition, newspapers were prohibited from publishing any but official statements, and a 9 p.m. to 5 a.m. curfew was set.

Arana extended the state of siege for another 30 days Dec. 13. Terrorist violence was reported to have caused 15 deaths during the initial 30 day state of siege period. (The curfew was lifted Jan. 30, 1971 although the state of siege was continued until Nov. 23, 1971.)

FAR leaders get Mexican asylum: Julio Eduardo Mendez Agualar, said to be a FAR leader, received political asylum in the Mexican embassy in Guatemala City, Guatemalan officials announced Nov. 18, 1970. Mendez Aguilar had been sought by the police. Another FAR leader, Jose Antonio Sierra Gonzalez, was reported Nov. 26 to have also been granted asylum in the Mexican embassy.

Assassinations. Opposition leader Adolfo Mijangos Lopez was shot and killed by gunmen Jan. 13, 1971. Mijangos was the leader in Congress of the opposition coalition group composed of the Democratic Revolutionary Union and the Christian Democratic party.

Labor leader Tereso de Jesus Oliva was shot and killed in Guatemala City Jan. 17. Oliva was head of the Confederation of Guatemalan Workers.

Terrorists entered the British consulate in Guatemala City Jan. 20 and shot and killed the consul's bodyguard.

Opposition Congressman Jose Luis Arriaga Arriola was shot and killed near his home July 6. Arriaga Arriola, 36, a member of the opposition Revolutionary party, was the third member of the current congress to be killed.

The second in command of the secret police, Rudy Hurtarte, and his assistant were assassinated when assailants in a passing vehicle shot the two near Hurtarte's home, it was reported Sept. 14.

Killings assailed abroad. The World Confederation of Labor, meeting in Brussels, charged in a statement Feb. 9, 1971 that "since individual and collective guarantees had been suspended in Guatemala Nov. 13, 1970, the 'forces of order' had assassinated by their own hands more than 600 persons." The labor group said that a "climate of terror" existed in the country.

Guatemalan Ambassador to Venezuela Francisco Consenza Galvez resigned in disagreement with the regime of President Carlos Arana, it was reported March 2. "I am unable to defend the current regime," Consenza Galvez said. "The government should not adopt the same tactics used by the [leftist] terrorists."

Jurists denounce terror—The International Commission of Jurists, in a communique reported in the French newspaper Le Monde July 29, denounced what it called "the reign of terror in Guatemala, where, after five years, more than 8,000 persons have been assassinated." According to the Commission, more than four assassinations were committed each day by rightist terrorist groups.

Alejos kidnapped. It was reported Aug. 4, 1971 that Roberto Alejos, 46, wealthy Guatemalan businessman and honorary chairman of the Fidelity National Bank of South Miami, Fla., had been kidnapped from his car in Guatemala City.

Alejos had been the government-backed presidential candidate in 1963 but the elections were never held because of a military coup. The Alejos plantation in Guatemala had been used to train the CIA-directed 1961 exile Bay of Pigs brigade for the invasion of Cuba.

Alejos was reported to have been released by his kidnappers Dec. 23.

An unidentified official was quoted by Le Monde Dec. 26 as saying that Alejos had been exchanged for 60 political prisoners. A family spokesman denied reports that a $500,000 ransom had been paid to the kidnappers, believed to be members of the Revolutionary Armed Forces (FAR).

The police had announced Aug. 27 that two policemen and a student who had been searching for Alejos had been assassinated on the outskirts of Guatemala City. A blind student who had accompanied the three was abducted by the killers.

In a related development, it was reported Aug. 6 that Guatemalan security forces had freed Victor Kaire, an important Guatemalan bank director who had been kidnaped in July. Kaire had been found in a small store outside Guatemala City. He was freed after an intense shoot-out, in which three kidnapers, members of the National United Revolutionary Front, were reportedly killed by armed troops.

Castaneda assassinated. Olivero Castaneda Paiz, a leader of the governing Movement for National Liberation and first vice president of Congress, was shot to death in Guatemala City June 25, 1972.

Castaneda had reportedly been accused of being a leader of The White Hand, a right-wing terrorist organization. His assassination ended a period of relative political peace among the country's various terrorist groups.

Other 1972 incidents. Among other incidents involving terrorists or terrorism in Guatemala during 1972:

The army announced Jan. 10 that a group of guerrillas had killed six members of a military patrol in Peten, escaping with arms seized from the dead soldiers.

Authorities claimed that Augusto Flores Rodriguez, reputedly second in command of a left-wing guerrilla group, had been killed in a clash with soldiers in the Peten region, the Miami Herald reported May 30.

One soldier was killed and five guerrillas were arrested when an army patrol clashed with a guerrilla detachment in the Peten region, near the Mexican

border, the London newsletter Latin America reported June 23. The army reportedly claimed to have found an important guerrilla base and arsenal in the region.

Francisco Lopez, reportedly the second in command of Guatemala's guerrillas, was captured in the Mexican border state of Chiapas, it was reported Aug. 4.

At least five persons were killed in a gun battle Oct. 15 as security forces rescued a kidnapped businessman in Guatemala City. Police said the businessman, Rodolfo Rosenberg, escaped unharmed.

Murder of Communists reported. The Cuban press agency Prensa Latina said Guatemalan guerrillas had kidnapped a policeman, Abel Juarez Villatoro, and forced him to reveal the fate of the eight leaders of the Communist Guatemalan Labor party (PGT) who disappeared in September 1972, the newsletter Latin America reported March 2, 1973.

Juarez reportedly said the PGT leaders—six men and two women—had been arrested by police, tortured for 48 hours, and then thrown into shark-infested Pacific waters from an air force plane.

The government had denied any knowledge of the victims' disappearance.

The government's move against the PGT leaders baffled the victims' relatives and other politicians, who considered the PGT membership moderate, the Times of the Americas reported April 4. The party reportedly had survived the government's 1971 anti-leftist campaign by pledging not to practice or advocate violence against authorities.

Deputy killed. Hector Solis Juarez, secretary of Congress, was shot to death by unidentified gunmen June 5, 1973.

Election controversy, violence. The government apparently used fraud to secure the victory of its presidential candidate in elections March 3, 1974, causing wide protests and a renewal of political violence.

High government, military and diplomatic sources had admitted the victory of retired Gen. Efrain Rios Montt of the National Opposition Front (FNO), according to numerous press reports. However, the government announced March 6 that retired Gen. Kjell Laugerud Garcia of the ruling Nationalist Coalition was the winner.

Official results gave Laugerud 260,313 votes, 41.2% of the total; Rios Montt 225,586 votes, or 35.7%; and Col. Ernesto Paiz Novales of the Revolutionary Party 145,967 votes, or 23.1%. Since no candidate won an absolute majority, the outgoing Congress, dominated by the government, proclaimed Laugerud the winner March 12.

The FNO claimed Rios Montt had won 44.8% of the vote, Laugerud 33.6% and Paiz Novales 21.6%, according to a report March 7. Its claim to victory had been bolstered March 4 by official returns from 373 of 493 precincts in Guatemala City, which gave Rios Montt 56% of the vote and Laugerud 28%.

Thousands of peasants armed with clubs and machetes were trucked into Guatemala City March 4 by members of the right-wing National Liberation Movement of the ruling coalition, to beat up students and journalists who supported Rios Montt. In the interior, four opposition members were murdered: FNO mayoral candidate Victor Manuel Monterroso was killed in the southern provincial capital of Cuilapa, and three students belonging to the FNO's Christian Democratic Party were found dead beside a highway in Zacapa Department.

Edmundo Guerra Theilheimer, a leftist leader unaffiliated with any of the presidential candidates, was machine-gunned to death by unknown rightists in Guatemala City March 11. Guerra, a lawyer who gave free legal advice to the poor and to the Committee of Relatives of Disappeared Persons, which held authorities responsible for the death or disappearance of hundreds of persons in recent years, had said before the election: "It doesn't make any difference who wins. Violence and repression will continue."

The Guatemalan Labor Party, eight of whose leaders had been murdered in 1972, had charged in February that rightist "death squads" had murdered at least 12 persons in January and February, the Cuban Press agency Prensa Latina reported Feb. 23.

Four Guatemala City newspapermen had been threatened by a "death squad" and eight radio stations in the capital had received government notice of cancellation of their right to broadcast, it was reported Feb. 23.

The Guatemalan Newspapermen's Association had reported shortly before the assassination that right-wing terrorists calling themselves the "Death Squad" had sent it a series of threatening letters, one of which read in part: "This is our final warning. Any further attacks in the press against the government, President [Carlos] Arana or President-elect [Gen. Kjell] Laugerud mean death—starting with the officers of [your] association."

Mario Monterroso Armas, a Guatemala City radio newscaster who had supported the opposition Christian Democratic Party in the March 3 vote, was murdered March 27.

Leonel Bojorges Gallardo, a former national police chief of detectives under President Arana, was shot to death by unidentified men in Guatemala City April 26. Col. Juan de Dios Aguilar, a wealthy landowner and PID presidential candidate in the 1966 election, was held March 27–April 23 by kidnappers who at one point demanded the return to Guatemala of retired Gen. Efrain Rios Montt, the opposition candidate in the March presidential election. Aguilar said his family had ransomed him.

The "Death Squad" claimed 10 more victims, most presumably killed for being petty criminals, according to reports April 16–May 24. Fifteen other persons were killed for apparently political reasons, some after being tortured, according to the French news agency Agence France-Presse May 4.

HAITI

Repression & Exile Activity

OAS Report Charges Terrorism. A report by the Organization of American States' Inter-American Commission of Human Rights charged the Haitian government with sanctioning a reign of terror and assassination in the country, Reuters reported Aug. 2, 1969.

The report, sent to governments of the OAS in July, was prepared from reports submitted by individual Haitians and associations. It described arbitrary arrests, disappearance of Haitian citizens and elimination of whole families. The OAS commission was not allowed to enter Haiti to verify the charges.

Exiles Cleared in Bahamas Murder. The death sentences of four Haitian exiles were voided April 8, 1969 by the Bahamas Appeals Court. The exiles had been convicted of murdering Haitian Consul Joseph Antoine Dorce June 7, 1968 on orders of the Haitian Coalition, a New York-based anti-Duvalier organization.

The Haitian Coalition Feb. 8 denied any role in the murder, though it admitted that the defendants were members of the organization.

Exile Camp Uncovered in Florida. Ten Haitians and two Americans were arrested in Florida March 12, 1969 on the discovery of what appeared to be a secret military training base for Haitian exiles.

The two Americans, thought to be in charge of the camp, were reported to be former members of the Green Berets, the U.S. Army force specializing in guerrilla warfare.

(The Haitian ambassador to the U.S., Arthur Bonhomme, said that his government knew of another training camp in Florida, about 60 miles from the one discovered, the New York Times reported March 14.)

Port-au-Prince Bombed. A four-engine Lockheed Constellation aircraft dropped six homemade bombs over Port-au-Prince June 4, 1969. The bombs—large oil drums filled with gasoline—started fires that resulted in three deaths, according to government reports. One bomb, which did not ignite, fell inside the grounds of Francois Duvalier's presidential palace. An anti-aircraft gun fired on the plane, which made two passes over the city.

A communique issued June 4 in Miami over the name of Haitian exile leader Rene J. Leon said that the Democratic Movement of Haitian Patriots "has placed its forces on Haitian soil." The statement did not reveal where or how an invasion had taken place, and there was no confirmation from Haitian or U.S. sources that exile forces had landed on the island. (The Miami Herald reported June 6 that an exile force, including at least two Americans, had left Florida during the last week of May bound for Haiti. The group of 20 was reportedly headed by Leon.)

A plane thought to be the one used in the Haitian raid made an emergency landing June 4 at a U.S. missile tracking base in the Bahamas. There were reports that it had been forced to land because of bullet holes in the fuel tank. The 10 persons aboard were charged with illegal entry by Bahama authorities June 5. Nine of them were returned to the U.S., and eight—six Americans and two Haitian exiles—were charged June 9 in U.S. District Court in Miami with violation of the U.S. Neutrality Act in connection with the Port-au-Prince bombing. Those charged included Leon, who had gone into exile in 1962 and had been sentenced in 1967 in connection with an abortive Haitian invasion attempt, and Gerald Smith, a Haitian who was arrested last March for involvement with the exile training camp discovered in the Florida Everglades.

U.S. envoy held, ransomed. U.S. Ambassador Clinton E. Knox was seized by three armed Haitians in Port-au-Prince Jan. 23, 1973 but released the next day in exchange for the release of 12 Haitian prisoners, safe conduct to Mexico and a $70,000 ransom.

Knox's captors were reported to have links with exile groups that had opposed the Haitian government for years. They said the persons released were political prisoners. The abductors and freed prisoners were flown to Mexico, where they were denied asylum Feb. 1. They then continued on to Chile, whose government gave them transit visas.

In Washington, a State Department spokesman said Knox's captors had demanded a $500,000 ransom, but this had been refused by Secretary of State

William P. Rogers. The spokesman said he did not know who paid the final ransom, but newspapers reported the $70,000 had been offered by French mediators during the tense all-night negotiations that preceded Knox's release.

Knox was seized as he drove to his residence in Port-au-Prince Jan. 23. He was forced at gunpoint into another car, in which he and his captors entered the residence grounds. Knox then telephoned the U.S. consul general in Port-au-Prince, Ward L. Christensen, who joined him at the residence and was held until the final agreement was reached with the kidnappers.

In New York, a Haitian exile group called the Coalition of National Liberation Brigades said that the released "prisoners have been under constant threat to be eliminated in case of any disorder in the country. And disorder there will be. ... The actual, archaic, farcical government, led by Clinton Knox and the State Department, must go."

The Haitian exiles—four men and a woman, most of them teachers—said Jan. 24 that they belonged to the National Antiduvalierist Movement, an organization without ideology or international political affiliations which sought only to free Haiti from the dictatorship of President Jean-Claude Duvalier. The kidnappers' leader was identified as Raymond Napoleon.

MEXICO

Many Guerrilla Bands Active

At least a half-dozen guerrilla-terrorist groups were active in Mexico during the early 1970s. As in other countries, the New York Times pointed out May 7, 1973, Mexico had "many leftist guerrillas . . . who may or may not be Communists and who periodically resort to terrorism to get money for arms or to call attention to their cause." The "guerrilla groups in various regions" were reported to "have little or no contact with one another," although some were alleged to receive aid and training from such foreign sources as the U.S.S.R. and North Korea.

Among Mexico's guerrilla-terrorist groups were the MAR (Movimiento de Accion Revolucionaria, or Revolutionary Action Movement, also called Movement for [or of] Revolutionary Action), the FUZ (Frente Urbano Zapatista, Zapata [or Zapatist] Urban Front) and the presumably Trotskyist FRAP (Fuerzas Revolucionarias Armadas del Pueblo, or People's Revolutionary Armed Forces).

5 Soviet diplomats expelled. The Mexican regime March 18, 1971 declared five members of the Soviet embassy in Mexico persona non grata and ordered them to leave the country "as soon as possible." The diplomats were Charge d'Affaires Dimitri Diakonov; First Secretary Boris Kolmiakov; Second Secretary Boris Voskovoinikov; Second Secretary Oleg Netchiporenko; and Alexandre Bolchakov, whose title was not given.

The Mexican expulsion order gave no reasons for the action, but press reports connected it with the arrests announced March 15 of 19 Mexican revolutionaries whose leaders, the government charged, had studied in the Soviet Union in 1963 and traveled to North Korea in 1968 and 1969 to study terrorism and guerrilla warfare.

Mexican Attorney General Julio Sanchez Vargas accused the Soviet Union of arranging and aiding the students' activities. The arrested revolutionaries said in a news conference March 16 that they were members of the Revolutionary Action Movement (MAR).

Mexican President Luis Echeverria explained March 20 that the Soviet diplomats had been expelled because to do otherwise could have brought on "tragic consequences, like in other countries."

Guerrillas accused in robberies. Mexico City Mayor Octavio Senties said in a TV statement July 22, 1971 that terrorists "with ties to the outside" had begun a campaign of assaults against banks, businesses and bus terminals in the city. He charged that the Movement of Revolutionary Action (MAR) had intended "to destroy society" and was responsible for the recent assaults.

Senties said the terrorist thefts "have all been executed in the same manner," by youths armed with machine guns or heavy rifles, using disguises and stolen cars.

The government had announced July 21 the capture of six men and a woman accused of robberies to finance terrorist activities. Those arrested had in their possession rifles, pistols, grenades and a large quantity of ammunition. The group was alleged to be part of a guerrilla organization that was centered in the state of Guerrero.

Government sources asserted Sept. 12 that five men and one woman who had robbed a bank in Leon Sept. 9 were members of the MAR.

President warns against subversives. In his first state of the union address since he assumed his office in 1970, President Louis Echeverria Alvarez warned Mexico's extreme leftists Sept. 1, 1971 against taking the law into their own hands and argued that violence would only lead to anarchy.

Echeverria also charged that many of the recent robberies in Mexico had been the work of subversive groups "connected with underground movements from abroad."

Terrorism. Among developments involving terrorism in Mexico:

Mario Renato Menendez Rodriguez, publisher of the leftist magazine Por que?, was arrested Feb. 12, 1971 and charged with financing guerrilla training camps in Tabasco and Chiapas states and with masterminding a number of terrorist bombings in Mexico City. Six other persons were also arrested in connection with the charges.

Melchor Ortega, 77, president of the ruling National Revolutionary party (1931–33), was shot and killed along with his chauffeur in an ambush north of Acapulco, it was reported March 10, 1971.

Guerrillas based in the mountains of Guerrero state were officially charged with kidnapping a wealthy banker and with distributing the ransom among the area's poor peasants, it was reported Sept. 11, 1971. The group's commander, Genaro Vasquez Rojas, was also held

responsible for the death of another kidnap victim and for 15 other robberies and kidnappings.

Industrialist kidnapped, released. Police reported that Julio Hirschfeld Almada, 54, industrialist and director of the nation's airport system, had been kidnapped Sept. 27, 1971 by three men and a woman.

Hirschfeld was released unharmed Sept. 29 after payment of 3 million pesos ($240,000).

Hirschfeld's abduction was originally blamed on the MAR. But the Washington Post Nov. 29 reported a shift of blame to a right-wing group, the FUZ (Zapata Urban Front), whose objective was to provoke government repression of the left. The FUZ later claimed credit for the kidnapping and was reported Nov. 27 to have announced that it had distributed $24,000 of the $240,000 ransom to the poor of Mexico City.

Prisoner exchange for kidnap victim. The Mexican government agreed Nov. 28 to exchange a group of political prisoners for the life of a kidnap victim, Dr. Jaime Castrejon Diez, rector of the State University of Guerrero who was kidnapped Nov. 19, 1971.

Castrejon Diez, millionaire owner of the Coca-Cola bottling concession in Guerrero, was released Dec. 1, two days after his family paid a $200,000 ransom and nine political prisoners (eight men and one woman) were flown to Cuba, where they were accepted by the Castro government for "humanitarian reasons," according to a Nov. 30 Havana Radio broadcast.

The abduction was believed to be work of a group of leftist rural guerrillas active in the mountains near Acapulco under command of a former schoolteacher, Genaro Vazquez Rojas. Five of the prisoners exchanged were said to be close associates of Vazquez Rojas and the woman was said to be his sister-in-law.

Priests explain crimes. The Miami Herald reported Feb. 25, 1972 that Bishop Manuel Talamas y Camanadari and the priests of his diocese had issued a statement in Ciudad Juarez attributing the recent outbreak of kidnappings and robberies to "a desperate struggle for freedom and justice."

The priests said incidents of violence since the student disorders of 1968 were not "isolated acts of common crime" but "links in an ever-expanding chain," and often "the dramatic outcries of men who, having been systematically barred from legal and democratic paths, have turned to violence as a means of dealing with an even greater violence."

The gap between rich and poor, the priests continued, was increasing daily, and people "are oppressed by an unjust system that denies them adequate participation at any level, economic, political or cultural."

Guerrilla leader killed. Guerrilla leader Genaro Vasquez Rojas died Feb. 2, 1972 in the state of Michoacan in what Mexican officials described as a car accident. Conflicting reports cited in U.S. newspapers Feb. 3 maintained, however, that Vasquez Rojas died in a shootout with agents of the Ciudad Hidalgo judicial police.

Vasquez Rojas had been sought by police since 1968, when he escaped from prison after serving two years of a life sentence for agitation and killing a policeman.

Vasquez Rojas had recently led the Southern Liberation Army (ELS), one of Mexico's most active guerrilla movements, which operated in the mountains of Guerrero.

Vasquez Rojas' death was followed by the discovery of ELS camps, stores and information networks, and by the arrest of eight members of the movement Feb. 8 in Chipalcingo. Rafael Equihua Palomares, described as Vasquez Rojas' second in command, was said to have revealed after his arrest that he had received guerrilla training in Nanking, China in 1969.

Soldiers ambushed. Ten soldiers were killed and two seriously wounded in the state of Guerrero June 25, 1972 in an ambush by alleged members of the Zapata Liberation Front.

Troops were killed Aug. 23 when guerrillas ambushed 2 army trucks in Guerrero. The Defense Ministry said Aug. 24 that seven soldiers had been killed, but the military commander in the area, Gen. Joaquin Solano, said Aug. 25 that 18 soldiers had died. Guerrilla leader Lucio Cabanas reportedly took credit for the ambushes in letters sent to five newspapers.

Peasants executed—Six peasants in the village of Peloncillo (Guerrero state) were executed by soldiers April 25, 1973 for allegedly sending food supplies to the guerrilla group headed by Lucio Cabanas, the mayor of the village reported. The official said the victims' wives and relatives had been forced to dig graves for them.

The executions reportedly followed the murder of a kidnapped local landowner by the Cabanas group after his family refused to pay $240,000 ransom.

Plane hijacked to Cuba. Four members of the Armed Communist League, a small guerrilla group, hijacked a Mexican airliner with 75 passengers in Monterrey Nov. 8, 1972. They then flew to Havana after obtaining arms, release of five imprisoned comrades, a government promise to drop charges against two fugitive comrades, and a ransom of about $330,000.

Cuba returned the plane and passengers Nov. 9, but kept the 11 guerrillas and the ransom. Mexico asked for extradition of seven of the guerrillas Nov. 16, but Cuba refused Nov. 30 on grounds that their action was "political."

The five prisoners released to the hijackers reportedly had been arrested in Monterrey Nov. 7 during a police search for guerrillas. Police action intensified in Monterrey and Mexico City Nov. 10. In reporting on the operation, the Mexican press admitted the existence of urban guerrillas for the first time.

Other developments. Among other events in 1972 involving terrorists and terrorism:

In Puebla July 25, university students demonstrated with teachers, peasants and workers to protest the murder, apparently by right-wing terrorists, of Joel Arriaga Navarro, a left-wing architect and headmaster of the local university's preparatory school.

Mexico's Independence Day celebrations Sept. 16 were marred by at least 12 bomb explosions in four cities that injured one person and caused considerable property damage. Seven of the blasts reportedly damaged U.S.-owned businesses.

Police had dismantled the People's Union, a small terrorist organization which had set off bomb explosions in several parts of the country over the previous few months, the French newspaper Le Monde reported Oct. 19.

U.S. envoy kidnapped, ransomed. The U.S. consul general in Guadalajara, Terrance G. Leonhardy, was kidnapped by leftist guerrillas May 4, 1973 but freed unharmed May 7 after the Mexican government agreed to a number of demands, including freedom and safe conduct to Cuba for 30 alleged political prisoners. Payment of $80,000 ransom was also reported.

The freed prisoners, 26 men and four women, arrived in Havana on a Mexican airliner May 6. They asserted that they would return to Mexico to fight the government. Mexican authorities called them "common delinquents," but press sources said most of them belonged to urban guerrilla groups, which had carried out other kidnappings and bank robberies. The best known of those released was Jose Bracho Campos, an associate of the late guerrilla leader Genaro Vasquez Rojas.

Leonhardy was kidnapped by members of the People's Revolutionary Armed Forces, who demanded May 5 that the government free the prisoners and transport them to Cuba; order the national press to publish a guerrilla communique; suspend the police and military search for Leonhardy; and allow the Cuban ambassador to go on television to confirm the safe arrival in Havana of the prisoners.

President Luis Echeverria Alvarez quickly agreed to meet the demands, saying his government prized human life highly. The U.S. reiterated its stance against yielding to extortion or blackmail for the release of officials abroad, and left the matter in Mexican hands.

The demands were met May 6, but Leonhardy was not released for another day, leading to speculation the guerrillas had asked other concessions from the government. The governor of Jalisco state, Alberto Orozco Romero, said May 8 that Leonhardy's wife had paid the guerrillas $80,000 ransom, which she borrowed from a local bank.

The guerrilla communique, published in the press May 6 and broadcast over television and radio, denounced Mexico's low health standards, its illiteracy and exorbitant credit rates, blaming the misery of impoverished workers and peasants on the concentration of wealth in the hands of a few, the outflow of Mexican capital abroad, and government repression of students, workers and peasants who tried to organize against authorities.

The guerrillas denounced the government for trying to "convince the people that we are common delinquents, hired killers, cattle rustlers, enemies of the country. Today, for the first time and not voluntarily, the mass media are serving the proletarian cause."

Guerrillas arrested. Jalisco State authorities Jan. 10, 1974 announced arrest of three leftist guerrillas, one of whom reportedly participated in the October 1973 kidnap-ransom of the honorary British consul in Guadalajara, Anthony Duncan Williams.

The guerrilla, identified as Jose de Jesus Ramirez Meza, reportedly admitted membership in the September 23 Communist League, held responsible for Williams' abduction as well as the October 1973 kidnap-murder of Mexican industrialist Fernando Aranguren.

Another guerrilla, Pedro Orozco Guzman, killed by police Dec. 24, 1973, confessed before dying that he had participated in the Williams and Aranguren abductions and the May 1973 kidnap-ransom of the U.S. consul general in Guadalajara, Terrance Leonhardy, according to the London newsletter Latin America Jan. 4.

U.S. aide murdered. The U.S. vice consul in Hermosillo (Sonora State), John Patterson, disappeared March 22, 1974 after leaving his consulate with an un-identified man. A note delivered to the consulate the same day said he had been kidnapped by the "People's Liberation Army." A mutilated body found in the desert near Hermosillo July 8 was posi-tively identified July 10 as that of Patter-son.

The U.S. consulate in Hermosillo had received a note the day Patterson vanished in which presumed kidnappers demanded a $500,000 ransom for the diplomat. Pat-terson's wife Ann subsequently said she had attempted to deliver the ransom money but had been unable to make contact with the abductors.

Mexican authorities July 10 asserted Patterson's kidnappers were not left-wing guerrillas, as some early reports had sug-gested, but persons from the U.S. seeking ransom. California resident Bobby Joe Keesee had been arrested in San Diego May 28 and indicted by a local grand jury June 7 on charges of causing Patterson's kidnapping.

Guerrero senator kidnapped. In what was described as the largest military operation in three decades, some 16,000 troops—one-third of the Mexican army—moved into the mountains of Guerrero June 27, 1974 to search for Sen. Ruben Figueroa, who apparently had been abducted by left-wing guerrillas led by Lucio Cabanas. Figueroa remained a captive for more than three months be-fore being released.

Figueroa, a local gubernatorial candi-date who advocated amnesty for rural insurgents, was kidnapped May 30 when he went into the mountains at Cabanas' invitation to negotiate a truce with Ca-banas' "Poor People's Party." An alleged party communique to the Acapulco press June 2 confirmed Figueroa's abduction and demanded that all troops and police be withdrawn from four Guerrero lo-calities as a first step toward negotiating the senator's release.

The government said June 4 it would comply with the alleged guerrilla demand, and Defense Minister Gen. Hermenegildo Cuenca Diaz asserted June 7 that "there isn't a soldier to be seen in the hills." However, student leaders claimed the sol-diers were merely deployed in civilian clothes, and a second alleged communique from Cabanas June 13 asserted soldiers were still "pursuing us, thus endangering the life of the man they want to rescue alive." Cuenca Diaz repeated June 14 that troops had been removed from the area.

President Luis Echeverria Alvarez ordered troops into the Guerrero moun-tains June 26 after the press received another alleged communique from Ca-banas making numerous demands, in-cluding a $4 million ransom for Figueroa's release, freedom for political prisoners and common criminals, delivery of 100 automatic rifles and 50 pistols, dis-tribution of tape recordings of speeches by guerrilla leaders and solution of numerous conflicts involving workers and peasants.

Attorney General Pedro Ojeda Pullada officially rejected the demands, asserting: "The people and the government do not make pacts with criminals. Public order cannot be negotiated."

Press sources expressed doubts about the authenticity of the June 26 commu-nique, noting Cabanas rarely made such unrealistic demands.

Figueroa was freed Sept. 8 during an alleged shootout between his captors and pursuing army troops.

Defense Minister Gen. Hermenegildo Cuenca Diaz said in a communique Sept. 8 that Figueroa and four persons kid-napped along with him escaped during a gun battle in the mountains of Guerrero State. Cuenca asserted soldiers killed or wounded a number of the abductors, members of Lucio Cabanas' Poor People's Party.

Subsequent press reports alleged that one of the captives, Luis Cabanas, a cousin of Lucio, had been fatally wounded in the shootout. (Luis Cabanas had ac-companied Figueroa into the Guerrero mountains May 30 as an intermediary in an attempt to arrange a truce between Lucio and the government.)

Cuenca's account of the Figueroa's es-cape was contradicted by an article prepared by the left-wing magazine Por que? and reported by Latin America. According to Por que?, Figueroa had been ransomed by his family, and he and his companions were being returned in the care of a group of peasants, who were attacked by the soldiers to give the appearance that Figueroa was being "saved."

President's kin kidnapped. In a 1974 incident, members of the leftist People's Revolutionary Armed Forces (FRAP) kidnapped President Luis Echeverria's father-in-law, Jose Guadalupe Zuno Hernandez, and held him for 11 days, during which Zuno made a tape recording praising his abductors and denouncing Echeverria's administration.

Zuno, a former Jalisco State governor who remained powerful in Mexican politics, was seized in Guadalajara Aug. 28. A FRAP communique received by the Mexico City newspaper Excelsior Aug. 30 threatened his execution unless the government paid a $1.6 million ransom, freed 10 political prisoners and flew them to Cuba, and authorized publication of a FRAP political statement in leading newspapers.

The government refused to negotiate with the guerrillas or meet their demands, in accordance with a policy set by Echeverria in 1973, after the FRAP secured the release of 30 political prisoners by kidnapping U.S. Consul Terrance G. Leonhardy. An official statement declared Aug. 29 that "the government does not negotiate with criminals."

Excelsior received a picture of Zuno in captivity and a tape recording of a conversation between Zuno and a FRAP member Sept. 6. In the recording, Zuno described his treatment by the abductors as "magnificent," praised the FRAP and leftist guerrilla leader Lucio Cabanas, and criticized the government for being "on the side of capitalist reaction."

Zuno was released Sept. 7. At a press conference the next day, he denied making the tape recording under duress and repeated his criticism of the government, which he said had "fallen under the control of the reactionary forces of the world." Zuno described his abductors as "confused boys who want to change the world but don't know how to do it," and

said they were not nearly "as dangerous for Mexicans as the CIA [U.S. Central Intelligence Agency], the Yankee imperialists and the capitalists who have respect for nothing."

The government announced the arrest of one of Zuno's alleged abductors Sept. 3 and 14 more Sept. 26.

Other 1974 incidents. Among developments involving terrorism in Mexico in 1974:

Guerrillas ambushed a police patrol outside Acapulco Jan. 14, killing three officers and taking one hostage.

In Oaxaca, presumed members of the September 23rd Communist League Jan. 19 abducted Raymundo Soberanis Otero, uncle of Guerrero Gov. Israel Nogueda Otero. League members asserted Feb. 26 that they had executed Soberanis "for being a bourgeois."

A policeman in Culiacan was kidnapped, tortured and killed, according to the Miami Herald Jan. 25.

The deputy mayor of Acapulco, Vicente Rueda Saucedo, was kidnapped Jan. 29 by avowed members of the "Revolutionary Armed Forces," and released Feb. 11 after payment of a $240,000 ransom. The abductors initially demanded $400,000 and release of some 50 peasants held since mid-1973 on suspicion of belonging to an armed band that had killed 30 soldiers.

Three peasant leaders in Guerrero State were killed apparently by assassins hired by landlords, it was reported Feb. 8.

Authorities reported seven bomb blasts in Guadalajara and Oaxaca, it was reported Feb. 26. Three of the targets were U.S.-owned firms—Pepsi-Cola, Coca-Cola and Union Carbide.

Jose Ignacio Olivares Torres, a leader of the September 23rd Communist League, was shot to death in Guadalajara, reportedly by a right-wing "death squad," according to the newsletter Latin America Feb. 15.

Salvador Alfaro Martinez, alleged leader of the September 23rd Communist League, was killed in a shootout with police outside Guadalajara May 1, according to police sources May 3.

The director of public security for Yucatan State and seven of his subordinates had been arrested on charges of assassinating Efrain Calderon Lara, a young law graduate who had been organizing workers in Merida into unions outside the Confederation of Workers of Mexico, the powerful labor organization allied with the ruling Revolutionary Institutional Party, it was reported May 12.

Pedro Sarquis, a Guadalajara millionaire kidnapped June 4, was found dead in a city street June 7. A note in his pocket explained he had died of a heart attack; it was signed by the "Salvador Allende Guerrilla Commando."

Francisco Preciado Arteaga, a Guadalajara student leader, and Jaime Lopez Salazar, an agronomy student and local soccer star, were shot to death June 27. Another student leader had been assassinated May 5, and two other students had been gunned down the week before the June 27 killings, according to the newspaper Excelsior June 28.

Unidentified persons set off bombs July 15 at Guadalajara headquarters of the ruling Revolutionary Institutional Party and at barracks of the 15th military zone, causing extensive property damage but no casualties.

Margarita Saad de Baz-Baz, kidnapped by women of the People's Revolutionary Armed Forces (FRAP) May 30, was found dead in Acapulco Sept. 13, one day after her family paid a $320,000 ransom. Police reports said she was strangled by her captors.

PERU

Terrorism Curbed

Guerrilla-terrorist activity in Peru was reported to be at a low level in the early 1970s as a result of forceful government action. The pro-Castro MIR (Movimiento de Izquierda Revolucionaria, or Leftist Revolutionary Movement) was said to have become "inactive" by 1974, while the ELN (Ejercito de Liberacion Nacional, or National Liberation Army) was described as "seriously weakened."

Death penalty for terrorists. The government Nov. 30, 1971 announced a law

establishing the death penalty for terrorists using "explosives or bombs." Other sanctions would include prison sentences of no less than 25 years in cases of attacks resulting in personal injury, and no less than 20 years, or more than 25 years in cases resulting in destruction or danger to property.

Terrorists arrested. The Interior Ministry said March 16, 1972 that 12 leftist terrorists accused of murdering two policemen, robbing several banks and organizing strikes had been arrested. The terrorists, allegedly members of the Maoist Revolutionary Vanguard, were charged with attacking the armed forces and the security of the state.

According to La Prensa of Buenos Aires March 17, the group was linked with recent mining and agrarian strikes in the north of Peru.

The regime said it had captured two groups of terrorists, among whose members were elements of the opposition American Popular Revolutionary Alliance party (APRA) and the extremist Trotskyist party, the Miami Herald reported May 20. It was the first time members of APRA had been accused directly of terrorist acts.

Guerrilla group broken up. The Interior Ministry said Aug. 3, 1972 that a guerrilla group operating in the northern department of Jaen had been broken up by security forces. Eight guerrillas were reported arrested, but seven others, including leader Gonzalo Fernandez Gasco, reportedly escaped.

According to the ministry, the band was connected with the Leftist Revolutionary Movement (MIR). However, MIR sources said Aug. 6 that the guerrillas were led by "dissidents" of the movement.

URUGUAY

Tupamaros Suppressed

The most famous of Latin America's guerrilla/terrorist groups is probably Uru-

*guay's Tupamaros, also known as the MLN
(Movimiento de Liberacion Nacional, or
National Liberation Movement). Deriving
their name from Tupac Amaru II, an Inca
chief who had rebelled against the Spanish
in Peru in the 1780s, the Tupamaros were
formed in 1962 as a Castro-type movement.
During their heyday, they attracted considerable acclaim in urban guerrilla circles
through such exploits as the kidnapping of
diplomats and the robbing of banks. Their
activities, however, were all but completely
suppressed as a result of a strong government anti-terrorist campaign that started in
1972 and apparently was one of the factors
that put Uruguay under virtual dictatorial
rule by mid-1973.*

Tupamaro Leader Arrested. Jorge
Manera Lluveras, reportedly a principal
leader of the Tupamaros, was arrested
March 21, 1969 in an action taken in
Montevideo by more than 1,000 police.
Eight other persons suspected of belong-
ing to the Tupamaros were also arrested.

Manera was accused of leading the
Aug. 7, 1968 kidnapping of Ulises
Pereira Reverbel, president of the state-
owned telephone and electricity service
and adviser to President Pacheco. (Pereira had been released unharmed after
five days following a Tupamaro announcement that the future safety of
public officials would depend "on the
behavior of the repressive forces and
the fascist groups at their service.")
Manera was also reported to have led
an armed attack Feb. 18, on the casino at
Punta del Este, where $220,000 was
stolen.

(The New York Times reported Jan.
23 that the Tupamaros was a well-dis-
ciplined urban guerrilla group numbering about 50 activitists and about 1,000
"support personnel," according to police estimates. The core of the organization was reported to include elements
of Uruguay's political and professional
elite, and members were believed to
hold important positions in ministries,
banks, universities and labor unions.
Operating with small, clandestine cells,
the group was reported to have organized
bombings, bank robberies, strikes and
riots.)

Town raided in honor of Che. In honor
of the second anniversary of the death of
Ernesto (Che) Guevara Oct. 8, 1969,
about 40 Tupamaros raided the town of
Pando, robbed three banks and seized its
main police station. In a gun battle with
police, three Tupamaros were reported
killed and 15 captured. A bystander and a
policeman were also reported killed. (The
Tupamaros were reported by the Washington Post Dec. 9 to have killed at least
six policemen since July. Their earlier
policies appeared to have emphasized
avoidance of bloodshed.)

Kidnapped banker released. Caetano
Pellegrini Giampietro, a prominent
banker and publisher of the newspapers
La Manana and El Diario, was released
Nov. 21, 1969 after being held for 73 days
by Tupamaros members. Pellegrini, 46,
was released for about $60,000 in
ransom, which had been donated, at the
insistence of the Tupamaros, to a medical clinic of a meat workers' union.

Pellegrini had been abducted from his
office Sept. 9. The incident took place
only hours after a violent clash between
police and striking employes who were
demonstrating in favor of 18 bank officials staging a hunger strike to protest
dismissal of numerous employes of
government-controlled banks.

In a clandestine radio broadcast Sept.
10, the Tupamaros threatened to kill
Pellegrini if the government of President
Jorge Pacheco Areco employed repressive measures against the striking
workers.

Terrorist attacks increase. Urban
terrorism was on the upswing in Montevideo following a guerrilla raid on a government armory late in May 1970.

Among the developments reported:

Thirteen female Tupamaros escaped
from Montevideo's women's prison
March 8 during a religious service.

Terrorists, identified by police as members of the Tupamaros, staged the largest
single robbery in Uruguay's history
April 5 and apparently escaped with
$400,000 in gold coins and equipment
from a property management firm. The

police April 17 arrested Juan Almiratti, said to be an important Tupamaros leader, in connection with the case.

Terrorists killed the chief of Uruguay's police intelligence unit, Hector Moran Charquero, April 13 in Montevideo. Moran Charquero headed a special anti-guerrilla police unit, which had recently been charged with torturing political prisoners.

Fifty members of the Tupamaros broke into a naval training center in Montevideo May 29 and seized more than 700 weapons and a large quantity of ammunition. The armed guerrillas, several wearing naval uniforms, overpowered the guards before the raid. There were no injuries reported.

One terrorist was killed, two wounded and several captured during gun battles with security forces May 31 as authorities searched for the Tupamaros involved in the raids. (Alberto Cia del Campo, a suspected Tupamaros leader, was arrested June 14 and charged with participating in the raid.)

A group of terrorists raided the Swiss embassy in Montevideo June 12, stealing documents, typewriters and a photocopying machine.

The Palestine Bank was robbed June 23, and terrorists fled with more than $72,000. A branch of the Union of Uruguayan Banks was robbed of $28,000 June 17.

Hector Amodio Perez, also known as Ernesto, was reportedly arrested in Montevideo July 1. Perez was said to be a top Tupamaro leader.

In a series of six attacks in Montevideo July 4, the Tupamaros killed one policeman, and wounded five others seriously. The attacks followed a report in the newspaper El Debate about the possibility of a truce between the government and the Tupamaros; the truce was supposed to have gone into effect July 4.

The Tupamaros continued their attacks July 11 and 12 with a series of raids on the homes of policemen. No injuries were reported but damage was done to each home.

'Tupamaros' censored. The government Nov. 30, 1969 had reaffirmed its prohibition of the use of the word "Tupamaros"

by the press and extended the censorship to include words such as "commandos," "ideological criminals," "cells," "extremists" and "subversives." Permissible descriptions included the words "delinquents" and "rapists." The government also had censored reporting of any guerrilla activities except as reported in official statements. Radio and TV broadcasts were also subjected to censorship.

The government June 25, 1970 suspended for five days the leftist newspaper El Popular and El Debate, the newspaper representing a sector of the opposition National Party. The papers were accused of "violation of security measures." El Debate had published the report on a possible truce with the Tupamaros and reportedly was about to publish strong charges made in parliament by Nationalist Deputy Alberto Gutierrez against President Jorge Pacheco Areco. According to Gutierrez, President Pacheco had personally ordered the killing of Ricardo Zabalza Waksman, a Tupamaro leader who reportedly took part in the raid on the town of Pando. Gutierrez also charged that corruption existed at the top of the special anti-guerrilla police force.

Foreign Diplomats Attacked

U.S.' Mitrione kidnapped and killed. Dan A. Mitrione, 49, a U.S. AID (Agency for International Development) official assigned as an adviser to the Uruguayan police, was kidnapped by members of the Tupamaros in Montevideo July 31, 1970. His body was found Aug. 10 in a stolen car in Montevideo. He had been shot twice in the head.

Brazilian Vice Consul Aloysio Mares Dias Gomide had been kidnapped the same day as Mitrione.

In apparently coordinated actions, the terrorists also attempted to kidnap two other U.S. diplomats—Michael Gordon Jones, 27, second secretary to the U.S. embassy in Montevideo, and cultural attache Nathan Rosenfeld, 48—but were unsuccessful.

In a statement delivered to the newspaper El Diario Aug. 2, the kidnappers demanded the release of all political prisoners in Uruguay as ransom for the two diplomats. However, in its first official comment on the abductions, the Uruguayan government Aug. 3 indicated that it was not yet ready to negotiate with the Tupamaros, although it did not rule out future negotiations.

In an earlier development, terrorists had kidnapped Judge Daniel Pereyra Manelli from his home in Montevideo July 28. Pereyra, a criminal court judge, was released Aug. 4. The judge conveyed a message to the government from the Tupamaros reiterating their demand that the political prisoners be released. The message also said that Mitrione, who had been wounded during the kidnapping incident, was "getting better," and that Gomide was "well."

Another American, Claude L. Fly, 65, an agricultural expert on contract to the Uruguayan government, was abducted Aug. 7.

The Tupamaros then warned Aug. 7 that Mitrione would be executed Aug. 9 if the Uruguayan government did not meet their demand to release all political prisoners, thought to number about 150. An anonymous telephone call to a radio station the afternoon of Aug. 9 announced that the execution had taken place and warned that the two other hostages would meet the same fate if the government continued its refusal to negotiate with the guerrillas.

President Jorge Pacheco Areco called Mitrione's death "the greatest attack this country's political institutions have faced in this century" and obtained Congressional passage of a measure suspending all individual civil rights for 20 days. Pacheco continued to refuse to free any prisoners, despite a threat Aug. 10 by the Tupamaros that they would kill Gomide if the government did not release the prisoners.

In a press speech Aug. 6, Pacheco had reiterated an Interior Ministry statement that the imprisoned Tupamaros were common criminals and could not be freed as political prisoners. Expressing sympathy for the hostages' families, Pacheco nevertheless affirmed that "as a president I have the supreme duty to maintain law, institutions and the intangible rights of legitimate justice."

U.S. State Department spokesman Robert J. McCloskey said Aug. 10 that the U.S. had maintained constant contact with the Uruguayan government throughout the incident but had not pressed for the release of the prisoners since it might have meant "great risks for all Americans overseas." He added that the State Department had taken a number of unspecified measures to increase the security of American diplomats abroad.

Brazilian Foreign Minister Mario Gibson Barbosa sent a sharp message to the Uruguayan government Aug. 10 requesting that no effort be spared in achieving Gomide's release.

In a massive manhunt Aug. 7, Uruguay police arrested several suspected Tupamaros leaders, including Raul Sendic, one of the founders of the guerrilla group, and Raul Bidegain Greissing, sought for kidnapings and bombings.

In three messages found Aug. 9, members of a so-called "justice squad" pledged to kill 50 "antisocial" persons for every foreigner killed by the terrorists and five for every policeman or soldier killed.

(Security officials March 20, 1973 announced the capture of four men said to have participated in Mitrione's kidnap-murder.

(Antonio Mas Mas, identified as a Spanish student who joined the Tupamaros while attending Montevideo University, was said to have killed Mitrione. His accomplices were identified as Henry Engler, Esteban Pereira and Rodolfo Wolf, arrested with him, and Armando Blanco, killed by police. Engler was said to have directed the abduction and ordered the killing.)

Government rejects ransom proposal— An offer by the Tupamaro guerrillas to release U.S. hostage Claude Fly in exchange for publication of a 1,200-word guerrilla manifesto was rejected by the government Sept. 20.

President Jorge Pacheco Areco Sept. 22 reiterated his refusal to offer any ransom for the release of Fly or Dias Gomide. Fly was reported to be ill and in need of hospital care. The guerrillas had said they would "immediately" set him free if their manifesto was broadcast over three specified radio stations and three television stations and published by six daily newspapers. The manifesto, which did not mention Dias Gomide, was critical of the Pacheco government and asserted that government officials had actually been carrying out "under the table" negotiations for the release of the two hostages, although publicly refusing to have any dealings with the guerrillas.

Since Mitrione's death, the Tupamaros had continued their antigovernment campaign with bombings, robberies and guerrilla raids. The government, for its part, made numerous arrests and continued to refuse to deal with the guerrillas. Among the developments:

Guerrillas seized a radio station Aug. 25, set off a bomb and fled. A terrorist group had taken over another radio station Aug. 21 in an unsuccessful attempt to broadcast an antigovernment statement.

Fifteen suspected Tupamaros were put on trial Sept. 2, following the sentencing of Tupamaro leader Raul Sendic and eight other guerrillas Aug. 31 to undisclosed prison sentences for "concealing knowledge" of the kidnappings and other charges.

Terrorists bombed six businesses and private homes Sept. 4 and machine-gunned the headquarters of the U.S. embassy Marine guard.

Tupamaros stole 176 pounds of dynamite and dozens of detonators from a quarry explosive store Sept. 8.

Terrorists raided a nightclub Sept. 19, locked three employes in a closet and set the building on fire. The employes broke out of the closet and extinguished the flames.

Seven police stations were attacked Sept. 21 with fire bombs, causing damages but no injuries.

Five male and four female Tupamaros robbed the Bank of the Republic early Nov. 13, taking jewels and cash whose value was ultimately reported to be $7.8 million. The guerrillas had kidnapped three bank officials and had used them as hostages to get into the bank. A bank employe apparently acted as an accomplice. The three bank officials and bank guards, who had been bound, were set free after the robbery.

Dias Gomide & Fly freed—Aloysio Mares Dias Gomide was released outside Montevideo by the Tupamaros Feb. 21, 1971. His wife, Maria Aparecida Dias Gomide, obtained his freedom after paying a ransom estimated at $250,000–$1 million.

Fly's wife, Miriam, and son, John, charged in Fort Collins, Colo. March 3 that the Uruguayan government and the U.S. State Department had refused to negotiate with the Tupamaros for Fly's release.

"There were no negotiations about his release," John Fly said. "It was just the fact that he had a heart attack and the Tupamaros were compassionate enough to release him." He continued: "I believe the refusal to negotiate is responsible for the death of Dan Mitrione and nearly for the death of my father."

Claude L. Fly, 65, was released by the Tupamaros March 2, 1971 after apparently suffering a heart attack while in their custody. The kidnappers left Fly on a stretcher in front of the British Hospital in Montevideo.

British envoy kidnapped. Tupamaros members kidnapped British Ambassador to Uruguay Geoffrey Jackson, 55, in Montevideo Jan. 8, 1971. They held him until Sept. 9.

The kidnappers, numbering about 20 and surrounding Jackson's car with five vehicles, abducted Jackson as he was being driven to the British embassy. His driver and bodyguards were dragged from the car and beaten.

In a note received by the government Jan. 10, the kidnapers made no specific ransom demand for Jackson but stipulated that the government open negotiations.

President Pacheco Areco asked Congress Jan. 11 for 90-day special police powers to aid in the search for Jackson's kidnappers. The 11-member Legislative Commission, serving during Congress' annual recess, complied with Pacheco Areco's request but reduced the duration of the emergency powers from 90 to 40 days.

Attorney general abducted. Tupamaros members kidnapped Uruguay's attorney general, Guido Berro Oribe, from his home in Montevideo March 10, 1971 and freed him March 22.

The attorney general was freed after being interrogated by a "people's tribunal" during which, according to his captors, he admitted that President Jorge Pacheco Areco had pressured the nation's public prosecutors to block the release of detained Tupamaros.

Berro Oribe was held in a "people's jail" in a cell next to British Ambassador to Uruguay Geoffrey Jackson.

Interior Minister Santiago de Brum Carbajal admitted March 24, after holding an interview with Berro Oribe, that "terrorist elements, without any doubt, have infiltrated the judicial power" of the country. De Brum Carbajal based his assertions on the fact that "the delinquents [Tupamaros] who interrogated Berro Oribe showed a knowledge of internal affairs which was very concrete and very detailed." He added that the "conspirators" had infiltrated other sectors of the government, including the executive branch.

Following Jackson's release Sept. 9, police said the ambassador had been freed on the steps of a parish church in a residential district in Montevideo. An unidentified woman caller advised the embassy of Jackson's release. The ambassador was picked up by British embassy officials and was taken to a hospital for a physical examination. He left Uruguay for Britain the next day.

The Tupamaros had issued a statement Sept. 8 saying that Jackson would soon be granted an "amnesty" since there was no further need to hold the ambassador in exchange for the release of "political prisoners." 106 Tupamaros had escaped from prison Sept. 6.

Other kidnappings. Among other terrorist kidnappings reported:

Ulyses Pereira Reverbel, director of the state-owned power and phone agency, was kidnapped by Tupamaros members March 30, 1971 and held until security forces freed him from a "people's jail" May 27, 1972. He had been kidnapped by the Tupamaros once before, in August 1968.

Alfredo Cambon, legal adviser to several large Uruguayan companies backed by American capital, was kidnapped June 23, 1971 and freed June 25. The left-wing OPR-33 (Organization of the Popular Revolution-33), named for 33 heroes of the 19th century independence movement, was allegedly responsible.

Argentine-born industrialist Jorge Berembaum, 24, was kidnapped by Tupamaros members July 12, 1971 and held until Nov. 26. In a ransom demand broadcast July 28, the kidnappers said that Berembaum's family, which owned Uruguay's biggest textile factories, would have to pay a million pesos ($300,-000) to textile workers' groups to compensate for recent factory closings.

In another guerrilla development, it was reported Oct. 23 that a group of armed Tupamaros kidnapped Jose Pereira Gonzalez, editor in chief of El Dia, a pro-government newspaper that had supported President Jorge Pacheco Areco's efforts to crush the Tupamaro organization.

French journalist Michele Ray, 34, was released Nov. 30 after being kidnapped and held for 38 hours by OPR-33.

Arrests & escapes. Lucia Topolansky, considered a key Tupamaros leader, was arrested in Montevideo Jan. 18, 1971.

Police announced Feb. 1 that Jessie Arlette Macchi, an important Tupamaro leader, had been arrested.

The arrests of two important Tupamaros were reported March 2. They were Maria Elida Serra de Devargas, 20, captured in Montevideo after a gunfight with police, and Nora Maneiro de Mansilla, 27, arrested in the city of Fray Bentos.

The police announced the escape May 26 of Juan Almiratti, 39, reportedly a top Tupamaros leader. Almiratti, a civil engineer, had been in Montevideo's Punta-Carretas prison. He had been arrested in April 1970 in connection with a robbery of a property management firm.

The government announced July 30 that 38 female Tupamaros had escaped from a maximum security prison in Montevideo and had been driven away in stolen cars. Police said the women escaped through a tunnel leading into the city's sewers. (One of the 38 escapees, Maria Teresa Labroca Ravellino, 39, considered a Tupamaros leader, was reported Oct. 5 to have been re-arrested in Montevideo.)

Tupamaros freed 106 male Tupamaros from the Punta-Carretas prison Sept. 6, 1971.

The escape was made through a 40-foot tunnel dug from a house across the street from the prison into a prison cell. The 111 prisoners, which included five "common criminals," then disappeared, presumably in automobiles or a bus.

Among the prisoners who escaped were Raul Sendic, one of the founders of the Tupamaros, and his two principal lieutenants, Jorge Manera Lluveras and Julio Marenales Sanez.

Two of the 106 escapees, Jorge Pedro Zabala and Angel Yoldi, described as Tupamaros leaders, were re-arrested Oct. 16 in the Paysandu district. Five more escapees were re-arrested Oct. 19 when police raided an alleged Tupamaros arsenal near Montevideo.

Tupamaros to Santiago. Ten Uruguayans detained in the military headquarters in Montevideo as Tupamaro guerrillas were deported to Chile, according to a report July 4, 1971.

The group, which included the wife and children of Raul Sendic, alleged leader of the Tupamaro movement, arrived with three-month tourist visas. One of the deportees said that "the authorities gave us the choice" of leaving the country or remaining in detention.

Chamber votes Pacheco impeachment. The Chamber of Deputies (lower house) voted July 23, 1971 to impeach President Jorge Pacheco Areco. It acted because the president July 15 had reinstated security measures that had been repealed by the General Assembly July 14.

Pacheco had justified his action on the grounds that he had "indisputable" proof "of the designs of certain groups and organizations to destroy the republican-democratic institutions and to attack inherent human rights," apparently referring to the Tupamaros.

The Senate decided Aug. 3 to set up a commission to investigate the Chamber's accusation that the president had violated the constitution.

The newly created commission was to give the president 10 days to answer the charges and defend his actions.

Pacheco Areco responded Aug. 4 to the commission's request by sending a brief note in which he reiterated an earlier message to the legislative general assembly justifying his reimposition of security measures—after the assembly had acted to lift them—as necessary to combat the "subversive plans" of the Tupamaro guerrillas. The president sent his interior minister, Danilo Sena, and his defense minister, Federico Garcia Capurro, to answer charges before the Senate commission, with instructions only to say that the Tupamaros posed a threat "to the security of the government."

Security Tightened

Armed forces in charge. President Pacheco Areco announced Sept. 9, 1971 that he had put the armed forces in full charge of fighting guerrilla subversion. The police had previously been charged with fighting the Tupamaros.

In a 15-minute radio and television address to the nation Sept. 11, Pacheco said his government would take even stronger measures against the Tupamaros. While he did not announce the new measures, he said he would "take all steps needed to defeat this subversion of your security."

Pacheco also assumed personal responsibility for the new anti-subversion measures.

Government candidate elected president. Amid bitter opposition accusations of electoral fraud, the government issued early figures Dec. 2, 1971 giving its Colorado party candidate, Juan Maria Bordaberry, a narrow 10,843 vote lead over National (Blanco) party candidate Sen. Wilson Ferreira Aldunate in the Nov. 28 presidential elections.

Ferreira had won the largest personal vote, but under the complex Uruguayan electoral system, votes cast for all candidates under the same party accrued to the leading party candidate.

Agriculture Minister Bordaberry, 43, a cattle rancher whose sole political venture prior to joining President Jorge Pacheco Areco's government was in a movement of the opposition National party, had been hand-picked as an alternate candidate by Pacheco.

Pacheco also ran for a second term but lost when voters rejected a constitutional amendment, voted on simultaneously with the Nov. 28 election, that would have removed the existing ban on a president succeeding himself.

Ferreira, who campaigned on a nationalist program (he would establish diplomatic relations with Cuba and nationalize the banks) and who had been promised a six-month grace period by the Tupamaros, charged the government Dec. 1 with electoral "fraud" and alleged "irregularities" in 38 Montevideo polling districts.

According to the Buenos Aires newspaper La Prensa Dec. 2, the Colorado party received 594,800 votes, the National party 583,957, and the Broad Front coalition 271,957, votes.

Majority support for the Colorados signified defeat for the Tupamaro-supported Broad Front.

Tupamaros end truce. The Tupamaros Jan. 6, 1972 announced the end of a truce they had declared for the presidential elections in November 1971.

After seizing a Montevideo radio station by force, they broadcast the announcement and blamed the government for the "civil war" affecting Uruguay, saying that it had run out of measures "to bring peace to the country."

Tupamaros raid industrial town—It was reported Jan. 6 that about 35 Tupamaros had seized weapons and dynamite in a raid on Paysandu, an industrial town 300 miles northeast of Montevideo. The raid had reportedly occurred three days before, but the action was held from newsmen by government censorship. An official in Paysandu said although the guerrillas virtually occupied some areas, the army subsequently regained control.

Other sources said the guerrillas took over the Paysandu airport and raided a police station, taking all its weapons. The raid signaled a change in Tupamaro strategy, switching attacks from Montevideo to more vulnerable towns in the interior.

State of siege regulations repealed. A joint session of Congress voted March 10, 1972 to cancel most of the curbs on civil liberties imposed by ex-President Jorge Pacheco Areco in June 1969.

Restrictions on union rights, freedom of the press and the right of public assembly were lifted, but a ban on news of guerrilla activities remained in effect, as did other state of siege regulations that were consigned to study by a 15-member inter-party commission. Congress also voted to free political prisoners by the end of April.

Shortly after the vote, Congress received a bill from President Juan Maria Bordaberry that would replace the Pacheco restrictions. The bill would empower the executive branch to declare parts of Uruguay military zones, mobilize citizens to the nation's defense and impose new controls on the press.

'State of war' declared. Congress declared a month-long "state of internal war" April 10, 1972 to help in the struggle against the Tupamaros. Tupamaros had killed four officials of Uruguay's anti-guerrilla campaign April 14, beginning a series of battles with police that left 19 dead within four days.

In ambushes in and near Montevideo April 14, Tupamaros killed police subcommissioner Oscar Delega, patrolman Alberto Leites, navy Capt. Ernesto Motto Benvenutto and former Interior Undersecretary Armando Acosta y Lara. Eight Tupamaros reportedly were killed in gun battles later that day when police invaded the districts in which the ambushes had taken place.

After an urgent Cabinet meeting April 14, Defense Minister Enrique Magnani announced that police had killed Raul Sendic, a founder of the Tupamaros. However, other sources could not confirm the claim. Interior Minister Alejandro Rivera later said that the Tupamaros' main strategist, Alberto Canadan Grajales, and another guerrilla leader, Tabare Rivero Cedres, had also been killed.

President Juan Maria Bordaberry requested the "state of war" powers and Congress granted them to the government April 15 after 20 hours of heated debate.

According to La Prensa of Buenos Aires April 16, the measure suspended individual liberties and placed the country under martial law. The government would be able to censor the press, declare curfews, search houses, detain or arrest persons and confiscate material at any time without judicial approval. Persons arrested would be tried in military courts and would not have the right to defense counsel.

'War' state extended—Congress voted May 15 to extend the "state of internal war" for 45 days, and it then voted June 30 to extend it for another 22 days and to suspend individual liberties for another 90 days. Bordaberry had requested an indefinite suspension.

During the Congressional debate June 30, Interior Minister Alejandro Rovira claimed that although the war measures had made possible military victories over the Tupamaros, the guerrillas were "not destroyed" and were "capable of rearming."

Rovira claimed that since the declaration of internal war April 15, authorities had conducted 1,093 raids, arresting 846 persons, killing 16, confiscating 317 firearms and finding 38 Tupamaro hideouts. However, Rovira's figures for all but arrests were lower than those announced by Defense Minister Enrique O. Magnani more than a month earlier.

Official hears 'death squad' testimony. Hector Gutierrez Ruiz, president of the Chamber of Deputies, was kidnapped by Tupamaros April 24, 1972 and released April 25 after hearing testimony from a captured police photographer on the existence in Uruguay of Brazilian-style political "death squads."

Gutierrez said April 25 that he had watched his captors interrogate the photographer, Nelson Bardesio, who confessed to membership in an unofficial police squad that killed suspected subversives. Gutierrez said he spoke to Bardesio several times and had the impression he was telling the truth.

(Tupamaros had sent open letters to congressmen the week before in which Bardesio gave details of some of the death squad murders in which he had participated, and asserted that three of

the officials killed by Tupamaros April 14 belonged to such bands.)

Bardesio had also claimed that the squads were backed by the Interior Ministry and had links with Brazilian and Argentine security forces.

The government had rejected Bardesio's claims, but opposition leader Wilson Ferreira Aldunate of the National (Blanco) party had supported them. Ferreira said he feared the death squads would attack not only Tupamaros but all sectors of the opposition, El Nacional of Caracas reported April 14.

(The Tupamaros were reported May 16 to have freed Bardesio.)

Tupamaro & counter-Tupamaro action. Among actions of the Tupamaros and of those fighting them during 1972's first half:

■ Two policemen and a civilian were killed Jan. 28 when Tupamaros attacked a police station in suburban Montevideo.

■ Two policemen were killed Feb. 14 when at least 40 Tupamaros raided a police station near the town of Soca, 30 miles north of Montevideo, and seized weapons.

■ Homero Farina, editor-in-chief of the pro-government newspaper Accion, was abducted in Montevideo Feb. 12 by six Tupamaros dressed in military and police uniforms. He was freed Feb. 29.

■ The Miami Herald reported March 3 that Miguel Shapire, editor of a book on the Tupamaros, had been sentenced to prison by a federal judge for "inciting to commit crimes" by "glorifying" the guerrillas.

■ Police announced March 4 that they had arrested Hector Amodio Perez, a founder of the Tupamaros and the presumed mastermind of the Punta-Carretas prison break.

La Prensa of Buenos Aires reported March 5 that Amodio Perez and several other Tupamaros had been arrested Feb. 25 in a Montevideo house in which police claimed to have found diagrams of the home of President Bordaberry.

■ Fifteen Tupamaros and 10 "common delinquents" tunneled their way out of the Punta-Carretas prison April 12.

■ Edda Fabbri Garrido, who had escaped from the Punta-Carretas jail in the Tupamaro women's prison break of July 1971, had been captured by security forces, El Nacional reported April 29. Police claimed to have arrested 10 other guerrillas on the basis of information obtained from her.

■ Tupamaros leader Nestor Peralta Larrosa was captured after "an intense search" in the state of Flores, military authorities announced May 3.

■ Julio Morato Manaro, a Montevideo physician, was shot and killed May 4 as he resisted attempts by a group of Tupamaros to kidnap him. The guerrillas reportedly sought a valuable collection of weapons owned by Morato.

■ A captured Tupamaro document indicated the guerrillas wanted to "maintain and develop relations" with revolutionary governments and movements throughout the world, authorities announced May 7.

The alleged Tupamaro document said the guerrillas would concentrate on strengthening relations with governments or movements in countries nearest Uruguay—Argentina, Brazil, Chile, Peru and Ecuador—and would stress four issues: arms, money, mobilization of combatants, and intelligence networks.

■ Alleged members of the Union of Antifascist Groups set off explosives at 11 different sites in Montevideo May 11.

■ Roberto Filipone Barbeito, described as an important guerrilla leader, was reported arrested May 16.

■ Four soldiers guarding the Montevideo home of the commander in chief of the army were shot to death by unidentified gunmen May 18.

■ Authorities announced June 14 that Leonel Martinez Platero, a top Tupamaro leader, had been killed by security forces at a beach resort near Montevideo.

■ Pedro Zabalza, called an important guerrilla leader, had been seriously wounded and captured along with seven other Tupamaros in the northwestern city of Paysandu, according to authorities June 16.

Authorities announced June 27 that 68 Tupamaros had been arrested in Paysandu. The army claimed to have found

several hideouts in the region in which arms allegedly smuggled in from Argentina and Chile were kept.

An army communique announced June 18 that 37 Tupamaros—among them four doctors and 12 schoolteachers —had been arrested in the north of Uruguay, near the Brazilian border.

■ Authorities said July 8 that 45 active Tupamaros and collaborators had been arrested in the state of Tacuarembo, 248 miles north of Montevideo. Among the collaborators was Fernando Secco Aparicio, a wealthy landowner and industrialist said to have been bankrolling the guerrillas.

Several Tupamaro underground hospitals had been dismantled and a medical communications network had been destroyed, according to military sources July 10.

■ One of the most important Tupamaro columns was practically destroyed July 17 when 39 guerrillas were arrested in the state of Rio Negro, 190 miles northwest of Montevideo, authorities announced. The group was reportedly led by Tupamaro founder Raul Sendic, who remained at large.

■ Carlos Alejandro Alvariza, a surgeon and alleged head of a Tupamaro medical team, was killed July 25 when he fell from a window while "trying to escape," military sources reported.

■ One Tupamaro was killed and two soldiers were wounded in a shootout in downtown Montevideo July 27. Julio Marenales Saenz, a founder of the guerrilla organization, was reportedly wounded and captured during the action.

'People's jails' & hospital captured. The Tupamaros May 27, 1972 suffered their worst setback since the government's declaration of internal war when security forces found one of their "people's jails" in Montevideo and freed two officials held there for more than a year. Eight guerrillas were reportedly arrested during the action.

The two officials were Ulyses Pereira Reverbel, head of the state telephone company, and ex-Agriculture Minister Carlos Frick Davie.

Authorities had said May 13 that they had discovered the people's jail in which guerrillas had been holding police photographer Nelson Bardesio but that Bardesio was rushed away just before they arrived. (Bardesio was freed shortly thereafter.)

Security forces discovered a well-equipped Tupamaro hospital in a Montevideo chemical fertilizer factory May 21.

'War' state lifted. The government July 11, 1972 lifted the existing "state of internal war" measures with the publication of a new national security law, passed the week before by Congress.

The new security law, introduced by President Juan Maria Bordaberry, placed subversive crimes under military jurisdiction, empowered army courts to hand down sentences of up to 30 years for subversion and provided for jail terms of up to two years for journalists committing "press crimes."

Congress voted Sept. 28 to extend the suspension of individual constitutional guarantees until Nov. 30, and it voted again to Nov. 30 to continue the extension until Feb. 15, 1973.

Tupamaro-army talks. It was reported that Tupamaros were secretly negotiating with members of the armed forces who were said to be as disillusioned with Uruguay's traditional politicians as the guerrillas. Jorge Batlle, a prominent politician and close associate of ex-President Jorge Pacheco Areco, recently had said he was worried that "the soldiers are not talking to us, the politicians, but they are talking to arrested Tupamaros in the military prisons," according to the London newsletter Latin America July 28, 1972.

Reports of contacts between the army and Tupamaros were said to have influenced President Juan Maria Bordaberry in a decision July 19 to dismiss Defense Minister Enrique O. Magnani. The defense minister had angered military officers by admitting that a Christian Democratic labor leader had been tortured to death at a military installation.

Sen. Zelmar Michelini of the leftist Broad Front confirmed Aug. 1 that there had been a July truce between Tupamaros and the army, during which guerrilla leaders negotiated with liberal army officers. The talks, Michelini said,

had encompassed "not only peace and the surrender of arms, but the social and economic situation of the country." The truce ended July 25 when Tupamaros shot and killed Col. Artigas Alvarez, chief of civil defense and brother of the commander in chief of the combined military and police forces.

According to the newsletter Latin America Sept. 1, the Tupamaro negotiators had been Mauricio Rosencoff and Eluterio Fernandez Huidoboro, who were released from prison for a few days to discuss the army's proposals with other guerrilla leaders. The Tupamaros apparently rejected the proposals, which reportedly entailed the surrender of all guerrillas in exchange for "lenient" treatment at the hands of military judges, and a number of social reforms similar to those proposed by Blanco presidential candidate Wilson Ferreira Aldunate in the 1971 election campaign.

Following the failure of the negotiations, military authorities were concentrating their attention on Rosencoff, who they believed played an important liaison role within the guerrilla movement, Latin America reported. Torture sessions—which had nearly killed Rosencoff in May—had resumed, but he was reportedly refusing to talk, the newsletter said.

Bordaberry, leftists meet—Growing fears of military involvement in politics had led President Juan Maria Bordaberry to meet recently with a delegation from the Broad Front, it was reported Aug. 18.

The meeting followed a show of force by the army in Congress Aug. 6. Under military pressure, Blanco and Colorado legislators had voted to remove the parliamentary immunity of Broad Front Deputy Washington Ferrer Almeida. The army claimed Ferrer was a Tupamaro collaborator, but Ferrer, who was in hiding, reportedly maintained the only evidence against him was a false confession obtained under torture when he was held in November 1971.

Sendic & other Tupamaro leaders captured. Raul Sendic, founder of the Tupamaros movement, was severely wounded (in the head) and captured by police in Montevideo Sept. 1, 1972. Two other Tupamaros surrendered.

Sendic, originally a rural labor union organizer, reportedly had played a leading part in developing the rural Tupamaro "columns," which began operations early in 1972. He reportedly had commanded the Rio Negro column in the western province of Paysandu, said to be the last of the rural groups to be broken up during the army's anti-guerrilla offensive.

Army and police communiques Aug. 4–Sept. 7 reported the arrests of 69 other Tupamaros—including three military officers and at least three guerrilla leaders—and the killing of six alleged guerrillas including one army officer. The captured leaders were said to be Alberto Mujica Cordano and Lucia Topolanski Saavedra, arrested Aug. 19, and Henry Willy Engler, reputedly the Tupamaro second-in-command, seized Aug. 17.

Despite their recent setbacks, the Tupamaros survived as a force, and some sources said recruitment was so brisk they lacked staff to assimilate all the volunteers, the London newsletter Latin America reported Sept. 1. The army's successes against the group in April–May reportedly had stemmed from one betrayal, by Tupamaro leader Hector Amodio Perez, who had revealed the locations of at least 30 guerrilla hideouts.

Authorities announced Sept. 18 that they had captured another important Tupamaro leader, Gabino Montes de Oca.

Other events. Among other developments involving terrorism and counterterrorism in Uruguay during 1972:

A new terrorist group calling itself the Armed Popular Front (FAP) issued a communique April 3 in which it vowed to combat "Zionist capitalism" and threatened to kill "the two strongest figures of Zionism" in Uruguay unless its demands for money were met by the Israeli Bank of Uruguay. The group took credit for the robbery of $5,000 from the bank March 21.

Terrorists presumed to be right-wing members set off explosives April 16 at three district offices of the Communist party, at the homes of three leftist politicians and the editor of a leftist magazine, and at Montevideo's Evangelical Methodist Church, which had been used in one of the ambushes. A bomb had gone off in the Soviet embassy in Montevideo April 15.

Soldiers killed seven Communists April 17 in a gunfight at party headquarters in Montevideo. The government initially claimed Tupamaros had taken refuge in the building but later said that police had been investigating a report that a gun had been thrown into the building, and the Communists inside had opened fire. Neighborhood residents charged, however, that the army began the shooting. Uruguay's press was not allowed to report the incident.

A French Roman Catholic priest, Rev. Louis Benaud, was arrested with eight other persons in the northern state of Salto Sept. 17 on charges of collaborating with Tupamaros. Benaud was in charge of a church-sponsored agrarian youth movement in the city of Salto.

A Molotov cocktail was thrown at the home of Broad Front Sen. Zelmar Michelini, who had consistently denounced the torture by security forces of captured Tupamaros and other political prisoners, it was reported Sept. 22. Unknown persons had fired at but missed Michelini's son as he returned home from school Sept. 6.

Officials said Sept. 24 that the armed forces had broken up a small left-wing guerrilla organization called the "December 22d Movement." The group allegedly had links with the Tupamaros.

Guarantees suspension extended. The Permanent Committee of the Executive Power, acting for Congress while both houses were recessed, voted Feb. 15, 1973 to extend the suspension of individual guarantees for 45 days.

Congress voted by 65–63 March 31, after more than 30 hours of debate, to extend the suspension for another 60 days.

The government's case was presented March 30 by Defense Minister Walter Ravenna and Interior Minister Nestor

Bolentini. In a four-hour speech, Bolentini argued that although the urban guerrilla movement was practically defeated, it should not be given an opportunity to reorganize.

Emergency measures imposed. President Juan Maria Bordaberry decreed emergency security measures June 1, 1973 after he lost his majority in Congress and the suspension of guarantees expired.

The measures, imposed indefinitely to combat alleged subversion, could be overturned by Congress. They allowed detention without trial, searches and arrests without court order, and partial press censorship. They were in force during most of the rule of Bordaberry's predecessor and political mentor, Jorge Pacheco Areco, when the Tupamaro guerrilla movement was much stronger.

Bordaberry asserted in a nationwide radio and television address later June 1 that subversion was "always latent" in Uruguay, and that guerrillas were currently regrouping in "hostile" countries.

Interior Minister Nestor Bolentini alleged in a newspaper interview June 10 that there was evidence of "new" subversive groups whose members were "trained abroad." He said the groups were distinct from Uruguay's "traditional" guerrillas—presumably the Tupamaros and the Popular Revolutionary Organization-33—but resembled them in wanting to reach power by force.

Chamber head ordered arrested. A warrant was issued Sept. 7, 1973 to arrest Hector Gutierrez Ruiz, president of the Chamber of Deputies, for alleged collaboration with the Tupamaro guerrilla movement. Gutierrez was in Buenos Aires, Argentina, where he fled immediately after President Bordaberry dissolved the Chamber in late June.

Charges against Gutierrez included changing into national currency $300,000 worth of gold and pounds sterling stolen by Tupamaros in 1971, and pretending to have been kidnapped by Tupamaros and given evidence of police "death squads" in 1972.

A second Chamber member, Hugo Batalla of the Broad Front, had been arrested Sept. 3 for alleged links to the Tupamaros but released Sept. 5 for lack of evidence. Military officials had claimed in announcing the arrest that arms and subversive literature had been found in Batalla's Chamber office.

VENEZUELA

Terrorism Declines

Terrorism in Venezuela seemed to be on the wane in the 1970s after flare-ups in the 1960s in which Cuba had often been assailed as the instigator. Douglas Bravo's FALN (Fuerzas Armadas de Liberacion Nacional, or National Liberation Armed Forces) and its FLN (Frente de Liberacion Nacional, or National Liberation Front) political arm seemed to be the major guerrilla/terrorist force in the late 1960s and early 1970s. Some strikes were also attributed to leftist splinter groups such as Zero Point (Punto Cero, also called People's Revolutionary Army) and Red Flag.

Constitutional guarantees suspended. Venezuelan President Raúl Leoni suspended constitutional guarantees Dec. 13, 1966 after terrorists killed a defense ministry lawyer and attempted to assassinate Gen. Roberto Morean Soto, chief of staff of the army. Francisco Astufillo Suárez, the slain lawyer, who had been a prosecutor of suspected terrorists, was killed by machinegun fire from a car as he left his home. Leoni announced the constitutional curbs—empowering the police to arrest without warrant, hold suspects without bail and enter suspected quarters without judicial permission—during a radio address in which he said Cuban Premier "Fidel Castro and his protectors" were behind the terrorist conspiracy.

Cuban Raid Charged. The government said May 12, 1967 that it had intercepted a landing party of 4 Cuban and 8 Venezuelan guerrillas May 8 and had killed or captured all 4 of the Cubans. The Venezuelans reportedly escaped inland to join a rebel group operating in the Bachiller Mountains.

Interior Min. Reinaldo Leandro Moro said May 12 that Cuban First Lt. Antonio

Briones Moxtoto, 27, had been shot to death and another Cuban had drowned in the landing attempt. Moro displayed 2 captured Cubans, Lt. Manuel Gil Castellanos, 25, and Pedro Cabrera Torres, 29, a marine militiaman. (Torres was found hanged in his Caracas prison cell June 2.) Moro said that the landing had taken place at Machurucuto, about 90 miles east of Caracas. The 2 captives admitted to newsmen that they had been sent to infiltrate the Venezuelans. Authorities said they had found supplies and a Russian rifle after the clash. $9,700 in U.S. currency was found on Briones' body.

The Cuban Communist party's Central Committee said May 18 that Cuba was "lending and will continue to lend aid to all those who fight against imperialism. . . ." The committee, acknowledging the Venezuelan charge, said that there was no "need to ask its permission or for forgiveness to fulfill its duty of solidarity with all the revolutionaries of the world, among them the Venezuelan revolutionaries, . . ."

Caldera Peace Offensive. Soon after his inauguration March 11, 1969, President Rafael Caldera Rodriguez opened a pacification campaign directed toward Venezuela's extreme leftist elements. Offering them a political alternative to violence, Caldera legalized the Venezuelan Communist Party and pledged amnesty for guerrillas willing to exchange their arms for constitutional political activity.

The six-year ban on the Communist Party was lifted March 26. The CP and the Movement of the Revolutionary Left (MIR) had been outlawed by President Romulo Betancourt in 1962 following a wave of terrorism.

The Cuban-supported guerrillas had been terrorizing the country intermittently since 1962. However, while still active, their success in recent months was reported to be negligible. Time magazine estimated May 2 that there were only 200 to 300 active guerrillas, divided into three factions.

Defense Minister Martin Garcia Villasmil said April 29 that no direct Cuban support of guerrilla activities in Vene-

zuela had been evident since November 1968 and that the attacks had been declining before then.

Guerrilla response to Caldera's amnesty proposal was mixed. There were reports that some negotiation between guerrilla and government representatives had begun.

Caracas newspaper Ultimas Noticias March 26 reported a telephone call from a man identifying himself as a spokesman for the FALN. The spokesman asserted that "guerrillas who accept the amnesty proposed by President Caldera will be shot."

A communique issued April 1 and signed by FALN stated that Elegido Sivada would represent more than 200 guerrillas in negotiations with the government.

The government April 9 said it had appointed a commission of mediators headed by Jose Cardinal Quintero, primate of Venezuela, and Luis Teofilo Nunez, editor of the newspaper El Universal, to talk with the guerrillas. The commission said guerrilla elements had indicated a desire for a ceasefire, the British journal Latin America reported April 18. The journal also reported that the government had temporarily called off its anti-guerrilla operations and had pledged to take no action against the guerrilla groups engaged in negotiations.

Following a meeting of guerrilla leaders, an FALN communique, issued April 14, declared: "The guerrillas will not surrender without conditions and will not lay down their arms under present circumstances." The communique called for unity among all "revolutionary movements" and charged that Caldera's policies were not "really different" from those of former President Raul Leoni. The communique was signed by guerrilla leaders Douglas Bravo, Francisco Prada, Freddy Carquez, Elegido Sivada, Ali Rodriguez, Julio Chirinos and Antonio Zamora.

Bravo vs. Castro. Douglas Bravo, in a manifesto received by Caracas newspapers Jan. 13, 1970, accused Cuban Premier Fidel Castro of "betraying proletarian internationalism" and accepting "the comfortable position of a Soviet satellite." Bravo, head of the FALN, charged that Castro had "suspended all aid to Latin American revolutionary movements" in order to concentrate solely on reinforcing the Cuban economy. Castro was also accused of favoring the Movement of the Revolutionary Left (MIR) and the Venezuelan Communist Party.

The Washington Post Jan. 27 cited reports that guerrilla leader Luben Petkoff had left the country for Cuba, accompanied by 24 Cuban and Venezuelan guerrillas. Petkoff reportedly had ideological differences with Bravo.

In an earlier development, FALN representatives were reported to have delivered to Caracas newspapers Jan. 8 a series of documents indicating that guerrilla leaders had agreed to purge their ranks and unify their revolutionary efforts. Citing a "summit meeting" of guerrilla chiefs held recently in the "mountains of the east," one of the documents announced the formation of a "Committee of Revolutionary Integration designed to resolve everything relating to the formation of the revolutionary party and army." The document was signed by Carlos (Geronimo) Betancourt, Douglas Bravo, Gabriel Puertas, Eliseo Ramos and Ali Rodriguez, "representing the fighters of the National Liberation Front-Armed Forces of National Liberation (FLN-FALN) and the Antonio Jose de Sucre guerrilla front [a militant MIR faction]." Betancourt, Puertas, Rodriguez and Ramos were named to compose the new committee.

Another of the documents indicated that guerrilla leader Freddy Carquez had been ousted from the FALN for "theft of large sums of money from the revolution." A third document reported the expulsion from the unified guerrilla group of Julio Escalona, MIR national command member, along with Marcos Gomez and Soto Rojas.

6 die in kidnap case. Police killed two suspected terrorists June 2, 1972 and another four June 4 as they searched unsuccessfully for Carlos Dominguez Chavez, a wealthy industrialist kidnapped June 2 by professed members of the left-wing Zero Point guerrilla organization. President Caldera called off the manhunt June 4 after an appeal from Dominguez to stay out of the case.

Dominguez Chavez was freed June 15 after his family paid a record $1.1 million ransom. The police, however, were not certain whether his abductors were terrorists or common criminals.

One report, cited by the newsletter Latin America June 23, claimed that the kidnapping had been organized by guerrilla leader Douglas Bravo. Another, in the London Times June 11, said authorities had identified the abductors as two ex-policemen, while a police report cited in El Nacional of Caracas June 18 said they were the same men who kidnapped Dr. Enrique Dao in 1971.

Meanwhile, The Red Flag, an extreme left-wing guerrilla group, claimed responsibility for the kidnapping, according to Latin America July 7.

A document attributed to guerrilla groups under the command of Douglas Bravo and Carlos Betancourt claimed 30

Velez exiled, others caught. Oscar Servando Velez Morillo, leader of the Zero Point terrorist organization, had been allowed to go into exile in Mexico, according to the Foreign Ministry June 13, 1972. He had taken refuge in the home of the acting Mexican ambassador in Caracas. However, both Venezuelan and Mexican sources emphasized that he had not been granted political asylum by Mexico.

Police announced July 25 that four Zero Point guerrillas, including Jose Rafael Toro Torres, one of the group's leaders, had been arrested in Barquisimeto.

(The arrest of urban guerrilla leader Maximo Canales had been announced Nov. 8, 1971.)

Guerrilla clashes reported. Guerrillas had renewed activities in the mountains of the western states of Lara, Falcon and Yaracuy, where they clashed several times with army troops, according to the London newsletter Latin America July 7, 1972. One group, operating on the Lara-Falcon border under the leadership of Honorio Jose Navarro, was said to have kidnapped several cattle ranchers.

Meanwhile, a raid by soldiers on a home in suburban Caracas June 17 reportedly uncovered a hideout of the left-wing Revolutionary Organization and quantities of explosives, machine guns and subversive propaganda. Seven alleged members of the group were arrested, but their leader, Julio Escalona, reportedly escaped.

Plane hijacked to Cuba. Four professed members of the People's Revolutionary Army (Zero Point) hijacked an airliner with 42 persons aboard May 18, 1973 and flew it to Cuba, where they asked for political asylum.

The hijackers, led by Zero Point leader Federico Bottini, seized the plane on a domestic flight from Valera to Barquisimeto. They claimed to have a bomb and threatened to blow up the aircraft unless the government released 79 "political prisoners."

The plane was ordered first to Curacao, where it refueled, then to Panama City, where five passengers were allowed to deplane, and then to Merida, on the Yucatan peninsula in Mexico. It continued early May 19 to Mexico City, where an official told the hijackers the Venezuelan government refused to discuss their demands.

The Mexican official, Miguel Nazar, persuaded the guerrillas not to destroy the plane and offered them either political asylum in Mexico or whatever assistance they needed to reach Cuba. They chose the latter, and the plane, with Nazar aboard, proceeded to Havana, where the hijackers were taken into custody by Cuban police. The plane and passengers were returned to Venezuela May 20.

Mexican Security Minister Mario Moya said May 19 that President Luis Echeverria Alvarez had kept in close touch with the situation, and had "emphasized that every effort should be made to preserve the lives of the innocent people aboard the plane." Mexico consistently had granted demands by hijackers and kidnappers to save lives but had dealt firmly with the culprits if they were caught.

The United States

RACIAL TERRORISM

Terrorists' Diverse Goals

Like virtually all terrorists, those accused of political violence in the U.S. during the 1960s and early 1970s have used force in the interest of what they considered the highest objectives.

Some black Americans have taken action because they hoped to right racial wrongs going back more than 400 years.

Some white Americans (whether Ku Klux Klan members or merely people whose thinking is indistinguishable from that of the KKK) have been equally self-righteous in their use of violence to defend their own racial (or other) cause against black, Roman Catholic, Jewish or government infringement.

Some American opponents of war (and specifically of U.S. actions in Indochina) have considered themselves justified in taking violent action to enforce a change in American policy or, at least, to give emphatic display of their feelings.

Some Americans (particularly some identified by the label "New Left") have acted violently for reasons similar to those of Latin American urban guerrillas. They hoped ultimately to change or overthrow the government and initially, at least, to make known their views and intentions to workers, students and others whom they considered their future allies.

The Black Panthers

Party's Start. Since its formation in Oct. 1966 by Huey P. Newton, 26, and Bobby Seale, 31, in Oakland, Calif., the militant Black Panther Party had become part of the national Negro movement. Its membership had swelled from a few hundred to several thousand persons with chapters in major U.S. cities, and some law enforcement officials were beginning to describe the movement as dangerously subversive and terroristic.

National interest in the Black Panthers was generated by Newton's trial and conviction for manslaughter in California and by the Presidential candidacy of Eldridge Cleaver, Panther "minister of information." Violent confrontations between Panthers and police had occured in California, New York and New Jersey and, charging police harassment and brutality, Panther leaders had issued repeated calls to Negroes to arm themselves for a struggle for liberation.

Newton was convicted of manslaughter Sept. 8, 1968 in the Oct. 28, 1967 fatal shooting of Oakland Patrolman John Frey, 23. Newton was sentenced Sept. 27 to 2–15 years imprisonment.

Oakland's Alameda County Courthouse, where the 7-week trial took place, was the scene of extensive "free Huey" demonstrations during the early days of the trial. 2,500 sympathizers marched on the courthouse July 15 when the trial began after 11 delays. Officials searched spectators and newsmen for weapons.

In addition to the murder charge, Newton had been indicted for assault with a deadly weapon against Patrolman Herbert Heanes, 25, who was wounded.

After a reversal in 1970 and a mistrial in 1971, however, the government decided to drop the case against Newton, and he was allowed to go free.

Newton took the stand Aug. 22 to deny that he had shot Frey. Most of his testimony was his explanation of his resentment against white society.

The California Court of Appeals reversed the conviction May 29, 1970 on the ground that the court should have told the jury that an acquittal was warranted if the jury accepted Newton's testimony that he was unconscious (as a result of a gunshot wound) when Frey was shot. Newton went on trial again in 1971, but the court declared a mistrial Aug. 8 after the jury deadlocked at 11 for conviction and one for acquittal. On a state motion Dec. 15, the case against Newton was then dismissed.

Search for Cleaver—Eldridge Cleaver, 33, author and recent Presidential candidate of the Peace & Freedom Party, was sought as a parole violator on a fugitive warrant issued Nov. 27, 1968 in San Francisco.

Cleaver had been free on parole after serving 9 years of a 14-year sentence on a 1958 conviction for assault with intent to kill. He had been rearrested Apr. 6 after being wounded in a Panther shootout with Oakland police. Cleaver's parole was immediately rescinded.

Cleaver was released June 12 on $50,000 bail by order of Superior Court Judge Raymond J. Sherwin, who criticized the cancellation of parole. Sherwin said that the cancellation had stemmed not from a failure of Cleaver's "personal rehabilitation," but from his "undue eloquence in pursuing political goals . . . offensive to many of his contemporaries." The State District Court of Appeals in San Franciso ruled Sept. 27 that Sherwin had acted beyond his authority in the case. This ruling was upheld by the California Supreme Court Nov. 20 when it refused to hear an appeal by Cleaver. U.S. Supreme Court Justice Thurgood Marshall Nov. 26 denied a request for a stay to prohibit officials from taking Cleaver into custody. The fugitive warrant was issued after Cleaver failed to surrender as ordered Nov. 27. He had said Nov. 24 that his only alternative was to "get out of the country."

Cleaver had been nominated for President by the Peace and Freedom Party Aug. 18 by a 3-1 vote over his major rival, former entertainer Dick Gregory, at the party's convention in Ann Arbor, Mich. Cleaver's campaign platform called for "the immediate withdrawal of U.S. troops from Vietnam." The more-than-200 convention delegates reflected their party's alliance with the Black Panthers by supporting "the right of armed self-defense" by "the oppressed peoples in America." Cleaver told newsmen in N.Y. City Oct. 11 that the purpose of his campaign was to "lay the base for a revolutionary movement that will unite black . . . and white radicals."

N.Y. 'Bomb Plot' Case. Twenty-one Black Panthers were indicted in New York April 2, 1969 on charges of plotting to set off bombs April 3 in five mid-town department stores, to dynamite the tracks of the Penn Central Railroad and to bomb a Bronx (N.Y. City) police station. District Attorney Frank S. Hogan, announcing the indictment, said that the militant Negroes had intended to destroy what they considered to be part of "the power structure."

Ultimately, 13 of those indicted went on trial, and all 13 were acquitted May 13, 1971.

In early morning raids following the indictments, the police had seized 12 of the defendants at their homes or at the homes of friends. The police said they had confiscated a quantity of firearms and explosives in making the arrests. Two defendants were already in jail in Newark, N.J. on robbery charges, and a third gave himself up to the police April 3. The remaining six defendants were being sought.

One of those arrested was Robert S. Collier, 32, who had served 21 months in jail after a 1965 conviction for conspiring to blow up national monuments, including the Statue of Liberty. Another was Joan Victoria Bird, 19, a student nurse who had been indicted Feb. 7 on a charge of attempting to murder two policemen in New York in January. Similar charges had been dropped against two other Panthers named in the April 2 indictment: Lumumba Abdul Shakur, 27, described as a Panther captain, and Clark Squares, 32. Also arrested were Michael Tabor (known also as Cetewayo), 23, described as a Panther captain; Shakur's wife, Afeni, 23; Walter Johnson (also known as Baba Odinga), 24, John J. Casson (Ali Hassan), 28, Alex McKiever (Catarra), 19, Eddie Joseph (Jamal Baltimore), 17, Richard Moore (Analye Dahruba), 25, and Curtis Powell, 33. Lonni Epps, 18, surrendered to the police April 3. Donald Weems (Kwesi Balagoon), 22, and Nathaniel Burns (Nathaniel Williams and Sekou Odinga), 25, were being held in Newark.

Those being sought were William King (Kinshasa), 31, Larry Mack, 23, Thomas Berry (Mshina), 26, Lee Roper (Shaba-Um), 22, and Lee Berry (Mkuba).

According to the police, the proposed targets of the conspiracy included the midtown stores of Macy's, Alexander's, Bloomingdale's, Korvette's and Abercrombie & Fitch; the tracks of the New Haven branch of Penn Central at six locations in Harlem; and, as a diversionary action, a police station in the Bronx.

Tabor and Moore disappeared during trial Feb. 6, 1971 and fled to Algeria. They forfeited bail totaling $150,000.

All 13 on trial, including Tabor and Moore, were acquitted May 13, 1971.

Carmichael Quits Party. Stokely Carmichael, prime minister of the Black Panther Party, resigned from the organization July 4, 1969. He announced his

resignation in a letter calling the organization "dogmatic" and condemning its tactics as "dishonest and vicious."

The black militant leader's letter was brought to the U.S. by his wife, singer Miriam Makeba. Mrs. Carmichael said her husband was in Conakry, Guinea, studying French.

Carmichael strongly criticized the organization's alliance with white radicals, claiming it would only lead to "complete subversion of the blacks by the whites through control of the black organization."

David Hilliard, chief of staff of the Panthers, said in Berkeley, Calif. July 5 that Carmichael's resignation from the militant organization "was not altogether a surprise." He rejected Carmichael's call for the party to sever all affliations with white radical groups. Hilliard said the party would continue to enlist white radical support.

Cleaver Vs. Carmichael. Eldridge Cleaver, the fugitive Black Panther Party minister of information, left his sanctuary in Cuba July 13, 1969 and arrived in Algiers July 15 for the Pan-African Cultural Festival. Stokely Carmichael also attended the festival.

Cleaver July 15 released a letter denouncing Carmichael's statement July 4 that the Black Panthers should be concerned primarily with the struggle of nonwhites against "Western imperialism." Cleaver asserted that "suffering is colorblind and that the victims of imperialism needed a unity based on revolutionary principles rather than skin color."

Carmichael replied July 23 that controversy within the Negro nationalist movement was "healthy," and that Cleaver's views were his "right." Carmichael said he had met privately with Cleaver to discuss their opposing views on the role of whites within the black nationalist movement.

Cleaver praised the Arab commando movement July 22 and denounced Israel as an American "puppet and pawn." The Black Panther leader made the remarks to Algerians gathered around the new Afro-American Information Center in Algiers. Cleaver said he supported the view of an Al Fatah official that

"Israel represents a new face of colonialism."

Panthers Sponsor Conference. The Black Panther Party sponsored a three-day meeting July 18–20, 1969 in Oakland, Calif., calling on the 3,000 Negro and white radicals participating to form a national Committee to Combat Fascism. Bobby Seale, chairman of the Panthers, said in the keynote address July 18 that its goal would be to work for community control of police departments across the nation. About 90 per cent of the delgates to the Panther-led conference were white.

Seale cited recent raids on Black Panther Party regional offices and mass arrests of student rebels as evidence that fascism was growing in the U.S.

Seale adjourned the convention July 20 with repeated assertions that the fight against "fascism" must be waged by a black-white coalition. He said racial confrontation had no place in the struggle.

Panthers Cited As Threat. Federal Bureau of Investigation Director J. Edgar Hoover said July 15, 1969 that among black militant groups, the Black Panther Party represented "the greatest threat to the internal security of the country." Hoover commented in the bureau's annual report for fiscal 1969. He accused the party of assaulting policemen and staging violent confrontations with federal authorities throughout the nation. The Panthers, according to Hoover, had sent their leaders to ghettos, universities and high schools to "preach their gospel of hate and violence."

The public opinion-sampling Harris Survey reported May 11, 1970 that 68% of the whites questioned in a poll conducted by the organization believed that the Black Panthers were "a serious menace to the country." The organization also reported that 81% of the whites surveyed believed that recent shootings of Black Panther officials had been "mainly the result of violence started by the Panthers themselves."

In another poll conducted by the Harris Survey, however, figures indicated that the Black Panthers were becoming increasingly more popular among blacks.

In a poll conducted for Time magazine, 25% of the blacks questioned said "the Black Panther philosophy is the same as mine." 64% of those blacks questioned also said that the Panthers had given the black community "a sense of pride."

FBI, state and local police officials had been charging for months that Black Panther members and other black "extremists" had started a campaign to murder policemen. According to some officials, policemen were shot down on the streets or lured into ambushes as part of this campaign. Black Panther members and sympathizers said that it was the police, instead, who had begun a drive to kill Black Panthers and other black militants.

Panther threat seen small. The House Internal Security Committee said Aug. 23, 1971 that the Black Panthers posed a physical danger to the nation's policemen but were "totally incapable of over-

The four Republicans on the committee indicated, however, that they objected to the moderate tone of the report. Reps. John M. Ashbrook (Ohio), John G. Schmitz (Calif.), Fletcher Thompson (Ga.) and Roger H. Zion (Ind.), contended that the majority report did not give "a clear understanding of the Black Panther Party as a subversive criminal group using the facade of politics as a cover for crimes of violence and extortion."

The majority report was defended by Rep. Richardson Preyer (D, N.C.), who headed a subcommittee that heard former Panthers testify about the party.

Preyer said in a separate report that it would be easy to write "a real zinger of a report" that would provoke greater public outrage, but it might also help revive the party by making martyrs of its leaders.

The majority report said that "the Black Panther Party, through its deliberately inflammatory rhetoric and through the actual arming and military training of its members, had contributed to an increase in acts of violence and constitutes a threat to the internal security of the United States." The report added, however, that the committee did not believe that the Panthers "constituted a clear and present danger to the continued functioning of the U.S. government or any other institutions of our democratic society."

Police-Panther Shootouts in Chicago.

Several gun battles took place between policemen and Black Panthers in Chicago.

Two Chicago policemen were killed and six wounded Nov. 13, 1969 during a gun battle between the police and Black Panther Party members. A 19-year-old youth associated with the Panthers was killed by the police after he allegedly shot a patrolman.

According to police reports the battle began when a police cruiser moved into Chicago's South Side to answer a distress call and was fired upon by snipers. A patrolman, Francis Rappaport, was killed by a youth a block from the police cruiser.

Rappaport's alleged killer, Spurgeon J. Winters, was shot and killed by other policemen. The original distress call had been telephoned by Winters' sister, who told police that the Panthers had come into the area with guns.

Patrolman John Gilhooley, who was wounded during the fracas, died later in a Chicago hospital.

Police in Chicago staged a pre-dawn raid on an apartment near Black Panther headquarters Dec. 4, 1969 and killed Fred Hampton, Illinois party chairman. The police also shot and killed Mark Clark, who was described by police as a leader of the Black Panthers in Peoria, Ill. Four others, two of them women, were wounded.

According to police reports, the raid was carried out on a warrant on the basis of information that Hampton's apartment was being used to stockpile weapons. The police asserted that when they knocked on the door a woman opened fire with a shotgun. Police said that at least 200 shots were fired during a "shootout" that lasted 10 or 12 minutes. Spokesmen for the Panthers Dec. 5 denied police accounts of the raid. They claimed that Hampton was "murdered in his bed" by police who opened fire as they burst through the door on what the Panthers termed a "search and destroy mission." The Panthers took newsmen through Hampton's apartment to support their argument that the only shooting was done by the police.

A black Chicago alderman and attorneys for the Black Panthers claimed Dec. 6 that an independent autopsy performed on Hampton's body "confirms our theory that he was murdered while he was asleep." The autopsy, performed by three white doctors, was held at the funeral home owned by Alderman A. A. Rayner, who had called for an investigation of the affair.

State Attorney Edward V. Hanrahan said Dec. 6 that Rayner was under investigation for his reputed connection with the Black Panthers. Hanrahan's office said Rayner had co-signed the lease on the Panther headquarters with a party official. Rayner confirmed this.

Bobby Lee Rush, the ranking officer in the Panther's Illinois office, surrendered to police Dec. 6. He had been sought on a warrant charging him with failing to register a weapon. The police said they had confiscated a derringer and several hundred rounds of ammunition during the raid.

A coroner's jury ruled July 21, 1971 that the killings of Hampton and Clark were justifiable. According to the testimony of several Chicago detectives who participated in the predawn raid, one or more persons in Hampton's apartment opened fire on the police.

The seven Black Panthers who had survived the Dec. 4, 1969 raid were indicted by a Chicago grand jury Jan. 30, 1970 on charges of attempted murder.

The indictments also charged the seven Panthers with armed violence. Indicted were Brenda Harris, Verlina Brewer, Blair Anderson, Ronald Satchell, Harold Bell, Deborah Johnson and Louis Truelock.

But the Illinois state attorney disclosed May 8 that all seven of the indicted Panthers had been freed and all criminal charges against them dropped.

State Attorney Edward V. Hanrahan said the seven had been released because there was not sufficient proof that any of them had fired a weapon at the police.

Hanrahan himself was among 14 law enforcement officials named Aug. 24, 1971 in a long-suppressed indictment handed down in Chicago on charges of conspiring to obstruct justice in connection with the 1969 raid.

The indictment was made public on orders issued Aug. 24 by the Illinois Supreme Court. Chief Criminal Court Judge Joseph A. Power, a former law partner of Chicago Mayor Richard J. Daley, had kept the indictment sealed since April, when it was prepared. Power had refused to accept the indictment because he contended that the grand jury had not heard all the pertinent witnesses and that it had been pressured into returning the true bills.

Others named in the indictment were an assistant state attorney, eight policemen who took part in the raid and four police officials who later conducted departmental investigations into the raid.

Chicago Police Superintendent James B. Conlisk Jr. was among five other Chicago law enforcement officials named as co-conspirators but not as defendants.

No specific allegations were made against Conlisk other than his listing as a co-conspirator who had knowledge of the alleged conspiracy to obstruct justice.

The indictment accused Hanrahan and the 13 other defendants of knowingly conspiring to obstruct justice by attempting to thwart criminal prosecution of the eight policemen who participated in the raid. The indictment also accused the 14 defendants of planting false evidence and conspiring to obstruct the legal defense of the seven Panthers who survived the raid.

Hanrahan was also accused by the grand jury of presenting evidence before another Cook County grand jury that "he knew or reasonably should have known to be false and inflammatory."

Hanrahan and his codefendants were acquitted Oct. 25, 1972. During the trial it was revealed that four of the Panthers who had survived the raid had given their lawyer written statements contradicting their grand jury testimony that they had not fired at the police.

Hilliard Accused of Threat to Nixon. David Hilliard, Black Panther chief of staff, was arrested by Secret Service agents in San Francisco Dec. 3, 1969 on charges of threatening the life of Presi-

dent Nixon. The charges stemmed from a speech Hilliard made during the Nov. 15 Moratorium Day peace rally at San Francisco's Golden Gate Park.

According to evidence presented to a federal grand jury, Hilliard called President Nixon "the man responsible for all the attacks on the Black Panther Party nationally." According to federal authorities, Hilliard was said to have added: "We will kill Richard Nixon."

Charles R. Garry, Hilliard's attorney, said Hilliard had actually said that "they (the Panthers) would kill Nixon or anyone else that stood in the way of their freedom."

A federal judge May 4, 1971 ordered Hilliard released because the government declined to divulge wiretap logs of conversations involving Hilliard.

Federal District Court Judge William P. Gray ordered the indictment dismissed and the Panther leader freed. When U.S. Attorney James Browning told the court that he was not authorized to make the logs available to Hilliard's lawyers, Gray ordered the case dropped.

Gun Battle in Los Angeles. Police in Los Angeles, armed with tear gas rifles, fought a four-hour battle with members of the Black Panthers Dec. 8, 1969 following a raid on the party's headquarters. Three policemen and three Panthers were wounded.

The police said they moved on the Panthers' office in search of a cache of illegal weapons and two party members wanted in connection with an assault charge. Two other buildings used by the Panthers were searched and seized without incident.

The police said they arrested 11 Panthers, including three women, at the party's headquarters and 13 others at the other two sites. According to police reports, the raiding parties seized two machine guns, three shotguns, several rifles and several hundred rounds of ammunition.

California State Sen. Mervyn Dymally denounced the raid as "part of a national plan of political repression against the Panthers." Dymally, whose constituency was the Los Angeles area in which the police raids took place, said the gun battle was not an isolated incident.

Police Harassment Reported. The American Civil Liberties Union Dec. 28, 1969 released a report of a documented survey of nine metropolitan centers that had led the organization to conclude that law enforcement agencies across the country were "waging a drive against the Black Panther Party resulting in serious civil liberties violations." The survey was prepared for submission to an independent commission headed by former Supreme Court Justice Arthur J. Goldberg and Roy Wilkens, head of the National Association for the Advancement of Colored People (NAACP).

The survey, covering police operations against the Black Panther Party, was conducted by ACLU affiliates in New York, Los Angeles, Chicago, San Francisco, Philadelphia and major metropolitan areas in Connecticut, Wisconsin, Indiana and Michigan. The data included alleged "repeated arrests" of members of the Black Panthers while they were circulating political literature and police raids on allegedly "specious charges."

Policemen shot in Philadelphia. One policeman was shot to death and six others wounded Aug. 29–31, 1970 in Philadelphia in a series of gun battles with members of the Black Panthers and a splinter group of another black militant organization.

Police Commissioner Frank L. Rizzo said Aug. 30 that the Aug. 29-30 shootings, which resulted in the death of a policeman and wounding of three others, had been attributed to a group called "The Revolutionaries," which he said had plotted to murder policemen.

Three other officers were wounded Aug. 31 when police staged raids at dawn on three Black Panther Party centers in search of a suspect wanted in connection with the earlier shootings. Gunfire was exchanged during two of the raids before the police used tear gas to rout the centers' occupants.

Rizzo said warrants for the raids had been obtained on the basis of information supplied by a suspect held in connection with the Aug. 29 slaying of Sgt. Frank Von Colln, 43. Von Colln was murdered in an isolated outpost in a public park after he had dispatched two other officers to investigate a report that a patrolman had been shot near the park.

Two other policemen had been wounded Aug. 30 when two men opened fire on their police cruiser and then fled when the officers radioed for assistance.

Panthers open Algiers office. Eldridge Cleaver, the self-exiled Black Panther leader, presided over the opening of the Panthers' first "international section" in Algiers Sept. 13, 1970. The Algerian government had formally accorded the Panthers the status of a "liberation movement." The Algiers office lasted for about 2½ years.

Pete O'Neal succeeded Cleaver as leader of the Black Panthers' international section in Algiers in 1971. The international section announced Sept. 29, 1972 that William R. Holder, a U.S. Army deserter who had hijacked an airliner to Algeria in June 1972, had in turn succeeded O'Neal as leader.

(The New York Times reported March 28, 1973 that the party's Algiers office had been abandoned and that the remaining members had apparently left Algeria. The Algerian government had restricted the party's activities after reports of internal Panther disputes.)

Panthers drop gun approach. Black Panthers co-founder Huey P. Newton said in a Jan. 30, 1972 interview that the party had abandoned the "pick-up-the-gun-now" approach in favor of community work and voter registration. Newton attributed the former violent approach to Eldridge Cleaver.

CIA disputed Panthers' foreign ties. The White House was told by the Central Intelligence Agency (CIA) in 1969 and 1970 that there was no substantial evidence to support Administration suspicions that the Black Panthers and other radical groups were being financed by foreign nations, the New York Times reported May 25, 1973.

However, the White House refused to believe the agency's evaluations and sent 35 Federal Bureau of Investigation (FBI) agents abroad to intelligence posts in 20 different countries.

The Times quoted one CIA analyst who worked on the studies as recalling: "We tried to show that the radical movements were home grown, indigenous responses to perceived grievances and problems that had been growing for years. We said the radicals were clean and that we couldn't find anything."

The CIA studied allegations of Algerian support for the Black Panthers. "Every intelligence agency said we think it's an interesting hypothesis but, by and large, the judgment of the intelligence community in 1970 was that there was no significant Algerian support for the domestic operations of blacks. History supports the judgment completely," a CIA source said, pointing out that the Panthers were ousted from Algeria in March.

San Rafael Judge Killed, Angela Davis Acquitted

Judge killed in courthouse shootout. Superior Court Judge Harold J. Haley, 65, and two San Quentin convicts were killed Aug. 7, 1970 in a gun fight after an attempted escape and kidnapping at the San Rafael, Calif. courthouse. Jonathan Jackson, 17, who had brought the guns used to force the judge and four other hostages out of the courtroom, was also killed in the shootout.

Marin County officials filed charges of kidnapping and murder Aug. 15 against Ruchell Magee, 31, a San Quentin convict who was in the courtroom as a witness and had been wounded in the gun battle. The same charges were brought against Angela Davis, 26, a black militant and Communist recently ousted from the University of California (Los Angeles) faculty. She had bought four guns brought into the courtroom by Jackson, identified as her frequent companion and bodyguard. Miss Davis and Jackson were both involved in raising money for the defense of the "Soledad Brothers,"

three blacks, one of them Jackson's brother, charged with killing a white guard at Soledad state prison. Police suggested that the kidnapping was part of a plot to exchange hostages taken at the San Rafael courthouse for the release of the Soledad Brothers, a theory supported by a reported quote from one of the kidnappers: "We want the Soledad Brothers freed by 12:30 today."

The gun battle began after the hostages were taken out of the courtroom—Haley with a sawed-off-shotgun taped to his neck —and forced into a rented van in the courthouse parking lot. The courthouse was surrounded by 100 law officers— sheriff's deputies and San Quentin guards. The shooting began when one of the prison guards tried to halt the van.

Witnesses were divided as to whether the firing first came from the gunmen or the guard who tried to halt the van. James W. Park, San Quentin associate warden, said Aug. 8 that prison policy was that "we will not let a prisoner here escape with a hostage. . . . Once you allow a hostage situation to work, then you'll be plagued with it forever, like airliner hijackings."

Angela Davis was seized by FBI agents Oct. 13 in a midtown New York City motel. She was acquitted by a Santa Clara County jury in San Jose, Calif. June 4, 1972 of all charges of murder, kidnapping and conspiracy in the case.

Other Black Militants

RAM Role Discounted. Atty. Gen. Nicholas deB. Katzenbach had testified before the House Un-American Activities Committee July 20, 1966 that the FBI "has no evidence" that recent racial outbreaks were incited by RAM (Revolutionary Action Movement), an organization reportedly headed by black expatriate Robert F. Williams, then a broadcaster from Havana. The alleged RAM connection with the riots had been reported in *Life* magazine.

RAM Suspects Convicted. Negro militants Herman B. Ferguson, 46, and Arthur Harris, 22, RAM members, were convicted in New York June 15, 1968 on charges of conspiracy to murder moderate Negro leaders Roy Wilkins of the NAACP and Whitney Young Jr. of the National Urban League. Ferguson and Harris were sentenced Oct. 3 to prison terms of 3½-7 years each. But State Supreme Court Justice Joseph M. Conroy ruled Oct. 17 that there was "reasonable doubt" that the 2 defendants had received a fair trial, and he authorized their release on bail. Conroy's ruling was based on the fact that the prosecutor had mentioned, in the jury's presence, the assassination of Sen. Robert F. Kennedy (D., N.Y.).

Cleveland slayings. A small band of armed black nationalists fought Cleveland police with rifles in the city's Glenville ghetto district the night of July 23–24, 1968. It was the first reported case in which black extremists had carried out threats to mount an attack in a major city.

7 persons were killed in the first wave of shooting between the group of nationalists and police. 3 of them were nationalists, 3 were white policemen, and one was a black who had attempted to aid the police. 3 more blacks were killed in other Cleveland shooting incidents the same night; an 11th person, also a Negro, was killed by a sniper in suburban Cleveland Heights July 26. 23 persons were wounded, more than 15 of them in the initial gunfight.

The shooting led to an explosion of racial tension in which burning and lootings brought an estimated $1.5 million worth of property damage. Although 3,100 National Guardsmen were sent to Cleveland, the relatively rapid restoration of order was widely credited to the efforts of the city's black mayor, Carl B. Stokes.

The initial attack was attributed to a small militant group called the Black Nationalists of New Libya, led by Ahmed (Fred) Evans, 37, an astrologer and then the director of an antipoverty project in the Glenville area. Evans surrendered to police late July 23, reportedly after his carbine had jammed during the fight. Although police said they had received prior warnings that coordinated

extremist attacks would occur in Cleveland, Detroit, Chicago and Pittsburgh July 24, the 3 other cities remained calm. It was reported later (July 28) that Evans had instigated the attack after being informed that he was being evicted from his home and his antipoverty project would not be permitted to move into premises promised to it.

Although reports conflicted as to exactly how the shooting began, press and news magazine accounts specified that the first shots were fired by a group of Evans' followers. According to a police summary of the events, issued July 31, a group of armed nationalists fired on police in a squadcar outside Evans' headquarters. The police, who had been keeping the headquarters under surveillance, radioed for reinforcements and then fled. A municipal tow truck attempting to remove an abandoned car from the section was fired on next, and the driver was wounded.

The police reinforcements, armed with semi-automatic weapons, arrived in the area and began returning the fire. The first fatalities, 3 policemen, the Negro aiding them and one nationalist, were killed in the early part of the gunfight. The bodies of 2 more extremists were found later in the ruins of one of the buildings; they had been killed by police bullets before the building was set afire and burned to the ground.

Acting while the Glenville gunfight was still underway and as rioting was beginning to spread to other nearby Negro ghetto communities, Mayor Stokes asked Ohio Gov. James A. Rhodes to send National Guardsmen to the city. Rhodes complied late July 23, and by the early morning hours of July 24 the first Guard units had entered Glenville. The gunfire and rioting had already halted, at least partially because of heavy rain that swept the city that night.

Commenting on the Cleveland violence July 27, Stokes was reported by *Time* magazine to have said: The Glenville outbreak was "uniquely different from any other in any other city in the country. The others were a spontaneous reaction to an unresponsive environment. But this was a small group of determined men who planned an attack on the police." (Phil Hutchings, newly-named program director of the Student Non-violent Coordinating Committee, told a New York press conference July 27 that the Cleveland eruption was "the first stage of a revolutionary armed struggle.") But Stokes said in a report released Aug. 9 that there was no "tangible" proof that the slain policemen had been lured into a trap. He said the trouble had sprung from a "spontaneous action," and there was no evidence to connect the shootings with recent sniping incidents in other cities.

Evans was found guilty of murder May 12, 1969 and was sentenced to die in the electric chair, but the sentence was not carried out. The jury found Evans guilty of 4 counts of first degree murder of 3 policemen and a civilian.

4 guilty in 'kill-a-cop' plot. Four young black men were convicted in New York May 13, 1971 of illegal possession of weapons and bombs that the prosecution said were to be used to "kill a cop a week." A fifth member of the so-called "Harlem Five" was acquitted.

The jury found Preston Lay Jr., 26, and Hannibal Thomas, 24, also known as Hannibal Ahmend, guilty of possession of a weapon, in reference to a rifle, and possession of a weapon, in reference to a bomb. Wallace Marks, 26, was found guilty on two counts of possessing a loaded pistol and bombs. Ebb Glenn was convicted of a single charge of possessing a weapon, in reference to bombs.

Lloyd Butler, 22, also known as Sayed Saladeen, was cleared of all seven counts. A sixth man, John Aykik Garrett, 26, was also charged in the case but Justice Arnold G. Fraiman dismissed the charges for lack of evidence.

Black extremists sought. A small, loosely-structured band of black extremists called the Black Liberation Army were believed to have been behind the shooting deaths of two New York City patrolmen Jan. 27, 1972.

The two slain men, Gregory P. Foster, 22, and Rocco Laurie, 23, were shot in the back, according to police, by at least three persons who continued to empty their guns into them while they lay dying on the street.

At a news conference Feb. 8, New York City Police Commissioner Patrick V. Murphy disclosed the names of four men being sought as suspects in the slayings.

One of the suspects, Ronald Carter, was killed Feb. 16 in a street gun-battle with police in St. Louis. Police recovered a pistol identified as the .38-caliber service revolver taken from Laurie's body.

Two other men were arrested following the St. Louis shootout. One of them, Henry Brown, was named in a warrant issued in New York Feb. 18 as one of the gunmen who killed Laurie and Foster.

De Mau Mau called killers. Eight members of a black terrorist gang called De Mau Mau were charged Oct. 15, 1972 in Chicago with the murders of nine whites in Illinois between May and September. The gang was said to be made up primarily of black Vietnam veterans.

All eight were in police custody. Six of the suspects were arrested Oct. 15. They were identified as: Reuben Taylor, 22; his brother Donald, 21; Michael Clark, 21; Nathaniel Burse, 23; Edward Moran Jr., 23; and Robert Wilson, 18, all of Chicago.

The other two suspects, Darrell Peatry, 20, and Garland Jackson, 22, surrendered Oct. 17.

Police said apparently not all of the eight had participated in all the killings.

Police said ballistic tests linked the nine murders, which occurred in the communities of Barrington Hills, Monee, Highland Park and Carbondale.

Cook County Sheriff Richard J. Elrod said Oct. 16 that the eight were apparently "roaming the countryside looking for someone to kill."

In a related development, the Pentagon said Oct. 18 that it had found "isolated instances" of existence of the De Mau Mau group at U.S. military installations.

Liberation Army member convicted. Clark E. Squire, a reputed member of the militant Black Liberation Army, was found guilty by a New Brunswick, N.J. jury March 11, 1974 of the murder of New Jersey state trooper Werner Foerster May 2, 1973. He was also convicted on four counts of assault, illegal possession of a weapon and robbery. He was sentenced to life in prison March 15.

Joanne D. Chesimard, reportedly a leader of the Black Liberation Army, was also accused of Foerster's murder. Her trial was severed from Squire's when she was found to be pregnant Jan. 26.

Chesimard and Fred Hilton, also an alleged member of the group, had been acquitted of bank robbery charges Dec. 28, 1973 by a New York City federal jury. A first trial had ended with jurors unable to reach a verdict.

During the incident in which trooper Foerster died, James F. Costen, former information minister for the Black Panthers faction loyal to Eldridge Cleaver, was shot to death by police.

Police claim army end—New York City Police Commissioner Donald F. Cawley had said Nov. 15, 1973 that the killing by police of Twymon Meyers "broke the back" of the Black Liberation Army. Meyers had been sought in connection with the slaying of two New York City policemen in January 1972 and several bank robberies.

A confidential report by the New York City Police Department, reported Nov. 16, 1973 by the New York Times, said at no time had there been more than "25 or 30 hard-core members" of the Black Liberation Army, although it might have had the support of 75 sympathizers.

Cawley cited seven group members who had died in shootouts with police and 18 others who were in custody awaiting trial on charges stemming from police shootings or bank robberies.

In San Francisco Oct. 27, 1973, Marilyn Buck, a 25-year old white, had been sentenced to 10 years in federal prison after being convicted of illegally procuring arms for the Black Liberation Army.

'Zebra' killings in San Francisco. San Francisco Mayor Joseph L. Alioto said April 17, 1974 that he had ordered police to stop, search and question all young black

men who appeared to match the description of a man thought responsible for a series of random shootings of whites that had resulted in 12 deaths in the past five months.

According to victims who survived, the shootings, 18 in all, were perpetrated by a young black man, who walked up to his targets and shot them in the back without warning. The weapon used, police said, was a .32-caliber automatic pistol.

Criticism of the police action began to build April 18. The Northern California chapter of the American Civil Liberties Union called the searches "a racist outrage and a massive violation of the constitutional rights of every black man in the city." Alioto defended his order concerning the killings—dubbed the "Zebra" killings because police communications regarding them had been handled over the Z police radio band—saying, "Extraordinary situations . . . call for extraordinary measures."

The controversy surrounding the case was heightened by a statement April 29 by Alioto that he believed the killers were members of a ring of black gunmen called the "Death Angels," who might have been responsible for as many as 80 "murderous assaults" on Californians since 1971. California Attorney General Evelle J. Younger said April 30 that he had no evidence to support Alioto's contention.

Four Black Muslims were indicted by a state grand jury May 16 on charges of murdering three white persons and conspiring to murder other whites at random. The killings cited in the indictment were among the "Zebra" killings.

Named in the indictment were Manuel Moore, 29, J. C. Simon, 29, Larry C. Green, 22, and Jessie Cooks. Cooks was currently serving a prison term for murder. The other defendants were among seven men arrested by San Francisco police May 1; four of the suspects seized in police dragnet were later released for lack of evidence. The seven men were all employed by the Black Self-Help Co., Inc., a small, Muslim-affiliated moving and storage firm in San Francisco.

Prior to the arrest of suspects May 1, U.S. District Court Judge Alfonso J. Zirpoli ruled April 25 that San Francisco police had violated the rights of 600 black men they had stopped and questioned in their investigation of the killings. Acting on a suit brought by the American Civil Liberties Union (ACLU), Zirpoli issued a temporary injunction forbidding the police from using their so-called "profile of the Zebra killer" as the sole basis for stopping a man for questioning.

The Ku Klux Klan
& Similar Terrorists

After a lull during World War II, the Ku Klux Klan, traditional source of violent repression of blacks, reappeared in the South as a welter of splinter groups and competing factions. In 1945 fiery crosses, a traditional Klan weapon of intimidation, burned in Tennessee, Alabama, Florida and as far North as New Jersey. Three years later a wave of kidnappings, floggings and cross burnings swept the Birmingham, Ala. area. 1950 saw the beginning of a two-year reign of Klan terror in North and South Carolina. The early years of the 1960s brought an intensified wave of bombings, assassinations, terror and race rioting to the South as an accompaniment to the growing civil rights movement.

House committee scores Klan. The House Un-American Activities Committee Oct. 24, 1966 issued a report denouncing the Ku Klux Klan as terrorists engaging in "threats, cross-burnings, the firing of churches and schools, bombings, beatings, maimings, murders."

According to the report, "secret Klan schools instruct in the fabrication of booby traps, bombs and Molotov cocktails and teach the use of bombs, firearms, judo and karate." It said there were about 15,000 Klan members in more than a dozen Klan organizations in at least 15 states.

The committee had reported Oct. 21 on 37 days of hearings:

"More than a dozen different Klan groups are presently active in at least 15 states," and "the largest of the Klan organizations now has units operating in at least 15 states."

"Secrecy is the cornerstone of the structure of klanism. Members must take an oath 'forever' to keep 'sacredly secret' within the Klan, and not to divulge to 'any person in the whole world,' all Klan 'matters

and knowledge' and to 'die rather than divulge same.' Information about treason, rape, and malicious murder only is excepted from the oath. This oath is considered by Klansmen to be superior to any other oath, in court or elsewhere. . . . In order to conceal the existence of units within the Klans as well as bank accounts and other matters, innocent-sounding cover names are used to create the impression that they are civic, improvement, sporting, or even rescue organizations. The largest existing Klan organization operates under the cover name 'Alabama Rescue Service.' . . . It maintains a bank account in this name and, in addition, authorized signatories on this account have used fictitious names as a further secrecy measure.

"Klans engage in . . . acts of violence to further their goal of white supremacy as well as other objectives. These acts, however, are not always racially motivated and sometimes are directed against citizens who are not racially oriented but who are conducting themselves to the dislike of the Klans, which take the law into their hands as vigilantes. . . .

"Klansmen frequently carry pistols, rifles, shotguns, and bombs on their persons and in their autos. . . . Radios and telephones are frequently used by Klans in their terroristic activities. Some Klan members have been issued federal licenses as gun dealers and have sold guns to members in wholesale lots. . . ."

7 convicted of 3 rights workers' murders. An all-white jury in Meridian, Miss. Oct. 20, 1967 convicted 7 white men of conspiracy in the 1964 murder of 3 civil rights workers near Philadelphia, Miss. 8 men were acquitted, and mistrials were declared in the cases of 3 men on whom the jury could not reach a verdict.

Those found guilty were: Cecil R. Price, 29, chief deputy sheriff of Neshoba County; Sam Holloway Bowers Jr., 43, imperial wizard of the White Knights of the Ku Klux Klan; Horace Doyle Barnette, 29, former Meridian automotive parts salesman; Jimmy Arledge, 30, a Meridian truck driver; Billy Wayne Posey, 30, Williamsville (Miss.) service station operator; Jimmie Snowden, 34, Meridian laundry truck driver; Alton Wayne Roberts, 29, Meridian mobile home salesman. All were freed on $5,000 bond each by Oct. 23.

The men were convicted of conspiring to deny "life or liberty without due process." The government charged that: (a) Price had arrested Michael H. Schwerner, 24, of New York, a white field worker for the Congress of Racial Equality (CORE); Andrew Goodman, 20, of New York, a white college student, and James E. Chaney, 21, of Meridian, a Negro plasterer; (b) Price held the 3 youths while a lynching party assembled;

(c) then Price released them and allowed them to be captured by the mob, which turned them over to gunmen to be murdered.

Those who were acquitted had not been accused of participating in the slayings. They were: Lawrence A. Rainey, 43, sheriff of Neshoba County; Bernard Lee Akin, 52, Meridian housetrailer dealer; Travis Maryn Barnette, 38, a Meridian auto mechanic; James Thomas Harris, 32, a Meridian truck driver; Frank J. Herndon, 48, Meridian drive-in restaurant operator; Olen L. Burrage, 37, Philadelphia (Miss.) trucking company operator and owner of the farm on which the bodies were buried; Herman Tucker, 38, Philadelphia contractor and builder of the dam in which the bodies were found; Richard Andrew Willis, former Philadelphia policeman.

During the trial Police Sgt. Carlton Wallace Miller, 43, testified Oct. 11 that he had joined the local klavern of the White Knights of the Ku Klux Klan in late March or April 1964 and had become a paid informer for the FBI the following September. Miller, who had been a member of the Meridian police force for 20 years, identified 11 of the 18 defendants as either members of the Klan or as having been present at Klan meetings. Miller said that most Klan discussions centered on opposition to integration. He said that at one meeting Edgar Ray Killen, who had recruited him for the Klan, explained the various kinds of "pressure" to be used against civil rights workers: "To begin with, we were to call them up or go see them, threaten them on the job, things of that nature," but the pressure would include "whippings, beatings. . . . After the pressure was applied and they didn't respond, then we were to apply physical pressure." Finally, he said, "there was elimination"; "that's a term for murdering them, killing them." Miller said Killen had once discussed a plan to "whip" Schwerner but later called it off; "Mr. Killen told us to leave him alone, that another unit was going to take care of him. His elimination had been approved of by the imperial wizard." Miller said that about a week after the 3 rights workers disappeared "Mr. Killen told me they had been shot

and were dead and were buried 15 feet in a dam." Miller testified that Killen said he had come to Meridian after receiving word by phone that the rights workers were in custody. According to Miller, Killen then contacted Frank J. Herndon, also a Klan member, and "got some boys together—and went to Philadelphia." Miller quoted Killen as saying that the rights workers had been run down after a 90–100-mph. highway chase.

Another former Klan member, James E. Jordan, was the government's key witness. He named 7 defendants as actual participants in the slayings. Jordan had been indicted in the same conspiracy charges but was not a defendant in the trial. Jordan described how Deputy Price had jailed the 3 youths, held them until the mob assembled, then released them only to recapture them after a highway chase. The youths, he said, were driven to the site of the slayings in the deputy's car. Jordan told the court that he was posted as lookout a short distance down the road. "I heard car doors slam, some loud talk that I could not distinguish, and then I heard several shots," he said. Then he walked down the road and found the youths on the ground, apparently dead. The Klansmen were "milling around," Jordan declared, but they removed the signs of the shootings. The bodies were put in the back of the station wagon, he testified, and were hauled to the dam in Neshoba County, where a bulldozer buried them. Jordan said that Sam Bowers, identified as imperial wizard of the White Knights, had approved the slayings. He reported that Bowers had said Schwerner was "a thorn in the side of everyone living, especially the white people, and should be taken care of."

The court Oct. 13 heard a statement signed by Horace D. Barnette, a defendant identified as a member of the lynching party. The statement charged Jordan with killing one of the rights workers. Henry Rask, an FBI agent, told the court that he had obtained the 10-page statement from Barnette during a 5-hour 56-minute session Nov. 20, 1964 at a motel near Springhill, La. Rask said that he and James A. Wooten, another FBI agent had talked with

Barnette Nov. 19, 20 and 21 and that Barnette had said the slayings "had been bothering him and he wanted to tell us about it."

Barnette's statement, read to the court by Asst. Atty. Gen. John Doar, said: The rights workers had been driven to the shooting site with Jordan. Schwerner was hauled from the back of the car and asked: "Are you that nigger lover?" Schwerner answered: "Sir, I know just how you feel." Then a mob member "took a pistol in his hand and shot Schwerner." "Schwerner fell to the left so that he was lying alongside the road, and Goodman spun around and fell back toward the bank in back." At that point Jordan stepped forward and said: "Save one for me." Jordan pulled Chaney out onto the road with him. "I remember Chaney backing up, facing the road and standing on the bank on the other side of the ditch, and Jordan stood in the middle of the road and shot him. Jordan then said: 'You didn't leave me anything but a nigger, but at least I killed me a nigger.'"

Dahmer suspects convicted. A jury in Hattiesburg, Miss. March 15, 1968 convicted Cecil Victor Sessum of first degree murder for his part in the firebomb death of Negro leader Vernon F. Dahmer Sr. Jan. 10, 1966. Sessum was sentenced to life imprisonment.

The state had charged that the attack on Dahmer was a Ku Klux Klan plot conceived because of Dahmer's efforts to encourage Negroes to register to vote. William I. Smith, an admitted Klan member also convicted in the case, received a life term July 19. Ex-Klan member Billy Roy Pitts, who pleaded guilty to both murder and arson, was sentenced to life in prison, and Lawrence Byrd was given a 10-year term Nov. 8.

Mistrials were declared in the murder trials of Henry Edward DeBoxtel Mar. 21, Charles Clifford Wilson July 28 and James F. Lyons Nov. 14. In each case the jurors could not agree on a verdict. The trial for arson of former Ku Klux Klan leader Sam H. Bowers Jr., had ended in a deadlock May 17 with 11 jurors voting guilty and one voting not guilty. Pitts, a key state witness in the trial, had

testified May 15 that Bowers had given the orders to firebomb Dahmer's house and kill him if possible.

Three more trials of Bowers on various charges connected with Dahmer's murder also ended in mistrials during 1968-9.

Prosecutor James Finch charged at a Jan. 21-25, 1969 trial that Bowers had "planned, directed, masterminded, instituted and inspired" the 1966 firebombing murder.

Billy Roy Pitts testified Jan. 23 that Dahmer's death had been planned at a meeting in which Bowers had insisted that the Klan deal with "that nigger Dahmer." According to Pitts, Bowers did not go along on the raid that ended in Dahmer's death but was to act as "backup man" if the murder attempt failed.

Charles Clifford Wilson had been convicted of Dahmer's murder Jan. 31, 1969 and was given a life sentence.

A federal jury in Meridian, Miss. acquitted three of 10 Ku Klux Klansmen May 10, 1969 of conspiracy charges in the Dahmer murder case. The jury returned verdicts of innocent for William Travis Giles, Frank Lyons and Lester Thornton. The jury was unable to reach a verdict on the other seven.

Plot Against Evers Foiled. A member of a Ku Klux Klan branch was arrested in Fayette, Miss. Sept. 9, 1969 as he drove a car filled with weapons into the parking lot of a store owned by Fayette Mayor Charles Evers. Several hours earlier, Evers, the first black mayor in Mississippi, had received several phone calls warning that an attempt would be made on his life. The arrest was made as Evers was standing in front of his supermarket.

Fayette Police Chief Robert Vanderson and his men arrested Dale Watson of Tupelo, Miss. after uncovering five guns in Watson's car. He was charged with carrying and concealing deadly weapons.

Federal Treasury Department agents Sept. 10 arrested two white men—Pat Massengale and Bobby D. Haywood-- suspected of conspiring to assassinate Evers. The agents arrested Massengale on charges of illegally transferring a .45-caliber Thompson sub-machine gun to another person. Bobby D. Haywood was described as a friend of Watson's.

5 guilty in Pontiac bus bombing. Detroit District Court Judge Lawrence Gubow May 21, 1973 found five ex-members of the Ku Klux Klan guilty of conspiracy in the plot to bomb school buses in Pontiac, Mich. during a busing controversy in 1971.

The five were found guilty of conspiring to interfere by force with the execution of a court-ordered desegregation plan and of conspiring to intimidate black children in the exercise of their right to attend public schools.

Those convicted, all Klansmen at the time of the bombing, were: Robert E. Miles, Alexander J. Distel Jr., Wallace E. Fruit, Raymond Quick Jr. and Dennis C. Ramsey. Miles had been the grand dragon of the Michigan Realm of the United Klans of America at the time of the bombing.

The ten vehicles, bombed Aug. 30, 1971, were part of Pontiac's fleet of 90 school buses being used to carry out a court-ordered integration plan involving the busing of 8,700 schoolchildren. The busing plan had triggered widespread community opposition.

The ex-Klansmen were convicted of plotting at a statewide meeting of the Klan in July to blow up the buses.

An affidavit filed in U.S. court in Detroit Sept. 10, 1971 said the Klansmen had also planned to "knock out" a power station in the Pontiac area as a diversion for a full-scale mortar attack on the city's 90-bus fleet.

NEW LEFT & ANTIWAR ACTIVISTS

Marcuse Threatened. Dr. Herbert Marcuse, 70, acknowledged philosophical Marxist and professor of philosophy at the University of California at San Diego (USCD), fled from his La Jolla home July 4, 1968 after a written threat on his life. But he returned unharmed in September after attending academic meetings in Europe during most of the summer. FBI agents in San Diego investigated the letter, postmarked July

1, which called him a "dirty Communist dog" and was reportedly signed "The KKK."

Author of such works as *One Dimensional Man*, Marcuse had been adopted by the international New Left as philosophical guide for the movement. The threatening letter, which warned him to leave the U.S., came amid a public controversy over his leanings and affiliations.

The chairman of the UCSD department of philosophy, Dr. Jason Saunders, said July 10 that Marcuse was "perhaps the most popular professor on campus." Saunders denied charges that Marcuse indoctrinated his students. A declaration adopted by UCSD professors Aug. 9 by 109–3 vote gave Marcuse their "complete support against the current attempts to silence him."

Marcuse, who came to the U.S. in 1934, was a high-ranking Government consultant in World War II and taught at Brandeis University before he came to UCSD in 1964. Although he wrote about life in terms of class struggle, he had not been considered a doctrinaire Marxist because he rejected the concept of the "working class" as a revolutionary agent. Instead, he looked to youth and oppressed minorities as instruments for change; he expressed support for "socially useful destructiveness," and he recommended "the withdrawal of toleration of speech and assembly from groups and movements which promote aggressive policies, armament, chauvinism, racial and religious discrimination, or which oppose the extension of public services" (from Marcuse's *A Critique of Pure Tolerance*). But Marcuse said in an interview that he "would restrict expression only in the case of movements which are definitely aggressive and destructive," for example, "the Hitler movement."

'Catonsville 9' Convicted. A U.S. District Court jury in Baltimore convicted a group of 9 Roman Catholic antiwar activists Oct. 16, 1968 of burning draft files May 17 after invading a Selective Service office at Catonsville, Md., a suburb of Baltimore.

Judge Roszel C. Thomsen Nov. 8 imposed sentences on the defendants ranging from 2 to 3½ years. The Rev. Philip Berrigan, 44, and Thomas Lewis, who both were serving 6-year terms for destroying Selective Service files in Baltimore Oct. 27, 1967, received 3½-year jail terms. 3-year prison terms were given to the Rev. Daniel Berrigan, brother of Father Philip, Thomas Melville, 37, a former Maryknoll priest, and George Mische, 30. The 4 other defendants received 2-year sentences. They were Marjorie Melville, a former Maryknoll nun and wife of Melville, Mary Moylan, 32, John Hogan, 33, a former Maryknoll brother, and David Darst, 26, a Christian brother.

12 Milwaukee Protesters Guilty. Twelve of the so-called Milwaukee 14 group of draft protesters were convicted of burglary, theft and arson May 26, 1969 in Milwaukee Circuit Court. The defendants were members of a group of Roman Catholics, including seven clergymen, charged with entering a Milwaukee selective service office Sept. 24, 1968, and seizing and burning thousands of draft files. The trial had opened May 12. Judge Charles L. Larson, 61, sentenced 11 of the 12 defendants to concurrent two-year jail terms and four years' probation June 6.

The defendants, who conducted their own defense, attempted to turn the trial into a forum for attacking the draft system and the Vietnam war. Larson ruled May 19 that the draft and the war were not relevant issues in the state trial but that the defendants could explain their motives for burning the draft records.

The 11 defendants sentenced June 6 were: Rev. Robert Cunnane, Stoughton, Mass.; Rev. Anthony J. Mullanoy, Boston; Brother Basil K. O'Leary, Wilnona, Minn.; James H. Forest, New York City; Robert E. Graf, Milwaukee; Rev. Lawrence E. Rosenbaugh, Milwaukee; Donald J. Cotton, Milwaukee; Rev. Alfred L. Janicke, Minneapolis; Fred J. Ojile, Minneapolis; Rev. James W. Harney, North Weymouth, Mass.; and Douglas Marvey, Minneapolis. The 12th defendant, Rev. John Higginbotham, 28, of St. Cloud, Minn., was sentenced to two years in prison June 20 after a delay granted so he could obtain counsel.

Detroit Bombings. Following a series of 8 bombings in the Detroit area, 11 young men and women described as "hippie types" were arrested Nov. 11, 1968 for conspiracy in what Detroit police called an "anti-establishment, anti-government" bombing plot. Lt. William McCoy of the city's Special Investigation Bureau said that there was no indication that the defendants were members of any formal organization. The bombing targets included a recruiting office of the Central Intelligence Agency, cars belonging to 3 policemen and an Army recruiter, a draft board office, a suburban school administration building and the University of Michigan Institute of Science & Technology.

SDS Origins & Offshoots. The most notorious of the New Left revolutionary and allegedly terroristic organizations of the 1960s and early 1970s was Students for a Democratic Society (SDS).

Nominally, SDS came into existence in 1959, but its background goes back to 1905 and to the Intercollegiate Socialist Society (ISS) founded then by Upton Sinclair, Walter Lippmann, Clarence Darrow and Jack London. The ISS underwent a reorganization in 1921 and became the League for Industrial Democracy (LID). Its youth wing was reorganized as the Student League for Industrial Democracy (SLID). SLID joined with the Communist-dominated National Student League (NSL) in December 1935 to form a "united front" under the title American Student Union (ASU).

After World War II, LID extracted the remains of SLID from the ASU merger (in 1946), and the civil rights movement brought new life to the youth group in the late 1950s.

A fresh reorganization transformed SLID into Students for a Democratic Society (SDS) in 1959. The organization made no real progress, however, until 1962, after its "Port Huron Statement," drafted by Tom Hayden and Al Haber, was adopted enthusiastically by the 45 delegates who attended the 1962 SDS convention at an AFL-CIO camp in Port Huron, Mich. Hayden, who delivered the statement, was elected SDS president. The statement, which called for "truly democratic alternatives" in the campaign against racial injustice, war and poverty, described violence "in social change or interchange" as "abhorrent."

At its 1968 national convention, held at Michigan State University in East Lansing June 10-15, delegates rejected proposals that would have turned SDS into an organized vehicle for revolution rather than a loosely structured foundation for building a radical movement. (But FBI Director J. Edgar Hoover charged in a report on FBI operations July 18 that workshops in "sabotage and explosives" had been conducted at the SDS conference.)

SDS splits in 1969—The SDS split into two rival factions during its 1969 national convention, held in the Chicago Coliseum June 18-22. Faced with a take-over threat by representatives of the Progressive Labor party and its allies from the Worker-Student Alliance, two of the three national SDS leaders and their followers walked out of the annual meeting June 20 and met separately in the First Presbyterian Church on the city's West Side. The split culminated a struggle within SDS between the smaller but well-organized PL faction and an anti-PL group at the convention called the National Office Collective.

Originally scheduled to open June 9, the convention had been postponed after SDS was denied use of more than 60 potential meeting sites at universities, colleges, auditoriums and union halls. Bernardine Dohrn, 27, SDS interorganizational secretary, said June 11 that the difficulty in finding a site was due to "federally masterminded pressure against radicals."

An estimated 1,100 to 1,500 delegates gathered at the Coliseum June 18 and passed resolutions to bar the "capitalist press" from the meetings.

Opposition to the PL faction centered around Miss Dohrn and Michael Klonsky, 25, SDS national secretary. This group believed that SDS should be mainly a student organization opposed to "imperialism" and supporting black liberation. The society's third national leader, Internal Education Secretary Fred Gordon, was a leading spokesman for the PL faction, which included about 600 delegates. The PL group, which labeled itself "Maoist," saw revolution in doctrinaire terms of class struggle. It charged the black power and student power move-ments were counterrevolutionary. The PL faction supported resolutions against the use of drugs and such "bourgeois" enterprises as Berkeley's "People's Park."

The National Office Collective, checked by the parliamentary skill of the PL faction, walked out of the Coliseum after an angry confrontation between Jules Cook, a Black Panther speaker, and Gordon, who condemned the Panthers as reactionary nationalists. The anti-PL faction, numbering from 500 to 1,000 delegates, met separately and returned to the Coliseum briefly about midnight June 21. Miss Dohrn mounted the podium and announced that the PL faction was expelled from SDS. The national office group retained control of the SDS membership files and treasury.

Both factions, each claiming the SDS label, announced national officers June 23. The national office group elected Mark Rudd, 22, leader of the 1968 Columbia University revolt, as its national secretary. Jeff Jones of New York was named interorganizational secretary and William Ayres, 24, internal education secretary. The PL group's officers, in corresponding posts, were John Pennington of Boston, Patricia Forman of San Francisco and Alan Spector.

Emergence of Weatherman—SDS' terrorist Weatherman faction appeared following the split at the 1969 convention.

The majority emerging from the convention took over the Chicago office as the Revolutionary Youth Movement (RYM), while the Progressive Labor faction seized control in Boston.

A further split in Chicago produced a RYM I and a RYM II. RYM II later became independent as simply Revolutionary Youth Movement.

RYM I became known as Weatherman, deriving its name from a position paper entitled "You Don't Need a Weatherman to Know Which Way the Wind Blows," a line from Bob Dylan's song "Subterranean Homesick Blues." The paper was written by Karen Ashley, Bill Ayers, Bernardine Dohrn, John (J.J.) Jacobs, Jeff Jones, Gerry Long, Howie Machtinger, Jim Mellen, Terry Robbins, Mark Rudd and Steve Tappis.

In the position paper, the Weatherman faction (later referred to as Weathermen and Weather Underground) described the "correct path" for revolution in the U.S. as action to "build a white movement which will support the blacks in moving as fast as they have to and are able to, and still itself keep up with that black movement enough so that white revolutionaries share the cost and the blacks don't have to do the whole thing alone."

Weatherman said in SDS' New Left Notes (June 18 issue) that alienated high school youths were the potential revolutionary class in the U.S. in addition to Third-World (minority) peoples. To win over the students, faction members believed they must prove that they were not timid intellectuals.

Weatherman 'Rage' in Chicago. Hundreds of Weatherman adherents staged demonstrations that they described as "days of rage" in Chicago Oct. 8–11, 1969 to coincide with the conspirary trial of eight antiwar protest leaders charged with fomenting disorders during the 1968 Democratic National Convention. The demonstrators chose the slogan "Bring the War Home" for their four-day campaign.

Helmeted Weatherman members clashed with police the night of Oct. 8 following a rally at Chicago's Lincoln Park. Sixty persons were arrested and three radicals were shot, one by a policeman who said he shot a demonstrator who had been clubbing him.

Police arrested 12 demonstrators Oct. 9 when 60 members of the Weatherman "women's militia" charged police lines after announcing that they would "destroy" a military induction center. Other arrests came during a police raid on a church in suburban Evanston early Oct. 11. Later that day, 103 demonstrators were arrested as they charged police lines in the heart of the Chicago business district. The resulting violence injured 24 policemen and scores of demonstrators.

The police said Oct. 13 that 290 had been arrested during the demonstrations. Two Weatherman leaders—Mark Rudd, the faction's national secretary, and Bernardine Dohrn, former SDS officer, were among those arrested.

Weatherman's rival RYM II faction also gathered in Chicago during the four days. They scored the Weatherman tactics as "adventuristic" and likely to alienate potential supporters among the working classes.

House Probes SDS. The House Committee on Internal Security began hearings June 3, 1969 on SDS activities.

New York Times reporter Anthony Ripley testified under subpoena June 3 that he was reluctant to appear before the committee because it would make it more difficult to cover "the radical community." He confirmed details he had reported on an SDS convention in 1968. He had quoted SDS Interorganizational Secretary Bernardine Dohrn as saying "I consider myself a revolutionary Communist." Earlier in the proceedings, Bradshaw Mallard, a Gainesville, Fla. policeman, had testified that SDS National Secretary Michael Klonsky had "openly admitted he was a Communist" during an April 11 speech at the University of Florida.

The Rev. Gerald F. Yates, a Georgetown University professor, testified June 4 that SDS had won an "indirect victory" for radicalism by forcing out "hundreds" of university presidents and deans who no longer "want to stand in the center of the shooting gallery and have their heads shot off." He mentioned James A. Perkins of Cornell and Buell G. Gallagher of City College of New York as two of many presidents forced to resign because of campus disruptions.

Weatherman Arrests in Cambridge. Twenty-three Weatherman members were arrested Nov. 18, 1969 in connection with a Nov. 8 sniper attack on the Cambridge, Mass. police headquarters. Eric Mann, 28, leader of the local Weatherman faction, was also arrested and charged with assault with intent to commit murder.

Judge M. Edward Viola dismissed the charges Nov. 29 against Mann and 20 of the group after a young prosecution witness testified that he had signed a statement implicating some of the Weathermen under threats from police. Five Weathermen were fined a total of $700 in district court in Boston Dec. 16 on charges arising from the incident. Two of the defendants received jail sentences.

N.Y. Bombing 'Plot.' The FBI Nov. 14, 1969 arrested three men and a woman and charged them with being radical-terrorists who had plotted and set off eight bombings in major corporate and government structures in New York City since July.

The suspects included Samuel Melville, the alleged ringleader, who the FBI said, fashioned the bombs from stolen dynamite. The others were George Demmerle, John D. Hughey 3d and Jane Lauren Alpert. Being sought was Patricia Swinton, who, the FBI said, had worked for the North American Congress of Latin America. The FBI said the organization "correlates research" on what the group calls "U.S. imperialism in Latin America."

The five suspects were charged with setting off or planting bombs in the following places:

July 27 -A United Fruit Company Pier on the Hudson River; Aug. 20—The Marine Midland Grace Trust Company Building on Broadway; Sept. 19 - The Federal Office Building at Federal Plaza; Oct. 7 The U.S. Armed Forces Examining and Entrance Station at Whitehall Street; Nov. 11—RCA Building at Rockefeller Plaza; General Motors Corporation Building on Fifth Avenue, and the Chase Manhattan Building at Chase Manhattan Plaza; and Nov. 12— The Criminal Courts Building and an Army truck parked near the 69th Regiment Armory.

(Melville, who later pleaded guilty, was killed Sept. 13, 1971 in the Attica, N.Y. prison uprising.)

'Bomb factory' destroyed. A series of dynamite explosions demolished a New York townhouse in the Greenwich Village area March 6, 1970 and killed three persons. Police said a revolutionaries' bomb factory was in operation in the four-story building. Two young women, one of them the daughter of a Midwest radio station president who owned the building, were reported to have fled the house as the first explosions rocked the building.

Police and firemen sifting through the rubble March 7-17 found the remains of three persons, one of whom remained unidentifiable. Police March 8 identified one of the victims as Theodore Gold, 23, believed to be a member of SDS' militant wing. Another victim was identified March 17 as Diana Oughton, 28, a member of SDS' Weatherman faction. A Weatherman statement published in May identified the third as Terry Robbins, a Weatherman who had been a Kent State University radical leader in 1968.

The two girls who fled the building were identified as Cathlyn Platt Wilkerson and Kathy Boudin. James P. Wilkerson, Cathlyn's father and owner of the demolished building, flew to New York March 11 and pleaded to his absent daughter to disclose the number of people in the townhouse at the time of the explosion.

The two missing girls had been ordered to appear in a Chicago criminal court in connection with the "four days of rage" staged by Weatherman in 1969.

Neither woman appeared in the Cook County court March 16. Their bail was ordered revoked and a warrant was issued for their arrest.

3 N.Y. buildings bombed. Scores of buildings were evacuated in New York March 12, 1970 after a series of explosions caused extensive damage in three mid-town big business skyscrapers. There were no injuries as the explosions shattered windows and walls at the home offices of Socony Mobil, General Telephone and Electronics, and International Business Machines (IBM). A terrorist group, calling itself "Revolutionary Force 9," claimed credit for the bombings. The group said in a letter that the three companies had been hit because they were "enemies of all life."

(A man was killed and several men injured March 28 by an explosion in a Lower-East-Side New York apartment. Police said they had found live bombs and bomb-making equipment in the debris.)

Illinois unit cites Weatherman threat. A report delivered to the Illinois Senate April 20 said that Weatherman posed "an immediate and long-range threat" to the internal security of the nation. The 750-page report, prepared by the staff of the Illinois Crime Investigation Commission, dealt with the Chicago "days of rage."

The report said the Weatherman faction had "risen beyond revolution to the level of anarchy" and was "in the business of fomenting discontent and revolution among America's youth." It connected the group with the international Communist movement but said no Communist financing was behind the Weatherman faction or SDS. The report noted that in 1969, $112,443 was deposited in an SDS account in Chicago's Manufacturers National Bank, compared with $99,679 the previous year.

Weatherman 'declaration.' The New York Times May 25 published excerpts from a statement that claimed to be a "declaration of war" issued by the Weatherman. The statement, received by the Times Chicago bureau, was identified by the senders as a transcript of a tape recording by Bernardine Dohrn, a leader of the group.

The statement warned: "Within the next 14 days we will attack a symbol or institution of Amerikan [a radical spelling used to suggest Nazi-like oppression] injustice. This is the way we celebrate the example of Eldridge Cleaver and H. Rap Brown and all black revolutionaries who first inspired us." (While there was no obvious Weatherman attack within the specified two weeks, a dynamite time bomb exploded in the New York City police headquarters [causing injury to at least seven people there] June 9, and the Associated Press received a handwritten communication signed "Weatherman" June 10 claiming that the group had planted the bomb because "the pigs in this country are our enemies.")

The statement said the Weathermen indicted in Chicago "move freely in and out of every city and youth scene in this country." The declaration claimed there were "several hundred members of the Weatherman underground.... In every tribe, commune, dormitory, farmhouse, barracks and townhouse where kids are making love, smoking dope and loading guns—fugitives from Amerikan justice are free to go." The statement said that Weatherman was "adopting the classic guerrilla strategy of the Vietcong and the urban guerrilla strategy of the Tupamaros [a Uruguayan revolu-

tionary organization] to our own situation here in the most technically advanced country in the world."

(The San Francisco Chronicle said July 28 that it had received a letter, signed "Weatherman Underground," which warned Attorney General John N. Mitchell: "Don't look for us, dog: we'll find you first." The letter was described by the senders as a "third communication," apparently referring to the May "declaration of war" and a second letter claiming credit for the bomb explosion in the New York City police headquarters. The letter, dated July 26 and also received by the New York Post, said the group was celebrating the 11th anniversary of the Cuban revolution. It said, "Everywhere we see the growth of revolutionary culture and the ways in which every move of the monster-state tightens the noose around its own neck.")

Weathermen indicted in bomb plots. A federal grand jury in Detroit indicted 13 Weathermen July 23, 1970 on charges of conspiracy to commit bombings through a nationwide underground of terrorists. By July 25, five of the defendants had been taken into custody.

The indictment charged that the conspiracy had been born at a December 1968 meeting in Flint, Mich. The charges traced the bombing plot through a February meeting in Cleveland and alleged bomb-making that resulted in the explosion that left three persons dead in New York.

The indictment charged: "It was part of the conspiracy that the defendants would organize a 'central committee' to direct underground bombing operations ... that this group would be assigned to Berkeley, Calif.; Chicago, Ill.; New York, N.Y.; and Detroit, Mich.; that clandestine and underground 'focals,' consisting of three or four persons, would be established; that the 'focals' would be commanded by the 'central committee' in the bombing of police and other civic, business and education buildings throughout the country." Justice Department officials said that the alleged "focals" were distinct from so-called Weatherman "affinity groups," which the organization used in street violence.

Named as defendants in the indictment were Mark W. Rudd, 23; Bernardine Dohrn, had disappeared. and Kathy Boudin, 27. All four had been named in the Chicago "Days of Ráge" indictment as was another defendant, Linda Sue Evans, 23, who had been arrested in New York City earlier in the year and released on bail. Also charged was Cathlyn P. Wilkerson, 26, who had been named as co-conspirator in the Chicago indictment and had disappeared after the March explosion in New York City, which destroyed a townhouse owned by her father.

Besides Miss Evans, defendants taken into custody by police were Russell T. Neufeld, 23, arrested in Chicago July 23; Dianne Marie Donghi, 21, arrested in New York City July 23; Robert G. Burlingham, 24, who surrendered in Boston; and Jane Spielman, 23, who surrendered in New York City July 25. The other defendants were Ronald D. Fliegelman, 26; Naomi E. Jaffe, 27; and Larry D. Grathwohl, 23.

Among 15 others named as co-conspirators in the indictment were at least two—Diana Oughton and Theodore Gold—who had been killed in the New York townhouse explosion. A third body found in the wreckage had not been identified, but Weathermen claimed it was Terry Robbins, also named as co-conspirator in the current indictment.

The grand jury cited 21 "overt acts" in carrying out the conspiracy but only connected the defendants with one actual bombing attempt, an abortive attack on a police association building in Detroit in March. Rudd was quoted as saying in a Cleveland speech Feb. 4 that "the Weathermen were going underground and would commit acts of assassination and bombings of police and military installations."

Assistant Attorney General Will Wilson, head of the Justice Department's Criminal Division, said July 23 that the defendants were the "top and core leadership" of the Weatherman faction.

Detroit District Court Judge Damon J. Keith Oct. 15, 1973 granted a government request to dismiss the charges because, the prosecution said, it could not comply with Keith's order to reveal whether "espionage techniques" had been used in obtaining evidence without compromising "foreign intelligence information deemed essential to the security of the United States."

Only six of the accused had surrendered or been captured: Robert G. Burlingham, Russell T. Neufeld, Mark Real, Dianne Marie Donghi, Linda Evans and Jane Spielman. The remainder, including Weathermen leaders Mark Rudd and Bernardine Dohrn, had disappeared.

Bomb penalties sought. President Nixon asked Congress March 25, 1970 to set severe penalties, including the death sentence, for the illegal use and transportation of explosives. He said he was asking for harsher federal laws to stem "an alarming increase in the number of criminal bombings in the cities of our country."

In a White House statement, Nixon said recent bombings were "the work of political fanatics" who must be dealt with as the "potential murderers they are." He proposed in his legislation that any individual "engaged in the transport or use of explosives" in violation of the proposed laws "be made subject to the death penalty if a fatality occurs."

The President said his purpose for bringing crimes linked with bombings under federal jurisdiction was to assist state and local governments combat the "multiplying number of acts of urban terror."

In a separate development, Nixon joined the Justice Department in asking Congress that "Molotov cocktails," homemade bombs made with gas-filled bottles and cloth or string wicks, be included in the categories now covered by existing antibombing laws.

Congressional hearings—Two congressional subcommittees held hearings July 15–22, 1970 and heard city, state and federal law enforcement officials testify that political, terrorist and criminal bombings had reached crisis proportions in some U.S. cities and on some college campuses.

Nearly all of the officials who appeared before the Senate's Investigations subcommittee and the House's Judiciary subcommittee No. 5 said federal legislation was needed to curb the sharp rise in bombings.

Sen. John L. McClellan (D, Ark.), who opened the Senate hearings July 15, said the wave of bombings "portend a very grave danger to our internal security and our peaceful way of life." Eugene T. Rossides, assistant secretary of the treasury, told the Senators at the opening session that "from January 1969 to April of this year ... this country suffered a total of 4,330 bombings, an additional 1,475 attempted bombings, and a reported 35,129 threatened bombings." Rossides said bombs had caused "at least 40 deaths and at least $21.8 million of property damage in the last 15 months."

New York City Police Commissioner Howard R. Leary told the Senators July 16 that since January 1969 there had been 366 bombing incidents in New York City, including those "of municipal and federal banks, religious houses of worship and commercial buildings as well as residential buildings used as 'bomb factories.'"

Assistant U.S. Attorney General Will Wilson testified July 17 that "the suppression of terroristic tactics is not a repression of free speech or the right to dissent or the right to protest." Wilson said most of the bombings were the work of "fanatics who are politically motivated..."

Charles A. O'Brien, chief deputy attorney general of California, offered a different view. He testified July 22 that the rising number of bombings was being perpetrated by people from all segments of society. He said that "bombs are playing a larger role in our society than simply as the deadly tools of political terrorists." O'Brien said there was hardly a segment of the American society—"white, black, poor, rich, middle class, educated and uneducated, right and left, native and immigrant, urban and rural—which is not represented among the bombers."

Nixon assails terrorism—President Nixon Sept. 16, 1970 again deplored "the spreading disease of violence" and "its use as a political tactic." Violence and terror, he said, "have no place in a free society.... In a system like ours, which provides the means for peaceful change, no cause justifies violence in the name of change."

Addressing a campus audience of some 15,000 in the Kansas State University fieldhouse at Manhattan, Kan., Nixon called for "an uncompromising stand against those who reject the rules of civilized conduct and respect for others, those who destroy what is right in our society and whose actions would do nothing to right what is wrong."

It was time, he said, "for the responsible university and college administrators, faculty and student leaders to stand up and be counted, because we must remember, only they can save higher education in America. It cannot be saved by government."

The President warned against "the acceptance of violence, the condoning of terror, excusing of inhuman acts in a misguided effort to accommodate the community's standards to those of the violent few."

The President also pressed these points in a letter to 900 university administrators and trustees, expressing concern over the tendency to lay the blame for campus disorders on federal domestic and foreign policies.

"There can be no substitute," he told them, "for the acceptance of responsibility for order and discipline on campuses by college administrators and college faculties." "Those who cannot accept that rule of reason, those who resort to the rule of force have no place on a college campus," he said.

The letter, made public Sept. 20, was accompanied by an article written by philosophy professor Sidney Hook of New York University and published in the Los Angeles Times Aug. 30. It was recommended by Nixon as "cogent and compelling." Hook said that it was "noisome hogwash" to contend that "the chief threat to academic freedom today comes from without and not from within." The problem and threat on campus, Hook said, was "academic disruption and violence which flow from substituting for the academic goals of learning the political goals of action."

This perverted the purpose of the university from a study of social and political problems into a political effort "agitating for the adoption of partisan political goals," Hook argued. He advocated university guidelines for expression of dissent, prompt punishment of violators and resort to civil authority in dangerous, violent campus situations involving "intervention by large outside nonstudent forces."

Man dies in Wisconsin blast. An early morning explosion tore apart the Army Mathematics Research Center at the University of Wisconsin (Madison) Aug. 24, 1970, killing a physics researcher and destroying most of the contents of the building, including a $1.5 million computer. The blast occurred at 3:42 a.m., two minutes after Madison police received an anonymous phone call warning that a bomb had been planted at the center.

Killed in the blast was Dr. Robert Fassnacht, 33, who had stayed late at the center to finish a research project in low-temperature physics. Four other persons were injured by the explosion, which destroyed trees and autos near the building and shattered windows 10 blocks from the campus. Edwin Young, university chancellor, said Aug. 25 the explosion "ruined the life work of five physics professors and wiped out the Ph.D. theses of two dozen graduate students."

Madison had been the scene of considerable turmoil and of a series of bombing incidents in recent years. The Mathematics Research Center had been the frequent target of antiwar demonstrators, who objected to research on campus under contract to the Army. However Dr. J. Barkley Rosser, director of the center, said Aug. 24 that the research was in applied mathematics and had "nothing to do with national defense."

Leaflets distributed in Madison Aug. 25 contained an explanation of the bombing offered by "We who understand and support the demolition of the Army Math Research Center." It charged that research at the center "has killed literally thousands of innocent people" and concluded, "if the military suppresses life and freedom, . . . we must suppress the military."

Similar motives were reported Aug. 27 in Kaleidoscope, an underground newspaper distributed on the campus. The paper said it had received a statement by telephone from "The New Year's Gang," which claimed responsibility for the bombing as "part of a worldwide struggle to defeat American imperialism." The name reportedly stemmed from an unsuccessful attempt to bomb an Army ammunition plant in Baraboo, Wis. Jan. 1. The statement said unless demands were met by Oct. 10, the group would take "revolutionary measures of an intensity never before seen in this country . . . open warfare, kidnaping . . . and even assassination." The newspaper said the explosion had gone off two minutes ahead of schedule and added that the gang "regrets the death of Robert Fassnacht."

The FBI filed charges Sept. 2 of conspiracy to bomb, sabotage and destruction of government property against Karleton Lewis Armstrong, 22, a former chemistry major at the university; his brother Dwight Alan Armstrong, 19, a high school dropout; Leo Frederick Burt, 22, a student at the university who had written for the campus newspaper, The Daily Cardinal; and David Sylvan Fine, 18, a Daily Cardinal staff member who formerly had been on the staff of a Students for a Democratic Society (SDS) publication at the University of Delaware.

The FBI identified the explosive in the blast as a mixture of nitrogen fertilizer and fuel oil, which had been planted in a rented van left beside the research center, and said Karleton Armstrong had bought fuel oil and nitrate fertilizer earlier in August.

The FBI cited a letter from Fine to a friend postmarked Aug. 28 New York City. The letter said Fine and Burt were headed toward Canada. It contained a document labeled "Communique from the underground number one—the Marion Delgado Collective." (Marion Delgado was a mythical revolutionary child popularized in the SDS publication, New Left Notes.) The document was an elaboration of the statement reported by Kaleidoscope.

Karleton Armstrong, arrested in Canada in 1972 and extradited to the U.S., pleaded guilty Sept. 28, 1973 to a reduced charge of 2d-degree murder. He was sentenced Nov. 1 to an "indeterminate" prison term not to exceed 23 years.

Bombings continue. Among other reports of terroristic bombings in 1970:

■A bomb explosion caused an estimated $200,000 worth of damage June 29 to a science building on the Drake University campus in Des Moines, Iowa.

■Bombs damaged two branches of the Bank of America June 19 in Berkeley, Calif. The explosions shattered dozens of windows but did little structural damage. No one was injured. The bombings were the latest in a series of violent acts against the nation's largest bank.

■A bomb exploded July 1 shattering windows and destroying reference material at the University of California's Center for South and Southeast Asia Studies in Berkeley.

■New York City police reported July 5 that a security policeman had uncovered 11 firebombs placed under five police cars in a fenced-in parking area. The police said the bombs, which were Molotov cocktails, had not exploded because they had been constructed with defective timing devices.

■Three persons were injured July 7 in New York City when a pipe bomb exploded at the Haitian consulate. A police inspector said damage was "minor." Two hours later explosive devices were found at the Portugese and South African government offices in New York City. The two bombs were defused by the police.

■Three explosions rocked the Camp McCoy Army base in Sparta, Wis. July 26 after an unidentified caller told camp authorities that a bomb had been planted on the base.

■Blasts Oct. 8 hit a courthouse in San Rafael, Calif., an ROTC building on the University of Washington campus in Seattle and a National Guard armory in Santa Barbara, Calif.

A fourth bomb was found and disarmed in a building at the University of California in Berkeley by an Army bomb squad.

No injuries were reported in the explosions, two of them preceded by telephone warnings. Property damage was extensive.

The bombings were believed by police to be the work of the Weatherman faction of the SDS. They came less than a day after a tape recorded message purportedly made by Bernardine Dohrn was played publicly at a news conference in New York. The message warned that a fall offensive by young revolutionaries was about to begin "that will spread from Santa Barbara to Boston, back to Kent [State] and Kansas."

■ Five buildings were hit Oct. 12 by dynamite blasts in Rochester, N.Y. The FBI joined county and city police in an attempt to find the terrorists responsible for the bombings, which damaged two downtown public buildings, two Negro churches and the home of a white union official.

■ An early-morning blast Oct. 14 ripped through Harvard's Center for International Affairs in Cambridge, Mass. The bomb exploded shortly after 1 a.m. when the center was closed. The blast, which injured no one, was preceded by a telephone caller who warned campus police "to get the janitor out of there. This is no joke." Responsibility for the bombing was claimed by the "Proud Eagle Tribe," which identified its members as "revolutionary women."

■ A virus research center at the Stanford Research Institute in Irvine, Calif. was demolished Oct. 18 by a blast which also destroyed a nearby greenhouse. No injuries were reported in the blast at the center, which had been a target of revolutionaries in 1969.

■ Two dynamite explosions Nov. 1 damaged a military induction center in Fresno, Calif. and the office of the Fresno Guide, a conservative triweekly newspaper.

■ Three persons were injured in an explosion Dec. 11 in the University of Kansas (Lawrence) computer center. The explosion came three minutes after a telephone call was received warning that a bomb was set to go off.

■ A bomb blew a hole in the roof of the Bank of America branch at Isla Vista, Calif. Dec. 15. The damaged building was a new structure built to replace one burned down earlier in the year during rioting at the nearby Santa Barbara campus of the University of California. (Fire had gutted a Bank of

America branch near the Irvine campus of the University of California Oct. 26. The burned building had been painted with various epithets, some reading "Death to the Pigs" and "All Power to the People.")

■ A firebomb exploded Dec. 15 in the Army Reserve Officers Training Corps offices on the University of Connecticut (Storrs) campus. Officials said there was modest damage to ROTC records. An apparent firebombing damaged the headquarters of the antipoverty agency in nearby Bridgeport Dec. 14.

6 seized in alleged bomb plot. Six persons were arrested in New York City Nov. 2 on charges of conspiracy to make bombs and commit arson and murder. Bronx County District Attorney Burton B. Roberts, who announced the arrests, said he had reason to believe that four of the suspects were "connected with the Weathermen."

Roberts told newsmen that the six were seized in raids on three different apartments, where police discovered books on explosives, materials to make bombs and maps of major buildings in New York and Chicago.

Roberts said the apartments had been under surveillance for three months and that evidence gained through court-sanctioned wiretaps and investigations by other agencies had convinced him that "this is a Weatherman operation." Those arrested were Donald Cavellini, 27, of New York; his twin brother William of Somerville, Mass.; Jefferson Bernard, 19, of Syracuse, N.Y.; Mrs. Beth Katz, 27, Timothy Doyle, 28, and his mother Mrs. Mary Doyle, 54, all of New York. Roberts said William Cavellini and Mrs. Doyle were not connected with the Weatherman faction.

Police hold Washington rally. Nearly 3,000 policemen from 25 states converged on Washington Oct. 14, 1970 for a noon rally on the steps of the Capitol to protest the increase in armed attacks on lawmen.

With a group of Congressmen in the crowd, the president of the Fraternal Order of Police (FOP) exhorted the policemen to bring pressure on their rep-

resentatives in Washington for legislation to give the police more power and reverse court decisions that he said "aid and abet criminals."

The FOP president, John H. Harrington, blamed the Supreme Court and the American Civil Liberties Union (ACLU) for violence by radical groups against policemen. Harrington, a 30-year veteran of the Philadelphia police, said that there was a national conspiracy by radical organizations to murder lawmen. He accused the Court and the ACLU of actions serving to coddle outlaws and extremists.

In an earlier appearance before the House Internal Security Committee, holding hearings on the Black Panthers, Harrington charged that "Communist backed" radical groups, like the Panthers, Students for a Democratic Society (SDS) and the Weathermen, were trying to terrorize Americans and topple the government. He blamed radicals for the murder of 20 policemen since January.

In a related development, Attorney General John N. Mitchell Oct. 23 discounted the idea that there was a national conspiracy hatched by the left to murder policemen. He told interviewers, however, that "constant repetition" of radical dialogue "has brought about more attacks upon police."

Mitchell, chiefs meet on terrorists. Attorney General John N. Mitchell met Oct. 30 with 13 high-ranking police officials from across the country to confer on terrorist bombings and attacks on police officers.

Mitchell said the exchange of intelligence information on terrorists had been discussed.

Asked if the terrorist activity was believed to be part of a national conspiracy, Mitchell responded: "We do not know of any total, national, combined synchronized conspiracy of terrorist groups. . . . But there are some of these anarchistic groups of nihilists acting on a national basis."

Hoover cites growing threat. Federal Bureau of Investigation (FBI) Director J. Edgar Hoover said Oct. 30 that activity by New Left extremist groups had increased and posed a growing problem for law enforcers. In the annual FBI report for the fiscal year that ended June 30, Hoover singled out the Weatherman faction as responsible for much of the recent terrorism.

Hoover said some elements of the New Left had gone underground to "set up communes and direct attention to guerrilla warfare." He said black militants also "conducted guerrilla-type warfare," mentioning such groups as the Black Panthers and the Detroit-based Republic of New Africa, a separatist organization.

Weatherman shift reported. A statement signed by Weatherman leader Bernardine Dohrn and reported by the New York Times Dec. 24, 1970 hinted movement toward a "cultural revolution" as an "alternative direction" to the "tendency to consider only bombings or picking up a gun as revolutionary."

The statement had been circulated by the Liberation News Service and had appeared in a number of campus and underground newspapers.

The statement said that the explosion in a New York City townhouse, in which three radicals were killed, "forever destroyed our belief that armed struggle is the only real revolutionary struggle."

The statement said: "It is time for the movement to go out into the air, to organize, to risk calling rallies and demonstrations, to convince that mass actions against the war and in support of rebellions do make a difference."

Above Miss Dohrn's name, the statement bore the words "Weather Underground," in contrast to "Weatherman Underground" identifying previous statements, a switch attributable to feminist influences in the movement.

Kidnap plot charged, 'Harrisburg 8' case ends in mistrial. FBI Director J. Edgar Hoover, testifying before a Senate Appropriations subcommittee Nov. 27, 1970, said that the FBI had uncovered a radical plot to kidnap a high government official.

Hoover alleged that Philip and Daniel Berrigan, two Roman Catholic priests currently in prison for destroying draft records, were leaders of the group, which he identified as the East Coast Conspiracy to Save Lives.

The FBI director said the "anarchist group," composed of Catholic priests, nuns and laymen, if successful in the kidnapping, "would demand an end to United States bombing operations in Southeast Asia and the release of all political prisoners as ransom." He also said the group "plans to blow up underground electrical conduits and steam pipes serving the Washington, D.C. area in order to disrupt federal government operations."

During his testimony Hoover said intelligence sources indicated that a White House aide had been intended as a possible victim of the plot. He later told reporters that other federal officials and foreign diplomats were potential targets.

William M. Kunstler and the Rev. William C. Cunningham, attorneys for the Berrigans, immediately branded Hoover's testimony as "a far-fetched spy story." They said if Hoover "had the evidence he claims to have," his duty would be to "see that the Berrigans and their alleged co-conspirators are prosecuted."

Six self-acknowledged members of the East Coast Conspiracy to Save Lives said Nov. 30 that the Berrigans had never belonged to their 11-member group and that they had never considered kidnapping or sabotage. At a Washington, D.C. news conference, the six said the group had been inactive since February 1970 when members had "liberated" draft files in Philadelphia and General Electric Co. records in Washington.

Philip Berrigan and five others were indicted Jan. 12, 1971 on charges of conspiring to kidnap Henry A. Kissinger, assistant to the President for national security affairs, and of plotting to blow up the heating systems of federal buildings in Washington. The six defendants were indicted by a federal grand jury in Harrisburg, Pa., near the federal prison at Lewisburg where Berrigan was imprisoned during part of the alleged conspiracy.

Also named as co-conspirators but not indicted were the Rev. Daniel Berrigan and six others.

The indictment stated that "dynamite charges were to be detonated in approximately five locations" in Washington underground tunnels on Washington's Birthday in February. It said that Philip Berrigan and the Rev. Joseph R. Wenderoth, 35, of Baltimore, also indicted, had investigated the city tunnel system as part of the plot. The indictment said the conspirators planned to kidnap Kissinger the next day.

Besides Berrigan and Wenderoth, the four others indicted were the Rev. Neil R. McLaughlin, 30, of Baltimore; Anthony Scoblick, 30, of Baltimore, a former priest; Eqbal Ahmad, 40, a fellow at the Adlai Stevenson Institute of Public Affairs in Chicago; and Sister Elizabeth McAlister, 31, of Marymount College (Tarrytown, N.Y.).

Along with Daniel Berrigan, the following persons were named co-conspirators: Sisters Beverly Bell, 43, and Marjorie A. Schuman, 47, both of Washington; William Davidon, 43, a professor at Haverford (Pa.) College; Thomas Davidson, 25, of Washington; Paul Mayer, 39, of Edgewater, N.J., a former priest; and Sister Joques Egan, 52, reported to be a member of the Religious Order of the Sacred Heart of Mary in New York.

A federal grand jury in Harrisburg April 3 issued a new indictment against Philip Berrigan and seven others on charges of plotting to kidnap Kissinger and to blow up heating tunnels in government buildings. The indictment superseded the one returned Jan. 12.

The new indictment named two additional defendants and broadened the charges to include a series of draft board raids. Attached to the indictment were two letters, allegedly exchanged by Berrigan and Sister Elizabeth McAlister, a nun who was also indicted. The letter attributed to Sister Elizabeth described a plan "to kidnap—in our terminology make a citizen's arrest of—someone like Henry Kissinger." Berrigan's alleged reply contained criticisms of the idea but added, "Nonetheless, I like the plan."

The indictment charged that Sister Elizabeth transmitted the letter in August 1970 to Berrigan in the federal prison in Lewisburg, Pa. The letter said that after the kidnapping was accomplished, the group would "issue a set of demands," including a halt to U.S. use

of B-52 bombers over North Vietnam, Cambodia and Laos and "release of political prisoners."

The letter said Kissinger would be held "for about a week" during which he would be tried and the trial filmed for the news media. The letter said, "There is no pretense of these demands being met and he would be released after this time with a word that we're nonviolent as opposed to you who would let a man be killed . . . so that you can go on killing."

The reply attributed to Berrigan objected that the plan was too "grandiose" and suggested ways to "weave elements of modesty into it." It also warned of the precedent of a kidnapping: "The first time opens the door to murder—the Tupamaros [guerrillas] are finding that out in Uruguay."

The two new defendants in the indictment were John Theodore Glick, 21, currently serving an 18-month sentence in federal prison (Ashland, Ky.) for a 1970 raid on federal offices in Rochester, N.Y., and Mary Cain Scoblick, 32, of Baltimore, a former nun.

The trial opened in Harrisburg Feb. 21, 1972, but a mistrial was declared Apr. 5 after the federal jury reported itself unable to reach a verdict on the charges of conspiracy to kidnap Kissinger, blow up heating tunnels and raid draft board offices. The jury, however, found Berrigan and Sister Elizabeth guilty of smuggling contraband letters at the Lewisburg federal prison. The government dropped the conspiracy charges Sept. 5, 1972.

Bomb explodes in Capitol. A powerful bomb exploded in the Senate wing of the Capitol at 1:32 a.m. March 1, 1971, 33 minutes after a phone warning that the blast would occur as a protest against the U.S.-supported Laos invasion. The explosion, in an unmarked, out-of-the way men's lavatory, damaged seven rooms. There was some damage as far as 250 feet away. No one was injured.

The telephone message to a Capitol operator warned: "This building will blow up in 30 minutes. You will get many calls like this, but this one is real. Evacuate the building. This is in protest of the Nixon involvement in Laos."

In letters postmarked March 1 after the bombing and sent to the New York

Times, the New York Post and the Associated Press, a group calling itself the Weather Underground claimed responsibility for the bombing. The letters, mailed from Elizabeth, N.J., said: "We have attacked the Capitol because it is, along with the White House and the Pentagon, the worldwide symbol of the government which is now attacking Indochina."

A subcommittee of the Senate Public Works Committee held a hearing March 2, called the day before by Sen. Jennings Randolph (D, W.Va.), chairman of the committee, to consider the "delicate matter" of protecting the Capitol "against attack while securing for all citizens total access to this symbol of liberty." Capt. Edwin Joyner, an Army bomb expert, told the Senators that the explosion could have been caused by 15–20 pounds of dynamite that could have been concealed in "an ordinary briefcase."

In other testimony, Capitol police Chief James M. Powell said 200–300 bomb threats had been received at the Capitol in the last few years. The Senators also heard from George M. White, the new architect of the Capitol, who said the blast apparently did not "damage the structural integrity" of the Capitol.

Leslie Bacon arrested, N.Y. bank bombing involvement—Leslie Bacon, 19, was arrested in Washington April 27 as a material witness "with personal knowledge" of the bombing of the Capitol. After her arrest, she was flown to Seattle April 29 where she appeared before a federal grand jury, which Justice Department officials said was investigating the bombing and other matters "relating to national security."

Although the Seattle grand jury sessions were closed, Miss Bacon was allowed to leave the room to consult with her lawyers before answering each question. Her lawyers said she was not asked about the Washington bombing until her second day of testimony, May 1. Reporting that she denied any knowledge of a plot to bomb the Capitol, Jeffrey Steinborn, one of her attorneys, denounced the probe May 1 as "a general fishing expedition into antiwar politics."

Miss Bacon refused to answer questions and pleaded the Fifth Amendment for the first time during her testimony May 2, when the questioning turned to a Dec. 4, 1970 attempt to bomb a New York City bank. Government attorneys, in a hearing May 3, sought a court order to force her to testify about "her participation in plans to bomb" the First National City Bank. The bombing was thwarted when undercover policemen arrested six persons, allegedly as they were planting the bomb.

(At the New York indictment of the six bomb plot suspects Dec. 8, 1970, it was alleged that they planned the blast as the first of a "series of heavy actions against the Establishment.")

Judge W. Boldt of U.S. District Court May 6 upheld the government's argument that Miss Bacon could not refuse on grounds of constitutional privilege to answer questions about the bombing because she waived her Fifth Amendment rights in the matter when she previously testified willingly about her part in the bomb plot. Boldt contended that the constitutional privilege existed for the witness's protection, "not for that of other parties."

Miss Bacon's lawyers said May 6 that she testified before the Seattle grand jury on the New York bombing, as ordered by the court, but refused to answer any other questions. In a statement read by her lawyers, she said "if they have a case against me, let them prove it without my help." Her statement also said that she had taken part in the early planning of the New York bombing but "withdrew from all plans more than a month before the actual attempt."

The six defendants in New York had pleaded guilty March 18 to conspiracy to fire-bomb or dynamite a branch of the First National City Bank and five other buildings, including one that contained the offices of President Nixon's former law firm, Mudge, Rose, Guthrie & Alexander. They had been arrested outside the bank on information supplied by an undercover patrolman who drove them to the site.

Before five of the six defendants were sentenced May 7, the defense pointed out that the defendants had been careful to avoid the possibility of injuring bystanders and that they had acted for political motives. State Supreme Court Justice Harold Birns, in imposing sentence, said the conspirators' "political beliefs in no way mitigate the enormity of the crime."

The youngest of the defendants, Christopher Trenkle, 20, was ordered to take a psychiatric examination before sentencing. Three defendants—Richard R. Palmer, 40, identified in the indictment as a Weatherman "recruiter," Sharon Krebs, 33, and Martin Lewis, 25—received the maximum sentence of four years each. The remaining two, sentenced to three years each, were Joyce Plecha, 26, and Claudia Conine, 23.

The Justice Department Nov. 1, 1972 dropped a conspiracy charge against Miss Bacon in the bank bombing case rather than reveal the contents of surveillance material.

Other bombings & arson. A federal grand jury in Madison, Wis. indicted three Army enlisted men Feb. 11, 1971 on charges of blowing up a telephone exchange, an electric substation and a water works at Camp McCoy, Wis. in July 1970.

Named in the indictments, believed to be the first charging soldiers in recent bombings, were Spec. 4 Stephen G. Geden, 21; Spec. 4 Thomas M. Chase, 21; and Spec. 4 Dannie E. Kreps, 21.

Geden, a Vietnam veteran, and Chase were under general court-martial charges at Fort Carson for participating in an unauthorized demonstration while in uniform. They were said to have distributed antiwar pamphlets.

■ An explosion at the Armed Forces Induction Center in Oakland, Calif. Feb. 4 broke 200 windows and tore doors off their hinges. A message received by the Oakland Tribune and signed "the Bay Bombers" read: "This is our reply to the invasion of Laos, in Cambodia, in Thailand, in Vietnam, and to the Pentagon's 'protective retaliation' policies." The Atlanta induction office was bombed Feb. 13, and Bucks County, Pa. draft files were burned Feb. 15 in Bristol.

■ Police sources charged that arson or fire-bombs caused blazes at the following

campuses: the Fletcher School of Law and Diplomacy at Tufts University (Medford, Mass.), where a blaze March 21 caused $75,000 damage; the University of Hawaii (Honolulu), where a March 5 fire caused by gasoline splashed around a campus building followed a fire the week before at a Reserve Officers Training Corps (ROTC) building; Cornell University (Ithaca, N.Y.), where a March 17 fire damaged a classroom used by the Air Force ROTC unit; the Santa Cruz campus of the University of California, where a fire April 8 destroyed the administration building and caused $500,000 of damage.

Bombs found in 8 banks. Ronald Kaufman, 33, a psychologist who was AWOL as an Army private, was indicted Jan. 13–19, 1972 in San Francisco, Chicago and New York on charges of placing time bombs in safe deposit boxes in eight bank branches in those cities.

The bombs, which were attached to nine-month timing devices, had been defused by police Jan. 7 after unsigned letters were received by several newspapers listing their precise locations. The letters, all identical, warned that the "Movement in Amerika" could "kidnap property" by planting powerful bombs in office buildings or highways under construction and reveal their location in return for the release of imprisoned radicals.

The Federal Bureau of Investigation said it identified Kaufman's fingerprints on applications for the safe deposit boxes. The suspect, who was still at large, was said to have been at one time an associate of Yippie leader Abbie Hoffman and, earlier, a member of Students for a Democratic Society.

A ninth bomb, mentioned in the letters, had exploded prematurely Sept. 7, 1971 at a San Francisco Bank of America branch.

Bomb damages Pentagon. An explosive device was detonated in a section of the Pentagon building early May 19, 1972. Damage was estimated at $75,000.

The Washington Post received a telephone call from someone identifying himself as "a Weatherman" and announcing the explosion just before it occurred. At the same time, the New York Post received a call saying the explosion was in honor of the birthday of the late North Vietnamese leader Ho Chi Minh, and directing the receiver to a phone booth where a six-page statement criticizing President Nixon's war policies was found. A similar statement was received later May 19 by the Washington Post, signed by "Weather Underground No. 12 " and bearing insignia identical to markings on 1971 Weather Underground letters claiming credit for a Capitol Building bomb.

The bomb was the 63rd to be exploded in a federal building since Jan. 1, 1970, according to the General Services Administration. Total damage costs were set at $829,400. According to Federal Bureau of Investigation figures reported May 20 there were 607 bombings in the U.S. and its territories in the first four months of 1972, killing 10 persons and injuring 56 others. The National Bomb Data Center in Washington claimed that "53% of the bombings have some sort of political motivation—right wing or left."

SLA kills black schools head. Marcus A. Foster, 50, black superintendent of schools for Oakland, Calif. since 1970, was killed Nov. 6, 1973 by gunmen who ambushed him and his deputy, Robert Blackburn, 38, as they left a local board of education meeting. Blackburn was wounded.

In a letter to an Oakland radio station, a group calling itself the Symbionese Liberation Army (SLA) said it had attacked Foster and Blackburn after a "court of the people" had found them "guilty of . . . crimes . . . against the children and the life of the people." These "crimes" included a school identity card system, a planned school system police unit and cooperation among police, probation officers and school officials.

An Alameda County coroner's report released Nov. 9 indicated that the cylinders of the bullets that had killed Foster had been hollowed out and cyanide crystals had been placed inside.

Russell Jack Little, 24, and Joseph Michael Remiro, 27, were arrested near Concord, Calif. Jan. 10, 1974 and charged with Foster's murder.

They were charged after a ballistics report indicated that the pistol found in Remiro's possession at the time of his arrest had been the gun used to kill Foster.

Shortly after Little and Remiro were arrested, a house in Concord was set afire. Police found in the house a large supply of weapons, ammunition, explosives, SLA literature and cyanide. The house had been rented by Nancy Ling Perry, 26, an alleged SLA member, who was seen driving away with several other presumed SLA members after the fire was started.

Novel cited as SLA name origin—"The Spook Who Sat by the Door," a novel written in 1959 by Sam Greenlee, probably served as the source for the term "Symbionese." The novel dealt with a small commando unit taking part in an uprising in Chicago's black ghetto. It mentioned the term "symbiology." According to SLA literature, the SLA was part of a Symbionese Federation of "members of different races and people and socialist political parties of the oppressed people of The Fascist United States of America. . . . The Symbionese Federation and the Symbionese Liberation Army is made up of the aged, youth and women and men of all races and people. The name Symbionese is taken from the word symbiosis and we define its meaning as a body of dissimilar bodies and organisms living in deep and loving harmony and partnership in the best interest of all within the body." The SLA said that its goals were: "To assure the rights of all people to self-determination and the rights to build their own nation and government. . . . To destroy all forms and institutions of Racism, Sexism, Ageism, Capitalism, Fascism, Individualism, Possessiveness, Competitiveness, and all other such institutions that have made and sustained capitalism."

SLA kidnaps Patricia Hearst. Patricia Hearst, 19, granddaughter of the late newspaper publisher William Randolph Hearst, was forcibly kidnapped from her Berkeley, Calif. apartment Feb. 5, 1974 by at least two women and two men, who were later identified as members of the Symbionese Liberation Army (SLA).

The SLA's role in the abduction was confirmed by a letter received Feb. 7 by Berkeley radio station KPFA-FM. The letter, containing a credit card issued in the name of Miss Hearst's father, Randolph A. Hearst, president and publisher of the San Francisco Examiner, said she was unharmed and in "protective custody."

The letter had at its top a seven-headed cobra, representing the SLA's seven goals of self-determination, cooperative production, creativity, unity, faith, purpose and collective responsibility.

According to police, a woman came to the door of Miss Hearst's apartment and asked to use the phone as her car had broken down. Two men with the woman forced their way into the apartment and dragged Miss Hearst to a waiting car. Before escaping in a hail of bullets they fired to ward off would-be pursuers, the kidnappers had beaten Miss Hearst's fiancé Stephen A. Weed, 26, semi-conscious for trying to interfere.

The kidnappers made their first demand known in a letter to KPFA Feb. 12. Accompanying the letter was a tape recording of Miss Hearst's voice saying she was all right and asking her father to meet her abductor's demands.

The kidnappers demanded that Hearst provide $70 worth of top quality free meat, vegetables and dairy products over a four-week period—commencing Feb. 19—to "all people [in California] with welfare cards, Social Security pension cards, food stamp cards, disabled veteran cards, medical cards, parole or probation papers and jail or bail release slips."

In addition to the tape recording of Miss Hearst's voice and the food-distribution demand, KPFA received a second tape recording, whose speaker called himself Field Marshal Cinque of the SLA and said he was black and the father of two children, who was "quite willing to carry out the execution of your daughter to save the life of starving men, women and children of every race."

Hearst said Feb. 13 that it was impossible to meet the demand. Later he said, "We'll set up some kind of food distribution system," but he warned "we can't meet the cost." (Estimates of the cost of giving $70 worth of food to all California's needy ran as high as $400 million.)

SLA leaders identified—Two escaped convicts were identified as leaders of the SLA. The San Francisco Chronicle reported Feb. 15 that Field Marshal Cinque was Donald D. DeFreeze, 30, who had escaped from the minimum security area of California's Soledad Prison March 5, 1973. Inmates at Soledad confirmed that the voice calling itself Cinque on the tapes sent to the Hearst family was that of DeFreeze. Also identified was Thero M. Wheeler, 29, who escaped from the medical facility at Vacaville State Prison in August 1973.

Wheeler and DeFreeze, who were at Vacaville in 1972, became involved with what was later to be the SLA through their participation in Vacaville's Black Cultural Association (BCA), a 100-inmate organization that concentrated on cultural programs, education and pre-release preparation for prisoners. Russell Jack Little, who was charged Jan. 24 with the murder of Marcus Foster; Little's wife JoAnn; and William Wolfe identified by police as an SLA member, gained access to the BCA as tutors.

Food plan starts—Randolph Hearst Feb. 19 announced details of a $2 million food giveaway plan aimed at obtaining the release of his daughter.

The announcement followed the receipt Feb. 16 of a second tape-recorded message from Patricia Hearst, in which she said that her abductors were not trying to be unreasonable in their demands. "It was never intended that you feed the whole state. Whatever you come up with is OK," she said. The SLA leader calling himself Field Marshall Cinque added, "We are quite able to assess the extent of your [Randolph A. Hearst] sincerity, and we will accept sincere efforts on your part."

The plan, modeled after the Neighbors in Need program established in Seattle in 1970 in the wake of widespread layoffs in the local aerospace industry, was to be run by A. Ludlow Kramer, Washington secretary of state, and Peggy Maze, director of Neighbors in Need. Aiding in the food distribution, which began Feb. 22 in San Francisco, was a coalition of activist groups: the American Indian Movement (AIM), the Black Teachers Caucus, Nairobi College of East Palo Alto, Calif., the United Prisoners Union, the National Welfare Rights Organization and the Glide Memorial Church of San Francisco, whose minister, Rev. Cecil Williams, was the recipient of the Feb. 16 SLA communique.

Hearst said Feb. 19 that he was putting up $500,000 of the $2 million to be spent for the giveaway, with the remainder supplied by the William Randolph Hearst Foundation.

Accusing Hearst of "throwing a few crumbs to the people," the kidnappers Feb. 21 demanded that another $4 million worth of food be added to the $2 million worth being distributed. The demand was voiced by Cinque in a tape-recorded message. Cinque said the Hearst empire had attempted to "mislead" and "deceive" the people "by claiming to put forth a good-faith gesture of $2 million."

Cinque said Patricia Hearst was being "maintained in ... [prisoner of war] status until such time as the status of our captured soldiers is changed. Should any attempt be made to rescue the subject prisoner [Patricia], or to injure or capture our captive soldiers, the subject is to be executed immediately."

The captive soldiers referred to by Cinque were Joseph Remiro and Russell Little, who were being held in San Quentin Penitentiary pending trial.

Hearst said Feb. 22, "The size of the latest demand ... is far beyond my financial capability. Therefore, the matter is now out of my hands." Hearst put his personal assets at about $2 million.

However, Charles Gould, publisher of the Examiner, said the Hearst Corp. was prepared to donate the $4 million to the food distribution effort—but only if Patricia Hearst were first released unharmed. "No other funds will be committed by the [Hearst] corporation or foundation under any circumstances."

The food giveaway, begun Feb. 22, suffered from poor organization and coordination. Trucks with food arrived at some of the centers several hours late, and the food had not been sorted into grocery bags. At the center in East Oakland, food was thrown from a truck into the crowd and the irate crowd threw the still-packed cases back at the truck. Fights broke out, and some members of the frustrated crowd began looting a supermarket near the distribution center.

A new distribution started Feb. 28 was, by contrast, rapid and orderly.

Patricia Hearst 'joins' SLA—Patricia Hearst, in a tape-recorded message received April 3, said she had "chosen to stay and fight" with the SLA for the "freedom of oppressed people."

Accompanying the April 3 tape was a color photograph of Miss Hearst, armed with a submachine gun, standing before a red flag bearing the SLA emblem of a seven-headed cobra.

Giving assurances she had not been forced to say anything on the tape, Miss Hearst criticized efforts by her parents to obtain her release. She called the food giveaway program intended to secure her release a "sham" and accused her parents of trying to deceive her and the SLA with statements of concern, when they were actually stalling for time.

Addressing her fiance, Stephen A. Weed, who was with her the night she was abducted at gunpoint by the SLA, Miss Hearst said: "You have been harassed by the FBI because of your supposed connections with so-called radicals, and some people have even gone so far as to suggest that I arranged my own arrest. We both know what really came down [happened] that Monday night. But you don't know what's happened since then. I have changed—grown. I've become conscious and can never go back to the life we led before. . . . My love . . . has grown into an unselfish love for my comrades here, in prison and on the streets."

Her strongest remarks were directed at her father, newspaper publisher Randolph A. Hearst: "Dad, you said that you were concerned with the life and interests of all oppressed people in this country, but you are a liar in both areas. . . . You, a corporate liar, of course will say you don't know what I am talking about, but I ask you then to prove it. Tell the poor and oppressed people of this nation what the corporate state is about to do. Warn black and poor people that they are about to be murdered down to the last man, woman and child."

Patricia Hearst in bank robbery?—The FBI said that cameras activated during the armed robbery of a San Francisco bank April 15 took photographs showing Patricia Hearst to be a participant.

The FBI said the robbery, which netted $10,960, was the work of the SLA. Two bystanders were seriously wounded when the robbers began firing wildly as they fled.

The degree of Miss Hearst's involvement was the subject of much public debate.

Eyewitness Edward Shea, a bank guard, said April 17 that Miss Hearst "absolutely was a participant" in the robbery. "She wasn't scared, I'll tell you that. . . . She had a gun and looked ready to use it. She had plenty of command in her voice. She was full of curse words. She let it be known that she meant business," Shea said.

The controversy surrounding Miss Hearst's involvement was fanned by Attorney General William B. Saxbe April 17 who said, "The entire group we're talking about [the SLA] is common criminals." Asked by reporters if he meant to include Miss Hearst, he answered, "And Miss Hearst is part of it."

A federal warrant for Miss Hearst's arrest as a material witness was sworn out April 15. Arrest warrants on bank robbery charges were issued for four alleged SLA members identified through the bank surveillance camera photographs. Named in the warrants were Donald D. DeFreeze (the SLA leader calling himself Cinque), Nancy Ling Perry, Patricia M. Soltysik and Camilla C. Hall. Including those who drove getaway cars, the robbery involved nine persons, police said.

Patricia Hearst, in a tape-recorded message received by the police April 24, said she had participated in the robbery of her own free will. She said it was "ridiculous" to believe that she had been brainwashed by the SLA.

Miss Hearst, who identified herself as "Tania" in the recording, spoke in what was described as a calm voice. At several points in the tape, she referred to her father as a "pig," an epithet she also used for Stephen Weed.

A federal grand jury in San Francisco June 6 indicted Patricia Hearst on charges of armed bank robbery. A second count in the indictment charged her with using a firearm to commit the robbery.

6 SLA members die in gunfight and fire. Six suspected members of the Symbionese

Liberation Army (SLA) died in a gun battle and ensuing fire that erupted after police surrounded their Los Angeles hideout May 17, 1974. Patricia Hearst was not present during the shootout.

A team of medical examiners from the Los Angeles County coroner's office identified the charred bodies found in the house as Donald D. Defreeze, Nancy Ling Perry, William L. Wolfe, Patricia Soltysik, Angela Atwood and Camilla Hall. Defreeze, Perry, Atwood and Hall apparently died from gunshot wounds, Wolfe and Soltysik from burns and smoke inhalation, the coroner's office said.

Los Angeles police had been alerted to the SLA group's whereabouts by the mother of one of the women living in the house in which the SLA members later died.

On the basis of the tip, 150 heavily armed police surrounded the house. With everyone in place, a police sergeant shouted on a bullhorn, "Come out with your hands up. The house is surrounded." The police waited, repeating the order five minutes later. When there was no response, an officer crept near the house and lobbed a canister of tear gas inside. Gun fire immediately erupted on both sides. The battle continued for at least an hour with both sides expending over 1,000 rounds of ammunition.

Finally, smoke began to pour from the house, apparently from a fire started by a tear-gas canister or an ignited SLA gasoline bomb. Flames rapidly engulfed the stucco house, and soon the gunfire from within ceased.

U.S. warrant seeks Patricia Hearst— The FBI May 19 issued a warrant for Patricia Hearst's arrest. It warned that she was "armed and very dangerous."

Also named in the warrant were William T. Harris and his wife Emily M. Harris, both suspected SLA members. A shoplifting incident May 16 involving the Harris' had first made police suspect that SLA operations had been moved to Los Angeles from the San Francisco area. After buying clothing at a Los Angeles sporting goods store, William 'Harris was stopped by a clerk who had n iced a pair of socks stuffed up one of Harris' sleeves. Outside the store, as the clerk struggled with Harris, a woman across the street opened fire with a machine gun. The Harris' and the gunwoman, later identified as Patricia Hearst, fled.

In their escape, the trio commandeered at least three cars at gunpoint.

They were presumed to be the last three living SLA members still at large.

PUERTO RICO

Terrorism in Name of Independence

Most Puerto Rican terrorism since the mid-1930s has been in the cause of independence from the U.S. This terrorism has not been confined to the island of Puerto Rico but has frequently spilled over onto the U.S. mainland.

Two spectacular acts of Puerto Rican terrorism took place in Washington in the 1950s:

(1) Two members of the Puerto Rican Nationalist Party (PRNP) tried Oct. 30, 1950 to assassinate President Harry S. Truman. The terrorists killed a Presidential guard and wounded two others, and one of the assassins was slain; but Truman was unharmed.

(2) Four PRNP members wounded five Congressmen on the floor of the U.S. House of Representatives March 1, 1954 by shooting at them from a House spectators' gallery.

A group of terrorists known as MIRA (defined variously as Movimiento Independentista [or Independiente] Revolucionario Armado, or Armed Revolutionary Independence Movement, and Movimiento Independencia Rebelde Armada, or Armed Rebel Independence Movement) has been blamed for more than 100 bombing and arson attempts against New York public buildings and department stores in 1970–1 as well as for numerous terroristic acts against targets in Puerto Rico.

A group known as CAL (Comandos Armados de Liberacion, or Armed Liberation

Commandos) has claimed to have destroyed millions of dollars worth of property owned by U.S. companies in Puerto Rico.

Bombings. U.S. businesses and military installations were the targets of 8 bombings in Puerto Rico Feb. 22–25, 1968. The bombings were believed to be the work of CAL. 3 bombs exploded Feb. 22 included one at the Strategic Air Command's Ramey Air Force Base (no damage reported). A police bomb expert was injured Feb. 23 while attempting to defuse a bomb on the Shell Oil Co. pipeline; 2 other bombs exploded along the line Feb. 25 without causing serious damage.

Three bombs exploded in garbage cans in various parts of San Juan Feb. 15, 1969. One went off outside the police traffic division in the borough of Hato Rey and destroyed two cars belonging to policemen; the second exploded minutes later outside the Government Development Bank in Santurce, and the third went off about an hour later in front of a Howard Johnson Hotel Restaurant in the Condado area. Five persons were injured in the bombings.

Bombs exploded at five hotels and a restaurant in San Juan Dec. 11, 1969. One tourist was slightly injured, but damage was described as light. Minutes before the bombings, two armed men broke into a radio station and forced the disc jockey to broadcast an announcement stating that a "revolution against Yankee imperialism begins tonight." Police arrested four Puerto Ricans Dec. 13 in connection with the incidents; they were identified as members of the Revolutionary Armed Independence Movement.

Police dismantled 51 bombs April 21, 1970 in a Navy relay power station near San Juan; two bombs exploded before they could be found, but damage was described as light. Police indicated that if the bombs had exploded, the blasts would have crippled most of the island's communication system.

A CAL statement Nov. 19, 1970 threatened San Juan's hotel section with a wave of terror bombings as part of its "war . . . against the Yanki invader."

"We said that it [the hotel section] would be a war zone and warned Puerto Ricans not to go there," the group claimed.

At least 14 bombs were exploded in San Juan during November, five of them in the hotel district Nov. 14. Few injuries were reported, and damage was described as light. In addition, a bomb exploded at the Dominican Republic consulate in San Juan Nov. 23, only hours after Dominican President Joaquin Balaguer had concluded a visit to Puerto Rico. No one was in the consulate at the time. An anonymous caller told United Press International that the CAL was responsible.

The crowning May 20 of Tanya Wilson, 21, of Honolulu as Miss USA of 1972 was marred by a series of explosions in the hotel in Dorado, Puerto Rico where the pageant was being held.

Other Areas

CANADA

Separatists Blamed for Bombings & Kidnappings

French Canadians in Quebec have long resented what some describe as second-class citizenship and economic and political inferiority to Canada's English-speaking majority. This resentment has led to separatist sentiments and has occasionally erupted in bombings and other terroristic actions. In 1970 separatists kidnapped a British diplomat and the labor minister of Quebec. The former was ultimately freed, the latter murdered.

Bomb Blasts. Several home-made bombs exploded late Dec. 31, 1968 in Ottawa and Montreal and caused some property damage but no injuries. Three other bombs were found in Ottawa mail boxes Jan. 2, 1969.

The Dec. 31 Ottawa blast, outside federal government offices, shattered windows in the building, knocked down power lines and left a five-foot crater in the street. Three other bombs exploded in Montreal, and a fourth device was dismantled near the mayor's office. (Two bombs had exploded Dec. 13, 1968 outside the homes of Montreal business leaders. Police linked the blasts with pronouncements by the extremist group Front de Liberation du Quebec and the Front de Liberation Populaire.)

Two Montreal youths, aged 13 and 16, pleaded guilty Jan. 8 to charges involving bomb explosions Jan. 5 near the St. Luc Secondary School and Jan. 6 near the home of Montreal Police Director Jean-Paul Gilbert. No one was injured in the blasts. Four other students confessed Jan. 10 to storing dynamite and detonators in St. Joseph's Oratory on Mount Royal.

Two more bombs exploded in Montreal Feb. 22 and 25, 1969.

The Feb. 22 explosion occurred in the basement of the Liberal Party's Reform Club while a private reception was taking place above; five persons were injured slightly. The other blast went off in the Queen's Printer book store, but an anonymous phone call had warned of the bomb's existence, and the store had been evacuated. The bomb exploded as the police were entering the store; no one was injured.

Shortly before the first blast, the Montreal Sunday newspaper Derniere Heure had received a copy of the March 1969 edition of Victoire, organ of the separatist Front de Liberation du Quebec (FLQ). The FLQ claimed responsibility for the current wave of bombing and warned: "During 1968 we tried to make people understand. During 1969 we will kill those who have not understood. Last warning." It pledged that the FLQ would soon launch Operation Westmount to begin the "systematic elimination of the English occupiers and their servants."

It asserted that the 1968 bombings were in retaliation for the life sentence imposed on Marxist revolutionary writer Pierre Vallieres, an FLQ leader convicted of manslaughter.

Montreal police raided a rooming house March 4 and arrested Pierre-Paul Geoffroy, 25, for the illegal possession of 161 sticks of dynamite, 100 bombs and other equipment used in making bombs. Geoffroy, who described himself as a Marxist revolutionary, admitted March 6 that he was a member of the FLQ and that he had taken part in assembling bombs that had exploded Feb. 13 at the Montreal Stock Exchange and Feb. 22 at the Reform Club. He denied planting the bombs himself; he said that the bomb used in the book store blast had been made in his apartment by someone else. Geoffroy pleaded guilty March 7 to 129 charges relating to 31 terrorist bombings during the past year. He was sentenced April 1 to 124 concurrent terms of life in prison and five five-year terms.

Defense building bombed. One woman was killed and two soldier guards were injured June 24, 1970 when a bomb blast ripped through a Defense Department building in Ottawa. The bomb exploded outside the communications room of the department, a restricted area. Mrs. Jeanne d'Arc St. Germain, a defense department clerk, was killed in the blast.

The explosion occurred on St. Jean Baptiste Day, a French-Canadian holiday that had frequently been an occasion for violence.

Laboratory tests conducted by special anti-terrorist squads confirmed that the workings of the bomb were similar to those used in the recent series of Montreal blasts, according to the police spokesman's announcement. Police had already attributed those bombings to terrorist groups.

The Front de Liberation du Quebec (FLQ) later claimed responsibility for the blast and for bombing a postal substation in Montreal.

The FLQ communique, distributed to Montreal news media June 30, said the separatist organization had planted the bombs to protest the firing of 435 mail truck drivers in the Montreal postal dispute.

(Montreal police defused a 150-pound bomb July 12, hours before it was set to explode outside the head office of the Bank of Montreal. The bomb, one of the largest ever found by Montreal police, was found in the trunk of a car by bank guards. The bomb was the fourth investigated in Montreal in a 48-hour period. One bomb killed a man July 11 when it exploded in his car. Another 40-pound bomb was found beside a branch of the Royal Bank of Canada and was dismantled by police 35 minutes before it was set to go off. Another was found in a Montreal suburb four hours after it was supposed to have exploded.)

Cross & Laporte Kidnapped, Laporte Slain

Separatists kidnap Cross & Laporte. Quebec separatists kidnapped the senior British diplomat in Montreal from his home Oct. 5, 1970. Notes found on the campus of the University of Quebec in Montreal linked the kidnapping to the Front de Liberation du Quebec (FLQ).

The FLQ demanded the freeing of 23 of its jailed members, $500,000 in gold, and safe passage to Cuba or Algeria in return for the release of James Richard Cross, 49, senior British trade commissioner in Quebec province and head of the British government office in Montreal.

Cross was seized by four or five men who entered his home at gunpoint and abducted him in a taxi.

The separatist group also called for reinstatement of certain post office workers who had lost their jobs earlier in 1970, and it demanded the publication by the police of the name and photograph of the informant whose tip led to a police raid on FLQ members June 21. They also demanded publication of a manifesto issued by the Front.

After a series of emergency meetings at the federal and provincial levels, the federal government announced Oct. 6 that "this set of demands will not be met." The announcement by External Affairs Minister Mitchell Sharp said Ottawa would not meet the demands in full but hinted that the government would consider a compromise.

The government Oct. 8 met one of the terrorists' demands when an announcer of the state-owned Canadian Broadcasting Corporation read on television a 1,400-word statement of the FLQ.

At a press conference Oct. 8, Robert Lemieux, a radical lawyer who had emerged as an unofficial spokesman for the FLQ, charged that the federal government was acting in "bad faith" and that police had violated the civil rights of numerous individuals called in for questioning.

Amid continuing extensions of the deadline for Cross' execution, a second cell of the Front de Liberation du Quebec Oct. 10 seized Quebec Labor Minister Pierre Laporte from his home. The FLQ, whose demands for Cross's release had dwindled to two, hiked the price for Laporte to the original set of demands put forth when Cross was first seized.

Before kidnapping Laporte, the FLQ had sent a "final" ransom note Oct. 9, demanding that the 23 prisoners be freed by 6 p.m. Oct. 10 or Cross would be killed.

The government reply to the demand was read over television Oct. 10 by Quebec Justice Minister Jerome Choquette. Choquette offered the kidnappers safe conduct to the country of their choice if they released Cross alive.

Minutes after the Choquette statement and the 6 p.m. deadline for Cross, two masked men armed with submachine guns forced Labor Minister Laporte into a car at his home in Montreal. The kidnappers identified themselves Oct. 11 as the Chenier cell of the FLQ (naming the kidnappers of Cross as the Liberation cell). The abductors said Laporte, 49, would be killed if the authorities did not agree by 10 p.m. to meet the ransom demands of the Cross kidnappers. A note in Laporte's handwriting pleaded with Premier Robert Bourassa to meet the Chenier cell's demands. "You have the power to decide on my life or my death," the letter said in part. "We are in the presence of a well-organized escalation . . . After me there will be a third and a fourth and a fifth."

Bourassa appeared on television at 9:55 p.m., five minutes before the deadline. He said the provincial government could not meet the terrorist demands before it was sure that the two captives would be freed. The premier asked the FLQ to get in touch with the government to give assurances that the two men would be released.

Police Oct. 11 arrested Lemieux, charging him with obstruction of their investigation into the kidnapings because of statements he had made at his press conferences.

The Quebec cabinet Oct. 12 appointed a Montreal lawyer, Robert Demers, to represent the cabinet in talks with Lemieux on the release of the two hostages. Both FLQ cells had said in messages earlier in the day that they wanted Lemieux to act as their intermediary in negotiations with the government. The talks opened Oct. 12 in the jail where Lemieux was being held. Lemieux was released Oct. 13.

The talks bogged down Oct. 14, however, with Lemieux complaining that he had still not received an answer as to whether or not the government would accede to the central FLQ demand and release 23 so-called "political prisoners." For its part, the FLQ refused, in a note found Oct. 14, to give any pledge for the safety of the kidnap victims other than a "solemn pledge to the people of Quebec." The provincial government had asked that each of the FLQ cells involved surrender one member as a guarantee.

In what appeared to be a final breakdown of the Lemieux-Demers talks, Lemieux charged Oct. 15 that police had discovered the location of the terrorist cell holding Laporte.

Meanwhile, radical students at the University of Montreal and the Montreal campus of the University of Quebec Oct. 15 passed strike resolutions and received support for their actions from a variety of labor and separatist groups. These all demanded the release of the 23 prisoners and denounced police and military repression. At the University of Quebec campus, students occupied the administrative offices and vowed to keep the campus shut until the FLQ demands were met.

In another development, Quebec Premier Robert Bourassa Oct. 15 asked Ottawa for troops to guard public buildings and the homes of public officials. The federal government responded to Quebec's request by flying in forces.

Bourassa, in what was termed a "final position" Oct. 15, refused to meet the FLQ demand for the release of all 23 prisoners but offered a counter-proposal to release five and to give safe passage to the kidnappers.

Prime Minister Pierre Elliot Trudeau Oct. 16 invoked the emergency War Measures Act for the first time in peacetime. Meanwhile, police fanned out across Quebec and seized an estimated 250 persons, among them Lemieux.

Under the Act, the FLQ was outlawed, and anyone who abetted the FLQ also became liable. In giving the government the power to do anything it "deems necessary for the security, defense, peace, order and welfare of Canada," the Act suspended civil liberties for many members and supporters of the militant separatist group and for possible witnesses in investigations. Trudeau promised that the powers would be withdrawn "as soon as it has been demonstrated that there is a cessation of the violence and threats of violence which made necessary their introduction."

Laporte murdered. Not long after midnight Oct. 18, Laporte's bloodstained body was found in the trunk of the car in which he had been kidnapped.

The discovery of Laporte's body followed an announcement late Oct. 17 by the Quebec government that detailed a plan to offer the kidnappers safe-conduct.

The plan offered immunity to the kidnappers if they brought themselves and the hostages to the Concordia Bridge on the grounds of the site of Expo '67. This spot would be treated as an extension of the Cuban consulate in Montreal, the statement said, and Cuban consular officials would take custody of the hostages until the kidnapers had arrived safely in Cuba. Transportation to Cuba would be provided.

Police Oct. 18 issued a bulletin for the arrest of Paul Rose, 27, and Marc Carbonneau, 37.

Police Oct. 19 discovered the house in which Laporte had been held hostage on an unpaved street in the Montreal suburb of St. Hubert. The police were led to the bungalow by a neighbor who recognized a televised picture of a suspect as one of the house's occupants. Investigation revealed that a man answering the description of Paul Rose had rented the house.

Mrs. Rosa Rose, mother of Jacques and Paul, testified Nov. 7 that she, her two sons, and Francis Simard had been traveling across the U.S. by automobile when news of the Cross kidnap became known. She said the three youths then "decided to return here in great haste." Mrs. Rose identified several blood-soaked fabrics as articles belonging to her sons or from her home.

Lortie arrested, confesses. Bernard Lortie, 19, was arrested by Montreal and Quebec police Nov. 6. He confessed at a coroner's hearing Nov. 7 to participating in Laporte's kidnapping, but he denied any part in Laporte's murder or in the kidnapping of James R. Cross.

At the inquest into Laporte's death, Lortie Nov. 7 described how he and three other members of the FLQ's Chenier cell —Paul and Jacques Rose and Francis Simard—had kidnapped Laporte. Lortie also gave names of alleged FLQ sympathizers, details of how the FLQ operated, meeting places, dates and other data.

Cross freed, kidnappers fly to Cuba. James R. Cross was released by his kidnappers unharmed Dec. 3, 1970. Three of the kidnappers and four of their relatives were flown to Cuba aboard a Canadian military plane in accordance with the terms of an agreement worked out earlier in the day by representatives of the Quebec government and the abductors.

Police spokesmen for the Royal Canadian Mounted Police (RCMP), the Quebec Provincial Police (QPP) and the Montreal police had announced Dec. 2 that investigators were "making headway" in the case. The police were then involved in a stakeout around 10949 Des Recollets Street in a Montreal working-class suburb. They had been led to the site a week earlier by tips pertaining to the whereabouts of Jacques Cossette-Trudel, whose name had been found written in the house where Laporte had been held and who was known to be the brother-in-law of Jacques Lanctot, prime suspect in the Cross kidnaping. Police located Cossette-Trudel and his wife, Lanctot's sister, and traced them to Des Recollets Street. They arrested the couple as they emerged from the house Dec. 2 and were thus able to affirm that Cross was held there.

Police then sealed off a six-block area in Montreal North around the house.

In the early hours of Dec. 3, the kidnappers sent a message that they were willing to negotiate. Federal troops and police reinforcements then moved into the sealed-off area; a police bomb squad was called in on the assumption, later confirmed, that the house was booby trapped.

Quebec Justice Minister Jerome Choquette led the negotiations, which were carried out by Robert Demers, acting for the government, and Bernard Mergler, a radical lawyer who represented the FLQ kidnappers.

With preliminary talks concluded at the hideaway house, the kidnappers drove Cross in a heavily booby-trapped car to the site of Man and His World on St. Helen's Island.

Cross was delivered to Ricardo Escartin, Cuba's acting consul in Montreal, at the Canadian Pavilion, which had been declared Cuban territory for the exchange.

A helicopter took the kidnappers and their relatives, who had joined them at St. Helen's Island, to Montreal's Dorval airport, where an RCMP plane took them to Cuba. Cross was held by Cuban officials in the Pavilion until the plane arrived in Cuba.

The seven persons on the military transport to Cuba were identified as Marc Carbonneau, 37, a Montreal taxi driver, sought by police in the kidnappings of both Cross and Laporte; Jacques Lanctot, 25, also a prime suspect; Lanctot's wife, Suzanne, and their child; Pierre Seguin, another alleged kidnapper; Jacques Cossette-Trudel, and Louise Cossette-Trudel.

The Cuban government emphasized that it had agreed to take the seven only at the request of Ottawa and for "humanitarian reasons." The official newspaper Granma stated: "The transfer of these people to our country happened following a formal request from the Canadian government to which the Cuban government agreed with a view to realizing the rescue of the British official."

(French authorities confirmed June 28, 1974 that Carbonneau, Lanctot and Seguin [alias Yves Langlois] had entered France through Czechoslovakia June 24 "through a security error."

(Paris police said June 24 they had no reason to arrest the kidnappers since there was no international warrant for their arrest. French officials indicated that a Canadian request for extradition would be denied because France did not extradite persons wanted in political cases.

(Canadian Prime Minister Trudeau, who had said June 24 that Ottawa would not seek extradition, reiterated June 26 that the 1970 guarantee of free passage protected the kidnappers from proceedings unless they reentered Canada.)

Commons approves antiterror bill. The House of Commons Dec. 1 approved an emergency powers bill introduced by the government to replace the War Measures Act invoked by Prime Minister Pierre Trudeau at the height of the Quebec kidnap crisis.

The bill, known as Public Order (Temporary Measures) Act, 1970, would continue to outlaw the Front de Liberation du Quebec (FLQ) and would extend the extraordinary powers used by Quebec police for the duration of the Act—until April 30, 1971.

The new bill was passed by a vote of 174–31.

(The government allowed the 1970 Public Order Act to expire on schedule April 30, 1971.)

Kidnap suspects captured. The three prime suspects in Laporte's kidnap-murder were captured Dec. 28, 1970 after a three-month manhunt that involved as many as 10,000 policemen and troops. Paul Rose, his brother Jacques and Francis Simard surrendered peacefully at an isolated farmhouse in St. Luc, about 30 miles north of the U.S. border. A fourth person, Michel Viger, 30, who had rented the house and allegedly aided the suspects, was also arrested.

The police, who had searched the farmhouse three times previously, had found the fugitives' shelter, a 25-by-four-foot chamber under the house, when they found a false panel in the farmhouse basement Dec. 27.

Jacques Ducros, a Montreal lawyer, was assigned by Quebec Justice Minister Jerome Choquette to meet with Dr. Jacques Ferron, a former separatist candidate, who acted on behalf of the suspects in negotiations aimed at their peaceful surrender. The three were known to have arms and food supplies in the shelter. The discussions reportedly centered on the question of bail for some 50 persons still held under war act emergency measures. Choquette reportedly assured the suspects he would withdraw his objections to bail. The three then surrendered without resistance.

The Rose brothers, Simard and Bernard Lortie were held at a coroner's inquest in Montreal Jan. 4, 1971 to be "criminally responsible" for Laporte's murder.

Police read into the inquest record Jan. 4 an unsigned statement they attributed to Simard. According to one policeman, Simard had made the statement "but refused to sign because he didn't want to further implicate himself."

The statement said that Simard and the Rose brothers killed Laporte after he tried to escape on the night of Oct. 16, 1970 from the bungalow in the Montreal suburb of St. Hubert where he was being held captive. Laporte was said to have cut himself on a broken window during the escape attempt and, Simard's statement said, "we decided to strangle him with the [religious] chain he had been wearing since his kidnapping." Simard allegedly said: "Paul, Jacques and I choked him. Politically we had to do it and we did. We are all equally responsible. We knew what we were doing."

According to the statement, Simard and the Rose brothers, with Lortie, had kidnapped Laporte to provide the FLQ with an alternate hostage to British trade commissioner Cross. They held that Cross had no connection with Quebec problems and should not be killed.

Paul Rose, convicted March 13, 1971 of noncapital murder, was sentenced to life imprisonment. He received a concurrent life sentence Nov. 30 on his conviction of kidnapping Laporte.

In summing up his own defense before the jury March 12, Rose said he was proud to have taken part in Laporte's kidnapping.

Simard, convicted May 20, 1971 of noncapital murder, also received a mandatory life sentence.

Lortie, convicted of the kidnapping charge, was given a 20-year sentence Nov. 2, 1971.

Jacques Rose was acquitted Dec. 9, 1972 of kidnapping and Feb. 22, 1973 of murder in the Laporte case.

FLQ leader defects. Pierre Vallieres, 33, announced his defection from the Front de Liberation du Quebec (FLQ) in December 1971. Vallieres had jumped bail in September while charged with counseling murder, kidnapping and sedition.

In an article sent to the Montreal newspaper Le Devoir, Vallieres urged all members and sympathizers of the FLQ to abandon terrorism tactics. He argued that terrorism only created support for repression by the Ottawa government, and that "the struggle of the Quebec masses is on the electoral plane." He called the FLQ outmoded.

(Vallieres surrendered to the Quebec provincial police Jan. 24, 1972. He received a one-year suspended sentence Oct. 4 on three charges of counseling political kidnapping.)

Canada & U.S. sign hijack pact. The U.S. and Canada signed in Washington Dec. 3, 1971 an extradition pact covering hijackers of aircraft and assailants of diplomats for the first time.

Signed by U.S. Secretary of State William P. Rogers and Canadian Secretary of State for External Affairs, Mitchell W. Sharp, the treaty denied hijackers and those committing crimes against foreign diplomats the privilege of claiming that their acts were political in character.

The pact, which listed 30 extraditable offenses, carried the usual provision that a person could not be extradited for a political offense.

The treaty placed emphasis on conspiracy to commit an extraditable offense, which would make possible the extradition of persons who conspired to commit a crime as well as those who did commit crimes.

Canada was the first country to accept the U.S. argument that hijacking should be exempted from the political protection clauses found in standard extradition treaties.

Toronto blast. Two people were killed March 18, 1972 by a terrorist explosion that destroyed a supermarket and travel agency in Toronto.

CYPRUS

Enosis Demand Spurs Terrorism

Terrorism has long been a fact of life in Cyprus, an island on which Cypriots of Greek and Turkish ancestry seem to be unceasingly at war with each other.

A newer element that caused fratricidal strife among Greek Cypriots is the dispute over enosis—the demand for union of Cyprus with Greece.

Gen. George Theodorus Grivas, who headed the successful 1955–9 underground struggle for Cyprus' independence from Britain, had assumed the leadership in the more recent campaign for enosis. Grivas' battle was fought not so much against the minority Turkish Cypriots, whose opposition was taken as a matter of course, as against the Cypriot government, dominated by Greek Cypriots and headed by President (Archbishop) Makarios. Grivas' campaign ended with his death in January 1974. And six months later Makarios was overthrown by the Cypriot National Guard under the leadership of pro-enosis Greek officers.

Grivas' enosis campaign had erupted in 1973 in a resurgence of terrorism, much of it blamed on his underground force, Eoka B (a name formed by the initials in Greek of the National Organization for Cyprus Strug-

gle), a new edition of Grivas' anti-British EOKA of the 1950s.

Terrorists strike. Armed men attacked a quarry near Limassol and stole dynamite and detonators Jan. 22, 1973. Other raids netted the guerrillas radio transmitters and weapons in the Limassol area Jan. 24 and Jan. 29–30.

The Greek government intervened in the upsurge of violence Feb. 1 with a statement deploring civil strife and urging Greek Cypriots "to recant and unite." The statement, attributed to a "qualified government source," did not blame any side for the current unrest. However, it was generally interpreted as a condemnation of the Grivas campaign.

Grivas' supporters attacked 20 police stations across the island and dynamited three of them at Famagusta Feb. 7. The raiders also stole weapons and uniforms. Police offered little resistance.

Presumed Grivas supporters were reported March 16 to have blown up three police stations and set off explosions in front of the homes of nine police officers. More than 20 bomb blasts before homes of Grivas supporters were reported March 17.

More than 21 bombings involving pro- and anti-Enosis forces were reported immediately before and during the celebration April 1 of the 18th anniversary of the Eoka guerrilla uprising against British rule in Cyprus.

An outspoken opponent of Gen. Grivas, George Photiou, was killed by three gunmen in the southern coastal town of Larnaca April 6. Thirty-two bombings against supporters of Grivas in Larnaca and two other coastal towns, Paphos and Limassol, were reported April 7–8. Archbishop Makarios admitted April 8 that government supporters were responsible for most of the blasts.

About 50 armed and masked men June 8 attacked a rural police station at Vatyli, 30 miles from Nicosia, wounding a policeman, and robbing and then dynamiting the building. The raid was the first in nearly two months by supporters of Grivas.

Two Greek Cypriot supporters of Makarios were shot to death June 22 by gunmen firing from a passing car in Limassol. Bombs exploded in the headquarters of the auxiliary police force in Nicosia the following day, causing heavy damage. At least seven other blasts in Nicosia June 23 damaged a number of cars. The Athens newspaper Estia blamed the attacks on Grivas' Eoka B.

A car bomb exploded near the House of Representatives in Nicosia Sept. 11, seriously injuring a nearby policeman.

Justice minister abducted. Justice Minister Christos Vakis was kidnapped from his home in Nicosia by two armed men in military uniforms July 27, 1973. (He was kept captive for a month.)

The tactical reserve police force rounded up more than 50 Grivas "activists" in pre-dawn raids July 29. Among those arrested were eight newsmen who worked for the island's three pro-Grivas newspapers. Two of the newspapers suspended publication after their offices were smashed, apparently by Makarios supporters.

The kidnapping sparked a stepped-up terrorist campaign, with bombs exploding in various parts of the island July 28–Aug. 1. An auxiliary police headquarters in Nicosia was bombed July 29, although a prior telephone warning prevented casualties. The chief of the police bomb disposal squad, Loizos Hajilouzou, was killed Aug. 1 while defusing a bomb planted in the western town of Morphou. The London Times reported Aug. 2 that nearly 100 bombs had been exploded by rival groups since the Vakis kidnapping.

A leaflet bearing Grivas' name was circulated Aug. 2, setting terms for the release of Vakis. These called for Makarios to choose between church and politics; the granting of "political freedoms"; new presidential elections; amnesty for all pro-Grivas prisoners; and reinstatement of Grivas men dismissed from the police and national guard.

Makarios rejected the conditions Aug. 3, and reiterated that he would "never give in to blackmail." In a signed, typewritten reply Aug. 4, Grivas threatened civil war unless Makarios resigned and called new elections.

Vakis was freed by his abductors Aug. 26. His kidnappers, supporters of Grivas, had said Vakis was ultimately responsible for the alleged ill treatment of political detainees. The government did not meet Grivas' demands for Vakis' release.

Top Grivas aide arrested—Police arrested Grivas' top aide, Stavros Stavrou, in a series of dawn raids in Limassol Aug. 9. Stavrou headed the military arm of Grivas' clandestine movement.

Several other members of the movement were also seized, including Dimitri Spourgidies, chief of Grivas' underground political organization in Limassol. Weapons and important documents were also found.

The government Aug. 10 reported details of an alleged plot by Grivas supporters to kill Makarios and seize power. The plan, outlining the ambush of Makarios on his daily drive through Nicosia to his office, was allegedly among the seized documents. Makarios Aug. 5 had disclosed another alleged assassination plot against him. Grivas' organization, Eoka B, distributed leaflets Aug. 12 denying the Aug. 10 allegations of an assassination plot.

Makarios assassination try fails. Archbishop Makarios escaped unhurt from what police described as an assassination attempt Oct. 7, 1973.

Four bombs exploded on a rural road near Famagusta, in eastern Cyprus, minutes before Makarios was scheduled to drive by.

Police arrested a Greek Cypriot in connection with the blasts. They said he was acting for a pro-enosis group.

Grivas dies. Gen. George Grivas, 75, leader of the guerrilla campaign for enosis, died after a heart attack at his hideout in Limassol Jan. 27, 1974.

President Makarios granted amnesty to Grivas' followers Jan. 28 and ordered the release of 100 jailed guerrillas. A statement attributed to Eoka B's new leadership later Jan. 28 suspended antigovernment operations "to provide the required time of peace for the sake of a responsible, positive and patriotic handling of the national issue."

More than 70,000 pro-enosis supporters attended the burial of Grivas at his
Limassol hideout Jan. 30 and vowed to
carry on the fight against Makarios. The
ceremony was conducted by former
Bishops Gennadios and Kyprianos,
Grivas supporters defrocked by a special
synod of the Greek Orthodox Church
called by Makarios in 1973.

Eoka B's Karousos ousted—George
Karousos, 47, a former Greek army major reportedly named by the late Gen.
George Grivas shortly before his death to
succeed him as leader of Cypriot guerrillas fighting for enosis, had been recently ousted from his post and forcibly
removed to Greece, the Athens newspaper
Estia confirmed March 1. Estia was
known to have close ties with Eoka B.

According to the New York Times
March 3, Karousos was seized for two
reasons: enosis hard-liners opposed Karousos' order for a halt to guerrilla activities, and Greek military leaders wanted
to gain control of Eoka B to curb Cypriot
militant leftists and Communists.

Makarios ousted in coup. Archbishop
Makarios was overthrown as president of
Cyprus July 15, 1974 by a military coup
staged by the Greek-officered Cypriot National Guard.

The 10,000-man Cypriot National
Guard, commanded by a contingent of
650 Greek officers, staged the coup early
in the morning of July 15.

The major fighting was in Nicosia
between the rebels and the tactical reserve
police force created by Makarios to fight
pro-enosis guerrillas and later used to
counter the pro-Athens National Guard.

The rebels broadcast a communique declaring the seizure of power to be an
internal affair. They also charged that
Makarios had been leading Cyprus into
civil war, apparently in reference to his
opposition to Greek Cypriots fighting for
enosis.

The rebels July 15 named a new president, Nikos Giorgiades Sampson, 38, a
Greek Cypriot newspaper publisher and
former terrorist once sentenced to death
by British colonial authorities for murder.
He was sworn in by Bishop Gennadios of
Paphos, who was named to replace Maka-

rios as head of the Cypriot church. Although a supporter of Eoka B, Sampson
was reported to have pledged to maintain
Cypriot independence.

(Makarios had supported enosis in the
1950s when the island was struggling for
independence from Britain, but once independence was achieved in 1960 he gave
only lip service to union with Greece. His
backing of enosis cooled further after the
military overthrew the Greek government
in 1967. The current junta strongman,
Brig. Gen. Demetrios Ioannides, who
came to power in another Greek military
coup in November 1973, was known to be
bitterly opposed to Makarios for his refusal to support enosis and his close ties
with Cypriot Communists and frequent
trips to Communist nations.)

Ambush of Makarios backer fails. Unknown gunmen failed in an assassination
attempt against Vassos Lyssarides, a
leading Greek Cypriot politician and supporter of Archbishop Makarios, in Nicosia Aug. 30, 1974.

Lyssarides, who was Makarios' personal physician and chairman of the
United Democratic Union of the Center,
a Socialist party, was slightly wounded.
Doros Loizou, secretary of the party's
youth section, who was driving the car in
which Lyssarides was riding at the time of
the assassination attempt, was killed. A
Greek Cypriot passerby was also shot
dead.

Later Aug. 30, Lyssarides expressed his
belief that the assassination attempt was
the work of Eoka B.

Guerrilla army formation reported.
Greek Cypriots were forming the Cyprus
Liberation Army (CLA), a CLA spokesman announced Aug. 27, 1974, for a
possible struggle with Turkish forces who
had invaded Cyprus after the ouster of
Makarios.

The spokesman said the guerrilla force
had already recruited about 300 armed
men, who were based in the Troodos
Mountains in the center of Cyprus. The
CLA included men from the Greek Cypriot National Guard, Eoka B and the
tactical reserve police force.

(According to a New York Times report Aug. 28, 18 CLA members had been sent to Lebanon the previous week for tactical training with Palestinian guerrilla groups.)

ETHIOPIA

Eritrean Terrorist Attacks

Ethiopian targets both in Ethiopia and abroad have come under terroristic attacks since 1961 by members of the Eritrean Liberation Front (ELF), a Muslim group formed in Cairo in 1958 to fight for Eritrea's independence from Ethiopia. By 1970 it was estimated that some 2,000 ELF members were under arms. The Sudanese government reported June 6, 1965 that it had found 18 tons of Czechoslovak arms on Sudanese territory intended for Eritrean rebels against Ethiopia. Some ELF members had received asylum in Syria, and Damascus radio Nov. 10, 1966 broadcast an ELF "military communique" claiming that the "Eritrean liberation army" had scored victories against Ethiopian military units in Eritrea in October.

Terrorism Intensified. ELF terrorists intensified their activities against Ethiopia beginning in 1967. Killings, plane hijackings and sabotage increased. In one suspected incident of sabotage, more than a million tons of gasoline and oil was destroyed Feb. 27, 1967 in an explosion at the Mobil terminal in Assab (Eritrea).

Anti-rebel activity by the government was also reported. As an apparent result of anti-insurgency efforts, *Le Monde* reported Sept. 20, 1967, 6 ELF leaders surrendered to Ethiopian authorities in Asmara. Freed under amnesty in accordance with a promise made by Ethiopian Emperor Haile Selassie, the terrorists told newsmen that they had received guerrilla training in Syria. They and 20 others, traveling on Syrian passports, had entered Eritrea via Jidda, Saudi Arabia and Port Sudan, they said. These admissions added credence to reports of Arab support of the guerrillas.

The *N.Y. Times* reported Sept. 27, 1968 that Eritrean guerrillas also had apparently lost many members because of defections and a loss of Arab aid since the Arab-Israeli war of 1967.

Ethiopian Planes Attacked. The ELF July 31, 1969 issued a communique warning travelers that they would risk their lives if they used Ethiopian Airlines. The ELF warned that it would resort to mid-air attacks in retaliation for Ethiopian air force attacks on Eritrean villages.

A bomb placed by ELF terrorists had damaged an Ethiopian Airlines Boeing 707 jet parked at Frankfurt airport March 11, and several German women who were cleaning the plane were injured. The Ethiopian Foreign Ministry March 13 blamed "certain hate-filled fanatical elements abetted by Syria" for the attack. The Addis Ababa daily Addis Zemen said in an editorial March 14 that a "Syrian-Arab organization" had claimed responsibility for setting the bomb. "This band of gangsters," the editorial said, "which works under Syrian direction, has been given the name the Syrian-Arab Movement for the Liberation of Eritrea. . . ."

An Ethiopian Airlines 707 was attacked June 18, 1969 by three ELF terrorists at Karachi, Pakistan. The plane's 15 passengers were in a transit lounge at the time of the attack, and no casualties were reported. The ELF attackers, all in their 20s, had arrived in Karachi from Beirut June 16.

(Police in Rome reported June 18 that an Eritrean student, Hagos Tesfai, was killed when a bomb he was preparing blew up in his room. Leaflets found in the debris announced an impending attack as the work of the Eritrean Liberation Front.)

Six students at Haile Selassie University in Addis Ababa and an official of the Ministry of Community Development Aug. 11 hijacked an Ethiopian Airlines DC-3 on an internal Ethiopian flight and forced the pilot to land in Khartoum. The ELF Aug. 12 took credit for the hijacking.

Three ELF guerrillas hijacked an Ethiopian DC-6 with 66 passengers aboard Sept. 13. The flight, bound for Djibouti from Addis Ababa, was forced to land in Aden. One of the hijackers, Mohammed Sayed, 18, was shot by an

Ethiopian secret police official who had been a passenger on the flight. The shooting occurred shortly after the plane landed. Police captured the other two.

Two armed ELF members aboard an Ethiopian Airlines Boeing 707 were killed Dec. 12 as the plane flew over southern Europe on the first leg of a flight from Madrid to Addis Ababa. The two who were armed with pistols and fused explosive devices, were slain by plainclothes security guards.

None of the 15 passengers or six crew were harmed.

Crew members said Dec. 12 that the men, who were carrying Senegalese and Yemeni passports, had intended to hijack the airliner to Aden in Southern Yemen, but a statement by the ELF in Damascus asserted that the two were ELF members who merely wanted to distribute leaflets to the passengers.

Madrid policemen disclosed Dec. 14 that an Ethiopian student arrested Dec. 10 in the Madrid airport was connected with the hijacking. The student, Ahmed Mohammed Ibrahim, 24, a suspected ELF member, had been carrying a suitcase containing explosives. Police sources said Ibrahim alleged that the plans included hijacking the plane for a flight over Paris and London to distribute leaflets, then destruction of the airliner with explosives in Copenhagen.

Seven armed ELF members were shot to death by Ethiopian security guards Dec. 8, 1972 when they tried to hijack an Ethiopian airliner between Addis Ababa and Paris. Two of the hijackers were women.

Assassinations. Ethiopian High Court Judges Zeroam Kofley and Hadgoug Gilliagabre, who had sentenced ELF supporters to death, were reported Nov. 27, 1970 to have been assassinated in a bar in Asmara.

It was also reported that Eritrean rebels Nov. 21 had killed Ethiopian army general Teshome Ergetu. Ergetu was on an inspection tour of the province. He was ambushed on a road in the northeastern section of the territory.

ELF rebels were believed responsible for the slaying in Asmara June 20, 1974 of

an adviser to the provincial governor and for the July 13 killing of Eritrean leader Hamid Feraeg Hamid, who had publicly opposed independence for the province.

Army losses. The ELF claimed that it had killed 20 officers and men of the Ethiopian army during actions in December 1973. A curfew had been imposed in Asmara, capital of Eritrea Province, Sept. 12, 1973, after the killing of Gen. Yelma, assistant commander of Ethiopian forces in Eritrea.

Eritrean rebels seize hostages. Three Americans and two Canadians, employes of Tenneco Ethiopia Inc., were captured by the ELF March 26, 1974. Their helicopter had crashed 45 miles northwest of the Red Sea port of Massawa where they had been prospecting for oil. The pilot was released June 26 with a ransom demand of $1 million to free the others. The remaining three were then released Sept. 10 with no disclosure of ransom payment.

ELF members also kidnapped a U.S. nurse, Deborah Dortzbach, from a provincial hospital in Ghinda May 27, at the same time killing a Dutch nurse, who died during a forced march. Diplomatic sources in Addis Ababa said May 31 that the ELF had stormed the hospital to secure medical aid for the prospectors.

Notes from the rebel group, delivered to the U.S. consulate in Asmara May 31, demanded an undisclosed quantity of medical supplies in exchange for Mrs. Dortzbach's freedom. The U.S. missionary group operating the Ghinda hospital had previously rejected the demand and closed the hospital in protest. Mrs. Dortzbach, six months pregnant, was released July 2.

The rebels kidnapped an Italian farmer from his Eritrean plantation June 4.

FRANCE

Minor Terrorism, Many Causes

France, where the term terrorist (terroriste) was coined (to describe agents or partisans of the revolutionary tribunal during the Reign of Terror), has been troubled by only minor acts of modern terrorism during the late 1960s and early 1970s. There have been occasional bombings by such nationality groups as Bretons, Basques, Corsicans and Occitans participating in what is generally considered autonomist rather than separatist movements. Some foreign terrorists have also been active in France during this period.

Bordeaux terrorists jailed. A state security court in Paris Dec. 18, 1968 sentenced seven members of the Revolutionary People's Front Group to prison terms ranging from 2 to 4 years for a series of bombings, thefts and incidents of arson committed in Bordeaux in June and July. 4 others received suspended sentences.

(A Gaullist party headquarters and a Renault auto showroom were among the targets of a series of bombings in Paris Dec. 8.)

Bretons seized. French police Jan. 1–14, 1969 arrested 28 suspected members of a nationalist group accused of engaging in violence to enforce their demands for autonomy for Brittany, France's northwesternmost province. About a ton of hidden explosives was seized. Among those arrested were four Roman Catholic priests.

The nationalist group was called the FLB (Front de Liberation de la Bretagne, or Liberation Front of Brittany). Its followers were said to be responsible for bomb attacks on public buildings in Brittany since the summer of 1967. The explosive raids against government buildings, tax offices and a police station had been stepped up in recent months.

Police investigating the blasts reported discovering Jan. 7 a charter of a self-styled Breton government in exile along with explosives and weapons. The cache was found near the Breton port of Lorient.

The leader of the Liberation Front, Yann Goulet, said in an interview published Jan. 13 in the weekly Nouvelle Observateur in Paris that the FLB's campaign of violence would be suspended when President de Gaulle visited Brittany Jan. 31–Feb. 2. But he warned that if de Gaulle "does not give the Breton people the freedom indispensable for their material and spiritual development, the tempo of military operations will only accelerate." Goulet, who lived in Ireland (the Breton language is similar to Gaelic), insisted that Brittany "is a nation and we will accept no compromise on this point."

The nationalist monthly L'Avenir de la Bretagne (Brittany's Future) declared in a statement published in Rennes Jan. 13 that nationalist violence was "a means and even a duty of self-defense" against "the regime that enslaves us." The statement was signed by the FLB, the National Political Council and the Breton Republican Army.

Thirteen persons, including three priests, were formally charged in Paris Jan. 14 with terrorist activities in Brittany. One of the defendants, René-Francois Vaillant, 41, a French-born Canadian, was accused of helping to blow up nine buildings, including a police station, government offices and a town hall at La Turballe, in the Nantes area. One of the priests arraigned was the Rev. Joseph Lec'hvien, 49, who had been arrested in Plesidy Jan. 13.

(The FLB took credit for some 200 bombings during the next four years.)

Bombing attacks. President Georges Pompidou appealed for public calm May 16, 1970 after a wave of unexplained bomb and arson attacks in Paris and other parts of France. The violence, attributed variously to left-wing and right-wing extremists, was directed against police stations, other public targets and the homes of Parliament members.

Pompidou asserted that it was "intolerable that some people, to drive home their ideas, . . . should attack persons and property." But he said it must not be assumed that every incident was "a criminal attack. We must remain calm and not believe that revolution knocks at the door."

Among the recent acts of violence: May 10—Bombs were thrown at police stations at Montpellier and Valras-

Plage. Both were unoccupied at the time. A bomb exploded at the entrance hall of a law court at Besancon, causing heavy damage. An explosion occurred outside the home of the assistant mayor of Cannes, shattering windows.

The police telephone system of a Paris police station May 11 was knocked out by a fire caused by a burning piece of cloth tossed through an open window. An explosive charge damaged an electric pylon in eastern France.

A bomb exploded May 15 outside the gas and electricity offices in Grenoble. The blast broke a water main and damaged windows and nearby parked cars.

A villa being built for a Gaullist deputy in a suburb of Lyons was destroyed by fire May 17. It was the third attack on property owned by members of Parliament within a week.

The Interior Ministry March 13 had announced the arrest of 20 radical militants on charges of terrorism and prohibited two antimilitarism meetings scheduled to be held in Paris March 14 and 17.

Thirteen of the militants had been seized on suspicion of participating in the burning of a flour mill at Corbeil March 6; the other seven had been accused of ransacking the town hall of Meulan the same day.

The antimilitary meetings were to be held to protest the imprisonment of three conscripts in Britanny Feb. 6 on charges of distributing leaflets calling for insubordination by other conscripts.

Extremist groups banned. The government June 28, 1973 banned two extremist groups on the right and left.

The move against the New Order, an extreme right-wing neo-Fascist group, and the Communist League, a Trotskyite movement, was apparently spurred by the June 21 violent clashes in Paris between leftist youths and the police. The confrontation had occurred when police tried to stop an attempt by leftists to halt a meeting of the New Order called to protest unlimited immigration to France of foreign workers.

The secretary general of the New Order, Alain Robert, 27, had been charged with illegal possession of arms

June 23, one day after police had raided the headquarters of both the New Order and Communist League and confiscated weapons. More than 20 persons had been charged for possession of arms.

Both the New Order and the Communist League were outgrowths of two extremist organizations banned in 1968 and 1969. The two newly banned groups each claimed 4,000 active members.

Blast kills 4 at Algerian consulate. A bomb exploded at the Algerian counsulate in Marseilles Dec. 14, 1973, killing four Algerians and injuring more than 20 others. The consul general, Ahmed Bakhti, had arrived a few minutes before the blast and was only slightly injured. The city had been suffering from racial tension since August when an Algerian stabbed a French bus driver to death.

13 terrorists arrested. Police announced the arrests Dec. 20, 1973 of 10 Turkish one Algerian and two Palestinian guerrillas who were said to be preparing terrorist attacks in Europe.

Police made most of their arrests in a villa in Villiers-sur-Marne southwest of Paris. They also seized there grenades, explosives, equipment to make bombs, false identity cards, passports and documents detailing terrorist plans. The 10 Turks were members of the Turkish People's Liberation Front, and the three Arabs claimed membership in the Popular Front for the Liberation of Palestine.

Separatist groups banned. The government Jan. 30, 1974 banned four separatist movements; three had claimed responsibility for bomb attacks and other violence. Those connected with violence were the two rival Breton groups, the Liberation Front of Brittany (FLB-ARB) and the left-wing Liberation Front of Brittany for National Liberation and Socialism (FLB-LNS), and the Corsican Peasant Front for Liberation (FPCL). The fourth was the Basque association "Enbata," which linked several political and cultural groups among the French-speaking Basques of southwest France.

The government accused the banned groups of permanent contacts with foreign political parties from whom, it claimed, they received money. Contacts were maintained, it charged, between the FLB and the banned Irish Republican Army, Enbatá and the outlawed Spanish Basque group ETA, and the FPCL and "certain Italian movements."

Eight persons suspected of membership in the FLB-LNS were arrested Jan. 29. (The group was suspected of being responsible for 10 bomb attacks since May 1973.) A Corsican business leader, Jose Stromboni, was jailed Jan. 26 and was released on bail Feb. 10 after being charged with illegal activities in connection with bomb attacks in Corsica.

Bombings in Corsica. Nine bombs exploded Jan. 3–4, 1974 in three towns of Corsica, a department of France, causing extensive damage but no injuries. The bombs were linked to the island's autonomy movements.

The FPCL claimed responsibility for three bomb attacks Feb. 21.

A bomb damaged a French jet airliner at Bastia airport March 22 and another explosion March 18 damaged the French Foreign Legion headquarters at Corte.

Premier Pierre Messmer warned March 26, at the close of a two-day visit to Corsica, that the government would quell "without pity" any resort to violence for political ends in the island and would combat "any attack on the unity of the French Republic."

Earlier March 26, a bomb blast attributed to Corsican militant autonomists had damaged a government building in Bastia a few hours after Messmer left it.

Six bombs exploded in Ajaccio, capital of Corsica, and elsewhere on the island the night of July 8–9, causing heavy damage but no injuries. Four of the attacks were directed against government buildings or banks. A group of Corsican militant autonomists, calling themselves "Giustizia Paolina," claimed credit for the blasts.

Several more blasts followed in Corsica during the next few days. The outlawed FPCL July 17 took responsibility for a bomb attack July 14 and immediately declared a bomb truce during the summer tourist season.

(A bomb explosion heavily damaged the city conference hall in Lyons Jan. 30, 36

hours before Premier Pierre Messmer was scheduled to deliver a speech in the building. There were no injuries.)

Bomb kills 2. Two persons were killed and 34 wounded Sept. 15, 1974 when a man threw a hand grenade into a crowd in the popular Paris "Drugstore Saint-Germain," a complex comprising a cafe, pharmacy and other shops. The attacker escaped.

An extreme right-wing organization, which called itself the Group for the Defense of Europe, claimed responsibility Sept. 18.

GREAT BRITAIN

Scattered Terrorist Acts

Most of the relatively few terroristic acts reported in Great Britain in this period were off-shoots of the Northern Ireland and Middle East conflicts. These incidents are recorded in this book in the sections covering the two issues. In addition, there was minor terrorism blamed on Welsh nationalists and on a group of revolutionary students going under the name The Angry Brigade. Four members of the latter group were convicted and jailed in 1972.

Welsh blasts as prince is invested. Charles Philip Arthur George was invested as Prince of Wales and Earl of Chester July 1, 1969 in ceremonies at Caernarvon Castle in Wales.

One man was killed by an explosion in Abergele, 30 miles from Caernarvon, only hours before the ceremony. Police suspected that the explosion might have been the work of Welsh nationalists protesting the investiture. The train carrying the royal family had been halted July 1 near Chester, England, when dummy explosives were found on the track. In Cardiff, 180 miles from Caernarvon, a bomb June 30 had exploded at a post office, but there were no injures. Just before the ceremony, an explosion went off on a railway siding on the outskirts of Caernavon. More than 2,500 policemen were on duty during the ceremony.

The Angry Brigade. Several bombings in the period 1968–71 were attributed to The Angry Brigade, described as a small, clandestine group of young revolutionaries.

Two bombs exploded Jan. 12, 1971 at the home of Employment Minister Robert Carr, but nobody was injured. The attack climaxed a day of labor protest against an industrial relations bill that Carr was piloting through Parliament. In a letter to London newspapers Jan. 14, The Angry Brigade took credit for the bombing.

A bomb exploded at a police computer center in London May 22. The blast damaged brickwork and shattered windows, but caused no injuries. The Angry Brigade took credit for the attack.

A bomb exploded at the home of William B. Batty, managing director of Ford's British subsidiary, in Essex June 22. The blast damaged the house but caused no injuries. The Angry Brigade said it was responsible.

In an attack in London, a bomb explosion damaged the apartment of Secretary of State for Trade and Industry John Davies July 31. Davies and his wife were not at home. A man later telephoned a newspaper and said the bomb had been planted by the Angry Brigade.

A bomb explosion damaged the top floors of the Post Office Tower in London Oct. 31, 1971, and another bomb exploded Nov. 1 at an army drill hall a quarter of a mile from London. The Angry Brigade took responsibility for both blasts.

Four alleged Angry Brigade members were sentenced to ten years in prison Dec. 6, 1972 after a jury found them guilty of conspiring to cause bomb explosions in Britain between 1968 and 1971. Four other accused persons were acquitted of the same charges.

Alert at London airport. London's Heathrow Airport was placed on major alert Jan. 5–7, 1974 to guard against terrorist attacks. Tanks, armored cars, 220 soldiers and 200 police participated in the alert at the airport, normally lightly guarded.

Authorities linked the action to their concern over increased Arab terrorist activities in Europe and reports that Arab guerrillas planned to attack aircraft at European airports with shoulder-mounted Soviet-made SAM-7 missiles. Other reports said SAMs had disappeared from Western military bases. Security measures were also tightened at other airports, including those at Rome, Paris and Brussels, it was reported Jan. 7.

3 charged with arms conspiracy—The airport alert came after a U.S. woman and two men were charged Jan. 4 with arms conspiracy in an alleged plot to attack Moroccan diplomats in London.

Allison Thompson, 18, of Santa Barbara, Calif.; Abdelkhir el-Hakkaoui, 25, of Morocco; and Athar Naseem, 21, of Pakistan had been detained by police since the end of December 1973 when Thompson was arrested at Heathrow in possession of five automatic pistols and more than 150 rounds of ammunition. Hakkaoui and Naseem had been students in Santa Barbara.

Another American citizen, Robin Oban, 25, was deported to the U.S. Jan. 6 after three days of questioning by British police in connection with the alleged antigovernment plot. She was not charged. FBI agents Jan. 5 had arrested Theodore Brown, 31 at Travis Air Force Base, Calif., and charged him with helping Thompson smuggle guns and ammunition to Britain.

Thompson was cleared by a jury in London of all charges in the arms smuggling and kidnap plot.

The two co-defendants accused with Thompson of plotting to kidnap a French official and hold him hostage for release of Moroccan political prisoners were sentenced. Hakkaoui was given a three-year sentence, Naseem a one-year term.

A U.S. federal prosecutor in Los Angeles said July 16 he had dropped charges against Thompson of violating the Neutrality and the Firearms Control Assistance Acts.

Tower of London blast kills 1. A bomb exploded without warning in a tourist-packed cellar armory at the Tower of London July 17, 1974, killing one person and injuring at least 36, many of them children.

The explosion occurred in the White Tower, the oldest of the 13 structures comprising the Tower of London. Little damage was done to the building, but part of the armory collection was damaged. The blast came one month after a bomb exploded in Westminster Hall, in the Houses of Parliament.

Earlier July 17, another bomb damaged a government tax office in south London.

A bomb exploded in a parking garage at London's Heathrow airport July 26 and four fire bombs were detonated in movie theaters in Birmingham July 31. There were no injuries.

GREECE

Terrorists Oppose Junta

Most of the terrorism reported in Greece during the late 1960s and early 1970s was described as activities in opposition to the military junta that had seized control of Greece in 1967 and that ruled until July 1974. Greece, however, was also the scene of acts of terrorism by forces campaigning for enosis (union of Greece and Cyprus) and by persons involved in the Arab-Israeli struggle; such developments are recorded in this book in the sections covering the Middle East and Cyprus.

Resistance bombings. A time bomb exploded Sept. 13 1969 in the office of the pro-government Athens newspaper Nea Politeia. There were no casualties, but damage was described as extensive.

Two more blasts caused damage at the City Hall and the neighboring central post office Sept. 22. Embassies and news agencies at the same time received a press bulletin from the Greek Democratic Movement, an antigovernment organization, reporting that it had set up "armed action groups."

A bomb Oct. 7 damaged the car of Panayotis Makarezos, brother of the minister of economic coordination. A spokesman for an underground organization, the Movement of National Resistance, claimed responsibility for the action.

27 convicted in sedition trial. A five-man military tribunal presiding over the trial of 34 Greeks charged with sedition April 12, 1970 sentenced the chief defendant to life in prison and returned guilty verdicts for 26 of the 33 others accused. The penalties were in every case lighter than those demanded by the prosecution.

The charges grew out of a "professors' bomb plot," which allegedly placed a number of bombs in the Athens area between January 1968 and August 1969. The alleged plot had been discovered in August 1969 when Dionysios Karayorgas, an economics instructor at the Panteios Graduate School, was seriously injured by a home-made bomb which exploded in his hands. The incident led to the discovery of a bomb workshop in Karayorgas' home.

In the sentences passed April 12, Karayorgas was sentenced to life in prison. Three other alleged ringleaders were given 18-year terms: George Mangakis, a professor; Spiridon Loukas, a chemist; and Jean Starakis, a Greek-born French journalist. (An April 12 report said Starakis, 28, had succeeded in smuggling a letter out of Greece recounting a series of tortures after which, he said, "I admitted everything they asked.")

Lt. Gen. George Iordanides, once Greece's representative to NATO, was sentenced to eight years. He was cleared of the charge that he was chief of an anti-regime organization. Three other defendants received prison terms of from 10 to 18 years and 19 others received terms of from one to eight years. Seven of the latter sentences were suspended. There were seven acquittals.

Mangakis had testified March 27 that he had been tortured until he had made a confession but that he later publicly denied the torture charge on a promise by security forces that his imprisoned wife would be released. (Mrs. Angeliki Mangakis, the daughter of Stylianos Gonatas, who was prime minister of Greece 1922-4, had been sentenced to four years in prison Aug. 27 for saying that her husband had been tortured by police.)

Nine more defendants also testified that they had been tortured.

In a surprise move April 5, the military prosecutor, Maj. Ioannis Liapis, accepted pleas by six defendants that their confessions to the police be disregarded as untruthful. Answering the plea, Liapis said: "Yes, I understand the reason. I can imagine what you have been through."

Explosions were reported in three areas of the Greek capital as the trial went into its fourth day March 30. The court heard testimony from five army officers testifying as prosecution witnesses who said the bombs were meant to "create fear among the citizens and cause impressions abroad."

Bombers score U.S. A bomb explosion May 14, 1971 killed a policeman and injured another near the statue of former U.S. President Harry S Truman in downtown Athens. The policeman was killed while trying to defuse the bomb.

A rightist underground organization, the "Free Greeks," had sent foreign correspondents a circular May 13 warning they would increase their activity against American institutions and property unless the U.S. government ceased support of the Greek regime. The circular said the group considered "the official American policy an enemy of the Greek people."

Bomb explosions in Athens Feb. 7 had damaged three cars, two owned by U.S. military personnel.

Bombs exploded in Athens April 26 in front of the headquarters of the General Confederation of Labor and of the U.S. Air Force group in Greece.

Bomb attacks in Athens the night of July 8–9 damaged a railway track and a tank-truck of the Esso-Pappas company.

A bomb exploded in the U.S. embassy in Athens Aug. 29, 1972, minutes after a warning was phoned to the Associated Press.

An anti-regime group called the Popular Revolutionary Resistance claimed responsibility Sept. 4. It also claimed credit for two bomb explosions in 1971 in connection with the visit of Vice President Spiro T. Agnew.

Seven U.S. official cars in the Athens area were damaged by explosions Jan. 18–20, 1974. Two underground groups, named "Laos (People) Number One" and "Laos Number 13," claimed responsibility for the bombings "in memory of the students killed last November by CIA agents."

Bomb suspects convicted. A special military tribunal in Athens Jan. 22, 1972 convicted eight men indicted as possessing and detonating explosive devices over the past two years.

The eight, alleged followers of exiled opposition leader Andreas Papandreou, included Ioannis Kyriazis and Iossif Valyrakis (son of a former Cretan member of Parliament) as the chief defendants. Kyriazis was sentenced to nine years in prison and Valyrakis to seven years imprisonment. Kyriazis admitted detonating two bombs in downtown Athens during October and December 1969. Valyrakis was charged with importing explosives from Sweden. Both men said they had been tortured.

Six co-conspirators were convicted as accomplices and received sentences ranging from 12–30 months. According to authorities, one received a suspended sentence, having "genuinely repented."

The court March 21 sentenced 11 of 15 defendants to prison terms ranging from one year's suspended sentence to eight years in prison on charges of illegal possession and use of explosives and of attempts to set up an underground resistance branch of the Panhellenic Liberation Movement (PAK), the expatriate group headed by Papandreou. Four of the defendants were acquitted.

Ioannis Koronaios, 55, a U.S.-born lawyer practicing in Athens, received the eight-year prison sentence. He had admitted in court March 18 that he had set off a bomb in 1970 in the gardens near the premier's Athens office, where Premier George Papadopoulos was conferring with U.S. Defense Secretary Melvin Laird. Koronaios said he had planted the bomb as a "symbolic protest because the United States remains silent about oppression in Greece." Koronaios accused the Greek military police of forcing his confession through torture.

Others sentenced included Xenophon Peloponnisios, a former civil servant, and Andreas Franghias, an electrical engineer, who were sentenced to six years and 4½ years imprisonment respectively. Both said they had been tortured in prison.

Other suspects tried. An Athens military court Aug. 4, 1972 sentenced five men to prison terms ranging from seven to 30 months and acquitted three other defendants of plotting to overthrow the government.

Seven of the defendants had denied the charges of setting up an urban guerrilla band and plotting violence to finance an attempted overthrow of the government. The eighth defendant and alleged leader of the group, Christos Ramadanis, had admitted on the first day of the trial Aug. 3 that robbery, bombing and kidnapping plans had been discussed, but he dismissed it as "idle, romantic talk." He denied charges they planned to kidnap John F. Kennedy Jr. on one of the boy's frequent visits to the Greek island of Skorpios, owned by his stepfather, Aristotle Onassis.

Ramadanis was sentenced to 39 months in prison and Georgios Boussiotis, described as his lieutenant, was sentenced to 18 months. The sentences of the three others convicted were subsequently suspended, the New York Times reported Aug. 6.

The court Jan. 20, 1973 sentenced five of 13 civilians on charges of conspiring to "kidnap ambassadors [U S Ambassador to Greece Henry Tasca] and hijack aircraft" as part of an alleged plot to arrange the prison escape of Alexandros Panaghoulis, jailed for attempting to assassinate Premier George Papadopoulos in 1968. All 13 of the accused were charged with belonging to the underground "Greek Resistance" anti-regime organization.

The chief defendant, Stathis Panaghoulis, brother of Alexandros, was sentenced to 4½ years in prison. Four others—including Lorna Caviglia Briffa, an Italian— were given jail terms of 15-30 months. Seven of the accused were given suspended sentences and one was acquitted. The unusually light sentences were thought to reflect the government's weak case.

Stathis Panaghoulis had denied all the charges and told the court Jan. 18 that he had been tortured by the police.

IRAN

Muslim & Communist Terrorists

Terrorists active in Iran recently have ranged in political orientation from conservative Shi'ites (a Muslim sect) of the National Liberation Movement to groups from the outlawed Tudeh (Communist) Party, which had split in 1965 into the pro-Peking Revolutionary Organization of the Tudeh Party and into a pro-Moscow faction. Maoist terrorists have been reported active in the Caspian province of Siakhal, and Southeast Iran's Baluchi Liberation Movement is said to be headquartered in Baghdad.

Farsiou assassinated. Gen Ziaddin Farsiou, chief of the Iranian military court, died April 11, 1971 after being shot by gunmen in Teheran April 7. Farsiou's son was wounded. Police named five suspects in the shooting. They were believed to be members of a Maoist group responsible for previous acts of terrorism.

Three guerrillas were shot to death in a gun battle with police in Teheran May 24. Six persons, including five policemen, were wounded. The fighting broke out when police and security units surrounded the guerrilla hideout. The men belonged to a nine-man Maoist group wanted for Farsiou's murder.

Guerrillas executed. Six guerrillas were executed by firing squad in Teheran March 1, 1972. One had been sentenced by a military court Jan. 31, and the five others had been condemned by the court the following day. They were among 23 defendants accused of anti-state activities, bank robbery, illegal possession of arms and membership in the outlawed Communist party. The 17 others received sentences ranging from one year to life imprisonment.

In another trial, a military tribunal Feb. 9 sentenced four guerrillas to life in prison and gave 16 others jail terms ranging from three to 10 years for anti-state activities.

Iranian authorities had disclosed Jan. 16 that one of the acts committed by some of the guerrillas was an attempt to kidnap U.S. Ambassador Douglas MacArthur II and his wife Nov. 30, 1971. The U.S. embassy said Jan. 18 that the MacArthurs were returning to their residence when their automobile was stopped by two other cars. Suspecting a kidnap attempt, the ambassador ordered his driver to proceed and the car broke through the ambush, the embassy said.

Five Iranians convicted of sabotage and terrorism were executed by an army firing squad Jan. 5, 1973. They were said to have admitted carrying out a number of acts, including placement of explosives in the office of the governor of northern Kurdistan region and of plotting to assassinate government officials there. They had been trained in Iraq.

Two persons charged with the August 1972 slaying of Gen. Saied Taheri, a senior police official, were executed by firing squad Jan. 11. The deaths of Mohammed Mosidi and Mohammed Bagher Abbasi brought to 56 the number of convicted guerrillas executed in the past 12 months. Both men also were accused of planting explosives in the British consulate in Teheran and of being involved in the sending of others to Palestinian commando training camps.

U.S. military aide slain. An Iranian terrorist shot and killed an American military adviser, Lt. Col. Lewis L. Hawkins, in Teheran June 2, 1973 and escaped on a motorcycle driven by a confederate.

Reza Rezai, suspected leader of the terrorist group that had murdered Hawkins, was killed June 15 by security forces that had surrounded his home. The pistol Rezai used in this shootout was found to have been a weapon taken the body of Gen. Taheri by his assassins.

Plot vs. Shah. The foiling of a plot to kidnap and assassinate Shah Mohammed Riza Pahlevi and his family was disclosed by the government Oct. 2, 1973.

A military court in Teheran Jan. 9, 1974 sentenced seven Tudeh Party members to death for their roles in the plot. Five others received prison terms of 3 to 5 years.

Officials said Iranian guerrillas had formulated their plans in the winter and spring of 1973 and the 12 had been arrested between April and October of that year. The guerrillas also had planned to kidnap five other persons, including a foreign ambassador, according to authorities. The prosecution said the hostages were to be held to enforce the release of political prisoners and the supplying of an escape plan.

ITALY

Rightist & Leftist Terrorism

Italy, with a strong Marxist movement and a history of Fascist rule, suffered both leftwing and rightwing terrorism in the late 1960s and early 1970s.

Terrorism in Milan. A bomb exploded Dec. 12, 1969 in the National Bank of Agriculture in Milan, killing 16 people and injuring 90. Three bombs were exploded in Rome the same day, causing injury to 17 persons, none seriously. One of the blasts occurred in the National Bank of Labor. The other two went off at the monument to King Vittorio Emmanuele II.

Police in both cities detained more than 100 persons identified with rightwing and left-wing movements. One of several extremist groups whose headquarters was searched by police for possible clues to the bombings was the Association for Cultural and Friendly Relations with the Chinese People's Republic in Rome.

President Giuseppe Saragat declared in a nationwide address that the bombings were "a ring in a chain of terrorist attacks that must be broken at all costs."

The police in Rome Dec. 16 charged Pietro Valpreda, a ballet dancer and anarchist, and eight others with participation in the Milan bombing. Five others, all linked to anarchist movements, were charged with mass murder Dec. 19 in connection with the incident.

Firebombs exploded Sept. 21, 1970 in three Milan churches, where police later found anticlerical leaflets signed by anarchists.

A Milan court May 28, 1971 sentenced three accused anarchists charged with 18 bomb explosions in 1968–69 to fines and prison terms ranging from three to eight years. The three other accused were acquitted. All six, who had been jailed in Milan, were immediately released from prison because of pardons granted by the court.

In March 1971 the Milan police had seized weapons and bomb parts traced to an ultra-leftist underground group. Known as the "Red Brigades," this group had claimed responsibility for a series of explosions, including a January 25 blast that had damaged Pirelli & Co.

Police in Milan clashed April 17, 1971 with extreme rightists. The violence occurred when police tried to disperse a neo-Fascist demonstration. The meeting had been banned after unidentified terrorists bombed the headquarters of the Socialist and Communist parties the previous night. Authorities blamed neo-Fascists for the explosion.

Pino Rauti, a member of the neo-Fascist Italian Social Movement (MSI) national executive, and two other extreme rightists were charged March 22, 1972 with roles in the 1969 bomb attacks in Milan and Rome for which Pietro Valpreda and other left-wing anarchists awaited trial. But Rauti was released from a Milan prison April 24 after a judge ruled there was insufficient evidence against him.

Luigi Calabresi, 35, chief of the political investigations section of Milan's police force, was shot to death May 17, 1972 by an unidentified gunman. Calabresi had headed the investigation of the 1969 bank bombing. Leftists had accused him of the death of an anarchist who had fallen or jumped from the window of Calabresi's office during interrogation.

Three senior police officials were indicted in Rome for concealing evidence that involved other persons in the Valpreda bomb case, the government announced Oct. 21, 1972. They were Elvio Catenacci, deputy chief of the national police; Antonino Allegra, head of the political office of the Milan police; and Bonaventura Provenza, head of the political office of the Rome police. But all three were exonerated in a report published by judicial investigators in February 1974. The investigators concluded that neo-Fascists were guilty of the bombing.

Two extremist right-wingers—Giovanni Ventura and Franco Freda—were indicted for organizing the 1969 Milan bomb blasts, the French newspaper Le Monde reported Aug. 30, 1972. (But Il Mondo June 12, 1974 quoted Defense Minister Giulio Andreotti as saying that a ministerial-level decision had been made to deny judiciary evidence obtained by the Secret Service indicating that extreme rightists had carried out the bombing.)

A policeman was killed and 14 others were injured by a grenade in Milan April 12, 1973 when violence erupted during neo-Fascist demonstrations. The violence broke out when local authorities banned a rally, organized by the MSI.

Two youths, both reportedly linked with MSI activists, were arrested for murder. Vittorio Loi was arrested April 14 and Maurizio Murelli April 16.

The arrests came as the National Right Wing—the official name for the parliamentary branch of the MSI—found itself increasingly accused of links with extreme rightist groups engaging in terrorism. MSI party leaders had always denied connection with them.

Premier Giulio Andreotti May 10 accused National Right Wing deputies of political responsibility for the death of the Milan policeman and backed proposals to try MSI leaders for allegedly re-constituting the banned Fascist party.

Four people were killed and more than 40 injured by the explosion of a grenade May 17, 1973 at the entrance of police headquarters in Milan at the end of a ceremony commemorating slain police official Luigi Calabresi.

Interior Minister Mariano Rumor and the national police chief, Efisio Zanda

Loy, had left the headquarters only minutes before the blast.

Immediately after the explosion, police arrested Gianfranco Bertoli, 40, identified by eyewitnesses as the thrower of the grenade. Bertoli, who had a long criminal record and alleged right-wing ties, described himself as an "individual anarchist."

A second suspect was arrested in Venice May 19, Mohammed Mansor Saeed, 35, an Arab.

A bomb damaged the Communist party offices in Milan Oct. 6. Leaflets on the premises claiming responsibility were signed by the Mussolini Action Squads. (SAM). SAM had also claimed responsibility for two bombs that exploded July 28 in the Milan offices of Mondadore, a leading publishing house, and of Edizioni Sapere, a left-wing publisher.

Bomb blasts April 23, 1974 damaged Milan's tax office and wrecked a building housing a Socialist Party office in Lecco, 30 miles north of Milan. Both explosions were attributed to a new underground right-wing group, the Black Order. The blasts were denounced by Communist and neo-Fascist newspapers.

Leftist publisher killed. The mutilated body of Giangiacomo Feltrinelli, 45, a leftist multi-millionaire publisher, was found March 15, 1972 under a dynamite-damaged power-line pylon near Milan. The body was positively identified as Feltrinelli's the following day.

Police hypothesized that Feltrinelli had been killed accidentally while preparing to blow up the power line. However, the extreme leftist Milan Student Movement charged March 16 that Feltrinelli had been murdered by extreme right-wingers seeking to discredit the left in the upcoming national elections.

An autopsy report March 18 said Feltrinelli had died from loss of blood caused by injuries suffered in an explosion. An official statement said Feltrinelli had also sustained injuries to the head and chest but noted that the time these injuries were inflicted was not determined.

Feltrinelli, a one-time Communist who had quit the party in 1956 and had subsequently become involved in revolutionary movements, had published Boris Pasternak's Dr. Zhivago.

Maoists jailed. Twenty-one Maoist extremists were sentenced April 18, 1973 in Genoa to prison terms ranging from one year to life on charges of kidnapping, robbing and killing to finance their group, known as the "October 22" group.

Mario Rossi, 22, leader of the group who shot to death a messenger in a robbery in September 1971, was sentenced to life imprisonment. Diego Vandelli, a former Fascist, received a 20-year sentence. One defendant was acquitted.

Prosecutor kidnapped—Genoa's deputy prosecutor, Mario Sossi, was kidnapped from in front of his home April 18, 1974. A terrorist organization called the Red Brigade later claimed responsibility and said he was being kept in a "people's jail" where he was awaiting trial by a "people's tribunal" for unspecified crimes.

Police reported May 6 that the kidnappers threated to kill Sossi unless eight members of the Maoist extremist "October 22" group were released from jail and flown to Cuba, North Korea or Algeria. Sossi had headed the prosecution of the group.

Sossi was released by his abductors May 23 after a court in Genoa had agreed to the kidnappers' demand for the release from prison of eight Maoist extremists on condition that Sossi be released first.

The Supreme Court June 18 overturned the decision to release the prisoners in exchange for Sossi's release.

U.S. facilities bombed. Four bombs damaged the offices of the U.S. firms of Honeywell, Inc., International Business Machines and the Bank of America and Italy in Milan and a Honeywell factory in a Milan suburb June 3, 1972.

Police said they did not know who was responsible for the blasts. Leaflets found at the bomb sites praised "the struggle of the Vietnamese people against American imperialism" and the victories "of the revolutionary and Communist army in Vietnam."

Three bombs exploded in Rome Jan. 11, 1974, heavily damaging offices of firms linked to the International Telephone & Telegraph Corp. A fourth bomb exploded in a Rome suburb, slightly damaging a truck owned by a telephone-line maintenance firm. Leaflets on the scene charged ITT with responsibility for the 1973 coup in Chile and for preparing, through telephone tapping, "a reactionary and fascist plot" in Italy.

Brecia bomb kills 7. A bomb exploded at an anti-Fascist rally in the northern industrial town of Brescia May 28, 1974, killing seven people and injuring 93.

The rally, attended by 3,000 workers and students, had been called by a local anti-Fascist committee to protest "obscure Fascist schemes" in connection with recent violence in the city. (In recent months, left-wing cooperatives and trade union buildings had been bombed and a neo-Fascist had been accidentally killed by a bomb he was carrying on his motor scooter.)

The leader of the neo-Fascist Italian Social Movement-National Right Wing, Giorgio Almirante, denied that his group, the nation's major neo-Fascist organization, was involved and denounced the blast as "a horrible crime in a moment of intolerable disorder."

A four-hour general strike was staged by Italy's three major trade unions May 29 to protest the blast. The strike shut down the state radio and television network, stores, government offices, public transportation, schools and universities, all entertainment places and the Milan Stock Exchange. Hundreds of thousands of persons participated in anti-Fascist rallies in Milan, Turin, Rome and elsewhere.

The May 29 demonstrations were marred by violence. Gasoline bombs were thrown at the Milan office of Iberia Airlines of Spain, protesters in several cities attacked the local offices of the Italian Social Movement-National Right Wing and were dispersed by police firing tear gas, and police cars were set on fire in Rome and Bologna.

After the Brescia bombing, police raided extreme leftist and rightist organizations. They arrested May 29 a doctor said to have Fascist sympathies and to be connected with the blast the previous day. An alleged member of a right-wing extremist group, the National Vanguard, was shot dead and two police were wounded in a remote mountain area near Rieti, about 50 miles north of Rome, May 30. Two other men surrendered uninjured. The gunfire exchange occurred as police were investigating reports of a paramilitary training camp in the vicinity. The police said they had found 100 pounds of explosives, many weapons and the equivalent of about $600,000, the latter thought obtained through kidnap ransoms.

The Cabinet May 30 ordered the formation of a special anti-terrorist unit to combat extremist violence. In raids in the Milan area and north of Rome, it was reported June 2, police captured documents and maps indicating that the Brescia bombing was part of a planned rightist terrorist offensive aimed at forcing a military take-over and bringing in a neo-Fascist government. The plans called for machine-gunning a labor demonstration in Milan, temporary occupation of the barracks of the paramilitary carabinieri police, destruction of roads, bridges and rail lines and assassination of prominent politicians.

Neo-Fascists killed. Two members of the neo-Fascist Italian Social Movement-National Right Wing were shot to death in the party's headquarters in Padua June 17, 1974. The extreme leftist Red Brigade later claimed responsibility.

Train bomb kills 12. A bomb exploded on a crowded train Aug. 4, 1974, killing 12 persons. A neo-Fascist terrorist group, the Black Order, claimed responsibility.

The explosion occurred as the train, which originated in Rome and was bound for Munich, West Germany, emerged from a tunnel between Florence and Bologna.

In a note Aug. 5, the Black Order said the bomb attack was designed "to demonstrate that we are capable of placing bombs where we want, at any time, in any place." The message said government members who were "bringing

Italy under Marxism by dissolving our organizations" must bear responsibility for the deaths. The Black Order was thought to be the successor of another extremist group, the New Order, which was banned in November 1973.

(A railroad engineer narrowly averted a crash April 21 when he halted his crowded train shortly before it would have hit a section of the Bologna-Florence track which had just been destroyed by terrorists.

(A Genoa court sentenced four rightist terrorists to prison terms of 14–23 years June 26 on charges of attempting to bomb a crowded train. The leader of the plot, Giancarlo Rognoni, who was tried in absentia, received the 23-year sentence.)

JAPAN

United Red Army Strikes

The only Japanese terrorist organization to achieve world notoriety is Rengo Sekigun (United Red Army, or URA, also called Japanese Red Army), which was formed in September 1969 by 400 radical members of the Zengakuren Socialist student league. The Red Army is best known for terroristic acts in cooperation with the Popular Front for the Liberation of Palestine (developments involving these acts are recorded in this book in the section devoted to the Middle East). In Japan, the Red Army was believed guilty of the murders of at least 11 police and defense officials as well as attacks on police, bank robberies and bombings.

Students hijack airliner. A Japan Air Lines plane with 122 passengers and seven crewmen was hijacked March 31, 1970 by nine Red Army members. The plane took them to North Korea April 3 after efforts to trick them into disembarking at Seoul, South Korea, had failed.

The students seized the jet minutes after takeoff from Tokyo on a domestic flight to Fukouka. Brandishing samurai swords and other weapons, they ordered it flown to Pyongyang, North Korea.

Capt. Shinji Ishida was able to persuade them that he did not have enough fuel, and at a stop in Itasuke Airport, near Fukouka, authorities secured the release of 22 women and children and an elderly male passenger.

The plane then left, apparently for Pyongyang, but landed later March 31 at Kimpo Airport in Seoul.

An elaborate ruse was attempted at Kimpo Airport to get the hijackers to believe they had landed in Pyongyang. North Korean flags were flown and officials and troops at the airport donned Communist uniforms. But the trick failed when hijackers questioned the supposed North Korean officials on points of Marxist doctrine and when one of them observed an American-made car. The students threatened to blow up the plane if any further attempt was made to thwart the hijacking.

During the bargaining sessions that followed, Japanese and South Korean authorities refused to allow the plane to leave for North Korea until the passengers were released. South Korean Defense Minister Chung Nae Hyuk, apparently with the concurrence of Japanese Transport Minister Tomisaburo Hashimote and Ambassador to South Korea Masahide Kanayama, warned the students to free the passengers.

On the evening of April 2, Shinjiro Yamamura, 36, the Japanese vice-minister of transport, offered to serve as a hostage on the trip to North Korea if the students, with whom he had been negotiating for two days, released the passengers and crew. The leader of the hijackers, Takamaro Tamiya, 27, asked that a Socialist member of the Diet, Sukeya Abe, be brought to the airport to verify Yamamura's identity. Abe also offered to go to Pyongyang, but, according to the New York Times April 4, South Korean officials opposed this on the grounds that he had been to North Korea the previous year.

The remaining 99 passengers and four stewardesses were released April 3, and the plane flew the hijackers to Pyongyang later the same day. (North Korea's ambivalence toward the Red Army members was indicated by a Pyongyang radio broadcast April 4 of a statement by KCNA, the North Korean news agency, which said that North Korea would not "play the role of the Japanese police" in guaranteeing the safety of the "Trotskyite" hijackers.)

The jet was returned to Tokyo April 5. Yamamura, the volunteer hostage, who was given a porcelain vase by the Diet for his services, said the hijackers "were very pleasant and polite companions" but were "like madmen" when opposed. The New York Times April 6 quoted North Korean broadcasts that day to the effect that the hijackers were "strangers who came uninvited" and that "our officials concerned will take appropriate steps after necessary investigation."

Plot foiled? Tokyo police Feb. 2, 1971 raided offices and meeting places of various New Left student groups, arresting five students and confiscating 1,366 weapons. The raids reportedly were aimed at forestalling an alleged plot by the United Red Army to kidnap government and business leaders.

Red Army kills 12 members. Tokyo police disclosed March 11, 1972 that URA "executioners" had murdered 12 of their rebel followers following mock trials ordered by their commander. Tsuneo Mori, 27, leader of the organization, confessed to the 12 killings and was placed under arrest with 13 other members.

The slayings came to light after police Feb. 28 had stormed a mountain lodge 90 miles northwest of Tokyo where the URA had held the caretaker's wife hostage for 10 days. Two policemen and a bystander were shot to death in the siege. Mori and four of his followers had fled to the lodge after police Feb. 19 had arrested nine URA members at the mountain resort of Karuizawa.

It was believed that the 12 slain radicals, nine of whose tortured bodies had been recovered in graves through March 12, were executed because of their opposition to the URA's revolutionary policies. Police said the organization had planned an armed attack on government leaders in April with the aim of establishing a "provisional revolutionary government."

Mori hanged himself in a Tokyo prison Jan. 1, 1973.

Tokyo bomb blast kills 8. The Mitsubishi Heavy Industries building in Tokyo was blasted by a bomb Aug. 30, 1974, killing eight people and injuring about 330. A few minutes before the explosion, a telephone call to the company's switchboard warned that two bombs had been set in front of the building and urged immediate evacuation of the offices.

Similar anonymous calls to Mitsubishi Electric, across the street, and later to a Mitsubishi office in Osaka warned that "tomorrow, we will carry out the same class struggle as we did in Tokyo this morning."

Police believed the Tokyo bombs, one of which was later found, were planted by left-wing radicals opposed to armaments production.

Hague embassy siege. Four United Red Army members surrendered Sept. 18, 1974 to Palestinian guerrillas in Damascus, Syria, where they had flown after releasing hostages whom three of the Japanese terrorists had held at gunpoint for four days at the French embassy in The Hague, Netherlands. The action by the three terrorists had won the release of a comrade from a French prison.

The Japanese guerrillas returned the $300,000 ransom they obtained from the French for release of the embassy hostages. Syria promised safe conduct for the terrorists to a country of their choice and left them in the custody of the Palestine Liberation Organization (PLO). The four terrorists had arrived in Damascus aboard a French Boeing 707 after flying from Amsterdam and refueling in Aden, Southern Yemen. Lebanon had refused the guerrillas permission to land.

Three of the terrorists had seized 11 hostages at the French embassy Sept. 13 and initially demanded a $1 million ransom and release of Yutaka Furuya, who had been arrested by French customs officials July 26 with three false passports, $10,000 in counterfeit money and documents that reportedly revealed plans for a terrorist campaign in France and elsewhere in

Europe. News reports indicated that France had deported up to nine Japanese nationals after Furuya's arrest.

Furuya was flown under police escort to Amsterdam's Schiphol Airport Sept. 13. The gunmen freed two women hostages Sept. 16 and released the other nine captives Sept. 17, including French Ambassador to the Netherlands Jacques Senard, after Furuya was freed and the French provided a Boeing 707 jet. Three of the hostages were freed at the embassy in The Hague and six at the airport.

The Paris office of the PLO denied Sept. 19 that its organization had asked Syrian authorities to hand over the Japanese guerrillas and said it "had nothing to do with The Hague affair."

NORTHERN IRELAND

War Against Partition

The creation of the Irish Free State in 1920 (and its transformation into the Republic of Ireland in 1949) failed to end a four-century-old struggle for Irish independence. While most of Catholic Ireland had left the British Commonwealth, the six most Protestant of Ulster's nine countries remained within the United Kingdom under the name Northern Ireland. On the surface, at least, the struggle often seemed to be as much a religious as a political one as Northern Ireland's Catholics, a minority in the six counties, charged that they were subject to political and economic discrimination because of their religion.

The Irish Republican Army (IRA), offspring of the 19th-century Fenians, had led the successful fight for southern Ireland's freedom. Although outlawed in both the Irish Republic and Northern Ireland, the IRA continued the struggle for a free and unified Ireland, and a major IRA tactic was terrorism. A split in the IRA started in 1964 with the formation of a "Provisional" IRA in Belfast. In September 1969 the Provisionals (or Provos) declared their group independent of the Dublin-led "Official" IRA. The Officials had adopted a Marxist orientation while the only clear political policy of the Provisionals was to liberate the six counties by force. Both IRAs have formed ties with Palestinian and other foreign terrorists. In

1969 a new wave of violence started, with Protestant as well as IRA extremists accused of atrocities, and ultimately the terrorism spilled over from Northern Ireland into the Irish Republic and Britain.

British troops began to guard public utilities, public service and government installations in Northern Ireland April 21, 1969 on the heels of violent clashes between Protestants and Catholics and three weeks after the outbreak of what became widespread sabotage. The troops had been requested by the Belfast government April 20 when it appeared that the Ulster constabulary force was unable to cope with the sabotage attacks.

Rioting, violence resumed. Fresh rioting and violence erupted in Northern Ireland at a heightened level in July–August 1970.

Thirty-one persons were injured, nine seriously, in an explosion of a bank in downtown Belfast July 16. It was the 55th explosion in Northern Ireland since Jan. 1 and caused the most injuries.

Two Ulster policemen died of injuries suffered Aug. 11 in a bomb explosion in Armagh County near the border with Ireland. The explosion occurred when the door of a stolen car was opened.

Commons gas bomb attack. The British House of Commons was thrown into an uproar July 23, 1970 when an Ulster Catholic in the chamber's visitors' gallery hurled two canisters of tear gas onto the floor. The bombs filled the chamber with thick white smoke, forcing evacuation of the hall. The Commons session was resumed later in the day.

After the incident, police arrested James Anthony Roach, 26, and accused him of violating the Firearms Act. Bowes Egan, an adviser to Parliament member Bernadette Devlin, a radical leader of Ulster Catholics, was arrested July 28 on charges of conspiring with Roach.

11 die in Belfast riots. At least 11 persons were killed in a new outbreak of clashes Feb. 3–9, 1971 between armed Catholic extremists and British soldiers in the Catholic districts of Belfast. Ulster officials and British Army officers blamed the outbreaks on the IRA.

The upsurge in violence began Feb. 3 as Roman Catholics used submachine guns, and threw bombs, grenades, stones and bottles at British troops during an arms search in the Clonard district of west Belfast. The soldiers, retaliating mainly with water cannon and rubber bullets, also returned fire six times. Seven soldiers were injured and more than 60 people arrested.

Maj. Gen. Anthony Farrar-Hockley, British commander of land forces in Belfast, Feb. 4 labeled the Clonard area a "harbor" of Provisional IRA leaders.

Acid and gasoline bomb attacks against the troops in Catholic districts continued Feb. 5. British soldiers were reinforced by an extra batallion of troops that day and by an armored scout car squadron commanded by the Duke of Kent.

The violence intensified Feb. 6 when four civilians and one soldier were killed in a street battle. Prime Minister James Chichester-Clark declared the same day that the armed battles represented "a trial of strength" between his government and the IRA and vowed that he would "not give in to intimidation."

Gun battles raged in the Ardoyne and Crumlin districts in Belfast Feb. 7, while in Londonderry rockthrowing rioters also battled British troops. The same day bombs exploded in the towns of Newry, Killeen, and Carrickmore, near the border of the Irish Republic.

A booby trap apparently intended for British soldiers killed five civilians Feb. 9 on a rural mountain road at Enniskillen. The victims were two British technicians for the British Broadcasting Corp. and three Irish construction workers.

British troops and Northern Irish police clashed with IRA extremists in Belfast Feb. 26-27. Two policemen were killed and four others wounded in a gun battle with terrorists in the Ardoyne district Feb. 26. Another policeman was injured when a bomb exploded outside a police station on the outskirts of Belfast. Gasoline bombs exploded throughout the city.

A gang of Catholics fire-bombed a two-man British military patrol in Londonderry March 1. One soldier was burned to death.

Three unarmed off-duty British soldiers were shot to death near a bar on the outskirts of Belfast March 10.

New security measures. Prime Minister James Chichester-Clark announced new security measures against IRA terrorists in Northern Ireland March 2, 1971. The measures included the dispatch to Northern Ireland of an extra battalion of British troops, raising the number there to about 8,000; maintenance of a permanent military presence in "riotous and subversive" IRA enclaves; "hot pursuit" of terrorists who engaged in armed violence; and the cordoning of areas to prevent terrorists from fleeing.

Wave of terrorist attacks. Large-scale terrorist attacks that resulted in several deaths and numerous injuries occurred from April through early July 1971. Some observers said the IRA may have embarked on a new policy designed to provoke British soldiers to retaliate against civilians.

Bombs exploded in downtown Belfast April 16. At least four persons were injured and the garage of a magistrate damaged.

Unknown gunmen ambushed a British army vehicle May 15 in downtown Belfast. A civilian was killed and two British soldiers and two civilians were wounded.

A British soldier was killed and two injured in an ambush of an army night patrol in Belfast May 21-22.

A bomb explosion in a British ex-servicemen's hall in the Belfast suburb of Suffolk May 21 injured about 30 persons.

A bomb exploded May 24 in a pub in a Protestant area of Belfast May 24. About 18 persons were injured.

Terrorists threw a bomb into a Belfast police station in a Roman Catholic area of Belfast May 25. One British soldier was killed and more than 20 persons injured, including policemen, soldiers and civilians.

Shortly before the May 25 bomb attack, Prime Minister Brian Faulkner had disclosed in Parliament that British soldiers had been authorized to shoot on sight anyone "acting suspiciously."

He said the army was "not prepared to take half measures with terrorists."

A series of bomb explosions struck Belfast June 5-6. At least eight persons were wounded. One of the bombs damaged a police station.

Two Catholic civilians were killed in Londonderry July 8 during a riot in which demonstrators threw bombs and the troops used live ammunition in retaliation.

The two deaths, which occurred on the fifth consecutive day of rioting in Londonderry, generated more violence. Londonderry youths threw rocks at British soldiers July 9 and tossed gasoline bombs in the streets. Rioters set fire to an American-owned factory, Essex International Brakelining, of Fort Wayne, Indiana. Extremists fired machine guns at British troops July 9-10.

About 11,000 soldiers and 4,000 police sealed off Catholic areas and prevented violence during Protestant Orange Order parades held July 12 to commemmorate the victory of Protestant William of Orange over Catholic forces in the battle of the Boyne. About 100,000 Protestants participated in the parades held throughout Northern Ireland.

Before the parades, which the Catholics regard as humiliating provocation, a series of bomb attacks July 12 had destroyed stores and damaged the central post office along the main parade route in Belfast. Nine persons were injured. Other bombings occurred in Belfast suburbs and outlying towns.

Away from the parade routes, a British soldier was killed by a sniper in a Roman Catholic neighborhood of Belfast July 12. Another soldier was killed in a Belfast ambush July 13. The IRA Provisional faction then claimed responsibility for the two deaths as a retaliatory action for the two killings in Londonderry.

Internment sparks riots. A new wave of rioting erupted Aug. 9, 1971 after the government invoked emergency powers of preventive detention and internment to crush IRA terrorists.

The crisis began with a series of dawn raids Aug. 9 when British army and police patrols seized more than 300 people for questioning. Later that morning, Prime

Minister Brian Faulkner announced that he had resorted to preventive detention and internment without trial of suspected IRA members.

Under the internment order, which was authorized by a Special Powers Act applicable only to Northern Ireland, people could be arrested and held for 48 hours—longer if necessary—without being charged.

The unrest—Rioting erupted in Belfast, Londonderry, Newry and Fermanagh immediately after the first dawn arrests Aug. 9, hours before Faulkner's announcement.

In Belfast, Roman Catholics set fire to buildings, hurled nail and gasoline bombs and exchanged gunfire with British troops. Twelve buses were hijacked. The city came to a standstill as pubs and restaurants shut down and public transportation ceased to run. Protestant families in predominantly Catholic neighborhoods and Catholic families in Protestant areas fled their homes. Protestants set fire to their own houses to insure that Catholics would not occupy them.

The commander of British army ground forces, Maj. Gen. Robert Ford, announced late Aug. 9 that the army had been engaged in "a constant war of attrition against terrorists." He reported the army and police had killed five men, two of them while raiding an army post in central Belfast.

In continued fighting Aug. 10, a British soldier was killed in Londonderry and at least four others were wounded by snipers there and in Belfast. Soldiers battled stone-throwing mobs in the primarily Catholic sections of Belfast with tear gas and rubber bullets. Bombs were thrown at a bank and a movie theater. Many cars were set afire and used as barricades.

At least four men were killed by British soldiers in gun battles with terrorists in Belfast Aug. 11. Arson and sniper fire erupted there, as well as in Londonderry and Armagh.

British troops Aug. 13 fought a gun battle with IRA suspects near the town of Newry, close to the border with the Irish Republic. Early the next morning, terrorists fired machine guns across the border at a police station in the frontier town of Belleek in Northern Ireland.

Terrorists blew up the gates of Belfast's heavily guarded Crumlin Jail Aug. 22, where nearly half of the 240 suspected terrorists were interned. Two prisoners and two prison officers were injured. It was the 11th explosion of the weekend.

A bomb exploded in the suburban offices of the Electricity Board of Northern Ireland in Belfast Aug. 25, killing one and injuring 35.

A British soldier was shot to death Aug. 29 and another wounded when their army patrol was ambushed by gunmen near the Northern Irish town of Crossmaglen near the border with the Irish Republic. The attack occurred after two armored patrol cars inadvertently crossed the border into the Irish Republic. The men fled back to Northern Ireland after hostile passersby burned one of the cars. The casualties occurred after the soldiers returned to Northern Ireland. The army claimed the shots were fired from within the Irish Republic.

Terrorists firing at British soldiers Sept. 3 in the Catholic Falls Road section of Belfast killed a 17-month-old girl.

A British soldier was killed Sept. 4 and two other soldiers injured when their scout car hit a mine at Bessbrook near the border with the Irish Republic.

Two young sisters, aged 15 and 12, were injured when a bomb exploded at a supermarket next to their home in Belfast Sept. 5.

A 14-year-old girl was killed in Londonderry Sept. 6 when she was caught in a gun battle between British soldiers and snipers.

A soldier was shot dead and two others were wounded in Belfast Sept. 17 while they were dismantling a gelignite bomb.

A British soldier was critically wounded Sept. 20 at an observation post in Londonderry by what the army said was a dumdum bullet, outlawed by the Geneva Convention on rules of warfare. The dumdum bullets split on impact, causing multiple wounds. The IRA claimed responsibility for the shooting, but denied use of a dumdum bullet.

219 persons interned. Prime Minister Faulkner announced Sept. 15 that he had signed internment orders for 219 of the approximately 240 persons detained since Aug. 9. The internment orders formally signified that the detainees could be held in prison without trial for an indefinite period.

Terrorism & counter-measures. An explosion in a Belfast bar frequented by Protestants killed two people Sept. 29, 1971. Both IRA factions (Official and Provisional) denied blame.

Terrorists shot to death Patrick Daly, 57, an Agriculture Ministry inspector, when he was caught in a gunfire exchange between British troops and IRA snipers in the Catholic Falls Road area of Belfast Oct. 3.

A bomb explosion in a shop in the Catholic Springfield Road area of Belfast killed one British soldier and wounded nine other soldiers and civilians Oct. 4.

Terrorists blew up a pumping station at a Belfast reservoir Oct. 8, causing extensive flooding and cutting water off from Catholic homes.

A bomb explosion in a bar frequented mainly by Belfast Catholics killed a woman and injured 14 people Oct. 9.

Unidentified army sources confirmed Oct. 12 that troops had been authorized to shoot across the border into the Irish Republic at armed men if their lives were endangered. In the past, troops were prohibited from opening fire if their shots were likely to cross the border.

British troops Oct. 13 began blowing up more than 50 secondary roads between Ulster and the Irish Republic in an effort to halt the flow of arms and guerrillas across the border.

Two Northern Irish plainclothesmen, members of the Royal Ulster Constabulary, were killed by machine gun in downtown Belfast Oct. 15.

A group called the Irish Republican Movement Oct. 16 claimed responsibility for the killing of the policemen. They said one of the policemen had been a member of a "police murder group" that had killed a man in Londonderry in 1969.

British soldiers Oct. 23 shot to death two sisters, ages 30 and 19, riding in a car in a Catholic district of Belfast. The sisters were reportedly members of the Clonard Women's Action Committee, a vigilante group that warned Catholic residents of army raids.

The army contended that shots had first been fired from the car, a claim denied by the driver and witnesses. Army officials explained that no weapons had been recovered from the car because hostile onlookers had prevented soldiers from reaching the vehicle immediately after the shooting.

A Protestant was found bound, gagged and shot to death in Belfast Oct. 26.

Two soldiers were killed when a bomb was thrown at an army observation post in Londonderry Oct. 27. The same day, a police sergeant was shot to death and a constable seriously wounded in an ambush on the outskirts of Belfast.

Fifteen Roman Catholic civilians, including two children, were killed Dec. 4 when a bomb destroyed a Belfast bar. It was the highest toll for a single terrorist incident in the more than two years of the province's civil unrest. Police hypothesized that the bar might have been used as a transfer point when the bomb exploded accidentally.

IRA terrorists Dec. 7-10 shot to death three members of the Ulster Defense Regiment—the equivalent of the national militia—in what was seen as a campaign to demoralize the volunteer force. Two of the victims were Catholic, one was Protestant. One of the Catholic victims was killed Dec. 9 in front of his five children in his Belfast home. The other killings took place in the villages of Clady and Curlough in Tyrone County.

A bomb explosion in a crowded shopping center in the Protestant Shankill Road area Dec. 11 killed two men and two children and injured at least 19 other persons.

The homes of five prominent Belfast residents in the exclusive Malone area came under bomb and gunfire attacks Dec. 14.

Suspects arrested. A suspected IRA leader, James Sullivan, was arrested Oct. 9, 1971 after a two-month police search.

Fifteen IRA suspects were arrested in police raids throughout the province Oct. 12. It was the second big raid within a week.

In a related development, a Belfast court Oct. 8 sentenced a man to 15 years' imprisonment and a woman to nine years on charges of exploding a bomb in a shopping arcade in July.

Provisional Sinn Fein strategy. Sean MacStiofain, Provisional IRA chief of staff, Oct. 24 told a Dublin annual conference of his group's political arm, the Provisional Sinn Fein, that the IRA campaign had "changed from a defensive to a retaliatory and offensive campaign in all parts of the occupied area of the North."

Ruairi O'Bradaigh, elected president of the Sinn Fein movement, defined the group's program: to bring down the Ulster government by making the province ungovernable; conduct an intensive campaign to force British withdrawal; and consider a temporary neutral peacekeeping force after success was obtained in the first two areas. Then the Sinn Fein would lead both northern and southern Irish in building a democratic Socialist Republic.

Arms shipments confiscated. Dutch police seized a 3½-ton cargo of Czechoslovak-made arms and ammunition on a Belgian charter plane at an Amsterdam airport Oct. 16. The arms were flown from Prague and were thought to be destined for the Irish Republican Army in Northern Ireland.

The official Czechoslovak press agency CTK Oct. 18 described as "without foundation" reports that Czechoslovakia had sent or sold the arms.

Rightist senator killed. Sen. John Barnhill, 63, a right-wing member of the ruling Unionist party, was shot to death and his house bombed Dec. 12, 1971.

Barnhill's wife charged the gunmen shot her husband as he opened the front door, then dragged his body into the living room, where they placed a bomb under his body.

The Official IRA Dec. 13 took responsibility for the killing and bombing but said it had intended only to destroy the house. The statement, issued in Dublin, said Barnhill had been shot after he attacked two IRA members who had asked him and his wife to evacuate the house because they planned to bomb it. The officials said the bombing was in "reprisal for the destruction of working-class homes throughout the province" by the British army.

Denouncing Northern Ireland's first political assassination since 1922, Prime Minister Brian Faulkner accused the Irish Republic Dec. 13 of offering a "safe haven" to the men responsible for the killing.

Shortly afterward, Irish Republic Prime Minister John Lynch condemned Barnhill's killing but denied that his government had sheltered the terrorists.

Londonderry Killings & Aftermath

13 slain in 'Londonderry massacre.' In the most violent clash between British soldiers and Ulster Catholics since the outbreak of civil unrest in August 1969, British paratroopers shot to death 13 civilians participating in a banned protest march in Londonderry Jan. 30, 1972.

The incident was denounced as a massacre by witnesses and defended by British army and government sources as justifiable defense in the face of violent provocation.

An immediate controversy arose over the events that led to the shootings, in which 15 demonstrators and one soldier were wounded.

Between 7,000 and 20,000 persons had participated in the Londonderry march, staged in defiance of the government's ban on all demonstrations, to protest the internment without trial of alleged terrorists. When the marchers found themselves blocked by army barricades, they proceeded to a meeting point in the Bogside, a Roman Catholic area, where Bernadette Devlin, Catholic civil rights leader and member of the British Parliament from Northern Ireland, was scheduled to address a rally. The demonstrators began to pelt the soldiers with stones, bottles and debris. The soldiers responded with gradually escalating violence, first spraying the demonstrators with purple dye and then firing rubber bullets and riot-control gas.

An army statement later said that more than 200 paratroopers were ordered forward and they had opened fire only after they came under nail bomb attack and sniper fire. The army said that over 200 rounds were fired indiscriminately at the soldiers during the 30-minute battle that followed and that soldiers had returned fire "only at identified targets." The British paratroop commander, Lt. Col. Derek Wilford, later said the troops had first been fired at by two snipers, both of whom were killed by the soldiers. He acknowledged that no weapons were found on the two bodies.

Witnesses, including several leading Northern Irish politicians and priests, countered with charges that the paratroopers had been the first to open fire and had fired directly into the crowd.

Widgery report—An official British inquiry into the "Londonderry massacre" issued a report April 19 that absolved the army of primary responsibility for the deaths. The report was immediately denounced by Northern Ireland's Catholics as a "white-wash."

Rejecting Catholic claims that the army had acted without provocation, the inquiry, conducted by Lord Widgery, Britain's lord chief justice, concluded that an IRA sniper had fired the first shot.

Widgery based his conclusion on the testimony of TV newsmen present during the incident and on his own deductive reasoning. Noting that soldiers initially had limited themselves to making arrests, Lord Widgery found "no reason to suppose that the soldiers would have opened fire if they had not been fired upon first."

Lord Widgery placed a major share of responsibility for the incident on the organizers of the march because "there would have been no deaths" if the organizers had not "created a highly dangerous situation in which a clash . . . was almost inevitable."

The army's share of responsibility, Lord Widgery said, stemmed from its decision to arrest "hooligans" participating in an illegal civil rights march rather than simply to contain the marchers. Without the arrest operation, he said, "the day might have passed without serious incident." Despite his finding that the firing by some troops had "bordered on the reckless" when four men were killed apparently "without justification" in Glenfada Park, Lord Widgery denied there had been any general breakdown in army discipline.

While generally backing the army, Lord Widgery nevertheless found no proof of the army's claim that soldiers had fired only at identified gunmen and bombers. He noted that no weapons were found by the army and none of the photographs of the march showed a civilian holding an object that could be identified as a firearm or bomb. He also noted the absence of injuries among the soldiers from firearms or bombs.

Despite the fact that none of the civilians killed or wounded were proved to have been shot while handling a firearm or bomb, Lord Widgery said there was "strong suspicion that some . . . had been firing weapons or handling bombs" during the afternoon. He based this conclusion on paraffin tests on the hands of the victims. Seven of those killed bore traces of lead particles indicating they had possibly handled firearms or been close to someone who did. A seventh victim was discovered to have had four nail bombs in his pockets, although two previous medical examinations had failed to turn up any such evidence.

Violence Spreads to London

7 killed near London. A bomb explosion Feb. 22, 1972 at the Aldershot army base, 35 miles from London, killed five waitresses, a gardener and an army chaplain. Seventeen other persons, 14 of them soldiers, were injured.

The Official IRA took credit for the blast as retaliation for the "Londonderry massacre."

The explosion ripped through the officers' mess of the parachute brigade that had been involved in the Londonderry shootings. The bomb had been planted in a car parked in front of the kitchen where the civilian staff was preparing lunch. The dining room was empty at the time of the blast.

Noel Jenkinson, 42, an IRA explosives expert, was sentenced in England to life in prison Nov. 14 after being found guilty of the bombing.

Other violence—Two British soldiers were killed Feb. 10 when a mine destroyed their patrol car near the border with the Irish Republic at Cullyhanna. Two other soldiers were killed by terrorists Feb. 13 and Feb. 16.

Police said that many of the victims had been lured by terrorists to the scene after misleading telephone calls had warned that bombs had been placed in a nearby street. (The IRA Provisionals March 23 took responsibility for the blast.)

A Roman Catholic bus driver was dragged from his bus by terrorists in Londonderry Feb. 16. His body was later found on the city outskirts, shot in the head. The victim was a member of the Ulster Defense Regiment.

A bomb explosion in a crowded Belfast restaurant March 4 killed two women and injured 136 other persons, 27 of them seriously. The bomb exploded without warning while afternoon shoppers were taking a tea break. Both the IRA Officials and the IRA Provisionals disclaimed responsibility for the blast and blamed Protestant extremists.

Another serious bomb explosion in a parking lot behind a movie theater in downtown Belfast injured 52 persons March 6, most of them women shoppers and office workers.

In an effort to halt the intensified terrorism in Belfast, Prime Minister Brian Faulkner March 8 imposed new security regulations that called for searching anyone entering public buildings, closing off some entrances and searching all shopping bags, briefcases or overcoats carried by store customers.

The Ulster Volunteer Force, an extremist Protestant group banned five years previously, responded to the terrorist campaign with a threat March 8 "to kill 10 IRA men for every policeman or soldier murdered in Ulster."

Two of three bombs mailed to three IRA offices in Dublin exploded March 20 after the packages in which they were contained were opened. Sean MacStiofain the Provisionals' chief of staff, was slightly injured.

Six persons, two of them policemen, were killed and 147 were injured March 20 when a 100-pound gelignite bomb hidden in a car exploded in a central Belfast street crowded with midday shoppers.

As part of the continuing bombing campaign, a bomb March 22 wrecked part of Belfast's biggest hotel, the Europa, injuring more than 70 persons.

Three soldiers and four civilians were killed April 7-13 as the IRA stepped up bombing and terrorism after a relative lull following the British government's March 30 takeover of direct rule in Northern Ireland.

A series of bomb explosions destroyed a $31 million textile complex under construction in Carrickfergus, near Belfast, May 1. One worker was killed and about 15 were injured, eight seriously.

Anti-Terror Action

8 IRA leaders arrested in Dublin. Signaling an apparent crackdown on the IRA guerrillas, Irish Republic police arrested eight IRA leaders in Dublin Feb. 23 under an act authorizing detention of suspects for 48 hours without charges. The action was ordered by Irish Republic Prime Minister John Lynch.

Among those detained for questioning were Cathal Goulding, chief of the IRA Official faction, and his son.

A tougher Irish Republic government policy had been indicated Feb. 20 when Justice Minister Desmond O'Malley told a conference of the ruling Fianna Fail party that the attorney general would order the retrial of certain persons who had been recently freed by "inexplicable" court decisions. His statement was thought to refer to a case in which illegal arms possession charges against seven IRA suspects were dismissed the previous week by a court at Dundalk because of insufficient evidence. The suspects included Anthony "Dutch" Doherty and Martin Meehan, two escapees from Crumlin Road prison in Belfast.

A Dublin court March 10 dropped charges against Goulding and three others after the prosecution failed to produce witnesses to testify against them. The defendants had been charged with membership in the IRA and illegal activities in connection with the group. The court March 27 dropped charges against Thomas MacGiolla, head of the Official Sinn Fein party (the political arm of the

Official IRA), because of insufficient evidence. MacGiolla had been accused of membership in an outlawed organization, attempts to raise an illegal military force and possession of incriminating documents.

IRA leader killed. Joseph McCann, 25, an Official IRA battalion commander, was shot to death by British troops in Belfast April 15, 1972 after he allegedly tried to escape an army patrol.

In subsequent violence, three British soldiers were killed and two others were wounded in Londonderry and Belfast April 16. The IRA official wing claimed responsibility for the killings and said they were in retaliation for McCann's death.

Protestants demand action against IRA. The Ulster Vanguard movement, an extreme right-wing Protestant group, warned April 30, 1972 that it would take "appropriate action" against Catholic terrorists unless Britain crushed the IRA. The threat, made in a letter delivered to British Prime Minister Edward Heath in London, charged that the IRA operated "without hindrance in many parts" of Ulster.

Amid mounting controversy over the "no go" sections of Northern Ireland's Roman Catholic districts where the IRA openly patrolled the streets and barred entry to British soldiers, ministers of the suspended provincial government urged Britain April 24 to launch a military offensive against the IRA strongholds in the Creggan and Bogside districts of Londonderry.

Terrorism mounts. A series of shootings and bombings beginning in mid-May 1972 heightened tensions between the Protestant and Roman Catholic communities. There were indications that both Protestant and Catholic gangs were committing terrorist deeds.

The violence began May 13 when a bomb exploded at a public house in the Ballymurphy area, injuring more than 60 persons. As others ran to help the injured, shots fired from the Springmartin district killed one Catholic civilian. News reports differed on the origin of the first shots, but they agreed that Protestants fired from Springmartin at the crowd in front of the public house and that the IRA returned fire from Ballymurphy. Catholics charged that Protestants had set the bomb to lure the Catholics into the open where they were easy targets. However, the army hypothesized the blast might have been caused by an IRA bomb that exploded by accident.

Two other civilians and a British soldier were killed later May 13 in separate incidents as gunfire erupted in other housing developments near the bombing scene. At certain points British troops were shot at by both Protestant and Catholics and reportedly returned fire in both directions.

In continued shooting May 14, one man was killed in the Springmartin district and a 13-year old girl was shot dead in Ballymurphy.

These were the first gun battles between Protestants and Roman Catholics since 1969.

Protestants temporarily barricaded about a dozen streets in the Woodvale area of Belfast May 14. The Ulster Defense Association (UDA), the militant wing of the extreme right-wing Protestant Ulster Vanguard movement, threatened to set up permanent "no go" areas in five weeks if Britain failed to curb the IRA and demolish the Catholic "no go" sections of Londonderry.

A bomb placed in a car outside a bar in the Protestant Sandy Row district of Belfast exploded May 15, injuring 17 persons. Four workers were shot outside a mainly Protestant factory in Belfast May 17, while a bomb exploded the same day in a car in a Protestant Belfast residential street, injuring 16 persons and damaging 20 homes. Protestant vigilantes, some of them hooded, set up wooden barricades near the scene of the blast later May 17. The same day British troops rescued three Protestants who had been kidnaped by IRA members and taken to the Catholic Turf Lodge area of Belfast.

A 15-year-old Protestant boy was shot dead in the Protestant Lower Falls area in Belfast May 18 by a sniper reportedly located in the neighboring Catholic area. A sniper fired six times into a crowd of Protestant high school students in Belfast May 19, but no one was injured.

A bomb explosion at an industrial plant in the Protestant Jennymount area of Belfast May 22 injured at least 60 persons, mainly Protestants.

William Whitelaw, British secretary of state for Northern Ireland, told the House of Commons May 18 that terrorist actions in Belfast and Londonderry indicated the IRA sought to provoke a Protestant backlash that would renew open sectarian violence in the province. He reiterated his intention to keep British soldiers out of the "no go" Londonderry areas.

9 die in Belfast bombings. Nine persons were killed and 130 injured in a mid-afternoon hour of at least 20 coordinated bombings in Belfast July 21, 1972. The IRA Provisionals took credit for the attack, said to be the most devastating since civil unrest began in 1969. The British administration immediately reversed its policy of restraint, intensifying military action against the renewed Provisional terrorist campaign.

Bus and railway stations, hotels, truck depots, a bank and a bridge were among the targets of the Belfast bombing attacks on what was dubbed "Bloody Friday." The worst toll occurred at a bus station, where at least five persons were killed. About six bombs exploded at about the same time in Londonderry and other places in Northern Ireland.

After the bombings, five other civilians were shot dead by snipers in Belfast July 21–22. Some of those shot were thought to be victims of Protestant revenge squads.

Perhaps 2,000 British soldiers moved into IRA strongholds in the Market, Lower Falls Road and other areas of Belfast July 22 to search for weapons, grenades and suspected terrorists.

The troops pursued their "search-and-arrest" tactics in Catholic districts throughout the week, seizing more than 700 pounds of explosives in an apparent guerrilla explosives factory in Belfast's Market area July 23 and another huge arms cache in Belfast's Turf Lodge area July 25.

UDA quits Ulster Vanguard. The Ulster Defense Association (UDA) announced July 23, 1972 that it was quitting the Ulster Vanguard in a policy dispute.

The UDA pledged July 24 an offensive against Provisional IRA strongholds "to try and convince the minority to desist from providing help and sanctuary to the Provisional IRA murderers."

Violence resumes. Terrorism was resumed in the second half of August 1972 after a temporary lull that started with the British decision to send troops into the IRA "no go" areas.

The worst bombing incident occurred when a bomb exploded prematurely in a Newry customs station Aug. 22. Eight persons were killed, including the two men who had planted the bomb, and five were injured. The police subsequently reported the discovery of the body of another victim, probably also an IRA member.

A bomb destroyed part of the Downpatrick race course near Belfast Aug. 26, killing three persons. Police theorized the victims were IRA terrorists who were planting the bomb.

(News reports speculated that the recent premature explosions were caused by the IRA's use of unstable chemical mixtures, including nitrobenzine and sodium chlorate, in the bombs. The IRA had apparently begun using the chemicals after army raids cut off gelignite supplies.)

In another incident, a bomb exploded in a Catholic church in East Belfast Aug. 20. The blast was subsequently attributed to Protestant extremists. No one was injured.

2 Protestants slain in clash with army. Amid a steady deterioration in relations between Northern Ireland's Protestants and the British army, two Protestant civilians were shot dead and two others wounded by paratroopers in a clash Sept. 7, 1972 in the Shankhill Road area of Belfast. The clash came after three successive nights of violence between civilians and soldiers in the Protestant area. It also followed on the heels of the announcement Sept. 4 by the Ulster Defense Association (UDA), the Protestant paramilitary group, that it had broken off "diplomatic relations" with the army because of "continual harassment" by the troops.

According to the army version of the Sept. 7 gun battle, Protestant gunmen opened fire on army patrols attempting to prevent UDA members from setting up a command post in front of a Shankill

Protestant groups form common front—Three right-wing Protestant organizations, the UDA, the Loyalist Association of Workers and the Ulster Vanguard movement, decided Sept. 11 to create a new inner council to coordinate their activities. They chose William Craig, leader of the Ulster Vanguard and a former Cabinet minister, to head the council.

Republic adopts anti-IRA bill after bombings. The Irish Republic's Dail (House of Representatives) Dec. 2, 1972 approved a bill giving the government expanded powers to combat the IRA. The measure was adopted a few hours after bombs killed two men in Dublin.

Before the bomb blasts, the bill seemed headed for certain defeat, which would have led to the dissolution of the Dail and new elections. The major opposition parties, Fine Gael and Labor, opposed the measure on the grounds it was repressive. The bill's major provision would change the rules of evidence to permit conviction of an IRA suspect based on a sworn "belief" of a senior police official that the suspect was an IRA member.

After the explosions occurred Dec. 1, the Dail recessed its heated debate on the question. When the 144-seat Dail reconvened, Patrick Cooney announced that his party, Fine Gael, "had decided to put nation before party" and would withdraw its amendment to kill the measure, clearing the way for passage. He said that most of the party's members had decided to abstain after the perpetrators of the blasts "were revealed as fellow travelers of the IRA."

The Provisional wing of the IRA denied all responsibility for the explosions. The Ulster Defense Association, the militant Protestant group in Northern Ireland, also denied any involvement.

The two blasts occurred within minutes of each other in a busy downtown Dublin area. The first bomb exploded outside Liberty Hall, headquarters of the Irish Congress of Trade Unions. One man was killed, 20 were injured, and the building was heavily damaged. The other bomb went off behind a department store, killing a man in a nearby office, and injuring many others.

The Senate passed the anti-terrorist bill early Dec. 3. President Eamon de Valera signed the measure into law later that day.

O'Bradaigh sentenced—Ruairi O'Bradaigh, president of Sinn Fein, the political wing of the Provisional IRA, was sentenced under the new law Jan. 11, 1973 to six month in prison. The Dublin special court had convicted him of being an IRA member after a senior police official had testified that he was.

(The Provisional Sinn Fein, meeting in Dublin Jan. 6, had elected Marie Drumm, 50, a Belfast housewife, as acting president of the organization while O'Bradaigh remained in prison.)

Anti-terrorist legal changes proposed. An official British commission recommended Dec. 20, 1972 the abolition of trial by jury in certain cases of suspected terrorists and urged that anyone found with or near a firearm should be considered guilty of illegal possession of that weapon until innocence was proved. The commission proposed that a judge from the High Court or county courts hear cases where trial by jury was suspended.

The other recommendations called for an increase in the powers of arrest for security authorities, more stringent bail conditions and maintenance of the detention policy. The measures would apply to both Catholic and Protestant extremists. The commission, headed by Lord Diplock, an appeals court judge, had been created in September to find an alternative to the executive internment policy and to explore ways to detain persons who planned terrorist activity but did not participate directly in the acts.

William Whitelaw, British secretary of state for Northern Ireland, announced acceptance in principle of all the recommendations Dec. 20.

New detention procedures approved—The House of Commons, by a 179–32 vote, approved a bill Dec. 11 approving new procedures to replace administrative internment without trial. The bill set a 28-day maximum limit on detention

of suspected terrorists after which the detainee would be sent to special commissioners who would either officially order their detention or free them.

New drive against 'random' assassins. William Whitelaw announced Dec. 6, 1972 the formation of a joint police and army task force to hunt down the persons responsible for the wave of "senseless, brutal and calculated murders" plaguing Northern Ireland.

His announcement followed the discovery of the body of the 106th victim of the assassinations in 1972. Seventy victims were Catholics, 36 Protestants.

The assassination campaign spread to the Irish Republic Jan. 1 with the murder of a young couple in Donegal County, near the border with Northern Ireland. The IRA Provisionals denied responsibility for the murders.

'72 casualty data reported. The death toll in Northern Ireland's civil unrest in 1972 totaled 467, more than double the fatalities of the previous three years combined, according to official figures in the London Times Jan. 2, 1973.

Of this number, 103 were soldiers, 14 were policemen, 3 were members of the Royal Ulster Constabulary Reserve and 24 were members of the part-time Ulster Defense Regiment. Authorities classified 121 of the deaths as assassinations, with 81 Roman Catholic and 40 Protestant victims. More than 3,400 people were injured during the year.

Since civil unrest began in 1969, the Times reported, 676 people had been killed, including 146 soldiers, and 2,627 explosions had occurred. The 3½-year fatality toll was higher than the total killed in the Irish civil war period in the 1920s, the New York Times reported Jan. 1.

Violence continues—Terrorist violence continued in the opening days of 1973:

A bomb explosion in a bar inside a Roman Catholic area of Belfast injured 25 persons Jan. 13.

Two officers of the Royal Ulster Constabulary were killed and two were injured Jan. 14 when a 20-pound bomb exploded beneath their car outside the main police station in Londonderry. Another policeman was killed and a fellow officer seriously injured when a land mine exploded under their jeep in County Tyrone, near the border with the Irish Republic. The Provisional IRA claimed responsibility for the Londonderry attack.

Amid the resumed wave of assassinations, a hand grenade was thrown at a bus load of Roman Catholic workmen Feb. 1, killing one man and injuring nine. The first British soldier to die in the civil unrest in 1973 was shot dead by a sniper the same day in Strabane.

The killings coincided with an upsurge in alleged IRA terrorist bombings—at least 20 in two weeks—the Washington Post reported Feb. 2.

The intensified violence had begun Jan. 29 when at least two Catholics—one a 14-year-old boy—were shot dead by terrorists. The IRA Provisionals had retaliated by killing a member of the Ulster Defense Association (UDA), a Protestant paramilitary organization. Deputy UDA chairman Thomas Herron, said Jan. 30 his group would no longer try to prevent assassinations of Catholics by Protestants, rescinding a short-lived curb announced early in January .

The worst violence occurred when nine people were killed and more than 20 wounded in Belfast Feb. 3-4. Six of the dead were killed by British soldiers Feb. 3 during a night of gun battles following an assassination in Belfast's New Lodge Road Catholic district. The other three were victims of assassination and machine gun squads.

Gunmen also opened fire from a passing car at a Roman Catholic soccer game Feb. 4, wounding three players. The attack was one of several during the week in which terrorists indiscriminately fired machine guns from speeding cars.

The violence continued Feb. 7 when Protestant snipers fired into a Belfast funeral procession of hundreds of Catholics following the coffins of three members of the IRA Provisionals. Two people, including an 11-year-old boy, were wounded.

U.S. veterans said to train IRA men— The London Sunday Telegraph published an article Feb. 18 saying at least 12 U.S. Vietnam veterans were training members

of the Provisional IRA, mainly in the Irish Republic. British intelligence officers said the report was "by and large well-informed," the news service United Press International (UPI) reported, although Provisional spokesmen denied the account. According to the Telegraph, Britain's internment of IRA explosives experts had forced the guerrillas to recruit Americans as military instructors.

The British intelligence officers also said that 90% of Provisional weapons came from the U.S., according to UPI.

The Protestant UDA had claimed to have recruited Americans to instruct its members in 1972.

Attacks in London & Abroad

London hit by bomb blasts. Two bombs exploded in London March 8, killing one man and injuring an estimated 200 other persons.

About 45 minutes before the first blast, which occurred in the afternoon, a telephone caller to the London Times gave the location of three automobiles containing explosives set to go off shortly.

The first bomb exploded in a car parked in front of the British army's central London recruiting office, near Trafalgar Square. The blast shattered windows of a nearby pub, the Agriculture Ministry and other government offices along Whitehall.

Ten minutes later, another bomb exploded in front of Old Bailey criminal court as police were trying to clear people from the area.

Another bomb was found and defused near the headquarters of the British Forces Broadcasting System. There were subsequent bomb scares at Windsor Castle, the offices of the London Times, the stock exchange and a score of other buildings.

Stiffer security measures were ordered in central London as the police erected barricades in front of the prime minister's residence and police searched parked cars near government buildings. Security checks had already been ordered at ports and airports after a bomb was defused outside Scotland Yard in the morning.

The police theorized that the IRA had set off the bombs to protest a referendum being held the same day in Northern Ireland. The referendum was aimed at determining whether the province would remain part of the United Kingdom or join the Irish Republic.

8 get life terms in London—Eight of 10 Provisional IRA members accused of the London bomb explosions in March were sentenced to life imprisonment in London Nov. 15. One of the defendants was given a 15-year jail term and another was acquitted.

(In another trial in England, an English-born Roman Catholic priest, Father Patrick Fell, was sentenced to 12 years' imprisonment in Birmingham Nov. 1 on charges of forming the Coventry unit of the IRA and of conspiring to commit arson and damage buildings.)

Referendum backs British tie. Northern Ireland Protestants voted overwhelmingly March 8, 1973 to remain part of the United Kingdom rather than join the Irish Republic. The referendum was boycotted by Catholics.

The IRA staged a heavy bombing campaign March 8, apparently in an attempt to disrupt the referendum.

Six bombs exploded in Belfast, and five in Londonderry, damaging stores, a pub and hotels. There were only a few minor injuries. A British soldier was shot dead, however, outside a polling station in a Catholic area of Belfast, and snipers shot at soldiers in two other incidents.

Protestant terrorists active. Patrick Wilson, a Belfast city councilman representing the SDLP and a senator in the former Ulster legislature, and a woman companion were stabbed to death in Belfast June 26, 1973.

A man claiming to represent Ulster's newest terrorist group, the Ulster Freedom Fighters, (UFF), said the group of Protestant extremists was responsible for the murders, but a later phone call claimed credit for the IRA.

The UFF surfaced about the time that splits were reported among the Protestant extremists.

Young Protestant militants claimed June 8 to have overthrown the leadership of the paramilitary Protestant extremist organization, the Ulster Defense Association (UDA), because they opposed what they considered the leaders' moderate policy. They wanted the UDA to retaliate for British arms raids on militant members in east Belfast. However, the militants' statement was never confirmed by the group's leadership, which was reported June 10 to be back in control.

Shortly after the alleged coup, Protestant gunmen fired at British troops in the Protestant Shankill Road area of Belfast June 10-11.

Two armed men forced their way into the Belfast home of Thomas Herron, a UDA leader, and killed his bedridden brother-in-law Michael Wilson June 15. The UDA said the IRA was responsible for the killing, but there was speculation it was the work of UFF extremists.

Two Roman Catholic men were found shot dead in the Belfast area June 16-17. A telephone caller claimed the murders were retaliation by the UFF for Wilson's murder. The UFF also said June 17 it had been responsible for three bombings in Belfast in the past week.

In the wake of the Wilson shooting, Herron was reported June 17 to have admitted that the UDA provided protection against hooligans to East Belfast pub owners. He denied the pub owners had been forced to pay, although a government spokesman described the activity as a "Mafia-type operation." There were reports of a pub being burned down when the owner refused to pay protection.

Bomb explosions tentatively attributed by the police to Protestants damaged two rural Catholic churches near the town of Ballymena, 20 miles northwest of Belfast, Aug. 22. A 600-pound bomb, one of the biggest in the four years of civil unrest, exploded Aug. 26 near a crowded Roman Catholic church in Ballycastle, County Antrim; four persons were injured.

IRA terrorism? The IRA Provisionals were thought to be behind a car bombing explosion June 12 in a crowded street of Coleraine, a predominantly Protestant university town, 50 miles north of Belfast. Six persons were killed and 33 injured.

The IRA was also believed responsible for the bombing of the Londonderry library June 23. No one was injured. Three men driving in County Tyrone, 25 miles south of Londonderry, were killed June 25 when a bomb exploded in their car. Police speculated they were planning to plant the bomb. The IRA Provisionals exploded a car bomb at Belfast airport June 29, injuring a few workers. A British soldier was shot dead in the Roman Catholic area of Ballymurphy July 1.

Terrorists exploded a 300–400-pound bomb in an army housing compound at Omagh, 25 miles south of Londonderry, Aug. 9, the second anniversary of the introduction of internment without trial in Northern Ireland. Sixteen women and children were injured and 50 houses damaged. The Provisional IRA claimed responsibility for the bombing and said that homes of the dependents of British troops stationed in Ulster would be considered legitimate targets for attack.

Six masked gunmen hijacked and booby-trapped a freight train near the border with the Irish Republic Aug. 16. British riflemen attempting to shoot the fuse off the explosives detonated the bomb and the train exploded. It was the first train hijacking in Ulster.

Two IRA Provisionals were killed Aug. 16 by a rocket that exploded as they were about to fire it at a police station at Pomeroy, 30 miles southwest of Londonderry. Four Soviet-made rockets and about 10 homemade missiles were fired by fellow Provisionals in the attack.

Fire & letter bombs in London. London was hit by fire and letter bombs beginning Aug. 18, 1973, when two bombs were first discovered in Harrods department store. The incidents were ascribed to the IRA.

Letter bombs were sent to the prime minister's official residence Aug. 21, to Conservative Party headquarters Aug. 22, to the London Stock Exchange and the House of Commons Aug. 24 and the Bank of England Aug. 25.

Most of the incendiary devices found in several department stores throughout the city were hidden in cigarette packages. Tourists and shoppers were stopped and searched in the central shopping district. False bomb warnings also plagued the city.

A letter bomb, sent to 10 Downing St. Aug. 21, was opened by a mechanical letter opener and "dealt with under normal security arrangements." A parcel bomb hidden in a booby-trapped book was defused Aug. 22 at Conservative party headquarters. Subway service was disrupted Aug. 23 when a bomb was found and defused at the Baker Street station minutes before it was timed to explode during the evening rush hour. A mail bomb was also defused the same day at the Ministry of Defense.

The first injuries resulted from the explosion Aug. 24 of a letter bomb in an office of the London Stock Exchange, where a chief administrative officer and his secretary were wounded. A secretary was also injured by a blast in the House of Commons the same day. Two other persons were injured, one critically, when a letter bomb exploded Aug. 25 in the Bank of England.

Bomb hits embassy in U.S.—A letter bomb, described by officials as similar to the ones discovered in London and attributed to the IRA, exploded in the British embassy in Washington Aug. 27, severing the hand of Nora Murray, secretary to the military attache. The explosion knocked out windows and damaged furniture in the sixth-floor office.

An embassy official said the letter was mailed in London and may have arrived in the U.S. on a Royal Air Force jet carrying mail and supplies for the embassy. He discounted reports that it had arrived in the diplomatic pouch. He said special security precautions around the embassy had begun last year "after we received more threats than usual."

The British Foreign Office in London Aug. 27 ordered extra security precautions for its diplomats around the world after the Washington incident.

Bombs hit other U.K. targets—The fire and letter bomb campaign continued in London, Birmingham, Manchester and abroad.

The major facts known by the police were that the detonators and plastic explosive used in the letter bombs were of Irish origin and that design of the bombs was associated with the Provisional IRA, the Washington Post reported Aug. 29.

Among the explosions:

Two bombs exploded in a bank doorway and outside another building in Solihull, near Birmingham, Aug. 29, slightly injuring three persons. A fire bomb burned a Birmingham shoe shop Aug. 30. A fire bomb injured four persons at Victoria rail station in London Sept. 8, and two other bombs struck King's Cross and Euston rail stations in London Sept. 10, the latter two injuring 13 persons, three seriously. There was only a three-minute warning in one of the Sept. 10 incidents and no warning in the other. Eight persons were reported injured when a bomb in a shopping bag exploded in a crowded London shopping area Sept. 12 and another bomb went off in the Chelsea district of London the same day. Three fire bombs had also exploded in store doorways in Manchester Sept. 8; another critically wounded an army disposal expert in Birmingham Sept. 17.

Letter bombs were intercepted unexploded at the British embassies in Paris Aug. 28 and Lisbon Sept. 17. Another letter bomb sent to a senior government official in Gibraltar was defused Sept. 17, and others addressed to Sir Christopher Soames, British representative to the European Economic Community (EEC), and to a member of the British permanent EEC delegation were defused by Brussels police Sept. 18. A letter bomb sent to the British embassy in Kinshasa, Zaire, exploded and injured a British security officer Sept. 17.

(The first fatality in the terrorist bombings that began in England in mid-August occurred Sept. 23 when an army officer died. He had tried to defuse a bomb in Birmingham a few days earlier.)

Twomey's escape. Seamus Twomey, chief of staff of the IRA Provisional wing, was arrested Sept. 1 in a farmhouse in County Monaghan, 15 miles from the border with Northern Ireland. Twomey, a native of Belfast, was charged in the Dublin Special Criminal Court with membership in the IRA and ordered jailed until Oct. 1. He was then sentenced in Dublin Oct. 8 to three years in prison for receiving stolen money and for being an IRA member.

Twomey and two other Provisional leaders escaped from Mountjoy prison in Dublin Oct. 31 in a hijacked helicopter.

The prisoners were airlifted from the prison exercise yard in a helicopter hired by a man with an American accent. He had directed the pilot to fly to the village of Stradbally, about 60 miles from Dublin, where two armed men boarded the craft and forced the pilot to fly to the prison. After snatching the prisoners, the gunmen flew to an abandoned race track a few miles away, where a car was waiting for the fugitives.

250 reported killed in '73. The number of 1973 fatalities in Northern Ireland's civil unrest totaled 250, compared with 467 in 1972, the New York Times reported Dec. 31. The death toll since 1969 was put at 928, including 204 British soldiers.

Air raid fails. IRA Provisional members Jan. 24, 1974 hijacked a helicopter in the Irish Republic and ordered the pilot to fly to Strabane, Northern Ireland, where they dropped two milk churns filled with explosives on a police station. The bombs, which missed their target, did not explode. The helicopter was flown back to the republic, and the terrorists escaped. It was the IRA's first air attack in Northern Ireland.

Terrorism in 1974. Terrorism stemming from the Northern Ireland issue continued on through 1974.

Two gunmen held up 13 electricity service workers on a lunch break in Belfast Jan. 31, told two Protestants to kneel and then machine-gunned the 11 standing Catholics. Two were killed and three wounded. The illegal Protestant Ulster Volunteer Force blamed the extremist splinter group, the UFF, for the attack, which came one day after the UFF refused to accept a UVF call for an end to sectarian murders.

The UVF ceasefire, announced Jan. 29, was in response to a decision by the IRA Provisionals Jan. 28 to halt murders of off-duty members of the part-time reserve Ulster Defense Regiment.

Three UVF leaders had secretly visited Dublin for discussions with IRA leaders, including Cathal Goulding, Official IRA chief of staff, it was reported Feb. 20.

They were said to discuss an end to sectarian assassinations. It was the first time Protestant and Catholic extremists had held discussions at the senior level, according to the report. The UVF leadership had recently adopted a Marxist ideology, also held by the Official IRA.

Former Home Secretary Reginald Maudling was slightly injured by a letter bomb in London Feb. 1, while a newly appointed circuit judge was slightly hurt by a letter bomb Jan. 30.

Police blamed IRA terrorists for a bomb blast in the National Defense College, in Latimer, Buckinghamshire, Feb. 12. Ten persons were injured, none critically.

SAS members on duty—About 40–50 former members of the Special Air Service (SAS), Britain's crack anti-terrorist unit, were serving as military undercover intelligence agents in Belfast and Londonderry, it was reported March 18. It was believed to be the first time the SAS had been involved in large-scale operations within the United Kingdom.

11 killed in British bus. Eleven persons were killed and 14 wounded Feb. 4, 1974. when a 50-pound bomb blew up a busload of British servicemen and their families as they were traveling through Yorkshire, Great Britain. The dead included an entire family—a soldier, his wife, and two children—and seven other soldiers.

Senator killed in Eire. William Fox, a Protestant senator, was shot dead March 12 near a farmhouse in Clones, close to the Northern Ireland border, where he was visiting his fiancee. Twelve masked men responsible for the killing also ransacked and burned the farmhouse.

IRA's plan. British Prime Minister Harold Wilson announced May 13, 1974 the capture of IRA documents revealing plans to seize control of key areas of Belfast. He said the documents showed that IRA terrorists planned a campaign to stir further sectarian hatred through indiscriminate violence. The IRA, according to the plan, would then move into Belfast as Catholic protectors and would occupy and control densely populated sections of the city. When forced by the British army to retreat, the IRA would burn the city.

An IRA spokesman acknowledged the document May 14 but said the scheme "was devised in the event of a civil war, not to provoke one."

Terrorist violence—A young Roman Catholic was shot to death in one of Belfast's Catholic areas April 20, bringing the official fatality toll to 1,000 since sectarian violence erupted in Northern Ireland in 1969.

The IRA was blamed for the firing of a Soviet-made ground-to-ground missile at a British army guardpost in a Catholic area of Belfast April 11.

Protestants were believed responsible for the bombing of a Roman Catholic-owned bar in Belfast May 2 in which five Catholics were killed. (Protestant extremists had announced at the end of April that they would resume the bombing of Catholic-owned bars.) The IRA admitted responsibility for a rocket attack on an Ulster Defense Regiment post in County Tyrone in which a woman member of the force was killed.

The home of right-wing Protestant leader William Craig was bombed in Belfast May 5. Craig was not at home, and his wife and two children were only slightly hurt.

Bomb attacks kill 30 in Eire. Bomb explosions in Dublin and Monaghan killed 30 persons and injured about 200 others May 17, causing more casualties than any attack since the start of Ulster's civil unrest in 1969.

Three car bombs exploded almost simultaneously and without warning in downtown Dublin at 5:30 p.m., the height of the city's rush hour. Twenty-three persons were killed immediately, and two more died later from injuries.

There was no official indication of who caused the attacks. The three cars containing the bombs had been stolen or hijacked in Northern Ireland and driven south.

Both the Provisional wing of the Irish Republican Army and the paramilitary Protestant Ulster Defense Association disclaimed responsibility.

A half hour after the Dublin explosions, a bomb exploded in front of a bar in Monaghan, 80 miles north of Dublin, killing five persons and injuring more than 20.

The government May 18 recalled its 340 soldiers with the United Nations forces in the Sinai Desert as part of the effort to intensify security along the border with Northern Ireland. Officials promised tighter security measures, including new border checkpoints and severe traffic restrictions in Dublin.

Protestant group takes blame—A new Protestant group, calling itself the Young Militants Association, claimed responsibility for the fatal car bombings in Dublin and Monaghan May 17, it was reported June 25. The terrorist group warned that it would retaliate in the republic for Irish Republican Army bombings in Northern Ireland.

IRA bombing campaign resumes. After a lull of more than a month, the IRA resumed its bombings June 13, 1974 when four incendiary bombs exploded in downtown Belfast department stores and a car bomb wounded a British military policeman.

Car bombs exploded in Armagh, Londonderry and elsewhere June 18–20. Twenty-two bomb attacks on more than a dozen towns and villages throughout the province had occurred since the resumption of the campaign. A policeman was killed in a letter bomb explosion in the town of Lurgan June 18.

The Provisional wing of the IRA June 19 claimed responsibility for the explosions and said the blasts were designed "to bring home to Britain our determination to intensify the war." The Provisionals said economic and military targets throughout the province would "come under constant attack" until Britain issued a declaration of intent to withdraw from Ulster and other demands by the Provisionals were satisfied.

A new development in the IRA bombing campaign was the use of so-called "proxy bombers"—innocent persons forced to drive bombs to their targets while the IRA held their relatives or friends hostage.

The IRA June 19 statement was issued the same day that a three-day conference of Protestant paramilitary groups ended. Although the west Belfast unit of the UDA had backed truce negotiations with the IRA, the other groups rejected such talks.

Two IRA guerrillas were killed by a premature explosion as they carried a bomb into a supermarket in Londonderry June 24.

IRA kills judge, magistrate—The IRA Provisional wing Sept. 16 killed a Roman Catholic county court judge and a Protestant magistrate at their homes in Belfast suburbs. The IRA later said it had warned both men that they were "part of the British war machine."

The judge, Roger "Rory" Conaghan, 54, frequently presided at trials of terrorists. The magistrate, Martin McBirney, was a lower echelon judiciary official.

Air strike fails—The Provisional wing of the IRA failed Sept. 29 in its second attempted air raid.

Four armed men ordered a flying instructor in the Irish Republic town of Dundalk, near the Ulster border, to fly two of them over a British army base in County Armagh, where they would drop four explosive canisters. Only one bomb was dropped, five miles from target, and the three others could not be pushed through a hatchway. At the same time, about 20 IRA guerrillas staged a mortar and machine gun attack against the post. There were no casualties, and all IRA attackers escaped.

PORTUGAL & AFRICA

African Territories Promised Freedom After Coup in Portugal

The civilian dictatorship that had ruled Portugal for more than 40 years was overthrown in a nearly bloodless military coup April 25, 1974. The revolt was fueled by a variety of economic, social and political dissatisfactions. Prominent among these causes was dismay at the dictatorship's colonial policies, which had resulted in long military struggles in Portugal's African territories against native rebels described by the Portuguese administration as ter-

*rorists but by sympathizers as freedom
fighters. Within weeks after the coup, the
successors to the Portuguese dictatorship
agreed to grant self-determination to the
African territories.*

Mondlane Killed. Dr. Eduardo Chi-
vambo Mondlane, 48, leader of the
Mozambique Liberation Front (Frente de
Libertacao de Mocambique, or FRE-
LIMO), died Feb. 3, 1969 when a
bomb exploded in a Dar es Salaam beach
house where he was working. Mondlane
had led the rebel organization, pledged
to free Mozambique of Portuguese rule,
since he had helped found it in 1964.
FRELIMO headquartered in Dar es
Salaam, and its more than 3,000 guerrillas kept some 40,000 Portuguese troops
active in the northern districts of Mozambique.

Tanzanian police speculated Feb. 5 that
the bomb had been mailed to Mondlane
in a package and that it had exploded as
he was opening it. No clues to the assassin were discovered in the rubble.

FRELIMO's executive committee
Feb. 12 elected the front's vice president,
the Rev. Uria Simango, a Methodist
minister, to succeed Mondlane. Simango
maintained a closer relationship with
the Chinese Communists than had the
Western-oriented Mondlane (who had
been educated in the U.S. and was a
Methodist layman). The executive committee's communique said that Simango
would hold the office until a permanent
president was chosen.

Kavandame Quits FRELIMO. The
Portuguese government announced April
5, 1969 that Lazaro Kavandame, chief of
the powerful Maconde tribe in Mozambique, had defected from FRELIMO.

Speaking at an April 12 news conference in Porto Amelia, Mozambique,
Kavandame claimed that FRELIMO had
used his people as "scapegoats of the
war." He said FRELIMO had received
arms from the U.S.S.R., Red China and
other Communist countries.

(The Voice of Freedom radio in
Mozambique reported April 8 that Kavandame, expelled by FRELIMO in

January, had fled to the Portuguese
with only a handful of followers. "His influence in the region is practically nil,"
the report added. "The population of
Mozambique considers him to be a
traitor to the cause of the Mozambican
people.")

Caetano Visits Africa. Premier Marcello Caetano visited the Portuguese
African territories of Portuguese
Guinea, Angola and Mozambique
April 14–21, 1969. With Caetano on
his trip, the first made by a Portuguese
premier to the Overseas Provinces, were
Overseas Territories Minister Joaquim
Moreira da Silva Cunha and Cesar
Moreira Baptista, secretary of state for
information. Caetano made his trip at a
time of continued guerrilla warfare in
all three of the territories; handling these
troubles took nearly 40% of the national
budget and about 120,000 troops (of
whom 1,868 had been killed in the fighting as of April 14, according to the
Portuguese Defense Ministry).

Addressing the Mozambique Legislative Council in Lourenco Marques
April 18, Caetano proposed increased
financial and administrative autonomy
for the territories in accord with their
economic and social needs. Throughout
his trip, however, Caetano had stressed
Portugal's firm determination to hold the
overseas territories.

FRELIMO Leaders Clash. Uria
Simango, one of FRELIMO's three
leaders, accused his two colleagues Nov.
4, 1969 of threatening to assassinate him.

Among his charges, Simango said that
Marcelino Dos Santos and Samora Moise
Machel had executed potential rivals
within the movement and had fostered
"tribalism and regionalism" and defections. Simango demanded negotiations
with those who had left the party and the
annulment of a decision to expel Mrs.
Janet Mondlane, American-born widow
of Eduardo Mondlane.

The leadership crisis ended May 22,
1970 with the election of Machel as
FRELIMO president and of Dos Santos
as vice president.

Cubans Fight in Guinea. The Portuguese government said Nov. 21, 1969 that Portuguese soldiers in Portuguese Guinea had captured Capt. Pedro Rodriquez Peralta, a Cuban army officer, during a clash with nationalist guerrillas. The Cuban had reportedly admitted that he and other officers had been commissioned by the Cuban government to serve with the Marxist PAIGC (Partido Africano da Independencia da Guine Portuguesa e das Ilhas de Cabo Verde, or African Party for the Independence of Portuguese Guinea & the Cape Verde Islands), an organization formed by Amilcar Cabral in 1956. PAIGC, based in Conakry, had led the armed insurrection in Portuguese Guinea since 1963.

Quarrel with Vatican. A sharp rift erupted between the Portuguese government and the Vatican July 1, 1970 when Pope Paul met three leaders of liberation movements in Portugal's African territories.

The three—Agostinho Neto of MPLA, the Movement for the Freedom of Angola; Amilcar Cabral of PAIGC, the African Party for the Independence of Guinea and Cape Verde; and Marcellino Dos Santos, head of FRELIMO, the Mozambique Liberation Movement – were in Rome to attend a conference sponsored by left-wing Italian groups. The three-day conference, on "solidarity with the peoples of the Portuguese colonies," had issued a final communique June 28 denouncing Portugal.

L'Osservatore Romano, the Vatican newspaper, made no direct reference to the Portuguese protest in an article July 3. Similarly, it made no reference to Dos Santos' comments, at a July 2 press conference, that the Pope had said the church "backed the struggle for . . . national independence" and that he would pray for the rebel leaders' cause. L'Osservatore said of the meeting: "The Holy Father greeted them [the three African leaders], and exhorted them to fidelity in the Christian principles in which they were educated." It noted that "the Pope, owing to his mission, receives all those who request the comfort of his blessing."

Premier Marcello Caetano announced July 7 that an explanation had come from the Vatican and that relations between Lisbon and the Holy See had returned to their old cordiality. Caetano said the Vatican had satisfactorily explained that there was "nothing political" in the Pope's audience with the three African leaders.

Palma sentenced in closed trial. Revolutionary leader Herminio da Palma Inacio was tried in absentia Jan. 7–Feb. 13, 1970 on a charge of committing the biggest bank robbery in Portuguese history. All press coverage of the trial was banned.

Twenty-three persons were incriminated in the theft of an estimated $1 million from the Bank of Portugal in Figueira-da-Foz in 1967. Palma had claimed responsibility for the theft.

Sixteen of the defendants were found guilty Feb. 13 and sentenced to prison terms ranging from six months to 20 years. Six of the seven principal defendants were sentenced in absentia, including Palma, who received a 16-year sentence.

Dissident group claims bombings. A series of bomb explosions affecting Africa-bound freighters and political and cultural installations marked the formation in 1970 of a new rebel group pledged to violence against "the colonial war machine of the fascist government."

The group, which called itself the Armed Revolutionary Action (ARA), issued a statement Oct. 27, claiming responsibility for two explosions aboard the cargo ship Cunene the day before. The Cunene, anchored at a Lisbon dock, regularly sailed the Portuguese-Africa run, carrying supplies for functionaries and military personnel of the Portuguese colonial presence in African territories. The ARA statement, distributed to foreign news agencies, said the Cunene had been "immobilized" because it helped "supply the war of colonial oppression."

A second explosion aboard the freighter Vera Cruz at Lisbon Oct. 29 resulted in the death of one dockworker. The ARA claimed responsibility for the action, charging that the Vera Cruz was used to transport troops to the African territories.

Three bombs exploded Nov. 20, damaging the U.S. cultural center in Lisbon, the Portuguese political police training school and a dock. One man was reported killed and four others injured. Police said the dead man, who could not be identified, was responsible for the bombing of the police school and was killed while trying to set a second charge.

The dock explosion, which caused extensive damage, resulted from a bomb placed in a metal suitcase. The suitcase was to have been loaded onto the liner Niassa, scheduled to leave for Africa Nov. 21 with soldiers aboard.

A Nov. 22 report said the director of Portuguese security police attributed the bombings to the ARA. Later, in a letter to the press, the ARA claimed responsibility for the three incidents, according to a Nov. 25 report.

Observers speculated that the ARA grew out of a split within the Portuguese Communist party between the orthodox Communist hierarchy and activists dissatisfied with the party's failure to organize to overthrow the dictatorship of Premier Marcello Caetano.

The Moscow-based party leadership transmitted its philosophy over Radio Free Portugal, broadcasting from Bucharest, with claims to be the "only voice of Portuguese resistance" and denunciations of the dissidents as "romantic revolutionaries." The dissident Patriotic Front, broadcasting from Algiers over the Voice of Liberty, accused the Portuguese party of "showing more interest in imposing its control over resistance organizations than in carrying out acts of resistance."

Security police linked the new ARA to recent infiltrations reported Oct. 27. The police said 30 armed men entered Portugal illegally in August. Three of them, arrested in September, were found to be armed with Czechoslovak weaponry and were carrying "a significant quantity" of munitions.

Guerrillas raid air base. Bomb explosions in a hangar at the Tancos air base, 100 miles northeast of Lisbon, destroyed six helicopters and two training planes March 9, 1971, according to an official communique. But ARA March 10, claiming credit for the strike, said it had destroyed at least 14 helicopters and three trainers.

The ARA said the action was to protest "the shameful colonial war . . . waged by the Portuguese fascists and colonialists against the peoples of Angola, Portuguese Guinea, and Mozambique . . ." The statement attributed the success of the operation to "growing anticolonialist feelings among Portuguese soldiers."

Bomb explosions interrupted communications between Lisbon and the rest of the world for nearly 12 hours June 3. The blasts occurred at a telephone substation in Sacavem, a suburb of the capital, and at the main Lisbon post office. ARA claimed responsibility for the blast June 7.

Zambia accused about kidnapings. Zambia and Portugal traded charges March 5-8, 1971 over 11 farm workers of Portuguese nationality said to have been kidnaped from Mozambique in January by members of COREMO, the Mozambique Revolutionary Council.

The Portuguese Foreign Ministry March 5 accused Zambia of responsibility for the incident. It said that five of the kidnaped men, all black Mozambicans, had escaped and one Portuguese had died.

Zambian Home Affairs Minister Lewis Changufu said March 5 that the captured Portuguese had never been in the country and his government had refused a COREMO request to bring the men into Zambia. Changufu March 8 accused Portuguese authorities of taking five Zambian hostages from villages along the Mozambique frontier.

In a related development, a March 29 bomb explosion in the Lusaka office of FRELIMO, the Mozambique Liberation Front, seriously injured Matteus Childende, an official of the organization, and damaged the building.

Caetano denounces terrorism. Premier Marcello Caetano, in a nationwide TV address June 15, 1971, urged the nation to unite in combating sabotage and terrorism. He disclosed that incidents, earlier reported as accidents, were actually the result of sabotage. One of the most serious was an explosion April 26 on board a ship off the Mozambique coast, resulting in the death of 23 crew members.

Subversion law invoked. The government's announcement that it would invoke Article 109 of the revised constitution to halt subversive acts was reported by the New York Times Nov. 17. The constitution authorized the government to take any measures necessary to curb subversion and provided for National Assembly debate in the event of prolonged incidents. The Times report said the government had asked the assembly to debate Portugal's "state of subversion."

The government acted following bomb explosions in the new North Atlantic Treaty Organization (NATO) headquarters outside Lisbon Oct. 27 and at a NATO military base at Caparica Nov. 8.

Arms bombed in Lisbon. A bomb explosion on the Lisbon docks Jan. 12, 1972 destroyed military equipment set for shipment to Portuguese troops in Africa. The ARA Jan. 13 claimed responsibility for the blast.

Mozambique truck blast. Portuguese army headquarters in Mozambique reported Feb. 10 that members of the Mozambique Liberation Front (FRELIMO) had blown up a truck the previous day in the vicinity of the Cabora Bassa Dam site, killing nine persons and wounding five others.

The report said that "with the complicity of some members of the population, who have no fixed abode in any village" the guerrillas had "managed to infiltrate a small group" in the Tete District, where the huge dam was being built across the Zambezi River.

Angolan nationalists unite. The two principal black liberation movements in Angola signed a pact Dec. 13, 1972 in Kinshasa, Zaire to form a united Supreme Council.

The merger brought together the Western-oriented Angolan National Liberation Front (FLNA) and the pro-Communist Movement for the Liberation of Angola (MPLA), headed by Angostinho Neto. Each side was to appoint 14 members to the ruling council and seven members each to the United Military Command and the Angolan Political Command. MPLA was to name the military leader and FLNA would choose the political chief.

Cabral killed in Guinea. Amilcar Cabral, who had headed the nationalist movement opposed to the government of Portuguese Guinea, was assassinated Jan. 20, 1973 before his home in Conakry capital of the Republic of Guinea.

The news was revealed in a radio speech Jan. 21 by Guinean President Sekou Toure, who said Cabral had been killed "in a cowardly and horrible manner" by "the poisoned hands of imperialism and Portuguese colonialism." The "principal killers" had been arrested soon after the assassination.

In a broadcast Jan. 22, Toure identified those responsible as Portuguese soldiers who had infiltrated Cabral's group, the African Party for the Independence of Guinea and Cape Verde (PAIGC), while posing as deserters. Toure said they confessed that they captured Aristide Pereira and several other top Cabral lieutenants and headed north in boats to Portuguese Guinea before being turned back to Conakry by naval vessels of the Toure government.

Bombs explode. Ten plastic bombs exploded at various public points in Lisbon Dec. 31, 1972 and 16 more went off Jan. 6, 1973. Pamphlets were found near each bomb opposing Portugal's Africa policies. Some of the leaflets were signed "revolutionary workers." Four children were injured in the explosions. Two months later two men were killed and eight injured when three bombs exploded at military offices in Lisbon March 9–10. There was no immediate evidence as to who had set the bombs.

FRELIMO strikes in Mozambique. According to an Aug. 10, 1973 report, a FRELIMO group had killed four people, injured 49 and kidnaped 62 in the Tete district.

In two similar follow-up operations in the Tete district reported Aug. 26 and Oct. 5, FRELIMO guerrillas killed 24 civilians, including some women and children. One woman reported her husband was executed by FRELIMO troops when he tried to escape, after the couple had been kidnapped and taken to Tanzania.

The Washington Post reported Sept. 4 that guerrillas were penetrating farther south into the country, and had seriously threatened security in the Tete region.

A high-ranking FRELIMO leader, Fackson Banda, surrendered to government authorities, it was reported Aug. 22.

LUAR arrests. The police said Jan. 19, 1974 that 29 members or associates of the rebel LUAR (Line of Revolutionary Unity and Action) had been arrested since apprehension of the group's leader, Herminio da Palma Inacio, Nov. 22, 1973.

According to police, the group had been responsible for bombings, and was planning an airplane hijacking and a bank robbery.

Conflict spreads. Clashes between the army and the Mozambique Liberation Front (FRELIMO) had increased in recent months, the Washington Post reported Jan. 29, 1974.

Guerrilla activities had spread from the northern and northwestern regions to central Mozambique, concentrating on railway connections, white-owned farms near the Rhodesian border and, in some instances, African villages considered unsympathetic to the liberation movement.

FRELIMO destroyed the northwestern village of Nhacambo in Tete Province Jan. 6, killing 17 tribesmen. Three other villages had also been attacked, the London Times reported Jan. 10.

The army garrison at Inhaminga, a town on the railway linking the seaport of Beira with Malawi, was attacked Jan. 27

for the second time in less than a week. Since Dec. 31, 1973, FRELIMO had engaged in a series of railway attacks, disrupting shipments and communications. Five people were killed in an attack near Beira, it was reported Feb. 18.

The London Times reported Feb. 12 that the government had moved approximately one million Africans into more than 1,000 "aldeamentos," protected resettlement villages, since the summer of 1973.

Because of increasing FRELIMO attacks, several Portuguese families living near the Rhodesian border had abandoned their farms and moved into Rhodesia, according to a Washington Post report Jan. 29.

Portuguese residents demonstrated in Beira and Lourenco Marques Jan. 18, demanding more government protection from the guerrillas and prompting Portugal to send its army chief of staff, Gen. Francisco Costa Gomes, to Mozambique to take charge of the situation.

Military rebellion fails. An estimated 200–300 members of the army's 5th Infantry regiment rebelled March 16, 1974. They surrendered without bloodshed after other military units refused to join them.

The rebels, led mainly by junior officers, were supporters of Gen. Antonio de Spinola, who had been dismissed as deputy chief of the general staff March 14 for writing a book that severely criticized Portugal's economic, social, political, military and diplomatic policies. Spinola was particularly critical of the government's colonial wars, arguing it could not win a military victory over rebel movements in Portugal's African territories.

The book, titled "Portugal and the Future," became an instant best-seller when it was published Feb. 22. It infuriated right-wing military officers and government officials, including President Americo Thomaz, who forced Premier Marcello Caetano to fire not only Spinola but his immediate superior, Gen. Francisco de Costa Gomes, who also called for modifications in the government's colonial policies.

Coup ends dictatorship. Rebel military officers calling themselves the Armed Forces Movement seized control of the government April 25, 1974, ending over 40 years of civilian dictatorship begun by the late Premier Antonio Salazar.

The coup reportedly was virtually bloodless and enjoyed widespread public support.

Premier Marcello Caetano and President Americo Thomaz were arrested, and leadership was assumed by a seven-man "junta of national salvation" pledged to bring democracy to Portugal and peace to its African colonies. The junta apparently was dominated by Gen. Antonio de Spinola.

Caetano's government policy had been aimed at retaining control by force of Portugal's African territories.

Liberation groups wary—In radio broadcasts April 26–28 from their headquarters in various African capitals, leaders of the rebel movements in Portugal's three African colonies expressed skepticism that the change of regime in Lisbon would substantially affect their activities.

While the groups hailed the coup because it removed the Caetano government, the spokesmen for the Front for the Liberation of Mozambique (FRELIMO), the Popular Movement for the Liberation of Angola (MPLA), the National Front for the Liberation of Angola (FNLA) and the African Party for the Independence of (Portuguese) Guinea and Cape Verde (PAIGC) all declared their opposition to the federative system of alliance with Portugal proposed by Gen. Spinola. [See above]

FRELIMO leaders said they expected no change in the government's policy and asserted, "We are not fighting to become Portuguese of black skin."

The MPLA announced that it would continue to strike at the Portuguese army and accused the coup of aiming to "perpetuate exploitation." The FNLA said it would be willing to negotiate with the new government, but only within "the historic context of total independence for Angola."

PAIGC forces vowed to step up their actions to "liquidate the largest possible number of Portuguese troops" and reiterated their opposition to any ties with Portugal.

Fighting resumes—After a post-coup combat lull, FRELIMO attacked a bus in northern Mozambique May 8, killing at least six passengers. One person was killed when the insurgents blew up a train on the Beira-Malawi line May 9.

FRELIMO announced May 8 that its forces had shot down two Rhodesian aircraft and captured the pilots April 20. Gen. Costa Gomes said May 13 that the rebels had used Soviet-made surface-to-air missiles in the attacks.

Groups of armed white civilians were patrolling the streets of Inhaminga in central Mozambique amid fears that FRELIMO would launch an intensified attack, according to a July 5 report. A major railway junction on the line connecting Tete, site of the Cabora Bassa dam, with Beira, Inhaminga had been hit frequently by guerrilla raids in recent weeks. Rebels had cut the rail link in four places along a 60-mile stretch June 14 and 26; the line connecting Tete and Malawi was also severed in a FRELIMO attack June 26. Three Portuguese soldiers had been killed in an ambush near Inhaminga May 28, while 30 Africans were reportedly kidnapped in a raid on a nearby cotton plantation May 29.

Lisbon opens talks with PAIGC. Portuguese Foreign Minister Mario Soares opened peace talks with representatives of the African Party for the Independence of (Portuguese) Guinea and Cape Verde (PAIGC) in London May 25. Soares had announced the talks May 17 following a meeting with PAIGC leader Aristides Pereira in Senegal. Earlier, the self-proclaimed government of Guinea-Bissau had called for negotiations with Portugal.

In an interview May 22- Soares said the scenario anticipated by Portugal for the political future of the African territories was "a cease-fire, self-determination [through a referendum] and independence," with the London talks to focus on the cease-fire. The negotiations bogged down, however, for the PAIGC had, according to the London Times May 27, established preconditions, including the recognition by Portugal of the "state" of Guinea-Bissau, a step that would effectively rule out the need for a referendum.

Luis Cabral, head of the Guinea-Bissau government, said in a May 27 radio broadcast that the guerrillas would resume combat if Portugal did not "respect our conquests." (According to the London Times May 28, the rebels controlled three-quarters of the territory.)

Lisbon-FRELIMO talks begin. Lisbon held "preliminary and exploratory" talks with the Front for the Liberation of Mozambique (FRELIMO) in Lusaka, Zambia June 5-6 in the first formal contacts between Portugal and the rebel movement.

Portuguese Foreign Minister Mario Soares headed Lisbon's delegation and greeted FRELIMO president Samora Machel June 5 with great warmth and emotion, saying: "We were and are objectively allied ... We two have enemies common to us both." (Soares, leader of the Portuguese Socialist Party, had been a fierce opponent of deposed Premier Marcello Caetano.)

Spinola cites independence options. Gen. Antonio de Spinola, provisional president of Portugal, in a major policy statement June 11, 1974 offered the African territories a choice of "federation, confederation, community or the mere existence of totally independent states." It was the first time he had noted the option of independence; previously he had spoken of "self-determination." However, Spinola continued to maintain that such a decision would be made in a referendum to be held following a gradual program of decolonization.

Spinola announced July 27 that Lisbon would start an immediate transfer of power in its African colonies beginning with Guinea-Bissau.

Guinea-Bissau free. Portugal formally recognized the independence of the Republic of Guinea-Bissau Sept. 10, as de Spinola handed the documents terminating five centuries of colonial rule

to Maj. Pedro Pires, who headed the new African state's delegation to Lisbon.

Mozambique government installed. An interim government provided for in an independence pact signed Sept. 7 by Portugal and the Front for the Independence of Mozambique (FRELIMO) assumed office in Lourenco Marques Sept. 20. Joaquim Chissano, FRELIMO's security operations chief and third-ranking leader, was sworn in as premier in the government which would rule until June 25, 1975 when full independence would be granted.

(FRELIMO forces began arriving in the capital Sept. 13; 200 troops patrolled and distributed food in black shantytowns to prevent further outbreaks of violence in the wake of the aborted attempt by whites to mount a coup.)

In a gesture which FRELIMO described as "the symbolic end" to the 10-year war for independence, the liberation movement freed 197 Portuguese soldiers from a camp in southern Tanzania and flew them to Mozambique Sept. 19.

FNLA halts fighting in Angola. Holden Roberto, president of the National Front for the Liberation of Angola (FNLA), announced Oct. 12 that the FNLA had agreed to suspend hostilities in Angola, effective Oct. 15. The announcement followed two days of talks with Portuguese officials in Kinshasa, Zaire where FNLA headquarters were located. The FNLA was the last of Angola's three liberation movements to agree to a halt in fighting.

Angola's provisional government had been sworn in Sept. 12.

THE PHILIPPINES

Red & Muslim Terrorism

The sporadic terrorism that frequently brings turmoil to the Philippines appears to be largely the work of Communist and Moslem rebel groups whose anti-government objectives frequently lead to close cooperation.

The oldest of these groups is the Huk (or Hukbalahap) movement, which originated in 1942 as the Communist-led Hukbo ng Bayan Laban sa Hapon (Anti-Japanese People's Army). The Communist Party reorganized the Huks in 1948 as its military arm under the name Hukbo ng Mapagpalaya ng Bayon (People's Liberation Army). By the late 1950s, however, the Huks were considered largely a collection of terrorist and criminal bands.

The Communists were also split into two parties, each called Partido Komunista ng Pilipinas (Communits Party of the Philippines), one being pro-Soviet, the other Maoist. In 1969 a Maoist splinter formed the New People's Army (NPA), headed by Commander Dante (Bernabe Buscayno). NPA cadres were reported to have infiltrated the Huks and the Muslim Independence Movement.

NPA loses leaders. Government troops said May 25, 1970 that they had killed two leading members of the New People's Army during a weekend battle. Another dissident was killed by colleagues while leading government troops to the guerrilla hideout of the 2,000-member group in central Luzon.

The government announced May 29 it had found the body of Arthur Garcia, 29, a top-ranking, Peking-trained guerrilla leader. The announcement said Garcia was slain in the course of "a deadly struggle for leadership" in the Maoist wing of the Communist Party. He was the second ranking officer of the New People's Party in central Luzon.

Huks also lose leaders. An old-guard Hukbalahap leader, Faustino del Mundo, surrendered to government soldiers Sept 16, 1970 after being sealed off in a tunnel between two houses. Del Mundo, alias Commander Sumulong, was captured with two aides.

The Hukbalahaps' top old-guard leader, Pedro Taruc, was shot to death Oct. 16 by two civilian informers who led an army unit to Taruc's house near Angeles City. (An unconfirmed report said Taruc had committed suicide on the approach of the informers; another report said he had been slain by his body-

guards who sought the $25,000 bounty offered for his apprehension, dead or alive.) The death of Taruc a month after the capture of del Mundo appeared to eliminate the leadership of the old-line faction among the Huks, leaving a new Maoist group in control.

Army reports said Taruc had been traced to his hideout by an army intelligence team. Local residents claimed that informers who led the army battalion to Taruc were members of the dead leader's own bodyguard.

Taruc, believed to be in his 60s, was secretary-general of the Communist party and "supremo" of the Hukbalahaps. But observers said Taruc's power had declined, and real control was in the hands of Del Mundo.

Bombs damage U.S. firms. The Manila headquarters of Esso and Caltex, two U.S. oil companies, were damaged by bombs Jan. 22, 1971. A Filipino employe was killed. Police said a note found near the Caltex office read "This is the anger of the Filipino people against American imperialism." It was signed "People's Revolutionary Front."

Weeks later a bomb exploded on the grounds of the U.S. embassy in Manila Feb. 12. Damage was minor and no one was hurt.

Terrorists disrupt Manila rally. Ten persons were killed and 74 were wounded by terrorist grenades at a pre-election rally of the opposition Liberal party in Manila Aug. 21, 1971.

Among the wounded were all eight senatorial candidates of the Liberal party who were to face the candidates of President Ferdinand E. Marcos' Nationalist party in November elections. Marcos suspended the campaign until his party and the Liberals decided how to proceed in the face of the violence.

In a nationwide radio and television broadcast Aug. 23, Marcos announced the indefinite suspension of the right of habeas corpus "for persons presently detained or those who might be detained for the crimes of insurrection or rebellion." Police were permitted to search without warrants and to detain suspects without charges.

The president attributed the Manila attack to a rebellious Marxist-Maoist force, which he said had the support of a foreign power. Marcos did not identify the group, but the Philippines Foreign Office said agents of the New People's Army had thrown the grenades.

The Manila blast was followed by sporadic bombing incidents.

Marcos asserted Aug. 26 that the emergency measures invoked had thwarted the Communists from a campaign of spreading terror. Marcos said an insurgent attack that day on a military command post proved that the Communist guerrillas had not given up their plans. Government officials said rebel raiders using grenade launchers Aug. 26 destroyed two air force combat helicopters at the military base in Isabela Province, 185 miles northeast of Manila.

Guerrilla forces struck again Sept. 8 at a government army unit in Isabela Province, killing six soldiers. A government spokesman said about 40 insurgents ambushed a weapons-carrier truck on a mission to search out and destroy the rebels.

Marcos' claim that Communists had been involved in the Manila incident was refuted Sept. 4 by Sen. José W. Diokno, a foe of the president. Diokno contended that the government military, or men trained by the military, were responsible for throwing two hand grenades at the rally. Diokno had resigned from the ruling Nationalist party in protest

Rebellion threat denied. A committee of the Philippines Senate reported Sept. 6 after a one-year study that "no clear and present danger of a Communist-inspired insurrection or rebellion" existed as President Ferdinand E. Marcos had charged. The report dealt with the situation in central Luzon, north of Manila, where Communist Hukbalahap insurgents had operated since World War II. The committee said it found that the immediate problem in central Luzon was lawlessness, poverty and government corruption.

Martial law declared. President Ferdinand E. Marcos declared a state of

martial law throughout the Philippines Sept. 23, 1972 to fight an alleged Communist rebellion "enjoying the active and moral support of a foreign power." Nearly 100 prominent persons, including a number of political opposition leaders, were arrested.

The emergency action followed an unsuccessful attempt Sept. 22 on the life of Defense Secretary Juan Ponce Enrile in Manila and a series of bombing incidents throughout the city. These developments came in the wake of what government leaders described as renewed Communist subversion and terrorist activity earlier in September.

The Defense Department said the attempted assassination of Enrile occurred when his automobile in Manila was overtaken by another car carrying heavily-armed men who fired about 30 bullets. The security men accompanying Enrile returned the fire but the assailants escaped. Targets of the bombing attacks in Manila included the city hall, public utility installations, department stores and three schools.

Previous incidents of unrest—Among the incidents of internal unrest in early September leading to President Marcos' decision to impose martial law:

Defense Secretary Juan Ponce Enrile warned Sept. 8 that the Maoist New People's Army (NPA), the military wing of the Communist party, was threatening open rebellion against the Manila government "24 hours a day." Enrile said the government was preparing for a "possible confrontation" with the rebels that could involve "actual street fighting either with small groups or in mass formations."

The defense department had disclosed Sept. 4 that captured NPA documents revealed a rebel assassination campaign that would include high government officials as targets.

In another incident attributed to the NPA, Manila was hit by a partial blackout Sept. 11 when at least two explosions struck the main office of the Manila Electric Co. and a power substation less than five miles away.

Marcos assassination plot. The government Oct. 17, 1972 announced four arrests in connection with an alleged

Communist plot to assassinate President Ferdinand E. Marcos.

Information Secretary Francisco S. Tatad said two men, a Filipino and a "non-Asian" foreigner, had been arrested Oct. 15 while trying to flee the country. The men, he said were preparing to escape by plane and boat, which were impounded by authorities. Two other persons, armed with rifles, had been arrested in a car parked inside the presidential palace grounds in Manila shortly before Marcos had issued his martial law proclamation Sept. 23, Tatad said.

Marcos' wife was stabbed and was seriously wounded near Manila Dec. 7. Her assailant was immediately shot and killed by guards assigned to protect her. The government charged Dec. 8 that the attack was part of a conspiracy to kill the president and his wife.

The would-be assassin was identified by the government Dec. 10 as Carlito Dimailig, 27. He slashed Mrs. Marcos on the hands and arms with a long knife as she was presenting awards for winners of a national beautification and cleanliness contest in Pasay City.

Two other participants in the ceremony, including Congressman Jose Aspiras, grappled with the assailant and were injured.

Marcos Jan. 7, 1973 confirmed a report that the government had crushed a Maoist plot to assassinate him, his wife and "key" military officers. Marcos said police had killed two Communists and arrested 30 others in thwarting the plot.

U.S. killer tied to anti-Marcos plot. A U.S. Senate Foreign Relations Committee report made public Feb. 17, 1973 said that an American had been hired in a Philippine right-wing plot to assassinate President Ferdinand E. Marcos and overthrow his government before the imposition of martial law in September 1972.

According to the report:

The trigger man was arrested by Philippine authorities and identified as August McCormick Lehman, whose name had first been given as Edward Lehman when seized in 1972. Two other Americans named in the plot were Lawrence Tractman and Robert Pincus. Key figures involved in the planned coup were Vice President Fernando Lopez, Sergio Osmena Jr. and Eleuterio Adevoso, an official of the opposition Liberal party. The plotters, largely retired army officers, formed a junta in 1969 to kill Marcos and seize his government. Adevoso led the group. Part of the plan called for Lopez to take over as caretaker president during the transition period. Osmena said "Washington authorities had been briefed and they showed great interest in the junta movement"

Rebel attack crushed. Government soldiers defeated a major rebel New People's Army attack in Mindanao Oct. 21–22, 1972. A force of 300 troops was flown to Marawi in Lanao Province to lift a rebel siege of a national police camp. About 100 paramilitary policemen had been pinned down all night by guerrilla fire.

Ten soldiers and 49 guerrillas were reported killed in the 24 hours of fighting. Information Secretary Francisco S. Tatad said the rebels, numbering 400 men, had stormed a road bridge leading to the police camp, where they killed five of six guards, and had overrun a nearby university campus at Marawi. Japan's ambassador, Tushio Urabe, had been caught up in the fighting at the campus, but later managed to escape. About 10,000 civilians were evacuated from Marawi Oct. 22.

Thousands of other civilians had been uprooted by the armed forces in areas where NPA guerrillas were active.

Government-Moslem rebel accord. A high-ranking Philippine military official Dec. 18, 1972 reported a peace pact between Moslem rebels and the armed forces in Mindanao.

Brig. Gen. Guillermo Pechache, deputy chief of staff for home defense, said Gen. Romeo Espino, chief of staff, had returned to Manila from the region and reported that the situation was being "gradually normalized" and that conflicts among "warring factions" of Moslems and Christians in the area had been settled peacefully.

The governor of Sulu, the island off the western coast of Mindanao, had reported that Moslem leaders had declared a temporary truce the previous week to give their followers a chance to turn in their weapons. Most of the rebels, however, were reported to be holding their arms.

The arms accord was reported Dec. 10 to have been reached in a meeting between President Ferdinand E. Marcos and a delegation of Moslem leaders.

Strife continued in southern Mindanao. Philippine troops Dec. 28 launched a major drive against rebel strongholds there. The offensive was aimed at recapturing villages under control of what the government described as foreign-trained secessionist rebels and Moslems allied with Communists.

A government report issued March 16, 1973 idenified the rebel leader as Nuraladji Misurai, "a known Communist Maoist." Some non-Moslem Communists from Luzon had joined the Mindanao rebels, the report said.

Rebel leaders captured. Government troops captured six leaders of the Communist New People's Army in 1973 near Manila. One of those seized was described as the fourth-ranking leader of the insurgents. The government news agency made the announcement May 29.

An armed forces report Jan. 12, 1974 said the NPA had regrouped after a brief disorganization and posed a new threat to national security. The NPA had expanded its rebellious activities in the Visayan Islands and Mindanao and had gained new footholds in Panay Island, Negros and a part of Mindanao, the report said.

RHODESIA

African (Black) Struggle for Majority Rule

Since its "unilateral declaration of independence" Nov. 11, 1965, the white minority government of Rhodesia has fought almost unceasingly against African (black) militants, whom it denounces as terrorists but whom sympathizers describe as nationalists struggling to win fair political representation for Rhodesia's black citizens, who comprise the overwhelming majority of the population.

Raids from Zambia. Zambia-based African nationalists in August 1967 began a series of what the Rhodesian government assailed as terrorist raids in Rhodesia.

Officials of 2 exiled Zambia-based nationalist groups—the Zimbabwe* African People's Union (ZAPU), which had been banned in Rhodesia, and the African National Congress of South Africa (ANC)—said in Lusaka Aug. 19 that their forces had killed 66 Rhodesian security force members Aug. 18 near the coal mining district of Wankie. ZAPU and ANC announced that they had formed a "military alliance" to overthrow the governments of Rhodesia and South Africa through guerrilla operations.

A Rhodesian government report Aug. 18 had said that 8 terrorists had been killed and 6 captured in clashes with security forces that day. Rhodesian casualties for the week had totaled 2 dead and 4 wounded, according to the report. A Salisbury announcement Aug. 19 said that about 30 armed terrorists had entered Rhodesia from Zambia the previous weekend. A later report said that 14 had been killed and that ANC membership cards had been found on their bodies.

A Rhodesian government statement Aug. 23 said 3 African terrorists from Zambia had been killed and one captured in a skirmish in Matabeleland. Government losses were listed at 2 dead.

Rhodesian security forces fought Aug. 23–25 with African infiltrators at Tjoloto and in the nearby Wankie game reserve, 60 miles northwest of Bulawayo. Rhodesian planes strafed rebel positions in the Wankie area Aug. 24. A South African police unit, flown from Johannesburg to Bulawayo Aug. 24, joined a Rhodesian police convoy bound for Tjoloto. Other South African police

---

*Zimbabwe, the name used by the African nationalists for Rhodesia, was the capital of an Iron Age culture that existed in the area in the period 1250–1750.

units reinforced Rhodesian security fighters flushing out guerrillas in the Wankie sector. South Africa was reported to have decided to help Rhodesia suppress the African nationalist uprising following reports that the infiltrators had marked South Africa as a prime target of their drive. African prisoners said they had been instructed to cross the Zambian-Rhodesian border near Livingstone, on the northern bank of the Zambezi River at the Victoria Falls, and then to cross into South Africa through Botswana. 9 African infiltrators had been arrested in Botswana Aug. 21, not far from the Wankie game reserve.

Rhodesian Deputy Prime Min. John Wrathall warned Aug. 25 that Rhodesia would take retaliatory action against Zambia unless the infiltration strikes ceased. Wrathall charged that the rebels were trained in Communist countries and were using Zambia as a base for their operations and for storing large quantities of arms and ammunition. The Rhodesian leader assailed the British government for not taking a stand against the terrorist attacks. "The silence is such as to make it plain that the British government is in favor of these activities, hoping that they will further its own economic offensive against Rhodesia," Wrathall asserted.

The Zambian government Aug. 27 denied that it was supporting the anti-Rhodesian guerrilla movement.

South Africa's police commissioner, Gen. John Keevy, denied Aug. 27 that his forces were involved in fighting the African guerrillas in Rhodesia or in Botswana. Keevy conceded that South Africa was "in close liaison" with authorities in those 2 countries and did not rule out future joint action.

The Salisbury government announced Aug. 27 that Rhodesian tribesmen were helping Rhodesian security forces to track down the remnants of an original 50-man guerrilla force in the Wankie-Tjoloto area. South African helicopters also were said to have joined Rhodesian aircraft in the search.

Salisbury announced Sept. 5 that security forces had killed 3 more terrorists; the guerrilla death toll in the past 3 weeks: 31. 7 Rhodesian security police were killed in the same period.

Britain Aug. 29 had rejected a Rhodesian note protesting the nationalist incursions from Zambia. The statement conceded that Lusaka at one time had sought to control the terrorist movement on its territory but currently was encouraging the attacks. According to the Rhodesian charge, Communist arms and equipment for the guerrillas were being funneled into Zambia through the African committee of the Organization of African Unity in Tanzania. Britain, the Aug. 29 Rhodesian note insisted, was obliged to use its influence to dissuade Zambia from aiding the guerrilla operations.

Rhodesian Prime Min. Ian D. Smith Aug. 30 assailed Britain for rejecting the Rhodesian note. Smith called London's move "a most blatant example of the British government assisting and indeed encouraging the action of terrorists against a friendly country."

Invaders Fought. Security forces were reported to have killed 22 African infiltrators in northern Rhodesia March 16–23, 1968.

The force of infiltrators, described as members of Rhodesia's outlawed ZAPU and Zimbabwe African National Union (ZANU), had entered Rhodesia from Zambia. The incursions were believed to have been spurred by the execution of several African convicts in Rhodesia earlier in March.

ZAPU's acting leader in Lusaka, James Chikerema, had said Mar. 19 that the purpose of the raids was to wrest control of Rhodesia from the white minority and to capture Ted Milton, the white Rhodesian hangman who had executed the Africans; Milton had since been dismissed from his post. Another statement by nationalist leaders in Lusaka Mar. 20 said ZAPU and ZANU had formed an alliance with the African National Congress of South Africa to wage a "second great offensive in the liberation war."

Security authorities April 27 reported fresh infiltration attacks by ZAPU and ZANU members from Zambia.

The Rhodesian security statement gave the location of 2 camps in Zambia allegedly used as staging grounds by the raiders for attacks on Rhodesia. After arriving from Tanzania, the armed African nationalists were stationed in the Nkomo camp, 16 miles northwest of Lusaka, and the Lithule camp, about 20 miles from Kuska, the report said.

Sithole Convicted. The Rev. Ndabaningi Sithole, leader of the ZANU, was convicted by Rhodesia's High Court Feb. 11, 1969 and sentenced to six years imprisonment at hard labor for plotting to murder Prime Minister Ian D. Smith, Justice Minister Desmond Lardner-Burke and External Affairs Minister Jack Howman. The trial had started Feb. 2.

Sithole, who had been held in detention since 1964 for alleged political offenses, was said to have written a letter instructing an unidentified African to hire three "hard-core criminals" to kill Smith and the two cabinet ministers. The letter, said to have been written in jail, was reportedly smuggled out of the jail by an African woman, who acted as Sithole's courier but actually was a police spy. She turned the letter over to the police.

After hearing the verdict, Sithole said he "dissociate [d] my name . . . from any subversive activities, from any terrorist activities and from any form of violence."

ZANU, meeting in Lusaka, Zambia, received March 8 a written appeal from Sithole for an intensified guerrilla struggle to "liberate" Rhodesia. The message was said to have been smuggled out of Sithole's jail in Salisbury

Nationalists Reprieved. The death sentences of 49 convicted African guerrillas were commuted to life terms March 7, 1969 by the Rhodesian Executive Council. The prisoners had been found guilty of bringing arms into Rhodesia from Zambia to carry on the nationalists' raids against the forces of the white minority government. In announcing the reprieve, the council said that the 49 men had been sentenced when the law made the death penalty mandatory for the specified crime but that parliament had since repealed the law.

Guerrillas resume raids. African nationalist forces in January 1970 carried out their first infiltration attacks in Rhodesia since mid-1968.

One guerrilla force crossed the Zambezi River from Zambia Jan. 3 and attacked a Rhodesian patrol launch, wounding a policeman.

Rhodesian officials reported that another nationalist band Jan. 16 raided the Victoria Falls airport and a detachment of South African police there. One infiltrator was killed and four South Africans wounded. ZAPU claimed in a statement issued in Lusaka, Zambia Jan. 18 that its forces had killed eight South Africans and five Rhodesian soldiers in the raid.

The government announced Jan. 26 that an African member of the Rhodesian security forces and three nationalists were killed in another battle in the Zambezi Valley. The infiltrators were said to include members of the South African ANC.

(Infiltration tapered off as the year advanced, however, and Prime Minister Ian D. Smith said Oct. 8, 1971 that no guerrillas had crossed into Rhodesia in the past 12 months. He added: "I believe this is the first clear year we have had since our declaration of independence.")

Liberation groups in Zambia merge. Two Rhodesian black liberation movements with offices in the Zambian capital of Lusaka joined forces Oct. 1, 1971 and chose a single leadership. The merger was between the Zimbabwe African People's Union (ZAPU) and the Zimbabwe African National Union (ZANU) to form the Front for the Liberation of Zimbabwe (FROLIZI). Shelton Siwela, 29, a former guerrilla commander with ZAPU, was elected chairman of the new group's Revolutionary Command Council, which included former Vice President James Chikerema and former National Secretary George Nyandoro (from ZAPU) and former Foreign Affairs Secretary Nathan Shamuyarira (from ZANU).

Edward Ndhlovu, who had served as ZAPU's deputy national secretary, denounced the new group Oct. 1 because it "does not have either the blessings of the peoples of Zimbabwe or those of their leadership" and because it was short of "the necessary military power which all true revolutionary movements cannot do without."

ZAPU and ZANU announced in Dar es Salaam, Tanzania March 23, 1972 that they had formed a "joint military command" to plan "revolutionary war" in Rhodesia.

Rhodesia closes Zambia border. Rhodesia closed its border with Zambia to all road and rail traffic Jan. 9, 1973 in retaliation for the killing of two South African policemen near there the previous day.

The policemen, who were aiding Rhodesian security forces in patrols against black nationalist guerrillas, were killed near Victoria Falls when their vehicle struck a land mine. Five other persons, including two more South Africans, were injured. A government spokesman explained that pamphlets "emanating from a terrorist organization operating from within Zambia were found at the scene of the incident."

Closure of the frontier was to be maintained, according to the spokesman, until Zambia gave "satisfactory assurances" it would take action against the guerrillas.

Zambian President Kenneth D. Kaunda said Jan. 10 that his country would maintain "solidarity with those gallant people struggling for their freedom" in southern Africa.

In a related development, Rhodesia was reported Jan. 6 to have moved additional army units to Centenary, in the northeast part of the country about 40 miles from the Mozambique border, following the killing in December 1972 of two members of a black guerrilla group that had fired on a local farmhouse and wounded a young girl.

Defense Minister Jack Howman, who had extended the period of national service in December from nine months to one year, said Jan. 6 that Rhodesia was also policing its border with Botswana because of "undoubted evidence of terrorists" operating from that country.

Smith on guerrillas. In a radio broadcast Jan. 18, 1973, Prime Minister Ian Smith admitted that Rhodesian blacks were supporting nationalist guerrillas who had entered the country recently from Mozambique.

Smith declared that for months terrorists had been "quietly and methodcially undermining the local population" by "intimidation at the point of a gun" and by bribing "a few witchdoctors of doubtful character."

As far as Zambia's connection with the guerrillas was concerned, Smith said Lusaka had "openly admitted" supporting the "international gangsters."

Smith claimed the Kaunda government was afraid to take action against the guerrillas, although "President Kaunda has already had occasion to arrest a large number of Rhodesian terrorists because they were siding with Zambians opposed to his government. For over a year now they have been incarcerated in a Zambian prison. Moreover, a batch of these prisoners were handed over to the Rhodesian authorities through mutual agreement at about the same time."

In Rhodesia, 11 blacks in Sinoia were given prison terms March 15 ranging from $3\frac{1}{2}$ to 10 years for assisting terrorists and failing to report their presence.

A Roman Catholic organization known as the Commission for Justice and Peace in Rhodesia, asked March 23 for an investigation of the government's policy of imposing heavy penalties on blacks accused of helping terrorists.

Rhodesia was reported Feb. 12 to have imposed its first collective fines against blacks suspected of helping guerrillas. Fines of $100, paid in cattle, were collected from a village in the Chiweshe tribal trust land, adjacent to Centenary, where schools and shops had been closed "for security reasons." A tribal leader, Chief Makope, was arrested.

Parliament approved a bill Nov. 8 providing the death penalty or life imprisonment for anyone who harbored rebels, failed to report their presence, or recruited or trained them. The law had been opposed by opposition black members of Parliament.

Killings, hangings reported—Three blacks who admitted bringing arms into Rhodesia to kill whites were hanged in Salisbury prison June 22. Three other blacks had been hanged in Salisbury May 21 after being convicted of murder for a guerrilla attack in December 1972.

Five blacks were executed Oct. 21 and Dec. 14 for killings connected with the rebellion.

A white farmer was shot dead by guerrillas June 7 on his farm about 70 miles north of Salisbury, bringing the total number of civilian whites reported killed by the rebels to 13. Four blacks and 13 members of the armed forces had also been killed by guerrillas.

Guerrillas kidnapped 282 children, teachers and nurses in two raids on a Roman Catholic mission in northern Rhodesia July 6, avowedly to train the children as guerrillas outside Rhodesia. Rhodesian security forces rescued all but 20 of those kidnapped by the next day.

Guerrillas held 31 of 93 children and young villagers Sept. 18 after kidnapping them in a raid from Mozambique. Some of those rescued by security forces said the captives might be taken to Zambia as guerrilla recruits.

Terrorists shot an African headman and hijacked four buses at the northeastern border, it was reported Aug. 20. It was thought to be the first time terrorists had hijacked buses.

Internal Affairs Minister Lance Smith asserted that primitive villagers were under "great pressure from terrorists and at times had to bow to their demands," according to a report released Aug. 21.

Smith said the government had resettled a large number of people from areas with terrorist activity.

Journalist sentenced. Peter Niesewand, a Rhodesian newsman, was sentenced in Salisbury April 6, 1973 to two years in prison at hard labor after he was found guilty of charges under the Official Secrets Act at a one-day trial in March.

John E. T. Hamilton, presiding magistrate, suspended one year of Niesewand's jail term on condition that the defendant not be convicted of a similar offense for three years because, he said, Niesewand had "acted openly and not in secret."

Although the charges against Niesewand were unspecified and his trial was held in secret, he was known to have been prosecuted under legislation making it a crime to publish information "calculated to be, or which might be, useful, directly

or indirectly, to any enemy." The act defined "enemy" as including any "hostile organization." Niesewand had reported the incursion into Rhodesia of black guerrillas entering the country from Mozambique.

Niesewand on guerrillas—The March issue of Africa Report, published in New York by the African-American Institute, carried a dispatch by Peter Niesewand mailed several days before his detention in which the journalist outlined the situation facing Rhodesian security forces along the country's northeastern border with Mozambique.

Niesewand contended the recent guerrilla incursions were carried out by ZANU (Zimbabwe African National Union) terrorists operating "in an extremely sophisticated manner" from Mozambique Liberation Front (FRELIMO) bases "so well equipped and entrenched that they even have cinema shows." The ZANU guerrillas had not entered Rhodesia from Zambia, Niesewand maintained, although ZAPU (Zimbabwe African People's Union) operatives regularly crossed from Zambia to plant land mines in Rhodesia.

Prime Minister Smith's decision to reopen the border with Zambia, closed to protest the Lusaka government's support for Rhodesian terrorists, therefore had "no bearing on the situation in the northeast, as the guerrillas there crossed from Mozambique." Niesewand continued:

"Had Mr. Smith felt able to disclose that the Portuguese territory had become self-sufficient as a rebel base, and that the insurgents operating in the northeast had never touched Zambia at all, he would not have lost as much political credibility internally. But on the other hand, he would have angered the Portuguese authorities, who are extremely touchy about their conduct of the Mozambique war, and who vehemently deny that FRELIMO is in control of any territory at all. Yet this is the position— and Mr. Smith chose to protect the Portuguese sensibilities, rather than his own political back."

Government broadens anti-rebel actions. Faced with increasingly bold guerrilla activities, the government moved to combat the insurgency during 1974.

A new military recruitment program announced Feb. 6 doubled the size of the army draft and instituted other measures to insure a bigger security force.

Guerrilla operations had changed the role of the army from a defensive to offensive unit, a government statement said.

Minister of Internal Affairs Lance Smith said a special militia, armed with shotguns, "the most effective anti-terrorist weapon for a civilian," would be formed on the Tribal Trust land reserved for Africans, it was reported Feb. 23.

More than 8,000 Africans living in the Mozambique border area were moved "with their consent" into "protected villages," the London Times reported Jan. 11. The transfer, along with a decision to strip bushes and trees that had provided cover for infiltrators, created a "no-go" 200-mile-long buffer zone as much as 10 miles wide. According to the Times, security forces would have the right to shoot anyone on sight in the area.

Guerrilla activities continue—Twenty guerrillas were killed in a border clash near Mount Darwin May 19. Army and police units were supported by air force planes in the confrontation which claimed the lives of several leaders of the Zimbabwe African National Union (ZANU). Seven children and four civilians "believed to be terrorists" were also killed during the incident, the government acknowledged May 31. Security forces killed two more civilians in the northeast June 4 and 12 rebels June 21. The government reported June 21 that 78 guerrillas had been killed since March. Fourteen rebels were killed in the Mount Darwin area in mid-August, it was reported Aug. 15, by Rhodesian security forces reinforced by aircraft strafing.

The government announced June 7 that five black guerrillas had been hanged in Salisbury.

A paper published by the London-based Institute for Strategic Studies claimed that Moscow and Peking had been providing training, armaments and financial assistance to the rebels, the London Observer reported Jan. 26. In attacks since 1972, guerrillas had used land mines, machine guns, automatic rifles, and 122-mm.

rockets, demonstrating a growing technical and strategic sophistication.

Baghdad Radio announced March 28 that Iraq had contributed $60,000 to the insurgency movement in Rhodesia.

60,000 Africans being 'resettled.' Rhodesian security forces announced July 25, 1974 that an entire community of about 60,000 was being moved from its present tribal trust land into 21 "protected villages" to deprive guerrillas of contact with the population and protect the people from terrorist harassment.

Security forces said the tribe's former homes in the Chiweshe Tribal Trust Land, about 40 miles north of Salisbury, could be seen from the fenced-in villages and that the people would not have far to walk to reach their fields.

Ivan Johnstone, district commissioner in charge of "Operation Overload," as the relocation program was called, said opposition to the resettlement had been encountered in only 17 of 189 kraals, the London Times reported July 28. According to an Aug. 15 report, the operation was virtually completed.

SOUTH AFRICA & SOUTH-WEST AFRICA (NAMIBIA)

Stern Action Curbs Terrorism

Dissent in South Africa usually meets with harsh repression. This official policy is often cited as a major factor in curtailing what might otherwise be much more terroristic and other anti-government action by the large African (black) majority resentful of the discrimination enforced by the white minority regime.

The African National Congress (ANC) has been a force for dissent in South Africa since 1912 although outlawed since 1960. Its leaders are reported to have included high-ranking Communists. The ANC formed the allegedly terrorist Umkhonto We Sizwe (Spear of the Nation) under the leadership of Nelson Mandela in 1961. The latter group was outlawed in 1963, but it remained active and was reported to have worked with such foreign African revolutionary groups as ZAPU of Rhodesia, FRELIMO of Mozambique and the MPLA of Angola.

The Pan-Africanist Congress (PAC), founded in 1959 by Mangaliso Sobukwe and banned the following year, is reported to have been Maoist since 1963, when it reorganized into cells and formed Poqo (Ourselves Alone), described as a terrorist-guerrilla group and outlawed in the year in which it was founded.

South-West Africa (named Namibia by the U.N. in 1968), ruled by South Africa (since 1915) despite U.N. demands (since 1968) that it give up control, has been the scene of revolutionary activity and sporadic terrorism. The South-West African People's Organization (SWAPO), a pan-Africanist organization founded by Sam Nujomo in the late 1950s to work for South-West African independence, is accused of terrorism.

In reaction to SWAPO activities, the South African government in 1967 enacted a "Terrorism Act" giving the government wide powers to act against suspected terrorists in South Africa and South-West Africa.

S-W Africans Sentenced. A Pretoria court convicted 30 South-West Africans Jan. 26, 1968 and sentenced them Feb. 9 to prison on charges of terrorism and membership in the banned South-West African People's Organization (SWAPO). All 30 came from the Ovambo section of South-West Africa.

19 of the defendants were sentenced to life terms, 9 to 20 years' imprisonment and 2 to terms of 5 years. 3 others, who had pleaded guilty to breaking parts of the Suppression of Communism Act, were given 5-year suspended sentences. (They had testified that several of their fellow defendants had been trained in guerrilla tactics in Communist China, the USSR, Tanzania, Ghana, Algeria and the UAR.) One African was acquitted Jan. 26, and judgment was suspended on another who was hospitalized. One of the original 37 defendants had died, and another had been acquitted before Jan. 26. (A South African appeals court Nov. 22 reduced the life sentences of five of those convicted to 20 years' imprisonment.)

In announcing the guilty verdicts Jan. 26, Judge Joseph F. Ludorf said: because the punishable acts "were committed before the [1967 terrorism] act passed by Parliament," and because "this is the first trial in which persons are charged with contravention of the act because of the retrospective effects thereof," "we have decided not to impose the death penalty in the case of any one of the accused." "The accused, because of their level of civilization, became easy misguided dupes of Communist indoctrination"; they had received "active financial and practical assistance" from the USSR, Communist China and other governments. (The prosecution had produced Soviet, Chinese and Czechoslovak weapons as evidence.) The defendants would not have begun "their futile and ill-conceived exploits" if they had not received "loud-mouthed moral support and incitement by representatives of foreign countries, and persons who published SWAPO newsletters...." SWAPO Pres. Sam Nujomo had ordered SWAPO's "Namibia liberation army" to invade South-West Africa.

Asking for mitigation of sentence, Toivo Herman ja Toivo, a former SWAPO secretary, told the court Feb. 1: South Africa was not ruling South-West Africa with the consent of the governed. "We find ourselves here in a foreign country, convicted under laws made by people whom we have always considered as foreigners." South Africa "has again shown its strength by detaining us for as long as it pleased, keeping some of us in solitary confinement for 300 to 400 days and bringing us to its capital to try us. It has shown its strength by passing an act specially for us and having it made retrospective." Toivo admitted assisting "these who had taken up arms" because "we believe that South Africa has robbed us of our country."

Announcing the sentences Feb. 9, Judge Ludorf said that the defendants' "actions were not those of 'freedom fighters' but of cowards, assassins and common criminals." Toivo was among the 9 sentenced to 20-year terms.

(The UN Security Council Jan. 25, without formal vote, had unanimously called on South Africa to release the 35 South-West Africans then on trial. The resolution charged that they were being tried under "arbitrary laws illegally extended" from South Africa to South-West Africa.)

In 1969 five more Ovambo tribesmen convicted of terrorist activities were sentenced to life imprisonment Aug. 22. A sixth received a term of 18 years. All were charged with conspiring to overthrow the white South African administration of South-West Africa under the aegis of SWAPO.

23 Rebels Jailed. The Pietermaritzburg Supreme Court sentenced 11 Africans to prison March 26, 1969 for attempting to overthrow the government. The defendants, who included one woman, were sentenced to terms of 10–20 years on charges of involvement in foreign Communist-led subversive groups and of training in guerrilla warfare in Ethiopia, Algeria, the U.S.S.R., Tanzania and Zambia.

Twenty-four black Africans from Graaf-Reinet district went on trial in Grahamstown Supreme Court June 23 on charges of belonging to Poqo. They pleaded not guilty to allegations that they had plotted to kill whites and blow up vital installations in Graaf-Reinet. In verdicts July 2, 12 were acquitted and 12 sentenced to terms of from one to seven years for membership in Poqo. All 24 were acquitted on the count of sabotage.

Political Arrests Continue. Forty persons were detained as political prisoners under the Terrorism Act after recent security raids, according to Cape Town Police Commissioner J.P. Gous June 15, 1969.

In a pre-dawn raid on the Bantu township of Soweto May 12, police arrested Mrs. Winnie Mandela, wife of Nelson Mandela, former African National Congress leader then serving a life sentence on Robben Island.

19 blacks acquitted, 1 sentenced. Nineteen black South Africans charged with carrying out black nationalist activities were acquitted Sept. 14, 1970. A 20th detainee, Benjamin Ramotse, held for a later appearance in court, was found guilty Sept. 29 and sentenced Sept. 30 to 15 years in prison.

The delayed trial had opened in Pretoria's Supreme Court Aug. 24. A 58-page indictment accused the 20 prisoners of plotting the violent overthrow of the South African government. Ramotse, listed as the chief accused, contended that he had been seized in neighboring Botswana by Rhodesian police and could not therefore legally be tried in Pretoria. The defense for the other prisoners focused on their contention that they were being tried for a second time on charges on which they had already been acquitted. (All 20 defendants and two others had been acquitted of the charges under the suppression of Communism Act in 1969. They had then been charged under the Terrorism Act with membership or support of the banned African National Congress, but the charges had been dropped Feb. 16, 1970, after which the accused had been rearrested immediately.)

The 19 had been detained 17 months; Ramotse claimed he had been held for 25 months.

In an 84-page decision on the pleas of the 19 defendants, Judge Gerrit Viljoen accepted the defense argument that the new charges were so substantially similar to the previous charges that the new trial was an "abuse of the process of the court." However, Viljoen rejected Ramotse's plea, saying his illegal arrest would not "affect the jurisdiction of this court."

Ramotse's trial resumed Sept. 24 with testimony from prosecution witnesses that Ramotse had trained in guerrilla warfare. He was found guilty on six counts under the Terrorism Act, including charges that he had trained as a guerrilla and had assisted in terrorist operations against Rhodesia and Zambia.

In another development, Mrs. Winnie Mandela, most prominent of the acquitted 19, was placed under house arrest Oct. 1. She was forbidden to attend social, political or instructional gatherings for five years and was restricted to her home from dusk to dawn on weekdays and public holidays. Mrs. Mandela had previously served a seven-year house arrest. Similar five-year bans on the other 18 acquitted were reported Oct. 2.

(Joel Carlson, defense lawyer for the case's defendants, escaped death Nov. 9 when a bomb concealed in a parcel mailed to his office failed to explode. The parcel bore Zambian stamps and a Lusaka postmark.)

Many arrested in terrorism raids. Twenty persons suspected of terrorism were arrested by security police in all parts of the country Feb. 18, 1971.

Those arrested, including teachers, lawyers and businessmen, were members of either the Non-European Unity Movement (NEUM) or the African Peoples Democratic Union of South Africa (APDUSA). Both organizations, legally operating in the country, had sought to make the franchise multiracial.

The police Oct. 24 raided homes in all parts of the country in an apparent effort to seize illegal political literature. One man taken into custody as a result of the raids died in disputed circumstances Oct. 27.

The police operation, carried out against the homes of 60 clergymen, university teachers, student leaders and newsmen, took place in Johannesburg, Cape Town, Durban, Port Elizabeth, East London and other cities.

The London Times Nov. 20 reported five more arrests for alleged terrorist activities in the past three days, and two more suspects were seized Nov. 22.

Land mines kill four. A land mine exploded May 22, 1971 in Namibia, killing two white South African policemen and injuring seven others, including two black trackers.

The incident occurred in the Caprivi Strip, an area of Namibia extending eastward to the Rhodesian border. It was believed to be the first time that guerrillas had inflicted fatalities in any territory controlled by South Africa.

Stephanus Lourens Muller, minister of police, said in the parliament in Cape Town May 24 that at the scene of the explosion six sets of footprints had been found leading northward into Zambia. The London Times reported May 24 that the mine was believed set by members of the South-West African People's Organization (SWAPO).

Land-mine explosions Oct. 4 and 5 in the Caprivi Strip killed a South African army officer and wounded four policemen, according to an announcement Oct. 5 by Prime Minister John Vorster.

The first blast, which occurred five miles west of Katima Mulilo, injured the policemen, who were riding in a motor vehicle. Capt. H. T. S. van Eeden was killed the following morning while on an inspection trip in the vicinity of the first explosion.

In disclosing the incident to members of his party's annual Transvaal Congress in Pretoria Oct. 5, Vorster repeated his government's warnings against "Communist-trained terrorists," saying they would be pursued "wherever they might flee. . . . This has therefore been done in this case, and should the pursuers be attacked, they will defend themselves. The responsibility in this case rests squarely on the shoulders of the country making available its territory for this sort of aggression."

Although Vorster's announcement was generally taken by the South African and foreign press to mean that government troops had entered Zambia in pursuit of the guerrillas, Vorster declared Oct. 6: "I never said that the police crossed the border."

Stephanus Lourens Muller, minister of police, underlined Vorster's earlier denial Oct. 7 when he remarked: "After the land-mine explosions, the police, as a matter of course, carried out follow-up work, but they definitely did not enter the territory of any foreign country in the process."

The London Times Oct. 8 reported that a spokesman for the SWAPO had claimed the previous day his group's guerrillas operated from Namibia rather than from Zambia.

Muller said Jan. 6, 1972 that a sergeant had been killed and three other policemen injured the previous day when a land mine exploded under the vehicle in which they were traveling in the Caprivi Strip.

Train wreck seen sabotage. Thirty-eight blacks were killed and another

174 injured March 31, 1972 when a train in which they were riding was derailed eight miles north of Potgietersrust in the Transvaal. Investigators discovered that the nuts and bolts fastening the rails had been removed.

Blacks convicted of terrorism. Thirteen black South Africans arrested in February 1971 were convicted April 4, 1972 of trying to secure money and recruits for guerrilla training and of plotting to overthrow the government with foreign help. They were sentenced April 6 to terms ranging from five to eight years.

Those convicted were APDOUSA and NEUM members. Their trial took place in August 1971.

Indians jailed for terrorism. Three men and a woman, all Indians whose trial began in June, were sentenced Nov. 1, 1972 to five years in jail for trying to overthrow the regime and for promoting the aims of the South African Communist party and the African National Congress, both outlawed organizations.

Right-wing extremists seized. Police officials in Cape Town arrested two men Oct. 9, 1972 in connection with actions of a group known as Scorpio which had engaged in bomb attacks against the homes of liberals. Among the targets had been Geoff Budlender, president of the student council at Cape Town University, and the Rev. Theo Kotze, a regional director for the Christian Institute.

Black jailed for 1967 Rhodesian raid. Fana Mzimela, a 34-year-old black said to have entered Rhodesia in 1967 and fought with guerrillas against security forces there, was sentenced Nov. 23, 1972, in Pietermaritzburg to 15 years in jail under the Terrorism Act.

Mzimela was accused of taking part in terrorist activities from 1962–72. He was also charged with membership in Umkhonto We Sizwe. State witnesses testified that Mzimela had been trained in China and Eastern Europe.

Six jailed in alleged plot. Two white foreigners and four black South Africans were tried under the Terrorism Act in November 1972, convicted of conspiracy to overthrow the government and sentenced to prison June 20, 1973.

An Australian, Alexandre Moumbaris, received a 12-year term, and John W. Hosey, of Northern Ireland, received a five-year sentence. The four blacks each received 15-year sentences.

Black leaders murdered. Abraham Tiro, a black former student leader who had been dismissed from a South African teaching post after clashes with school officials over apartheid, was killed by a parcel bomb in Botswana, it was reported Feb. 6, 1974.

John Dube, an official of the African National Congress of South Africa, was killed and two others injured by an explosion in a Zambia building housing various southern Africa opposition groups, it was reported Feb. 12.

SWAPO head seized. David Meroro, national chairman of the South-West Africa People's Organization (SWAPO), an opposition group, was arrested in Windhoek, South-West Africa (Namibia) by South African police Feb. 8, 1974.

(It was reported June 16 that South Africa had begun to recruit, arm and train blacks for army and police antiterrorist units to protect the northern border regions. The announcement, made by Minister of Police John Kruger, was a significant departure from the all-white defense force policy previously in effect.)

SOVIET UNION

Jewish Militants Active

If there is terrorism in the Soviet Union, reports of it fail to seep through the communications barrier that surrounds the U.S.S.R. but that is pierced frequently by samizdat ("self-published" writings of dissenters) and manuscripts that the gov-

ernment apparently does not want published. Outside of the country, acts of anti-Soviet terrorism sometimes take place. In recent years, Soviet officials, traveling performers and facilities have been targets of harassment and several bombings, especially in the U.S., by Jewish militants incensed at Soviet mistreatment of Jews who seek to emigrate from the U.S.S.R. A U.S. organization most frequently accused of this anti-Soviet activity is the Jewish Defense League (JDL), a force of young Jews that a Brooklyn rabbi, Meir D. Kahane, had originally recruited to protect New York Jews from muggers and anti-Semitic attacks.

Embassy bombed. A bomb of undetermined origin exploded at the Soviet embassy in Washington Feb. 21, 1968 at about 5:45 a.m. No one was injured. Amb.-to-U.S. Anatoly F. Dobrynin was among several persons in the embassy at the time. The bomb apparently was placed on the window sill of a ground-floor office, which suffered considerable damage.

Strong protests, charging that police protection was inadequate, were made by the Soviet Union in Washington and Moscow. An early statement from Tass, official Soviet press agency, that the bombing "could have been committed only with the connivance of the American authorities," was described by White House Press Secy. George Christian as "utterly ridiculous."

JDL activity blocks Bolshoi tour. Anti-Soviet harassment by Jewish militants in 1970 threatened U.S.-Soviet cultural exchanges.

The U.S.S.R. Dec. 11 canceled a planned 1971 tour of the U.S. by the Bolshoi Theater's opera and ballet companies because of what it called "provocations by Zionist thugs."

The reference was to a Nov. 25 bomb explosion at the Soviet airline (Aeroflot) and tourist office in New York and a Nov. 20 sit-in at the Washington office of the Soviet news agency Tass, staged by eight college students believed to be members of the Jewish Defense League. The eight were arrested Nov. 20 and charged with unlawful entry.

No injuries were reported in either incident.

After the bomb explosion Nov. 25, Rabbi Meir Kahane, national director of the JDL, said no one in his group had taken part but that he "heartily applauded" the incident. U.S. State Department spokesman John King said Nov. 25 that the Nixon Administration "strongly condemns such irresponsible acts of violence and considers them injurious to the interests of the U.S."

The Bolshoi cancellation was announced in Moscow to U.S. Ambassador Jacob D. Beam in a note read by Vasily V. Kuznetsov, Soviet first deputy foreign minister. Kuznetsov declared that despite Soviet protests U.S. officials "have not taken necessary measures to stop these criminal actions, thereby encouraging them. . . . The provocations not only create obstacles to the implementation by Soviet institutions in the U.S. of their official functions, and threaten to disrupt measures within the sphere of cultural exchange, but also endanger the personal safety of Soviet citizens."

The scheduled tour by the entire Bolshoi Theater, arranged by U.S. impresario Sol Hurok, was regarded as the feature attraction of the current U.S.-Soviet cultural exchange pact.

The Times of London later Dec. 11 quoted a JDL spokesman in New York as having said of the tour's cancellation: "Our actions here against official harassment of Jews in the Soviet Union were very influential."

Soviet performance disrupted. The performance of a Soviet dance troupe in New York was disrupted Jan. 28 1971 by a bomb threat and the opening of ammonia bottles.

The Siberian Dancers and Singers of Omsk halted their performance at Carnegie Hall while police searched the auditorium in response to a telephone message by a man who identified himself as a member of the Student Struggle for Soviet Jewry.

Members of the Jewish Defense League Jan. 20 had conducted a sit-in at the New York offices of Columbia Artists Management, Inc., the organization booking the Siberian Dancers tour.

State Department spokesman Robert J. McCloskey had warned Jan. 26 against any efforts by "irresponsible elements" to disrupt the tour.

Soviet warns on Jews' harassment. In a note handed to State Department officials Jan. 4, 1971, the U.S.S.R. charged the U.S. with "conniving at criminal actions" committed by "Zionist extremists" against Soviet representatives in the U.S.

The Soviet note asserted: "Zionist extremists not only interfere with the normal functioning of Soviet representatives in the U.S., but also venture to threaten openly Soviet diplomats and other Soviet citizens with physical reprisals." The note said that the U.S. had failed to provide normal working conditions for Soviet officials and it should "not expect that such conditions will be provided for U.S. premises in the Soviet Union."

(The Soviet delegation to the U.N. charged Jan. 5 that in a demonstration outside the Soviet Mission to the U.N. Dec. 27–28, 1970 by JDL members, a bottle thrown through a window had injured a staff member and wakened a child.)

The Soviet protest Jan. 4, delivered in writing by Ambassador Anatoly F. Dobrynin, was immediately rejected by U. Alexis Johnson, the acting secretary of state. State Department spokesman Robert J. McCloskey said Jan. 5 that "deplorable as actions against the Soviets in the U.S. are, they are acts of misguided individuals, and the U.S. government is acting progressively to prevent further actions of this kind." McCloskey emphasized "that we are deeply concerned and shocked at the open threat of possible retaliation against American interests in the Soviet Union." He noted that two U.S. diplomats in Moscow had recently received threatening phone calls at home and added that, because the diplomats' phone numbers were unlisted, it "would seem implausible to us that such threats could be carried out short of or without official backing."

Five Soviet delegations presented petitions to the U.S. embassy in Moscow Jan. 7 against the harassment of Soviet representatives in the U.S.

Soviet Foreign Minister Andrei A. Gromyko delivered "a stern protest" Jan. 8 to U.S. Ambassador Jacob D. Beam over a bomb explosion in Washington that day.

Mark R. Palmer, a U.S. embassy officer in Moscow, was lectured in the street by Soviet citizens Jan. 6. A similar incident occurred Jan. 7 with Erastus Corning 3d, Moscow representative for Pan American World Airways.

The cars of three U.S. newsmen in Moscow were vandalized Jan. 9 and 10. Thompson R. Buchanan, political officer at the U.S. embassy in Moscow, protested the incidents Jan. 11. Buchanan was told there would have been no harassment had U.S. authorities provided regular working conditions for Soviet diplomats.

Yehuda-Leib Levin, Moscow's chief rabbi, delivered a letter of protest to the U.S. embassy Jan. 12 in which he deplored the Jewish Defense League campaign. The letter said: "Soviet Jews do not want the help of unsolicited protectors and Fascist Jews."

President Nixon was reported Jan. 12 to have declared the previous day that bomb attacks against Soviet buildings in the U.S. were "morally wrong." In an answer to letters from Jewish leaders condemning the attacks, Nixon declared: "All decent and law-abiding Americans share your outrage at recent criminal acts of violence against Soviet facilities in this country."

Nixon sent 60 federal guards Jan. 17 to protect the Soviet U.N. Mission in New York.

Kahane halts harassment. JDL leader Meir Kahane Jan. 19, 1971 declared an "indefinite moratorium" in his organization's campaign, which had been announced Jan. 10, to "follow, question and harass" Soviet diplomats in New York. The harassment had provoked a retaliatory campaign against U.S. diplomats in Moscow, and the situation was worsened by a Jan. 8 bomb explosion outside a Soviet cultural building in

Washington and the smashing of a window Jan. 15 at the New York office of the Soviet airline Aeroflot.

In his Jan. 19 statement, Kahane declared: "If we don't see any results, we'll go back to our harassment." The remark was made as Kahane entered a New York criminal court to face charges of disorderly conduct, resisting arrest and obstructing governmental administration.

(Meir Kahane was convicted Feb. 23, 1971 in New York of obstructing governmental administration and disorderly conduct during demonstrations in 1969. Kahane had been arrested again in New York Feb. 15 outside the Soviet Mission to the U.N. and charged with harassment and verbal abuse. He had declared an end the previous day to a moratorium on JDL harassment of Soviet diplomats.)

Kahane term suspended. Kahane got a five-year suspended sentence, was fined $5,000 and placed on probation for five years in New York July 23, 1971 for his role in a plot to manufacture explosives.

Kahane had entered a plea of guilty July 9 following a pretrial hearing on an indictment returned May 13 accusing him and six other JDL members of conspiring to violate federal gun laws.

Two other members of the JDL, Chaim Bieber and Stewart Cohen, also received suspended sentences and fines for their roles in the bomb plot. U.S. District Court Judge Jack B. Weinstein gave Bieber a three-year suspended sentence, fined him $2,500 and placed him on probation for three years. Cohen was sentenced to a three-year suspended jail sentence, fined $500 and placed on probation for three years.

Soviet office bombed in N.Y. A bomb exploded April 22 at the New York offices of the Amtorg Trading Corp., the Soviet trading agency. No one was injured in the blast, which damaged the building. The incident drew an official Soviet protest April 24.

Approximately 20 minutes before the explosion, the Associated Press and United Press International received warning telephone calls from a man who used slogans of the JDL. The JDL denied responsibility for the bombing later April 22.

George Bush, U.S. representative at the U.N., telephoned Yakov A. Malik, the Soviet delegate, to express regrets.

Bush declared: "I appeal to all the extremists and their followers to abandon their barbaric tactics—tactics that can only lead to a deterioration of decent relationships between countries."

In Moscow April 24, U.S. Ambassador Jacob D. Beam was summoned to the Soviet Foreign Ministry to receive a protest from Vasily V. Kuznetsov, the first deputy foreign minister.

Other bombings—Among other anti-Soviet bombings in 1971:

Three gelignite bombs were thrown at the Soviet embassy in Canberra Jan. 17. Some windows were broken, but no injuries were reported. The police arrested two Bulgarians in connection with the bombing.

An explosion damaged the Soviet trade delegation's building in Amsterdam April 15. Four of the 20 occupants and a passerby were injured. The bomb also damaged the neighboring U.S. consulate. The Soviet embassy in The Hague immediately protested. Police arrested an American Jew living in the Netherlands as a suspect. A board attached to the gate of the building bore the words in English, "Never again! Let my people go!"—JDL slogans.

An unexploded bomb was found June 12 at the Soviet Union's estate in Glen Cove, N.Y. Police said a faulty timing device had prevented the bomb from exploding.

3 admit bombings. Three JDL members pleaded guilty in federal court in New York Sept. 26, 1972 to charges stemming from two anti-Soviet bombings.

Sheldon Siegel, 26, pleaded guilty to conspiring to bomb and make two bombs planted at the Soviet Union's trade agency, Amtorg, in April 1971.

Eileen Garfinkle, 21, and Jacob Weisel, 25, pleaded guilty to illegal possession of dynamite, some of which was used in a bomb planted at the Soviet estate in Glen Cove, N.Y.

Bomb kills Hurok employe. A woman employe of Sol Hurok Enterprises, which booked Soviet artists for U.S. concerts, was killed Jan. 26, 1972 and 13 other persons, including Hurok, were injured when what police believed was an incendiary device exploded in the group's offices in New York. The blast and fire followed by several minutes a similar detonation at Columbia Artists, another talent-booking organization located a few blocks away.

The Associated Press and the National Broadcasting Company received anonymous telephone calls shortly after the explosions from a person who declared that the fires had been set to protest the "deaths and imprisonment of Soviet Jews" for which "Soviet culture is responsible." The caller ended his message with the JDL slogan "Never again!" (Rabbi Meir Kahane said Jan. 26 in Jerusalem that the persons responsible for the incidents were "insane." Kahane added: "It isn't the first time our slogan has been used. I know our group wouldn't do this.")

Witnesses at Columbia Artists said the bombs apparently had been set by two young men, "clean-cut and white."

The woman killed in the Hurok office's bombing was Iris Kones, a receptionist.

Anti-Soviet bomb plot in U.S. Acting Attorney General Richard G. Kleindienst announced May 24, 1974 the arrest May 23 of four JDL members while assembling bombs to be used in blowing up the residence of the Soviet mission to the United Nations at Glen Cove, N.Y.

Kleindienst said the four, who were held without bail on state and federal charges of conspiracy and possessing a bomb, were arrested at Lido Beach Jewish Center on Long Island after an anonymous telephone call had been made to Nassau County police. Directions leading to nearby Glen Cove were found in possession of the men, who were identified as Mark I. Binsky, David Levine, Robert E. Fine and Ezra S. Gindi.

Legislation requested—George Bush, U.S. representative at the U.N., asked Congress March 16 for legislation making it a crime to harass foreign diplomats. Bush, testifying before a House judiciary committee, enumerated "senseless acts of violence" that had taken place in New York. He declared: "Bricks have been thrown through windows, paint has been thrown against walls of buildings, motor oil has been placed in car radiators, burning rags in gas tanks and Molotov cocktails have been thrown at mission vehicles. . . ."

Kahane sentenced. A Jerusalem district court convicted Rabbi Meir Kahane June 27, 1974 of trying to harm Israeli-American relations by conspiring to blow up foreign embassies in Washington but acquitted him of charges of conspiring to murder and kidnap Soviet and Arab diplomats in the U.S. He received a two-year suspended sentence June 28.

Kahane had admitted urging JDL members in the U.S. to blow up the Soviet and Iraqi embassies in Washington and financial institutions in New York that had ties with the Soviet Union.

SPAIN

Basques Fight Regime

Spanish authorities have accused anarchists, Communist and Catalan separatists of acts of terrorism, but the most prominent terrorist group is the Basque separatist organization ETA (Euzkadi ta Askatasuna, or Basque Nation and Freedom). The ETA is reported to have split into several factions, some of which are said to cooperate with Communist and other terrorist groups.

Bombs planted on Spanish planes. Bombs planted in luggage were placed aboard planes of Iberia Air Lines in four European cities May 10, 1970.

In Geneva, 50 passengers were removed minutes before an incendiary device exploded in the baggage compartment of an Iberia DC-9. A baggage check had been called when officials discovered one suitcase too many aboard the plane, but it was an anonymous phone call which caused the order for evacuation.

Fire bombs intended for placement aboard Iberia planes also exploded in the airports at Amsterdam and Frankfurt.

A telephone warning tipped off agents at London's Heathrow Airport; they discovered' a fire bomb in a suitcase aboard a loaded Iberia plane.

A telephoned bomb threat in Basel, Switzerland delayed takeoff of another Iberia liner May 11. A Barcelona-bound plane was also delayed May 11 when an anonymous caller said a fire bomb was aboard.

Observers May 10 had speculated that the bomb-plantings were the work of opponents of the Franco regime. Anonymous callers in New York May 11 claimed the bombs were planted by anti-Castro Cuban nationalists protesting Spain's trade with Cuba. In Paris, the Basque and Spanish Republican governments in exile denied any connection with the attempts, according to a May 12 report.

Basques convicted, death sentences commuted. A five-man military tribunal in Burgos Dec. 28, 1970 pronounced death sentences on six of 16 alleged Basque terrorists. The major defendants were convicted of assassinating Meliton Manzanas, chief of the political police in Guipuzcoa province, in 1968.

Generalissimo Francisco Franco Dec. 30 commuted the death sentences.

Three of the six defendants had been sentenced twice to the death penalty by the Burgos tribunal. Nine other defendants including two women and two Roman Catholic priests—received sentences ranging from 12 to 70 years. Two of those sentenced to double death sentences also received 30-year jail terms. A 16th defendant was acquitted.

The sentences handed down by the Burgos military tribunal:

Francisco Izco, 29, charged with actually shooting police official Militon Manzanas—death, commuted by Franco Dec. 30; Eduardo Uriarte, 25- -death, commuted; Joaquim Gorostidi, 26—death, commuted; Francisco Larena, 25—death, commuted; Mario Onaindia, 22—death, commuted; Jose Dorronsoro, 29—death, commuted. Izco, Uriarte and Gorostidi had also received second death sentences on general charges of banditry. All six were ordered by the tribunal to pay an indemnity of $14,285 to Manzanas' widow.

The six were scheduled to have been executed by firing squad Dec. 31. Under Franco's commutation order, each death sentence was changed to a 30-year prison term. Izco, Uriarte and Gorostidi, who received double death terms, would have a 60-year sentence, plus additional terms of from 20 to 30 years which each of the six received. However, under current Spanish law no one could spend more than 30 years in prison.

The other sentences handed down by the Burgos tribunal:

Rev. Juan Echave—50 years; Rev. Julian Calzada —12 years; Juana Dorronsoro, Izco's wife—50 years; Iciar Aizpurua, Gorostidi's wife—15 years; Jesus Abnisqueta—62 years; Victor Arana -70 years; Antonio Carrera—12 years; Enrique Guesalaga—50 years; Gregorio Lopez Irasuegui—30 years; Maria Aranzazu Arruti, wife of Lopez Irasuegui - acquittal.

The 105-page sentence contained a long indictment of the ETA. The sentence said the ETA was a "separatist Marxist terrorist organization . . .whose purposes were to . . . destroy by violence the organization of the state, dismember a part of the national territory by subversive actions, terrorism, armed warfare and social revolution." The document charged that ETA had relations with "revolutionary groups abroad, with Communist parties . . . and others characterized by their animosity toward Spain." All the defendants in the trial, charged with "murder and banditry," had admitted membership in the ETA and Marxist political beliefs, but they had denied any involvement in the murder.

Bonn consul kidnapped, then freed. Eugen Beihl, 59, West German honorary consul and representative of several German industrial concerns, had been kidnapped from his home in San Sebastian in the heart of the Basque country Dec. 1, during the Burgos trial.

Beihl was released Dec. 25 and driven to Wiesbaden in West Germany by executives of the Second West German Television Network (ZDF) who had arranged for his release. Two ZDF technicians who were held hostage were freed in France Dec. 26 after Beihl's safe arrival in Germany.

The release and its timing, just in time for Christmas day, were designed "to show first our people, then the world, that ETA is not an irresponsible, fanatical and bloodthirsty band," according to a statement issued by the organization in France

Dec. 25. The communique added, however, that there would be reprisals if the Burgos tribunal handed down any death sentences.

Beihl told a nationwide West German television audience that he had been captured and held in an unknown place by masked, armed men. Asked about his attitude toward the Basque movement, Beihl said: "I am no enemy of the Basques. I am even their friend."

Industrialists kidnapped. Lorenzo Zabala, was kidnapped by ETA members near Bilbao Jan. 19, 1972 and freed Jan. 22.

He was released after his instruments company agreed to rehire 120 of 183 dismissed workers, increase wages by nearly $4 weekly and grant workers a voice in management decisions. Police also acceded to a demand for the release of two priests and 10 workers arrested during the hunt for the kidnappers.

Felipe Huarte was kidnapped by four ETA members from his Pamplona home Jan. 17, 1973 and released Jan. 25 after one of his factories agreed to a labor settlement and his family paid 50 million pesetas ($800,000) in ransom.

The ETA had released a statement in France claiming responsibility and issuing a set of demands, including the rehiring of 114 workers who had been dismissed for staging a strike at Torfinasa, a Huarte subsidiary, a $47 per month wage increase at the affected plant, fully paid sick leave and a one-month annual vacation.

Huarte's company agreed almost immediately to rehire the men and accepted the other terms Jan. 25. Huarte's family, one of Spain's leading industrial families, reportedly paid the ransom to ETA agents in France. (The government Jan. 31 revoked the labor concessions as granted under duress.)

The Spanish government had concentrated thousands of Civil Guards in the mountains north of Pamplona in a search for the kidnappers, but Huarte was released on the French border near the city of Irun.

In a related development, a military court in Bilbao sentenced four Basques to prison for 12–17 years Jan. 25 for complicity in Zabala's kidnapping. Seven defendants were acquitted for lack of evidence. The kidnappers themselves were still at large.

2 Basques sentenced. A military court in Santander March 17, 1972 sentenced Jesus Ibarguchi San Pedro and Luis Maria Aizpurua, both allegedly ETA members, to 20-year prison terms and $720 fines each on charges of terrorism. The defendants were accused of planting a bomb at the headquarters of the Falange party's youth group at San Sebastian in 1967.

France bans ETA. The French government banned ETA Oct. 8, 1972 and ordered seven Basque exiles to leave France.

The move climaxed a gradual crackdown on the Basques by French authorities, a policy spurred by increasing cooperation between the two governments. The anti-Basque crackdown had led to sharp protests by the Basques living in southwest France, culminating in the bombing of the sub-prefecture in Bayonne in September.

French consulate set afire. The French consulate in Saragossa was set afire Nov. 2, 1972, and the consul, Roger Tur, died Nov. 7 of injuries suffered in the blaze. Two others were also injured.

According to initial Spanish press reports, three persons identifying themselves as Basque separatists entered the consulate Nov. 2, tied up the consul and two employes, set the fire and fled.

A military court in Saragossa sentenced five members of a leftist student group to 30-year prison terms Feb. 1, 1973 for their role in setting the fire. The trial brought out that the consulate had not been bombed as initially reported.

During trial, the students said they had acted in protest against the French government ban on Basque separatists residing in France.

The prosecutor claimed that the members of the group, called the Hammer and Sickle Collective, had been responsible for 15 crimes in one year, including a bank holdup. He said the fathers of three defendants were career officers, one a high level civil servant and one a prominent journalist in the governing party press.

A sixth defendant was acquitted.

Basque leader killed. Eustaquio Mendizabal, leader of the military wing of the ETA, was killed in a gunfight with police April 19, 1973 in a village near Bilbao. Police said Mendizabal, wanted in connection with three major political kidnappings since 1970, was killed while attempting to escape.

Cifra, the semi-official news agency, implied that Mendizabal's whereabouts had been disclosed to police by fellow activists after a dispute over disposal of $800,000 in ransom paid for the release of industrialist Felipe Huarte in January.

Premier assassinated. Premier Luis Carrero Blanco, 70, was assassinated in Madrid Dec. 20, 1973, apparently by Basque nationalists.

Carrero, his chauffeur and a police guard were killed by an explosion that lifted their car five stories off the street and into the courtyard of a church where the premier had just attended mass.

A statement issued in the name of the ETA in Bordeaux, France took credit for the assassination, which it said was done in revenge for the killing of nine Basque militants by the government and to fight repression in Spain.

During the Madrid funeral procession for Carrero Dec. 21, many of the thousands of regime supporters who lined the routes demanded that the army seize power and that "Reds" be killed. Archbishop Vicente Cardinal Enrique y Tarancon, other bishops and Papal Nuncio Msgr. Luigi Dadaglio were subjected to insults and threats.

Anarchist garroted. Salvador Puig Antich, a 26-year-old Catalan anarchist sentenced to die for killing a policeman in 1973, was garroted in the Barcelona city jail March 2, 1974.

It was the first execution with political overtones and the first by garroting since two Catalan anarchists were garroted in August 1963. The garrote was a centuries-old Spanish torture and death device consisting of an iron collar tightened around a victim's neck until he died of either strangulation or a broken spine.

University students clashed with police in Madrid and Barcelona March 4 after demonstrating against Puig Antich's execution. In Madrid, students rioted after police invaded the campus and dispersed protesters. In Barcelona, demonstrations were held in the two universities and the city's streets, with students hurling gasoline bombs and burning a car. Demonstrations continued the next day in the two cities and spread to Bilbao and San Sebastian.

Franco was believed to have been under great pressure from police, army and right-wing groups to deny clemency for Puig Antich, according to the New York Times March 3.

In an apparent effort to depoliticize Puig Antich's execution, the government March 2 also garroted Heinz Chez, a stateless person of Polish origin condemned to die for shooting a civil guard near Tarragona in December 1972. The death sentence of a third convicted police killer, civil guard Antonio Franco Martin, was commuted to life imprisonment.

Puig Antich had received his death sentence Jan. 9 and simultaneously was sentenced to 30 years in jail for bank robbery.

Two teen-aged accomplices, who along with Puig Antich were charged with membership in the Iberian Liberation Movement, a leftist splinter group, were sentenced to five and 30 years respectively for the robbery. Antich and one of the other defendants admitted membership in the group.

Appeals for clemency for Puig Antich had been made by the governments of Denmark, West Germany, the Netherlands, Belgium, France and Italy, according to the Washington Post March 3.

Other appeals had come from the Geneva section of the Human Rights League Feb. 14, from the Spanish General Council of Lawyers Feb. 15, from the French Communist Party Feb. 20, from Christopher Soames, vice president of the Executive Commission of the European Economic Community, Feb. 21, and from some 300 Madrid intellectuals March 1.

Thousands of persons demonstrated in Barcelona and Paris Feb. 21 to demand clemency. A number of bombings inside and outside Spain, also apparently protesting Puig Antich's death sentence, had been reported earlier.

Bombs exploded Feb. 8 at a monument to pro-Franco war dead in Badalona, near Barcelona, and inside a police station in Martorell, also near the Catalan capital. A Molotov cocktail was hurled at an Air France office in Barcelona the same day.

Bombs were set off Feb. 16 at a Spanish tourist office and a Spanish bank in Brussels, Belgium. The same day a fire set by arsonists damaged a Spanish travel agency in Frankfurt, West Germany.

Banker abducted. Angel Suarez, head of the Paris branch of the Bank of Bilbao, was kidnapped from his French home May 3, 1974. The anarchist Internationalist Revolutionary Action Group (GARI) announced its responsibility May 7 and made a series of demands for Suarez' release, including the freeing of political prisoners in Spain—particularly Santiago Soler Amigo, an ILM member said to be in poor health—and publication of anarchist communiques in Spanish newspapers.

Suarez was released May 22 after the payment of about $700,000 in ransom.

TURKEY

Leftist Terrorism

Several leftist terrorist groups have been active in Turkey. The best known is the Turkish People's Liberation Army (TPLA), made up mainly of students and said to have formed ties with such foreign guerrilla organizations as Uruguay's Tupamaros. Also active was Dev-Genk, the Turkish Revolutionary Youth Federation.

4 kidnaped U.S. airmen freed. Four U.S. airmen kidnaped by leftist extremists were released unharmed March 8. 1971. Both the U.S. and Turkey had refused to yield to ransom demands.

The airmen—Sgt. James J. Sexton, and Pvts. Larry J. Heavner, Richard Caraszi, and James M. Gholson—had been kidnaped by five armed men March 4 as they drove from a radar base outside Ankara to their billets. Setting a March 6 deadline, the kidnapers demanded $400,000 as the ransom price for not shooting the airmen. The police March 4 arrested one of the kidnap suspects, Mete Ertekin, 24, a student at the Middle East Technical University in Ankara. His arrest prompted an additional demand by the kidnapers for his release.

In a manifesto delivered to the semiofficial Turkish news agency and a radio station the same day, the Turkish People's Liberation Army, a new leftist guerrilla group, claimed responsibility for the kidnaping as well as for two bank robberies, recent bomb explosions and the armed kidnaping of another U.S. serviceman, Sgt. Jimmy Ray Finley, in Ankara Feb. 15. (Finley was released unharmed 17 hours after his abduction from a U.S. Air Force base on the outskirts of Ankara.) The group called for armed struggle to liberate Turkey from Americans and other "enemies" of the nation.

More than 2,000 policemen and militiamen searched for the kidnapers in Ankara. They surrounded the campus of the Middle East Technical University March 5, touching off riots in which at least one student and one policeman were killed and 20 students injured. The police used tear gas bombs to dislodge students who barricaded themselves in the school buildings with dynamite, guns and fire bombs. About 200 students were arrested.

Kidnaped Israeli diplomat killed. The body of the Israeli consul general in Istanbul, Ephraim Elrom, was found May 23, 1971 in Istanbul six days after he had been kidnaped by four leftist terrorists. He had been shot three times in the head.

The crisis began May 17 when four armed terrorists raided Elrom's residence and bound and gagged 12 persons before the diplomat returned home for lunch. After a brief struggle, Elrom was dragged away to a waiting car.

The Turkish People's Liberation Army (TPLA) took responsibility. It threatened to kill Elrom, 58, unless "all revolutionary guerrillas under detention" in Turkey were released by the evening of May 20. The government immediately rejected the demands and began an intensive search for the kidnaped diplomat and his abductors.

The government said the kidnapers probably belonged to the militant leftist Turkish Revolutionary Youth Federation (Dev-Genc), which had been banned May 12 by court order. A member of Dev-Genc, Omer Ayna, had been arrested after an armed holdup of an Istanbul bank May 3. Many members of Dev-Genc were thought to belong to the TPLA, which in turn was said to have links with the anti-Israeli Popular Front for the Liberation of Palestine. The government had recently alleged that extreme leftists had received guerrilla training in Arab countries.

(Three members of Dev-Genc were apprehended May 8 while attempting to cross the frontier into Syria. They reportedly confessed plans to receive training in guerrilla warfare by Arab militants in Syria.)

Deputy Premier Sadi Kocas reiterated in the Senate May 18 that the government had "no intention of bargaining with a handful of adventurers." He also announced the arrest of a major suspect, Ayhan Yalin.

The police found Elrom's body May 23 in an apartment only 500 yards from the Israeli consulate. A police doctor estimated death had occurred the previous evening—well after the expiration of the original deadline.

Premier Nihat Erim promised that those responsible for the kidnap-murder would be "dealt with most severely." He said the government was "determined that Turkey will not become a country ruled by anarchists and terrorists."

Press reports said May 24 that within the past week the government had held for questioning nearly 1,000 persons, including leftist university professors, writers and other intellectuals; many were quickly released.

Martial law authorities announced May 24 they were seeking nine university students—eight men and a woman—in connection with the murder. The same day the police said that three persons taken into custody May 23 had confessed participation in planning the kidnaping

and in watching the Elrom apartment and the Israeli consulate.

Hostage rescued, guerrilla killed. Sibel Erkan, 14, the daughter of an army major, was rescued June 1, 1971 from two armed leftist guerrillas who had held her hostage since May 30. One of the guerrillas, Huseyin Cevahir, was killed in a police shootout and the other, Mahir Cayan, was seriously wounded. The men were members of the Turkish People's Liberation Army and were wanted in connection with the kidnap-murder of Ephraim Elrom.

The guerrillas had seized the girl May 30 and held her hostage in her own house after permitting her mother and brother to leave. They threatened to kill her unless they were granted safe passage out of Turkey. Police and troops surrounded the house and, after a 51-hour siege, assaulted the apartment. A postmortem revealed 23 bullet wounds in the body of Cevahir. Cayan, wounded, tried to flee but yielded to police when confronted by an angry mob. One policeman was wounded in the battle.

Acuner's immunity lifted. The Senate July 2, 1971 lifted the immunity of Senator Ekrem Acuner, accused of organizing a leftist terrorist group that engaged in robberies and sabotage. Thirteen other persons were accused in connection with the case. Acuner had been made a senator for life for his role in the 1960 coup.

A former parliament member, Irfan Solmazer, was jailed by an Istanbul military court June 21 on charges of collaborating with Acuner in subversive and terrorist activities.

Terrorism. Among other developments involving terrorism in Turkey during 1971:

Bombs exploded in the headquarters of Turk-Is, the Confederation of Turkish Trade Unions, in Istanbul Jan. 18.

A bomb explosion destroyed the Kennedy Memorial at the Middle East Technical University in Ankara Feb. 15.

Students, armed with guns, dynamite and gasoline bombs, clashed with police at Hacettepe Medical University in Ankara Feb. 19. At least 20 persons were injured and 200 arrested. The battle began when police attempted to search for arms in the university.

An Ankara military court July 1 sentenced Sar Kuray, son of a former governor of Ankara, and Ruhi Koc to eight and 15 years' imprisonment respectively for bombing the residence of a general in April.

Terrorists exploded bombs at the U.S. consulate, a branch of the American-Turkish Trading Bank, and offices of the right-wing Ankara newspaper Dunya March 14.

15 arrested on escape plot charge. Fifteen persons were arrested on charges of plotting to rescue 26 accused terrorists on trial in Istanbul, it was announced Oct. 21, 1971.

The announcement said the group had plotted to kidnap senior NATO officers, government and public officials and prominent businessmen, whom they planned to hold for ransom in exchange for the accused on trial.

The trial of 26 persons accused of membership in the Turkish People's Liberation Army had opened in Istanbul Aug. 16. They were charged with attempting violent overthrow of the government, setting up secret organizations, and possessing or using arms to establish a single class rule. Thirteen persons were accused of taking part in the kidnap-murder of Elrom.

Terrorist suspects escape. Five members of the Turkish People's Liberation Army escaped Nov. 30, 1971 from a maximum security military prison in Istanbul.

One of the escapees, Ulas Bardakci, an alleged participant in Elrom's kidnap-murder, was reported shot and killed in a clash with police on the Bosphorus shores Feb. 19, 1972. A second escapee, Ziya Yilmaz, also accused in the Elrom case, was captured in the Feb. 19 clash and was given a death sentence by an Istanbul military court March 17.

10 terrorists, 3 hostages killed. Heavily armed police and soldiers killed 10 leftist terrorists hiding in a mountain shack March 30, 1972, reportedly after the terrorists killed two Britons and a Canadian being held hostage for the release of three leftist terrorists sentenced to death.

The government reported the hostages had been shot in the head with their hands tied behind their backs before police rushed the shack, located in the village of Kizildere, about 60 miles south of Unye on the Black Sea. The troops then opened fire with rockets and small arms, killing the 10 terrorist members of the Turkish People's Liberation Army (TPLA). Among the 10 were Mahir Cayan, a suspect in the kidnap-murder of Israeli consul Ephraim Elrom, and Cihan Alptekin and Omer Ayna. All three had escaped from prison in November 1971.

The hostages—Gordon Banner and Charles Turner, of Britain, and John Stewart Law, of Canada—had been kidnaped from their apartment by five terrorists March 26. They were employed as NATO civilian technicians at a Turkish air force radar base at Unye.

The government had refused to bargain with the terrorists either for the release of their condemned comrades or for the kidnapers' subsequent demand for safe passage out of Turkey once the police surrounded their hideout.

Interior Minister Ferit Kubat, who had personally supervised the assault on the shack, announced in the National Assembly March 31 that one of the kidnapers, Ertugrul Kurkcu, had been captured alive near the house.

It was disclosed March 31 that a letter allegedly written by the terrorists and found in the house had said the hostages were killed because they were "English agents of the NATO forces which occupy our country, and . . . we consider it our basic right and a debt of honor to execute them."

General shot; army put on alert. Four gunmen shot and wounded Gen. Kemalettin Eken, the commander of the Turkish national police, in an apparent kidnaping attempt in Ankara May 4, 1972.

Eken and four other persons were wounded in the shootout outside the general's home. Police said one of the assailants was killed and another captured. Reports linked the shootings to the extreme leftist Turkish People's Liberation Army.

Hijackers free hostages & plane. Four Turkish guerrillas May 4, 1972 dropped their demand for the release of three condemned militants and released unharmed about 68 passengers and crewmen of a DC-9 Turkish Airlines twinjet they had hijacked on an Ankara-Istanbul flight May 3.

The hijackers, armed with pistols and hand grenades, had forced the plane to fly to the airport in Sofia, Bulgaria, where they threatened to blow up the jet and everyone aboard unless the Turkish government agreed to their demand.

The Turkish government refused to bargain with the hijackers but said it would agree to asylum for the guerrillas in Bulgaria if they released the passengers and crew and left the plane unharmed. The four were granted political asylum in Bulgaria after their surrender.

The hijackers—three students and an electrician—had extended their ultimatum deadline several times.

The hijacking followed the approval April 24 by the National Assembly and May 2 by the Senate of death sentences passed by a military court on the three leftist guerrillas—Deniz Gezmis, Yusef Aslan and Huseyin Inan. President Cevdet Sunay ratified the death sentences May 3. (The parliamentary and presidential ratification of the death sentences had followed the revocation April 8 by the Constitutional Court of earlier death sentences against the guerrillas because of faulty drafting of the execution order.)

3 guerrillas hanged. Three members of the Turkish People's Liberation Army were hanged May 6, 1972 in an Ankara prison. The three—Deniz Gezmis, 25, Yusef Aslan, 25, and Huseyin Inan, 22, —were convicted of kidnaping 3 U.S. servicemen in 1971 and of trying to overthrow the government.

Several bombs exploded in Ankara and Istanbul May 7, in apparent retaliation for the executions. Four persons were injured, one allegedly a bomb-thrower. The Turkish tourist office in Stockholm

was bombed May 3, reportedly in response to the Ankara parliament's ratification of the death sentences.

Hijackers surrender in Bulgaria. Four hijackers surrendered to authorities in Sofia Oct. 23, 1972 after being granted political asylum in Bulgaria. The hijackers, reportedly university students, freed 60 hostages held aboard a jet they had seized Oct. 22 en route from Istanbul to Ankara and forced to fly to Sofia.

The surrender followed the Turkish government's refusal to grant the hijackers' demands for release of 12 leftist prisoners, abolition of the strike ban in martial law areas, greater freedom in the universities, land reform and end of the "anti-democratic" articles in the constitution.

The hijackers had threatened to blow up the jet and the hostages if their demands were not met.

Officials slain in U.S. The Turkish consul general in Los Angeles and his deputy were shot dead at a hotel luncheon Jan. 27, 1973 by an Armenian who claimed members of his family had been killed in Turkey.

The shooting occurred in the Biltmore Hotel in nearby Santa Barbara, where the officials were attending a luncheon. Mehmet Baydar, the consul general, died almost instantly and Bahadir Demir, deputy consul general, died shortly after arrival at a local hospital. Both had been shot in the head. Witnesses said Gourgen M. Yanikian surrendered to authorities.

WEST GERMANY

Baader-Meinhof Group Accused

An outbreak of terrorism in West Germany in 1972 was largely blamed on the leftist-anarchist Rote Armee Fraktion (Red Army Faction), more widely known as the Baader-Meinhof group. Although the group's leaders, Andreas Baader and Ulrike Meinhof, were arrested in 1972, it was believed to be still active.

Wave of terrorist bombings. A wave of terrorist bombings swept through West Germany May 11–24, 1972.

A series of explosions May 11 killed U.S. Army Lt. Col. Paul A. Bloomquist, 39, and injured 13 other persons, five seriously, at the headquarters complex of the 5th U.S. Army Corps in Frankfurt. The bombs heavily damaged the officer's club behind the main building.

The German Press Agency office in Munich received a letter May 15 from the "Petra Schelm Command" of the "Red Army Faction" claiming responsibility for the bombing in retaliation for the "bomb blockade of the U.S. imperialists against North Vietnam." The note demanded an end to the mining of North Vietnamese harbors and immediate withdrawal of all U.S. troops from Indochina.

Two bombs exploded May 12 at police headquarters in Augsburg, while shortly afterwards another powerful blast struck the Munich criminal police headquarters about 25 miles away.

A bomb explosion May 15 severely injured Mrs. Gerta Buddenberg, 53, the wife of Judge Wolfgang Buddenberg, who had been investigating the activities of the Baader-Meinhof group. The bomb exploded as Mrs. Buddenberg turned the ignition key in her car parked at her home in Karlsruhe.

Two bombs exploded at the Hamburg headquarters of the right-wing Axel Springer newspaper and magazine publishing concern May 19, injuring 15 employes, at least six seriously. The bombs exploded in midafternoon when 3,000 employes were at work.

Two bombs placed in parked cars exploded within seconds of each other inside the U.S. Army's European headquarters in Heidelberg May 24, killing an army officer and two soldiers and injuring five other persons. The explosions ripped a hole in the wall of a data processing building.

Interior Minister Hans-Dietrich Genscher confirmed, in a television interview later May 24, that suspects sought in the recent terrorist attacks were linked to the Baader-Meinhof gang.

(The next month, Genscher, presenting a report on 1971 West German counter-intelligence activities to newsmen, said June 3 that agitation by leftist, rightist and foreign extremists had increased in West Germany.

(Genscher reported that right-wing agitation groups had increased from 108 in 1970 to 123 in 1971, and under a collective title of the New Right, had devoted most of their energies to their fight against the government's policy of detente. He said terrorist acts attributed to the New Right more than doubled from 53 in 1970 to 123 in 1971. Left-wing agitation groups, Genscher reported, had been responsible for 555 "terror acts" in 1971, with 390 groups identified as active, compared with 250 in 1970. He said foreign agitators had increased the number of their active groups from 100 in 1970 to 220 in 1971. Of these, 47 were terrorist-oriented.)

Terrorist chief captured. State and federal police captured Andreas Baader and two other Baader-Meinhof group leaders in Frankfurt June 1, 1972. Other gang members arrested were Holger Meins, 30, and Jan-Carl Raspe, 27.

Baader was shot in the hip by police in a shootout that occurred when police surrounded a garage used as the hideout. (Baader had been hunted by West German police since 1970 when masked gang members freed him in a spectacular jail break in Berlin. He had been sentenced for setting fire to a department store in 1968.)

Another allegedly "hard core" gang member, Gudrun Ensslin, 31, was arrested by police June 7 in a downtown shopping center in Hamburg.

Meinhof arrested. Ulrike Meinhof, 37, the object of an intensive police search as a founder of the Baader-Meinhof group, was arrested in a Hanover suburb June 15, 1972. Gerhard Mueller, 23, was arrested with her.

Police June 19 arrested another member of the group, Siegfried Hausner, 21.

Mahler jailed. Horst Mahler, 36, a lawyer, was sentenced Feb. 26, 1973 to 12 years in prison by a West Berlin court. He was convicted of helping to found the Baader-Meinhof urban guerrilla group and planning and participating in three armed robberies in Berlin in 1970.

YUGOSLAVIA

Croatians Attack Regime

Yugoslavia's Communist regime has faced repeated terrorist attacks by members of the Croation independence group Ustashi. These attacks have taken place both inside Yugoslavia and abroad.

Envoy assassinated in Sweden. Vladimir Rolovic, Yugoslavia's ambassador to Sweden, died April 15, 1971 in Stockholm as a result of bullet wounds inflicted April 7 by two Croatian terrorists.

The assailants, later identified as Andjelko Brajkowic and Miro Barzico, entered the embassy on the pretext of obtaining passports and shot Rolovic a number of times. Mira Stemphihar, a secretary, was wounded trying to protect the ambassador.

Two Ustashi members had occupied the Yugoslav consulate at Goteborg for 24 hours Feb. 10 and threatened to kill hostages unless a Croatian militant under death sentence in Belgrade was released. Rolovic had told the men the Yugoslav government rejected their demands. They later released the hostages and were jailed.

The Yugoslav Federal Executive Council protested the attack on Rolovic April 7 in a note transmitted to the Swedish government representative in Belgrade later that day by Mirko Tepavac, Yugoslav foreign minister. The note cited the Goteborg incident as well as previous warnings to the Swedish government about the existence of emigre organizations. Sweden's "tolerance" of "the so-called political activity of these terrorist groups" was described as "totally impermissible and dangerous" and likely to have "grave consequences for the friendly relations between the two countries."

Brajkowic, Barzico and a third man suspected of aiding them were charged with murder April 16 in a Stockholm court. Lars Bergmark, Barzico's lawyer, had told reporters April 12 that the men planned to kidnap the ambassador and exchange him for militant Croats in Yugoslavia but that Rolovic drew a gun.

Brajkowic and Barzico were sentenced by the Stockholm city court July 14 to life imprisonment.

Also sentenced for complicity in the case were Marinko Lemo and Stanislav Milicevic, each given two-year terms. Ante Stojanov, the group's leader, was given four years. The London Times said July 14 that the five had planned to form a terrorist group that would punish people in Sweden working for Yugoslavia against Croation factions.

Croatian terrorists killed. An estimated 30 Croatian terrorists, thought to have come from abroad, were reported killed by security forces by July 28, 1972 after entering the country earlier in the month. The intruders were described as members of the Ustashi.

The Croatians were understood to have come from Australia, where as many as 250,000 persons of Yugoslav origin were living, and to have crossed the border from Austria. They then overpowered a truck driver and forced him to take them to the region of Bugojno, northwest of Sarajevo, in Bosnia-Herzegovina. The driver apparently escaped and was able to warn the police, who sent soldiers to the area where the Croatians were hiding.

The first official account of the incident came July 3 with the announcement that 17 "known Ustashi terrorists and criminals" had been killed and that two others had escaped. The Yugoslav news agency Tanyug said July 26 that 13 government soldiers, including a captain, had been killed in the shooting and that the two infiltrators who initially escaped were now dead. Tanyug reported July 28 that Croatian government forces "successfully liquidated" the "eight terrorists who crossed to this republic's territory" after their group had been "smashed" in Bosnia-Herzegovina. No government version of the events attempted to explain the mission of the terrorists, although some press sources charged that Sweden and West Germany, as well as Australia, were harboring substantial numbers of Ustashi.

Croats surrender in Spain. Nine Croatian extremists surrendered to authorities at Madrid airport Sept. 16, 1972, hours after arriving aboard a DC-9 jetliner they had hijacked from Sweden.

The incident began Sept. 15 when three armed Ustashi members hijacked a Scandanavian Airlines System (SAS) plane bound from Goteborg to Stockholm and forced it to land at Malmo. The hijackers demanded that in exchange for the lives of the plane's 79 passengers and four crewmen the Swedish government release seven Croatian prisoners, including two men convicted for the 1971 murder of the Yugoslav ambassador to Sweden.

After an emergency Cabinet session, Premier Olof Palme ordered the prisoners taken to the Malmo airport, where Justice Minister Lennart Geijer conducted negotiations with the hijackers. When three prisoners had been exchanged for 30 passengers, the terrorists demanded about $200,000 but settled for half that amount before completing the exchange. One of the prisoners refused to join the hijackers.

The hijackers and crew then flew to Madrid. There followed another three hours of negotiations with Spanish officials, much of which reportedly passed with the Croatians arguing among themselves The men were believed to have surrendered partly because they thought few countries would accept them.

The official Yugoslav news agency Tanyug blamed the hijacking Sept. 16 on the "benevolent and tolerant attitude" of the Swedish government toward the Ustashi living and working in Sweden.

Ustashi in Australia. Australian Attorney General Lionel Murphy presented 56 official documents in Parliament March 27, 1973 and called them "incontestable evidence" that the Ustashi operated out of Australia. Declaring that the "toleration of terrorism in this country is over," he outlined plans to introduce anti-terrorist legislation and said he had already recommended deportation of certain immigrants.

Murphy criticized the former Liberal-Country coalitions for tolerating the Croatian groups and called former Attorney General Ivor Greenwood in the McMahon coalition "an active protector" of right-wing terrorists. Greenwood denounced Murphy's charges as "malicious abuse of parliamentary privilege."

(The previous government had denied the Yugoslav government's assertion that Croatian terrorist groups existed in Australia.)

Murphy named the Croatian Revolutionary Brotherhood, the United Croatians of West Germany and the Croatian Revolutionary Organization as the main terrorist groups in Australia.

Police raided the homes of about 80 Yugoslavs in Sydney April 1 and charged at least 12 persons with possession of firearms and explosives and assaulting policemen.

Murphy was given a vote of confidence April 10 in the House of Representatives after a debate on his handling of operations involving Croatian terrorists. The House vote came after the Senate had passed a censure motion April 5.

Murphy was censured by the Senate, 29–25, after he replied to his detractors in a bitter speech. He said "even in the last few days"—a reference to the police roundup of alleged terrorists in Sydney and Wollongong—evidence of terrorist organizations had been uncovered.

The motion against the attorney general also accused him of misleading the Senate by disclosing only selected documents found in the March 16 raid on the offices of the Australian Security Intelligence Organization (ASIO).

In the House debate, Prime Minister Gough Whitlam April 10 expressed "complete confidence" in Murphy.

Whitlam had told the House April 3 that the reason for the raid was a document from the ASIO files that indicated a "conspiracy" among public servants to conceal truth about Croatian terrorist activities in Australia. He was referring to a report, found by Murphy on a surprise visit to the ASIO Office in Canberra March 16, which covered a meeting on terrorism.

The report said a foreign affairs official had contended that Murphy's statement should not contradict an earlier reply to a Yugoslav government protest that the Croatians were being trained in Australia. That reply had denied there was evidence to support the Yugoslav allegation. The subsequent raid on the ASIO offices disclosed facts to the contrary, according to Whitlam.

Croatian terrorists executed. Three Ustashi members who had sneaked into Yugoslavia in 1972 had been tried and executed, the Belgrade government announced April 12. The announcement was the first public indication there had been any survivors of the incident.

The three men, all naturalized Australian citizens, were described as members of the Croatian Revolutionary Brotherhood. They were identified as Djuro Horvat, Vejsil Deskic and Mirko Vlasnovic. The sentence of a fourth detainee, Ludvig Pavlovic, reportedly was reduced to 20 years in jail because he gave a full confession.

Australian Prime Minister Gough Whitlam sent a protest note to the Yugoslav government April 13 saying he had expected the dead men to receive the same protection given Australian nationals anywhere in the world.

International Action

U.N. Discusses Problem

A United Nations committee began consideration of the matter of international terrorism during 1973. Observers asserted, however, that early U.N. action on the issue was unlikely because the positions of member nations were too widely and strongly contradictory.

U.N. to probe terrorism. The U.N. General Assembly Sept. 23, 1972 had placed on its agenda an amended version of a proposal by Secretary General Kurt Waldheim that it act on terrorism. The issue was assigned to the Legal Committee.

The item, passed 66–27 with 33 abstentions, embodied Jamaican and Saudi Arabian amendments that would focus the debate on international terrorism and widen its scope to include its underlying causes. The measures were credited with eroding African and Arab opposition to a discussion of terrorism.

In its final version, the item called for "measures to prevent international terrorism which endangers or takes innocent human lives or jeopardizes fundamental freedoms, and study of those underlying causes of terrorism and acts of violence which lie in misery, frustration, grievance and despair, and which cause some people to sacrifice

human lives, including their own, in an attempt to effect radical changes."

Waldheim's original item, passed Sept. 22 by the Assembly's General Committee, had called for "measures to prevent terrorism and other forms of violence which endanger or take innocent human lives or jeopardize fundamental freedoms."

The Jamaican amendment added the word "international" before "terrorism" and deleted "and other forms of violence," alleviating the fears of moderate African states that the item could be used against African liberation movements. The Saudi Arabian amendment required study of the problems underlying terrorism.

Eight Arab states voted against the final version, four abstained, and Jordan voted in favor. Sixteen African nations voted no, 13 abstained, and six voted in favor.

The Soviet bloc abstained from the final vote, and China and Cuba voted no. The Soviet abstention reportedly reflected concern over terrorism and wishes to protect Waldheim's position— said to be seriously undermined by the controversy over the terrorism debate— and remain flexible in dealings with the U.S. China, however, had been against Waldheim's original item on grounds that "it is perfectly just for oppressed nations and peoples to use revolutionary violence against the violence of imperialism, colonialism, neocolonialism, racism and Israeli Zionism."

Rogers asks 1973 parley—U.S. Secretary of State William P. Rogers urged the U.N. Sept. 25 to convene a meeting early in 1973 with power to define and set up the legal basis for forceful action to end terrorism.

Addressing the General Assembly on the first day of its general debate, Rogers asked the U.N. to be "the driving force for the specific and vigorous steps that are required" to arrest the "growing assault on international order with which we are all faced."

The U.S. simultaneously distributed among the 132 member countries at the U.N. a draft convention that spelled out in legal terms what constituted international terrorism and defined legal jurisdiction. The convention, to be considered at the proposed 1973 conference, provided for the prosecution or extradition of persons who killed, seriously injured or kidnaped innocent civilians in a foreign state for the purpose of harming or obtaining concessions from another state or from an international organization.

Stressing what he called the U.N.'s obligation to take action on terrorism, Rogers said "the issue is whether the vulnerable lines of international communication—the airways and the mails, diplomatic discourse and international meetings—can continue without disruption, to bring nations and peoples together. All who have a stake in this have a stake in decisive action to suppress these demented acts of terrorism."

Citing a wide range of terrorist acts in different countries, Rogers said: "we are all aware that . . . many criminal acts of terrorism derive from political origins. We recognize that issues such as self-determination must continue to be addressed seriously by the international community. But political passion, however deeply held, cannot be a justification for criminal violence against innocent persons."

(Rogers also announced that Interpol, the international police organization, had approved a U.S.-sponsored resolution urging its 110 member nations to intensify their efforts to combat "non-political" terrorism. A U.S. official said the resolution had been worked out with Israeli and Arab police leaders, and was "acceptable to all." It cited "certain aspects of modern international criminality, such as the holding of hostages with the intention of perpetrating blackmail or other forms of extortion" which Interpol members could act against within the limits of organization rules barring involvement in political, religious or military matters.)

As Rogers spoke, tight security precautions were again in effect at the U.N. and foreign consulates in New York, which had received a flood of threats of violence. A special 40-man detachment of the U.S. Executive Protection Service had been sent from Washington to bolster regular police protection of diplomats, and security checks were stringent.

Gromyko assails Arab terrorists—In the strongest Soviet criticism of Arab terrorism, Foreign Minister Andrei Gromyko told the General Assembly Sept. 26 that some Palestinian terrorists had turned to "criminal actions."

Gromyko called for an end to Israeli occupation of Arab territory, reiterating the Soviet Union's support of "the just struggle of the Arab people of Palestine for the restoration of their inalienable rights recognized by the United Nations." But he added, "it is certainly impossible to condone the acts of terrorism by certain elements from among the participants in the Palestinian movement which have led, notably, to the recent tragic events in Munich."

"These criminal actions," Gromyko said, "deal a blow also to the national interests and aspirations of the Palestinians; these acts are used by the Israeli criminals in order to cover up their bandit-like policy against the Arab peoples."

Gromyko also criticized acts of terrorism affecting diplomats, airplane hijackings, and general "acts of violence which serve no positive ends and cause loss of human life."

Study set—The Assembly Dec. 18 adopted a resolution calling for establishment of a 35-nation committee to consider reports by member countries on the causes of international terrorism and ways of finding an effective solution to the problem.

The measure, passed 76–35 with 17 abstentions, was sponsored by Arab and African countries and opposed by many Western powers. Its opponents had proposed that after a period of preliminary study an international conference be held to draw up a convention aimed at bringing an end to international terrorism.

Speaking in favor of the final resolution, an Iraqui representative said it respected the rights of people to self-determination and national liberation "and in no way can be interpreted to limit the rights of people" to free themselves from foreign bondage. The British representative, Sir Colin Crowe, maintained the measure was "seriously defective," and contained language that "could be taken to suggest that recourse to violence may be legitimate in the exercise of the right to self-determination."

Terrorism committee opens talks. The Special Committee on International Terrorism opened a four-week meeting at United Nations headquarters in New York July 16, 1973 with delegates of all 35 member nations attending.

The committee had a wide mandate from the 27th General Assembly to discuss international terrorism and its "underlying causes," and to make concrete recommendations to the 28th assembly, scheduled to open in September. It had before it observations submitted by 38 governments with varying views on the issue.

A Syrian statement asserted "the international community is under legal and moral obligation to promote the struggle for liberation and to resist any attempt to depict this struggle as synonymous with terrorism and illegitimate violence."

On the other hand, Japan stressed the "immediate peril endangering innocent lives and fundamental human rights," and urged the U.N. to "make every effort to avoid a situation where the adoption of preventive measures is hampered by delay in studying the underlying causes" of terrorism.

The Japanese view was echoed July 24 by the U.S. representative, W. Tapley Bennett Jr., who urged the committee to focus its attention on "the most serious criminal threat" and avoid "extended conceptual controversy" and the "consideration of abstract definitions."

The British representative, John R. Freeland, joined Bennett in his call for action, stressing that the study of terrorism's underlying causes was "inevitably a long-term matter" and should not "become a brake on progress with measures to protect the innocent."

The General Assembly Dec. 7 postponed until 1974 its debate on terrorism, ostensibly because of a lack of time for debate by the Legal Committee before the Assembly session ended Dec. 18. Israel charged the move showed U.N. helplessness and unwillingness to tackle the issue.

Arab delegates did not participate in the debate.

Bouteflika backs 'violence.' The 19th General Assembly opened Sept. 17, 1974 with a strident address by its president, Algerian Foreign Minister Abdelaziz Bouteflika.

Bouteflika, unanimously elected president as the 13-week Assembly session began, said he accepted the office as a representative of "generations of freedom fighters who contributed to making a better world with weapons in their hands." He asserted these fighters had shown that "revolutionary violence is the only way for peoples to liberate themselves."

Bouteflika assailed "modern capitalist exploitation" and the so-called detente between the U.S. and the Soviet Union, which, he asserted, had created an international order with a fragile balance of power which could easily be shattered.

Bouteflika defended the right of Palestinians "to freely exercise their right to self-determination " and warned that the international community would not accept a "Middle East bargain" in which "the conquered territories [were not] returned."

Bouteflika praised Portugal for beginning to free its African colonies, and asserted that the people of Indochina had defeated the "aggressors," presumably the U.S.

No Action on 'Skyjackings'

Western governments, airlines and airline pilots were unsuccessful in their proposals for strong U.N. action to curb a major terrorist tactic—the hijacking of airliners.

ICAO to Weigh Hijackings. The 27-member governing council of the International Civil Aviation Organization voted March 3, 1969 to consider the subject of "unlawful interference" with airliners. The proposal, which provided for discussions of hijackings and armed attacks against aircraft, was submitted Feb. 24 by the U.S., Australia, Brazil, Britain, Canada, West Germany, France, Japan and the Netherlands.

In a separate action Feb. 21 a legal subcommittee of ICAO completed the draft of a convention dealing with illegal seizure of planes. The convention said hijackers should be prosecuted in the country where they land or extradited to the country from which they came; but neither action would be mandatory under the convention.

The International Air Transport Association, representing 103 scheduled airlines had asked governments of its member airlines Jan. 13 to "seek U.N. action in regard to armed intervention involving aircraft in scheduled service."

The International Federation of Airline Pilots Associations (IFALPA), representing 44,000 pilots in 54 countries, March 26 adopted a resolution threatening reprisals against states that refused to institute "appropriate punishment" against hijackers. The resolution, approved in Amsterdam, the Netherlands, at IFALPA's 24th conference, authorized the association's officers: (a) to ban all air traffic into the offending nation; (b) to coordinate with other organizations in limiting air traffic and in restricting movement of air and surface cargo to and from the state; (c) to call a worldwide strike of 12–24 hours to call public attention to the "pressing problem of air safety."

'Hijacking' on Agenda. The General Committee, organizing body for General Assembly sessions, decided without objection Oct. 9, 1969 to urge inclusion of the question of aircraft hijacking in the Assembly's agenda and to allocate the item to the Sixth (Legal) Committee.

The General Assembly passed the measure Oct. 10. Only Cuban Ambassador Ricardo Alarcon Quesada opposed the recommendation.

The item—the 105th on the agenda—was proposed under the title "Piracy in the Air" by 12 delegations Oct. 3. Objections were raised by members of Arab states to use of the word "piracy," and by Soviet Ambassador Jacob A. Malik who charged that "some circles" were carrying out "tendentious and noisy propaganda . . . for unsavory political purposes."

The suggestion of Barbados that the item be entitled "Forcible Diversion of Aircraft" was modified by Nigeria, and the item was adopted as "Forcible Diversioon of Civil Aircraft in Flight."

Pilots stage 24-hour strike. Airline pilots around the world staged a one-day stoppage June 19, 1972 to press for more stringent international sanctions against hijacking and sabotage of aircraft.

It was the first time international pilots had organized to stop air travel on the world's carriers.

The pilots' strike was organized by the International Federation of Air Line Pilots' Associations, an umbrella group of national pilots' unions. Ola Forsberg of Finland, president of the international group, called the work stoppage "a successful expression of extreme concern." Specifically, the pilots were seeking to have the U.N. Security Council direct the International Civil Aviation Organization, a 124-member body, to begin setting up the necessary machinery to enforce antihijacking accords.

The pilots' strike had the most impact abroad, where air travel in more than 30 countries was shut down. In almost all of Western Europe, save Great Britain, air traffic was at a virtual standstill.

Of the Communist-bloc nations, only pilots of Yugoslavia and Czechoslovakia showed support for the strike. Yugoslavia's pilots remained on the ground while pilots in Czechoslovakia took part in a one-hour work stoppage.

Among the major non-Communist nations whose pilots were nonparticipants in the strike were Australia, countries of the Arab world, the Philippines and Japan.

The hopes of the strike's organizers for a shutdown of air service in the U.S. were severely damaged after the U.S. airlines obtained temporary injunctions barring their pilots from joining the work stoppage.

Security Council condemnation. The U.N. Security Council June 20, 1972 issued a strongly worded consensus statement condemning aircraft hijacking and calling on all nations to deter and prevent such acts.

The council's agreement fell far short, however, of adopting the position sought by the International Federation of Air Line Pilots Associations, which represented the various worldwide pilot groups. The federation had asked the U.N. to declare hijacking a threat to international peace and security and to demand enforcement of antihijacking accords.

But after 10 days of private meetings, the 15-member Security Council agreed on the consensus statement instead. The agreement was drawn up in private to avoid debate over such matters as what to do with hijackers whose deeds had political overtones.

The council called upon all states "to take all appropriate measures within their jurisdiction to deter and prevent such acts [hijackings] and to take effective measures to deal with those who commit such acts."

Conference fails to adopt treaty. A special 15-nation conference on aircraft hijacking met for two weeks in Washington in September 1972 without agreeing on the terms of a new international treaty against air piracy and sabotage.

The new treaty was fashioned by the U.S., Canada, Great Britain and the Netherlands as a compromise measure after some nations sharply opposed the terms of the original draft.

The rewritten treaty outlined the machinery under which signatory nations could collectively investigate whether another nation had improperly failed to punish or extradite airplane hijackers or saboteurs. Under the original treaty, proposed when the conference opened Sept. 4, much stronger sanctions would have been imposed against nations failing to punish or extradite airplane terrorists.

The original treaty was scrapped after it evoked opposition of the representatives from the Soviet Union, France and Great Britain.